THE SONNET

THE SONNET

THE SONNET

STEPHEN REGAN

UNIVERSITY PRESS

OXFORD
UNIVERSITY PRESS

Great Clarendon Street, Oxford, OX2 6DP,
United Kingdom

Oxford University Press is a department of the University of Oxford.
It furthers the University's objective of excellence in research, scholarship,
and education by publishing worldwide. Oxford is a registered trade mark of
Oxford University Press in the UK and in certain other countries

© Stephen Regan 2019

The moral rights of the author have been asserted

First Edition published in 2019

Impression: 1

All rights reserved. No part of this publication may be reproduced, stored in
a retrieval system, or transmitted, in any form or by any means, without the
prior permission in writing of Oxford University Press, or as expressly permitted
by law, by licence or under terms agreed with the appropriate reprographics
rights organization. Enquiries concerning reproduction outside the scope of the
above should be sent to the Rights Department, Oxford University Press, at the
address above

You must not circulate this work in any other form
and you must impose this same condition on any acquirer

Published in the United States of America by Oxford University Press
198 Madison Avenue, New York, NY 10016, United States of America

British Library Cataloguing in Publication Data
Data available

Library of Congress Control Number: 2018953773

ISBN 978–0–19–289307–9 (hbk.)
978–0–19–883886–9 (pbk.)

Printed and bound by
CPI Group (UK) Ltd, Croydon, CR0 4YY

Links to third party websites are provided by Oxford in good faith and
for information only. Oxford disclaims any responsibility for the materials
contained in any third party website referenced in this work.

For Eleanor

I' benedico il loco e 'l tempo e l'ora
che sì alto miraron gli occhi mei

Acknowledgements

Acknowledgements are due to *The Robert Frost Review*, *The Yearbook of English Studies*, and *CounterText*, in which extracts from three chapters have previously appeared. *The Sonnet* has been a long time in the making, and I owe a great debt of thanks to friends and colleagues who have offered help and guidance along the way. I am especially grateful to Ted Chamberlin and Lorna Goodison for their unwavering support and enthusiasm, and to Terry Eagleton for many years of friendship and encouragement. Ewan Fernie, Bernard O'Donoghue, and Ron Schleifer all generously took time to read and comment on parts of the book, and I am hugely thankful for their many helpful suggestions and illuminating insights. For various acts of kindness and advice, I am deeply indebted to Sue Asbee, Chris Bissell, Tom Bristow, Lars Burman, John Davison, Maura Dooley, Rachel Falconer, Deanna Fernie, Helen Habibi, Hugh Haughton, David Johnson, Laura McKenzie, Michael Parker, Jahan Ramazani, Stephen Reimer, Nicholas Roe, Dan Ross, Kiernan Ryan, Yasmine Shamma, Alison Shell, Katherine Skaris, Terence Spencer, and Colm Tóibín. The preparation of the book was overseen with great care and thoughtfulness by Aimee Wright at OUP. I am grateful to Timothy Beck for his excellent copy-editing and Kate Legon for her meticulous indexing. I have been blessed with the best and most patient of editors in Jacqueline Norton.

I should like to thank my colleagues at Durham University for their constant support and good will. It has been a great pleasure to work closely with Michael O'Neill, whose studies of poetry and poetic form have been an inspiration. I have learned a good deal along the way from Paul Batchelor, Robert Carver, Stefano Cracolici, David Fuller, Jason Harding, Barbara Ravelhofer, Gareth Reeves, Barry Sheils, and Patricia Waugh. Financial assistance for permissions and artwork was kindly provided by the research committees of the Department of English Studies and the Faculty of Arts and Humanities at Durham University, and I am grateful for the advice and support of successive directors of research: John Nash, Fiona Robertson, Corinne Saunders, and Sarah Wootton. I wish to thank the Department of

English at Harvard University for granting me a research fellowship to work on the book, along with many opportunities for stimulating discussion. In particular, I should like to record my gratitude to Helen Vendler for her illustrious work on Shakespeare and Keats, as well as many other poets, and to Stephanie Burt, whose critical studies of the sonnet have been invigorating and enlightening.

The book draws on conversations and correspondence with several of the poets whose work appears in its pages, and I should like to express my thanks to Ciaran Carson, Wendy Cope, Douglas Dunn, Alan Gillis, Robert Hampson, Tony Harrison, Seamus Heaney, Andrew McNeillie, Andrew Motion, Paul Muldoon, Don Paterson, Tom Pickard, and Anne Stevenson. I wish to record my heartfelt thanks to Derek Walcott, with whom I spent many happy hours in St Lucia, reading sonnets aloud and from memory against the gentle hush of the Caribbean Sea... 'words which love had hoped to use | Erased with the surf's pages'.

★ ★ ★

Every effort has been made to trace and contact copyright holders prior to publication. If notified, the publisher will be pleased to rectify any errors or omissions at the earliest opportunity. I am grateful for permission to reproduce the following excerpts:

- Reprinted by permission of Farrar, Straus, and Giroux: 'Sonnet' [1979] from *The Complete Poems 1927–1979* by Elizabeth Bishop. © 1979, 1983 by Alice Helen Methfessel. 'X' from 'Glanmore Sonnets' from *Opened Ground: Selected Poems 1966–1996* by Seamus Heaney. © 1998 by Seamus Heaney. Excerpts from 'Inauguration Day: January 1953', 'Night Sweat', and 'The Dolphin' from *Collected Poems* by Robert Lowell. © 2003 by Harriet Lowell and Sheridan Lowell. 'Lull' from *Poems: 1968–1998* by Paul Muldoon. © 2001 by Paul Muldoon. 'Quoof' and 'Why Brownlee Left' from *Selected Poems 1968–2014* by Paul Muldoon. © 2016 by Paul Muldoon.
- 'Lay Your Sleeping Head, My Love', and 'Brussels in Winter', © 1940 and renewed 1968 by W. H. Auden; 'The Secret Agent', © 1934 and renewed 1962 by W. H. Auden; 'Sonnets from China XXI: To E. M. Forster', © 1945 by W. H. Auden, renewed 1973 by The Estate of W. H. Auden; and 'In Time of War' from *W. H. Auden Collected Poems* by W. H. Auden,

ACKNOWLEDGEMENTS

© 1976 by Edward Mendelson, William Meredith, and Monroe K. Spears, Executors of the Estate of W. H. Auden. Used by permission of Random House, an imprint and division of Penguin Random House LLC. All rights reserved.

- Edmund Blunden, 'Vlamertinghe: Passing the Chateau' from *Undertones of War*, Penguin Books.
- 'Prayer' from *Mean Time* by Carol Ann Duffy. Published by Picador, 2013. © Carol Ann Duffy. Reproduced by permission of the author c/o Rogers, Coleridge & White Ltd, 20 Powis Mews, London W11 1JN.
- '1798' from *The Alexandrine Plan* (1998) and 'Au Cabaret-Vert', *Collected Poems* (2008) by Ciaran Carson, by kind permission of the author and The Gallery Press, Loughcrew, Oldcastle, County Meath, Ireland.
- Ken Edwards, 'Darkly Slow' and 'His Last Gasp (2)', *eight + six* (2003), by permission of the author.
- Robert Hampson, from 'Reworked Disasters or: Next Checking Out the Chapmans' Goyas', *The Reality Street Book of Sonnets*, ed. Jeff Hilson (London: Reality Street, 2008), by permission of the author and the publisher.
- *Landing Light* by Don Paterson. Published by Faber and Faber Ltd, 2003. © Don Paterson. Reproduced by permission of the author c/o Rogers, Coleridge & White Ltd, 20 Powis Mews, London W11 1JN and Faber and Faber Ltd.
- 'The Kaleidoscope' and 'Sandra's Mobile' by Douglas Dunn from *Elegies* (© Douglas Dunn, 1982) are printed by permission of United Agents <www.unitedagents.co.uk> on behalf of Douglas Dunn.
- 'Why Brownlee Left', 'Lull', 'Quoof' from *New Selected Poems* by Paul Muldoon, by permission of Faber and Faber Ltd.
- Seamus Heaney, 'Glanmore Sonnets' from *Field Work* (1979), and 'Fosterling' from *Seeing Things* (1991), by permission of Faber and Faber Ltd.
- 'Autumn Refrain' from *The Collected Poems of Wallace Stevens* by Wallace Stevens, © 1954 by Wallace Stevens and copyright renewed 1982 by Holly Stevens. Used by permissions of Alfred A. Knopf, an imprint of the Knopf Doubleday Publishing Group, a division of Penguin Random House, LLC. All rights reserved and by permission of Faber and Faber Ltd.

ACKNOWLEDGEMENTS

- Wendy Cope, 'Faint Praise' and 'The Sitter' from *Two Cures for Love: Selected Poems 1979–2006* (2008) by permission of the author and Faber and Faber Ltd.
- Wendy Cope, 'Strugnell's Bargain', by permission of the author.
- The poems of Patrick Kavanagh are reprinted from *Collected Poems*, edited by Antoinette Quinn (Allen Lane, 2004), by kind permission of the Trustees of the Estate of the late Katherine B. Kavanagh, through the Jonathan Williams Literary Agency.
- Eleanor Brown, Sonnets 3 and 33 in *Maiden Speech* (Bloodaxe, 1996), by permission of the publisher.
- Anne Stevenson, 'Sonnets for Five Seasons' from *Poems 1955–2005* (Bloodaxe, 2004) by permission of the publisher.
- Elizabeth Jennings, 'A Sense of Place' and 'Sources of Light' from *The Collected Poems*, Carcanet Press.
- Michael Longley, 'Ceasefire', 'The Vision of Theoclymenus', and 'The Beech Tree' from *Collected Poems*, © Michael Longley 2006.
- 'Heroic'. © 1998 by Eavan Boland, 'Yeats in Civil War', from *New Collected Poems* by Eavan Boland. Copyright © 2005, 2001, 1998, 1994, 1990, 1987, 1980, 1975, 1967, 1962 by Eavan Boland. Used by permission of W. W. Norton & Company, Inc.
- 'next to of course god america I'. © 1926, 1954, © 1991 by the Trustees for the E. E. Cummings Trust. © 1985 by George James Firmage, from *Complete Poems: 1904–1962* by E. E. Cummings, edited by George J. Firmage. Used by permission of Liveright Publishing Corporation.
- 'Exequy' (from the Italian of Petrarch) translated by Derek Mahon from *Echo's Grove* (2013) by kind permission of the author and The Gallery Press, Loughcrew, Oldcastle, County Meath, Ireland.
- 'The Mayflower', 'Sonnet to Eva', and 'Aftermath' from *The Collected Poems of Sylvia Plath*, edited by Ted Hughes. © 1960, 1965, 1971, 1981 by the Estate of Sylvia Plath. Editorial material © 1981 by Ted Hughes. Reprinted by permission of HarperCollins Publishers.
- Edwin Morgan, 'Glasgow Sonnets', *Collected Poems*, by permission of Carcanet Press Limited.
- Andrew McNeillie, 'Glyn Dwr Sonnets', *Slower*, by permission of Carcanet Press Limited.

ACKNOWLEDGEMENTS

- Siegfried Sassoon, 'Remorse', 'Two Hundred Years After', 'Trench Duty', 'A Subaltern'. © Siegfried Sassoon by kind permission of the Estate of George Sassoon.
- Geoffrey Hill, from 'Requiem for the Plantagenet Kings', 'Funeral Music', 'Lachrimae', and 'An Apology for the Revival of Christian Architecture in England' from *Broken Hierarchies: Poems 1952–2012*, edited by Kenneth Haynes, by kind permission of the Estate of Geoffrey Hill.
- Tony Harrison, 'On Not Being Milton', 'Book Ends', 'Continuous', and 'Marked with D' from *Selected Poems*, by kind permission of the author.

Contents

Introduction	1
1. The Renaissance sonnet	15
2. The Romantic sonnet	80
3. The Victorian sonnet	123
4. The Irish sonnet	158
5. The American sonnet	220
6. The modern sonnet	286
Epilogue: The sonnet and its travels	392
Bibliography	403
Index	419

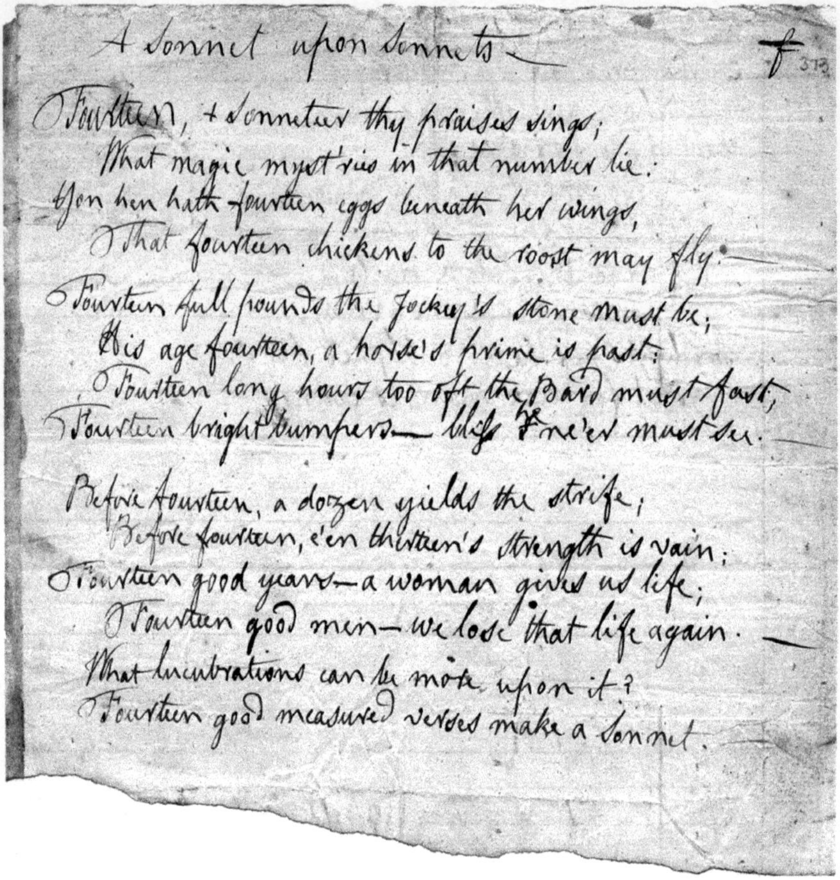
A Sonnet upon Sonnets—

Fourteen, a Sonneteer thy praises sings;
What magic myst'ries in that number lie:
Yon hen hath fourteen eggs beneath her wings,
That fourteen chickens to the roost may fly.—
Fourteen full pounds the Jockey's stone must be;
His age fourteen, a horse's prime is past;
Fourteen long hours too oft the Bard must fast;
Fourteen bright bumpers—bliss he ne'er must see.
Before Fourteen, a dozen yields the strife;
Before fourteen, e'en thirteen's strength is vain;
Fourteen good years—a woman gives us life;
Fourteen good men—we lose that life again.—
What lucubrations can be more upon it?
Fourteen good measured verses make a Sonnet.

Figure 1 Robert Burns, 'A Sonnet upon Sonnets', by kind permission of the National Trust for Scotland.

Introduction

The form of the sonnet

The sonnet is one of the oldest poetic forms and also one of the most widely travelled. Over several centuries it has come to be associated with intense imaginative life, and with an intimate exploration of thought and feeling. Although it has a well-established place in English poetic tradition, the sonnet is also a resilient and versatile form that continually invites experimentation and renewal. Some of the best-known poems in English are sonnets—among them 'Ozymandias', 'The Windhover', and 'Leda and the Swan'—and the most accomplished sonnets are poems, like these, that capture some profound and far-reaching vision, a powerful revelation, or a startling insight, in the space of just fourteen lines.[1] The challenge of finding an appropriate voice or capturing an impression within that circumscribed space continues to give the sonnet a special appeal among writers and readers alike. Primarily a love poem, the sonnet has extended its remit over the centuries, to become not only the pre-eminent form for the poetry of sexual desire and disillusionment, but also a form ideally suited to religious devotion, elegiac mourning, political protest, philosophical reflection, and topographical description. What distinguishes the sonnet over the course of its development, however, is not so much its variety of subject matter as its powerfully condensed expression of ideas and emotions, and its elaborate use of rhyme and rhythm for eloquent, persuasive speech.

   The sonnet is a *lyric* poem, and like other kinds of lyric poetry it appeals to its readers through those special qualities peculiar to the genre: brevity,

---

[1]. Percy Bysshe Shelley, *The Major Works*, ed. Zachary Leader and Michael O'Neill (Oxford: Oxford University Press, 2009), p. 198. Gerard Manley Hopkins, *The Major Works*, ed. Catherine Phillips (Oxford: Oxford University Press, 2009), p. 132; W. B. Yeats, *The Major Works*, ed. Edward Larrissy (Oxford: Oxford University Press, 2008), p. 112.

musicality, and intimacy. At the same time, the sonnet acquires its special distinctiveness by accommodating the rhythms and stresses of the speaking voice within its prescribed form. The brevity of the sonnet is one of its chief hallmarks, aptly summed up by the great Scots poet, Robert Burns, in the fourteenth line of his 'Sonnet upon Sonnets': 'Fourteen good measur'd verses make a sonnet'.[2] Even when the sonnet form is playfully curtailed to eleven or twelve lines (as it is by Gerard Manley Hopkins and W. B. Yeats) or willfully extended to sixteen lines (as it is by George Meredith and Tony Harrison), the experiment is measured against that time-honoured requirement of fourteen lines. Most practitioners of the sonnet, however, would probably claim that a little more elaboration is needed by way of definition. What gives the sonnet its structural identity, as we will see, is not just the number but also the deployment of its lines. The sonnet is a dynamic form, and its energy and momentum are generated through the articulation of carefully weighted structural components. The traditional division of the sonnet's fourteen lines into units of eight and six (an octave and a sestet) opens up considerable intellectual and emotional possibilities in terms of playing off one kind of statement or expression against another. The further division of fourteen lines into units of four and three (quatrains and tercets) multiplies these possibilities, encouraging a close correlation between intricate form and complex thought.

Burns speaks of *measured* lines, suggesting metre and musicality, and traditionally the measure associated with the sonnet written in English has been the staple line of iambic pentameter, a ten-syllable line with alternating stresses, as with this opening line from Shakespeare's Sonnet 104: 'To **me**, fair **friend**, you **never can** be **old**'.[3] Some of the most imposing effects in sonnet writing, however, have come from poets varying the stress patterns, either by crossing these with other modulations found in the speaking voice or by introducing different metrical patterns that disrupt the basic iambic rhythm. Burns himself ironically evades the good measured verse associated with the English sonnet, and lets his syllables spill over in a casually relaxed imitation of actual speech: 'Fourteen good measur'd verses make a sonnet'. Musicality in the sonnet is also produced by rhyme, and once again there is considerable room for variation and experimentation in the space of just

---

2. Robert Burns, *Poems and Songs*, ed. James Kinsley (Oxford: Oxford University Press, 1971), p. 357.
3. William Shakespeare, *The Complete Sonnets and Poems*, ed. Colin Burrow (Oxford: Oxford University Press, 2008), p. 589.

fourteen lines, with the octave-sestet and quatrain-tercet divisions encouraging patterns that can be adhered to or denied, in keeping with the subject matter and the function of each individual sonnet.

Just as important to the lyric appeal of the sonnet as its brevity and musicality is its intimacy. Though usually less obvious than its other qualities, the intimacy or 'interiority' of the sonnet is a vital part of its repertoire of effects. As Helen Vendler reminds us, lyric poems are principally poems of self-definition and self-declaration, and they avail themselves of a wide range of speech acts or utterances, including apology, celebration, command, consolation, debate, declaration, description, explanation, invitation, invocation, lament, meditation, narration, prayer, reproach, surmise, warning, and yearning. What characterizes the lyric poem above all else is its 'active process of thinking', and the sonnet arguably exemplifies this quality of lyric thinking, of 'thought made visible', more powerfully and persistently than any other poetic form. What Vendler memorably describes as 'the performance of the mind in solitary speech' in Shakespeare's sonnets holds good for many sonnets written earlier and later, encouraging us to appreciate the sonnet form as an intense kind of verse soliloquy.[4]

The lyrical qualities of brevity, musicality, and intimacy brought to fruition in the sonnet form can be readily observed in a poem written by John Keats in January 1818:

> When I have fears that I may cease to be
>   Before my pen has glean'd my teeming brain,
> Before high-piled books in charactery,
>   Hold like rich garners the full ripen'd grain;
> When I behold, upon the night's starr'd face,
>   Huge cloudy symbols of a high romance,
> And think that I may never live to trace
>   Their shadows, with the magic hand of chance:
> And when I feel, fair creature of an hour,
>   That I shall never look upon thee more,
> Never have relish in the faery power
>   Of unreflecting love;—then on the Shore
> Of the wide world I stand alone, and think
> Till love and fame to nothingness do sink.[5]

---

4. Helen Vendler, *Poets Thinking: Pope, Whitman, Dickinson, Yeats* (Cambridge, MA: Harvard University Press, 2004), p. 6. *The Art of Shakespeare's Sonnets* (Cambridge, MA: Harvard University Press, 1997), p. 2.
5. John Keats, *Poetical Works*, ed. H. W. Garrod (Oxford: Oxford University Press, 1970), p. 366.

The sonnet is movingly candid in declaring its fears of premature death and its anxious hopes of fulfilment in love and literary fame. What is most striking, though, is the way in which these fourteen lines vividly convey the subtle processes of thought and feeling. There is an articulate energy here, shaping the linguistic contours of the poem in a way that resembles the play of mind. The opening line is starkly and intimately in keeping with the brief duration of the sonnet itself, and the idea of imminent demise is carried through in the emphatic 'Before' and the repeated temporal clauses, 'When I behold' and 'when I feel'. Each 'when' marks the beginning of a quatrain, corresponding to a new phase of thought, and the third 'when' (line 9) also initiates a movement or turning from 'think' in the octave to 'feel' in the sestet, and from the speculative 'never live' to the more immediate 'never look'. We return to 'think' at the precarious end of the penultimate line, where the sonnet dramatically depicts the solitary mind in communion with itself. Keats shows us how the sonnet form is perfectly suited to an exploration of troubling, painful contraries, and how its tightly compressed shape paradoxically enables imaginative vistas of sublime intensity.

Keats's 'wide world' recalls the opening lines of Shakespeare's Sonnet 107 ('Not mine own fears, nor the prophetic soul | Of the wide world dreaming on things to come...'), and there is much that looks back to Shakespeare in this poem, including its temporal phrasing, its quatrain divisions, and its rhyme scheme.[6] This was, in fact, the first sonnet in which Keats fully attempted the Shakespearean form, with its alternating rhymes and closing couplet. Like many sonnets, including those of Shakespeare, it reveals a strong preoccupation not just with love and death, but with writing and reading, and with the value of poetry itself in a world overshadowed by ultimate 'nothingness'. At the same time, we can find in Keats's sonnet those qualities that perhaps belong more obviously to Romantic poetry, including its emphasis on what it is to 'feel' as well as think. We can also note those stylistic flourishes that are peculiarly Keats's own, including the strong caesura in line 12 and the fluent enjambment that follows, both of which allow for a subtle modulation of rhythm in the closing lines, and so avoid too neat a concluding statement in the couplet. In reading sonnets, we need to be alert both to convention (what is clearly tried and tested) and to innovation (what is generally untried and untested), and so it helps to be acquainted with the history and development of the form. Even when they

---

6. *The Complete Sonnets and Poems*, ed. Burrow, p. 595.

appear to be radically transgressive and disruptive, sonnets are often shaped by ideas and techniques that are already part of tradition.

The origins of the sonnet

The sonnet originated in Italy as early as 1230, acquiring its basic form in the writings of a small group of poets working at the court of Emperor Frederick II of Sicily. The poetic template of fourteen lines with an intricate rhyme scheme has been attributed to Giacomo da Lentino, the emperor's notary and legal assistant, who composed twenty-five sonnets with distinctive patterns of rhyme, either *abab abab cde cde* or *abab abab ccd ccd*.[7] The repetition and variation of rhyme, indicated here by the spacing, suggests that, from the outset, the sonnet was designed as a form with a dynamic internal structure: an octave (eight lines) and a sestet (six lines), which can be further divided into two quatrains (four lines) and two tercets (three lines). Literary historians refer to the 'invention' of the sonnet, rightly crediting its earliest practitioners with a degree of ingenuity, but in subject matter, at least, it was very likely inspired by the yearning love lyrics of the eleventh-century Provençal troubadour poets. Technically, the octave of the sonnet resembles the eight-line Sicilian peasant song known as the *strambotto*, and the sestet might well have been adapted from the existing *canzone*, another song-like form with stanzas of seven to twenty lines. In any case, the addition of the sestet to the octave, with a clearly marked turn or *volta* between them, creates a form more akin to speech than song, a discursive structure encouraging the progression of thought in meditation, reflection, and intellectual debate.

The name 'sonnet' comes from the Italian *sonetto*, a diminutive version of *suono*, meaning 'sound', and the idea of the sonnet as a small space or echo chamber for the sounding voice has inspired many of its finest achievements. The sound of the human voice, with all its various nuances and inflections, has informed and shaped the sonnet from the beginning. In court circles throughout Europe, eloquence was equated with power, an opportunity for the courtier to establish a position of respect and influence through elaborate and persuasive speech. Sonnets came to be associated with pleading and

---

7. Michael R. G. Spiller, *The Development of the Sonnet: An Introduction* (London: Routledge, 1992), p. 13.

bargaining, the eloquent speech of the lover functioning as an intimate enactment of larger power relations in court society. One of the persistent features of the sonnet is the assertion of a dramatized self or persona, a speaking voice that appeals to an imagined listener through a carefully staged set of arguments and explanations. Among a narrow social elite trained in law and philosophy, the sonnet functioned as an exercise in rhetorical persuasion and as an intellectual game or pastime. Sonnets were exchanged and circulated in a spirit of dialogue and competition, initially among small literary coteries in southern Italy, and then throughout Britain, France, Spain, and other parts of Europe.

The perfection of the Italian sonnet is generally associated with the work of its two greatest exponents, Dante Alighieri and Francis Petrarch (Francesco Petrarco), though the form was well established by the time they came to use it. Dante and Petrarch succeeded in elevating the sonnet as a form dedicated to the sorrows and sacred mysteries of love, and their influence on the so-called 'amatory tradition' lasted throughout the Renaissance and well into the nineteenth century. Shelley, in his inspiring 'Defence of Poetry' (1821), acknowledged Petrarch's poems as 'spells, which unseal the inmost enchanted fountains of the delight which is in the grief of love', and claimed that 'Dante understood the secret things of love even more than Petrarch'.[8] What Dante and Petrarch also established in the history of the form is the idea of the sonnet as part of a series or sequence that allows for narrative expansion and makes possible what we might now see as psychological exploration or emotional autobiography.

Dante's *Vita Nuova* (*c.*1292) incorporates twenty-five sonnets and a small number of other poems within an autobiographical and critical prose narrative recording the poet's childhood encounter with Beatrice and his flourishing love for her throughout his adult life. The apotheosis of Beatrice, the *donna angelicata* of the later *Divine Comedy*, instils the sonnets with an unprecedented emotional intensity and visionary beauty. The skills of rhetoric and verbal articulation associated with the early Italian sonnet are given a new lucidity and brilliance characteristic of the *dolce stil nuovo* ('sweet new style') of Dante's generation of poets. By the time Petrarch started writing sonnets in the 1330s, the sonnet form was already a century old and highly sophisticated as a poetic instrument of reasoning and argumentation. His *Rime Sparse*

---

8. Percy Bysshe Shelley, *The Major Works*, ed. Zachary Leader and Michael O'Neill (Oxford: Oxford University Press, 2003), p. 674.

('Scattered Verses'), also known as the *Canzoniere*, is a collection of 317 sonnets set alongside other poetic forms, including madrigals and ballads. Ostensibly addressed to Laura de Sade, who was born in Avignon and died there of the Black Plague in 1348, the sonnets have an extraordinary power to convey the pleasures and torments of love, and they do so with an intense and sensitive understanding of the divided self that would strike many readers as paradigmatically modern. Without the spiritual resolution of Dante's *Vita Nuova*, Petrarch's sonnets confront the fierce tensions and contraries endured by the self in its quest for beauty and love. In candidly depicting the painful suffering of love, as well as its glorious pleasures and desires, and in fashioning a speaker sometimes on the edge of incoherence and breakdown, Petrarch provided the most powerful inspiration for the love poetry of Renaissance Europe.

What came to be known as the Petrarchan sonnet consists of an octave in enclosed or envelope rhymes rather than in open or alternating rhymes (*abbaabba* rather than *abababab*) and a sestet typically rhymed *cdecde* or *cdcdcd* (occasionally with another variation such as *cdedce* or *cdeced*). The open octave (*abbaabba*) was already being used by Guittone d'Arezzo and other poets of the *stilnovisti* well before the end of the thirteenth century, but Petrarch is generally credited with having consolidated the Italian form, bringing it to a new standard of technical expertise in his *Rime*. As John Fuller points out, 'The essence of the sonnet's form is the unequal relationship between octave and sestet', and that structural relationship has enormous semantic potential in terms of how a sonnet might progress and open up multiple perspectives and interpretive possibilities.[9] The bipartite structure of octave and sestet allows for a number of possible intellectual and emotional developments, including observation and conclusion, and statement and counter-statement, with the turn between the eighth line and the ninth line signalling a shift in mood or opinion, or else an intensification or reaffirmation of an existing idea or feeling.

Within this larger structural framework, however, the quatrain and tercet subdivisions encourage a more complex and complicated set of relationships. The first quatrain, for instance, might ask a question or propose an idea that the second quatrain then answers or elaborates upon. The first tercet then proceeds to prove the point or test its veracity, while the second tercet moves towards resolution and conclusion. The logical procedures of the

---

9. John Fuller, *The Sonnet* (London: Methuen, 1972), p. 2.

sonnet are reinforced by prosody, in that the eight lines of closed rhyme in the octave have a steady movement induced by repetition, while the sestet is likely to appear unpredictable, as well as more intense and urgent, with three rhymes in six lines coming quickly after two rhymes in eight. Within the compressed space of the sonnet, the distribution of pauses induced by mid-line punctuation and the pace resulting from the alternation of run-on lines and end-stopped lines are all the more effective in channelling and controlling the flow of thought and meaning. What the sonnet demonstrates very clearly and decisively is the dynamic relationship between form and subject matter.

It was not until the early sixteenth century that the sonnet became established in the vernacular languages of Britain, France, and Spain. The Petrarchan sonnet enjoyed a new lease of life in courtly circles, often introduced by diplomats travelling between Italy and other European countries. The first sonnets in English were written by Sir Thomas Wyatt and Henry Howard, Earl of Surrey, both closely associated with the court of Henry VIII. Some of these sonnets are rough translations and versions of Petrarch's *Rime*, but in their concern with decorum, conduct, and eloquence they articulate the values and attitudes of English court life. The courtly discourse of these early English sonnets, brimming with dedications and compliments, reveals a strong commitment to ideals of honour and service, but it also brings with it an underlying anxiety about position and status, and (especially in Wyatt's writings) a deep sense of political insecurity.

Wyatt not only imported the Petrarchan sonnet into Britain but also introduced a major structural change, reorganizing the sestet so that it functioned effectively as a third quatrain with a closing couplet: *abba abba cddc ee* (as the spacing here suggests). This innovation subtly alters the dynamics of the sonnet, giving it force and progression as an instrument of reasoning and disputation, with the couplet sometimes serving as a witty apophthegm or proverbial maxim, an opportunity for the display of courtly wisdom and worldliness. Where the couplet coincides with a sense unit or stands as an independent syntactical entity, its clinching effect is all the more emphatic and decisive. Michael Spiller sees Wyatt's technical handling of the sonnet in relation to 'a secular world of practical courtly reality', with the couplet helping to shape a preoccupation with 'the practical wisdoms of secular humanist court life'.[10]

---

10. Michael Spiller, *Early Modern Sonneteers: From Wyatt to Milton* (Tavistock: Northcote House, 2001), p. 20.

Surrey further amended the structure of the nascent English sonnet by adopting alternating rhymes in the octave, and by introducing a greater variety of rhyme words than the Italian sonnet possessed, so facilitating the challenge of rhyming in English: *abab cdcd efef gg*. This is the form that came to be known as the English or Shakespearean sonnet, even though it would be another half century or so before Shakespeare widely popularized the form and employed it with an unprecedented stylistic brilliance in his *Sonnets* (1609). Wyatt and Surrey never saw their sonnets in print, but their poems were collected and published by Richard Tottel in a volume titled *Songes and Sonettes, written by the right honorable Lorde Henry Haward late Earle of Surrey, and other* (1557), later referred to simply as *Tottel's Miscellany*.

The history of the sonnet in Britain in the later part of the sixteenth century, from Wyatt and Surrey to Shakespeare, is dominated by the huge success and popularity of the sonnet sequence. The holy sonnets in *A Meditation of a Penitent Sinner* (1560) by Anne Lok (also spelled Locke) constitute the first sequence in English, but the tradition of passionate, erotic sonnets in a narrative or autobiographical sequence is prompted by Thomas Watson's eighteen-line (sonnet-like) love poems in *Hekatompathia* (1582). The final decade of the sixteenth century witnessed some of the most prolific and inventive sonnet writing of the Elizabethan period, with Sir Philip Sidney's *Astrophil and Stella* (1591) and Edmund Spenser's *Amoretti* (1595) among its notable achievements. Samuel Daniel's *Delia* (1592) and Michael Drayton's *Ideas Mirrour* (1595), later retitled *Idea*, went through numerous editions and reprints in the late 1590s and early 1600s, testifying to the growing readership and popular interest that the sonnet attracted at the time.

For all the imaginative ambitiousness and dramatic potential invested in the sonnet sequence, it is invariably the local stylistic effects of individual sonnets that readers respond to and recall. One of the most frequently anthologized sonnets from Drayton's *Idea* shows how well a single love sonnet can make an impact, even when abstracted from its sequence:

> Since there's no help, come let us kiss and part.
> Nay, I have done: you get no more of me,
> And I am glad, yea glad with all my heart
> That thus so cleanly I myself can free.
> Shake hands for ever, cancel all our vows,
> And when we meet at any time again,
> Be it not seen in either of our brows
> That we one jot of former love retain.
> Now at the last gasp of love's latest breath,

> When, his pulse failing, passion speechless lies,
> When faith is kneeling by his bed of death
> And innocence is closing up his eyes,
> Now, if thou would'st, when all have given him over,
> From death to life thou might'st him yet recover.[11]

What Drayton captures so well here, in a style that we also find in the sonnets of Sir Philip Sidney and John Donne, is the impression of a passionate, personal outburst and dramatic confrontation. The lively colloquial tenor is maintained through repeated imperatives and associated gestures ('Come let us kiss... Shake hands for ever...'), as well as through the short, impassioned exclamations, 'Nay' and 'yea'. The sonnet vividly contrasts the torments of an enslaving love with its miraculous recovery, just as it shows us both the speaker's proud disdain and his desperate hopes. There is obvious wit in the shape and direction of the sonnet, in the way that it begins with a strong sense of closure—'You get no more of me'—and closes with a possible new beginning. There is a touch of comic farce, as well, in the scuttling personifications of love, passion, faith, and innocence. All of these stylistic effects, however, are carefully orchestrated within the overriding formal structure provided by the octave-sestet division and the quatrain-couplet sub-division. The first quatrain (*abab*) issues a strong declaration of parting, and the second quatrain (*cdcd*) reiterates and intensifies it. The turn between octave and sestet is clearly indicated by the temporal marker, 'Now', repeated emphatically at the beginning of the closing couplet. The third quatrain (*efef*) moves towards the final extinction of love, but dramatically suspends the process through the repeated conjunction 'When', allowing the couplet (here syntactically connected rather than independent) to effect a further turn and assert the possibility of recovery.

Before the 1590s, the term 'sonnet' appears to have been used very loosely in England to describe any short lyric poem. It was also conveniently grouped with 'songs', as in the title of John Donne's *Songs and Sonnets* (1633), a book which, strictly speaking, contains no sonnets at all. The Elizabethan poet George Gascoine was clearly alert to the possible confusion regarding the English sonnet, helpfully offering one of the earliest definitions of the form in 1575:

> Then have you sonnets: some think that all poems (being short) may be called sonnets, as in deed it is a diminutive word derived of *sonare*, but yet I can best

---

11. *The Oxford Book of Sonnets*, ed. John Fuller (Oxford: Oxford University Press, 2000), p. 35.

allow to call those sonnets which are of fourteen lines, every line containing ten syllables. The first twelve do rhyme in staves of four lines by cross metre, and the last two rhyming together do conclude the whole.[12]

What Gascoine confirms here, and what is clearly borne out in the work of Drayton and Shakespeare and others, is that the sonnet gradually becomes established in England as a form with particular structural characteristics: not just a short poem of fourteen lines, but one with strong internal dynamics, deriving from strictly observed line length and rhyme scheme, and from the interplay of its constituent parts. To appreciate the special appeal of the sonnet most fully, and to measure its ambitions and achievements, we need to regard it both synchronically (identifying common and persistent structural features) and diachronically (observing how it evolves under changing social conditions). The fascination of the sonnet for readers and writers alike is that it calls for discipline and constraint while simultaneously inviting endless permutation and innovation.

The politics of the sonnet

The aim of this book is to provide the first comprehensive study of the sonnet in English from the Renaissance to the present, both attending to the distinctive structural qualities of the sonnet as demonstrated in specific examples by notable poets, and exploring the ways in which the sonnet form registers the clashes and collisions of history, from the English Civil War and the revolutionary politics of the Romantic period to the First World War and the violent conflicts of the modern world. It considers the sonnet in terms of *attitude*, *address*, and *adaptability*. It asks in relation to *attitude* what kind of structural identity the sonnet has. What ways of thought and feeling are characteristic of the form? What can it do that the limerick or the villanelle, for instance, might not be able to accomplish? The book further explores, in terms of *address*, how the sonnet approaches its subject matter. How does it speak about particular kinds of experience, and how does it appeal to its listeners? The principal concern of the book is with the *adaptability* of the sonnet, with its prolonged use and persistence over several centuries, and with its transmission as a poetic form across geographical, as

---

12. George Gascoine, 'Certain Notes of Instruction', *Elizabethan Critical Essays*, ed. Gregory Smith (Oxford: Oxford University Press, 1904), vol. 1, p. 55. Spelling has been modernized.

well as historical, terrain. The methods used are those of historical formalism, which involves some lengthy and detailed exposition of individual sonnets at the level of diction, syntax, rhyme, and rhythm, as well as attention to the specific social and political circumstances in which the poetry was composed.

The development of the sonnet can be explained, to some extent, by genre theory, which has shown how certain kinds of literature are given to historical variation and transformation. The idea that genres are mutable lends credence to the argument that the sonnet is a versatile and flexible instrument that can be modified in shape according to its function. The poetic form that comes to be known as the sonnet is already a generic mixture, which is yet another reason for treating with caution any suggestion of a 'true' or 'legitimate' sonnet form that ought to take priority over transgressive or illicit types. As Jahan Ramazani has thoughtfully noted in *Poetry and its Others* (2014), 'Genres change as they absorb and resist other genres'.[13] This intergeneric dialogue exists between different poetic forms—between the sonnet and the elegy, for instance, or even the sonnet and the novel—but it extends to formal relationships between poetry and many other forms of discourse, including letters, sermons, prayers, songs, political speeches, journalism, and the news. The sonnets discussed in this book have a surprisingly wide and ambitious generic reach, sometimes purporting to be 'epic' poems (as with Patrick Kavanagh's sonnet of that title), and sometimes entering into dialogue with popular song and recitation, religious liturgy, political debate, and news reports (even the shipping forecast). A key argument in the kind of dialogic poetics proposed in *Poetry and its Others* is that 'individual works both activate and press against the genre assumptions brought to bear on them'.[14] This, too, has been a guiding principle in seeking to show how the sonnet form has been both adopted and perpetually renewed.

In seeking to show how the sonnet develops over several centuries, the book is careful not to suggest some manifest evolution of the form or to imply that there is a gradual refinement of its stylistic repertoire as it becomes more widely used. It does, however, try to show the diverse ways in which the sonnet has been brought into play, whether as love poem or elegy, and it offers a critical evaluation of the rhetorical achievements of the form. One of the insights to be derived from this kind of genre-based study is that

---

13. Jahan Ramazani, *Poetry and its Others: News, Prayer, Song, and the Dialogue of Genres* (Chicago: University of Chicago Press, 2014), p. 5.
14. Ramazani, *Poetry and its Others*, p. 4.

sonnets are often inspired by other sonnets, to the extent that individual poems and groups of poems appear to be in conversation with each other. To trace the influence of Milton in the sonnets of Shelley and Wordsworth and Tony Harrison, or to note the ways in which Edna St Vincent Millay and Sylvia Plath resist the sonnet strategies of their poetic predecessors, is to have a better understanding of the sonnet tradition as a whole.

Sonnets respond to other sonnets, but they also respond to social and historical actualities in ways that are perhaps more difficult to determine. It is tempting to suggest, in a grand teleological sweep, that the sonnet begins life in the realm of love poetry and shifts its allegiance to politics, and that a prestige form with its origins in European courtly society ends up as a protest poem on the streets of America. To move swiftly from Sir Philip Sidney's *Astrophil and Stella* to Claude McKay's 'America' might give us reason to think so. What a broad historical study of this kind reveals, however, is that the sonnet has always been deeply implicated in politics, and always uneasily preoccupied with power. The brevity and dialectical structure of the sonnet are well suited to political intervention and debate, and there are many distinguished examples of sonnets (by Milton, Shelley, Wordsworth, Keats, Tennyson, Auden, and others) that show how a form often associated with private introspection can modulate into public outcry and polemic. The sonnet is well disposed to political debate precisely *because of*, and not *in spite of*, its lyrical qualities. The solitary mind that informs the sonnet is often disenchanted with the world, desiring a better place and time. In its brief glimpses of futurity, the sonnet cannot help but prompt reflection on the meaning and value of the world around it, and many sonnets measure their own soaring imaginative aspirations against the vanity and hollowness of worldly power. Even while questioning their own artistic durability, Shakespeare's sonnets repeatedly inveigh against the might of princes and kings, setting their own lyrical beauty against material wealth.

Studying the history of the sonnet over several centuries prompts a decisive rethinking of the maps we make of poetry. With this kind of long perspective, we can better appreciate and explain the achievements of poets who belong indubitably to that much-contested territory, the literary canon. At the same time, there is an opportunity to bring into focus some extraordinary poetic accomplishments that have tended to be forgotten or neglected. It is only when we survey the field in this way that we grasp the full significance of Elizabeth Barrett Browning's *Sonnets from the Portuguese* (1847), not only as a bold intervention in the tradition of sonnet writing by a Victorian woman writer, but as the first major sequence of love sonnets published in English since the Renaissance. In the same way, it is only by challenging some of the critical orthodoxies about the demise of lyric poetry in the twentieth century that we can fully appreciate the audacious talent of Edna St Vincent Millay or the stylistic adventurousness of Robert Frost. In this study, Frost emerges as one of the most distinguished practitioners of the sonnet in English, deserving extensive critical attention. More surprising, perhaps, Rupert Brooke is also given serious consideration as a poet whose experiments with the sonnet vastly exceed what might be suggested by his best-known work, 'The Soldier'. We can readily acknowledge in a broad historical study of this kind how the sonnet both accommodated and resisted the violence of the First World War, and how it maintained its appeal for poets such as Wilfred Owen and Ivor Gurney. That knowledge, in turn, helps us to explain why the sonnet had a special attraction for later poets such as W. H. Auden, Geoffrey Hill, and Tony Harrison, all of whom regard the sonnet as a form deeply inscribed by the experience of war.

The study of the sonnet is, in the end, a study of poetry at its most intense. Sonnets, perhaps more than other forms of poetry, reflect on their own making and their own being. The writing of sonnets engenders new and different forms. The sonnets of Keats provide the constituent verse elements for his better-known odes, while the sonnet sequences of Wordsworth on nature and liberty acquire an epic ambitiousness that generates his great autobiographical work, *The Prelude*. In the later nineteenth century, George Meredith writes a troubled sonnet sequence of unhappy love that comes to resemble a French realist novel, while Gerard Manley Hopkins subjects the religious, devotional sonnet to formal pressures exceeding even the daring innovations of John Donne's magnificent *Holy Sonnets*. Auden's sonnets written in China are an integral part of an experimental travelogue co-authored with Christopher Isherwood. The prolific sonnets written by Sylvia Plath and Philip Larkin as youthful aspiring poets can be seen to underpin the virtuosic handling of line and metre and rhythm in their later work. Tony Harrison's masterwork is purposefully titled *from The School of Eloquence* to suggest that this is a sonnet sequence still in the process of composition and one that might never be completed. The sonnet will never cease to surprise its readers in its endless inventiveness, so that even if we never settle on a single, satisfactory definition of the sonnet, we can at least be sure of its continuing vitality.

I

The Renaissance sonnet

The flourishing of the English Renaissance sonnet from the early 1500s to the mid-1600s owes much to the cultural endeavours of two courtiers in the reign of Henry VIII: Sir Thomas Wyatt and Henry Howard, Earl of Surrey. Although their sonnets were small in number and modest in scope, they effectively established a strong tradition of sonnet writing in English that would persist well beyond their own short-lived careers. Wyatt and Surrey were instrumental in promoting and popularizing the work of Petrarch through their lively translations and versions of his work, but in the process they also modified the established Italian sonnet structure in ways that would allow the English vernacular tongue to speak most eloquently in verse. What becomes known as the English sonnet is not a sudden discovery, but the product of exploratory stylistic endeavour and a continual reaching for a credible speaking voice that might be accommodated within the basic fourteen-line structure inherited from Italian poets. About half of Wyatt's sonnets (17 out of 33) are versions of Petrarch's poems. Some of these are close translations, while others are loose adaptations based on memorable words and phrases.[1] We can learn a good deal about the development of the English sonnet and its relationship with the Italian form by looking carefully at particular instances of translation and imitation.

Sir Thomas Wyatt and Henry Howard, Earl of Surrey

Wyatt's sonnet beginning 'The long love that in my thought doth harbour' is a line-by-line translation of Petrarch's *Rime* 140, and a brief analysis of

---

1. Quotations from Petrarch are from *Canzoniere*, ed. and translated by Anthony Mortimer (London: Penguin, 2002). Quotations from Wyatt are from *Collected Poems*, ed. Joost Daalder (London: Oxford University Press, 1975). Page numbers are given within brackets in the text.

the two poems together is revealing in terms of the dynamics of form and content.

> Amor, che nel penser mio vive et regna
> e 'l suo seggio maggior nel mio cor tene,
> talor armato ne la fronte vene;
> ivi si loca et ivi pon sua insegna.
>
> Quella ch'amare et sofferir ne 'nsegna
> e vol che 'l gran desio, l'accesa spene
> ragion, vergogna, et reverenza affrene,
> di nostro ardir fra se stessa si sdegna.
>
> Onde Amor paventoso fugge al core,
> lasciando ogni sua impresa, et piange et trema;
> ivi s'asconde et non appar più fore.
>
> Che poss'io far, temendo il mio signore,
> se non star seco infin a l'ora estrema?
> Ché bel fin fa chi ben amando more.   (77)
>
> The long love that in my thought doth harbour
> And in mine heart doth keep his residence,
> Into my face presseth with bold pretence,
> And therein campeth, spreading his banner.
> She that me learneth to love and suffer
> And will that my trust and lust's negligence
> Be reined by reason, shame and reverence,
> With his hardiness taketh displeasure.
> Wherewithal unto the heart's forest he fleeth,
> Leaving his enterprise with pain and cry,
> And there him hideth, and not appeareth.
> What may I do, when my master feareth,
> But in the field with him to live and die?
> For good is the life ending faithfully.   (4)

One of the obvious structural features that the sonnets share is a strong turn, marking in both poems a shift from bold declaration to pained abandonment, but within the octave-sestet division (8 + 6) it is possible to discern a further division of both sonnets into two quatrains and two tercets (4 + 4 + 3 + 3). These sub-divisions correspond in both cases to a clear progression of images and ideas: the military metaphor of Love coming forth in armour and setting up his banner; the displeasure of the beloved, who teaches 'reason, shame and reverence'; the retreat and hiding of Love; and the closing commitment to a life of loyalty. The four-part arrangement suggested by syntax and punctuation is supported in Petrarch's sonnet by an equivalent rhyme scheme: *abba abba cdc cdc*. In Wyatt's sonnet, however, there is a slight variation, so that the rhyme scheme doesn't quite match the divisions suggested by syntax: *abbaabbacdccdd*. By simply substituting Petrarch's final *c* rhyme with a *d* rhyme, Wyatt produces a closing couplet. In this instance, however, the strength of the couplet is not pronounced, partly because it is ushered in by the preceding couplet with feminine rhymes ('appeareth'/'feareth') and partly because it depends on the enjambment between lines 12 and 13. Syntactically, we have a two-line question followed by a single line of reflection. As with Petrarch's original, the ending is subdued.

In other respects, Wyatt's translation shows signs of individuality and creative freedom. The neatly alliterative 'long love' in the opening line looks forward to the wit and daring of the metaphysical poets, especially John Donne and Andrew Marvell, and this boldness is generally in keeping with Wyatt's determination to give love a more vivid realization and physical presence than it assumes in the work of his Italian predecessor. The verb 'harbour' serves this purpose, suggesting a more homely and familiar location than the regal setting of Petrarch's sonnet, in which love 'lives and reigns' ('vive et regna') in the speaker's thoughts. The image of 'the heart's forest' in the sestet of Wyatt's sonnet has no equivalent in Petrarch's poem.

What Wyatt appears to be drawn to in this and other versions of Petrarch's sonnets is the implied emotional turbulence and instability of love. There is a powerful duality here between candid declaration and shamed concealment that structures other sonnets by Wyatt, including his best-known translation of Petrarch, 'Whoso list to hunt'. This time, the engagement with Petrarch is so profound and the imaginative conception so striking that what results is much more than a literal translation. Petrarch's *Rime* 190 records the magical appearance and disappearance of a white doe, the sacred emblem of the Goddess Diana and here an emblem of the speaker's own beloved Laura. The poem emphasizes the unripe season of love and evokes its sense of a fading vision through the turning away of the midday sun and the speaker falling into water. There is no suggestion of a hunt and no suggestion of pained defeat and weariness, such as we find in Wyatt's version of the poem. What in Petrarch is construed as delight is transformed in Wyatt's sonnet into disappointment. The metaphor of the hunt both conveys the impression of struggle and turns the private, meditative vision of Petrarch's poem into a public arena.

> Whoso list to hunt: I know where is an hind.
> But as for me, alas I may no more:
> The vain travail hath wearied me so sore,
> I am of them that farthest cometh behind.
> Yet may I by no means my wearied mind
> Draw from the deer, but as she fleeth afore
> Fainting I follow. I leave off therefore,
> Sithens in a net I seek to hold the wind.
> Who list her hunt, I put him out of doubt,
> As well as I may spend his time in vain,
> And graven with diamonds in letters plain
> There is written her fair neck round about:
> '*Noli me tangere*, for Caesar's I am,
> And wild for to hold, though I seem tame.' (7)

Wyatt's sonnet stresses the vain nature of pursuit and the painfulness of desire. It tends towards a critical, almost cynical, analysis of the seemingly endless chase rather than an awed fascination with the mysteries of love. In both poems Caesar effectively issues an edict of chastity, but while in *Rime* 190 he appears as an all-powerful God, conferring freedom as well as expecting obedience, in Wyatt's sonnet he is more evidently a political ruler with a lust for physical possession. Wyatt's adoption of the vulgate Latin *Noli me tangere* from John (20:17) recalls Christ's appearance before Mary Magdalene after his resurrection and seems to reinforce an ethic of Christian trust and obedience, but the emphatic declaration, 'Caesar's I am' and the strongly physical 'wild for to hold' collide with this suggestion and point surreptitiously towards the political and sexual intrigues of Wyatt's own time. Not surprisingly, many commentators have identified Caesar as Henry VIII. F. W. Bateson, in a popular introduction to English poetry written in 1950, confidently announced that 'Wyatt's hind is Anne Boleyn, who was almost certainly his mistress before she was appropriated by Henry VIII', and many critics and editors of Wyatt's poetry have endorsed this view.[2] Though undoubtedly the poem derives from considerations of power and privilege *outside* Petrarch's *Rime* 190, its enduring appeal has much to do with its reluctance and inability to be explicit. The rhetorical devices it employs are subtly allusive and indirect. An eagerness to associate the poem with the immediate circumstances of Wyatt's alleged affair with Anne Boleyn prior to her marriage with the monarch detracts from its more general and far-reaching

---

2. F. W. Bateson, *English Poetry: A Critical Introduction* (London: Longman, 1950; 1966), p. 101.

concern with sexual and political contestation, but also inhibits an adequate understanding of how the poem functions as a sonnet.

In one of the most influential and persuasive readings of Wyatt's poetry, Stephen Greenblatt argues that the power of implication in the writing is heightened by Wyatt's ambassadorial experience, and that, in many ways, the poems are themselves acts of diplomacy. He finds a plausible link between erotic disillusionment in Wyatt's poems and his acquaintance with techniques of doubleness and deception in the diplomatic service. This recognition complicates our responses as readers to the voices that we detect in the poems, and also alerts us to the possibility of masquerade and indirection. Greenblatt's analysis of 'Who so list to hunt' valuably draws attention to the way in which 'The whole poem is caught up in a series of suspensions, or alternatives, in *passages* from one state to another.'[3] The speaker of the poem is suspended between renunciation and continued commitment to the hunt, while the woman pursued (the metaphorical hind) appears to be both wild and tame. Disillusionment with the operations of political power and the competition for position and status finds a powerful outlet in the conventions of the love lyric and the voice of the cautious, disappointed lover.

Renaissance diplomacy intensifies an already heightened awareness among poets of the politics of language and the subtle skills of rhetorical contrivance. As we have seen, the sonnet form is already deeply implicated in courtly power relations by the time it reaches Renaissance England. Petrarch's pictorial and descriptive opening to *Rime* 190 gives way in translation to a strong rhetorical immediacy and pointed address. The confident assertion of Wyatt's opening line, however, is quickly undermined by the exclamatory 'alas' and the diminution of what follows. The sonnet remains suspended, as Greenblatt suggests, between renunciation and commitment.

The strong sense of compactness and tightness in the poem is assisted by a fondness for alliterative lines. 'Hunt' and 'hind' in the opening line have a pleasing phonological likeness, and we then have in quick succession a related set of pairings in 'means' and 'mind', 'draw' and 'deer', and 'Fainting I follow'. Structurally, the sonnet makes strategic use of both the octave-sestet division and the quatrain-couplet arrangement dictated by the rhyme scheme. Petrarch's sonnet has its *volta* effectively marked by the letters on the collar

---

3. Stephen Greenblatt, *Renaissance Self-Fashioning: From More to Shakespeare* (Chicago: University of Chicago Press, 1980), p. 147.

of the animal—'Nessun mi tocchi'—but Wyatt's sonnet delays its '*Noli me tangere*' until the further turn provided by the closing couplet. The octave-sestet division in Wyatt's sonnet repeats the opening announcement in 'Who list her hunt', but this time the stirring suggestions of romantic encounter and amatory quest are emphatically denied. The unlikely prospect of possessing the hind is reinforced by the typographical and phonological similarities in the closing line of the octave and the closing line of the sestet: 'hold the wind' and 'wild for to hold'. What Wyatt bequeaths to later English writers of the sonnet is a strongly marked progression of thought and feeling, assisted by prominent conjunctions—'But... Yet... And'—which coincide with line openings. He also shows a fondness for the mid-line caesura, here effectively capturing the speaker's stops and starts in lines 6 and 7.

Wyatt's rhyme scheme preserves the *abbaabba* octave of the Petrarchan sonnet, but makes a decisive adjustment in the sestet, replacing *cdecde* with *cddcee*. In this instance, the closing couplet is neatly introduced by the preceding line, 'There is written', and takes on the force of declaration. 'Am' and 'tame' are full rhymes for Wyatt, but the rhetorical conclusiveness of the poem derives in part from a slight irregularity in the number of syllables in the closing couplet, and from a crucial pause in the final line. The control of syntax through punctuation and the tendency to play off syntactical features against metrical patterns become familiar aspects of English sonnet writing after Wyatt. If Wyatt can be credited with having made 'the first formal change in the structure of the sonnet since its invention in southern Italy in the early thirteenth century', he also deserves recognition for his daring political move in writing a thinly veiled allegory of monarchic power and the dangers of courtly life.[4]

Like Wyatt, Surrey tries his hand at the sonnet form in a small number of poems modelled on Italian examples (including a version of Petrarch's *Rime* 140 discussed above, p. 16). Whereas Wyatt infuses the originals with his own distinctive boldness, vigour, and urgency, Surrey is apt to cultivate a smoother, more elegant, and refined alternative. One of Surrey's best-known sonnets, 'Set me whereas the sun doth parch the green', is a loose translation of Petrarch's *Rime* 145, 'Ponmi ove 'l sole occide i fiori et l'erba':

> Set me wheras the sonne dothe perche the grene,
> Or whear his beames may not dissolve the ise;
> In temprat heat wheare he is felt and sene;

---

4. Michael Spiller, *The Development of the Sonnet: An Introduction* (London: Routledge, 1992), p. 84.

> With prowde people, in presence sad and wyse;
> Set me in base, or yet in highe degree,
> In the long night, or in the shortyst day,
> In clere weather, or whear mysts thikest be,
> In loste yowthe, or when my heares be grey;
> Set me in earthe, in heaven, or yet in hell,
> In hill, in dale, or in the fowming floode;
> Thrawle, or at lage, alive whersoo I dwell,
> Sike, or in healthe, in yll fame or in good:
> Yours will I be, and with that onely thought
> Comfort my self when that my hape is nowght.[5]

Although the language of Surrey's sonnet is appealingly conversational, it retains some of the structural features of the original, especially the repeated imperative, 'Set me'. Petrarch opens lines 1, 5, 9, and 12 with 'Ponmi' ('place me'), explicitly drawing attention to the quatrain-tercet units and playing down the octave-sestet division. Surrey sets up a similar momentum based on the commanding verb at the opening of lines 1, 5, and 9, but the structural pattern he emphasizes is that of three quatrains and a closing couplet. In place of Petrarch's familiar *abbaabbacdcdcd*, he gives us *ababcdcdefefgg*. The function of the couplet is to introduce and declare a commitment to an addressee who is significantly absent in Petrarch's sonnet: 'Yours will I be.' More decisive in structural terms, however, is the inspired decision to arrange the rhymes in an alternating (rather than enclosed) pattern and to introduce a change of rhyme in the second quatrain of the octave (*cdcd*). This is the structure that many later sonnet writers, including Shakespeare, would employ, and the one that would generally be acknowledged as 'the English sonnet'.

Petrarch's sonnet and Surrey's version are notably concerned with the whims of hap or fortune, though line 5 of Surrey's poem resonates with the brisk epithets of English social hierarchy: 'Set me in base, or yet in highe degree'. The vocabulary reminds us that, from the very outset, the sonnet was implicated in power relations, and that its subsequent shaping was political, as well as poetical. When Richard Tottel published his influential collection of *Songes and Sonettes* in 1557, strongly promoting the sonnet in English, he set Surrey in 'highe degree', giving his work prominence over that of Wyatt in the ordering of the book and titling the first edition *Songes*

---

5. Henry Howard, Earl of Surrey, *Poems*, ed. Emrys Jones (Oxford: Clarendon Press, 1964), pp. 2–3. Further page numbers are given within brackets in the text.

and Sonettes, written by the ryght honorable Lorde Henry Haward late Earle of Surrey, and other. The poems included in *Tottel's Miscellany* (as it became known) suggest, however, that Surrey's social privileges did not render him immune to anxieties about rank and fortune. A number of the sonnets by Surrey are lover's 'complaints' in which 'desire' might be understood more generally in terms of the poet's social aspirations and ambitions. The sonnets speak eloquently of pained rejection and despair, of how 'the spote of change infects the mynd', and of how 'My service thus is growne into disdayne' (3). The mood of the sonnets, shifting anxiously between joy and sorrow, dejection and hope, is aptly and memorably summed up in Surrey's confession of 'doutfull ease' (4). Neither Wyatt nor Surrey lived to see their sonnets in print, and it is largely due to Tottel that their troubled legacy survives. Wyatt spent several months of 'doutfull ease' in the Tower of London in 1536 and died in 1542, and Surrey was executed on charges of treason in 1547. The foundations for an English sonnet had been established, and what remained was the question of its aggregation: how to collect and organize sonnets for printing and reading. The idea of a 'sonnet sequence' in English would be taken up by later poets, including Sir Philip Sidney and Lady Mary Wroth.

Sir Philip Sidney

Sir Philip Sidney's reputation as the very epitome of the Renaissance courtier—soldier, scholar, poet, lover—is still so strong and alluring as to encourage a largely biographical reading of his sparkling sonnet sequence, *Astrophil and Stella*. There is a persistent critical tendency to regard the most innovative and dynamic aspects of the sequence as profoundly expressive of a complex and extraordinary personality. The sonnets appear to endorse a biographical reading, both emphasizing a candid and confessional revelation of personal conflicts and crises, and freely alluding to contemporary social and political events. Familiar places and people are invoked to create a strong semblance of actuality, and this includes both a playful use of the name Philip (Sonnet 83) and a provocative (and potentially libellous) series of puns on the married surname (Rich) of Penelope Devereux, daughter of the First Earl of Essex, who is commonly thought to have inspired the sonnets in 1581–2.

What makes *Astrophil and Stella* such an original and compelling achievement, however, is not its daring exposure of some real-life love affair, but the technical expertise with which it adopts and transforms existing conventions of love poetry, audaciously sustaining a sequence of 108 sonnets and 11 'songs'. The subtlety and complexity of the sequence are such that autobiography takes its place as just one of many frames or conventions by which experience is registered and explored throughout the poem. The self-conscious construction of a personality and a speaking voice is fundamental to the poem's critical preoccupation with truth and fiction. The poem openly acknowledges that speaking from the heart is, itself, a familiar convention, and indeed much of the enduring interest and appeal of *Astrophil and Stella* derives from its metapoetic activity, including its persistent reflection on its own making and its own material existence as writing. While ostensibly recording the unrequited love of Astrophil, the star lover, for Stella, the distant star, the sonnet sequence repeatedly draws attention to its own fictions and fabrications.

To read *Astrophil and Stella* as autobiography or even as semi-autobiography is to risk diminishing its intense fascination with the processes of poetic creativity and composition. While at one level the poem subtly effaces any distinction between poet and persona, it also creates a degree of ironic distance between them, so that the first-person voice, the plausible 'I' of the poem, remains an unstable entity, always subject to critique and exposure. This inherent instability extends to the very title of the poem. Is it *Astrophil and Stella* or *Astrophel and Stella*? There is no evidence to suggest that Sidney himself devised a title for the sequence. 'Astrophil' appears in the eighth and ninth songs in the manuscript, but *Astrophel and Stella* was chosen as the title for the first edition in 1591, five years after Sidney's death. Astrophil neatly combines the Greek words for 'star' and 'love', at the same time as echoing the poet's forename, while Astrophel ('star-leaf') appropriately suggests a bitter plant.

Although the sonnet sequence traces Astrophil's developing love for Stella through moments of hopefulness to ultimate disappointment, it is less a narrative than a dramatic composition. Thomas Nashe, in the preface to the first edition, described the sequence as 'the tragicomedy of love…performed by starlight'.[6] While this memorable encomium doesn't fully register the energetic range and shifts of perspective in the sequence, it does acknowledge both the strong sense of performance and the underlying comic irony that

---

6. Gregory Smith (ed.), *Elizabethan Critical Essays* (Oxford: Oxford University Press, 1904), vol. 2, p. 223. Spelling has been modernized.

help to sustain it. On several occasions, Stella is made vividly present in narrative cameos—out riding in the sun in Sonnet 22, for instance, or sailing on the Thames in Sonnet 103—but much of the sequence is a dramatization of attitudes, ideas, and feelings in the first-person voice of Astrophil. Not all of the sonnets are addressed to Stella, though all recall her or reflect upon her; some are addressed to an unnamed friend, while others function as soliloquies to be overheard by imagined listeners. Sidney's sequence is both a scholarly adaptation of the Petrarchan model and a striking departure from it. Like the *Rime* of Petrarch, it interweaves songs with sonnets and other lyric forms, and it presents a speaker who gives extravagant praise to the woman he loves in elaborate figures of speech.

At the same time, Astrophil is intent on disowning Petrarch and establishing a new standard for the love poetry of his time. It is Petrarch's influence that he is made to denounce in Sonnet 6, in which he distances himself from those poets who speak 'Of hopes begot by fear, of wot not what desires, | Of force of heavenly beams, infusing hellish pain, | Of living deaths, dear wounds, fair storms and freezing fires.'[7] More generally, Astrophil is inclined to distrust the entire tradition of courtly love poetry and its classical models. Sonnet 15 is explicitly addressed to his aspiring contemporaries:

> You that do search for every purling spring
>   Which from the ribs of old Parnassus flows;
>   And every flower, not sweet perhaps, which grows
> Near thereabouts, into your poesy wring;
> You that do dictionary's method bring
>   Into your rhymes, running in rattling rows;
>   You that poor Petrarch's long-deceased woes
> With new-born sighs and denizened wit do sing:
>   You take wrong ways, those far-fet helps be such
>   As do bewray a want of inward touch:
> And sure at length stol'n goods do come to light.
>   But if (both for your love and skill) your name
>   You seek to nurse at fullest breasts of fame,
> Stella behold, and then begin to endite.   (158–9)

Here, there are at least three popular poetic trends that Astrophil cautions his listeners against: an excessive overuse of water and flower imagery derived from classical models; a heavy employment of alliteration; and an overblown

---

7. Sir Philip Sidney, *The Major Works*, ed. Katherine Duncan-Jones (Oxford: Oxford University Press, 2008), p. 155. Further page numbers are given within brackets in the text.

imitation of Petrarchan conceits in love poetry. The sonnet is both a declaration of Stella's unrivalled beauty and an insistence on a new and individual (rather than inherited) poetic style. Much later in the sequence, in Sonnet 74, Astrophil neatly reiterates the importance of originality: 'I am no pick-purse of another's wit' (184). Of course, this emphasis on truth and originality is, itself, highly contrived. Even while Sonnet 15 seeks to rise above 'poor *Petrarch's* long-deceased woes', it remains indebted to the Petrarchan model in its deployment of rhymes: *abbaabbaccdeed*. The sestet introduces a variation on the standard Petrarchan rhyme scheme, but avoids the closing couplet that had come to be associated with the English sonnet in the hands of Wyatt and Surrey. What is characteristic of Sidney's style is the strong syntactical composition of the sonnet and the tendency to maximize the possibilities opened up by the divisions and sub-divisions of octave and sestet, quatrains and tercets. There is a strong rhetorical pattern created by the second-person address, and this neatly coincides with lines 1, 5, 9, and 13, as if the sonnet were sub-divided into three quatrains and a couplet (4 + 4 + 4 + 2). However, the rhymes run counter to this expectation, creating a momentary discomfiture. The turn at line 9 is skilfully accomplished, with the sestet announcing a contrary direction as Astrophil berates his contemporaries: 'You take wrong ways...'.

Although it is customary to claim that Sidney employs an Italian octave and an English sestet in his sonnets, there is in fact a good deal of variety and experimentation in his use of rhyme. The octave tends to follow the familiar *abbaabba* arrangement or a variant using just the two rhyme words (*abababab* or *ababbaba*), while the sestet adopts the *cdcdee* pattern favoured by Wyatt, occasionally introducing variants such as *ccdeed*, *cddcee*, *ccdccd*, and *cdcdcd*. The majority of the sonnets (85 out of 108) end with a rhyming couplet, and over half (59) follow the pattern *abbaabbacdcdee*. However, there are some notable variations, such as Sonnet 89, which relies entirely on the words 'night' and 'day', creating an appropriately repetitive rhyme scheme: *abbaabbaababab*. Some sonnets, such as 1, 76, and 102, employ a twelve-syllable (alexandrine) line.

Sidney is credited with having written the first major sonnet sequence in English, but his most significant contribution to the sonnet form is the innovative and versatile use of a syntax and diction approximating to the rhythm of the actual spoken voice. In this, he sets a new standard of poetic eloquence quite at odds with the ornate, embellished diction associated with the courtly love tradition. Sonnet 55 bids farewell to borrowed words and phrases, especially those of a melancholy cast, and insists on a native English idiom that is both pleasing and direct.

> Muses, I oft invoked your holy aid,
>   With choicest flowers my speech to engarland so
>   That it, despised in true but naked show,
> Might win some grace in your sweet skill arrayed;
> And oft whole troops of saddest words I stayed,
>   Striving abroad a-foraging to go,
>   Until by your inspiring I might know
> How their black banner might be best displayed.
>   But now I mean no more your help to try,
>   Nor other sugaring of my speech to prove,
>   But on her name incessantly to cry:
> For let me but name her, whom I do love,
>   So sweet sounds straight mine ear and heart do hit
>   That I well find no eloquence like it.   (174)

Here, the sonnet form itself is brought into the skilful service of a new eloquence. The sestet boldly turns from the muses of classical tradition towards the simple naming of Stella. The closing couplet, with its sibilant penultimate line and monosyllabic force, emphatically suggests the kind of poetic renovation that Sidney considers desirable. The word 'eloquence' draws attention to itself by being the only word of more than one syllable in the closing couplet.

The vigorous diction, the frequent shifts in register, and the lively rhythms of vernacular speech all help to sustain the sequence and create the impression of Astrophil speaking with a present-tense immediacy. As Spiller has pointed out, one of the frequent rhetorical devices in the sequence is the use of apostrophe. Although the lyric apostrophe is a well-established convention, summoning the attention of a person or thing, and usually implying the presence of a listener, it takes on a new quality in *Astrophil and Stella*: 'the impression is one of excited and constant movement, and a certain extravagance of gesture'.[8] One of the most compelling instances of this apostrophizing tendency can be found in the frequently anthologized Sonnet 31, addressed to the moon:

> With how sad steps, O moon, thou climb'st the skies;
> How silently, and with how wan a face.
> What, may it be that even in heav'nly place

---

8. Spiller, *The Development of the Sonnet*, p. 109.

>   That busy archer his sharp arrows tries?
>   Sure, if that long-with-love-acquainted eyes
>   Can judge of love, thou feel'st a lover's case;
>   I read it in thy looks; thy languished grace
>   To me, that feels the like, thy state descries.
>   Then even of fellowship, O moon, tell me,
>   Is constant love deemed there but want of wit?
>   Are beauties there as proud as here they be?
>   Do they above love to be loved, and yet
>   Those lovers scorn whom that love doth possess?
>   Do they call virtue there ungratefulness?   (165)

What makes this such a captivating sonnet is its combination of a highly structured syntax and a seemingly easeful, even casual, conversational flow. The fanciful conceit of a melancholic moon is rendered plainly in the simplicity of 'sad steps' and eased along acoustically through the accompanying sibilance of 'skies' and 'silently'. The impression of an immediate spoken address depends, paradoxically, on a high degree of verbal contrivance and organization. The obvious parallel structure in 'how sad steps', 'How silently', and 'how wan a face' gives structural coherence to the opening lines, reinforced by the internal rhyme of 'how' and 'thou'. The sonnet is heavily punctuated with rhetorical questions and implied exclamations, creating an impression of agitated speech. The word 'Sure' at the beginning of line 4 is typical of the intimate and familiar way in which the moon is addressed in Sonnet 31, but this is immediately followed by the strikingly compressed and heavily pre-modified 'long-with-love-acquainted eyes', once again suggesting an unusual combination and interdependence of the casual and the contrived.

Sonnet 31 appears relatively stable and regular in rhyme and metre, but there are subtle tensions and variations throughout. The opening line is smoothly iambic, but thereafter the stresses pull towards the flow of speech rather than metre. The structure appears to observe the traditional octave-sestet division and to allow within this for a further division of three quatrains and a rhyming couplet: *abbaabbacdcdee*. The syntax coincides with the rhyme scheme in the octave, and the turn is clearly marked by the introduction of the word 'Then' at line 9 and the repetition of the apostrophe, 'O moon'. The sestet, however, is highly intricate. Although the rhyme scheme suggests a 4 + 2 arrangement (quatrain and couplet), the syntax pulls away from this to create a competing pattern of 3 + 3, consisting of alternating two-line and one-line questions. Furthermore, the sudden introduction of the conjunction, 'and yet', in line 12 has the force of a premature additional turn as we reach the closing couplet. Consequently, the final two lines do not constitute a couplet in terms of sense, even though they rhyme. The climax of the sonnet extends across the closing *three* lines and acquires momentum from the syntactical parallel between lines 12 and 14: 'Do they above love...Do they call...?'.

Sidney's technique of relentlessly counterpointing rhyme and syntax enables his bold and iconoclastic exploration of conventional attitudes to love. In some respects, Astrophil's address to the moon is absurd and ludicrous, but it also invites a measure of sympathy and recognition. The comic irony that ensues from Astrophil's identification and attempted dialogue with a seemingly abject moon both revitalizes a well-worn convention in love poetry (the equation of the moon with constant love) and initiates an intellectual analysis and comprehension of love *on earth*. The wordplay in lines 12–13 ('love...loved...lovers...love') is so compressed as to warrant a close investigation and prompt the enquiry: what *is* love, and how *should* it be reciprocated?

That Stella's 'Vertue' might, in fact, be an obstacle to love rather than consonant with it, is an idea that occurs very early in the sequence. Rather than following the Petrarchan code of conduct and pursuing a transcendental ideal of love, *Astrophil and Stella* eschews metaphysics and explicitly confronts the nature of sexual desire. As Alan Sinfield has argued, there is 'a powerful sexual component' in Astrophil's love for Stella, and this is evident right from the beginning of the sequence, though sometimes disguised in the language of *double entendre*.[9] A struggle between 'Vertue' and 'Desire', which reason is incapable of resolving, is established within the first ten sonnets of the sequence. Sonnet 4 candidly dismisses institutionalized virtue, and asserts the sensuality of the lover: 'Churches or schools are for thy seat more fit: | I do confess—pardon a fault confessed— | My mouth too tender is for thy hard bit' (154). The conflict of Vertue and Desire reaches a new intensity in Sonnets 71 and 72. The first of these strives to accept the neo-Platonic wisdom of equating love with beauty, truth, and goodness, but Desire breaks through and demands to be fed: 'So while thy beauty draws the heart to love, | As fast thy virtue bends that love to good. | But ah, desire still cries: "Give me some food"' (182). Here, an unconventional and outspoken attitude to physical love clearly disrupts the sonnet form. An abrupt and emphatic

---

9. Alan Sinfield, 'Sexual Puns in *Astrophil and Stella*', *Essays in Criticism* 24 (1974), 341.

line in Sonnet 72 ostensibly bids farewell to Desire—'I must no more in thy sweet passions lie'—and yet desire is reinstated all the while (182). The declaration that 'Virtue's gold now must head my Cupid's dart' (182) reasserts an obvious phallic symbol, as does the phrase 'so soft a rod' (183) in Sonnet 73. The closing couplet in Sonnet 72 is a curious rhetorical structure, both strongly asserting the banishment of desire and painfully questioning whether such an action is possible: 'But thou, desire, because thou would'st have all, | Now banish art—but yet, alas, how shall?' (182).

As well as possessing a thinly veiled sexual vocabulary, *Astrophil and Stella* also contains a more explicit declaration of intense passion and sexual longing. Sonnets 79 to 83 form an extended meditation on the sensuous pleasures of kissing that is arguably without parallel in Renaissance sonneteering. Each sonnet evokes the joy of kissing in single lyrical lines that are among the most memorable in the entire sequence: 'Cease we to praise, now pray we for a kiss' (186); 'Sweet lip, you teach my mouth with one sweet kiss' (186); 'I will but kiss, I never more will bite' (187). In Sonnet 81, Stella blushingly refuses Astrophil's poetic homage to her lips. Line 9 has a clearly marked turn ('But she forbids...'), but Astrophil's passion is so strong and insistent that it prompts a further turn:

> But my heart burns, I cannot silent be.
>   Then since (dear life) you fain would have me peace,
>   And I, mad with delight, want wit to cease,
> Stop you my mouth with still, still kissing me.   (187)

The imperative force of the closing line is perpetuated by the passionate punning of 'still, still', with the two meanings of stillness and continuity pulling against each other in a way that threatens to defy grammar altogether.

The closing sonnet in this brief paean to kissing (79–83) is a comic address to Stella's pet sparrow, also called Philip (Pip or Philip being a common name for a small bird). The sonnet accuses the bird not only of seeking 'favour' and having 'ambitious thoughts', but of kissing Stella in lecherous fashion. It closes with an unmistakable warning: 'Leave that, sir Phip, lest off your neck be wrung' (187). Even in this touching, light-hearted sonnet, there is evidence that love and desire in *Astrophil and Stella* cannot easily be abstracted from a broader social and political milieu in which ambition, reward, and social status are highly valued. As we have seen with Wyatt, the role of the lover and the role of the courtier or diplomat are often blurred, and what purports to be private and personal can be seen to have analogies within the public sphere. Often, the sexual desire of the fervent lover and the worldly ambition of the aspiring courtier turn out to be one and the same. What unites them is the language of courtship: a discourse of service, dedication, and flattery. The sonnet is a form in which these writers might eloquently strive for self-improvement and worldly gain, but also declare their feelings of disappointment and rejection, by subtly utilizing the conventions of the love lyric.

Arthur Marotti, in his influential essay on the political encoding of love poetry, argues that in *Astrophil and Stella*, Sidney 'crafted a sonnet sequence as a form of mediation between socio-economic or socio-political desires and the constraints of the established order'.[10] He finds a close analogy between erotic forwardness and political forwardness, between the sexually assertive lover and the actively ambitious courtier, suggesting that the candid expression of sexual desire is effectively an outlet for social and economic frustration. Marotti reminds us that in the 1580s Sidney was 'a fiercely ambitious courtier who faced the reality of a failed political career', and he speculates that Lady Penelope Rich served as 'a fit symbol of his unattained and unattainable social and political goals'.[11] Insisting too strongly on the biographical circumstances of *Astrophil and Stella*, though, he gives an overdetermined reading of the sequence in which Sidney and Astrophil are all but identical. Even so, his essay is valuable in reminding us that the politics of the Elizabethan court were often turbulent and divisive. We need to exercise caution in thinking about the sonnet as an aristocratic form, since its early practitioners in England quickly discovered that it could provide a space for dissident voices and for sentiments that ran counter to the prevailing moral and political values of the time.

It is not necessary to fasten *Astrophil and Stella* in a tight relationship with the events of Sidney's life to perceive that the sonnet sequence involves a crisis of identity, and that this might have as much to do with social ambition as with sexual desire. A strong feature of *Astrophil and Stella* is its tendency to insist on love as a personal aspiration and potential fulfilment beyond the interference of the court, only to reveal that love has already been regulated. What seems at first a private vision turns out to be a public spectacle. In Sonnet 23, the 'curious wits' and 'fools' of court notice the melancholy cast

---

10. Arthur F. Marotti, '"Love Is Not Love": Elizabethan Sonnet Sequences and the Social Order', *ELH* 49 (1982), 399.
11. Marotti, "'Love Is Not Love'", 400.

in Astrophil's eyes. Some believe that he is preoccupied with poetry, while others think that he is concerned with matters of state. The 'harder judges' blame ambition, 'Scourge of itself, still climbing slippery place', but Astrophil throws out all speculation and insists that his thoughts belong entirely with 'Stella's eyes and Stella's heart' (162). Sonnet 27 similarly sets the private experience of love against the world of gossip and rumour. Denying accusations of selfish pride, Astrophil does confess to 'one worse fault, ambition', that makes him overlook his friends, but the closing line of the sonnet insists that this ambition is entirely in the service of Stella's 'grace' (163). The more Astrophil protests against the judgement of his peers, presenting his love as separate and removed, the more his distinction between private and public experience falters and collapses. Sidney's technique in other sonnets is to use the closing couplet as a way of asserting the primacy of Astrophil's love over the trivialities and petty intrigues of court. In Sonnet 30, the pressing concerns of international politics are presented as trifling distractions from Astrophil's complete absorption in thoughts of Stella:

> Whether the Turkish new moon minded be
>   To fill his horns this year on Christian coast;
>   How Pole's right king means, without leave of host,
> To warm with ill-made fire cold Muscovy;
> If French can yet three parts in one agree;
>   What now the Dutch in their full diets boast;
>   How Holland hearts, now so good towns be lost,
> Trust in the pleasing shade of Orange tree;
>   How Ulster likes of that same golden bit
> Wherewith my father once made it half tame;
> If in the Scottish court be welt'ring yet;
> These questions busy wits to me do frame.
>   I, cumbered with good manners, answer do,
>   But know not how, for still I think of you.   (164)

The sonnet reveals the likely affairs of state in 1582, including the Turkish plan to capture Spain, the Polish invasion of Russia, the instability caused by political factions in France and Scotland, and the political relations with Ulster, where Sidney's father, Sir Henry Sidney, had earlier imposed his will as governor of Ireland. What gives the sonnet momentum is the contrast between the hectic calendar of political events and the still constancy of Astrophil's love for Stella, and between the uncertain, speculative nature of affairs of state ('Whether...How...If...What now...How...How...If...') and the simple declaration of love in the closing couplet, especially in the final six words: 'for still I think of you.' Ironically, of course, Astrophil's 'good manners' and his casual, unconcerned response to world events are an indication of how he remains firmly tied to court, even while appearing to dissociate himself from its affairs.

However much *Astrophil and Stella* strives for an ideal of love that transcends the politics of court, what the sonnets repeatedly show is the extent to which that yearning is itself shaped and informed by prevailing hierarchies of power. Sonnet 69 is remarkably explicit in this respect, contrasting its own 'low' style with the 'high' happiness of love acknowledged and returned. The imagery is conventional—winter turns to spring and joy is extravagantly figured in 'oceans of delight'—but the dominant trope is that of the political state:

> O joy too high for my low style to show;
>   O bliss, fit for a nobler state than me;
>   Envy, put out thine eyes, lest thou do see
> What oceans of delight in me do flow.
> My friend, that oft saw through all masks of woe,
>   Come, come, and let me pour myself on thee;
>   Gone is the winter of my misery,
> My spring appears; O see what here doth grow!
>   For Stella hath, with words where faith doth shine,
> Of her high heart giv'n me the monarchy;
> I, I, O I may say, that she is mine.
> And though she give but thus conditionally
>   This realm of bliss, while virtuous course I take,
>   No kings be crowned, but they some covenants make.   (181)

An identification between the affairs of the heart and the affairs of the court is neatly captured in 'a nobler state' and 'this realm of bliss'. The very highest love, of course, is equated with the absolute power of the monarchy. However, in seeking to find some metaphorical equivalent for the conditions imposed upon his love by Stella, Astrophil reveals that bliss does not, in fact, blind him or isolate him from the pragmatic operations of political power: 'No kings be crowned, but they some covenants make.'

The structure of *Astrophil and Stella* is flexible enough to accommodate a relentless shifting between hopeful, idealistic yearning and cynical, disillusioned rejection. We might easily regard the sonnet sequence as tending towards despair and disappointment, but this underestimates the intensity of emotional fluctuation that persists through to the closing sonnets. Sonnet 104 is proof enough that the sequence does not simply settle for rejection and resignation. Even while declaring his 'sorrow's eloquence' from within the 'dungeon dark' of painful separation, Astrophil turns on the 'Envious wits' and 'Fools' of court, reasserting his love for Stella. Here, the sestet works resourcefully to conjure up a hopeful image of Astrophil passing by Stella's 'happy window' with 'stars upon mine armour' (208).

Sonnet 107 seeks to mitigate love's disappointment by offering in its place the ideal of service. Stella is now seen to exercise the powers of a princess and a queen, while Astrophil commits himself as her lieutenant in an undefined 'great cause' (211). To the very end of the sequence, the values of the court determine the nature and course of the love depicted. The sonnets have an ironic and uneasy relationship with the court, which complicates any assessment of their political relevance and significance. If *Astrophil and Stella* confirms that the English sonnet has its origins in an essentially aristocratic social order, it also demonstrates how the sonnet can be deftly turned towards subversion and critique.

Edmund Spenser

For poets writing at the end of the sixteenth century, *Astrophil and Stella* undoubtedly provides a poetic standard for what the sonnet sequence can achieve in the exploration and expression of love's many moods. The potential of the sonnet for both lyrical intensity and narrative continuity finds ample scope in Edmund Spenser's *Amoretti* ('small love tokens'), a sequence of 89 sonnets deriving from his courtship of Elizabeth Boyle during his time as a colonial administrator in Ireland. The sonnets were probably written between 1591 and 1594, and presented to his future wife as a nuptial gift, along with his *Epithalamion*.[12] Spenser's sequence is altogether more equable and restrained than Sidney's sometimes pyrotechnic production, reaching as it does towards the acceptance and accommodation of sexual desire within Christian marriage, though it is not without the occasional extravagance and hyperbole. If it lacks the brilliant repertoire of rhetorical devices and colloquial nuances of its predecessor, it excels in the steady progression of a subtle and fluent syntax.

---

12. All quotations from *Amoretti* are from *The Poetical Works of Edmund Spenser*, Vol. 1: *Spenser's Minor Poems*, ed. Ernest de Sélincourt (Oxford: Clarendon Press, 1910).

What Spenser shares with Sidney is a persistent and self-reflexive preoccupation with the act of writing, and a sophisticated awareness of how the first-person voice might be constructed and modulated throughout a lengthy sequence of poems. Both sequences present us with a poet-lover for whom writing is inseparable from loving. In the *Amoretti*, however, heart and art are intensely conjoined. The opening dedicatory sonnet happily brings together the 'Leaues, lines, and rymes' of poetry in a determined effort to please the poet's beloved:

> Happy ye leaues when as those lilly hands,
>   which hold my life in their dead doing might,
>   shall handle you and hold in loues soft bands,
>   lyke captiues trembling at the victors sight.
> And happy lines, on which with starry light,
>   those lamping eyes will deigne sometimes to look
>   and reade the sorrowes of my dying spright,
>   written with teares in harts close bleeding book.
> And happy rymes bath'd in the sacred brooke,
>   of *Helicon* whence she deriued is,
>   when yet behold that Angels blessed looke,
>   my soules long lacked foode, my heauens blis.
> Leaues, lines, and rymes, seeke her to please alone,
>   whom if ye please, I care for other none.   (372)

There is a neatness and elegance in the opening sonnet, especially in the convergence of the three discrete but closely linked quatrains in the closing couplet. 'Leaves, lines, and rymes' is clearly designed to please the ear with its deft phonetic shift from alliteration to assonance. Each quatrain praises the beauty of the recipient, imagined in the act of resting—her 'lilly hands', her 'lamping eyes', and 'blessed looke'—while at the same time recording the poet-petitioner's anguish and sorrow. Throughout the sequence, the turbulence of the lover's heart finds some outlet and repose within the poet's art. The sonnets are remarkable for their depiction of a speaker with a vivid inner life and a 'self' that can be shaped and 'fashioned'. Sonnet 8, for instance, points unmistakably to the depths of thought and feeling in a surprisingly modern lover: 'You frame my thoughts and fashion me within, | you stop my toung, and teach my hart to speake.' Similarly, Sonnet 45 suggests through the brilliant image of a crystal glass that the self can be perceived and understood in various ways. Even more striking is the sonnet's subtle distinction between inner and outer selves:

> Leaue lady in your glasse of christall clene,
>   Your goodly selfe for euermore to vew,
>   and in my selfe, my inward selfe I meane,
>   most liuely lyke behold your semblant trew.   (394)

The attainment of a shared and secure sense of self is vital to the concept of love that emerges in the *Amoretti*, and both the design of individual sonnets and the larger structure of the sequence convey a sense of steady progression and unfolding realization.

The distinctive rhyme scheme of the Spenserian sonnet, derived from the stanzaic arrangement of the *Faerie Queene*, contributes to the overall impression of stability and assurance within the sequence, even when the seas of love are rough:

> Lyke as a ship that through the Ocean wyde,
>   by conduct of some star doth make her way,
>   whenas a storme hath dimd her trusty guyde,
>   out of her course doth wander far astray.
> So I her star, that wont with her bright ray,
>   me to direct, with cloudes is ouercast,
>   does wander now in darknesse and dismay,
>   through hidden perils about me plast.
> Yet hope I well, that when this storme is past
>   my *Helice* the lodestar of my lyfe
>   will shine again, and looke on me at last,
>   with louely light to cleare my cloudy grief.
> Till then I wander carefull comfortlesse,
>   in secret sorrow and sad pensiuenesse.   (388)

Sonnet 34 amply demonstrates the possibilities of the Spenserian rhyme scheme: *ababbcbccdcdee*. The interlacing rhymes both emphasize the quatrain as a unit of thought and effectively suggest progression of thought across the fourteen lines of the sonnet. This effect is enhanced by a typography that employs both indentation and lower-case lettering to give visual emphasis to the 4 + 4 + 4 + 2 arrangement of lines. What Sonnet 34 also shows is Spenser's fondness for analogical reasoning, with the key terms of comparison and deduction—'Lyke . . . So . . . Yet . . . Till . . .'—clearly corresponding to the structural pattern of the sonnet. Although a turn is initiated by the word 'Yet', this is not so much a new direction of thought as a firm insistence on waiting patiently for the sky to clear. Whatever storms might cause the lover to wander, the abiding impression is one of intellectual resourcefulness and emotional control.

The image of the lover as a lone ship in search of a guiding star is, of course, part of a familiar and well-established set of conventions in Renaissance love poetry. There are many conventional tropes of this kind in the *Amoretti*, including the oft-invoked Petrarchan contrast of cold and heat: 'My loue is lyke to yse, and I to fyre' (30). The occasional hyperbole and rhetorical extravagance in a sonnet sequence that is otherwise dignified and restrained in its outlook has led some readers to ask if Spenser sometimes indulges in irony and parody. Louis Martz has persuaded many readers that there is a playful, light-hearted side to Spenser's poetry but it might also be argued that the Petrarchan motifs in his *Amoretti* have a strategic function in terms of establishing the various concepts of love (and their literary counterparts) that the poet-lover must confront and assimilate on his way to a more mature realization and fulfilment of desire.[13]

It is much too simple, however, to assume that Spenser's amatory sequence progresses smoothly and confidently or that the *Amoretti* charts a clear and victorious progression from frustrated physical yearning to a happy reconciliation of sense and spirit. One of the foremost authorities on the Elizabethan sonnet, J. W. Lever, argues that 'Spenser's poetry was largely concerned with a denigration of the romance cult of courtly love and the substitution of a new theme: the triumph of virtuous courtship in betrothal and holy matrimony.' There is no doubt, as Lever claims, that the sequence is informed by Spenser's Protestant teaching, 'with its emphasis upon the individual conscience and on the merit of sacramental marriage', but his reading of the *Amoretti* too easily resolves the tensions and complexities of love that the speaker confronts in his education of the heart.[14]

There is, as several critics have pointed out, a highly developed and intricate relationship between the sequential design of Spenser's sonnets and the Christian calendar. Despite the absence of any obvious narrative plotting in *Amoretti*, we can trace the passage of twelve months between Sonnet 3 and Sonnet 62, both of which acknowledge the arrival of a new year. An important state of transition occurs between Sonnet 57 and Sonnet 67, in which archetypal lovers' dilemmas are confronted and overcome. The speaker seeks peace with his 'Sweet warriour' (400), the lover's ship survives

---

13. Louis L. Martz, 'The *Amoretti*: "Most Goodly Temperature"', in *Form and Convention in the Poetry of Edmund Spenser*, ed. W. Nelson (New York: Columbia University Press, 1961), p. 150.
14. J. W. Lever, *The Elizabethan Love Sonnet* (London: Methuen, 1956; 1978), p. 136.

the storms and finds 'the happy shore' (403), and the huntsman finds that the wild beast he has been pursuing is really a 'gentle deare' (405). Sonnet 68 is a resounding celebration of Easter Day, proclaiming the unity of human and divine love: 'So let vs loue, deare loue, lyke as we ought, | loue is the lesson which the Lord vs taught' (405). It might seem that this is the ultimate insight that the lovers can gain, and that what the sequence depicts is 'the condition of assured courtship awaiting its consecration in marriage'.[15] In fact, the sequence is remarkably explicit in its realization that the promise of legitimation in Christian marriage does not absolve the poet-lover of his restless, 'wanton' thoughts.

In Sonnet 76, the speaker lavishly praises his lover's breasts, but what the language of the sonnet signifies is not the spiritual and physical assurance that comes with Christian marriage, but rather the continuing frustration and desire of the lonely male poet. Far from being obediently reconciled to Christian ideals of love, the sonnet flagrantly adopts traditional religious concepts to describe the sensuous delights of the body. The woman's 'Fayre bosome' is 'the paradice of pleasure, | the sacred harbour of that heuenly spright', while the poet-lover envies his thoughts their resting place between these heavenly breasts, regretting that he 'neuer was so blest'. While Spenser's sequence differs significantly from Sidney's *Astrophil and Stella* in its realization of mutual affection and impending marriage, it is not without its tensions and complications, and these persist throughout the sequence, overshadowing the final sonnets and ultimately displacing celebration with lament.

The overarching structure of *Amoretti* allows for a growing sense of reciprocal desire and simultaneously shows this mutual love being tried and tested by slander and separation. Despite its calendrical structure, the sequence is not constructed in a simple linear fashion. If there is progression in the poet-lover's understanding of love and his eventual betrothal to the woman he desires, there is also a profound sense of mutability and a persistent longing for security. Nor is there any clearly articulated narrative, although three sonnets (12, 16, and 75) all begin 'One day'. On these occasions the casual, colloquial nature of the expression prepares us for something uneventful, only to lead us into the realm of amazement. The supreme instance of this

---

15. Lever, *Elizabethan Love Sonnet*, p. 100.

occurs in Sonnet 75, in which a seemingly commonplace event takes on the power of epiphany:

> One day I wrote her name vpon the strand,
>   But came the waues and washed it away:
>   agayne I wrote it with a second hand,
>   but came the tyde, and made my paynes his pray.
> Vayne man, sayd she, thou doest in vaine assay,
>   a mortall thing so to immortalize,
>   for I my selue shall lyke to this decay,
>   and eek my name bee wyped out lykewize.
> Not so, (quod I) let baser things deuize
>   to dy in dust, but you shall liue by fame:
>   my verse your vertues rare shall eternize,
>   and in the heuens wryte your glorious name.
> Where whenas death shall all the world subdew,
>   our loue shall liue, and later life renew.   (409)

As Andrew Hadfield notes in his excellent biography of the poet, it is very likely that Spenser spent time with Elizabeth on the strand of Youghal, close to where she lived, and that their marriage took place there, too. The biographical interest lends additional charm to what is probably Spenser's 'most famous sonnet'.[16] What makes this such a compelling poem, however, is the startling transition it makes from 'One day' to the vastness of eternity within the space of fourteen lines. The dynamics of the sonnet form are exploited here with maximum intensity. The first-person voice is strongly present in the opening line of both the octave and the sestet, and in this instance the turn is firmly indicated as the speaker rejects the pessimism of his beloved and exchanges his hopeless signature in the sand for a glorious inscription in the heavens.

Writing and loving are closely aligned as we enter the dialogue of the lovers and move from 'her name' to 'my name' to 'your glorious name', each quatrain carefully registering the poet's instinct to preserve his love in the fundamental gesture of naming. Although Spenser employs a more archaic diction than we find in Sidney's *Astrophil and Stella* ('eek' and 'quod' sounding strange to the modern ear), the sonnet has a relaxed colloquial appeal. This is partly the effect of lines 2 and 4 creating the impression of returning waves through simple repetition: 'but came the waues...but came the tyde'. The most striking feature of the sonnet, however, is its bold attempt to stage a dialogue between the lovers within the small compass of its fourteen lines.

---

16. Andrew Hadfield, *Edmund Spenser: A Life* (Oxford: Oxford University Press, 2012), p. 308.

The Spenserian rhyme scheme works to great advantage here, both propelling the narrative through repeated sounds and building an elaborate structure that might hold good for all future generations of readers.

Despite the growing anticipation of a happy resolution, then, the closing sonnets shift the *Amoretti* into a minor key. Sonnet 86 is surprisingly candid in its condemnation of a 'Venemous toung…that didst with guile conspire | in my sweet peace such breaches to haue bred' (414). There is no explicit connection between these feared breaches and the separation of the lovers in the closing three sonnets. It is rather that the sonnets together concede that there will be challenges and hardships along the way. It is also the case that the conventions of the love sonnet require an absent lover to generate an eloquent yearning for presence. As Michael Spiller suggests, Spenser both acknowledges and transmutes the convention by offering us a profound sense of separation, but one that is relieved when the sonnets are read in conjunction with his celebratory *Epithalamion*. He ends his sonnets 'with one of the most intensely realized absences in the whole of English literature'.[17] The separation of the lovers is beautifully intimated through the memorable image of the dove awaiting its mate in the encroaching darkness.

> Lyke as the Culuer on the bared bough,
>   Sits mourning for the absence of her mate:
>   and in her songs sends many a wishfull vow,
>   for his returne that seemes to linger late.
> So I alone now left disconsolate,
>   mourne to my selfe the absence of my loue:
>   and wandring here and there all desolate,
>   seek with my playnts to match that mournful doue:
> Ne ioy of ought that vnder heaven doth houe,
>   can comfort me, but her owne ioyous sight:
>   whose sweet aspect both God and man can moue,
>   in her vnspotted pleasauns to delight.
> Dark is my day, whyles her fayre light I mis,
>   and dead my life that wants such liuely blis.   (416)

The sonnet moves with impressive fluency, gathering momentum across its three clearly marked quatrains and culminating in the resounding closing couplet with its resigned suspension of death in life. The simplicity of the opening simile is matched by the simplicity of the pervasive imagery of light and darkness. The sonnet gains cohesion from a repeated series of

---

17. Michael Spiller, *Early Modern Sonneteers: From Wyatt to Milton* (Tavistock: Northcote House, 2001), p. 44.

short alliterative phrases, each of which furthers the emotional emphasis on loneliness and pain: 'bared bough', 'linger late', 'mourne to my selfe', 'Dark is my day'. The rhymes are dove-like in their open vowel sounds, especially in the gentle combination of love—dove—hove—move. The octave rhymes 'disconsolate' and 'desolate', producing a plangent echo in 'late...late...late'. The enjambment is light and easeful, giving the sonnet great fluency within its otherwise tightly ordered structure. Even so, the chained rhyme of Spenser's sonnets is often beguiling, and we need to be alert to 'the subtleties...under a very smooth and melodious surface'.[18]

As the sequence reaches a close, Spenser asks in Sonnet 80 for leave to 'sing my loues sweet praise' before returning to the major task of completing *The Faerie Queene* (411). This is one of several references to his travels in 'Faery Land'. Sonnet 33, addressed to his friend Lodovick Bryskett, acknowledges the debt he owes to Queen Elizabeth, 'that most sacred Empresse my dear dred', and also records his troubled thoughts about finishing the poem (388). Sonnet 74 pays tribute to 'three Elizabeths'—his mother, his love, and 'my souereign Queene most kind, | that honour and large richesse to me lent' (408). Marotti is inclined to see these various references to *The Faerie Queene* and royal patronage as an indication of Spenser's anxieties over social status. Presenting himself within the *Amoretti* as England's national poet and a royal client was a way of 'proclaiming artistic authority in a world that insistently frustrated his economic and political ambition'. Marotti suggests that the 'amorous mutuality' of the sonnets—the idea of marrying for love rather than social and economic prestige—suggests 'advancement by merit rather than by birth or influence'. In the *Amoretti*, then, Spenser achieves 'the moral and literary prestige that could partly compensate for his socio-economic disadvantages'.[19] The envious slander at the end of the sequence is a stern reminder of the world of social competition and its inevitable frustrations and disappointments.

If the politics of Renaissance love poetry are subtly encoded in Spenser's *Amoretti*, they find their most explicit and tormented expression in the poems of Fulke Greville, 'servant to Queen Elizabeth, councillor to King James, and friend to Sir Philip Sidney' (as his own modest epitaph describes him).[20] Greville's *Caelica*, a collection of 109 short lyric poems, of which 41

---

18. Spiller, *Early Modern Sonneteers*, p. 42.   19. Marotti, "'Love Is Not Love'", p. 416.
20. Fulke Greville, *Selected Poems*, ed. Neil Powell (Manchester: Carcanet, 1990), p. 21. Further references are to this edition of the poems.

are sonnets, was probably written over a period of twenty years between the late 1580s and the early 1600s. In keeping with the love poems of the time, *Caelica* presents a relationship between lover and mistress in which devotion, loyalty, and service are also political expectations binding subject and ruler, courtier and monarch. Greville's poems are unusual, however, in their resolute refusal to conceal the extent of their author's political disillusionment. In seeking to articulate a profound dissatisfaction with the corruption and dissimulation of court relations, Greville pushes the conventions of love poetry to the point of abandonment. As David Norbrook has argued, both Sidney and Spenser seek to reconcile the inherited conventions of courtly love with the demands of a Protestant conscience, but Greville's conscience turns him towards denunciation of a social system that thrives on fear and insecurity.[21] Not surprisingly, inherited Petrarchan and neo-Platonic ideals are severely displaced. The second poem in *Caelica*, which is also the first sonnet in the collection, opens with a peculiarly violent image of passion as a dog tearing out the lover's heart and spilling his blood and bowels. The lover's cry for death in the opening line of the sestet seems perversely premature: 'Kill therefore in the end, and end my anguish.'[22]

The opening poems of *Caelica* are strongly Anacreontic (repeatedly invoking Cupid and his mother Venus), but one of the late sonnets (LXXXIV) is curtly dismissive.

> Farewell sweet boy, complain not of my truth;
> Thy mother lov'd thee not with more devotion;
> For to thy boy's play I gave all my youth,
> Young master, I did hope for your promotion.
>
> While some sought honours, princes' thoughts observing,
> Many woo'd fame, the child of pain and anguish,
> Others judg'd inward good a chief deserving,
> I in thy wanton visions joy'd to languish.
>
> I bow'd not to thy image for succession,
> Nor bound thy bow to shoot reformed kindness,
> Thy plays of hope and fear were my confession,
> The spectacles to my life was thy blindness:
>   But Cupid now farewell, I will go play me,
>   With thoughts that please me less, and less betray me. (97–8)

---

21. David Norbrook, *Poetry and Politics in the English Renaissance* (Oxford: Oxford University Press, 1984; 2002), p. 140.
22. Greville, *Selected Poems*, p. 26.

Here, the discourse of love is noticeably entangled with the vocabulary of social status—promotion, honours, succession—and also marked by fear and suspicion of betrayal. The opening address seems light-hearted and colloquial, but the mood throughout is sardonic. The speaker can no longer hold to an innocent vision of love or expect love to be untainted by court preferment. Greville seems intent on denying the sonnet its customary lyrical smoothness (the third quatrain is especially jarring), though ironically the closing couplet is admirably eloquent in its final farewell to love.

Although the Renaissance love sonnet lingers on for some time (Michael Drayton helps to keep it alive by continually revising his 1594 sequence *Idea*), it might be argued that with Greville's *Caelica* the potential of the sonnet as an amatory form is severely questioned and undermined. David Norbrook claims convincingly that Greville's radical politics are often at odds with his religious convictions, and that his Protestantism eventually urges within him a resigned acceptance of the way things are.[23] If the tension leads to a rejection of conventional love poetry, it also produces the sublimely hellish darkness in one of the final and most memorable sonnets in the collection:

> In night, when colours all to black are cast,
> Distinction lost, or gone down with the light;
> The eye a watch to inward senses plac'd,
> Not seeing, yet still having power of sight,
>
> Gives vain alarums to the inward sense,
> Where fear stirr'd up with witty tyranny,
> Confounds all powers, and thorough self-offence,
> Doth forge and raise impossibility:
>
> Such as in thick depriving darknesses,
> Proper reflections of the error be,
> And images of self-confusednesses,
> Which hurt imaginations only see;
>   And from this nothing seen, tells news of devils,
>   Which but expressions be of inward evils.   (110)

This deeply troubled sonnet seems to render the dark night of the soul, but its inability to see things clearly issues from an unspecified 'fear' and 'hurt'. The sonnet can barely contain the tensions it generates: the ungainly rhyme of 'darkness' and 'self-confusednesses' pushes the resources of the form to extremity. If the world of power relations is deceptive and treacherous, so

---

23. Norbrook, *Poetry and Politics*, p. 145.

too is the 'inward sense', and this strong suspicion of 'self-offence' and 'inward evils' makes the sonnet unrelievedly bleak. In his valuable edition of Greville's *Selected Poems*, Neil Powell notes the 'uncannily "modern" psychological perspective' in this sonnet and comments on how the language 'enacts the stages of a mental process'.[24] Although Greville has been unjustly neglected, he amply demonstrates the capacity of the sonnet as a form that is highly attuned to the play of mind and the subtle adjustments of voice and feeling. Marotti speculates that Greville probably switched from writing amorous verse to composing religious and philosophical poetry around 1603: 'With the death of Elizabeth and the accession of a king interested in religious and philosophical verse and prose, love poetry no longer served as a major literary means of expressing social, economic, and political ambition.'[25] The reasons for the shifts are surely more complicated than that, but Greville's example seems to usher in a new set of possibilities for the sonnet, preparing us for the radical political sentiments of John Milton and (much later) the tormented religious conscience of Gerard Manley Hopkins.

William Shakespeare

The Sonnets of William Shakespeare, the largest single collection of sonnets in the English Renaissance repertoire, were published in 1609, a decade after the Elizabethan vogue for writing sonnet sequences had reached its zenith. It is not known for certain when the Sonnets were written, whether they derived from actual relationships in Shakespeare's life, or whether Shakespeare authorized their ordering, their printing, and their dedication to the enigmatic Mr W. H. It seems likely that the Sonnets were composed in groups, though not in the order in which they appear in the 1609 printing, with the earliest group dating from 1591–5 and the latest from 1598–1604.[26]

The extraordinary state of affairs to which the Sonnets allude—a sexual triangle involving the poet/speaker's passionate and disappointed love for a beautiful young man and a dark-haired, dark-eyed woman, both of whom prove false—gives the poetry a powerful emotional intensity and a strong

---
24. Neil Powell, Introduction to Greville, *Selected Poems*, p. 19.
25. Marotti, "'Love Is Not Love'", p. 420.
26. The main critical concerns prompted by the Sonnets, including their compositional history, their biographical significance, and their formal achievements, are dealt with lucidly and thoroughly by Paul Edmondson and Stanley Wells in *Shakespeare's Sonnets* (Oxford: Oxford University Press, 2004).

sense of intrigue unparalleled in sonnet sequences of the time.[27] The painful and prolonged meditation on sexual betrayal that preoccupies many of the Sonnets inevitably prompts a desire among readers for some narrative coherence or some clear correspondence between the troubled circumstances of the poems and events in Shakespeare's life. At the same time, as Colin Burrow has wisely noted, the Sonnets themselves seem to relish uncertainty, and are perhaps most profitably read in terms of how they evade and frustrate, rather than conform to, a linear narrative: 'They are a structured miscellany of recurrent themes, passions, and thoughts, rather than a story or a mathematically ordered sequence.' The wonderful compensation for the 'empirical uncertainties' in Shakespeare's Sonnets is the 'delighted mystification' that they 'repeatedly invite'.[28]

The first 126 sonnets are ostensibly addressed to a young man in terms of endearment that range from 'tender churl' to 'lovely boy', but the epithets fluctuate as feelings of respect and admiration collapse into jealousy and hurt. If the praise and devotion accorded the young man by the speaker suggest a relationship based on patronage, the sharp reproach and ironic sting in many of the Sonnets serve to complicate that view. The pervasive erotic imagery and sexual wordplay of the Sonnets might render 'friendship' euphemistic, but the shifting terms of address and the unstable rhetorical features of the Sonnets make it exceedingly difficult to define the addressee with any confidence or certainty. This first set of sonnets contemplates the nature of beauty and how it might survive in the face of 'Time's fickle glass, his sickle hour', though its subject matter is remarkably diverse compared with that of earlier sonnet sequences. It closes with an envoy, Sonnet 126, an appropriately curtailed sonnet of six pentameter couplets, which in the original Quarto printing included two pairs of italic parentheses in place of the missing closing couplet. Sonnets 127 to 152 are similarly preoccupied with beauty, but turn their attention to a mistress who has come to be known as the 'Dark Lady', though that appellation never appears in the sequence. This second set of sonnets is unmatched in sequences of the time for its potent mix of passionate adoration and bitter

---

27. Edmondson and Wells offer a salutary reminder that some of the opening 126 sonnets 'could relate to either a male or a female' and that the later sonnets apparently addressed to a 'Dark Lady' are 'not necessarily about one and the same person'. See *Shakespeare's Sonnets*, p. xiii.
28. Colin Burrow, Introduction to William Shakespeare, *The Complete Sonnets and Poems* (Oxford: Oxford University Press, 2002), p. 118. All quotations from Shakespeare's Sonnets are from this edition.

reproach, as it simultaneously praises the physical attractions of the mistress and castigates her for her promiscuity and deceit. The sequence closes with two sonnets (153–4) on Cupid, which both function as a coda to the poems addressed to the mistress and allow for modulation between the sequence and the poem in rhyme-royal, *A Lover's Complaint*, with which it was printed in 1609.

In a tradition of sonnet writing so powerfully shaped by Petrarchan ideals of love, the introduction of a fundamentally flawed and untrustworthy lover is a bold innovation. Shakespeare goes even further in his exploration of a debased and conflicted love, and for the first time in the history of the sonnet presents *two* unworthy recipients of the speaker's devotion. Helen Vendler astutely notes that the speaker's erotic relationships involve different kinds of sexual passion, and that their intense combination is, in itself, unusual. The first set of sonnets is preoccupied mainly with sexual infatuation and registers this through the agency of the gazing eye, making a fetish of the young man's countenance, while the second set suggests a potent link between the speaker's sexual arousal and the promiscuity of his mistress. The sonnet sequence is idiosyncratic, not least in its attribution of these complex sexual passions and anxieties to a single intelligence, but its most important innovation is the refinement of a poetic method and technique through which the speaker's resulting anguish and self-reproach might be articulated. Vendler's main concern is not so much with the thematic originality in Shakespeare's *dramatis personae*, as with 'the newly complex system of expression, unprecedented in the Renaissance lyric, through which he could, accurately and convincingly, represent and enact that arousal and that self-loathing'. In this respect, 'Shakespeare's speaker, alone with his thoughts, is the greatest achievement, imaginatively speaking, of the sequence.'[29]

What has come to be known as the Shakespearean sonnet form—three quatrains with alternating rhymes and a closing couplet—was not in itself an innovation. Surrey had already established the rhyme scheme (*ababcdcdefefgg*) and shown how contrary patterns of thought might be developed in the sonnet by playing off the flexible four-part structure of quatrains and couplet (4 + 4 + 4 + 2) against the octave-sestet division. So, too, had Sidney already demonstrated in *Astrophil and Stella* how the rhythms of everyday speech might be employed in the dramatization of the speaker's changing

---

[29]. Helen Vendler, *The Art of Shakespeare's Sonnets* (Cambridge, MA: Harvard University Press, 1997), pp. 17–19.

moods of love. Shakespeare's Sonnets, however, possess much greater structural versatility and metrical subtlety than is found in the sonnets of his predecessors. As George Wright has noted, the metrical art of Shakespeare's Sonnets might not appear to be radically different from that of *Astrophil and Stella*, but 'the arguments are marked by less exclamation and self-interruption and by more continuous and more philosophical reflection; and the treatment of feeling finds phrases that convey still more subtle nuances'.[30] What is new in Shakespeare's handling of the form is both the metrical subtlety and the powerful dynamic interplay he brings to the constituent parts of the sonnet, so that every word and line and sentence is vibrant with meaning. As Spiller remarks, 'if the shape is conventional, the movement imparted to it is not'.[31] Shakespeare's method is one of intensification at every level—phonetic, semantic, syntactic, rhythmic—so that what emerges is both strikingly novel in terms of style and profoundly mimetic of a complex analytical mind in dialogue with itself.[32]

Sonnet 18 remains one of the most popular and memorable of the Sonnets, not least because it grants what seems like privileged access to the subtle movements of a mind rehearsing an intimate conversation. This is true, to some extent, of all the Sonnets, but Sonnet 18 has an apparent simplicity and immediacy of address that make it appear more than usually candid and forthright. Although it is frequently anthologized out of sequence or read in isolation, it gains momentum and intensity in relation to the sonnets that surround it. As commentators frequently point out, Sonnets 1–17 constitute an unusual and compelling sub-set or group in which the speaker urges his friend to marry and perpetuate his existence by fathering a child. Against the doubtful value assigned to poetry as memorial in Sonnet 17, 'Who will believe my verse in time to come' (415), Sonnet 18 reasserts a commitment to futurity and a belief in the persistence and durability of poetic creation. Sonnet 18 is also free of the corrosive fear and suspicion that soon begin to undermine the speaker's trust in his friend. Its unsuspecting innocence, troubled only by the shadow of boastful Death, is undoubtedly part of its continuing appeal:

30. George Wright, *Shakespeare's Metrical Art* (Berkeley: University of California Press, 1988), p. 76.
31. Spiller, *The Development of the Sonnet*, p. 159.
32. In what remains one of the most striking and influential accounts of the Sonnets, Joel Fineman claims that Shakespeare simultaneously reconfigures the declining tradition of 'the poetry of praise' and devises a new kind of post-Renaissance poetic subjectivity or 'selfhood'; see *Shakespeare's Perjured Eye: The Invention of Poetic Subjectivity in the Sonnets* (Berkeley: University of California Press, 1986), pp. 1–3.

> Shall I compare thee to a summer's day?
> Thou art more lovely and more temperate:
> Rough winds do shake the darling buds of May,
> And summer's lease hath all too short a date;
> Sometime too hot the eye of heaven shines,
> And often is his gold complexion dimmed,
> And every fair from fair sometime declines,
> By chance or nature's changing course untrimmed:
> But thy eternal summer shall not fade,
> Nor lose possession of that fair thou ow'st;
> Nor shall Death brag thou wand'rest in his shade,
> When in eternal lines to time thou grow'st.
>   So long as men can breathe or eyes can see,
>   So long lives this, and this gives life to thee.   (417)

The process of intensification can be seen at once, as we slip from the pleasantry of 'a summer's day', a proverbial image of perfection, into a more sober reflection on 'summer's lease', and even as the loosely colloquial 'lovely' stiffens into the more restrained 'temperate'. The opening line is startling in its singularity and its direct rhetorical address, though also self-consciously poetic as it embarks upon the primary act of simile-making. The brilliance of that opening line is that it looks two ways at once: though brightly contemplative and buoyant, it hints at inevitable disappointment in the brevity of a single day. The sonnet begins its act of rhetorical persuasion by assuming that the answer to its opening question is both 'Yes' and 'No'. The question initiates the structure of equivalence and contradiction, parallelism and antithesis, which generates so much of the intense linguistic energy in the Sonnets. Within twelve lines, we are imaginatively transported from 'a summer's day' and 'summer's lease' to the wide expanse of 'eternal summer' and 'eternal lines', from the transient beauty of nature to the seeming permanence of art. The opening simile modulates into metaphor, and then into increasingly elaborate figures of speech, as the sun is first imagined as 'the eye of heaven' and then more fully personified (and likened to the young man) through 'his gold complexion'. The imagery of light persists in line 8, which in its broad suggestiveness hints at both the decline of natural beauty when left uncultivated and also the guttering light of a candle left 'untrimmed'. The further decline of light is subtly intimated in 'fade' and 'shade', as the sestet begins to assert the lasting power of poetry against the encroaching darkness.

  Sonnet 18 clearly illustrates the compositional strength and resilience of Shakespeare's Sonnets, inviting comprehension and interpretation on several levels at once. The octave-sestet division, firmly indicated by the conjunction 'But', suggests an overarching conceptual turn from statement to counterstatement, from perceptions of physical beauty and its impermanence to intimations of art and immortality. Working both with and against this two-part structure is the four-part structure suggested by the arrangement of three quatrains and a closing couplet. In the first quatrain, a question is asked and immediately answered; in the second quatrain, the theme of physical diminution is elaborated; in the third quatrain, an assertion is made against the remorseless passage of time through the momentary stay of paradox ('eternal summer'); and in the closing couplet, a more reasonable and less extravagant formulation of longevity is contemplated through the life-enhancing powers of art and poetry. The structural principle of contrast is augmented by the principle of expansion in a way that serves to deepen and intensify possible readings of the sonnet.

As well as manipulating the structural components of the sonnet for maximum rhetorical and expressive effect, Shakespeare is more than usually agile among sonneteers of his time in appropriating and exploiting the vocabulary (and, by implication, the attitudes and values) associated with the diverse discourses of religion, law, patronage, commerce, exploration, astronomy, and prophecy. The confined space of the sonnet enables a highly dense semantic and phonetic patterning in which words find both equivalence and contradiction as they enter into new and unexpected combinations. The resourcefulness of Shakespeare's diction is such that a single word—'untrimmed'—acquires in its context a bewildering range of horticultural, biblical, and nautical associations. This kind of wordplay is not incidental or occasional in Shakespeare's Sonnets, but structurally pervasive and habitual, skilfully exemplifying the rhetorical device of *paronomasia*. The purposeful collocation of Sonnet 18 is seen at play in the subtle shift from 'summer's day' to 'summer's lease', from the colloquial and everyday to the more specialized and contrived, with the season now figured as property and possession, leased or let for a limited period of time. The idea of 'possession' resurfaces in line 10, in relation to the impending loss of the friend's fair beauty. Line 7, 'And every fair from fair sometime declines', gains strength from lexical compression and also from the alliterative play of the *f* sound. Fairness is similarly contracted to 'fair' in line 10, as if enacting its own foreshortening, while 'ow'st' is a contraction of 'ownest' (possession) with a hint of 'owing' (repayment). The tantalizing paradox of 'eternal summer' holds in suspension the sonnet's search for a way of reconciling a desire for permanence with an acceptance of inevitable loss, gently modulating into 'eternal lines' with its happy suggestion of procreation within poetic creation.

The wonder of the closing couplet is that it seems to hold out a glimpse of immortality through the efficacy of lyric verse without ever explicitly making such an ambitious claim for poetry. Rather, it works through an act of rhetorical persuasiveness. The neatness of the parallel phrase 'So long' appeals simultaneously to the eye and the ear, seeming to resolve the preceding dilemmas by allowing 'So' to carry the double meaning of 'as' and 'therefore'. Each word in the final couplet is a monosyllable, which gives a strongly emphatic movement to the closing lines, as does the simple rhyming couplet, simultaneously re-uniting us with the initial 'thee' in the opening line. The final line is a perfectly regular verse of iambic pentameter, and its momentous caesura not only brings 'this' act of writing to the fore, but also induces the ideal reflection of life and art—'lives this, and this gives life'—that it aspires to. Although the closing lines appear to celebrate the permanence of art over life's mutability, and are frequently read in terms of that simple binary, there is nothing 'triumphal' about them. What they testify to is not so much the miraculous transcendence of poetic art, since poetry depends on speakers and listeners for its own life, but rather 'the fragile strength of art before its extinction'.[33]

If Shakespeare's Sonnets represent a significant development in tradition, both in exploring a complicated triangular relationship and in depicting a love that proves to be hurtful and corrosive, they are also remarkable for the candour with which they expose the distinctions of wealth and status that separate the speaker and the young man. The Sonnets move repeatedly, as Sonnet 18 does, from potential disappointment towards moments of revaluation and tentative affirmation, but they can never eradicate the gnawing awareness of social and economic inequities that stand in the way of any wholehearted idealization of love. There is an understandable temptation among readers to applaud the eternizing impulse of the Sonnets, their seeming universal preoccupation with the transcendent value of love and art in the face of time and death, without proper regard for their explicit acknowledgement of material wealth and social influence, and the complicating role that these have in determining the course of love and friendship. We might go further than this and say that the Sonnets are notable for their high estimation of the durability and worth of poetry as a testament of love

33. Vendler, *The Art of Shakespeare's Sonnets*, p. 122.

precisely because they push against, and find it difficult to ignore, the worldly values of rank and power. They assert an alternative idea of power that is boldly measured in opposition to the short-lived supremacy of kings and tyrants.

The vocabulary of favour, honour, and fortune has an elasticity in the Sonnets that allows it to stretch between intimate, amatory forms of address and the more public and devious world of court politics. Sonnet 25 is notable for its subtle reckoning of personal honour in opposition to the public record of titles and military achievements:

> Let those who are in favour with their stars
> Of public honour and proud titles boast,
> Whilst I, whom fortune of such triumph bars,
> Unlooked for joy in that I honour most.
> Great princes' favourites their fair leaves spread
> But as the marigold at the sun's eye,
> And in themselves their pride lies burièd,
> For at a frown they in their glory die.
> The painful warrior famousèd for might
> After a thousand victories, once foiled
> Is from the book of honour razèd quite,
> And all the rest forgot for which he toiled:
>   Then happy I that love and am beloved
>   Where I may not remove, nor be removed.   (431)

'Favour' in the opening line anticipates 'favourites' and acts as a hinge between the workings of astrology and those of a monarchical social order. If 'stars' initially seems to present the social hierarchy as natural and irrefutable, it also troublingly suggests that power and success owe much to chance. The diminishing sunlight from 'the eye of heaven' in Sonnet 18 reappears here in the striking simile of the marigold opening to 'the sun's eye' and closing in its disappearance. The versatile 'frown' is both an image of declining light and a potent reminder of the fickleness of favouritism. In a poem in which we cannot be altogether sure of the value of 'honour', even the greatness of 'Great' princes is cast in doubt. The closing couplet, with its double rhyme on 'love' and 'remove' (full rhymes in Shakespearean English), appears to assert a private ethic of trust and reciprocity against the inconstant world of public affairs, with 'not remove' (staying firm and true) seeming to earn for the speaker the right not to be 'removed' from the love of his friend. However, the euphemistic language of political extirpation ('removed' from office or favour), coupled with the unfortunate medical connotations of being removed or 'flushed' from the system, has clearly already infiltrated the discourse of love, and there is no easy separation of private and public ethics. In this respect, the couplet is a matter of wishful thinking rather than resolute belief.

Much of the pathos of the Sonnets derives from the speaker's abject condition, and a reading of the poems as a collection reveals that abjection to be a consequence of economic insecurity and social degradation, and not simply disappointment in love.[34] David Schalkwyk, in his excellent account of the complicated relationship between love and service in the Sonnets, goes so far as to designate the speaker as 'the poet-servant'. He claims that 'The constitutive tensions of the sonnets to the young man arise from the poet's consciousness of his social inferiority, on the one hand, and his desire for an intimate, affective relationship, on the other.'[35] Words like 'disgrace' and 'outcast' in Sonnet 29 are the inverse of 'favour'. As with Sonnet 25, the lexis of fortune and fate initially conceals a deep-seated complaint about the distribution of privilege and wealth. However we interpret the troubling 'cries' of the sonnet, it clearly has a range and complexity of meaning that far exceed the speaker's personal 'state' of mind:

> When in disgrace with Fortune and men's eyes
> I all alone beweep my outcast state,
> And trouble deaf heaven with my bootless cries,
> And look upon myself and curse my fate,
> Wishing me like to one more rich in hope,
> Featured like him, like him with friends possessed,
> Desiring this man's art, and that man's scope,
> With what I most enjoy contented least;
> Yet in these thoughts myself almost despising,
> Haply I think on thee, and then my state
> (Like to the lark at break of day arising)
> From sullen earth sings hymns at heaven's gate.
>   For thy sweet love remembered such wealth brings
>   That then I scorn to change my state with kings.   (439)

'State' functions like the word 'honour' in Sonnet 25, giving lexical cohesion to the verse through repetition, but also subtly shifting its application from an intimate, personal context to a more obvious social and political realm.

---

34. Ewan Fernie argues persuasively that 'shame' (in all its socio-economic and moral complexity) is a powerful motivating force in the Sonnets. See *Shame in Shakespeare* (London: Routledge, 2002), especially pp. 91–5.
35. David Schalkwyk, *Shakespeare, Love and Service* (Cambridge: Cambridge University Press, 2008), p. 116.

It gains prominence in Sonnet 29 as a repeated rhyme word, so that the rhyme scheme (unusually) becomes *ababcdcdebebff*. There is a further, internal rhyme, with the third and final 'state' in the closing line echoing the preceding rhyme of 'state' and 'gate' in lines 10 and 12. The 'outcast state' in the second line of the octave is momentarily relieved by the aspiring 'state' of happiness in the second line of the sestet, but at the very end of the sonnet the implications of 'state' alter considerably through association with 'kings', inviting thoughts of power and wealth, and not just personal happiness. At one level, then, the sonnet seems to exalt the value of the friend's 'sweet love' over merely pecuniary wealth, even over the vast fortunes of the most powerful men on earth, but at another level it seems unable to ignore the importance of material possession and prosperity.

One way of understanding the sonnet, as John Barrell has argued, is to appreciate the extent to which words and phrases like 'bootless cries', 'rich in hope', 'friends', 'art', and 'scope' might function as an index of both personal relations and economic relations. Together, he claims, these words and phrases 'cohere and co-operate to define the historical moment of their utterance, and to specify within that moment, the social position of the narrator who utters them'.[36] The discourse of patronage (or lack of patronage) that Barrell identifies, with helpful illustrations from other Elizabethan and Jacobean texts, exhibits itself in such a way that the poetry of complaint becomes part plea for recognition and part critique or censure of a system that fails to distinguish between moral and material worth and worthlessness. Barrell's argument extends persuasively to questions of editing, since his contention is that to remove the brackets around the line '(Like to the lark at break of day arising)' and to insert a comma after 'sullen earth' (as some modern editors have done) is to change the tenor of the sestet significantly. The Quarto printing, he insists, suggests that the speaker's 'state' remains firmly attached to 'sullen earth', from which it directs its songs at 'heaven's gate', rather than achieving some glorious transcendence. The neatness of the simile 'Like to the lark' does not readily convey what kind of 'arising' might be involved here (is it spiritual or material or both?). Barrell also notes how the metaphor of 'heaven's gate', through its close proximity to 'sweet love', bestows a God-like power upon the giver of that love. He adds, persuasively, that this recognition of the speaker's subtle manipulation of the discourse of patronage in no way diminishes the pathos of the sonnet.[37]

---

36. John Barrell, *Poetry, Language and Politics* (Manchester: Manchester University Press, 1988), p. 21.
37. Barrell, *Poetry, Language and Politics*, pp. 34, 24, 42.

As we have seen with Sonnet 18, the value and worth of poetry that the speaker impresses upon the young man and offers in exchange for his trust is its lasting power, its capacity for creating an image of love and devotion that will persist throughout the ages. Many of the Sonnets are explicit and assertive in the way that they measure the achievements of verse against material and worldly success, not necessarily to claim the supremacy of one over the other, but rather to explore and complicate the relationship between them. A familiar strategy in the Sonnets is to render poetry as epitaph: a tribute more gracious and durable than tombs and monuments, but one nevertheless concerned with 'praise' and 'posterity'. Poetry is then granted a value and a power exceeding the best efforts of princes to memorialize themselves, as in Sonnet 55:

> Not marble, nor the gilded monuments
> Of princes shall outlive this pow'rful rhyme,
> But you shall shine more bright in these contents
> Than unswept stone besmeared with sluttish time.

Even so, as the closing couplet somewhat awkwardly concedes, that judgement is qualified by the final Judgement at 'the ending doom', and so, too, are any further thoughts of 'arising': 'So, till the judgement that yourself arise, | You live in this, and dwell in lovers' eyes' (491). However much we might be tempted to read the Sonnets primarily as an assertion of creative power over mutability and decay, that simple opposition is repeatedly intensified and complicated by considerations of agency and power that are social, political, and economic. In Sonnet 64, there is both a plangent expression of loss and an undisguised social disdain for 'The rich proud cost of outworn buried age' and 'sometime lofty towers' brought down by Time. The sonnet opens, like Sonnet 29, with a temporal reckoning of fortune, but carries this through to the sestet and opens it out into a general meditation on mutability:

> When I have seen such interchange of state,
> Or state itself confounded to decay,
> Ruin hath taught me thus to ruminate,
> That Time will come and take my love away.   (509)

The 'interchange of state' refers to the encroachment of sea on land in the preceding lines, but the sonnet's acknowledgement of 'the kingdom of the shore' immediately turns that elemental imagery towards considerations of political power. At an abstract level, 'interchange' suggests both swapping and transformation, but it also carries legal and political connotations that suggest the transfer of property and government, just as 'state itself' in the next line prompts the idea of 'commonwealths brought to nothing'. 'Ruin' (both physical decline and personal misfortune) is phonetically captured in 'ruminate', and the hint of a half rhyme gives the line an adroitness and self-containment that makes any elaboration seem superfluous. The realization of how our material circumstances condition our thought is far more radical and unsettling than the simple proposition that follows it.

Often, lines that seem to operate at the level of generality, reflecting on common human truths and dilemmas, turn out to have more specific social and historical references, or present themselves (as do the lines on 'interchange of state') in a teasingly multivalent way that overlays one set of meanings with another. The playful, entertaining way in which Shakespeare writes of shadow and substance embraces both idealist philosophical assumptions about the nature of truth and materialist concerns about wealth and worth. Sonnet 37 presents the speaker as 'decrepit' and lamed by Fortune, but taking 'comfort' from the young man's 'worth and truth'. The sestet boldly announces, 'So then I am not lame, poor, nor despised, | Whilst that this shadow doth such substance give' (455). The element of surprise that accompanies the paradoxical figure of a shadow providing substance initially deters us from appreciating the diverse range of meanings it embodies. The shadow or image of the young man gives nourishing life or substance to the speaker (extending the earlier metaphor in which the speaker's love is 'engrafted' to the young man's 'store' of virtues and possessions), and it also proves the truth of his being. At the same time, 'substance' gains obvious material suggestions through association with words like 'wealth', 'store', and 'abundance'. The young man is a man of substance, just as he is a man of parts (cohering in his shadow or image), of which the speaker hopes to claim a part. Similarly, 'shadow' extends itself across the page, with the speaker manifestly in the shadow of his fortunate friend, but also like a 'poor player' or shadow acting out a part, as well as expecting one.

In Sonnet 53, the Platonic relationship of shadow and substance is once again playfully invoked, and once again there is a semantic drift that has to do with wealth and patronage. To many modern readers familiar with the psychological insights of Freud and Jung, the opening lines have a startling contemporaneity, as if venturing a daring new theory of personality: 'What is your substance, wherof are you made, | That millions of strange shadows on you tend?' (487). As John Kerrigan remarks, the implication of 'strange' seems to be that, although the shadows 'do not belong to the young man, they are pieces of him, fragments and flawed reflections'.[38] If the young man is admired in earlier sonnets for his several 'parts', he is here presented as mysteriously and intriguingly irreducible. Shadows 'tend' on him in the sense of congregating or moving in his direction, tending to resemble him, but also in attending to his needs (waiting in service). As numerous commentators have pointed out, 'shadows' plausibly alludes to lackeys and parasites, giving added significance both to 'substance' and to 'every shadow lend'. The second and third quatrains of the sonnet (lines 5–12) heap extravagant praise upon the young man and his androgynous beauty, skilfully elaborating the idea that every act of verbal or artistic representation, be it depicting Adonis, Helen, or the changing seasons, is a poor imitation or derivative of the single, original thing of beauty. The closing couplet seeks to reconcile the abiding paradox that the young man is both archetypal (with all fine forms seeming to partake of his beauty and worth) and unique: 'In all external grace you have some part, | But you like none, none you, for constant heart' (487). For all its philosophical subtlety and its deft play with ideas of imitation, the sonnet is shaped by considerations of patronage. The young man's 'external grace' involves not just 'elegant refinement of manner' but 'willingness to grant favours'. The consonance that Vendler notes between 'substance' in the first line and 'constant' in the last might well be read in terms of the habitual tendency of the Sonnets to represent what appear to be economic relations as 'natural' personal relations.

An awareness of the extent to which Shakespeare's Sonnets inflect the language of love and devotion with historically rooted concerns about wealth and social standing (and the lack of these) in no way diminishes their power and eloquence as poetry, or their capacity to speak movingly to readers across several centuries. What is truly radical about the Sonnets, and what constitutes a vital part of their legacy in the hands of later poets such as Shelley and Auden, is their extraordinary grasp of contingency—their moments of sudden realization that the course of history might well be diverted by the 'millioned accidents' that 'Creep in 'twixt vows, and change decrees of kings'. No doubt, a strong sense of insecurity and uncertainty keeps the intelligence that informs the Sonnets sharply focused on the 'course of alt'ring things' (Sonnet 115, 611). What marks the difference between 'this poor rhyme' in Sonnet 107 (595) and 'this pow'rful rhyme' in Sonnet 55 (491)

---

38. John Kerrigan (ed.), *William Shakespeare: The Sonnets and a Lover's Complaint* (Harmondsworth: Penguin 1986; 1999), p. 237.

might, crudely put, be money, but it is also the tremendous sense of futurity, the sense of a history not yet written, that the Sonnets collectively reach towards. Sonnet 107, more than any other sonnet in the collection, seems uplifted and inspired by the anticipatory illumination of a world to come that Kiernan Ryan finds so compelling in the plays.[39] Even while disavowing 'the prophetic soul | Of the wide world', the sonnet allows itself the luxury of 'dreaming on things to come', with the speaker confidently forecasting that he, and not just the putative friend or patron, will 'live' in verse. The strongly subjunctive mood that characterizes the closing couplet in so many of the Sonnets is all the more remarkable in a poem that has so often been singled out for its apparent chronicling of contemporary historical actualities:

> Not mine own fears, nor the prophetic soul
> Of the wide world, dreaming on things to come,
> Can yet the lease of my true love control,
> Supposed as forfeit to a confined doom.
> The mortal moon hath her eclipse endured,
> And the sad augurs mock their own presage.
> Incertainties now crown themselves assured,
> And peace proclaims olives of endless age.
> Now with the drops of this most balmy time
> My love looks fresh, and death to me subscribes,
> Since, spite of him, I'll live in this poor rhyme,
> While he insults o'er dull and speechless tribes.
>   And thou in this shalt find thy monument,
>   When tyrants' crests and tombs of brass are spent. (595)

The eclipse of the 'mortal moon' has prompted much debate among editors and critics of the Sonnets, who have variously pointed to the defeat of the Spanish Armada (drawn up in crescent formation) in 1588; the eclipse (much feared) that passed without incident in 1595; the so-called 'grand climacteric' (the sixty-third year) of Queen Elizabeth in 1595–6; and the rumour that the queen (popularly associated with Cynthia, the goddess of chastity and the moon) was seriously ill in 1599–1600. However, there is extensive evidence, much of it compiled by John Kerrigan, to support the case that Sonnet 107 relates to the death of the queen and the accession of James I in 1603 (with 'olives of endless age' alluding to the efforts of the king's supporters to present his reign as one of peaceful prosperity).[40] The dating of the sonnet

---

39. Kiernan Ryan, *Shakespeare* (Basingstoke: Palgrave, 1989; 2002), p. 176.
40. Kerrigan, *William Shakespeare*, pp. 313–20.

as a Jacobean poem of the early 1600s supports the speculation that 'confined doom' refers to a literal imprisonment (possibly that of the Earl of Southampton, who was released from the Tower in 1603, or that of the Earl of Pembroke, released from the Fleet prison in 1601). If this and other Sonnets prompt intense historical speculation, they also impress upon their readers a powerful and compelling intuition of a history not yet written, of a future time 'When tyrants' crests and tombs of brass are spent'.

John Donne, George Herbert, William Drummond, and Lady Mary Wroth

It might seem from the intense concentration on religious self-expression in the poetry of the early seventeenth century, especially in the work of John Donne and George Herbert, that the development of the sonnet at this time reflects a general turning away from secular to sacred experience. It would be much too simple, however, to assume that the exhaustion of Petrarchan themes and ideals of love prompts a shift from physical to spiritual preoccupations in sonnet writing. What proves to be most interesting is the inter-relationship of amatory and religious forms of the sonnet, and the extent to which the rhetoric of desire and despair can be variously manipulated within ostensibly different kinds of passionate address. As Helen Wilcox notes, 'It is a sign of the profound interconnection of secular and sacred experience in Donne's work that, while his love poems in the *Songs and Sonnets* include no formal sonnets, his devotional poetry embraces this poetic form most closely associated with the Petrarchan tradition of earthly love.'[41] 'Devotion' is the mediating term that allows so many religious sonnets to function as love poems to God—wildly and extravagantly in the sonnets of Donne, candidly and imploringly in the sonnets of Herbert. Even when seeming to reject the worldly love sonnet, Herbert engages with its strategies and conceits in dynamic ways, subtly reconfiguring Petrarchan concepts to better serve his God.

The sonnet is flexible enough and amenable enough to allow the familiar forms of address in love poetry to be translated into spiritual meditation and prayer. The conversational address to God, fluctuating between praise

---

41. Helen Wilcox, 'Devotional Writing', in *The Cambridge Companion to John Donne*, ed. Achsah Guibbory (Cambridge: Cambridge University Press, 2006), p. 150.

and plea, and embracing fears, hopes, and desires, is a compelling aspect of the religious sonnet, giving it a powerful, dramatic appeal. At the same time, as Louis Martz has convincingly shown, the sonnet form is particularly well disposed to the poetry of meditation, with the tripartite structure set up by the quatrain divisions neatly corresponding to the three-part spiritual meditation advocated by Ignatius Loyola, founder of the Jesuits.[42] In addition, the language of paradox and hyperbole, so artfully wrought by sonneteers in the pursuit of love's definition, lends itself superbly well to the anguished exploration of sin and redemption, death and resurrection. The intensification of stylistic traits and attributes inherent in the love sonnet, as well as a declared departure from them, seems to encourage Donne, Herbert, and others to strive for astonishing new levels of technical achievement within a form already recognized as an index of rhetorical finesse: 'A recurring concern of the sonneteers is the extent to which their own skills are stretched in their impossible desire to speak of and to God.'[43]

It is worth remembering that the religious sonnet in England dates back to 1560 and the publication of *A Meditation of a Penitent Sinner* by Anne Lok, and that holy sonnets were written by both Protestant and Catholic writers in the late 1500s and early 1600s, among them Henry Constable, Henry Lok, Barnabe Barnes, William Alabaster, and Nicholas Breton. *A Divine Centurie of Spirituall Sonnets* by Barnabe Barnes (1595) testifies to the popularity of religious sonnet sequences in the period, though smaller, prayer-like groupings of sonnets were also composed for meditative purposes. Donne's 'La Corona' is a sequence of seven sonnets, a meditation on the life of Christ, in which images of weaving construct 'a crown of prayer and praise', while the interlocking of first and last lines sets up a liturgical, Rosary-like pattern of repetition and circularity.[44] The opening sonnet plays with the various connotations of 'crown' and 'crowning', freely exchanging the poet's crown of bays for Christ's crown of thorns and the hope of resurrection in a 'crown of glory'. Written sometime between 1607 and 1609 (the year in which Shakespeare's Sonnets were published), 'La Corona' might have been produced for the spiritual benefit of Magdalen Herbert (the mother of

---

42. Louis L. Martz, *The Poetry of Meditation* (New Haven: Yale University Press, 1955), p. 43.
43. Helen Wilcox, 'Sacred Desire, Forms of Belief: The Religious Sonnet in Early Modern Britain', in *The Cambridge Companion to the Sonnet* (Cambridge: Cambridge University Press, 2011), p. 152.
44. Quotations from John Donne's sonnets are from *John Donne*, ed. John Carey (Oxford: Oxford University Press, 1990).

George Herbert). The sonnets employ an inventive crossing of Italian and English rhyme schemes, with *abbaabba* in the octave and either *cddcee* or *cdcdee* in the sestet, ensuring that there is always a closing couplet, but occasionally an additional rhyming couplet in lines 10–11. The same deployment of rhymes appears in the nineteen *Holy Sonnets* composed by Donne between 1610 and 1619. These later sonnets, among the best known and greatly admired of all Donne's poems, do not form a sequence, but together they constitute a powerful grouping of religious sonnets and demonstrate some of the most technically adventurous uses of the form in its entire history.

The imaginative daring and linguistic intensity of Donne's sonnets are well represented in the sonnet summoning angels to announce the Last Day:

> At the round earth's imagined corners, blow
> Your trumpets, angels, and arise, arise
> From death, you numberless infinities
> Of souls, and to your scattered bodies go,
> All whom the flood did, and fire shall o'erthrow,
> All whom war, dearth, age, agues, tyrannies,
> Despair, law, chance, hath slain, and you whose eyes,
> Shall behold God, and never taste death's woe.
> But let them sleep, Lord, and me mourn a space,
> For, if above all these, my sins abound,
> 'Tis late to ask abundance of thy grace,
> When we are there; here on this lowly ground,
> Teach me how to repent; for that's as good
> As if thou hadst sealed my pardon, with thy blood.   (175)

The sonnet is composed as a three-part meditation, opening with a scene of contemplation, moving into comprehension, and closing with contrition. What is most striking, however, is Donne's compelling imaginative attempt to picture the Last Judgement within the circumscribed space of the opening eight lines, and the sheer verbal energy with which this vision is conveyed. Drawing provocatively on myths and maps of the earth's shape and magnitude, the sonnet uses paradox to tease and confound the mental reckoning of its readers, just as 'numberless infinities' tests the mind's capacity to comprehend the action of the soul in returning to the body on the final day. The strategic placing of imperative verbs, combined with strident enjambment, gives power and authority to the verse, with the peremptory 'arise, arise' coming between the prolonged vowel music of 'blow' and 'go'. The second quatrain is densely and bewilderingly packed with images of the dead, a veritable catalogue of misfortune and inevitability stretching from the biblical flood to the apocalyptic destruction of the earth by fire. The urgency of the call is reinforced by the anaphoric repetition of 'All whom' and by the alliterative alignment and tight compression of past and future tenses: 'the flood did, and fire shall o'erthrow'. The clamour of the quatrain is gently relieved, as we move towards the sestet, by the sudden, touching acknowledgement, in a second-person address, of those still living at the time of the Last Judgement: 'you whose eyes | Shall behold God, and never taste death's woe.'

With the prayer-like turn, the sonnet enacts a dramatic reversal of its powerful opening call for the end of the world, and the speaker now registers a sober and sombre awareness of his own urgent need for repentance: 'But let them sleep, Lord, and me mourn a space'. The strong imperatives of the octave modulate into a plea, and the sonnet reverts from the visionary, apocalyptic geography of the opening to the humble and abject condition of 'this lowly ground'. The transition is marvellously performed by the strong mid-line caesura and the striking deictic placement of 'there; here' in line 12, setting up the closing couplet in which the speaker seeks to earn the pardon and forgiveness promised in Christ's sacrifice. The idea of pardon 'sealed' or confirmed is given palpable form in the associated image of a seal in blood. For all its apparent humility and capitulation in the face of ultimate authority, the sonnet retains its imaginative daring in the amiable discourse with which it conducts its colloquy with God, and in the speaker's bold suggestion that Judgement might be delayed to let him 'mourn a space'.

Donne's legacy for later sonnet writers—for soldier poets such as Wilfred Owen, as much as for religious authors such as Gerard Manley Hopkins—has much to do with the subtle rhetorical contrivance by which he controls and contains the most extreme anxieties and fears. His achievement is partly a matter of address, as with the masterful personification of Death in 'Death be not proud, though some have called thee | Mighty and dreadful'. What seems at first to be a chiding, declamatory voice takes on great tonal complexity, by turns chastising and confiding, steadily accumulating conviction through the simple, repeated conjunction 'And', and through the curt rhetorical question, 'why swell'st thou then?' If the sonnet is an elaborate verbal performance, excelling in the language of paradox and embracing both lyrical musing and dramatic speech, it also functions as a small sermon, exploring and communicating the mysteries of our being: 'One short sleep past, we wake eternally, | And death shall be no more, Death thou shalt die' (175–6).

Donne's startling achievement is to compose a series of holy sonnets that exceed some of the most candid secular love poetry of the time in their vivacious physicality, sexualized language, and erotic imagery. The obvious and immediate tension between sacred and sexual longing is gripping and profound. At the same time, the innovative nature of these sonnets derives from intricate technical devices and effects at the level of diction, syntax, metre, and rhyme. The opening of one of Donne's most celebrated sonnets is a triumph of poetic violence, giving hyperbolic force to the gentle, appealing image of Christ knocking imploringly at the door of the sinner's heart in Revelation 3:20. Part of the novelty has to do with Donne's dismissal of intermediaries and his direct address to the three persons of the Trinity at once, but the innovation is also audible, conveyed through the reversed foot of the opening word and the cluster of stressed syllables in the second line: 'Batter my heart, three-personed God; for you | As yet but knock, breathe, shine, and seek to mend.' It is only when we reach the second quatrain that we can fully appreciate the daring nature of the opening conceit and the phallic image of the battering ram directed at a heart in siege. The language of warfare is skilfully intertwined with the charged vocabulary of sexual desire, while freedom and purity are envisaged within the fierce language of paradox: 'Take me to you, imprison me, for I | Except you enthral me, never shall be free, | Nor ever chaste, except you ravish me.' Syntactically, the rhyming couplet depends on the preceding line and what it articulates is continuing struggle rather than confident resolution. The speaker's appeal to his maker to 'bend | Your force, to break, blow, burn, and make me new' is vigorously acted out in the making of the sonnet itself (177–8).[45]

Donne brings about a decisive re-direction in the history of the sonnet form through a radical appropriation of the erotic love lyric for a new and intense kind of religious, meditational poetry. George Herbert, cautiously following his footsteps, begins his poetic career with two notable sonnets in which he querulously inveighs against 'those many Love-poems, that are daily writ and consecrated to *Venus*', and asks his God, 'Why are not *Sonnets* made of thee?'[46] As with Donne, a dramatic tension is created between secular

---

45. In a stimulating reading of Donne's sonnet, Ewan Fernie reminds us that the speaker who cries out for divine possession is already betrothed to the Devil, and that Donne therefore courts 'a degree of scandalous equivalency between these traditionally opposed powers'. See *The Demonic: Literature and Experience* (London: Routledge, 2013), p. 221.
46. Quotations from George Herbert's sonnets are from *The Works of George Herbert*, ed. F. E. Hutchinson (Oxford: Clarendon Press, 1941).

and sacred images and vocabularies, but a different kind of dynamic ensues. For all their colloquial vigour, metaphorical ingenuity, and argumentative skill, Herbert's sonnets work towards the rejection of elaborate, hyperbolic tropes of love and the achievement of a contrasting plain and simple style. The two early sonnets were sent as a New Year's gift to his mother in 1610, when Herbert was just 16 and in his first year as a student at Cambridge. In the accompanying letter to his mother, he declares his resolution to consecrate his abilities in poetry to God's glory. His determination to 'look towards *God* and *Heaven*' clearly informs the paired sonnets, with one seeming to answer and placate the agitated questions of the other:

> My God, where is that ancient heat towards thee,
>   Wherewith whole shoals of *Martyrs* once did burn,
>   Besides their other flames? Doth Poetry
> Wear *Venus* Livery? only serve her turn?
> Why are not *Sonnets* made of thee? and layes
>   Upon thine Altar burnt? Cannot thy love
>   Heighten a spirit to sound out thy praise
> As well as any she? Cannot thy *Dove*
> Out-strip their *Cupid* easily in flight?
>   Or, since thy wayes are deep, and still the same,
>   Will not a verse run smooth that bears thy name?
> Why doth that fire, which by thy power and might
>   Each breast does feel, no braver fuel choose
>   Than that, which one day Worms may chance refuse?
>
> Sure, Lord, there is enough in thee to dry
>   Oceans of *Ink*; for, as the Deluge did
>   Cover the Earth, so doth thy Majesty:
> Each Cloud distills thy praise, and doth forbid
> *Poets* to turn it to another use.
>   *Roses* and *Lillies* speak thee; and to make
>   A pair of Cheeks of them, is thy abuse.
> Why should I *Womens eyes* for Chrystal take?
> Such poor invention burns in their low mind
>   Whose fire is wild, and doth not upward go
>   To praise, and on thee, Lord, some *Ink* bestow.
> Open the bones, and you shall nothing find
>   In the best *face* but *filth*, when, Lord, in thee
>   The *beauty* lies in the *discovery*.   (206)

There is a high degree of technical proficiency and adventurousness in these sonnets, suggesting that Herbert has shrewdly noted and skilfully emulated the colloquial vigour of Sidney, the coursing enjambment of Donne, and perhaps even the neatly turned quatrain and couplet structures of Shakespeare, whose sonnets had only just recently appeared in print. The opening sonnet establishes an intimate address with God, but works primarily through repeated rhetorical questions, breaking up the congruence of line and sense by introducing a high degree of enjambment and strong mid-line pauses. The force of complaint delays the turn until line 10, but when it does arrive, it settles into a mimetic metrical smoothness, aided by the felicitous couplet in the opportune rhyme scheme (*ababcdcdeffegg*): 'Or, since they ways are deep, and still the same, | Will not a verse run smooth that bears thy name?' The prevailing conceit is that of fire: the sonnet contrasts the burning passion of love with the holy fires of martyrdom, briefly diverting into metaphors of flight and running water before reasserting the fiery power of the divine spirit over merely physical and fleshly devotion.

The second sonnet perpetuates the fire metaphor, but also introduces a self-reflexive interest in the proper uses of ink. Once again, it is as if the passionate lines of enquiry and retort cannot be neatly contained within the quatrain divisions suggested by rhyme, and they keep spilling over, as line 4 so flagrantly does. Accordingly, while there is a notional 4 + 4 + 4 + 2 structure suggested by the placement of rhyme, the sentence structure and punctuation dictate a different (5 + 2 + 1 + 3 + 3) deployment of lines. The closing couplet is relieved of any suggestion of easy resolution or complacent summing up by its syntactical adhesion to the preceding line 12. The sonnet closes with an unforgettable meditation on the mortal remains within the grave, faithfully contrasting physical decay with the spiritual renewal of Christ's resurrection. The shock of '*filth*' found in the fairest face is gently relieved by the wonder of '*discovery*', subtly conveying both the revelation associated with Christ's empty tomb and the rewards of a slow and patient uncovering or disclosing of the truth.

In addition to these two early New Year's sonnets, Herbert wrote fifteen sonnets that were printed in his posthumous collection of poems, *The Temple* (1633). The form tends to be Shakespearean or a variant of this (*ababcdcdeffegg*), and sometimes fewer rhymes are used, but the sonnets always close with a couplet. The sonnet provides an ideal space for the characteristic movement in Herbert's poems, from expostulation and elaborate conceit to humility and chastened simplicity. 'Prayer (1)' demonstrates this movement superbly well, initiating a reflection on the meaning of prayer that matches some of the metaphysical poets' definitions of love in its subtlety and ingenuity:

> Prayer the Churches banquet, Angels age,
>   Gods breath in man returning to his birth,

> The soul in paraphrase, heart in pilgrimage,
> The Christian plummet sounding heav'n and earth.

In swift succession, the sonnet considers prayer as spiritual food or sustenance, as a meditation on the timeless existence of the angels, as God's animating breath, as the clarifying expansion of the soul and the spiritual journey of the heart, and as a device or tool for measuring the distance between earth and heaven ('sounding' subtly suggesting both exploration and speech). As the sonnet proceeds, however, the definitions become ever more elaborate and clever, so that the search for the most fitting way of describing prayer begins to resemble an intellectual game or riddle. Lacking a main verb, the sonnet stacks up its definitions, one or two to a line, but it seems to get no nearer to a comprehensive account of its subject. The sestet tries a different tack, proposing abstract states and conjoined single words as epithets of prayer: 'Softness, and peace, and joy, and love, and blisse', but still the sonnet calls out for more exalted definitions. Although the sestet strives to see prayer as 'Heaven in ordinarie' (ordinary things, as well as the Ordinary daily mass), it reaches out in a final imaginative burst of invention towards the extraordinary and the exotic. The great achievement of the sonnet is in the skill and control with which it gives free rein to imaginative extravagance, before the sudden pause and quiet declaration of a more humble and satisfying concept of prayer in the closing half line:

> The milkie way, the bird of Paradise,
>   Church-bels beyond the starres heard, the souls bloud,
>   The land of spices; something understood.   (51)

In just two words, Herbert arrives at an appreciation of prayer as that which is beyond definition, with the vagueness but essentiality of 'something' eschewing all previous elaborate descriptions and 'understood' standing firmly for contrite recognition and personal conviction in communion with God.

'Redemption' shows how well Herbert could fit a parable-like narrative to the three quatrains and closing couplet of the English sonnet, enacting a three-part journey in which the speaker seeks to renew the terms of his faith or 'lease' and does so through a powerful and extraordinary encounter with his 'Lord':

> Having been tenant long to a rich Lord,
>   Not thriving, I resolved to be bold,
>   And make a suit unto him, to afford
> A new small-rented lease, and cancel th' old.

With simple economy of diction and syntax, Herbert creates a speaker who is earnest but misguided, and the sonnet is once again a lesson in humility. The speaker's searching brings him back to earth and to a more considered awareness of 'greatness':

> I straight returned, and knowing his great birth,
>   Sought him accordingly in great resorts;
>   In cities, theatres, gardens, parks, and courts:
> At length I heard a ragged noise and mirth
>   Of theeves and murderers: there I him espied,
>   Who straight, *Your suit is granted*, said, & died.   (40)

The sestet turns on the idea of straightness, contrasting the anxious, self-seeking nature of the speaker's 'straight' return (direct and at once) with the 'straight' (right and proper, as well as immediate) granting of his suit by the crucified Christ. There is a stunned realization of the enormity of Christ's sacrifice in the sudden reporting of his death, as well as an awed apprehension of its mystery. There is a profound acknowledgement, too, of the social radicalism of Christ's message and its shunning of worldly power. The startling discovery of Christ among the sinners and the outcast is powerfully rendered in the transposed epithet of 'ragged noise and mirth'. At the same time, Herbert gently prises the sonnet form away from the centres of courtly power and opens it to a devotional conscience that cannot help but challenge social distinctions and inequities.

'The Answer', one of Herbert's most formally accomplished sonnets, shows yet another devotional purpose that the form might serve by couching its spiritual enquiry in the style of a near confessional:

> My comforts drop and melt away like snow:
> I shake my head, and all the thoughts and ends,
> Which my fierce youth did bandie, fall and flow
> Like leaves about me: or like summer friends,
> Flyes of estates and sunne-shine. But to all,
> Who think me eager, hot, and undertaking,
> But in my prosecutions slack and small;
> As a young exhalation, newly waking,
> Scorns his first bed of dirt, and means the sky;
> But cooling by the way, grows pursie and slow,
> And setling to a cloud, doth live and die
> In that dark state of tears: to all, that so
>   Show me, and set me, I have one reply,
>   Which they that know the rest, know more then I.   (169)

The sonnet candidly and poignantly records a moment of painful exposure, when the speaker's youthful energies and assurances seem to have melted away or fallen like autumn leaves, and his spiritual quest for improvement and redemption seems to stall, leaving him stagnating in a 'dark state of tears'. Once again, the sonnet eschews the social niceties associated with worldly power and possession in its rueful recollection of 'summer friends, | Flyes of estates and sunne-shine'. Like Shakespeare's Sonnet 121, 'The Answer' initially seems anxious to defend its speaker's reputation against charges of personal misconduct, but Herbert's sonnet is altogether different, both in its syntactical manoeuvres and in its spiritual resolution. The search for an answer to the dilemmas of existence pushes the syntax of the sonnet over the usual quatrain divisions and over the octave-sestet division, so that the movement and direction of the poem have to be registered with special care. The insertion of 'But' in line 5 and then again in line 7 leaves us wondering where the turn might be, but then it suddenly appears with the brilliant metaphysical conceit of the self as 'a young exhalation' rising skywards like vapour from the earth. The use of the colloquial 'pursie' (swollen or puffy), like the earlier 'bandie' (toss to and fro), helps the sonnet to retain a colloquial intimacy while rising towards revelation. With a dramatically powerful use of *aposiopesis* (a shift from speech to silence), the sonnet breaks off its thought processes with the word 'tears', struggling to recover its momentum in the repeated address of line 5, 'to all'. The answer promised by the title proves opaque and unyielding, with the internal rhymes of 'so', 'Show', and 'know' effectively offsetting any inclination towards complacency or easy resolution. The sonnet provides its answer by withholding it, revealing a speaker who is wiser than he initially seemed in his patient acceptance of what cannot be known.

Some credit for revitalizing the sonnet in the seventeenth century should be given to William Drummond, Laird of Hawthornden Castle and estate in Midlothian, Scotland. An avid reader, with a large private library of European literature, Drummond infused his sonnets with allusions, quotations, and translations, easefully demonstrating his knowledge of English, Italian, French, and Spanish poetry. He was, as he himself noted, the only British poet to have followed Petrarch in composing a sequence of sonnets addressing a loved one *in vita* and *in morte*. However, his most original and imposing work is to be found in the spiritual poems, printed in the third section, 'Urania', of his *Poems* (1616) and in the later *Flowers of Sion* (1623).

As with Donne, there is a linguistic brilliance prompted by the sublime apprehension of heaven and its angels:

> To spreade the azure Canopie of Heauen,
> And spangle it all with Sparkes of burning Gold,
> To place this ponderous Globe of Earth so euen,
> That it should all, and nought should it vphold:
> To giue strange Motions to the Planets seuen,
> And *Ioue* to make so meeke, and *Mars* so bold,
> To temper what is moist, drie, hote, and cold,
> Of all their Iarres that sweet Accords are giuen.
> LORD, to thy Wit is nought, nought to thy Might,
> But that thou shouldst (*thy Glorie laid aside*)
> Come basely in Mortalitie to bide,
> And die for them deseru'd eternall Plight,
>   A Wonder is, so farre aboue our Wit,
>   That *Angells* stand amaz'd to thinke on it.[47]

The repeated infinitive underscores the mystery and wonder of God's creation, as well as the imaginative challenge in trying to write about it. The opening is beautifully embellished and sensuously evocative, with the alliterative trio of 'spreade' and 'spangle' and 'Sparkes' reinforcing a strong physical impression of colour and light and warmth. Like Donne, Drummond teasingly blends a contemporary scientific discourse of planetary motion and geographical climate with common wisdom and popular myth. The rhyme scheme—*abababbacddcee*—is a hybrid form favoured by Drummond, allowing for both the elegant envelope rhymes of the Petrarchan model and the emphatic closing couplet of its Shakespearean counterpart. In a strikingly innovative move, the sonnet lengthens out its enquiry into the wonder of creation by extending the breathless syntax of the octave (a single sentence) to line 9, when it first tentatively addresses the Lord of creation. Accordingly, the turn is effectively delayed until line 10, when the speaker sees, in sharp contrast to the glorious maker, a God 'Come basely in Mortalitie to bide'. The sonnet ascends to rhetorical heights in its vision of creation and its colloquy with God, but it just as surely comes back to earth with its deflationary closing couplet, simultaneously elevating and undermining poetic wit, and cleverly displacing human thought and amazement on to the attendant angels.

---

47. *The Poetical Works of William Drummond of Hawthornden*, ed. L. E. Kastner (Manchester: Manchester University Press, 1913), vol. 1, p. 87.

A later sonnet, 'The Booke of the World' (Sonnet vi in *Flowers of Sion*), brings Herbert, rather than Donne, to mind, both in its simple, homely conceit of the world as a book and in its humility in the face of God's truth and beauty. As with Herbert's poems, the sonnet presents a searing criticism of human vanity and egotism, but one that clearly has a particular relevance for the writer whose bookish preoccupations are a cause of spiritual neglect:

> Of this fair Volumne which wee World doe name,
> If wee the sheetes and leaues could turne with care,
> Of Him who it correctes and did it frame,
> Wee cleare might read the Art and Wisedome rare?
> Finde out his Power which wildest Pow'rs doth tame,
> His Prouidence extending euerie-where,
> His Iustice which proud Rebels doeth not spare,
> In euery Page, no, Period of the same:
> But sillie wee, like foolish Children, rest
> Well pleas'd with coloured Velame, Leaues of Gold,
> Faire dangling Ribbones, leauing what is best,
> On the great Writers sense nee'r taking hold;
>   Or if by chance our Mindes doe muse on ought,
>   It is some Picture on the Margine wrought.[48]

Once again, Drummond employs a hybrid sonnet form with both Petrarchan and Shakespearean elements (*abababbacdcdee*), starting with a reasoned, allegorical premiss, proceeding to a heightened declaration of God's power and providence in the second quatrain, and then using the turn to enforce a critique of our human propensity to value pleasure over sense. The closing couplet resists censure on the grounds of its rhythmic neatness, because it is, itself, an act of censure. The rather pat couplet spells out the spiritual instruction that we are too easily distracted by marginal and inessential things. The reference to 'proud Rebels' recalls the fallen angels and reminds us of a God who exercises both power and providence, but in retrospect it might also alert us to Drummond's Royalist politics. If Drummond seems at some distance, culturally and politically, from Milton, it is nevertheless important to note how effectively his spiritual sonnets demolish social hierarchies in their all-encompassing critique of 'sillie wee'. Already, by the early 1600s, the

---

48. *The Poetical Works of William Drummond of Hawthornden*, ed. L. E. Kastner (Manchester: Manchester University Press, 1913), vol. 2, p. 8.

sonnet has moved a long way from its court origins and has become adept at addressing a much broader potential readership. It might seem fitting, then, that it was Milton's nephew, Edward Phillips, who in 1656 edited and published a major edition of Drummond's *Poems*, helping to keep his work in circulation.

It was in familiar court circles, however, that Lady Mary Wroth composed what is generally seen as the last of the English Petrarchan sonnet sequences. As the daughter of Robert Sidney and the niece of Sir Philip, she was exceptionally well placed to make a strong impression on the development of the English sonnet. *Pamphilia to Amphilanthus* (1621) appears relatively late, after the vogue for amatory sonnet sequences in seventeenth-century England has begun to die down, but it is the first to provide an extended exploration of female subjectivity.[49] Amphilanthus is probably based on William Herbert (assumed by some to be the dedicatee of Shakespeare's Sonnets), who became her lover after the death of her husband in 1614, though (as with the Sonnets) such speculation does little to enhance an appreciation of the complex ideas of love that inform the sequence. If the speaker of these painful sonnets strives for autonomy, she also reveals a deep-seated sense of powerlessness and enforced passivity. Wroth's radical contribution to the tradition of sonnet writing might well be in the candid declaration of distress, as much as in the yearning for fulfilment. Diana Henderson observes how 'her female subject usually remains in the shadows, aligned with darkness and pain', and Heather Dubrow notes 'the exceptionally melancholic tone of her sonnets'.[50] As Dubrow has argued, it would be unwise to classify the sonnets as either Petrarchan or anti-Petrarchan, since part of their distinctive achievement is to confound these categories and move beyond them into an altogether richer and more complicated depiction of female desire.

From the opening dream vision onwards, the sonnets in *Pamphilia to Amphilanthus* seem intent on both embracing and disrupting familiar Petrarchan conventions. The speaker dreams of her heart being 'martyred' and hopes on waking for relief, only to find that the pain is real and unabated. The

---

49. Quotations from the sonnets of Lady Mary Wroth are from *Lady Mary Wroth: Poems*, ed. R. E. Pritchard (Keele: Keele University Press, 1996).
50. Diana E. Henderson, 'The Sonnet, Subjectivity and Gender', in *The Cambridge Companion to the Sonnet* (Cambridge: Cambridge University Press, 2011), p. 58. Heather Dubrow, *Echoes of Desire: English Petrarchism and its Counterdiscourses* (Ithaca and London: Cornell University Press, 1995), p. 138.

sequence acquires a powerful intensity by aligning Petrarchan imagery (such as that comparing the beloved with the beauty of the stars) with the language and ideas of religious, devotional verse. Sonnet 41 is an inspired and moving address to the stars, all the more remarkable for the way in which it enthusiastically upholds and then steadily devalues 'Heaven's glory' in comparison with earthly love:

> You blessèd stars, which do Heaven's glory show,
>   And at your brightness make our eyes admire:
>   Yet envy not, though I on earth below,
>   Enjoy a sight which moves in me more fire.
>
> I do confess such beauty breeds desire,
>   You shine, and clearest light on us bestow,
>   Yet doth a sight on earth more warmth inspire
>   Into my loving soul, his grace to know.
>
> Clear, bright and shining as you are, is this
>   Light of my joy, fixed steadfast, nor will move
>   His light from me, nor I change from his love,
>   But still increase as th'height of all my bliss.
>
> His sight gives life unto my love-ruled eyes,
>   My love content, because in his, love lies.   (69)

The address to the stars recalls the passionate stellar sonnet written by her father, Robert Sidney: 'You purest stars, whose ever dying fires | Deck heavenly spheres, and rule the world below.' At the same time, Wroth's poem is reminiscent of Sir Philip Sidney's Sonnet in *Astrophil and Stella* ('With how sad steps'), and the rhyme scheme (*ababbaabcddcee*) is one of the Italian-English variants favoured by her uncle. What is unusual here is the pervasively religious vocabulary—'blessèd', 'Heaven's glory', 'confess', 'soul', 'bliss'—but also the unexpected expression of contentment in the closing couplet. Very soon after, in Sonnet 43, the speaker is plunged into a miserable darkness: 'And darkness must these poor lost rooms possess, | So be all blessèd lights from henceforth hid' (72). The co-existence of a seemingly secure emotional vantage point and a helpless state of dejection undoubtedly creates some difficulties of interpretation for readers of the sequence, but for the speaker of these deeply conflicted sonnets such contradiction is a way of being. If *Pamphilia to Amphilanthus* pushes Petrarchan and anti-Petrarchan discourses as far as they will go in its turbulent exploration of desire and disappointment, it also shows contentment and constancy to be ideals worth striving for amidst so much agitation and distress.

John Milton

John Milton's sonnets come at the end of a remarkable Renaissance flowering of English lyric poetry, but in many ways they signal a dramatic and decisive turning point in the history of the form. What we hear in Milton's sonnets is no longer the courtly discourse of patronage and favour, but the steady, implacable reasoning of a radical Puritan Republican—not just the voice of a fastidious religious conscience, but the voice of political liberty and civic humanism. Most of the sonnets were composed between 1642 and 1655, and they are steeped in the politics of the English Revolution. If they register the shock of civil war and the difficult interregnum of Cromwell's Commonwealth, they also constitute a courageous and forthright appeal for individual freedom and peaceful resolution. In this respect, the sonnets share the heroic grandeur of Milton's better-known epic poetry.[51]

Milton's sonnets are remarkable in other ways, too. They consistently follow the Petrarchan model, making them unusual among English sonnets of the Renaissance period, and five of the early sonnets (together with a near-sonnet or Canzone Stanza of fifteen lines) are written in Italian. Sonnet 1 is written in English, though like the Italian compositions (also dating from around 1629), it shows the strong influence of the love poetry of Petrarch and Dante. Purportedly addressed, like its companion pieces, to a young Italian woman called Emilia, the sonnet invokes the nightingale as the harbinger of love:

> O nightingale, that on yon bloomy spray
>   Warblest at eve, when all the woods are still,
>   Thou with fresh hope the lover's heart dost fill,
> While the jolly hours lead on propitious May,
> Thy liquid notes that close the eye of day,
>   First heard before the shallow cuckoo's bill
>   Portend success in love; O if Jove's will
>   Have linked that amorous power to thy soft lay,
> Now timely sing, ere the rude bird of hate
>   Foretell my hopeless doom in some grove nigh:
>   As thou from year to year hast sung too late

---

51. Quotations from John Milton's sonnets are from *John Milton*, ed. Stephen Orgel and Jonathan Goldberg (Oxford: Oxford University Press, 1991).

> For my relief; yet hadst no reason why,
>   Whether the muse, or Love call thee his mate,
>   Both them I serve, and of their train am I. (30)

The speaker declares his dual allegiance to both love and poetry, and this strong ethic of service anticipates the religious and political duty that informs the later sonnets: 'Whether the muse or Love call thee his mate, | Both them I serve, and of their train am I.' As Douglas Bush remarks, the early sonnets 'attest the young Milton's considerable mastery of Italian and the Italian sonneteers' language of love', but other Italian influences, poetic and critical, were to have a profound effect on both his outlook and his style.[52] The influence of Torquato Tasso's *Sonneti Eroici* is evident in the sonnets dedicated to prominent statesmen (Oliver Cromwell, Thomas Fairfax, and Henry Vane), and to friends from Milton's youth (Edward Lawrence and Cyriack Skinner). The most significant and lasting Italian influence, however, is that of Giovanni Della Casa, whose *Rime e Prose* (1563) Milton obtained in 1629 and began to emulate in the gravity of tone and elaborate syntactical manoeuvres of his later sonnets. In the end, it is not the Italian poetry of amatory idealism that Milton strives to follow, but the Italian poetry of civic humanism and political virtue.

Although there have been several attempts to present Milton's sonnets as a sequence or to organize them into thematic and chronological groupings, they clearly declare themselves as occasional sonnets which coincide with notable events in the poet's personal life and political career. One of the best-known sonnets, apparently written to mark the occasion of Milton's twenty-third birthday on 9 December 1631, was found among the manuscripts now housed in the Library of Trinity College, Cambridge, included as part of a draft letter to a friend who had urged the poet to take holy orders. The sonnet, by Milton's own admission, contains 'some nightward thoughts' in which he dwells on a 'certaine belatedness' in himself:

> How soon hath time the subtle thief of youth,
>   Stol'n on his wing my three and twentieth year!
>   My hasting days fly on with full career,
>   But my late spring no bud or blossom shew'th.
> Perhaps my semblance might deceive the truth,
>   That I to manhood am arrived so near,
>   And inward ripeness doth much less appear,
>   That some more timely-happy spirits endueth.

---

52. Douglas Bush (ed.), *Milton: Poetical Works* (Oxford: Oxford University Press, 1966), p. 79.

> Yet be it less or more, or soon or slow,
>   It shall be still in strictest measure event,
>   To that same lot, however mean or high,
> Toward which time leads me, and the will of heaven:
>   All is, if I have grace to use it so,
>   As ever in my great task-master's eye.   (34–5)

The floral imagery of personal and spiritual progress is reminiscent of Herbert, and the sonnet form is modestly Petrarchan (*abbaabbacdedce*), carefully observing the *volta* between octave and sestet, as well as the sub-divisions of quatrains and tercets within them. Even so, the measured seriousness and gravity of tone, and the chastened, austere diction, are unmistakably Milton's own. Although the sonnet eschews a rhyming couplet, the closing lines have the force and conviction of epigram, in part because of the chime of 'grace' and 'great'. Simplicity of expression is combined with a vision of infinite possibility: 'All is, if I have grace to use it so, | As ever in my great task-master's eye.'

Milton's modification of Italian sonnet practice into a mature and highly wrought style of his own is powerfully illustrated in Sonnet 16, sometimes sub-titled 'On his blindness', and thought to have been written soon after the onset of blindness in 1652. What is immediately striking is the palpable tension between the pent-up energy of the run-on lines and the frustrating suspension of meaning. It is as if the sonnet structure is only barely able to contain the insistent pressure of the speaker's urge for meaning:

> When I consider how my light is spent,
>   Ere half my days, in this dark world and wide,
>   And that one talent which is death to hide,
>   Lodged with me useless, through my soul more bent
> To serve therewith my maker, and present
>   My true account, lest he returning chide,
>   Doth God exact day-labour, light denied,
>   I fondly ask; but patience to prevent
> That murmur, soon replies, God doth not need
>   Either man's work or his own gifts, who best
>   Bear his mild yoke, they serve him best, his state
> Is kingly. Thousands at his bidding speed
>   And post o'er land and ocean without rest:
>   They also serve who only stand and wait.   (81)

The opening line is an echo of Shakespeare's Sonnet 15 ('When I consider everything that grows'), but the pace and movement of the verse across quatrain and tercet divisions is altogether different, not least because of the high degree of enjambment. As Spiller points out, Milton's sonnet is a poem of 'life-reckoning', though it is not necessary to calculate some exact figure for 'half my days' to appreciate the intense self-searching it enacts.[53] The verb 'consider' speaks eloquently of the sonnet's sombre reflective capacity. Even so, that musing opening line has no obvious or immediate verbal fulfilment. The structure encourages us to seek completion of the statement, but what we find instead is a series of sub-clauses or dependent statements, introduced by conjunctions and other connectives—'Ere', 'in', 'And', though', 'and', 'lest'—extending all the way through the octave. The main verb in the octave does not occur until line 8, 'I fondly ask', and is then briskly followed by the conjunction 'but', as if precipitating the *volta* prematurely. Barrell notes that the question asked in the octave is complicated not just by the delayed verb, but by the seeming paradox (angled as if trying 'to catch God out') of being expected to do day work in the dark: 'Doth God exact day-labour, light denied'.[54]

The sonnet works obliquely through scriptural reference. There are two biblical allusions, both drawn from parables in Matthew 25, which give authority to the sonnet's prevailing imagery of light and darkness. The first is taken from the parable of the wise and foolish virgins, in which the image of a lamp burning is equated with unswerving faith and the need to stand in readiness for the arrival of the Lord. The 'spent' light in line 1 implies near despair as well as physical darkness. The second reference is to the parable of the talents and the story of the unenterprising servant who fails to invest his talent (or silver coin). Like the servant in the parable, Milton's speaker is cast into darkness. The poem itself functions as a kind of parable in which the poet 'fondly' (foolishly) queries God about his duty. Patience is personified as a voice who 'soon replies' (appropriately breaking in before the sestet) and calms the speaker's initial anxieties.

What makes the first few readings of the sonnet seem difficult and confused is the experience of holding several pieces of information in mind while the main statement remains incomplete. This delaying technique creates suspense, which is highly appropriate since the sonnet's meaning turns on the experience of waiting. The convoluted and protracted syntax imitates the speaker's frustrated mental reckoning, before giving way to the more direct and simplified reply of 'patience' in the sestet. Milton's suspended

---

53. Spiller, *The Development of the Sonnet*, p. 192.
54. Barrell, *Poetry, Language and Politics*, p. 53.

syntax places further demands on its readers through the use of *ellipsis*, where words appear to have been omitted in the interests of compression ('though my soul [is] more bent'), and *hyperbaton*, where the word order is inverted for emphasis ('this dark world and wide'). Significantly, the final line, which carries the weight and authority of a proverb, is the only one in the sonnet that can be read as a single conceptual unit. The Petrarchan rhyme scheme ensures that we have to wait for the final rhyme of 'state' and 'wait' to be fulfilled. Milton's readiness to stand and wait is not an idle condition but a braced attention to the working out of God's will. The ideal of service that the sonnet envisages is both religious and political, anticipating the establishment of a paradise on earth. The vision of angels in their 'Thousands' is sublime, but the ethic of duty underpinning it is firmly rooted in Milton's civic humanism. In the context of the English Revolution, the reference to God's 'kingly' state is an ironic reminder of that other 'kingly' state—the monarchy of Charles I—that foundered on its own corruption when the king was executed in 1649.

The powerful potential of the sonnet as a vehicle of political and religious protest is nowhere better seen than in Milton's sonnet 'On the Late Massacre in Piedmont'. Directing its political invective through impassioned prayer, the sonnet sanctions vengeance by appealing to the Book of Revelation. The poem was composed soon after 24 April 1655, when the Duke of Savoy's Italian troops massacred the Vaudois (also known as the Waldensians), a Protestant sect considered by Milton and his contemporaries as the representatives of 'pure' or 'primitive' Christianity. Cromwell took up the cause of the Vaudois, and Milton, as Secretary, drafted letters of protest to European heads of state, and an address to the Duke of Savoy. Notwithstanding the political and religious complexities of the event, the sonnet registers its protest both eloquently and urgently:

> Avenge O Lord thy slaughtered saints, whose bones
>   Lie scattered on the Alpine mountains cold,
>   Even them who kept thy truth so pure of old
>   When all our fathers worshipped stocks and stones,
> Forget not: in thy book record their groans
>   Who were thy sheep and in their ancient fold
>   Slain by the bloody Piedmontese that rolled
>   Mother with infant down the rocks. Their moans
> The vales redoubled to the hills, and they
>   To heaven. Their martyred blood and ashes sow
>   O'er all the Italian fields where still doth sway

> The triple tyrant: that from these may grow
> A hundredfold, who having learnt thy way
> Early may fly the Babylonian woe.   (80)

Although the sonnet deploys its quatrains strategically, reinforcing the opening imperative with a double plea in line 4 ('Forget not...record'), it nevertheless adopts the surging syntax employed in Milton's other sonnets, playing off strongly marked caesurae against an irrepressible enjambment. Consequently, the turn between octave and sestet is effaced in the interests of a reiterated plea. The syntactical striding on is especially effective here, since it coincides with the appalling image of mother and infant rolling down the rocks, and with the reverberating echo of their cries 'redoubled' across lines 8–10, from 'hills' to 'heaven'. The desultory opening picture of scattered bones is then relieved by the redemptive imagery of 'martyred blood and ashes' that God might 'sow' (the birth of a new generation of followers is registered in the rhyme with 'grow'). The powerful sway of papal Rome is embodied in the 'triple tyrant' (the Pope with his three-tiered crown) and the 'Babylonian woe' (the city of oppression and evil in Revelation). The terrible shock of slaughter and the possible blow to belief are gently eased by the lightness and deftness of 'Early may fly', but the elevated style of the sonnet cannot altogether mitigate its painful and persistent woe.

Although he wrote just a small number of sonnets, Milton can be credited with having given to the form a new and serious political function. What makes his sonnets so original and imposing is their combination of a complex syntactical armature and a fierce, forthright stance on questions of liberty. Milton's political sonnets seem far removed from the courtly discourse of an earlier generation of Renaissance poets. Caught up in the rapidly changing balance of power in the Civil War years and the political settlement that followed, the sonnets are courageously outspoken on matters of individual conscience and social justice. Two sonnets from 1645–6 reflect upon Milton's divorce tracts and their controversial reception, tilting the verse towards political satire. The first of these, 'A book was writ of late called *Tetrachordon*', records with amusement and dismay the difficulty some readers had with the name (a four-note scale, alluding to the four places in scripture relevant to the question of divorce), comically rhyming the offending word with 'pored on', 'word on', and 'Gordon' (78). The second sonnet ('On the Same') is caustically satirical, recalling how the poet's well-meaning cry for the people to cast off restraints on personal liberty (specifically those relating to marriage) is greeted with a bestiary of protest:

> I did but prompt the age to quit their clogs
> By the known rules of ancient liberty,
> When straight a barbarous noise environs me
> Of owls and cuckoos, asses, apes and dogs.

The animal imagery is perpetuated in the allusion to Matthew's Gospel (7:6) and the familiar notion of wasted effort in 'casting pearl to hogs', but as it slips from octave to sestet, the sonnet tautens and the tone becomes more solemn, as the speaker gravely contemplates how far off liberty remains, 'For all this waste of wealth, and loss of blood' (79).

Three sonnets, addressed in turn to Thomas Fairfax, Oliver Cromwell, and Henry Vane, reveal how boldly and comprehensively Milton adopted the sonnet to affairs of state. Alike in their modes of address and rhetorical persuasion, each sonnet opens by naming the intended recipient, bestowing praise upon them, and then proceeding through elaborate grammatical manoeuvres to declare what must be done in the interests of establishing and maintaining peace. Although this model of public solicitation and statesmanlike advice can be found in the Italian Renaissance sonnet, Milton's sonnets look back (as some of Andrew Marvell's poems do) to the much earlier example of Horace. The sonnet to Fairfax, allegedly written soon after the siege of Colchester in 1648, celebrates military achievement ('Fairfax, whose name in arms through Europe rings') before asserting at the opening of the sestet, 'O yet a nobler task awaits thy hand'. Shakespeare's Sonnets look in awe upon the wealth and power of kings, but now it is 'jealous monarchs' and 'remotest kings' who look with 'amaze' on successive republican victories over royalist forces. There is admonition, as well as praise, in the sonnet, and it looks forward, beyond war, to that time when 'truth, and right from violence be freed'. In the event, Fairfax went into retirement after the execution of the king, though Milton's premonitions of how 'public faith' would have to contend with 'public fraud' are borne out in the later sonnets of 1652 (85).

As Barrell notes, the 'heroic' sonnets for Cromwell and Vane belong to a particular (and particularly fraught) phase of the Revolution, which included 'attempts in the early 1650s to set up an established church and restrict the religious toleration which Milton, Cromwell, and Vane all defended'. He argues persuasively that from the initial vocative, 'Cromwell, our chief of men', the name and the achievements are carried forward, as if language and syntax are enacting the inexorable force that Cromwell represents: 'The name sets up a syntactical obligation, which sooner or later must be discharged.' However, if the syntax serves 'to represent and reinforce the overmastering power of that individual will', it also leaves room for a tactful intervention.[55] John Carey acknowledges that Cromwell was 'in favour of unlimited liberty of dissent', but thinks that this sonnet 'urges him away from establishment altogether'.[56] The delayed turn, midway through line 9, asserts on behalf of peace, 'yet much remains | To conquer still'. The main verbal connection that the name of Cromwell finds, however, is the imperative in the closing lines (notably, the only rhyming couplet among the sonnets Milton wrote in English): 'Help us to save free conscience from the paw | Of hireling wolves whose gospel is their maw' (85). The sonnet to Vane employs a similarly dense and winding syntax, suspending the main verb until line 11, but this time the emphasis is upon intelligent statesmanship rather than military prowess: 'Vane, young in years, but in sage counsel old.' The sonnet effects its delayed turn through the verb 'to know', bringing into satisfying view what it is that Vane has 'learned': 'Both spiritual power and civil, what each means, | What severs each' (86). The sonnet's tribute to Vane and its hopes for a better, more peaceful, state speak eloquently across the years, undiminished by the knowledge of Vane's execution ten years later, with the restoration of Charles II.

It was not the political loss of an unprecedented opportunity for establishing paradise on earth, but the personal loss of his second wife, Katherine Woodcock, that prompted Milton in 1658 to write one of the greatest sonnets in English.[57] Here, the syntax is not disposed towards the resolution of political and religious struggles, but rather indicative of the poet's painful articulation of grief and loss, intensified by a double darkness. The diversions into classical and biblical myth momentarily restrain, but cannot ultimately impede, the speaker's passionate longing for 'full sight' of his dead wife. The tight space of the sonnet proves the ideal place for 'this tough, severe, slightly pedantic, but miraculously tender voice',[58] as it recalls the ghostly image of the poet's dead wife:

55. Barrell, *Poetry, Language and Politics*, p. 57.
56. John Carey (ed.), *Milton: The Complete Shorter Poems* (Harlow: Longman, 1997), p. 328.
57. In the light of claims that the poem might have been written for the poet's first wife, Mary Powell, Stephen Orgel and Jonathan Goldberg tactfully suggest that 'it might be worth entertaining the possibility that Milton is thinking of both his marriages in the poem'. See *John Milton*, p. 784.
58. Spiller, *Early Modern Sonneteers*, p. 89.

> Methought I saw my late espousèd saint
>> Brought to me like Alcestis from the grave,
>> Whom Jove's great son to her glad husband gave,
>> Rescued from death by force though pale and faint.
> Mine as whom washed from spot of childbed taint,
>> Purification in the old law did save,
>> And such, as yet once more I trust to have
> Full sight of her in heaven without restraint,
> Came vested all in white, pure as her mind:
>> Her face was veiled, yet to my fancied sight,
>> Love, sweetness, goodness in her person shined
> So clear, as in no face with more delight.
>> But O as to embrace me she inclined
>> I waked, she fled, and day brought back my night.   (82)

Milton seems, for a moment, to return to the dream visions of Dante and Petrarch that inspired his early sonnets, but his vision is unique. The opening line, 'Methought I saw my late espousèd saint', is distinguished by its way of seeing (seeing in blindness, as well as in dream or imagination), by its acknowledgement of marriage to its subject, rather than desire for the unattainable, and by its wonderful collusion of 'espousèd' and 'saint' (both the visible, virtuous saint of Puritan theology and a saint blessed in heaven). The first quatrain invokes a comparison with Euripides' Alcestis, rescued by Hercules from the grave, while the second quatrain turns to the Old Testament (Chapter 12 of Leviticus) and the idea of being 'saved' through ritual purification after childbirth. These classical and biblical allusions serve to elevate the dead woman, while allowing the speaker a momentary sense of distance from his loss, but the turn in the sonnet is used to powerful effect to return us to the startling vision of the opening line and the angel-like woman who 'Came vested all in white'. The repetition of 'face' quite possibly alludes to Saint Paul's First Epistle to the Corinthians (13:12), in which having looked 'through a glass darkly', we are assured of one day having a vision that is 'face to face'. The closing apostrophe is a startling admission of desire collapsing into disappointment, though tantalizingly held for the duration of the word 'inclined'. The word 'blind' is not mentioned, though it hovers over the ending, as if seeking a closing couplet. Day brings back not light, but 'night', evacuating the earlier promise of 'sight' and 'delight'. In this final sonnet, also one of the final English sonnets of the entire Renaissance period, Milton establishes his legacy for future exponents of the form, and shows himself to be not only a formidable wielder of the political sonnet but also a consummate artist of the elegiac sonnet.

2

The Romantic sonnet

The sonnet revival that took place just over a century after the death of John Milton coincided with the dawn of the Romantic movement in the 1780s and 1790s. It was also generated, to a large extent, by the increasing prominence of women writers in the literary culture of the time, most notably Anna Seward (1742–1809), Charlotte Turner Smith (1749–1806), and Helen Maria Williams (1761–1827). Women writers were acutely responsive to the new emphasis on 'sensibility' and the expression of private modes of thought and feeling in late eighteenth-century poetry, and the sonnet came to be seen (in the words of Charlotte Smith) as 'no improper vehicle for a single Sentiment'.[1] The sonnet was thought to be the ideal form for momentary but intense explorations of personal loss, disappointment, loneliness, and despair. One of the distinguishing characteristics of sonnets by women writers of the late eighteenth century is the vivid and powerful realization of mood through the exploration of landscape, both sublime and picturesque. In their heightened fascination with the emotional associations of particular landscapes (mountains and seashores, especially), and in their imaginative identification with particular birds and flowers (the nightingale and the poppy among them), these sonnets strikingly anticipate and shape some of the major preoccupations of the Romantic movement.

Anna Seward, Charlotte Smith, and Helen Maria Williams

In their politics, the women sonneteers of the late eighteenth century are prototypically Romantic, sharing with Wordsworth and Coleridge both

---

1. Charlotte Smith, Preface to the first and second editions of *Elegiac Sonnets* (1784), *The Poems of Charlotte Smith*, ed. Stuart Curran (New York and Oxford: Oxford University Press, 1993), p. 3.

blissful idealism and abject disillusionment in their shifting responses to the French Revolution. Here, too, the sonnet is brought into service, with its Miltonic modes of public address renewed. Anna Seward's 'Sonnet to France on her Present Exertions' was among the first poetic responses in English to the French Revolution when it appeared in the *Gentleman's Magazine* in 1789.

> Thou, that where Freedom's sacred fountains play,
>   Which sprung effulgent, though with crimson stains,
>   On transatlantic shores, and widening plains,
>   Hast, in their living waters, washed away
> Those cankering spots, shed by tyrannic sway
>   On thy long drooping lilies; English veins
>   Swell with the tide of exultation gay
>   To see thee spurn thy deeply-galling chains.
> Few of Britannia's free-born sons forbear
>   To bless thy cause; cold is the heart that breathes
>   No wish fraternal. France, we bid thee share
> The blessings twining with our civic wreaths,
>   While Victory's trophies, permanent as fair,
>   Crown the bright sword that Liberty unsheathes.[2]

Seward's imagined landscape includes the 'transatlantic shores and widening plains' of revolutionary America, as well as revolutionary France. The sonnet is stiffly rhetorical in some respects (the lofty personification of Freedom, Victory, and Liberty is an obvious instance of its conventionality), but it is also technically adventurous and strikingly radical in its politics. There is a strident energy in the run-on lines, with both the octave and the sestet acquiring a charge that helps to offset the formality of the address. This is partly aided by the unexpected shift from *abba* to *abad* in the second quatrain of what is otherwise a Petrarchan sonnet. Although Seward later moderated her revolutionary political ideals, the closing line of this 1789 sonnet is a bold indication of her early commitment to the cause of Liberty.

In other sonnets written in the 1780s and 1790s, Seward shows an acutely sensitive response to the seasonal changes of the landscape and a striking facility for registering the corresponding moods of the onlooker. The early stirrings of the Romantic movement are clearly evident in those sonnets

---

2. *The Collected Poems of Anna Seward*, ed. Lisa L. Moore (Abingdon: Routledge, 2016), vol. 1, p. 140. Page numbers for further quotations are given within brackets in the text.

that acknowledge the power and sublimity of nature, vividly recording the sounds, as well as the sights, of the English landscape. Seward, like other women poets of the time, shows a particular fondness for the atmospheric seashore. In the sonnet that opens 'On the damp margin of the sea-beat shore', the speaker is compelled 'To listen with deep thought those awful sounds' and compares the delight of 'the furious main', communicated through 'my rapt spirit and my thrilling heart', with 'the softer joys green vales impart' (226). The sonnet form lends itself especially well in this instance to the intense candour of the speaker's personal feelings, with the relentless enjambment hurtling over quatrain divisions and powerfully registering an excited apprehension of sublime beauty.

Seward is perhaps best known for 'Sonnet: To the Poppy', which effectively subverts a long tradition of love poems honouring the rose, and gives dubious recognition instead to the scarlet flower that was to become such a prominent motif in the work of later Romantic and Decadent poets:

> While summer roses all their glory yield
>   To crown the votary of love and joy,
>   Misfortune's victim hails, with many a sigh,
> Thee, scarlet Poppy of the pathless field,
> Gaudy, yet wild and lone; no leaf to shield
>   Thy flaccid vest that, as the gale blows high,
>   Flaps, and alternate folds around thy head.
>   So stands in the long grass a love-crazed maid,
> Smiling aghast; while stream to every wind
>   Her garish ribbons, smeared with dust and rain;
>   But brain-sick visions cheat her tortured mind,
> And bring false peace. Thus, lulling grief and pain,
>   Kind dreams oblivious from thy juice proceed,
>   Thou flimsy, showy, melancholy weed.   (213)

The personification of the poppy as 'a love-crazed maid' at the turn between octave and sestet shows qualities that are characteristic of this sonnet as a whole: a vivid handling of metaphor and an impressive technical proficiency. The rhymes are deft and subtle ('Joy' rhymes with 'sigh', and 'head' with 'Maid'), and the syntax is alert and adroit. The sonnet ends with a rhyming couplet, but the force of the conclusion is generated by the caesura and the ensuing half line that precede the couplet.

Sewards's nearest poetic peer was Charlotte Smith, whose earliest sonnets were printed in the *European Magazine* in 1782. *Elegiac Sonnets* appeared in 1784 and went through eleven editions up to 1851, with translations in

French and Italian.[3] Although melancholy is the prevailing mood, the sonnets are notable for their variety of subject matter and their technical resourcefulness. Several poems are either versions of well-known sonnets by Petrarch, such as Sonnet XIII—'Oh! place me where the burning noon | Forbids the wither'd flower to blow' (21)—or meditations on familiar Petrarchan themes. Sonnet III, 'To a nightingale', is prompted by Petrarch's nightingale that sweetly weeps ('Quel rosigniol, che si soave piange'), but the emotional intensity anticipates the writings of John Keats:

> Poor melancholy bird—that all night long
>   Tell'st to the Moon thy tale of tender woe;
>   From what sad cause can such sweet sorrow flow,
> And whence this mournful melody of song?
> Thy poet's musing fancy would translate
>   What mean the sounds that swell thy little breast,
>   When still at dewy eve thou leavest thy nest,
> Thus to the listening night to sing thy fate. (14)

The octave, which is printed as two typographically distinct quatrains, adopts Petrarchan envelope rhymes (*abba cddc*), but the sestet is firmly Shakespearean. The closing couplet, with its lyric apostrophe to the bird and its rapt identification with the nightingale as 'martyr of disastrous love', reveals how potently the sonnet embodies the intense subjective yearning that came to be associated with Romanticism: 'Ah! songstress sad! that such my lot might be, | To sigh, and sing at liberty—like thee!' (14). Sonnet VII, 'On the departure of the nightingale', is even more striking than the earlier poem in its anticipation of Keats:

> Sweet poet of the woods!—a long adieu!
>   Farewel soft minstrel of the early year!
> Ah! 'twill be long ere thou shalt sing anew,
>   And pour thy music on 'the night's dull ear'.
> Whether on spring thy wandering flights await,
>   Or whether silent in our groves you dwell,
> The pensive Muse shall own thee for her mate,
>   And still protect the song she loves so well.
> With cautious step the love-lorn youth shall glide
>   Thro' the lone brake that shades thy mossy nest;

---

3. Quotations from Charlotte Smith's *Elegiac Sonnets* are from *The Poems of Charlotte Smith*, ed. Stuart Curran (New York and Oxford: Oxford University Press, 1993).

> And shepherd girls from eyes profane shall hide
>   The gentle bird, who sings of pity best:
> For still thy voice shall soft affections move,
> And still be dear to Sorrow and to Love! (17)

This time, the sonnet is consistently Shakespearean in its rhyme scheme, and there are echoes of Shakespeare in 'night's dull ear' (from the Prologue to *Henry V*). Even so, there are other influences at play, especially that of Milton. Line 7 echoes Milton's first sonnet ('Whither the Muse or Love call thee his mate, | Both them I serve, and of their train am I').[4]

Milton is also a presiding spirit in Sonnet VIII, 'To spring', especially in the liberties it takes with syntax:

> Again the wood, and long-withdrawing vale,
>   In many a tint of tender green are drest,
> Where the young leaves, unfolding, scarce conceal
>   Beneath their early shade, the half-form'd nest
> Of finch or woodlark; and the primrose pale,
>   And lavish cowslip, wildly scatter'd round,
> Give their sweet spirits to the sighing gale.
>   Ah! season of delight!—could aught be found
>   To soothe awhile the tortured bosom's pain,
>   Of Sorrow's rankling shaft to cure the wound,
>   And bring life's first delusions once again,
> 'Twere surely met in thee!—thy prospect fair,
> Thy sounds of harmony, thy balmy air,
> Have power to cure all sadness—but despair. (17–18)

Although the rhyme scheme is Shakespearean at the outset, it collapses with the Miltonic sweep from octave to sestet. The sestet retains the *d* rhyme, giving prominence to 'wound', and then substitutes a triplet in place of the traditional couplet, producing *ababcdcdedefff*. The rhymes are intricately played off against the hurtling syntax, so that what appears to be a celebration of the power and promise of spring is suddenly undercut by the single word 'despair'. As with the closing line of Sonnet III, the dash is deftly placed. The closing line carries an echo of *Paradise Lost*, Book IV (155–6).[5] In its pensive, elegiac mood, the sonnet lives up completely to the title of the volume.

---

4. *John Milton*, ed. Stephen Orgel and Jonathan Goldberg (Oxford: Oxford University Press, 1991), p. 30.
5. *John Milton*, ed. Orgel and Goldberg, p. 424.

The mood is darker still in Sonnet XLII, 'Composed during a walk on the Downs, in November 1787', with its ominous opening images of 'The dark and pillowy cloud' and 'sallow trees' grieving 'o'er the ruins of the year' (40). In Sonnet XLIV, 'Written in the church-yard at Middleton in Sussex', the sea and wind conspire to expose a scene of chilling Gothic horror:

> Press'd by the Moon, mute arbitress of tides,
>   While the loud equinox its power combines,
>   The sea no more its swelling surge confines,
> But o'er the shrinking land sublimely rides.
> The wild blast, rising from the Western cave,
>   Drives the huge billows from their heaving bed;
>   Tears from their grassy tombs the village dead,
> And breaks the silent sabbath of the grave!
> With shells and sea-weed mingled, on the shore,
>   Lo! their bones whiten in the frequent wave;
>   But vain to them the winds and waters rave;
> *They* hear the warring elements no more:
> While I am doom'd—by life's long storm opprest,
> To gaze with envy on their gloomy rest.   (42)

In a note accompanying the sonnet, Smith casually explains that the wall of the churchyard at Middleton has been entirely swept away, many of the graves broken up, and the remains of bodies interred washed into the sea. The power of the sonnet, however, derives not from its alarming account of graves emptied into the sea and bones scattered on the shore, but from its even more alarming suggestion that to be among the village dead is an enviable prospect.

The fearful sublimity and the insistent death wish in *Elegiac Sonnets* point to the emerging dark side of Romanticism, but the more tranquil elements in Smith's poetry, especially in her numerous songs of praise to the River Arun, set the tone for a growing tradition of river sonnets that includes William Lisle Bowles's 'To the River Itchin, near Winton', Samuel Taylor Coleridge's 'To the River Otter', and William Wordsworth's River Duddon sonnets. Wordsworth read *Elegiac Sonnets* as an undergraduate in 1789 and visited Smith in Brighton on his way to France in 1791. He received from Smith a letter of introduction to another political radical and writer of sonnets, Helen Maria Williams, though he was not to meet Williams until 1820, on a later visit to France.

Despite her strong support for the French Revolution, her long residence in France, and her acquaintance with William Godwin, Thomas Paine, and

Mary Wollstonecraft, Williams was drawn to the sonnet as a vehicle of private memory and personal sentiment rather than political engagement. Although she gives the sonnet tradition an infusion of exotic imagery in poems such as 'Sonnet: To the Torrid Zone', 'Sonnet to the Calbassia Tree', and 'Sonnet: To the White Bird of the Tropic', it is her sonnets recalling the English landscape of her childhood for which she is best remembered. The English sonnets are 'on a single sentiment': 'To Love', 'To Hope', 'Disappointment'. Her 'Sonnet: To the Strawberry' favourably contrasts the 'Plant of my native soil' with the more exotic lime and guava, recalling 'The vanished hours of life's enchanting spring'.[6] 'Sonnet: To the Curlew' is an elegant Petrarchan composition, evoking the loneliness and melancholy that make the curlew a 'congenial bird':

> Sooth'd by the murmurs on the sea-beat shore,
> His dun-grey plumage floating to the gale,
> The Curlew blends his melancholy wail
>   With those hoarse sounds the rushing waters pour.
>   Like thee, congenial bird! my steps explore
> The bleak lone sea-beach, or the rocky dale,—
> And shun the orange bower, the myrtle vale,
>   Whose gay luxuriance suits my soul no more.
> I love the ocean's broad expanse, when drest
>   In limpid clearness, or when tempests blow:
> When the smooth currents on its placid breast
>   Flow calm, as my past moments us'd to flow;
> Or when its troubled waves refuse to rest,
>   And seem the symbol of my present woe.   (77–8)

Like Smith, Williams is temperamentally drawn to 'the sea-beat shore' and 'rocky dale', finding in remote and deserted landscapes an objective correlative for troubled memories and obscure sorrows. The gradual shift of attention from bird to self in the octave is followed by a more emphatic first-person declaration of likeness at the turn to the sestet, while the insistent temporal constructions ('when drest...when tempests blow...') convey the instability of both inner and outer landscapes. All of this is neatly done within the formal constraints of the sonnet.

---

6. *Romantic Women Poets, 1770–1838: An Anthology*, ed. Andrew Ashfield (Manchester: Manchester University Press, 1995), p. 77. Further quotations from the poems of Helen Maria Williams are from this anthology, and page numbers will be given in brackets within the text.

William Bowles and Samuel Taylor Coleridge

Together, Seward, Smith, and Williams help to revive the English sonnet and establish it as a principal form for the Romantic movement. Samuel Taylor Coleridge, in announcing the desirable scope and function of the sonnet in 1797, points to those characteristics that women writers of the decade had been actively promoting: 'In a Sonnet then we require a development of some lonely feeling, by whatever cause it may have been excited; but those Sonnets appear to me the most exquisite, in which moral Sentiments, Affections, or Feelings, are deduced from, and associated with, the scenery of Nature.' A few years earlier than Wordsworth, then, Coleridge discerns in the sonnet a form that might prove amenable to their distinctive Romantic philosophy of mind and nature. 'Such compositions', Coleridge goes on to say, 'create a sweet and indissoluble union between the intellectual and the material world.'[7] He acknowledges Charlotte Smith as one of the major practitioners of the time, but his own experiments with the form probably owe more to the example of William Lisle Bowles.

Jonathan Wordsworth claims that Bowles was 'a sort of John the Baptist to Coleridge—except that Coleridge started by worshipping him'.[8] If any baptism took place, it was surely a baptism in English river water. The seemingly natural, spontaneous flow of thought and feeling, combined with a relaxed, colloquial diction, attracted Coleridge to Bowles's *Fourteen Sonnets* (1789). The fluidity of these sonnets, their ease in establishing analogies between the contours of the landscape and the workings of the mind, is exemplified in those poems dedicated to English rivers, including the Tweed and the Wenbeck. Bowles had probably acquired this watery impulse from his Oxford tutor, Thomas Warton, whose sonnet 'To the River Loden' is still a fashionable anthology piece, though Charlotte Smith (as we have seen) had already written numerous tributes to the River Arun. Bowles gives coherence to his collection of sonnets by describing them (in keeping with the fashion of the day) as 'picturesque' poems from a recent tour, and maintaining the editorial fiction that they were 'found in a Traveller's Memorandum-Book'.

---

7. Samuel Taylor Coleridge, Introduction to *Sonnets from Various Authors* (Bristol: privately printed, 1796), pp. 1–2. In *Coleridge's Responses*, Vol. 1: *Coleridge on Writers and Writing*, ed. Seamus Perry (London: Continuum, 2008), p. 4.
8. Jonathan Wordsworth, Introduction to William Lisle Bowles, *Fourteen Sonnets, Elegiac and Descriptive, Written during a Tour* (London: Dilly, 1789). Facsimile edn (Oxford: Woodstock Books, 1991), p. i.

Among the initial fourteen sonnets (expanded to twenty-one in a later edition) are picturesque descriptions of Scotland and Northumberland ('At Bamborough Castle'), melancholy reflections on leaving and returning to England ('On Dover Cliffs'), and occasional meditations on conventional themes ('To Time', 'To Evening'). The qualities that Coleridge admired are amply evident in Sonnet VIII, 'To the River Itchin, Near Winton':

> Itchin, when I behold thy banks again,
> Thy crumbling margin, and thy silver breast,
> On which the self-same tints still seem to rest,
> Why feels my heart the shiv'ring sense of pain?
> Is it, that many a summer's day has past
> Since, in life's morn, I carol'd on thy side?
> Is it, that oft, since then, my heart has sigh'd,
> As Youth, and Hope's delusive gleams, flew fast?
> Is it that those, who circled on thy shore,
> Companions of my youth, now meet no more?
> Whate'er the cause, upon thy banks I bend
> Sorrowing, yet feel such solace at my heart,
> As at the meeting of some long-lost friend,
> From whom, in happier hours, we wept to part.[9]

A familiar idea of returning with renewed insight to a place already imprinted with a strong sense of attachment is invested here with an especially poignant and intimate series of reflections. The 'crumbling margin' is a touching detail that delicately combines the physical actuality of the riverbank and the speaker's painful apprehension of loss. The rhetorical control is impressive. The sonnet is structured around a series of imploring questions that extend across the octave-sestet division ('Is it...? Is it...? Is it...?'), prompting a late turn after line 12. This unusual structural shift is reinforced by a novel rhyme scheme that stresses the 12 + 4 dynamic rather than the usual 8 + 6 arrangement, strategically introducing a couplet in lines 9–10 and giving weight to a closing quatrain: *abacddceefgfg*.

Even a brief glance at Coleridge's 'Sonnet: To the River Otter' reveals what he enthusiastically responded to in Bowles's poem:

> Dear native brook! wild streamlet of the West!
> How many various-fated years have past,
> What happy, and what mournful hours, since last

---

9. William Lisle Bowles, *Fourteen Sonnets, Elegiac and Descriptive, Written during a Tour* (London: Dilly, 1789). Facsimile edn (Oxford: Woodstock Books, 1991), p. 9.

> I skimmed the smooth thin stone along thy breast,
> Numbering its light leaps! yet so deep imprest
> Sink the sweet scenes of childhood, that mine eyes
>   I never shut amid the sunny ray,
> But straight with all their tints thy waters rise,
>   Thy crossing plank, thy marge with willows grey,
> And bedded sand that, veined with various dyes,
> Gleamed through thy bright transparence! On my way,
>   Visions of childhood! oft have ye beguiled
> Lone manhood's cares, yet waking fondest sighs:
>   Ah! that once more I were a careless child![10]

Coleridge repeats the intimate opening address to the river in the earlier sonnet, but also echoes some of the memorable descriptive detail, including the 'tints' of light on water, the 'margin' or 'marge' of the river banks, the speaker's heartfelt 'sighs', and the perception of the river's smooth surface as a nurturing 'breast' (reinforcing for Coleridge the suggestion of a return to innocent childhood). In other respects, however, Coleridge's poem is more intellectually engaging and also more stylistically complex and syntactically adroit than Bowles's sonnet. The correspondence between the flow of the river and the workings of the mind is highly developed in the later sonnet, so that the 'beeded sand...veined with various dyes' becomes an organic image of memory, and the 'bright transparence' of the river a beautifully radiant description of the imagination at work.

The strong import of childhood and childhood experience gives added poignancy to Coleridge's sonnet, with the skimming of the stone across the water initiating the process of numbering that begins with 'light leaps' and ends with lost years. There is a temporal suspension at the heart of the sonnet, gently facilitated by the subtle shifts of tense and the complicated syntactical twists of lines 2–11. The transition from past scenes to present imaginings, from the life of nature to the life of the mind, is vividly enacted in lines 6–8, with 'mine eyes | I never shut' carrying all the verbal force of both definite past tense and habitual present-tense activity, although the full significance of that 'never shut' is teasingly withheld until the end of the octave: 'But straight with all their tints the waters rise.' The present-tense 'rise' marvellously coincides with the imagined moment of poetic repossession of the river, while the 'crossing plank', so decisively situated between

---

10. Samuel Taylor Coleridge, *The Major Works*, ed. H. J. Jackson (Oxford: Oxford University Press, 2008), p. 6.

octave and sestet, provides a way forward—an imaginative point of transition between past and present, allowing the poem to hold both childhood memories and life's continuing journey in imaginative harmony. A sighing for the vanished past is accompanied by a firm acknowledgement of the beguiling 'visions of childhood', so that the closing line appears without indulgence or sentimentality: 'Ah! that once more I were a careless child!'

William Wordsworth

Having promoted a new respect for the sonnet, and having prompted several of his contemporaries, including Robert Southey and Charles Lamb, to publish sonnets on various topical subjects, Coleridge abruptly abandoned interest in the form at the end of the 1790s. In November 1797 he submitted for publication three sonnets in the name of Nehemiah Higgenbottom, wickedly parodying the 'elaborate and swelling language and imagery' that he himself had encouraged in sonnets of the time.[11] In a curious reversal of Coleridge's attitude to the sonnet, his friend and collaborator William Wordsworth began by considering the form 'egregiously absurd', but then became the most ardently enthusiastic and prolific sonneteer among the Romantic poets.[12] There is no doubt that Wordsworth was influenced by Coleridge's advocacy of both the topographical or prospect sonnet and the sonnet on eminent characters and public themes. Between 1802 and 1846, he produced over five hundred sonnets, arranging and re-arranging them in groups and sequences, including 'memorials of various Tours', 'The River Duddon Series', and 'Ecclesiastical Sonnets', so that these collections would reveal 'the growth of the poet's mind' in a way that paralleled and complemented the epic ambition of *The Prelude*.[13]

It is understandable, perhaps, that a poet who sought to establish a new model of poetic diction based on the rhythms of actual, local speech should be wary of the high-flown eloquence of the sonnet. Wordsworth's turning to the sonnet coincides not only with his reconsideration of poetic form after *Lyrical Ballads*, but with his deepening political anxieties and fears in

---

11. *Coleridge's Responses*, ed. Perry, p. 46.
12. Cited by Stuart Curran in his excellent account of Wordsworth's treatment of the sonnet, in *Poetic Form and British Romanticism* (New York and Oxford: Oxford University Press, 1986), p. 39.
13. William Wordsworth, *The Major Works*, ed. Stephen Gill (Oxford: Oxford University Press, 2008), p. 375.

the aftermath of the French Revolution. In both cases, the example of John Milton was to prove decisive. Wordsworth claimed in a letter to Walter Savage Landor that his reawakening of interest in Milton's sonnets occurred when his sister read the poems to him one afternoon in 1801 (though Dorothy's Journal suggests that the date was 21 May 1802):

> I had long been well acquainted with them, but I was particularly struck on that occasion by the dignified simplicity and majestic harmony that runs through most of them,—in character so different from the Italian, and still more so from Shakespeare's fine Sonnets. I took fire, if I may be allowed to say so, and produced three Sonnets the same afternoon, the first I ever wrote except an irregular one at school. Of these three, the only one I distinctly remember is 'I grieved for Buonaparte'.[14]

Recalling that occasion some twenty years later, Wordsworth remembered being 'singularly struck with the style of harmony, and the gravity, and republican austerity' of Milton's sonnets.[15] Throughout the rest of his career, he gave careful thought to the component parts of the sonnet and to the various ways in which the sonnet might be structured. In a letter written in spring 1833, he explains his preference for the Miltonic sonnet over the usual Italian form. The sonnet, he thinks, 'like every other legitimate composition, ought to have a beginning, a middle, and an end—in other words, to consist of three parts, like the three propositions of a syllogism'. The Italian sonnet, however, is 'best fitted to a division of the sense into two parts, of eight and six lines each'. The great attraction of Milton's sonnets is that they carry the sense across the turn between octave and sestet. Wordsworth's conviction is that this 'overflow' serves 'not merely to gratify the ear by variety and freedom of sound, but also to aid in giving that pervading sense of intense Unity in which the excellence of the sonnet has always seemed to me mainly to consist'. Wordsworth's distinctive

---

14. *The Letters of William and Dorothy Wordsworth: The Later Years*, ed. E. de Sélincourt (Oxford: Clarendon Press, 1939), vol. 1, p. 71. Wordsworth's comments are reprinted as 'Note to "Miscellaneous Sonnets"' (1843), in *Wordsworth's Poetical Works*, vol. 3, ed. E. de Sélincourt (Oxford: Clarendon Press, 1940), p. 417. For Dorothy's dating of the reading of Milton's sonnets, see *Journals of Dorothy Wordsworth*, ed. Mary Moorman (London: Oxford University Press, 1971), p. 127. As Stuart Curran points out (*Poetic Form and British Romanticism*, p. 228), there are in fact four sonnets among Wordsworth's juvenilia, the earliest being 'Sonnet on Seeing Miss Helen Maria Williams Weep at a Tale of Distress', composed in 1787. See *Wordsworth's Poetical Works*, 'Poems Written in Youth, Poems Referring to the Period of Childhood', ed. E. de Sélincourt (Oxford: Clarendon Press, 1940), p. 269.
15. *The Letters of William and Dorothy Wordsworth: The Later Years*, ed. E. de Sélincourt (Oxford: Clarendon Press, 1939), vol. 1, p. 71.

contribution to the theory of sonnet writing—a striking instance of Romantic aesthetics—is to imagine an even more profound sense of unity, so that the sonnet is no longer comprehended as a series of syntactical building blocks but rather as a natural, organic sphere, like a drop of dew: 'Instead of looking at its composition as a piece of architecture, making a whole out of three parts, I have been much in the habit of preferring the image of an orbicular body,—a sphere—or a dew-drop.'[16]

Wordsworth's remarks elsewhere suggest that the initial attraction of Milton's sonnets was their capacity for accommodating a range of poetic effects within a tightly confined space. There is an admiration for Milton's powers of compression in the observation that his sonnets have 'an energetic and varied flow of sound crowding into narrow room more of the combined effect of rhyme and blank verse than can be done by any other kind of verse I know'.[17] The appeal of a narrow room provides the motivating impulse in the Prefatory sonnet—a sonnet about the sonnet—that Wordsworth attached to his first major grouping of sonnets in *Poems, in Two Volumes* (1807).

> Nuns fret not at their Convent's narrow room;
> And Hermits are contented with their Cells;
> And Students with their pensive Citadels:
> Maids at the Wheel, the Weaver at his Loom,
> Sit blithe and happy; Bees that soar for bloom,
> High as the highest Peak of Furness Fells,
> Will murmur by the hour in Foxglove bells:
> In truth, the prison, unto which we doom
> Ourselves, no prison is: and hence to me,
> In sundry moods, 'twas pastime to be bound
> Within the Sonnet's scanty plot of ground:
> Pleas'd if some Souls (for such there needs must be)
> Who have felt the weight of too much liberty,
> Should find short solace there, as I have found.   (286)

This sonnet was probably composed in late 1802, not long after Wordsworth 'took fire' from hearing his sister read Milton's sonnets.[18] The lessons learned

---

16. *The Letters of William and Dorothy Wordsworth: The Later Years*, ed. E. de Sélincourt (Oxford: Clarendon Press, 1939), vol. 2, pp. 604–5.
17. Wordsworth, in a letter written in 1802, cited in William Wordsworth, *The Major Works*, ed. Stephen Gill (Oxford: Oxford University Press, 2009), p. 710. Unless otherwise indicated, quotations from Wordsworth's sonnets are from this volume.
18. See n. 14 above.

on that occasion are immediately apparent. The poem adopts a familiar Petrarchan rhyme scheme—*abbaabbacddccd*—but syntactically it overruns and effaces the division between the opening quatrains and (even more emphatically) between octave and sestet. The general principle of conducting 'an energetic and varied flow of sound' within a tightly confined space is evident from the outset. The sonnet opens with a striking spondaic (rather than the usual iambic) rhythm, and then proceeds to set up a strong and insistent pattern of sound through anaphoric repetition, syntactic parallelism, and emphatic pauses.

There are three parts to the sonnet, 'like the propositions of a syllogism'. Lines 1–7 expand from the initial conception of an enclosed contemplative life exemplified by nuns and hermits to the intellectual life of students and the labouring life of spinners and weavers. In each case, there is an ideal of freedom within confinement, though this is amplified as we move from nuns who 'fret not' to labourers who are 'blithe and happy'. The caesura in line 5 establishes a close correspondence between human and natural endeavour. The suggestion of bees that 'soar for bloom' being murmurously content in the small space of flower petals is neatly compacted in the interplay of alliterative and assonantal effects between line 5 and line 7. The second proposition occupies only a line and a half, but it has a crucial, pivotal function: 'In truth, the prison, into which we doom | Ourselves, no prison is'. The division between octave and sestet is marked by the internal reflection of 'prison' and 'no prison' (neatly encapsulating the overall tenor of the sonnet), but the expectation of a clearly marked structural *volta* is cleverly confounded by the false turns, one unconventionally early (at the beginning of line 8) and one unconventionally late (in the middle of line 9). The final proposition (lines 9–14) asserts the value of the sonnet's 'scanty plot of ground' for writers and readers alike. The unashamed subjectivity ('and hence to me') is reminiscent of the 'Lucy' poems in *Lyrical Ballads* ('But she is in her grave, and, oh | The difference to me'). The purpose here, however, is to insist on the validity of the poet's experience of 'short solace', at the same time as recognizing and sanctioning the need for such solace among the general public.

If Wordsworth's 1807 volume of poems offers itself as a model of literary achievement within the tight confines of lyric form, it also provides a political corollary by tacitly suggesting a way of contending with the political constraints of the post-revolutionary years. The urgency of the moment and the simultaneous embrace of both poetic and political imperatives is conveyed in the acknowledgement of 'some Souls (for such there needs must be) | Who have felt the weight of too much liberty'. To speak of liberty in the decades immediately following the French Revolution was to activate a set of highly controversial ideas about the nature and meaning of political freedom, extending all the way from John Locke to Edmund Burke. To see this sonnet as marking a turn from revolutionary to reactionary politics in Wordsworth's own career would, however, be much too simple. Its function is to mark the beginning of an extensive sequence of sonnets in which the process of reflection and retrospection, rather than terminal disillusionment, is the salient characteristic, and in which a tentative and changing assessment of international politics is accompanied by a self-conscious search for an appropriate poetic form. The appeal of the sonnet sequence in this turbulent context is that it allows for moments of insight and apprehension in individual poems, while also permitting expansion and redefinition along the way.

The sonnet extolling the virtues of a chastened freedom that inhabits a narrow room and a scanty plot of ground serves as a preface to both groupings of sonnets in *Poems, in Two Volumes: Part the First: Miscellaneous Sonnets and Part the Second: Sonnets Dedicated to Liberty*. These sonnets were later regrouped under new or slightly different headings, but in their 1807 presentation they constitute a significant reworking of the two principal modes of sonnet writing that Wordsworth had inherited from Coleridge: the topographical or prospect sonnet and the topical or political sonnet. Stuart Curran points out that the 'Miscellaneous Sonnets' are typically Petrarchan, while the 'Sonnets Dedicated to Liberty' are much more emphatically Miltonic.[19] There is a corresponding distinction between the private, introspective mode of the first part and the public, polemical mode of the second. Frequently, however, any such distinction breaks down and what the sonnets are seen to share is a cautious reassessment of both the workings of the imagination and the possibilities of civic liberty in the uncertain political climate of the early 1800s.

'To the River Duddon' strongly recalls the river poems of Coleridge and Bowles, but Wordsworth's sonnet is noticeably chastened and subdued. The octave opens with a promising salute to the mountain stream and the solitary places through which it flows, but the sestet registers a deep sense of desertion, as if the river flows on regardless of its onlookers: 'Thee hath

---

19. Curran, *Poetic Form and British Romanticism*, p. 42.

some awful Spirit impelled to leave, | Utterly to desert, the haunts of men, | Though simple the Companions were and few' (306). This is not the only note of discontent and dissatisfaction in the 'Miscellaneous Sonnets'. From the outset, it seems as if the sonnets are prepared for disappointment, cautiously limiting the boundaries of the imagination and checking any impulse to excess. The opening sonnet seems at first to give free scope to the vernal impulse: 'How sweet it is, when mother Fancy rocks | The wayward brain, to saunter through a wood!' The closing lines suggest, to the contrary, that Fancy can overwhelm the wanderer with its combination of dream and gleam: 'at last in fear I shrink, | And leap at once from the delicious stream' (268). The shrinking here reveals a wariness about the play of the mind and the senses, but it also indicates that the small scale of the sonnet provided restorative moments of encounter and exploration while Wordsworth prepared the ground for his more ambitious epic work.

These are sonnets that are acutely aware of their own relation to tradition, and critically aware of their own perceptual processes. The sonnet 'Composed after a Journey across the Hamilton Hills, Yorkshire' and its immediate successor (Sonnets 3 and 4) are quite unlike any of the earlier Romantic prospect sonnets, even though Wordsworth is clearly indebted to that tradition initiated by Charlotte Smith and others. What is most striking about Sonnet 3 is its immediate denial of the anticipated pleasures of the prospect, and its robust refusal to settle for any substitute conjured up in clouds. The poem's disappointed admission that the pleasures of the prospect have been lost to darkness gives it an unusual place in the tradition of topographical sonnets:

> Ere we had reached the wished-for place, night fell:
> We were too late at least by one dark hour,
> And nothing could we see of all that power
> Of prospect, whereof many thousands tell.
> The western sky did recompence us well
> With Grecian Temple, Minaret, and Bower;
> And, in one part, a Minster with its Tower
> Substantially distinct, a place for Bell
> Or Clock to toll from. Many a glorious pile
> Did we behold, sights that might well repay
> All disappointment! and, as such, the eye
> Delighted in them; but we felt, the while,
> We should forget them: they are of the sky,
> And from our earthly memory fade away. (287)

The strong sense of a chastened vision and a corresponding commitment to earth-bound actuality runs through other sonnets written in the early 1800s. In a strangely self-reflexive way, Sonnet 4 is remarkably explicit about its own 'unstable' thought. It takes as its staring point the closing lines of Sonnet 3 and offers further meditation on the 'proper' scope of vision and memory. The cloud illusions, though not lacking in beauty, are dispelled for their aery insignificance:

> The Grove, the sky-built Temple, and the Dome,
> Though clad in colours beautiful and pure,
> Find in the heart of man no natural home:
> The immortal Mind craves objects that endure:
> These cleave to it; from these it cannot roam,
> Nor they from it: their fellowship is secure.   (287)

The immediate biographical circumstances of early October 1802 help to explain why Wordsworth was so intent on witnessing 'that power | Of prospect' in Sonnet 3, and why he gives such strength of commitment to the heart as home, to objects that endure, and to the ideal of secure fellowship in this Hamilton (later 'Hambleton') sonnet. Sonnet 3 was composed, Wordsworth claims, 'on a day memorable to me—the day of my marriage'. As he points out, 'The horizon commanded by those hills is most magnificent', but what the poem recalls is his abject disappointment at being denied the sight of that magnificent view as night closed in. As John Kerrigan notes, an awareness of Wordsworth's recent marriage gives a special poignancy to the sonnet.[20]

That Wordsworth envisaged his earliest sonnets as a travelogue connecting private and public themes is amply borne out by the Hambleton Hills sonnets and other poems in the 1807 volume. One effect of this design is to allow individual sonnets to clarify moments of reflection and stillness within an overall framework that allows for movement and progression. The tension between perpetual motion and momentary stillness is powerfully and memorably captured in the sonnet 'Composed Upon Westminster Bridge':

> Earth has not any thing to shew more fair:
> Dull would he be of soul who could pass by
> A sight so touching in its majesty:
> This City now doth like a garment wear

---

20. John Kerrigan, 'Wordsworth and the Sonnet: Building, Dwelling, Thinking', *Essays in Criticism* 35.1 (1985), 45.

> The beauty of the morning; silent, bare,
> Ships, towers, domes, theatres, and temples lie
> Open unto the fields, and to the sky;
> All bright and glittering in the smokeless air.
> Never did sun more beautifully steep
> In his first splendor valley, rock, or hill;
> Ne'er saw I, never felt, a calm so deep!
> The river glideth at his own sweet will:
> Dear God! the very houses seem asleep;
> And all that mighty heart is lying still!   (285)

The title itself deserves some scrutiny. It suggests 'upon' in more than just the conventional sense of being 'about' Westminster Bridge. If Wordsworth's own recollections are to be taken as a true record, the poem was 'Composed on the roof of a coach, on my way to France Sept 1802'. Some readers of the sonnet have fastened upon this hint of imminent departure from England as a way of explaining and justifying Wordsworth's unexpected reverence for the beauty of the city. Dorothy's journal suggests that very likely the poem was *conceived* at the end of July 1802, but possibly it was not *composed* until some time after their return at the end of August that year.[21]

The perception of purity, of a city scene transfigured by light to the extent of becoming like 'one of nature's own grand spectacles' undoubtedly helps to explain the appeal and popularity of the poem. Even so, there is an enigmatic quality in the writing, induced in part by the use of negative superlatives, strikingly so in the opening line and even more emphatically in the thrice repeated 'never' in the sestet. What the sonnet also adds to the journal account is a strong association between seeing and feeling, and this, too, is intensified in the relationship between octave and sestet, with 'A sight so touching' being amplified in 'Ne'er saw I, never felt'. In this respect, the sonnet might be seen as a characteristically Wordsworthian composition, a concentrated instance of deeply felt sensation, and of emotion recollected in tranquillity.

---

21. The journal entry brilliantly captures the vision of London shared by brother and sister in the early morning of 31 July 1802 and appears to be the genesis of the poem: 'It was a beautiful morning. The City, St Paul's, with the River and a multitude of little Boats, made a most beautiful sight as we crossed Westminster Bridge. The houses were not overhung by their cloud of smoke and they were spread out endlessly, yet the sun shone brightly with such a pure light that there was even something like the purity of one of nature's own grand spectacles.' *Journals of Dorothy Wordsworth*, pp. 150–1. In some editions of Wordsworth's poetry, the sonnet is dated 3 September 1803, possibly the date of completion.

Cleanth Brooks, in one of the most influential critical studies of Wordsworth's Westminster Bridge sonnet, claims that the poem acquires its power, paradoxically, through a style of writing that at first seems flat and unremarkable. According to Brooks, there is nothing brilliant or strikingly realistic in the opening images of London. Wordsworth 'simply huddles the details together' and we get 'a blurred impression—points of roofs and pinnacles along the skyline'. What gives the poem its special appeal is its 'sense of awed surprise' that 'the city should be able to "wear the beauty of the morning" at all'. The poem's profound insight is that the city is not merely mechanical—it participates in the life of nature—and this leads Brooks to consider the strange suggestions of sleeping and death in the closing lines: 'It is only when the poet sees the city under the semblance of death that he can see it as actually alive—quick with the only life which he can accept, the organic life of "nature."' His essential point is that 'paradox is the language appropriate and inevitable to poetry', but for all his concern with the ideal poem as a 'well-wrought urn', he gives no consideration at all to Wordsworth's handling of the sonnet form.[22]

'Composed Upon Westminster Bridge' adopts one of the most familiar Petrarchan rhyme schemes—*abbaabbacdcdcd*—but it invests this simple pattern with elements of rhythmic surprise and variation. The unadorned simplicity and colloquial tenor of the opening two lines, giving emphasis to 'Earth' and 'Dull', are reminiscent of the *Lyrical Ballads*. The enjambment of lines 2–3, lines 4–5, and lines 6–7, played off against the strongly marked caesura in line 5, prepares us for the more expansive visionary mode and revelation in the sestet. The word 'Open' carries us magically from earth to sky in a brilliant moment of imaginative transportation. The city might be conceived in broad brush strokes, as a generalized plurality of landmarks, but the sonnet's great achievement is to convey that multiplicity so compactly and economically. The brisk run of descriptive nouns—'Ships, towers, domes, theatres, and temples'—is echoed in the sestet in 'valley, rock, or hill', and there is a further structural equivalence between the closing 'all' in the octave and the closing 'all' in the sestet, enriching the sonnet's sense of the plenitude and potential of city life.

The crucial mediating figure between these signifiers of city and country life is, of course, the river, with all its symbolic associations of connection and continuity. If Wordsworth's poem is one of the great city sonnets, it is

---

22. Cleanth Brooks, *The Well Wrought Urn* (London: Dennis Dobson, 1949), pp. 5–6.

also the highpoint of a great English Romantic tradition of river sonnets, reaching back to the work of Bowles and Coleridge. It is the easeful movement of the river that prevents the closing lines from settling into petrifaction. Brooks and other critics, including J. Hillis Miller, have pointed out that the city, at the close of the sonnet, appears to be both sleeping and dead, but to insist too strongly on this intimation is to detract from the sonnet's powerful acknowledgement of latent or dormant potential in 'that mighty heart'.[23] If there is a monumental stillness about the city, there is also a vivid realization of what is *still* going on.

The moment of 'passing by', whether in July or September of 1802, assumes an even greater significance in the larger structural context of Wordsworth's journeying sonnets of the time. The bridge, with the river flowing sweetly beneath it, is an imaginative point of transition, an in-between place for momentary reflections. To suggest that the deep calm of the poem conceals political anxieties attendant on the leaving of England for France might be to make Westminster Bridge carry too much symbolic weight. It might be better, then, to suppose that the poem was composed, in more settled circumstances, on Wordsworth's return from France. However, the poem embraces a perspective that is strangely both before and after the moment of departure.

Tempting as it might be to lift this sonnet clear of historical and political entanglements, and to regard it as a moment of solitary rapture and private reflection, we need to remind ourselves that its thoroughfare is Westminster, a seat of government since the eleventh century, and the place where parliamentary debates about freedom were conducted. Like many of the 'Sonnets Dedicated to Liberty', this one looks at England in the aftermath of the French Revolution and finds appropriate images of both thwarted and unrealized potential in the stillness of a mighty heart. That Wordsworth's reflections are, in part, reflections on the revolution in France is confirmed by the potent Burkean rhetoric that gives the sonnet its syntactical armature. The poem echoes one of the most famous passages in Burke's *Reflections on the Revolution in France*—his lyrical lamentation on the death of Marie Antoinette. Burke's delighted vision of the dauphiness underpins Wordsworth's evocation of the 'majesty' of the city, and his memory of her 'glittering like the morning star' just above the horizon is neatly transposed into the image of the city skyline, 'All bright and glittering in the smokeless air'. Burke's appeal, like

---

23. J. Hillis Miller, *The Linguistic Moment* (Princeton: Princeton University Press, 1985), p. 73.

Wordsworth's, is to the heart, and to what the heart can withstand: 'what a heart must I have, to contemplate without emotion that elevation and that fall'.[24] His strictures on the unfeeling spectator give rise to Wordsworth's 'Dull would he be of soul who could pass by…'.

The sonnet's striking image of the city wearing the beauty of the morning 'like a garment' restores 'the decent drapery of life' rudely torn away by revolution in Burke's panegyric, while the gliding river recalls Burke's living stream and his potent warning that 'when your fountain is choked up and polluted, the stream will not run long, or not run clear with us, or perhaps with any nation'.[25] Within the sonnet's Burkean reflections, there is relief at the discovery of continuing organic life in the heart of the nation, momentarily stilled as it might be. There is also a continuing trust in the imagination. If the adoption of the sonnet form is, in some ways, a cautious occupation of a manageable artistic space, it nevertheless allows for moments of visionary expansiveness and revelation.

'Composed Upon Westminster Bridge', so deftly poised between England and France, between private meditation and public life, suggests that there are clear areas of overlap and continuity between the Part One 'Miscellaneous Sonnets' and the Part Two 'Sonnets Dedicated to Liberty' in their 1807 arrangement. The point is borne out by two other memorable sonnets in Part One: 'The world is too much with us' and 'It is a beauteous evening'. In the first of these, the voice of civic conscience upbraids a public that is more intent on materialistic gain than in learning from nature:

> The world is too much with us; late and soon,
> Getting and spending, we lay waste our powers:
> Little we see in nature that is ours;
> We have given our hearts away, a sordid boon!

Here, the poet speaks on behalf of a community whose powers of perception and apprehension have been squandered, and whose feelings for the natural world have been laid waste: 'It moves us not.' In its general disapprobation for a society so 'out of time', and in its plea for a more authentic mode of being, the sonnet anticipates 'London, 1802'. Milton's influence is already at work here in the syntactical crescendo in the sestet, and in

---

24. Edmund Burke, *Reflections on the Revolution in France*, ed. L. G. Mitchell (Oxford: Oxford University Press, 1993), pp. 75–6.
25. Burke, *Reflections on the Revolution*, p. 80.

the summoning of Proteus from the sea, with its distant echo of *Paradise Lost* (3.603–4):

> Great God! I'd rather be
> A Pagan suckled in a creed outworn;
> So might I, standing on this pleasant lea,
> Have glimpses that would make me less forlorn;
> Have sight of Proteus coming from the sea;
> Or hear old Triton blow his wreathed horn.   (270)

In Miltonic style, the *volta* is effectively delayed until the middle of line 9, though it is clearly signalled by the turn from 'we' and 'us' to 'I', confirming the poet's role as witness and spokesman for the community. Like the 'Dear God' of the Westminster Bridge sonnet, the address is both an expression of deeply felt emotion and a sign of the poet's continuing search for some benevolent Deity, even if this necessitates the acceptance of Pagan attributes.

In the sonnet that follows, there is a strong assurance that 'the mighty Being is awake', and that nature and human nature are alike divine:

> It is a beauteous Evening, calm and free;
> The holy time is quiet as a Nun
> Breathless with adoration; the broad sun
> Is sinking down in its tranquillity;
> The gentleness of heaven is on the Sea:
> Listen! The mighty Being is awake
> And doth with his eternal motion make
> A sound like thunder—everlastingly.
> Dear Child! Dear Girl! that walkest with me here,
> If thou appear'st untouched by solemn thought,
> Thy nature is not therefore less divine:
> Thou liest in Abraham's bosom all the year;
> And worshipp'st at the Temple's inner shrine,
> God being with thee when we know it not.   (281)

The structure here is more obviously Petrarchan than that of the previous sonnet. In keeping with the calm mood of the opening lines, the octave gently conforms to the usual pattern of two distinct quatrains, though the sound of everlasting thunder is powerfully rendered in the sudden caesura marked with a mid-line dash. The *volta* is a turning to a dear companion, reminiscent of the turning to Dorothy at the end of 'Lines written a few miles above Tintern Abbey', except that the child here appears 'untouched by solemn thought', and so the poet, as so often in these sonnets, can only invest his trust and hope in a perceived potential. That the sonnet was probably composed in August 1802 during Wordsworth's sojourn in France, and very likely prompted by his reunion with his 9-year-old daughter, Caroline, is a further reason for thinking that the division of the early sonnets into two parts does not entirely efface their common concerns. This is, after all, a sonnet that contemplates, in its opening line, what it is to be 'free'.

The 'Sonnets Dedicated to Liberty' have a striking immediacy and coherence that come from their vivid response to English–French politics in the post-revolutionary years. The collection opens significantly with the poet looking back at England from the French coast as the light declines. With the exception of the 1860 postscript (Sonnet 26), all of the sonnets were composed between May 1802 and October 1803. One of the unfortunate consequences of Wordsworth's later regrouping and expansion of the sonnets under 'Poems Dedicated to National Independence and Liberty' was the dissipation of the initial urgency and immediacy that makes the sonnets appear written 'to the moment'. As Curran points out, the poems capture the public ambivalence that accompanied the Treaty of Amiens (25 March 1802 to May 1803).[26] The collective endeavour of the sonnets is to rediscover and redefine the spirit of liberty in the post-revolutionary years. If this entails a swelling of patriotic emotion, as England's civic and cultural achievements are measured against the tide of tyranny in Napoleonic France, it also generates the occasional fierce criticism of stagnation and neglect at home, most notably in 'London, 1802'. The formal achievement of the sonnets is to allow for moments of reflection on these ambivalent, conflicting views of liberty, while at the same time offering a sense of progression and direction.

It seems fitting that the opening sonnets in the collection should offer a perspective on liberty from the seaside town of Calais, as if that marginal position afforded an appropriate mental space for looking back, both at the contemporary England across the water and at the pre-revolutionary France that Wordsworth visited a decade earlier. The opening poem, 'Composed by the Sea-Side, near Calais', a reworking of Coleridge's 1790 sonnet 'To The Evening Star', sees in the glorious 'Fair Star of Evening' shining over England, a fitting portent of national destiny. The Miltonic surge of the sonnet across the octave-sestet division and its excited, exclamatory diction give the poem a buoyant start but cannot altogether conceal the underlying

---

26. Curran, *Poetic Form and British Romanticism*, p. 46.

tension and fear. The address to the star, forming an extended turn in lines 6 to 9, is offered as a reassertion of the sonnet's initial perception, but it also introduces a note of caution: 'Thou, I think, | Should'st be my Country's emblem' (281). For all its insistence on the star as an image of national unity ('one hope, one lot, | One life, one glory!'), the sonnet closes with lingering uncertainty and circumspection.

The sonnets written in France, including 'Calais, August, 1802', cast shame on the 'feeble Heads' bowing before a tyrannical regime, and ruefully contrast the sombre reality of the present with the revolutionary hopes of the past (280). In Sonnet 3, addressed to his undergraduate friend and travelling companion, Robert Jones, Wordsworth sets the hollow greeting heard on the road from Calais to Ardres, '*Good morrow, Citizen!*', against his memory of the 'festivals of new-born Liberty' which he witnessed with Jones in the autumn of 1790 (282). Napoleon's rise to power provides the impulse for several of the sonnets on liberty, most obviously Sonnet 4 ('I grieved for Buonaparte'), the first to be written under the potent influence of Milton. If Milton's example shapes the rhetorical structure of the sonnet, including its anguished opening questions and its insistent assurances, it also informs the sonnet's sense of what constitutes 'True Power' and good conduct (267). The proclamation of Napoleon as First Consul of the Republic for life in August 1802 is the subject of Sonnet 5 ('Calais, August 15th, 1802'), in which the 'pomps and games' of the present are contrasted (across octave and sestet) with 'Another time' when 'The senselessness of joy was then sublime!' (283). Three sonnets consider the consequences of Napoleon's rule for the liberty of nations outside of England and France. Sonnet 6 mourns the extinction of the Venetian Republic after Napoleon's occupation of Venice, 'the eldest Child of Liberty', in May 1797 (268), while Sonnet 7 pays tribute to the king of Sweden for his principled resistance to Napoleon. Sonnet 8 praises the imprisoned governor of St Domingo, Toussaint L'Ouverture, for his opposition to Napoleon's edict re-establishing slavery in Haiti. In all three sonnets the ideal of liberty persists, despite Napoleon's abuses of power.

Sonnet 10, 'Composed in the Valley, near Dover, on the Day of Landing', renews the spirit of patriotism evident at the outset, this time responding with relief and gratitude to particular national qualities and characteristics, including the boys in 'white-sleeved shirts' playing in the meadow: 'All, all are English.' In view of the latest strictures on England's degradation and decline, the exuberant exclamation, 'Thou art free | My Country!', might seem premature (284). That the sonnets need to be read as part of a continuing meditation rather than in isolation is confirmed by the dampened spirit of 'London, 1802':

> Milton! Thou should'st be living at this hour:
> England hath need of thee: she is a fen
> Of stagnant waters: altar, sword and pen,
> Fireside, the heroic wealth of hall and bower,
> Have forfeited their ancient English dower
> Of inward happiness. We are selfish men;
> Oh! raise us up, return to us again;
> And give us manners, virtue, freedom, power.
> Thy soul was like a Star and dwelt apart:
> Thou hadst a voice whose sound was like the sea;
> Pure as the naked heavens, majestic, free,
> So didst thou travel on life's common way,
> In cheerful godliness; and yet thy heart
> The lowliest duties on itself did lay.   (286)

Here, a conventional Petrarchan structure (*abbaabbacddece*) is given distinctive Miltonic inflections. Although the sonnet retains a clear division between octave and sestet, the strong control exerted over the syntax by mid-line and end of line pauses leads to a satisfyingly articulate and authoritative conclusion in the closing three lines. The virtues that Wordsworth recognizes in Milton—the assured righteousness and undemonstrative humility—are reminiscent of the 'dignified simplicity and majestic harmony' that he so admired in Milton's sonnets when he heard his sister read them earlier that year. The acknowledgement of Milton's virtues relieves the negative picture of England as 'a fen | Of stagnant waters' in the octave, and this is aided by the important shift from stasis to motion in the sestet: 'So didst thou travel on life's common way'. At the same time, the 'majestic' scene of London and its 'mighty heart' in the Westminster Bridge sonnet now seem to be constricted, finding potential in one man only. As if in recognition of that desultory fact, Sonnet 16 announces that 'Great Men have been among us' and adds to the list, 'the later Sydney, Marvel, Harrington, | Young Vane, and others who call'd Milton Friend' (276). Sonnet 17 equates the spirit of freedom with speaking 'the tongue | That Shakespeare spake', as well as holding 'the faith and morals... | Which Milton held', though the presiding influence in this sonnet is most likely Edmund Burke (276).

It is difficult to offer any clear and decisive assessment of Wordsworth's politics in a collection of sonnets so fraught with tension, ambivalence, and uncertainty. Individual sonnets are charged with conflict, both psychological and social, while the larger structure allows for reconsideration and continued meditation, rather than insisting on any simple linear progression of thought and feeling. Stephen Gill claims that in 1802–3, 'Wordsworth remained true to the republican ideal that had fired him a decade before, but the evidence was overwhelming that France was diverging further and further from it.'[27] Other critics have seen a falling off, in both political zeal and poetic style, in the 'Sonnets Dedicated to Liberty'. John Lucas finds Wordsworth's Miltonic rhetoric unconvincing, 'part of a lapse into nostalgia', and evidence that Wordsworth was now left without a language appropriate to the occasion. Lucas claims that 'The publication of *Ecclesiastical Sonnets* in 1822 marks Wordsworth's full retreat into an essentially anti-democratic monarchism', but he detects a divergence from Milton's republicanism much earlier than that: 'The result is that support for Milton becomes very difficult, except where he can be seen as a master of style alone, his politics ignored.'[28]

One telling indication of Wordsworth's transformed political sentiments can be found in the sonnet titled '1830', included in later collections of 'Miscellaneous Sonnets':

>   Chatsworth! thy stately mansion, and the pride
>   Of thy domain, strange contrast do present
>   To house and home in many a craggy rent
>   Of the wild Peak; where new-born waters glide
>   Through fields whose thrifty occupants abide
>   As in a dear and chosen banishment,
>   With every semblance of entire content;
>   So kind is simple Nature, fairly tried!
>   Yet He whose heart in childhood gave her troth
>   To pastoral dales, thin-set with modest farms,
>   May learn, if judgment strengthen with his growth,
>   That, not for Fancy only, pomp hath charms;
>   And, strenuous to protect from lawless harms
>   The extremes of favoured life, may honour both.

The sonnet was written in November 1830, during (or shortly after) a journey that Wordsworth made from Westmorland to Cambridge, stopping in Derbyshire to admire the house and estate of the Duke of

---

27. Stephen Gill, *William Wordsworth: A Life* (Oxford: Oxford University Press, 1990), p. 209.
28. John Lucas, *England and Englishness* (London: Hogarth Press, 1990), p. 119.

Devonshire.[29] The opening apostrophe echoes that of 'London, 1802', but the political allegiances now seem very far removed from Milton's republicanism.[30] The 'stately mansion' provides 'strange contrast' with the humble dwellings in the Peak District, and the sonnet strives awkwardly to justify and naturalize that contrast. The turn between octave and sestet suggests a process of growth in learning and judgement for one whose childhood was spent in 'pastoral dales', but what that process entails is an acceptance of 'pomp', along with the class distinctions and social divisions implied in 'The extremes of favoured life' in England in 1830. Ironically, the sonnet's Miltonic rhetoric now speaks on behalf of established authority and serves an earnestly conservative political vision.

Percy Bysshe Shelley

Wordsworth's revival of the sonnet form was decisive and long lasting, and his influence as a sonnet writer extended well into the nineteenth century, with Matthew Arnold being a notable admirer. One indication of his popular success was the publication in 1838 of *The Sonnets of William Wordsworth: Collected in One Volume*, with a prefatory acknowledgement to John Milton. By this time, however, Wordsworth's achievements as a sonnet writer had already been outstripped by other distinguished exponents of the form. The task of keeping alive the republican spirit of Milton fell to Percy Bysshe Shelley. Although relatively few in number compared with Wordsworth's vast outpouring, Shelley's sonnets impressively fuse a zealous political radicalism with a daring technical expertise.[31] The sonnet 'To Wordsworth', written in 1814–15, suggests how far the older poet had fallen in Shelley's estimation, but it also provides an early instance of Shelley's own adept and distinctive handling of the sonnet form:

> Poet of Nature, thou hast wept to know
> That things depart which never may return:

---

29. Wordsworth, '1830', *The Sonnets of William Wordsworth: Collected in One Volume* (London: Edward Moxon, 1838), p. 103.
30. John Lucas offers an incisive reading of the Chatsworth sonnet in the light of Wordsworth's politics in the 1830s (developing the arguments proposed in *England and Englishness*) in 'England in 1830—Wordsworth, Clare, and the Question of Poetic Authority', *Critical Survey* 4.1 (1992), 62–6.
31. Quotations from Shelley's sonnets are from Percy Bysshe Shelley, *The Major Works*, ed. Zachary Leader and Michael O'Neill (Oxford: Oxford University Press, 2003).

> Childhood and youth, friendship and love's first glow,
> Have fled like sweet dreams, leaving thee to mourn.
> These common woes I feel. One loss is mine
> Which thou too feel'st, yet I alone deplore.
> Thou wert as a lone star, whose light did shine
> On some frail bark in winter's midnight roar:
> Thou hast like to a rock-built refuge stood
> Above the blind and battling multitude:
> In honored poverty thy voice did weave
> Songs consecrate to truth and liberty,—
> Deserting these, thou leavest me to grieve,
> Thus having been, that thou shouldst cease to be.   (91)

The opening address is reminiscent of Wordsworth's summoning of Milton in 'London, 1802', and the striking image of Wordsworth as 'a lone star' recalls the tribute paid to Milton in that poem ('Thy soul was like a Star'). Whereas Wordsworth had sought to revive the spirit of Milton, Shelley mourns with bitter irony the premature 'death' of Wordsworth. The characterization of Wordsworth as the poet of loss and sorrow, finely registered in the sonnet's rueful echoes of 'Lines written a few miles above Tintern Abbey' and 'Ode: Intimations of Immortality', is turned against him so that the 'Poet of Nature' is now himself one of those departed things which 'never may return'. The closing lines carry an echo of one of Wordsworth's 'Sonnets Dedicated to Liberty': 'Men we are, and must grieve when even the Shade | Of that which was great, is passed away.' These lines are from a sonnet, 'On the Extinction of the Venetian Republic' (268), and Shelley's perception of fading glory intensifies the saddened acknowledgement of Wordsworth as political renegade. That acknowledgement is given force through form: the turn from octave to sestet, with its insistent repetition of what Wordsworth has until recently stood for, holds out hope of some recuperation right until the dashing of that possibility at the end of line 12. The rhyme scheme similarly moves in Shakespearean fashion towards resolution, but introduces a rhyming couplet surprisingly early (lines 9–10), as if structurally acknowledging the foreshortening of Wordsworth's career.

Shelley's awareness of the polemical force that might be generated through the tightly compressed form of the sonnet is evident in two early compositions which date from August 1812: 'Sonnet: On Launching Some Bottles Filled with Knowledge into the Bristol Channel' and 'Sonnet: To a Balloon, Laden with Knowledge'. As Michael O'Neill points out, these two sonnets illustrate the importance that Shelley attached to the dissemination of radical political ideals, and they amply convey his 'enthusiasm for unfettered communication of ideas'.[32] In both poems there is an implicit connection between small containers of potentially explosive knowledge (bottles and balloons) and the small but potentially powerful form of the sonnet. Both poems experiment with rhyme schemes that modulate between Petrarchan and Shakespearean patterns, and both make effective use of a resounding closing couplet. Shelley's fierce commitment to liberty contrasts strongly with Wordsworth's more circumspect vision in his 1807 sonnets. Although his early handling of the sonnet form is mannered and hyperbolic, it powerfully conveys his hatred of 'tyrant-hearts' and 'tyrants' gilded domes' (9).

In 'Ozymandias', written in late 1817, Shelley's condemnation of tyranny is all the more effective for its restrained avoidance of clamorous rhetoric. The sonnet acquires a serene detachment by presenting a story within a story, and allowing the broken image of the mighty ruler to resonate within the reader's consciousness. It functions through ironic implication rather than moral insistence. The diction and structure of the sonnet are commensurate with the starkness and bareness of the wrecked colossus and the desert landscape:

> I met a traveller from an antique land
> Who said—'Two vast and trunkless legs of stone
> Stand in the desert. Near them, on the sand,
> Half sunk, a shattered visage lies, whose frown,
> And wrinkled lip, and sneer of cold command,
> Tell that its sculptor well those passions read
> Which yet survive, stamped on these lifeless things,
> The hand that mocked them and the heart that fed;
> And on the pedestal these words appear:
> "My name is Ozymandias, King of Kings:
> Look on my Works, ye Mighty, and despair!"
> Nothing beside remains. Round the decay
> Of that colossal Wreck, boundless and bare
> The lone and level sands stretch far away.' (198)

The sonnet alludes to the fall of Pharaoh Ramses II (1279–1213 BC), and was probably inspired by Shelley's reading of Diodorus Siculus, the Greek historian, and by his acquaintance with contemporary travel writings

---

32. Michael O'Neill, *Percy Bysshe Shelley: A Literary Life* (Basingstoke: Macmillan, 1989), p. 20.

about Egypt. The poem invites us to reflect on the vanity of worldly glory, but it also tacitly acknowledges the survival and persistence of art in what remains of the sculptor's work. If, in some ways, 'Ozymandias' is the fulfilment of Shakespeare's Sonnet 107, with its anticipation of that time 'When tyrants' crests and tombs of brass are spent', it is, in other ways, a peculiar and distinctive achievement.[33] The rhyme scheme is neither Shakespearean nor Petrarchan (*ababacdcedefef*), and the usual quatrain divisions are effaced by the verbal energy of the traveller's tale. There is an undemonstrative turn between octave and sestet, marked by the semicolon at the end of line 8 and the introduction of the words on the pedestal in line 9, but the crucial shift of perspective begins in the middle of line 12 with an emphatic caesura. The rhythmic interplay of alliteration and enjambment in the closing lines reinforces the sonnet's compelling vision of infinitude.

The abuse of kingly power by George III and his dissolute sons prompts the forceful opening lines of 'Sonnet: England in 1819'. Although written without any assurance of publication in Shelley's own lifetime (it was withheld until 1839), it remains one of the most urgent and stirring political sonnets ever conceived:

> An old, mad, blind, despised, and dying King;
> Princes, the dregs of their dull race, who flow
> Through public scorn,—mud from a muddy spring;
> Rulers who neither see nor feel nor know,
> But leechlike to their fainting country cling
> Till they drop, blind in blood, without a blow.
> A people starved and stabbed in th'untilled field;
> An army whom liberticide and prey
> Makes as a two-edged sword to all who wield;
> Golden and sanguine laws which tempt and slay;
> Religion Christless, Godless, a book sealed;
> A senate, Time's worst statute, unrepealed—
> Are graves from which a glorious Phantom may
> Burst, to illumine our tempestuous day.   (446)

The drumroll of the opening line, with its insistent plosives falling heavily on 'King', prepares us for the suspended verbal action that gives the sonnet its powerful political appeal. The delayed verb is preceded by a catalogue of

---

33. William Shakespeare, *The Complete Sonnets and Poems*, ed. Colin Burrow (Oxford: Oxford University Press, 2008), p. 595.

ills—not just the Peterloo massacre of peaceful protestors earlier that year, but the continuing injustices perpetrated by Parliament—and these are now seen starkly and grimly as graves. The brilliance of the sonnet is in the transformative rhetoric which carries the momentum all the way through to the final verb 'Burst', simultaneously echoing with positive force those plosive *b*s and *d*s that dominate the opening.

F. R. Leavis drew attention to what he considered 'the pathetic weakness of the final couplet' in his influential chapter on Shelley in *Revaluation* (1936), and numerous critics have since commented on the apparent hesitation or despair suggested by the qualifying 'may'.[34] The positioning of that word in such a tightly constructed sonnet is an indication of its urgency rather than its uncertainty; it goes beyond 'might' to register the sense of a revolutionary spirit already empowered and ready to act. John Lucas sums this up well when he comments that 'both words ['may' and 'Burst'] are heavily stressed: they operate in perilous balance'.[35] The rhyme scheme is once again strikingly independent and unorthodox: *abababcdcdccdd*. As well as making a powerful impact through two closing couplets, the sonnet inverts the usual octave-sestet relationship, as if structurally enacting the revolution anticipated in its closing lines.

The 'tempestuous day' of 'England in 1819' is given sublime expression and a further burst of illumination in Shelley's 'Ode to the West Wind', begun in Florence later that year. The Italian cultural and political context gives way to a more comprehensive and prophetic heralding of freedom, with the West Wind suggesting (among other possibilities) the spirit of American freedom carried over the Atlantic. If the poem has all the grandeur and spaciousness associated with the ode as a celebratory form, it might be that it also represents Shelley's most adventurous experiment with the sonnet. Each stanza consists of four tercets and a couplet, fusing the dynamics of the English sonnet with those of the Italian *terza rima* employed by Dante. If this arrangement effectively conveys the impression of speed and forward movement, it also creates a strongly liturgical or prayer-like structure, harnessing repeated imperatives in its litany to the spirit of freedom. Although his 'Ode to the West Wind' is not usually discussed in histories of the sonnet, Shelley succeeds in revitalizing both the religious and political functions of the form in one magnificent orchestration.

---

34. F. R. Leavis, *Revaluation* (Harmondsworth: Penguin, 1994), p. 189.
35. Lucas, *England and Englishness*, p. 124.

John Keats

Shelley's poetry gives a fierce new energy to the sonnet as a form well suited to the expression of political subject matter, and it carries forward the work of Milton and Wordsworth, but that legacy can be observed elsewhere in second-generation Romantic poetry. It flares brightly, for instance, in Byron's sonnet 'On Chillon':

> Eternal Spirit of the chainless Mind!
> Brightest in dungeons, Liberty, thou art;
> For there thy habitation is the heart—
> The heart which love of thee alone can bind.[36]

The hatred of tyranny and the commitment to political freedom shared by Byron and Shelley also resound throughout the early sonnets of John Keats, though literary criticism has been slow to acknowledge the radical, progressive elements in Keats's poetry.[37] In what is likely his earliest sonnet, probably written in April 1814, Keats marks the end of war with France and records the demise of Napoleon's power.

> O Peace! and dost thou with thy presence bless
>   The dwellings of this war-surrounded Isle;
> Soothing with placid brow our late distress,
>   Making the triple kingdom brightly smile?
> Joyful I hail thy presence; and I hail
>   The sweet companions that await on thee;
> Complete my joy—let not my first wish fail,
>   Let the sweet mountain nymph thy favourite be,
> With England's happiness proclaim Europa's Liberty.
>   O Europe! let not sceptred tyrants see
> That thou must shelter in thy former state;
>   Keep thy chains burst, and boldly say thou art free;
> Give thy kings law—leave not uncurbed the great;
> So with the horrors past thou'lt win thy happier fate!   (419)

This early sonnet 'On Peace' extends the concerns of Wordsworth in his 'Sonnets Dedicated to Liberty', and it also echoes Milton's 'L'Allegro' in

---

36. Lord Byron, *The Complete Poetical Works*, ed. Jerome J. McGann (Oxford: Clarendon, 1992), vol. 4, p. 3.
37. Quotations from the sonnets of John Keats are from *Poetical Works*, ed. H. W. Garrod (Oxford: Oxford University Press, 1970).

depicting Liberty, the favourite companion of Peace, as a mountain nymph. The vigilant welcoming of new opportunities for freedom in Europe is in keeping with the political stance of Leigh Hunt, whose essays in the *Examiner* were known to Keats. The sonnet dispels the myth that Keats had no interest in politics, and it also shows a remarkable degree of stylistic experimentation at an early stage in his career. The irregular Shakespearean rhyme scheme (*ababcdcdddedee*) contradicts the common view that Keats wrote only Petrarchan sonnets until early 1818. The opening two quatrains follow the usual Shakespearean pattern, but the sonnet then deviates with a Miltonic crescendo that cuts across the expected turn between octave and sestet. The delayed turn at line 10 is given additional weight by the triple '*d*' rhyme, prolonging the buoyant expression of liberty. The mood of excited celebration and expectancy is heightened further by the additional syllables in line 9 and line 14 (a stately alexandrine).

Keats's close friend, Charles Cowden Clarke, claimed that Leigh Hunt's journal, the *Examiner*, 'no doubt laid the foundation of his love of civil and religious liberty'.[38] Although Keats did not meet Hunt until October 1816, his commitment to the radical political tradition that Hunt espoused is strongly signalled in the sonnet 'Written on the Day that Mr Leigh Hunt Left Prison'.

> What though, for showing truth to flatter'd state,
>   Kind Hunt was shut in prison, yet has he,
>   In his immortal spirit, been as free
> As the sky-searching lark, and as elate.
> Minion of grandeur! think you he did wait?
>   Think you he nought but prison walls did see,
>   Till, so unwilling, thou unturn'dst the key?
> Ah, no! far happier, nobler was his fate!
> In Spenser's halls he strayed, and bowers fair,
>   Culling enchanted flowers; and he flew
> With daring Milton through the fields of air:
>   To regions of his own his genius true
> Took happy flights. Who shall his fame impair
> When thou art dead, and all thy wretched crew?   (34)

Hunt was released from prison on 2 February 1815, after serving a two-year sentence for having written a libellous attack on the Prince Regent. The sonnet directs its finely tuned accusatory rhetoric at those minions of power

---

38. Walter Jackson Bate, *John Keats* (Cambridge, MA: Harvard University Press, 1963), p. 25.

who have supported the abuse of freedom. Its sentiments recall Wordsworth's lines on confinement and imaginative freedom ('Nuns fret not at their convent's narrow room'), but the soaring inspiration and energetic syntax undoubtedly derive from 'daring Milton'.

The imaginative flight envisaged for Hunt in his reading of Milton is experienced by Keats himself in several notable encounters with works of literary genius. One of the distinguishing features of his sonnets is the quality of revelation and wonder associated with reading, nowhere better seen than in the sonnet, 'On First Looking into Chapman's Homer', printed in the *Examiner* in December 1816. Here, a sense of stunned amazement is vividly realized, with the sonnet turning on the analogy between the scope of the literary imagination and the boundlessness of astronomical and geographical discovery:

>Much have I travell'd in the realms of gold,
>　And many goodly states and kingdoms seen;
>　Round many western islands have I been
>Which bards in fealty to Apollo hold.
>Oft of one wide expanse had I been told
>　That deep-brow'd Homer ruled as his demesne;
>　Yet did I never breathe its pure serene
>Till I heard Chapman speak out loud and bold:
>Then felt I like some watcher of the skies
>　When a new planet swims into his ken;
>Or like stout Cortez when with eagle eyes
>　He star'd at the Pacific—and all his men
>Look'd at each other with a wild surmise—
>　Silent, upon a peak in Darien.　　(38)

If the sonnet looks into the literary past, at the great achievements of Homer translated by the Renaissance poet and dramatist, George Chapman, it also looks out at what is still to be encountered. Andrew Motion offers an astute commentary on this 'forward-looking' dimension of the poem, but notes as well that the sonnet 'qualifies its excitement'. The title suggests that Keats had 'come late to high culture' and 'could not read Homer in the original Greek'. He suggests that the sonnet 'for all its wonderfully bold energy, succumbs to a moment of awkward translationese ("pure serene")'.[39] In fact, 'pure serene' is Coleridge's description of the sky in his memorable account of 'sky-pointing peaks' in his 'Hymn Before Sun-Rise, in the Vale of

39. Andrew Motion, *Keats* (London: Faber, 1997), p. 112.

Chamouni' (1802).[40] It shows Keats absorbing and assimilating the poetic diction of his contemporaries and making it his own.

Rather too much has been made of Keats's other sources: William Robertson's *History of America* (1777), which he read at school, and J. Bonnycastle's *Introduction to Astronomy*. Keats very likely confused Balboa's first sight of the Pacific from the isthmus of Darien with Cortes's distant view of Mexico City, but what is most remarkable is the way in which the sonnet conveys the excited exploration of sky and sea, opening out into its final moment of breath-taking sublimity. The conventional Petrarchan form (*abbaabbacdcdcd*) is given confident and articulate control, with every other line of the octave establishing a significant pause. What initially looks like a premature turn with the emphatic 'Yet' at the beginning of line 7 makes the actual turn ('Then felt I...') all the more powerfully expressive. The sonnet turns from hearing to seeing, from the 'loud and bold' voice of Chapman to the stunned silence of the explorers, but what enables that final expression of astonishment and wonder is the syntactical fulfilment of the final four lines and the strategic placing and timing of dramatic pauses after 'surmise' and 'silent'. In fourteen lines, Keats brilliantly conveys his rapturous appreciation of the epic reach of Homer, giving the classical landscape of sky and sea and mountain a romantic sublimity that strikingly suggests the infinite capacity of the imagination. The act of 'looking into' Chapman's Homer is transformed from cursory bibliographical inspection to transfixed amazement.

A measure of the distance travelled in Keats's intellectual development can be found in the space between that 'first' excited encounter with Homer in translation in October 1816 and the chastened experience described in the later sonnet, 'On Sitting Down to Read *King Lear* Once Again', composed in January 1818. As Curran notes, the 'use of the sonnet to record, or enact, an artistic experience...took Keats far beyond the conventional in response'. Like the earlier sonnet, the *King Lear* poem is 'a revelation of the psychology of aesthetic experience', but what it demonstrates most emphatically is Keats's maturing awareness and appreciation of Shakespearean tragedy.[41] In both poems there is ambition and aspiration tempered by a characteristic humility and a candid acknowledgement of personal shortcomings. The genesis of the

---

40. Coleridge, *The Major Works*, p. 118.
41. Curran, *Poetic Form and British Romanticism*, p. 52.

King Lear sonnet is recorded in a letter from Keats to his brothers, George and Tom, on 23 January 1818, in which the poet writes movingly of 'a very gradual ripening of the intellectual powers'.[42] This time, serene and golden and far away things are explicitly associated with Romance and a literary experience that must now give way to the humanizing effects of tragedy:

> O Golden tongued Romance with serene Lute!
>   Fair plumed Syren! Queen of far away!
>   Leave melodizing on this wintry day,
> Shut up thine olden Pages, and be mute:
> Adieu! for, once again, the fierce dispute
>   Betwixt damnation and impassion'd clay
>   Must I burn through; once more humbly assay
> The bitter-sweet of this Shakespearian fruit:
> Chief Poet! and ye Clouds of Albion,
>   Begetters of our deep eternal theme!
> When through the old oak forest I am gone,
>   Let me not wander in a barren dream,
> But, when I am consumed in the fire,
> Give me new Phoenix wings to fly at my desire.   (380)

The critical transition between two literary styles and between different literary modes of apprehending the world is neatly captured in the formal shift from a Petrarchan octave to a Shakespearean sestet (*abbaabbacdcdee*), and also in the announcement of a turning to Shakespeare, in which Keats imagines burning through the troubled nature of existence towards a new conception of the poet's role. As Helen Vendler notes, Keats both bids farewell to Spenserian Romance and provides a critique of his own early poems, including the numerous sonnets he had written in Petrarchan fashion. The extended closing line is a measure of the poem's painful struggle towards a new imaginative realization of the worth and value of poetry, but it also 'looks back in homage to the hexameters with which Spenser ends his stanzas in *The Faerie Queene*'.[43]

The temporal phrasing ('when I') recalls Shakespeare's Sonnets, and it echoes throughout the first of Keats's sonnets to adopt the Shakespearean rhyme scheme in its entirety:

---

42. *John Keats*, ed. Elizabeth Cook (Oxford: Oxford University Press, 1990), p. 374.
43. Helen Vendler, *Coming of Age as a Poet: Milton, Keats, Eliot, Plath* (Cambridge, MA: Harvard University Press, 2003), p. 66.

> When I have fears that I may cease to be
>   Before my pen has glean'd my teeming brain,
> Before high-piled books in charactery,
>   Hold like rich garners the full ripen'd grain;
> When I behold, upon the night's starr'd face,
>   Huge cloudy symbols of a high romance,
> And think that I may never live to trace
>   Their shadows, with the magic hand of chance;
> And when I feel, fair creature of an hour,
>   That I shall never look upon thee more,
> Never have relish in the faery power
>   Of unreflecting love;—then on the shore
> Of the wide world I stand alone, and think
> Till love and fame to nothingness do sink.   (366)

The quatrain divisions and the turn are clearly marked by a parallel syntactical structure ('When I have fears...When I behold...And when I feel'), and the sonnet strives for a strongly intensified impression of personal feeling and thinking.

    Literary fame and romantic love, the subjects of the first and third quatrains, are closely embraced in the second quatrain in the idea of 'a high romance' and in the imagined tracing of shadows that both writing and loving entail. Intellectual 'ripening' within the constraints of mortality is once again the impulse behind the sonnet, as the alliterative harvesting imagery of 'glean'd' and 'garners' and 'grain' makes clear. The sestet picks up the sad but stoical 'never live' in 'never look', opening out the fears of untimely death and unfulfilled ambition into a more settled philosophical reflection on self and world. The 'wide world' in the penultimate line declares an allegiance with the 'wide world, dreaming on things to come' in Sonnet 107, but Shakespeare's prophetic idiom gives way to a distinctively muted existential musing.[44] At the same time, the sonnet avoids the 'pouncing' effect of the Shakespearean couplet by introducing a strong mid-line caesura and allowing the enjambment of lines 12–14 to emulate the flow of thought. The liminal 'shore' between mind and world, and life and death, reinforces the desolate solitude of the closing lines, steadily dissolving the phonetic attraction of the preceding 'hour', 'more', and 'power'. The coastal image also beautifully conjures up an impression of the sun setting over water, gently relieving the final and inevitable 'sink' into 'nothingness'.

---

44. *The Complete Sonnets and Poems*, ed. Burrow, p. 595.

Keats finely and subtly develops the meditative, philosophical cast of the Romantic sonnet, and he also brings to it a linguistic and emotional intensity unrivalled among his contemporaries. Although he wrote only fifty-three sonnets, these show an extraordinary concentration of purpose, a lively appreciation of the versatility of the form, and a readiness to experiment with its rhythmic possibilities. The radical political vision of the early sonnets is not dispersed, but re-directed into energizing the sonnet in such a way that it might become more inclusive and more generally representative of human suffering and struggle. If the sonnets are self-consciously alert to their own studied literariness and their own ambitious imaginative endeavours, they are also poignantly vulnerable and acutely exposed to common human failings and limitations. In opening the sonnet further to a 'sharing of common feeling' and consequently 'humanising its diction', Keats makes a profound contribution to the democratizing of the sonnet in the Romantic period.[45]

John Clare

The challenge of democratizing the sonnet further, to the point where its language would become continuous with the energies and textures of actual living speech, would fall to John Clare, one of the most undeservedly neglected poets in the history of English poetry. Clare's fervent admiration for Keats is evident in one of his earliest sonnets, 'To the Memory of John Keats', written soon after the poet's death in 1821:

> The world, its hopes, and fears, have pass'd away;
> No more its trifling thou shalt feel or see;
> Thy hopes are ripening in a brighter day,
> While these left buds thy monument shall be.[46]

Clare's tribute recalls the sonnet 'When I have fears that I might cease to be', but it looks back through Keats to Shakespeare, both in its formal design and in its preoccupation with monuments. The turn asserts in its address to Keats, 'Thou shalt survive' (64). A continuing indebtedness to Keats is recorded in 'The Nightingale', a sonnet written over twenty years later (June 1844), though Clare tellingly shifts perspective from his own charmed

---

45. Vendler, *Coming of Age as a Poet*, p. 46.
46. John Clare, *Selected Poems*, ed. J. W. Tibble and Anne Tibble (London: Dent, 1975), p. 64.

listening of the 'unseen' bird to that of the ploughman returning home at dusk.[47] The sonnet closes with a mellifluous flourish of Keatsian lyricism ('Still sings the nightingale her soft melodious song'), but in other respects Clare shows himself to be a very different kind of writer: an attentive, ecological poet, enthused and inspired by the manifold processes of nature and weather, by the relationships between insects, flowers, birds, animals, and people, and by the land as a place of work. The sonnets inspired by his intimate knowledge of rural life—sonnets like 'The Primrose', 'The Yellow-hammer', 'The Vixen', 'The Mole-catcher' and 'Mouse's Nest'—are startlingly vivid vignettes of the English countryside at a critical point of social change. Although largely forgotten for the best part of the century that followed, they are simply without comparison in English poetry.

Like his near contemporary, George Crabbe, Clare was strongly opposed to the kind of pastoral poetry that idealized rural life and labour, and strenuously resisted the temptation to join those poets 'who dream of rural ease, | Whom the smooth stream and smoother sonnet please'.[48] As an agricultural labourer, he knew the realities and hardships of the English countryside, and the sonnets he wrote can hardly be described as 'smooth'. At the time Clare published his first book of poems, *Poems Descriptive of Rural Life and Scenery* (with Keats's publisher, John Taylor) in 1820, the acts of enclosure had already transformed large stretches of common land into private property. The process seriously affected the parish of Helpston where he lived, and dramatically altered the landscape he knew. Not only did the redefinition of 'property rights' make villagers trespassers on their own land; it profoundly unsettled their sense of security and identity. In Clare's sonnets the relationship between self and place is a matter of intense and sustained engagement.[49] His deep sense of local attachment is immediately apparent in the rooted vernacular sounds and precise naturalist observations of poems like 'Emmonsails Heath in Winter':[50]

---

47. John Clare, *Major Works*, ed. Eric Robinson and David Powell, with an Introduction by Tom Paulin (Oxford: Oxford University Press, 2008), p. 356.
48. George Crabbe, *The Complete Poetical Works*, ed. Norma Dalrymple-Champneys and Arthur Pollard (Oxford: Clarendon Press, 1988), vol. 1, pp. 174–5.
49. I am indebted to John Barrell for his highly perceptive account of Clare's response to the changing landscape of his times in *Poetry, Language and Politics* (Manchester: Manchester University Press, 1988), pp. 100–36.
50. *Major Works*, ed. Robinson and Powell, p. 212 (but printed below from the manuscript).

> I love to see the old heaths withered brake
> Mingle its crimpled leaves with furze and ling
> While the old heron from the lonely lake
> Starts slow and flaps its melancholly wing
> And oddling crow in idle motion swing
> On the half rotten ash trees topmost twig
> Beside whose trunk the gipsey makes his bed
> Up flies the bouncing woodcock from the brig
> Where a black quagmire quakes beneath the tread
> The fieldfares chatter in the whistling thorn
> And for the awe round fields and closen rove
> And coy bumbarrels twenty in a drove
> Flit down the hedgerows in the frozen plain
> And hang on little twigs and start again

The extent to which Clare draws on regional speech necessitates a glossary in which editors and critics of the poetry are likely to include 'brake' (bracken or fern); 'crimpled' (crumpled and crimped); 'furze' (gorse); 'ling' (heather); 'brig' (bridge); 'awe' (an abbreviation for the hawthorn berry); 'closen' (small enclosures of land); and 'bumbarrels' (long-tailed tits). Among the other non-standard linguistic features in Clare's sonnet is its total lack of punctuation. As well as disregarding minor items of punctuation such as the apostrophe in 'heath's' and 'tree's', Clare omits all commas and full stops. In the manuscript he indicates the conjunction 'and' with an ampersand. It is clear, however, that as well as evincing a strong sense of attachment to the land, Clare's sonnets also reveal a strong sense of attachment to a long tradition of oral poetry, including folk-songs and ballads. Part of Clare's distinctive achievement is in wedding this oral tradition of song and recitation to the conventional form of the sonnet as it generally appeared in print, thereby reinvigorating the sonnet tradition.

The sonnet opens with a declaration of personal affection for the heath and the creatures that dwell there, but the sentence structure, with its run-on lines and lack of punctuation, makes it difficult, at first, to see what connection exists between the speaker and the place. The 'while' in line 3, for instance, seems to link both 'I' and the 'leaves' in the first two lines with 'the old heron': something is happening to both the speaker and the heath *while* the heron is flying. Similarly, line 5 is likely to catch us off balance because of its surprising diction and its unusually compact expression (seeming to prolong the opening sentiment, as if saying, 'And [I also love to see] an odd-looking crow swaying on the top of a tree'). The overall effect, though, is of simultaneous impressions, of an intense and complex relationship between the speaker and the place. Michael O'Neill sums up the extempore effects of Clare's sonnets very persuasively when he notes that they are 'organized in ways that give priority to the accidental and chanced-upon, and spurn syntaxes of co-ordinated order in favour of a poetics close to the improvisatory'.[51]

The sentence structure of 'Emmonsails Heath in Winter' moves towards a pause or close at the end of line 7 ('the gipsey makes his bed'), but there is no loss of momentum, and nor is there any obvious sense of division between octave and sestet, even though there is a kind of turn at the beginning of line 8. The abrupt and unexpected observation, 'Up flies the bouncing woodcock', introduces a new series of impressions linked with repeated conjunctions. The rhyme scheme is both familiar and strange. It starts out with a Shakespearean quatrain, but then appears to lose its way (*ababbcdcdeffgg*), before restoring a sense of harmony with two rhyming couplets (not noticeably pronounced because of the strong enjambment in the sonnet). The isolated, unrhymed word 'thorn' seems out of place, though its presence is mitigated by the phonetic recall of the opening participles and the anticipation of the closing *ain* sounds. What is not voiced, but gently suggested, is pain. There is no concluding commentary or summary: the sonnet reaches a close at the end of fourteen lines, but it also retains its sense of immediacy with the present-tense 'start again' (in the sense of 'fly off'). It is almost as if the poem wishes to 'keep things going' in a closely observed integration of speaker and place, whatever else is happening to the landscape. Despite the lively activity of the scene, there is a peculiar sense of stasis created by the description of the winter landscape—'withered', 'crimpled', and 'frozen'—and in a similar way the sonnet mingles evident pleasure with an underlying melancholy.

The politics that stir beneath Clare's sonnets emerge from deeply felt tensions between attachment and exclusion, possession and loss, and freedom and constraint. They surface with an alarming cry of injustice in 'England, 1830', one of the most anguished and outspoken sonnets on the oppressive class politics of the late Romantic period:

---

51. Michael O'Neill, 'The Romantic Sonnet', in *The Cambridge Companion to the Sonnet*, ed. A. D. Cousins and Peter Howarth (Cambridge: Cambridge University Press, 2011), pp. 186–7. Also see Andrew Hodgson's fine essay on the subtlety of Clare's handling of the sonnet: 'Form and Feeling in John Clare's Sonnets', *John Clare Society Journal* 31 (2012), 51–66.

> These vague allusions to a country's wrongs,
> Where one says 'Ay' and others answer 'No'
> In contradiction from a thousand tongues,
> Till like to prison-cells her freedoms grow
> Becobwebbed with these oft-repeated songs
> Of peace and plenty in the midst of woe—
> And is it thus they mock her year by year,
> Telling poor truth unto her face she lies,
> Declaiming of her wealth with gibe severe,
> So long as taxes drain their wished supplies?
> And will these jailers rivet every chain
> Anew, yet loudest in their mockery be,
> To damn her into madness with disdain,
> Forging new bonds and bidding her be free?[52]

The political circumstances to which the sonnet refers are those of the Swing Riots, prompted by a long history of grievances among agricultural workers in south-east England, including the Enclosure Acts, the Poor Law, the tithe system, and the lowering of wages with the introduction of the threshing machine.[53] The radical political sentiment and the rhetorical power of the sonnet look back to Milton, but the immediate poetic model is Shelley's 'England in 1819'. The imagery of prison-cells, chains, and bonds recalls Shelley's emancipatory politics, but so too does the radical redeployment of the sonnet form. Like Shelley, Clare sets up a rhyme scheme that suggests a turning upside down of octave and sestet (*abababcdcdefef*), and like Shelley he loads the pentameter line with loud plosives, bringing these into play in the closing, rather than the opening, lines of the poem. The sonnet speaks eloquently on behalf of 'poor truth', blasting hypocrisy and deceit, and exposing the hollow, contradictory aspirations of a ruling class that proclaims the freedom of the nation.

By the end of the decade, the 'madness' and confinement of 'England, 1830' had taken on a disturbing personal and psychological significance, and Clare's deep sense of social alienation was now intensified by an acute identity crisis. Later, as an inmate in Northampton General Lunatic Asylum in the mid-1840s, he produced the desultory but moving 'Sonnet: "I Am"', appended to the better-known lyric poem 'I Am'. The heaviness of being that is emphasized in the repeated phrase 'I only know I am'

---

52. *Selected Poems*, ed. Tibble and Tibble, p. 194.   53. Lucas, 'England in 1830', pp. 65–6.

is forlornly contrasted with the poet's earlier transcendentalist yearnings. Shelley's skylark is evoked for a moment, as the sonnet recalls a free spirit, 'like a thought sublime...Spurning earth's vain and soul debasing thrall'. Once again, the sonnet surges with the rhythmic force of two rhyming couplets, but this time the effect is one of calculated bathos: 'But now I only know I am,—that's all.'[54] Clare's work remained in obscurity until the publication of *The Poems of John Clare* in 1935, but his sonnets are assuredly among the most original and arresting examples of the form in English.

54. *Major Works*, ed. Robinson and Powell, p. 362.

3

The Victorian sonnet

A glance at the few scattered sonnets that appear in the collected poems of Alfred Tennyson and Robert Browning might be cause for thinking that the Victorian sonnet is an outmoded form, possessing neither the impassioned rhetoric nor the bold thematic diversity that Romantic poets were able to bring to 'the Sonnet's scanty plot of ground'.[1] Wordsworth's prolific output as a writer of sonnets after 1802 did not always have a salutary influence on his successors and there are dozens of half-hearted imitations of his best-known efforts in the genre. In addition to the many contrived and uninspiring sonnets about the sonnet in the later nineteenth century, there are numerous Victorian anthologies of sonnets, introductions to the sonnet, and scholarly essays on the history of the sonnet.[2] Much of this material is laboured and prescriptive, conveying a general impression that the sonnet, while undoubtedly popular, has ceased to have a vital, dynamic connection with contemporary culture.

In recent years, however, modern criticism has taken issue with the idea that the Victorian sonnet is antiquated and derivative, and has sought to emphasize what is most innovative in nineteenth-century examples of the form. Jennifer Ann Wagner, for instance, argues that later nineteenth-century poets were empowered rather than overwhelmed by Wordsworth's immense and authoritative control of the form, and that they considerably extended the intellectual and aesthetic preoccupations of the Romantic sonnet. In *A Moment's Monument: Revisionary Poetics and the Nineteenth-Century English Sonnet*, she traces what she sees as 'the second life' of a form that had enjoyed its original heyday three centuries earlier. She argues persuasively that 'the

---

1. *William Wordsworth*, ed. Stephen Gill (Oxford: Oxford University Press, 1984), p. 286.
2. See Alison Chapman, 'Sonnet and Sonnet Sequences', in *A Companion to Victorian Poetry*, ed. Richard Cronin, Alison Chapman, and Antony H. Harrison (Oxford: Blackwell, 2002), pp. 99–114.

history of the sonnet in the nineteenth century is more than a decorative strand in this century's textual history', and she shows how the sonnet becomes the exemplary form for poets who are deeply preoccupied with ideas of subjectivity and temporality. Even so, she claims that there is a diminution of the political force of the Romantic sonnet, and that 'the sonnet is not as primary an arena for politics in the late nineteenth century as it had been previously'.[3]

We need, perhaps, to broaden our conception of politics if we are to appreciate the full extent to which Victorian poets modified the sonnet form in response to their own most urgent social and cultural needs. What proves to be most interesting is the way in which the dialectical structure of the sonnet suggests to writers a way of confronting and exploring the controversial issues of the time, including problems of democracy and social class. The ideas that were to coalesce in Matthew Arnold's *Culture and Anarchy* also found an outlet in a series of sonnets that Arnold composed at moments of personal and social crisis in the 1840s and 1860s. These are profoundly political poems, even if their politics are essentially reformist rather than revolutionary. In terms of sexual politics, too, Victorian sonnets are often surprisingly adventurous. George Meredith's *Modern Love* was condemned with such virulence when it first appeared in 1862 that it came to be seen as a threat to the moral well-being of the nation.[4] There is no simple distinction to be made in Meredith's case between sexual politics and politics proper. His sonnet sequence is one of the most candid and provocative accounts of marital failure in nineteenth-century literature and a daring disavowal of all that the love sonnet had previously celebrated and enshrined.

There are complex and intriguing political affiliations in the devotional sonnets of Gerard Manley Hopkins, including those written in Dublin during a time of burgeoning Irish nationalism. If 'Felix Randal' ennobles the life of a Liverpool labourer, 'Tom's Garland' recoils in fear from the spectacle of working-class discontent and mass unemployment. As we will see, it is part of the special appeal of Hopkins as a sonnet writer that he can be at once the most anarchic and the most conservative of poets.

---

[3]. Jennifer Ann Wagner, *A Moment's Monument: Revisionary Poetics and the Nineteenth-Century English Sonnet* (London: Associated University Presses, 1996), pp. 12, 128.
[4]. See *Meredith: The Critical Heritage*, ed. Ioan Williams (London: Routledge and Kegan Paul, 1971), pp. 92–107.

Alfred Tennyson and Robert Browning

There is certainly some truth in the claim that what preoccupies the Victorian sonnet is a self-reflexive concern with subjectivity and moments of heightened consciousness, and the argument would appear to be borne out by the handful of sonnets for which Tennyson and Browning are remembered. The strange, exploratory sonnets in Tennyson's *Poems, Chiefly Lyrical* (1830) and *Poems* (1832), along with the uncollected sonnets of the 1830s, generally answer to Charles Tennyson's description of 'a characteristic mood of depression and self-depreciation' in the early work.[5] Nearly all are irregular sonnets, freely crossing Italian and English rhyme schemes. The subjective, introspective nature of the sonnets is amply conveyed by the sonnet beginning, 'Me my own Fate to lasting sorrow doometh'. The sonnets are revealing in the context of other early Tennyson poems such as 'Mariana' and 'The Lady of Shalott', not least for the way in which they interpret and expand Romantic, especially Keatsian, images and motifs. Consciousness of place is strongly imbued with the experience or foreboding of disappointed love:

> Check every outflash, every ruder sally
>   Of thought and speech; speak low, and give up wholly
>   Thy spirit to mild-minded Melancholy;
>   This is the place. Through yonder poplar alley,
> Below, the blue-green river windeth slowly,
>   But in the middle of the sombre valley,
>   The crispèd waters whisper musically,
>   And all the haunted place is dark and holy.
> The nightingale, with long and low preamble,
>   Warbled from yonder knoll of solemn larches,
>   And in and out the woodbine's flowery arches
>   The summer midges wove their wanton gambol,
> And all the white stemmed pinewood slept above—
>   When in this valley first I told my love. (323)

Here, the energetic imperatives of Keats's 'Ode on Melancholy' ('Then glut thy sorrow on a morning rose, | Or on the rainbow of the salt sand-wave') give way to abject resignation and withdrawal.[6] At the same time, Tennyson

---

5. Charles Tennyson (ed.), *Unpublished Early Poems by Alfred Tennyson* (1931), cited in *The Poems of Tennyson*, ed. Christopher Ricks (Harlow: Longman, 1987), vol. 1, p. 317. All quotations from Tennyson's sonnets are from the Ricks (three-volume) edition of the poems.
6. John Keats, *Poetical Works*, ed. H. W. Garrod (Oxford: Oxford University Press, 1970), p. 220.

establishes his own distinctive poetic landscape with its 'poplar alley' and 'sombre valley', as well as his own inimitable nocturnal music: 'And all the haunted place is dark and holy.' The sonnet was published in the *Englishman's Magazine* in 1831 and again in *Friendship's Offering* in 1832. It was not included in the 1832 *Poems*, though lines 2–3 were adapted for use in 'The Lotos-Eaters' (108–9). Tennyson's friend, Arthur Henry Hallam, wrote to the publisher, Edward Moxon, on 24 July 1831: 'I am glad you like the Sonnet: I do not doubt it will attract attention.' Hallam might well have been referring to the striking plethora of feminine rhymes, but no doubt the candid confession of troubled love was also a talking point. Tennyson claimed, in retrospect, that the sonnet was never intended for publication and wished that it had been 'suffered to moulder in the dead body of the experiodical'.[7]

It is in keeping with Tennyson's tentative exploration of his potential readership, as well as with the flexible appeal of the sonnet form itself, that two sonnets in the 1832 *Poems* should be dedicated to the cause of political liberty and national self-determination. 'Sonnet written on hearing of the outbreak of the Polish Insurrection' and 'Sonnet: On the Result of the Late Russian Invasion of Poland' were very likely inspired by the sonnets to Kosciusko written by Keats and Coleridge during the Polish insurrection of 1794, though they respond with alacrity to the immediate occasion of the November Uprising against the Russians in 1830: 'Arise, brave Poles, the boldest of the bold' (498). The second sonnet, with its resounding opening cry from *Revelation* (vi. 10), is unmistakably modelled on Milton's sonnet 'On the Late Massacre in Piedmont', and it shows in its taut rhetorical questions and suspended syntax how effectively Tennyson has absorbed the stylistic qualities that make for an urgent political address: 'How long, O God, shall men be ridden down, | And trampled under by the last and least | Of men?' (499).

Even so, it is the sonnet as love lyric that draws Tennyson's interest and feeds most decisively into his later work. Two sonnets allegedly addressed to Arthur Hallam, whom Tennyson met in 1829, are notable for their tender, confiding expression of love and desire. As Christopher Ricks points out, the first of these ('If I were loved, as I desire to be') 'anticipates the mood and thought of *In Memoriam*', especially in the strategically placed turn with its memorable image of physical union ('claspt hand-in-hand with thee').[8]

---

7. *The Poems of Tennyson*, ed. Ricks, p. 322.
8. *The Poems of Tennyson*, ed. Ricks, vol. 1, p. 386.

It is likely, too, that Tennyson's facility in handling the Petrarchan quatrain gives shape and buoyancy to the *In Memoriam* stanza. The second sonnet, beginning 'As when with downcast eyes we muse and brood', is notable for its dreamy states of 'mystical similitude' and its intense psychological mirroring of speaker and friend: 'Opposèd mirrors each reflecting each' (500).

Tennyson's enchanting lyric, 'Now sleeps the crimson petal', is occasionally extracted from *The Princess* (1847) and included in sonnet anthologies, though the poem is essentially an unrhymed fourteen-line composition that gathers momentum through sustained anaphoric and epistrophic effects rather than through the more usual observation and modification of the sonnet's structural dynamics:

> Now sleeps the crimson petal, now the white;
> Nor waves the cypress in the palace walk;
> Nor winks the gold fin in the porphyry font:
> The fire-fly wakens: waken thou with me.
>
> Now droops the milkwhite peacock like a ghost,
> And like a ghost she glimmers on to me.
>
> Now lies the Earth all Danaë to the stars,
> And all they heart lies open unto me.
>
> Now slides the silent meteor on, and leaves
> A shining furrow, as thy thoughts in me.
>
> Now folds the lily all her sweetness up,
> And slips into the bosom of the lake:
> So fold thyself, my dearest, thou, and slip
> Into my bosom and be lost in me.[9]

As a fantasy of female submissiveness, the poem might be said to conform very well (thematically, at least) with a long tradition of love sonnets from the Renaissance onwards. Structurally, however, it raises some pertinent questions about what constitutes a sonnet, other than the basic requirement of fourteen lines in iambic pentameter. Tennyson's lyric certainly possesses a strong sense of design, but the typographical layout is in keeping with its repeated insistence on the present moment of fulfilment rather than with any perception of finely poised oppositions or logically constructed arguments. The deployment of lines (4 + 2 + 2 + 2 + 4, rather than 8 + 6 or 4 + 4 + 4 + 2) suggests that the poem is weighted rather differently from the traditional

---

9. *The Poems of Tennyson*, ed. Ricks, vol. 2, p. 284.

Renaissance or Romantic love sonnet. The unwavering present-tense observations of a drowsy world, the simple but strategic conjunctions, and the incantatory repetition of line openings and line endings all work to enhance the poem's seductive close.

Browning, as an admirer of Shelley, was clearly aware of how the sonnet might be prised away from its aristocratic, courtly origins and put to the service of radical political causes. His own modest attempt at writing a political sonnet is cautiously egalitarian rather than revolutionary. The uncollected poem, 'Why I Am a Liberal', deftly balances the vagaries of fortune against a more principled ideal of Liberty.[10] The turn from octave to sestet marks the sonnet's acknowledgement of the limitations of a laissez-faire politics and asserts the importance of inalienable rights: 'But little do or can the best of us: | That little is achieved through Liberty.' As the title of the sonnet suggests, the rhetorical impulse is towards declaration and explanation rather than incitement. The poem dutifully answers itself with a flatly assertive 'That is why'. 'Why I Am a Liberal' lacks both the rhetorical command and the powerful political vision that Shelley was able to summon in his sonnets, but it nevertheless provides an indication that the sonnet continues to provide a space, not just for thoughts of love, but for meditations on the problems of democracy.

Browning's 'Now' (from *Asolando*, 1889) shares the intensity and inwardness of Tennyson's lyric, 'Now sleeps the crimson petal', and it achieves this through an intricate modification of the Petrarchan sonnet form, bringing the third rhyme word unexpectedly forward (the rhyme scheme is *abbcacdedefggf*). Where Tennyson repeatedly uses line endings to emphasize the first-person pronoun, Browning effectively conveys the turning from 'you' to 'me' at the very centre of the poem. Lines 8 and 10 end with 'me', while line 9 (the structural 'turn' of the sonnet) also begins with 'me':

> Out of your whole life give but a moment!
> All of your life that has gone before,
> All to come after it,—so you ignore
> So you make perfect the present,—condense,
> In a rapture of rage, for perfection's endowment,
> Thought and feeling and soul and sense—
> Merged in a moment which gives me at last
> You around me for once, you beneath me, above me—

---

10. Robert Browning, *The Major Works*, ed. Adam Roberts and Daniel Karlin (Oxford: Oxford University Press, 2005), p. 572.

> Me—sure that despite of time future, time past,—
> This tick of our life-time's one moment you love me!
> How long such suspension may linger? Ah, sweet—
> The moment eternal—just that and no more—
> When ecstasy's utmost we clutch at the core
> While cheeks burn, arms open, eyes shut and lips meet.[11]

Browning's sonnet is remarkable for the way in which it creates 'a moment's monument', both acutely registering the impulse to preserve the experience of 'ecstasy' and simultaneously acknowledging the need to let it go. In a breathlessly elliptical and densely parenthetical style, the sonnet opens up long perspectives on a 'whole life' and fastens vividly and erotically on the passing moment. The love sonnets of Tennyson and Browning neatly encapsulate those stylistic features for which the two poets are renowned: one tending towards mellifluousness and ornamentation, the other striving for the impact and immediacy of actual speech. Both poets are drawn to the concentrated form of the sonnet, but within the space of a single short poem their pronouncements on love are likely to appear insubstantial or merely whimsical. A more discursive, expository treatment of love requires the expansiveness of a sonnet sequence: Elizabeth Barrett Browning's *Sonnets from the Portuguese*, Christina Rossetti's 'Monna Innominata', Dante Gabriel Rossetti's *The House of Life*, and, perhaps most importantly, George Meredith's *Modern Love*.

Elizabeth Barrett Browning, Christina Rossetti, and Dante Gabriel Rossetti

Elizabeth Barrett Browning's *Sonnets from the Portuguese*, her sequence of forty-four Petrarchan sonnets published in 1850, is usually regarded as the first amatory sonnet sequence in English to be published since the Renaissance, and an important stimulus for sonnet writing more generally in the Victorian period.[12] It is also, of course, a striking extension of that crucial shift of perspective engendered in the sonnets of Lady Mary Wroth in England and Vittoria Colonna in Italy, by which the woman, traditionally the idealized object of desire, is empowered to speak of her own most intimate thoughts

---

11. *The Complete Works of Robert Browning*, ed. Ashby B. Crowder and Allan C. Dooley (Athens, TX: Baylor University Press, 2011), vol. 17, p. 11.
12. Quotations from Elizabeth Barrett Browning's sonnets are from *The Poetical Works of Elizabeth Barrett Browning* (Edinburgh: W. P. Nimmo, Hay, and Mitchell, 1903).

and feelings. Biographical readings recounting Elizabeth Barrett's romantic courtship with Robert Browning and the couple's elopement to Italy are apt to sentimentalize the sonnets, and what we lose sight of is the startling immediacy of the woman's voice addressing her lover, sometimes excitedly, as in Sonnet 33—'Yes, call me by my pet-name! let me hear | The name I used to run at, when a child' (455), and sometimes more pensively, as in Sonnet 35—'If I leave all for thee, wilt thou exchange | And *be* all to me?' (456). For all their life-like conversational intimacy, the sonnets need to be appreciated for their technical and stylistic virtuosity, and for the subtle ways in which they both look back to Renaissance models and develop an independent poetic voice. The Brownings were, themselves, apprehensive about the publication of the sonnets, and presenting them as if part of an imagined dialogue with the Portuguese poet, Luís de Camoens (like the earlier poem 'Catarina to Camoens') was clearly an attempt at concealment, encouraging some readers to believe that the sonnets were, in fact, translations.

The intense biographical speculation about *Sonnets from the Portuguese* has also been responsible, to some extent, for the relative neglect of the earlier sonnets in *Poems* (1844). These early poems, among them 'The Soul's Expression','On a Portrait of Wordsworth by R. B. Haydon','Tears', 'Grief', and 'Finite and Infinite', show Barrett Browning adopting Romantic concepts of beauty, sublimity, and infinity, and tempering them with a Christian fortitude and humility. Other early sonnets, all of them Petrarchan, including 'The Poet' and 'The Prisoner', as well as the sonnets to George Sand and Mary Russell Mitford, clearly anticipate the strong sense of confinement, the Romantic motif of thoughts as flowers, and the impassioned enquiry into the role of the woman poet in the 'Portuguese' sonnets. Of particular note is the sonnet simply titled 'Love', which turns from 'mere' life's fulfilment in the octave to the enthralling possibility of love's fulfilment in the sestet, and asks what happens when 'a soul, by choice and conscience, doth | Throw out her full force on another soul' (440).

Sonnets from the Portuguese conveys a yearning for what that early sonnet, 'Love', defines as 'life in perfect whole'. Like Shakespeare's Sonnets, the sequence both invites and dispels a search for narrative coherence, working principally through heightened moments of lyric expressiveness and dramatic speech. Sonnet 28, as Stephanie Burt has persuasively shown, draws powerfully on the resources of the dramatic monologue, as the speaker settles down to read a cache of love letters:

> My letters! All dead paper, mute and white!
> And yet they seem alive and quivering
> Against my tremulous hands, which loose the string
> And let them drop down on my knee to-night.

The exclamation marks, the ellipses, the casual asides, and the italicized extracts from selected letters all contribute to the dramatic nature of the sonnet, as they do in the dramatic monologues of Robert Browning.[13] The repeated demonstratives ('This said...This said...And this...') keep our focus on the letters, but what they cumulatively work towards is the tantalizing withholding of revelation: 'And this...O Love, thy words have ill availed | If, what this said, I dared repeat at last!' (453). There is wit, as well as passion, in this elegant curtailment. In an excellent study of Barrett Browning's artful handling of genre, Rebecca Stott has shown how the 'intensely conversational quality' of the courtship letters is also evident in *Sonnets from the Portuguese*. She claims that the innovative urge of the sequence is not simply to invert the traditional relationship between 'the male speaking subject and the silent female object of desire', but rather to establish a 'new love of equals' within a duet-like play of voices. In this respect, what the sonnet sequence achieves is a new epistemology of love: the declaration of a knowledge and experience of love 'based on dialogue and conversation and shared thoughts and preoccupations'.[14]

Sonnet 43, the best-known and most frequently anthologized sonnet in the sequence, makes its appeal through what initially might appear to be a simple, passionate declaration of love, but its achievement is in its handling of form and its subtle creation of an intimate, confiding voice:

> How do I love thee? Let me count the ways.
> I love thee to the depth and breadth and height
> My soul can reach, when feeling out of sight
> For the ends of Being and ideal Grace.
> I love thee to the level of every day's
> Most quiet need, by sun and candlelight.
> I love thee freely, as men strive for Right;
> I love thee purely, as they turn from Praise.
> I love thee with the passion put to use

---

13. Stephanie Burt and David Mikics (eds), *The Art of the Sonnet* (Cambridge, MA: Harvard University Press, 2010), p. 162.
14. Simon Avery and Rebecca Stott, *Elizabeth Barrett Browning* (Harlow: Longman, 2003), p. 126.

> In my old griefs, and with my childhood's faith.
> I love thee with a love I seemed to lose
> With my lost saints!—I love thee with the breath,
> Smiles, tears, of all my life!—and, if God choose,
> I shall but love thee better after death.   (458–9)

Like Shakespeare's Sonnet 18, the poem opens with a question and proceeds to answer it with elaborate images of measurement and value, intensifying the expression of love as it does so. The technique, however, is enumerative rather than contrastive. It works by listing the number of ways (eight altogether) in which the speaker of the sonnet conceives of her love. Consequently, there is no obvious turn between octave and sestet, and no obvious sense of progression from quatrain to quatrain. Rather than proceeding by logical reasoning and argumentation, the sonnet offers a sustained and impassioned declaration of love that runs across all fourteen lines. The sonnet acquires its emotional intensity from its repeated stress on a single phrase: 'I love thee'. Six lines begin 'I love thee', while another three include the words within their structure. The form is not one of simple incantation, however, and there is nothing mechanical in the verbal repetition. Instead, the interplay of rhymes and the alternation of end-stopped and run-on lines give the sonnet a powerful, energetic movement.

Compared with Shakespeare's highly figurative sonnets, Sonnet 43 has little imagery, and the diction is relatively plain and unadorned. Images of space ('depth and breadth and height'), and of time ('sun and candle-light'), are used very subtly in the octave to intensify the idea of a love that is both spiritual and physical, both yearning for infinity and yet answering each day's earthly needs. This love is given 'freely' and 'purely', instinctively and unselfishly. The sestet proposes an additional four ways of loving—with all the passion spent on past hopes and sorrows; with the intensity of religious devotion; with all the emotions of an entire life; and with eternal togetherness in heaven. There is a hint of an earlier religious despair in 'a love I seemed to lose | With my lost saints', but the speaker's new love provides a reason for trusting in eternal life. Intellectual and emotional honesty, rather than piety, is what the sonnet finally achieves. What gives Sonnet 43 its stature and appeal is its confident declaration of a woman's right to speak of love. It perfectly exemplifies Isobel Armstrong's characterization of *Sonnets from the Portuguese* as a sequence working towards 'expansion' and 'going beyond the limit of definition'. In doing so, the sonnets enact in formal terms a dissolution of customary restrictions and inhibitions, breaking into 'new areas of being'.

They effectively 'chart the struggle of the feminine subject to take up a new position which is free of dependency'.[15]

Like *Sonnets from the Portuguese*, Christina Rossetti's sonnet sequence 'Monna Innominata' challenges convention by reversing the usual roles and allowing the 'unnamed lady', one of the many anonymous women in the history of the sonnet, to address an absent man. In her preface to 'Monna Innominata', Rossetti refers to Petrarch's Laura and Dante's Beatrice as women who have 'come down to us resplendent with charms, but...scant of attractiveness'. A more tender portrait might have been created, she suggests, if such women had spoken for themselves. She acknowledges the example of 'the great Poetess of our own day and nation', but suggests that if Elizabeth Barrett Browning had been 'unhappy instead of happy', she might have created a more persuasive female persona, 'worthy to occupy a niche beside Beatrice and Laura'.[16] Part of Rossetti's motivation here is to write about love without resorting to the techniques of concealment and indirection that Barrett Browning had found necessary to protect her relationship, and to create a voice that speaks without disguise about a woman's feelings of emptiness and desolation. The differences between the two sonnet sequences are also determined by differences of religious conviction. In *Sonnets from the Portuguese* the speaker finds a way of reconciling earthly and heavenly aspirations, but in 'Monna Innominata' the conflict between physical and spiritual love continues unresolved. The speaker in Rossetti's sequence finds consolation, but the sonnets are riven with feelings of separation and unfulfilment. Hers is a troubled art of self-postponement.

'Monna Innominata' consists of fourteen sonnets—a sonnet of sonnets—written between 1866 and 1881. Each sonnet carries an epigraph consisting of two quotations, one from Dante and one from Petrarch, simultaneously linking the sequence to illustrious Italian predecessors and suggesting a critical engagement with that legacy. In the same way, the sonnets pay tribute to the Petrarchan tradition by repeating familiar rhyme schemes, but they also perform an intricate and unusual set of variations on those rhyme schemes (especially in the sestets of the sonnets), as if probing and testing the possibilities of rhyme. Sonnet 4, for instance, has both alternating and enclosed rhymes in the octave, incorporating a third *c* rhyme, and it also repeats the *a* rhyme from the octave in the sestet: *ababccbdeadae*. The opening and closing

---

15. Isobel Armstrong, *Victorian Poetry: Poetry, Poetics and Politics* (London: Routledge, 1993), p. 356.
16. Christina Rossetti, *Poems and Prose*, ed. Simon Humphries (Oxford: Oxford University Press, 2008), p. 227. Quotations from the poetry are from this edition.

sonnets of the sequence are meditations on waiting and uncertainty, and if they show a close familiarity with Petrarchan motifs and conventions, they also acknowledge how those conventions have already been received and modified in English Renaissance poetry. Sonnet 1 deftly catches the temporal expectancy and attendant frustrations so familiar in *Astrophil and Stella* ('come not yet', 'come again', 'come not'), and registers its pains and pleasures in a striking lunar simile: 'My hope hangs waning, waxing, like a moon | Between the heavenly days on which we meet.' The sonnet's declaration of love marries the hyperbolic, global vision of *Antony and Cleopatra* with the prophetic hope of Shakespeare's Sonnet 107: 'For one man is my world of all the men | This wide world holds' (227–8). The bewildered loss of song in Sonnet 1 anticipates the more desolate and terminal silence of Sonnet 14:

> Youth gone, and beauty gone if ever there
> Dwelt beauty in so poor a face as this;
> Youth gone and beauty, what remains of bliss?
> I will not bind fresh roses in my hair,
> To shame a cheek at best but little fair,—
> Leave youth his roses, who can bear a thorn,—
> I will not seek for blossoms anywhere,
> Except such common flowers as blow with corn.
> Youth gone and beauty gone, what doth remain?
> The longing of a heart pent up forlorn,
> A silent heart whose silence loves and longs;
> The silence of a heart which sang its songs
> While youth and beauty made a summer morn,
> Silence of love that cannot sing again.   (234–5)

The bleak resignation towards which 'Monna Innominata' tends is distilled in the occasional sonnets, including 'Rest' and 'Remember', which are among her best-known, if generally unappreciated, work. Criticism has not been kind to Rossetti, routinely characterizing these sonnets as morbid, introspective, and derivative. As Diana Henderson notes, critics have been slow to acknowledge and appreciate 'the meditative beauty and craft of her haunting sonnets'.[17] The sonnets in 'Later Life: A Double Sonnet of Sonnets' (1881), prompted by Rossetti's fiftieth birthday in 1880, are much more various and 'more fully Victorian' than those in 'Monna Innominata'. Sonnet 17 in the sequence seems, initially, to speak with the weariness and enervation of

---

17. Diana E. Henderson, 'The Sonnet, Subjectivity and Gender', in *The Cambridge Companion to the Sonnet*, ed. A. D. Cousins and Peter Howarth (Cambridge: Cambridge University Press, 2011), p. 61.

Tennyson's 'Mariana' or 'The Lady of Shalott'—'I am sick of where I am and where I am not'—only to dispel the growing ennui and issue a sociable greeting more reminiscent of Browning: 'Oh weary impatient patience with my lot!— | Thus with myself: how fares it, Friends, with you?' (255).

Dante Gabriel Rossetti, like his sister, was conversant with Italian literary tradition, and his deep immersion in the legacy of Petrarch and Dante is immediately apparent in *The House of Life*, his sequence of 103 sonnets written between 1848 and 1881. Equally, the memorializing tendency of Shakespeare and the aesthetic intensity of Keats play over the sonnets, giving them a dense pattern of intertextual reference and self-conscious artistry.[18] Ostensibly a set of love lyrics with autobiographical origins in Rossetti's relationships with Elizabeth Siddall and Jane Morris, the sonnets are more specifically and self-reflexively concerned with the artistic challenge of how to render the experience of love in lasting artistic form. As the title suggests, it is the architectonics of form rather than any narrative or dramatic exposition of life's events that preoccupies the poetry. *The House of Life* is notable, among other things, for having established the term 'sequence' (rather than 'series') as a description of a number of interlinked sonnets, and for having formulated one of the most memorable definitions of a sonnet:

> A Sonnet is a moment's monument,—
>   Memorial from the Soul's eternity
> To one dead deathless hour. Look that it be,
> Whether for lustral rite or dire portent,
> Of its own arduous fulness reverent:
>   Carve it in ivory or in ebony,
>   As Day or Night may rule; and let Time see
> Its flowering crest impearled and orient.
>
> A Sonnet is a coin: its face reveals
>   The soul,—its converse, to what Power 'tis due:—
> Whether for tribute to the august appeals
>   Of Life, or dower in Love's high retinue,
> It serve; or, 'mid the dark wharf's cavernous breath,
> In Charon's palm it pay the toll to Death. (127)

From the outset, Rossetti's sonnet is implicated in a code of service and reverence that takes it back to its Italian courtly origins. At the same time, its preoccupation with its own formal properties signals the growing appeal of

---

18. Unless otherwise indicated, quotations from the sonnets of Dante Gabriel Rossetti are from his *Collected Poetry and Prose*, ed. Jerome McGann (New Haven: Yale University Press, 2003).

aestheticism at the end of the nineteenth century. One of the functions of the prefatory sonnet is to reflect upon the use and value of the sonnet form, and to assert that its worth lies partly in its own 'arduous fulness'. Rossetti's fierce concentration on the sonnet as both mystical vision and artistic object necessitates a language that tends towards paradox and contradiction. Many sonnet writers, including Shakespeare, have acknowledged the sonnet's peculiar power to give lasting form to transient and fugitive impressions, but few have captured that capacity with the striking force of 'a moment's monument'. To those sonnets that have pictured the black ink of writing on a white page as a durable image of poetry's persistence through time, Rossetti adds the memorable visualization of the sonnet as an artistic object carved 'in ivory or in ebony'. The light-dark imagery, echoed in 'Day or Night', is a reminder that the sonnet serves both life and death, simultaneously celebrating the fullness of experience manifested in love and mourning its inevitable loss. The duality of Rossetti's vision is intensified in the sestet, with its assertion that 'A Sonnet is a coin': it has material worth and exchange value, but it bears the imprint of the soul and pays what is 'due' to Life and Love and Death.

The relentless personification of Love makes Rossetti's sequence appear curiously archaic and other worldly, but it also serves to remind us of the close parallels between *The House of Life* and Dante's *Vita Nuova*, which Rossetti had translated into English in 1861. Following Dante, Rossetti composes a meditation on the changing course of love, and on love's many moods and manifestations, but what makes his sequence distinctive and modern is its unusually explicit and sometimes intensely sexual rendering of its subject matter. 'Nuptial Sleep' must have surprised many Victorian readers in its ardent physicality:

> At length their long kiss severed, with sweet smart:
>   And as the last slow sudden drops are shed
>   From sparkling eaves when all the storm has fled,
> So singly flagged the pulses of each heart.
> Their bosoms sundered, with the opening start
>   Of married flowers to either side outspread
>   From the knit stem; yet still their mouths, burnt red,
> Fawned on each other where they lay apart.
>
> Sleep sank them lower than the tide of dreams,
>   And their dreams watched them sink, and slid away.
> Slowly their souls swam up again, through gleams
>   Of watered light and dull drowned waifs of day;

> Till from some wonder of new woods and streams
> He woke, and wondered more: for there she lay.   (130)

The sonnet was singled out for condemnation by Robert Buchanan in his notorious attack on Pre-Raphaelite poetry, 'The Fleshly School of Poetry', in 1871. Buchanan's article accused Rossetti of having made explicit 'the most secret mysteries of sexual connection', and having done so with 'so sickening a desire to reproduce the sensual mood' and 'convey mere animal sensations' that readers would 'surely shudder at the shameless nakedness'.[19] Rossetti's measured reply, 'The Stealthy School of Criticism' (a reference to Buchanan's cowardly use of a pseudonym), pointed out that 'Nuptial Sleep' was but one 'sonnet-stanza' of a larger poem that showed unmistakably that 'the passionate and just delights of the body' were but 'naught if not ennobled by the concurrence of the soul at all times'.[20] Perhaps the most illuminating contemporary criticism of Rossetti's poetry, however, came from Walter Pater, who claimed that, in his opposition to Manichean dualities of spirit and matter, Rossetti was returning poetry to a quality of vivid conception close to that of Dante: 'Like Dante, he knows no region of spirit which shall not be sensuous also, or material.'[21]

Pater was alert, as well, to the 'pictorial genius' of Rossetti's work and to 'the painter's sensuous clearness of conception'. Among Rossetti's most highly accomplished sonnets are those that bear some special ekphrastic relationship to paintings by notable Renaissance artists, including Leonardo Da Vinci, Sandro Botticelli, and Giorgione. Several of Rossetti's best-known Pre-Raphaelite paintings, including *Found, Astarte Syriaca, Lilith,* and *The Girlhood of Mary Virgin*, are accompanied by sonnets, reminding us that Rossetti's creation of double works of art is 'one of the signature innovations of his highly inventive career'.[22] *Proserpine* is an especially powerful example of Rossetti's intense fusing of pictorial and verbal art, with the sonnet 'Proserpina' inscribed in Italian on the canvas and reproduced in English in the frame. As Jerome McGann instructively notes, with Rossetti's sonnets for pictures, 'we always have to deal with three aesthetic events: the picture itself, the sonnet itself, and the liminal event that emerges from their dialectical

---

19. Robert Buchanan, 'The Fleshly School of Poetry', *Contemporary Review* (1871). Reprinted in *The Victorian Poet: Poetics and Persona*, ed. Joseph Bristow (London: Croom Helm, 1987), p. 145.
20. Rossetti, 'The Stealthy School of Criticism', *Athenaeum* (1871). Reprinted in *The Victorian Poet: Poetics and Persona*, ed. Joseph Bristow (London: Croom Helm, 1987), p. 147.
21. Walter Pater, *Appreciations, with an Essay on Style* (London: Macmillan, 1907), p. 213.
22. Jerome McGann, *Dante Gabriel Rossetti and the Game That Must Be Lost* (New Haven: Yale University Press, 2000), p. 108.

relation'. 'Proserpina' calls for a heightened aesthetic response: 'to the conceptual aspects of the picture and to the iconographical features of the text'.[23] The sonnet recalls 'the flowers of Enna' and the 'drear | Dire fruit' (the pomegranate) that has occasioned Proserpina's imprisonment in Hades, but what it also does, in a startling way, is to allow Proserpina to speak in a tender human voice of her banishment from earth: 'how far away, | The nights that shall be from the days that were' (195).

Two sonnets in *The House of Life*, 'Soul's Beauty' and 'Body's Beauty', were written to accompany the paintings titled *Sibylla Palmifera and Lilith*. The poems are a powerful verbal exploration of the iconography associated with mythical accounts of female beauty, similar in their subtle contemplative style to Pater's famous poetic tribute to the Mona Lisa in his *Studies in the History of the Renaissance* (1873). 'Body's Beauty' summons Lilith through familiar emblems of the snake, the bright web, and the rose and poppy, but it makes its impact most forcefully and unforgettably through the closing image of youthful love destroyed in Lilith's enchanted hair: 'so went | Thy spell through him, and left his straight neck bent | And round his heart one strangling golden hair' (162). It is difficult, however, to underestimate the impact that 'Soul's Beauty' had on a later generation of poets, including the Decadent poets of the 1890s. Beauty, in the octave, is 'enthroned' amidst terror and mystery, recalling the sublime countenance of Moneta in Keats's 'The Fall of Hyperion', but in the sestet the fixed gaze of beauty gives way to a more energetic personification, with the poet-painter in passionate pursuit of a fleeting, elusive ideal:

> This is that Lady Beauty, in whose praise
>   Thy voice and hand shake still,—long known to thee
>   By flying hair and fluttering hem,—the beat
>   Following her daily of thy heart and feet,
>   How passionately and irretrievably,
> In what fond flight, how many ways and days! (161)

The word play, the internal rhyme, and the wavering fricatives all contribute to the awe-struck vision of Beauty in flight. An earlier line in the sonnet, 'I drew it in as simply as my breath', both describes the speaker's awe-struck response to the gaze of Beauty and imagines that Beauty being 'drawn' by the artist. Similarly, the 'beat' of the poet's heart is also a rhythmic measure of his verse, giving movement to his metrical 'feet'.

---

23. McGann, *Dante Gabriel Rossetti*, pp. 171–2.

Rossetti was not as far removed from the realm of political populism as *The House of Life* might suggest. The earliest sonnets in the sequence date from that great year of European revolution, 1848, and there are occasional sonnets from that time to suggest that Rossetti was intent on exploring the possibilities of the sonnet both as a devotional, amatory form and as the vehicle of popular political sentiment. 'At the Sunrise in 1848' appears to celebrate republican achievements—'God said, Let there be light! And there was light'—only to re-assert the allusion to Genesis at the end of the poem as a way of cautioning 'Man' against the usurpation of God's word. If the poem is one of liberal political optimism, it also draws on Christian authority to moderate its message, expressing fear that future generations might have need to ask, 'What the word *king* may mean in their day's task'.[24] 'Vox Ecclesiae, Vox Christi', purportedly written in 1849 in the disappointing aftermath of revolutionary struggle, follows Milton's sonnet 'On the Late Massacre in Piedmont', drawing its rhetorical power from Revelation and from a surging syntax that cuts impatiently across the usual quatrain divisions. This time, the Church is condemned for having blessed the weapons and condoned the acts of counter-revolutionary violence.[25] Rossetti's political scepticism and disillusionment is even more strongly marked in the sonnet 'On Refusal of Aid Between Nations', occasioned by the non-intervention of other European nations in the struggle of Italy and Hungary against Austria. The strongly negative declarations in the octave recall Shelley's 'Political Greatness', but the appeal to an avenging God once again looks to Milton for authority. Rossetti resorts to an apocalyptic idiom, not just to register the violent conflict across Europe ('Not that the earth is changing, O my God! | Nor that the seasons totter in their walk'), but to convey his deep dismay that 'Man is parcelled out in men'. The sestet concludes that the defeat of political ideals by stubborn self-interest is reason enough for dwelling on the terminal destruction of the earth: '"He is he, I am I." By this we know | That the earth falls asunder, being old' (189). The pessimism of the poem is such that its verbal energy steadily seeps away after the rhetorical outcry of the opening line. If this makes for an uninspiring, etiolated poetry, it also fittingly describes the political disappointments of 1849.

---

24. Dante Gabriel Rossetti, *The Complete Poetical Works of Dante Gabriel Rossetti*, ed. William M. Rossetti (Boston: Little, Brown, and Co., 1907), p. 287.
25. *The Complete Poetical Works*, ed. Rossetti, p. 304.

Matthew Arnold

The political upheavals of 1848–9 provide an appropriate starting point for a discussion of Matthew Arnold's sonnets, though Arnold is notably more responsive than Rossetti to the political sonnets of the Romantic poets. Just as 'The Scholar-Gipsy' and 'Thyrsis' reverberate with the Keatsian sensuousness that Arnold elsewhere admonished, so too do the sonnets appear to exceed themselves in their affirmative echoes of those Romantic authors from whom Arnold, in his critical essays, was at pains to distance himself. This is not to suggest that Arnold was avowedly in support of the more revolutionary tendencies in Romantic poetry. The political relationship with Wordsworth, especially, is complex, and it often manifests itself in terms of a chastened, circumspect view of human liberty. Among Arnold's 1849 sonnets are several conventional pieces dedicated to Shakespeare, to Emerson, and to the Duke of Wellington, but there is also a small group of sonnets clearly inspired by the political events of 1848—by revolution in France and by the powerful surge of the Chartist movement in Britain.

Arnold's 'Quiet Work' (simply titled 'Sonnet' in *The Strayed Reveller, and Other Poems*, 1849) responds to the 'fitful uproar' of 1848 with a call for patience and repose that draws extensively on Romantic ideals of harmonious integration with Nature.[26] The opening is strongly Wordsworthian—'One lesson, Nature, let me learn of thee'—but so, too, is the modified Petrarchan form of the sonnet, with its introduction of a third rhyme in the octave (*abbaaccadefdef*). The repeated emphasis on 'toil', 'labour', and 'work' keeps the class conflicts of the 1840s in view, but the labourers that the sonnet most admires are Nature's 'sleepless ministers', the stars. Here, the sonnet effectively consolidates a range of well-established Romantic motifs, all of which reinforce the ideal of quiet work: 'the secret ministry of frost' in Coleridge's 'Frost at Midnight', the 'silent tasks' in Wordsworth's 'Gipsies', and the 'patient, sleepless eremite' in Keats's 'Bright star' sonnet.[27]

If Arnold draws on Romantic precursors to underwrite the quietistic politics of this early sonnet, he can also at times be prompted into more radical

---

26. *Arnold: The Complete Poems*, ed. Kenneth Allott (London: Longman, 1965; 2nd edn, ed. Miriam Allott 1979), p. 112. All other quotations from Arnold's poems are from this edition.
27. Samuel Taylor Coleridge, *The Major Works*, ed. H. J. Jackson (Oxford: Oxford University Press, 2008), p. 87; William Wordsworth, *The Major Works*, ed. Stephen Gill (Oxford: Oxford University Press, 2008), p. 332; Keats, *Poetical Works*, ed. Garrod, p. 372.

political gestures that suggest the influence of Shelley rather than Wordsworth. His sonnet 'To a Republican Friend, 1848' has its origins in his extensive correspondence with Arthur Hugh Clough, but the specific date (added to the title when the poem was reprinted in 1853) also establishes that great year of revolution and political upheaval as a crucial context for understanding the poem. The prevailing conditional tense appears to echo Clough's remark in March 1848, 'If it were not for all these blessed revolutions, I should sink into hopeless lethargy',[28] but just as surely it echoes Shelley's 'Ode to the West Wind':

> God knows it, I am with you. If to prize
> Those virtues, prized and practised by too few,
> But prized, but loved, but eminent in you,
> Man's fundamental life; if to despise
>
> The barren optimistic sophistries
> Of comfortable moles, whom what they do
> Teaches the limit of the just and true
> (And for such doing they require not eyes);
>
> If sadness at the long heart-wasting show
> Wherein earth's great ones are disquieted;
> If thoughts, not idle, while before me flow
>
> The armies of the homeless and unfed—
> If these are yours, if this is what you are,
> Then am I yours, and what you feel, I share.   (108)

The rhyme scheme here constructs a hybrid Petrarchan-Shakespearean form, both retaining the formal elegance of the envelope rhymes in the octave and making resourceful use of the emphatic closing couplet: *abbaabbacdcdee*. Arnold creates a powerful and imposing tension in the sonnet by running repeated conditional phrases ('If to prize...if to despise...If sadness...If thoughts...If these...if this...') against the confident certainty of the opening and closing lines, with their positive declaration of solidarity. 'I am with you' is intensified in the candid, epistolary signing off, 'Then am I yours'. In a style that recalls Shelley's 'England in 1819', the sonnet rebukes the comfortable and complacent upholders of the establishment and mourns the neglect of truth and justice. The parenthetical insertion at the end of the octave is especially reminiscent of Shelley. Although democracy was often

---

28. *The Complete Poems*, ed. Allott, p. 107.

negatively portrayed as a flood and a deluge, as well as a militant force, Arnold's perception of a starving, vagrant underclass is both stark and sympathetic.

Arnold's correspondence with Clough clearly shapes the strong sense of dialogue within and between the sonnets of the 1840s and lends them a conversational ease. The second sonnet to his republican friend, simply titled 'Continued', has an air of cautious reassessment, if not recantation:

> Yet, when I muse on what life is, I seem
> Rather to patience prompted, than that proud
> Prospect of hope which France proclaims so loud.   (108)

This time, the voice is at a distance from the republican politics espoused by Clough. The second sonnet responds pessimistically to the idea of an imminent revolutionary change, seeming to postpone equality until we are 'left standing face to face with God'. The turn from octave to sestet reinforces this conviction: 'Nor will that day dawn at a human nod.' Even so, the idea of humanity 'bursting' through its mundane concerns with 'plot and plan' to achieve eventual liberty is strongly Shelleyan (109). In the light of these two sonnets and their dialogue with both Clough and Shelley, it would seem unwise to make any definitive pronouncement on the politics of Arnold's poetry in the late 1840s. What the sonnets reveal is the profound instability and disquiet that flow through Arnold's thoughts about the place of poetry in modern culture and about its social and moral responsibilities at this unnerving time.

Arnold's conviction that the sonnet was still available for public and political intervention is evident as late as 1863, when he came to write a pair of sonnets titled 'East London' and 'West London', both of which were published in *New Poems* (1867) and then in successive editions of Arnold's poems in 1868 and 1869. These, of course, are the years in which Arnold's meditations on culture and anarchy are at their most intense, and we need to read these sonnets in the context of the growing campaign for political reform if we are to appreciate them fully. 'West London' is remarkably candid in its depiction of class conflict, subtly utilizing the resources of the sonnet to draw attention, not just to obvious disparities between rich and poor, but to the utter destitution of 'the homeless and unfed' in the most fashionable part of the city:

> Crouched on the pavement, close by Belgrave Square,
> A tramp I saw, ill, moody, and tongue-tied.
> A babe was in her arms, and at her side
> A girl; their clothes were rags, their feet were bare.

>   Some labouring men, whose work lay somewhere there,
>   Passed opposite; she touched her girl, who hied
>   Across, and begged, and came back satisfied.
>   The rich she had let pass with frozen stare.
>
>   Thought I: 'Above her state this spirit towers;
>   She will not ask of aliens, but of friends,
>   Of sharers in a common human fate.
>
>   She turns from that cold succour, which attends
>   The unknown little from the unknowing great,
>   And points us to a better time than ours.'   (526)

The conventions of the Petrarchan sonnet are very deftly employed here, with the octave-sestet and quatrain-tercet divisions being used for maximum political effect. Each verse section of the poem contains a particular observation or perception. The sonnet turns effectively from the speaker's casual observation to his concentrated thought, at the same time demonstrating the difference between the destitute woman's 'tongue-tied' condition and his own refined and elegant speech. Even more impressively, the sonnet slips from the narrative past to the imposing present, before closing with a strikingly prophetic awareness of social change. There is evidence here that the sonnet form, carrying with it the inspiring rhetoric of Milton and Shelley, functions in a way that enables a more radical and emancipatory politics than we are accustomed to finding in Arnold's writings of the 1860s.

George Meredith

It is worth noting that while Arnold perpetuates and reworks the tradition of the political sonnet, he does not employ the sonnet form for the more private, introspective musings of the Marguerite poems, even though these have an epistolary mode of address not unlike the sonnets addressed to Clough ('To Marguerite—Continued' is indicative of this tendency). It is difficult to conceive of Arnold venturing into the confessional, revelatory discourse associated with the sonnet sequences of Elizabeth Barrett Browning, or Dante Gabriel Rossetti, or, indeed, of George Meredith. There are moments in Meredith's *Modern Love* when his disenchanted protagonists seem to show the 'palsied hearts' symptomatic of 'this strange disease of modern life', but in other respects his sonnet sequence is far too iconoclastic for Arnold's liking.[29] The title of Meredith's sonnet sequence is deeply ironic, for the lovers in question, however enlightened they may appear to be, are still bound by convention and hypocritically conceal their broken marriage: 'Each sucked a secret, and each wore a mask' (30). Here, the isolation that Arnold writes of in his Marguerite poems has become a chronically destructive condition.

Meredith's sixteen-line sonnet is a highly flexible and versatile form that clearly suits the skills of a writer habitually attuned to the technical resources and demands of realist fiction. The enlargement of the form allows for narrative expansion of the episodic action within the individual sonnets and it opens up space for the play of dialogue. At the same time, Meredith does observe the familiar conventions of sonnet writing, judiciously exploiting the tension between rhythmical structure and syntactical structure, and also making strategic use of the characteristic turn or *volta*. The rhyme scheme is *abbacddceffeghhg*. The greater variety of rhymes than we usually find in the sonnet, either in its English or Italian variants, considerably eases the requirements of narrative progression. This arrangement also conveniently avoids the epigrammatic neatness associated with the Shakespearean closing couplet.

The fictional qualities of *Modern Love* are evident not just in the sustained narrative framework of the sequence and its highly developed dialogue, but also in the diction and syntax of individual sonnets. One of the most innovative features of the sequence is its accommodation of long, syntactical units, more readily associated with the realist novel than with lyric poetry. Complex sentences are run across the four constituent quatrains of each sixteen-line sonnet, creating a strong sense of propulsion and also dislocation. Sonnet I provides an excellent example of the characteristic interplay of syntactical and rhythmical structures in the sonnet sequence as a whole:

> By this he knew she wept with waking eyes:
> That, at his hand's light quiver by her head,
> The strange low sobs that shook their common bed,
> Were called into her with a sharp surprise,
> And strangled mute, like little gaping snakes,
> Dreadfully venomous to him. She lay
> Stone-still, and the long darkness flowed away
> With muffled pulses. Then, as midnight makes

---

29. Quotations from George Meredith's sonnets are from *Modern Love*, ed. Stephen Regan (Peterborough: Monitor House, 1988). See also *The Poems of George Meredith*, ed. Phyllis Bartlett (New Haven: Yale University Press, 1978).

> Her giant heart of Memory and Tears
> Drink the pale drug of silence, and so beat
> Sleep's heavy measure, they from head to feet
> Were moveless, looking through their dead black years,
> By vain regret scrawled over the blank wall.
> Like sculptured effigies they might be seen
> Upon their marriage-tomb, the sword between;
> Each wishing for the sword that severs all.   (29)

Even though the rhyme scheme suggests that the individual sonnets are structured around a series of quatrains, the syntax in this opening sonnet moves headlong across the first six lines. It also ends in the middle of a line, creating a strong caesura and setting up the steady enjambment of lines 6–12. These opening six lines owe more to the realist novel than the traditional love sonnet. Characteristic of Meredith's language is the strongly emphatic and dissonant connective 'that' at the beginning of line 2, upsetting any expectations of lyric melody and establishing a more vernacular idiom. The most enigmatic aspect of the poem's narrative structure is its use of both third-person and first-person voices, sometimes within the same sonnet. In Sonnet III, for instance, the omniscient mode is suddenly transposed into an insistent first-person presence: 'See that I am drawn to her even now' (30). Sonnet IV then returns, rather puzzlingly, to the more detached third-person viewpoint. This alternation of perspectives initially suggests a framing device, with a dramatic monologue or monodrama being enclosed by a more objective testimony. However, the opening and closing shifts of perspective can be readily understood in terms of a single, protean consciousness in a profound state of distraction, desperately confronting the circumstances of an appalling personal tragedy. This, too, is part of the poem's indubitable modernity.

As it progresses, *Modern Love* moves through a bewildering variety of literary modes—dramatic, pictorial, allegorical, and elegiac—and these are often strangely at odds with the realist elements that predominate. The opening sonnet's capitalized 'Memory' and 'Tears', for instance, seem luridly allegorical, and there are also touches of melodrama in this and other sonnets. The poem is both lyrical and anti-lyrical, sometimes shifting abruptly from metrical smoothness and regularity to highly convoluted syntax and elliptical phrasing. It repeatedly draws attention to its own discordant tendencies and linguistic peculiarities, with the husband sarcastically declaring at the end of Sonnet XXXIII: 'Strange love talk, is it not?' (45). The curiously hybrid language of the sequence is in keeping with the powerful clash of ideas and values that Meredith's lovers struggle to resolve. If the lovers are 'modern' in their determination to base their conduct on new ideas of human physiology and psychology, they are also inveterate traditionalists, instinctively reverting to older models of human progress and development in times of crisis. Sonnet XXX amply demonstrates the extent to which the lovers are caught between a progressive, evolutionary discourse and an older, biblical wisdom:

> What are we first? First, animals; and next
> Intelligences at a leap; on whom
> Pale lies the distant shadow of the tomb,
> And all that draweth on the tomb for text.
> Into which state comes Love, the crowning sun:
> Beneath whose light the shadow loses form.
> We are the lords of life, and life is warm.
> Intelligence and instinct now are one.
> But Nature says: 'My children most they seem
> When they least know me: therefore I decree
> That they shall suffer.' Swift doth young Love flee
> And we stand wakened, shivering from our dream.
> Then if we study Nature we are wise.
> Thus do the few who live but with the day:
> The scientific animals are they.—
> Lady, this is my sonnet to your eyes.   (44)

The self-conscious incongruity of the closing line is a measure of the distance between inherited poetic tradition and the prevailing evolutionary discourse of the 1850s and 1860s. The linguistic devices of the sonnet that have persisted all the way from the Renaissance to the nineteenth century as a standard of what love poetry should be are now seen to be drastically, even comically, anachronistic. The unusual collocation that comes from infusing the traditional language of love poetry with empirical scientific discourse is brilliantly captured elsewhere (Sonnet XIV) in the husband's disillusioned homage to his 'gold-haired lady's eyeballs pure' (36). A relentless displacement of conventional poeticizing is one of the hallmarks of Meredith's radical appropriation of the love sonnet. Repeatedly and obsessively, *Modern Love* draws upon a poetic idiom that is patently derivative and self-consciously 'literary', only to debunk it as grotesquely archaic and inadequate to the times.

The poem's modernity is seen, as well, in its exploration and authentication of sexual jealousy and anger, and in the provocative association it establishes between sexual repression and neurotic behaviour. Initially, the husband's agitation is seen to emerge from the friction between his continuing sexual desire for his wife and his moral revulsion at her suspected infidelity, but an additional source of frustration is his struggle against conventional outrage, to the point where he theatrically invokes and then censors his own role as the injured and vengeful partner, as in Sonnet VI: 'Behold me striking the world's coward stroke' (32). A painful sense of self-division accompanies this fitful role-playing. The husband is by turns sarcastic and pitiful, tender and indignant, bitterly hostile and warmly generous, striving to 'ape the magnanimity of love' (30). The strongly interrogative nature of the husband's address suggests a radical crisis of identity and a desperate need for reassurance over the disruption of his marriage: 'But where began the change; and what's my crime?' (34). There are numerous dramatic asides that reinforce this impression of personal instability, as the husband pauses to address himself, his wife, or an imaginary audience: 'Am I failing?' (43); 'What's my drift?' (44).

That the wife's adultery is one of the causes of marital breakdown is implied as early as Sonnet II—'This was the woman; what now of the man?'—but much of the dramatic power of *Modern Love* stems from the husband's reversion to the most blatant stereotypes, as he struggles to achieve a more equable and emancipated view of women. Accordingly, the wife in the poem is viewed as both divine and malignant, both queen of heaven and sinful transgressor: 'A star with lurid beams, she seemed to crown | The pit of infamy'; 'Poor twisting worm, so queenly beautiful'; 'Devilish malignant witch! And oh, young beam | Of heaven's circle-glory' (30, 33). The complexity of the poem, however, is such that the husband is acutely and ironically aware of his own idealizing and debasing tendencies. There are moments when the husband reveals an acutely ironic sense of the mundane world of household matters: 'She issues radiant from her dressing room, | Like one prepared to scale an upper sphere: | —By stirring up a lower, much I fear!' (32). The comic rhyme here suggests an instinct for bathos remarkably similar to that of T. S. Eliot in his dramatic monologues, 'The Love Song of J. Alfred Prufrock' and 'Portrait of a Lady'.[30]

The wife in *Modern Love* is more reminiscent of the psychologically complex New Woman of the later decades of the nineteenth century than of any obvious female stereotype. Unlike many of her predecessors in sonnet sequences, she has the capacity for speech, a sarcastic sense of humour, and

---

30. Isobel Armstrong argues persuasively that, in a complicated way, *Modern Love* is a comic poem and she reads it in the light of Meredith's 'Essay on the idea of comedy and the uses of the comic spirit' (1877). See *Victorian Poetry: Poetry, Poetics and Politics* (London: Routledge, 1993), pp. 440–59.

a lively intelligence. Meredith's flair for social comedy is once again apparent: 'Once: "Have you no fear?" | He said: 'twas dusk, she in his grasp; none near, | She laughed: "No surely; am I not with you?"' (33). Even so, the response of the wife to her husband's affair suggests that she, too, is far from emancipated in her state of modern love. Meredith referred to *Modern Love* as 'a dissection of the sentimental passion of these days', perhaps tactfully playing down its autobiographical elements, but also emphasizing its broad cultural relevance.[31] The husband's sentimentality, frequently the target of the poem's biting satire, is evident in his continuing idealization of 'Love's inmost sacredness' and his inability to accept the loss of the heavenly splendour it once bestowed upon his life:

> Is my soul beggared? Something more than earth
> I cry for still: I cannot be at peace
> In having love upon a mortal lease.
> I cannot take the woman at her worth!   (43)

While wishing to respond intelligently and sensitively to the pressures of marital breakdown and estrangement, the husband cannot entirely abandon the idea of love as sacred and immortal. In a powerfully compelling way, the poem associates the husband's crisis of belief with a more general intellectual crisis in the wake of evolutionary theory. 'Out in the yellow meadows' of spring, the husband recalls a time when love seemed to confirm his place in a purposeful and benevolent world: 'What's this when Nature swears there is no change | To challenge eyesight? Now, as then, the grace | Of heaven seems holding earth in its embrace' (34). The 'spiritual splendour' and 'the consecration of the Past' have been displaced, but the latent religious vocabulary here suggests both a former happiness in love and a former belief in a divinely ordained universe. In its rueful and ironic echoes of Wordsworthian sublimity, the poem reveals its own tormented post-romantic sensibility: 'The "What has been" a moment seemed his own: | The splendours, mysteries, dearer because known, | Nor less divine' (31).

The deep sexual disillusionment in *Modern Love* coincides with a widespread epistemological crisis and a critical turning from a confident apprehension of 'Nature's holy plan' to an appalled awareness of 'Nature red in tooth and claw'. The poem nevertheless suggests the possibility of a close alignment and integration between human needs and desires and a newly emerging conception of the natural environment. This tentative rapport

---

31. *The Letters of George Meredith*, ed. C. L. Cline (Oxford: Clarendon Press, 1970), vol. I, p. 160.

finds its most serene expression in Sonnet XLVII, which Swinburne thought was the finest sonnet in the sequence ('a more perfect piece of writing no man alive has ever turned out'):[32]

> We saw the swallows gathering in the sky,
> And in the osier-isle we heard them noise.
> We had not to look back on summer joys,
> Or forward to a summer of bright dye:
> But in the largeness of the evening earth
> Our spirits grew as we went side by side.
> The hour became her husband and my bride.
> Love that had robbed us so, thus blessed our dearth!
> The pilgrims of the year waxed very loud
> In multitudinous chatterings, as the flood
> Full brown came from the West, and like pale blood
> Expanded to the upper crimson cloud.
> Love that had robbed us of immortal things,
> This little moment mercifully gave,
> Where I have seen across the twilight wave
> The swan sail with her young beneath her wings.   (52)

Here, at a late stage in the sequence, husband and wife find an unexpected moment of harmony, gratefully sharing the present moment rather than dwelling obsessively on the past. The scene of contemplation conveys the quiet inevitability of change in its delicate, transient images of light and water, and in the subtle suggestiveness of swallows and swans in flight. In this brief interlude, the poem extols the idea of blood kinship with the earth, but the blood-stained crimson clouds also have an ominous significance. The recovery of emotional stability is only partial, and the tranquil scene is all the more poignant in that it precedes, and perhaps even precipitates, the desperate suicide of the wife.

Throughout *Modern Love* there is an insistent parallel between the breakdown in communication between husband and wife and the seeming refusal of Nature to render any coherent meaning to human perception. The poem's final magnificent image gives tragic recognition to the waves of destiny, whose consequences are powerfully felt but only dimly comprehended:

> In tragic hints here see what evermore
> Moves dark as yonder midnight ocean's force,
> Thundering like ramping hosts of warrior horse,
> To throw that faint thin line upon the shore!   (54)

32. *Spectator*, 7 June 1862.

Modern Love lays bare the troubled sexual ethics of its time with a boldness and adventurousness unmatched in Victorian poetry. In doing so, it decisively transforms the poetic diction habitually associated with the sonnet, exposing and displacing the most stultifying and artificial aspects of convention, but also ambitiously enlarging the narrative possibilities of the sonnet sequence. It is not just the disturbing frankness with which the poem dissects 'the sentimental passion' of its day that distinguishes it from other sonnet sequences such as Dante Gabriel Rossetti's *House of Life* or Elizabeth Barrett Browning's *Sonnets from the Portuguese*; it is also its imaginative capacity to look beyond the ideological constraints of its own time towards a future in which men and women will live with a greater sense of confidence, equality and freedom.

Gerard Manley Hopkins

After the publication of *Modern Love,* Meredith continued to write sonnets in the usual fourteen-line form, sometimes sending them to national newspapers such as the *Daily Chronicle* as a way of intervening in public debates. 'The Warning' and 'Outside the Crowd', both written in 1896, take a strong stand against British colonial aggression, the former intent on exposing 'This little Isle's insatiable greed | For Continents'.[33] By the time Meredith came to write these late political sonnets, his experiments with sixteen-line and fourteen-line compositions had already been overtaken and surpassed by those of another prolific and prodigious writer of sonnets, one whose work was to remain in relative obscurity until 1918. Among Victorian poets, Gerard Manley Hopkins stands alone as the most technically proficient and most radically innovative in his use of the sonnet form. It is part of his interest and appeal as a writer of sonnets that Hopkins is also the most stringent and most exacting of poets in terms of observing and respecting the mathematical proportions of the sonnet. If Meredith is essentially concerned with expansion, and with the narrative, dialogic potential of the sonnet form, Hopkins is preoccupied with intensification, and with the discipline and dynamism of the sonnet's constituent parts. Where Meredith dramatically transforms the love sonnet, fusing it with realist fiction to give a bold and unillusioned view of sexual ethics, Hopkins produces the most powerful and compelling religious or devotional sonnets since those of John Donne and George

33. *The Poems*, ed. Bartlett, vol. 2, p. 780.

Herbert. In very different ways, Meredith and Hopkins decisively alter the standard of poetic diction customarily associated with the sonnet, though both writers appear to be drawing on the rhythms and cadences of actual speech in their striking experiments with the form.

Hopkins's undergraduate essay 'On the Origin of Beauty', a Platonic dialogue purportedly written for Walter Pater in 1865, considers the idea that beauty derives from a complex relationship between regularity and irregularity, likeness and difference. In a passage of the discussion that bears on the proportions of the sonnet, Hopkins proposes through the presiding Professor of Aesthetics (probably based on John Ruskin) that 'there is a relation between the parts of the thing to each other and again of the parts to the whole, which must be duly kept'. The sonnet illustrates this formal principle, in that 'It must be made up of fourteen lines: if you were to take a line out, that would be an important loss to the structural unity.' Similarly, in contemplating the 'emphasis of pathos' to be found in the rhyming couplet of a Shakespearean sonnet, the essay considers the relation of the parts to each other and of the parts to the whole: 'On the one hand the sonnet would lose if you put two other lines instead of that couplet at the end, on the other the couplet would lose if quoted apart, so as to be without the emphasis which has been gathering through the sonnet.'[34]

Some fifteen or sixteen years later, Hopkins was to offer similar pronouncements on the sonnet form in a letter to Richard Watson Dixon, carefully distinguishing between the Shakespearean sonnet and the Italian sonnet, 'which is the sonnet proper'. He considers the Shakespearean sonnet 'a very beautiful and effective species of composition in the kind' and adds that, 'though simpler, it is as strict, regular and specific as the sonnet proper'. Crucially, the Shakespearean sonnet has 'the division into the two parts 8 + 6, at all events 4 + 4 + 4 + 2', and this division is seen by Hopkins as 'the real characteristic of the sonnet'. Mathematically, the form might be regarded as an unsymmetrical equation 'in the shape $x + y = a$, where x and y are unequal in some simple ratio'. Musically, it might be regarded in terms of major and minor scales. Paradoxically, it is largely owing to his self-confessed 'dogmatic' views about the exact proportions of the sonnet that Hopkins is compelled to produce such powerful and energetic versions of his own.[35]

---

34. *The Notebooks and Papers of Gerard Manley Hopkins*, ed. Humphry House (London: Oxford University Press, 1937), pp. 70–2.
35. *The Correspondence of Gerard Manley Hopkins and Richard Watson Dixon*, ed. Claude Colleer Abbott (London: Oxford University Press, 1935; 1955), pp. 71–2.

There are three main phases of sonnet writing in Hopkins's poetic career. The earliest phase is confined to a single year, 1865, when Hopkins is preparing to enter the Catholic Church. It includes some soul-searching devotional sonnets, such as 'Myself unholy', 'Let me be to Thee', and 'See how Spring opens'. The second phase, 1877 to 1879, coincides with Hopkins's final year at St Beuno's in Wales (1877 was the year he was ordained) and his brief return to Oxford as curate at the church of St Aloysius. This middle phase includes some of his most innovative and exuberant sonnets, including 'God's Grandeur', 'The Windhover', 'Hurrahing in Harvest', and 'Pied Beauty'. The third and final phase is that of the late 1880s, when Hopkins is living in Dublin. It includes the so-called 'sonnets of desolation' or 'terrible sonnets', probably composed in 1885, as well as some 'extended' sonnets, such as 'Spelt from Sibyl's Leaves', 'Tom's Garland', and 'That Nature is a Heraclitean Fire'.[36]

Despite his high regard for the Shakespearean sonnet, it is the Petrarchan or Italian sonnet, 'the sonnet proper', that most appeals to Hopkins when he first begins to try his hand at the form. 'See how Spring opens', written in June 1865 when he was on the verge of conversion to Catholicism, shows an impressive control of the form, though the poem is much more conventional and stable than the sonnets Hopkins would write in the year of his ordination as a priest:

> See how Spring opens with disabling cold,
> And hunting winds and the long-lying snow.
> Is it a wonder if the buds are slow?
> Or where is strength to make the leaf unfold?
> Chilling remembrance of my days of old
> Afflicts no less, what yet I hope may blow,
> That seed which the good sower once did sow,
> So loading with obstruction that threshold
>
> Which should ere now have led my feet to the field.
> It is the waste done in unreticent youth
> Which makes so small the promise of that yield
> That I may win with late-learnt skill uncouth
> From furrows of the poor and stinting weald.
> Therefore how bitter, and learnt how late, the truth!   (68)

The rhyme scheme here is one of the simplest Petrarchan types—*abbaabbacdcdcd*—and the octave and sestet offer a clear conceptual development,

---

36. Quotations from the poems of Gerard Manley Hopkins are from *The Major Works*, ed. Catherine Phillips (Oxford: Oxford University Press, 2009). Page numbers will be given within brackets in the text.

from the imperative opening, through rhetorical questions and expressions of regret, towards a painful realization and acceptance of the truth. If Hopkins adopts 'the sonnet proper', however, he does so with a strong awareness of how Milton had employed the Italian form. The opening line recalls the 'late spring' of Milton's sonnet on his twenty-third birthday ('How soon hath Time') and there are echoes of other Milton sonnets in the use of scripture (the parable of the good sower appears in Matthew 13 as well as Luke 8, the Gospel reading for 25 June in the *Book of Common Prayer*). The compression and inversion of 'learnt-late skill uncouth' are also reminiscent of Milton, as are the numerous clauses that swell the ponderous syntax. Most impressively, however, Hopkins follows Milton in allowing the syntax to surge across the octave-sestet division, powerfully and mimetically crossing the threshold that has, for so long, been loaded with obstruction. Even at this early stage, Hopkins both observes the structural relationship of octave and sestet and shows a freedom of invention. As a meditation on his delayed conversion to the Catholic faith, the sonnet carries hope and promise, however muted. At the same time, as Norman White has pointed out in his biography of Hopkins, the 'self-denigration' in this and an earlier sonnet, 'Myself unholy', anticipates the terrible crisis in the sonnets written twenty years later.[37]

The most fertile time for Hopkins's experimentation with the sonnet was undoubtedly the year of his ordination, 1877, when his contemplation of his dual vocation as priest and poet was at its most intense. In the eight months between February and September of that year, Hopkins produced some of the most astonishingly innovative sonnets ever written, including 'God's Grandeur', 'The Starlight Night', 'As kingfishers catch fire', 'The Sea and the Skylark', 'The Windhover', 'Pied Beauty', 'The Caged Skylark', 'Hurrahing in Harvest', and 'The Lantern out of Doors'. Throughout these sonnets, there is an insistent acknowledgement of God's presence in the world and of the spectator's instinct to praise God for the mysteriousness and multifariousness of his creation. Hopkins told Robert Bridges that 'The Windhover' was the best thing he had written, and much of its power derives from the tremendous compression that Hopkins is able to bring to the sonnet form without it collapsing completely under the turbulent force of its own idiosyncratic diction and rhythm:

> I caught this morning morning's minion, king-
>   dom of daylight's dauphin, dapple-dáwn-drawn Falcon, in his riding
>   Of the rólling level ùnderneath him steady áir, and stríding

37. Norman White, *Hopkins: A Literary Biography* (Oxford: Clarendon, 1992), p. 117.

High there, how he rung upon the rein of a wimpling wing
In his ecstacy! Then off, off forth on swing,
    As a skate's heel sweeps smooth on a bow-bend: the hurl and gliding
Rebuffed the big wind. My heart in hiding
Stirred for a bird,—the achieve of, the mastery of the thing!
Brute beauty and valour and act, oh, air, pride, plume, here
    Buckle! AND the fire that breaks from thee then, a billion
Times told lovelier, more dangerous, O my chevalier!

No wónder of it: shéer plód makes plóugh down síllion
Shine, and blue-bleak embers, ah my dear,
    Fall, gáll themsélves, and gásh góld-vermílion.   (132)

Despite the extensive critical commentary that 'The Windhover' has received, very little of it has been concerned with the poem as a sonnet. In some respects, it observes the familiar Petrarchan form of fourteen lines rhyming *abbaabba cdc cdc*, except that the sestet is visibly displayed as two tercets. The rhymes in the octave are alternating male and female rhymes, though of course it might be argued that the same 'ing' rhyme word is simply maintained throughout. The repeated participles have an accelerating effect on the poem's momentum. Where Hopkins makes a radical departure from convention is in greatly lengthening the number of syllables per line, while tending to retain the usual five stresses associated with iambic pentameter. The resulting large number of unstressed syllables creates a highly energetic and syncopated sprung rhythm, so powerfully driven that it splits the word 'kingdom' across the ending of the first line and sets up a forceful enjambment throughout the rest of the sonnet.

    As Norman White observes, 'The excitement and high-pitched intensity of the octave is effected by a madrigal medley of sound devices: nearly every line has its characteristic one, two, or three consonants', and in the first two lines, in particular, these take the form of alliterative 'adjectival clusters'.[38] The self that catches sight of the kestrel in the opening line of the octave reappears in the closing line, confessing a secret admiration for the bird: 'My heart in hiding | Stirred for a bird'. It would be too simple to see this notion of 'hiding' in terms of the conflict between the poet's perception of sensuous, physical beauty and the priest's apprehension of the spiritual beauty of God's creation, but there is undoubtedly a tension between the 'Brute beauty' of the bird and what Hopkins later terms 'God's better beauty, grace'. The poem observes the turn from octave to sestet characteristic of the sonnet

---

38. White, *Hopkins: A Literary Biography*, p. 282.

proper, but also energetically sustains it, so that the capitalized conjunction in the second line of the sestet seems to carry the force of the traditional *volta*. All of the majestic qualities of the bird are seen to coalesce or 'buckle' in the sestet as the bird falls to earth (with 'buckle' semantically anticipating 'collapse'). At the same time as recognizing the bird as Christ's chivalric messenger, the poem is drawn towards a humble recognition of vocational hardship. Just as the sheer plod of the ploughman makes the ploughshare shine as it cuts through the earth, so the priest's daily toil will be dedicated to the greater glory of God. The sestet slows into a more meditative mood, with the punctuation in the closing line allowing for the brilliant climactic image of the crucifixion in 'gásh góld-vermílion'. The affectionate address, 'ah my dear', so reminiscent of George Herbert's devotional poems, suggests that 'The Windhover' is, above all, a love sonnet dedicated 'to Christ our Lord'.

In the elegiac sonnet, 'Felix Randal', Hopkins once again takes the measure of his own vocation in relation to a traditional craft involving hard, physical labour. The poem falls slightly outside the three main phases of sonnet writing outlined above and was occasioned by the death of a young blacksmith, Felix Spencer, one of Hopkins's parishioners in the Liverpool slums where he was working in 1880. Although the sonnet is noticeably more subdued than 'The Windhover', it uses the same technique of extending the sonnet line and introducing a sprung rhythm. Here, the alexandrine measure gives a more stately movement to the line (Hopkins marks six stresses rather than five), while the carefully observed divisions both within and between octave and sestet also contribute to the dignified, elegiac mood:

> Félix Rándal the fárrier, O is he déad then? My duty all énded,
> Who have watched his mould of man, big-boned and hardy-handsome
> Pining, pining, till time when reason rambled in it and some
> Fatal four disorders, fleshed there, all contended?
>
> Sickness broke him. Impatient, he cursed at first, but mended
> Being anointed and all; though a heavenlier heart began some
> Mónths éarlier, since I had our swéet repríeve and ránsom
> Téndered to him. Ah well, God rést him áll road éver he offénded!
>
> This séeing the síck endéars them tó us, us tóo it endéars.
> My tongue had taught thee comfort, touch had quenched they tears,
> Thy tears that touched my heart, child, Felix, poor Felix Randal;
>
> How far from then forethought of, all thy more boisterous years,
> When thou at the random grim forge, powerful amidst peers,
> Didst fettle for the great grey drayhorse his bright and battering sandal!
>
> (150)

The 'O' in the opening line effectively combines a conventional, literary expression of grief with the muted surprise that often enters casual conversation. In the same way, the sonnet repeatedly crosses a highly stylized poetic diction with a local speech derived from Lancashire dialect. 'Mended' is exactly right as a way of describing the blacksmith's change of heart, just as 'fettle' (still in use in the north of England) is a putting right and a restoring to a good state. 'Ah well, God rest him all road ever he offended' effectively catches the rhythm and stress of local speech. As Tom Paulin suggests, 'Anyone who enjoys the extremes of impulsive affection and vitality in regional speech is bound to notice that Hopkins's inner ear is awash with an infinite and exquisite sense of unique vocal patterns.'[39] Much of the poem's verbal energy, however, issues from particular kinds of phonetic heightening, including internal rhyme ('cursed at first') and repeated consonantal and assonantal chiming. Some of the most vigorous linguistic effects derive from neologisms such as 'hardy-handsome' or from a revitalized archaic diction. James Milroy points out that 'sandal', as a surprising substitute for 'shoe', is an example of Old English or Old Norse kenning.[40] Paulin's claim is that Hopkins's privileging of demotic speech is in keeping with the enlarged democratic sympathies that came from his immersion in working-class culture in Liverpool, Glasgow, and Dublin. At the same time, simply by dedicating the sonnet to a Liverpool labourer, Hopkins makes a vital contribution to the transformation of a poetic form that for centuries had been the preserve of an aristocratic elite. The structure of the sonnet, and not just its diction, carries the force of that transformation, placing the speaker's perception of common humanity at the critical turn from octave to sestet. The sonnet moves from the sudden death of Felix Randal to his recent illness and his dwindling strength, but the final tercet recovers from the more distant past a bright sustaining memory, heroic and mythological in its proportions, and magnificently rolls it out in that long closing line, with its powerful alliteration and internal rhyme.

Hopkins's conversion to Catholicism undoubtedly had complicating political consequences. Paulin believes that Hopkins's vocation brought him into closer contact with human suffering and broadened his political awareness: 'By refusing the self-defining solitudes of Protestant individualism, he came to sympathize with the deprivations of powerless working people.'[41]

39. Tom Paulin, *Minotaur: Poetry and the Nation State* (London: Faber, 1992), p. 90.
40. James Milroy, *The Language of Gerard Manley Hopkins* (London: André Deutsch), p. 140.
41. Paulin, *Minotaur*, p. 91.

'Felix Randal', however, harks back to a disappearing agrarian economy, while the later sonnet 'Tom's Garland' fearfully contemplates the militant 'packs' of unemployed labourers who 'infest the age' (178). Ironically, in Dublin at a time when Home Rule for Ireland is being vigorously debated, the English Hopkins reverts to 'self-defining solitude' and the sonnet now becomes the appropriate form for registering private torment and frustration. That his exile in Ireland intensified the spiritual anguish that Hopkins experienced in the 1880s is evident in the sonnet that opens, 'To seem the stranger lies my lot, my life | Among strangers'. The poem echoes John Clare's lyric, 'I am', most emphatically at the turn from octave to sestet: 'I am in Ireland now; now I am at a third | Remove' (166). The chiasmus in the line reinforces the strong sense of alienation and self-division in the sonnet, while the 'third | Remove' suggests successive stages of isolation and difference: from family and then from the wider Anglican community by virtue of conversion to Catholicism, and then from the Irish by virtue of being English.

'I wake and feel the fell of dark' is very likely the sonnet that Hopkins claimed, in a letter to Robert Bridges, he had 'written in blood'.[42] It, too, echoes Clare's strange lyric at its turn, but this time the realization of self is bitter and burning: 'I am gall, I am heartburn' (166). These Dublin sonnets of desolation are markedly different in style and vision from either 'The Windhover' or 'Felix Randal'. As Daniel Harris argues, Hopkins's late sonnets 'did not manifest...that inscaping of Christ in nature which had formerly been his joy; nor did they serve a communal function by implicitly ministering to an imagined congregation'. Instead, they show 'a sudden and darkly brilliant heightening in Hopkins's scope and linguistic incisiveness', tending towards nightmare and breakdown.[43] While Hopkins was to carry on experimenting with the sonnet, creating in 'Spelt from Sibyl's Leaves' what he called 'the longest sonnet ever made', the impulse of his final efforts carries the sonnet towards modernist fragmentation and towards a dark psychological intensity that has rarely been equalled in the form.[44]

---

42. *The Letters of Gerard Manley Hopkins to Robert Bridges*, ed. Claude Colleer Abbott (Oxford: Oxford University Press, 1935; 1955), p. 219.
43. Daniel Harris, *Inspirations Unbidden: The 'Terrible Sonnets' of Gerard Manley Hopkins* (Berkeley: University of California Press, 1982), pp. xiii–xiv.
44. *The Letters of Gerard Manley Hopkins to Robert Bridges*, ed. Abbott, p. 245.

4

The Irish sonnet

A crucial point of mediation between the English sonnet and its Irish counterpart occurred with the publication of Thomas MacDonagh's *Literature in Ireland: Studies Irish and Anglo-Irish* just a few months after his execution in May 1916 for his part in the Easter Rising. MacDonagh was a brilliant student of Elizabethan poetry (he wrote his MA thesis at University College, Dublin, on the Elizabethan lyric), and his book contains a dedicatory sonnet for George Sigerson, a leading advocate of the Irish Literary Revival, praising Sigerson as 'Patriot and Sage, Bard of the Gael and Gall'.[1] Prefacing a book on Irish writing with a sonnet might seem an ironic gesture when we recall that the refinement of the English Renaissance sonnet that begins with Sidney's *Astrophil and Stella* in 1591 coincides with one of the most decisive phases of English colonial settlement in Ireland, but MacDonagh's book was to prove massively influential in showing how English lyric forms might be fused with Irish poetic forms like the *aisling* (or dream vision) in the creation of a new and distinctive Anglo-Irish poetry. In his introduction, MacDonagh points to Keats's sonnet, 'On First Looking into Chapman's Homer', as an exemplary instance of the cultural diversity and inclusivity—classical, Renaissance, and Romantic—that modern Irish literature might emulate. In terms of language, however, what MacDonagh terms 'the Irish mode' is a way of writing in English that catches the rhythms of Irish music or Anglo-Irish speech in its rhythms, rather than attempting to follow the usual metrical patterns of English verse.[2] Though far more revolutionary than W. B. Yeats in his nationalist politics, MacDonagh shared with Yeats a

---

1. Thomas MacDonagh, *Literature in Ireland: Studies Irish and Anglo-Irish* (London: T. Fisher Unwin, 1916), p. vi.
2. MacDonagh, *Literature in Ireland*, pp. 6–8.

belief in 'a national tradition, a national literature, which shall be none the less Irish in spirit from being English in language'.[3]

Sonnets had been written in Ireland, and about Ireland, from the time of Spenser onwards. The English topographical sonnet, popular in the eighteenth century, has a notable variant in Mary Tighe's Killarney sonnets in 1800, though there is little in these picturesque sonnets, apart from their titles, to suggest their Irish provenance. John Kells Ingram published a popular volume of *Sonnets and Other Poems* in 1900, but the sonnets generally lack the stirring political rhetoric that had given his 'Memory of the Dead' such powerful appeal in the context of the Young Ireland Movement in the 1840s. 'National Presage', the most explicitly political sonnet in the collection, adopts a modified Petrarchan form, and uses the octave-sestet division to look backwards then forwards, imagining Ireland's children as they 'Turn to the future'.[4] The opening quatrain is strident in its declaration of what appears to be nationalist sentiment ('Unhappy Erin, what a lot was thine! | Half-conquered by a greedy robber band; | Ill govern'd with now lax, now ruthless hand'), but as the sonnet proceeds, it turns its attention from colonial oppression to the failings of nationalist politics, unhappily rhyming 'pseudo-patriot league' with 'faction and intrigue'. The sestet addresses Ireland 'in the coming time', surely but vaguely expecting 'something great'. Although confidently and assertively Irish, as it turns from a 'mournful history' to a 'mystic faith sublime', the sonnet announces its national origins and aspirations without any striking formal innovation.

W. B. Yeats

One of the most decisive poetic achievements of W. B. Yeats, as Helen Vendler has clearly demonstrated, was to modernize the sonnet and at the same time make it distinctively Irish. Arguing that 'the sonnet compelled from Yeats both his literary allegiance and his nationalist disobedience', she shows with meticulous detail how the Irish poet renewed the form, between the romantic sentimentality of his 1886 Petrarchan sonnet 'Remembrance' and the modernist freakishness of his 1938 hexameter sonnet, 'High Talk'.[5]

---

3. John Kelly and Eric Domville (eds), *The Collected Letters of W. B. Yeats*, Vol. 1: *1865–1895* (Oxford: Oxford University Press, 1986), p. 338.
4. John Kells Ingram, *Sonnets and Other Poems* (London: Adam and Charles Black, 1900), p. 76.
5. Helen Vendler, *Our Secret Discipline: Yeats and Lyric Form* (Oxford: Oxford University Press, 2007), p. 147.

Her claim that Yeats often demonstrated an acute awareness of the structural possibilities and dynamics of the form in poems that are almost sonnets (twelve or thirteen lines) is borne out by his brisk curtailment of Pierre Ronsard's sonnet, 'Quand vous serez bien vieille', in an English version of twelve lines (a pentameter douzain) titled 'When You are Old'. If Yeats initially seems wary of the strong binary element of the Petrarchan sonnet and more interested in the possibilities of the Shakespearean quatrain, he also seems given to wilful transgression, as with the thirteen-line 'sonnet manqué', 'The Fascination of What's Difficult'. Vendler gives ample evidence of the ways in which Yeats makes his sonnets 'Irish' through myth and allusion, as well as through new hybrid forms that are structurally emblematic of their Anglo-Irish origins, but what is also worth noting is how phonetically the sonnets advance 'the Irish mode' proposed by MacDonagh, revitalizing the English pentameter line through the imposing and distinctive rhythms of Irish song and speech.[6]

As well as being a persistent form in Yeats's long career, the sonnet also bends to meet and accommodate events in each new phase of artistic development, from the early Celtic Twilight of the Irish Literary Revival to the frenzied modernist extravagance of the posthumous *Last Poems* (1939). 'The Harp of Aengus', written in 1900 as a prologue for the dramatic poem *The Shadowy Waters* (1906), is a meditation on the magic and wonder of love, using the unrhymed sonnet form to emulate the incantatory music and vivid presentation of Irish storytelling. Like 'The Song of Wandering Aengus', the sonnet draws on legends of the Celtic God of youth, beauty, and poetry, but it uses the octave-sestet relationship to explore the sad separation of Edain and Angus, as well as their mutual creativity:

> *He made a harp with Druid apple-wood*
> *That she among her winds might know he wept;*
> *And from that hour he has watched over none*
> *But faithful lovers.*[7]

In its making, the harp becomes emblematic of Irish art as well as of national yearning for freedom. The dramatically foreshortened closing line gives prominence to 'faithful lovers', while letting the remaining silence and blankness speak eloquently of an uncertain future. Two slightly later love sonnets, 'The Folly of Being Comforted' (1902) and 'Never Give all the Heart' (1905),

---

6. Vendler, *Our Secret Discipline*, p. 164.
7. W. B. Yeats, *The Poems*, ed. Daniel Albright (London: Dent), p. 114.

both published in the collection *In the Seven Woods* (1907), suggest how quickly the poet's wild love for Maud Gonne turned to disillusionment, while also tacitly acknowledging, in their own formal accomplishment, that great art has its origins in 'the foul rag and bone shop of the heart'.[8] Both sonnets are written in relentless rhyming couplets. One employs dramatic dialogue in which the heart cries out against the comforting notion that time heals loss, rupturing the sonnet form at line 6 and appending an isolated remorseful couplet, while the other makes its complaint in brisk tetrameter, enacting a premature turn that divides the sonnet in two and mournfully repeats what has already been said: 'O never give the heart outright'.

The title poem of *In the Seven Woods* is crucially important in the history of the sonnet in Ireland, as it turns from pastoral musing to political indignation, and at the same time shakes and roughens the sonnet form itself. Colm Tóibín has offered a compelling reading of the poem, noting that its specific dating of August 1902 coincides with the British-Israelite excavation of Tara, regarded by Yeats and other Revivalists as a desecration of an ancient Irish monument associated with the high kings of Celtic Ireland.[9] The dating also alludes to the coronation of Edward VII, the son of Queen Victoria, whom Yeats and his contemporaries considered vulgar and dissolute. The poem seeks sanctuary in the Seven Woods of Lady Gregory's estate at Coole Park, hoping to 'put away | The unavailing outcries and the old bitterness | That empty the heart', and turning for a brief respite from contemporary political events: 'I have forgot awhile | Tara uprooted, and new commonness | Upon the throne and crying about the streets.' Against that dismal state of affairs, Yeats arms himself with thoughts of 'that Great Archer' (Sagittarius) who 'but awaits His hour to shoot', thereby promising a different political destiny.[10]

Tóibín is surely right to establish a further connection between Yeats's composition of 'In the Seven Woods' and his writing of an introduction to a selection of the poems of Edmund Spenser in the same year (1902). Commenting on Spenser's *View of the Present State of Ireland* (1596), Yeats recalls the Elizabethan poet's description of the 'wandering companies that

---

8. *W. B. Yeats*, ed. Edward Larrissy (Oxford: Oxford University Press, 1997), p. 180. Further quotations from the poems of W. B. Yeats are from this edition.
9. Colm Tóibín, 'As Things Fall Apart: The Response to Violence in the Work of W. B. Yeats and James Joyce', Plenary Lecture at the Annual Conference of the European Society for the Study of English, National University of Ireland, Galway, 25 August 2016. I am grateful to Colm Tóibín for kindly allowing me access to his unpublished lecture.
10. The text of 'In the Seven Woods' quoted here is from *The Poems*, ed. Albright, p. 103.

keep the wood' and how the native Irish were deliberately starved as a salient part of colonial policy: 'Out of every corner of the woodes and glynnes they came creeping forth upon theyr hands.' In the Seven Woods, in stark contrast, Yeats finds momentary contentment, but also reasserts the freedom of a 'wild heart'. His handling of the sonnet form is similarly wild. In the essay on Spenser, he claims that the English poet wrote 'many intolerably artificial sonnets', and not surprisingly his own efforts divert considerably from that particular English model of sonnet writing.[11] The iambic metre is repeatedly disrupted, as is any semblance of a coherent rhyme scheme. 'Quiet' and 'heart' find phonetic and semantic togetherness, as do 'bitterness' and 'commonness', but in other respects the sonnet veers wildly from any formal rhyme scheme. It similarly violates the customary division of octave and sestet by letting the syntax run on across the turn, and beginning line 9 with the ungainly connective 'Because'. With this unruly political sonnet, Yeats's poetry is suddenly on 'the streets', anticipating the violent action that would hurl 'the little streets upon the great' in 'No Second Troy' just six years later (42). In the meantime, Yeats's political indignation would be intensified by the deep dismay he came to feel towards the growing philistinism of the audience he wished to write for.

Two sonnets from the period leading up to the Easter Rising of 1916 record Yeats's disappointment with the people for whom he had hoped to create a national poetry and a national theatre, registering in the compact space of fourteen lines those sentiments so candidly expressed in a later reflective poem, 'The Fisherman': 'What I had hoped' twould be | To write for my own race | And the reality' (69). 'At the Abbey Theatre', a key poem in Yeats's transition from the Celtic Twilight to the more public and urbane (and occasionally bitter) writing that characterizes *The Green Helmet* (1912), is another imitation of Ronsard, though it opens with an address to Craoibhin Aoibhin, the pen name of Douglas Hyde, the Gaelic scholar and fervent nationalist. This time, Yeats writes a true Shakespearean sonnet, carefully observing rhyme scheme, line length, and metre, but the language is so vigorously colloquial that it cannot be easily contained within the usual quatrain divisions. The subject is the capricious appetite of Dublin audiences at the Abbey, one moment complaining of high-minded abstraction—'When we are high and airy hundreds say | That if we hold that flight they'll leave the place'—and the next moment rejecting an 'art of common things,

---

11. W. B. Yeats, *Essays and Introductions* (London: Macmillan, 1974), pp. 373–4, 362.

| So bitterly, you'd dream they longed to look | All their lives through into some drift of wings' (44–5). The rhythms of Yeats's own Anglo-Irish speech course through the sonnet and are especially evident in the ironic handling of the modal auxiliary verb ('you'd dream'), heard again in the elegiac 'September 1913' ('You'd cry...'). Having once vowed with Verlaine to 'wring the neck of rhetoric',[12] Yeats now discovers the power of dramatic speech compressed within the sonnet form and unleashes a series of rhetorical questions at his fickle national audience, meeting mockery with mockery, and again anticipating 'September 1913':

> Is there a bridle for this Proteus
> That turns and changes like his draughty seas?
> Or is there none, most popular of men,
> But when they mock us, that we mock again? (45)

Yeats's triumph of denunciatory rhetoric in the sonnet form is undoubtedly his 'Closing Rhymes' (initially titled 'Notoriety') in *Responsibilities* (1914). The notoriety in question is the unwanted celebrity status bestowed on the poet by the popular press (allegedly in a carping magazine article written by George Moore), and Yeats responds (having first invoked the 'reed-throated whisperer', inspiration) with a magnificent single suspended sentence, lifting himself 'Beyond the fling of the dull ass's hoof'. The sonnet has a Shakespearean octave with virtuosic rhymes ('whisperer'/'air'; 'once'/'companions') and a Petrarchan sestet that skilfully prolongs the syntactical complexity and suspension. Helen Vendler astutely notes that Milton is 'the unseen presider' over its public discourse and its energetic array of subordinate clauses.[13] The sonnet turns towards forgiveness, but opens out into an elevated rhetorical defiance of cheap criticism, galvanizing itself with both scornful resentment and stoical endurance: 'till all my priceless things | Are but a post the passing dogs defile.'

The most startling experiments that Yeats attempts with the sonnet form occur in the 1920s in response to political violence in the modern world, as his poetry acutely registers the impact of the First World War, revolution in Russia, and the Easter Rising and War of Independence in Ireland. In keeping with the cyclical theory of history outlined in his extraordinary work of arcane philosophy and penetrating insight, *A Vision*, Yeats sees a powerful antithetical force sweeping away the civilization of the previous two thousand years and supplanting it with a new and brutal world order.

---

12. W. B. Yeats (ed.), *The Oxford Book of Modern Verse* (Oxford: Clarendon Press, 1936), p. xii.
13. Vendler, *Our Secret Discipline*, p. 169.

'The Second Coming' fearfully imagines the birth of Christ and the promise of resurrection displaced by some 'rough beast', as it 'Slouches towards Bethlehem to be born' (92). Seamus Deane sees the poem's anarchic vision as a product of 'the pan-European militarization of politics that put an end to nineteenth-century liberalism', but he also perceptively notes how its mythical pattern of birth and rebirth is subtly conveyed through the dynamics of the sonnet form. Significantly, the speaker's presence in the poem is made manifest at that 'strategic moment' when it turns from an opening octave, not towards a resuming sestet, but towards the convulsive birth of an entirely new sonnet.[14] The astounded vision of what Vendler aptly terms the 'monstrous' sonnet is communicated through a rapt blank verse that begins as if striving for rhyme but quickly abandons the project, as if imitating the disintegrating world around it.[15]

'Leda and the Swan' depicts another violent conception in the mythological rape of Leda by Zeus, leading to the birth of Helen and the tumultuous events of the Trojan War. Taking its narrative framework from Greek legend and augmenting it with precise visual details drawn from Michelangelo's famous painting of the subject, the poem vividly imagines and recreates the encounter of bird and woman in a taut and fractured sonnet:

> A sudden blow: the great wings beating still
> Above the staggering girl, her thighs caressed
> By the dark webs, her nape caught in his bill,
> He holds her helpless breast upon his breast.
>
> How can those terrified vague fingers push
> The feathered glory from her loosening thighs?
> And how can body, laid in that white rush,
> But feel the strange heart beating where it lies?
>
> A shudder in the loins engenders there
> The broken wall, the burning roof and tower
> And Agamemnon dead.
>   Being so caught up,
> So mastered by the brute blood of the air,
> Did she put on his knowledge with his power
> Before the indifferent beak could let her drop?   (112)

---

14. Seamus Deane, *Strange Country: Modernity and Nationhood in Irish Writing Since 1790* (Oxford: Clarendon Press, 1997), pp. 172, 175–6.
15. Vendler, *Our Secret Discipline*, p. 170.

The powerful chiastic plosives—'sudden blow' and 'beating still'—are played out in a mesmerizing series of strongly physical descriptions—'bill' and 'breast' and 'body', 'broken wall' and 'burning roof', and 'brute blood of the air'—until the terrifying 'drop' at the end of the poem. The strange ambivalent image of 'great wings beating still' captures the wild, energetic movement of the swan's wings as it steadies itself above her, while also conveying the transfixed vision of Leda herself. At the same time as suggesting the stillness of a painting, that momentous opening line serves as a forecast of a history that is still going on. The tightly compressed form of the sonnet allows Yeats to alternate with alarming speed between the graphic bodily depiction of 'the staggering girl'—'her thighs', 'her nape', 'her helpless breast'—and the sublimely enigmatic appearance of the omnipotent swan-god rendered through 'dark webs', 'feathered glory', and 'white rush'. An agitated, energetic movement is created through the syncopated, anapestic rhythms that course through the verse. The hybrid Shakespearean/Petrarchan form (*abab cdcd efgefg*) aptly conveys the bewildering union of Leda and the swan, while giving a strange complexion to the traditional role of the sonnet as a love poem. The turn climactically coincides with 'A shudder in the loins', but the poem's most striking structural achievement is the inspired shattering of the sestet, as the sonnet moves forward in history to envisage the violence of the Trojan war and the death of Agamemnon, and then pauses dramatically before turning to its troubled meditation on knowledge and power. Both the octave and the sestet end with unfathomable questions, as the sonnet tries, initially, to imagine the physical experience of Leda, and then wonders if Leda (in that moment of being both 'caught' and 'caught up') 'put on' the intellectual power of Zeus, enabling her to see into the future.

Like 'The Second Coming', 'Leda and the Swan' employs what T. S. Eliot termed 'the mythical method' as a way 'of controlling, of ordering, of giving a shape and a significance to the immense panorama of futility and anarchy which is contemporary history'.[16] It, too, has its murky origins in Yeats's excited but apprehensive response at the prospect of revolutionary turmoil and the imposition of totalitarian power. He explained to Lady Gregory that the poem had been inspired by his 'long belief that the reign

---

16. T. S. Eliot, '*Ulysses*, Order, and Myth', *Dial* 75 (1923), pp. 480–3. Reprinted in *Selected Prose of T. S. Eliot*, ed. Frank Kermode (London: Faber, 1975), p. 175.

of democracy was over for the present, and in reaction there will be violent government from above, as now in Russia, and is beginning here'.[17] That he saw the poem as illustrating his belief in antithetical cycles of history is clearly evident in the original title 'Annunciation', and in the title of the chapter, 'Dove or Swan', where it later appeared in *A Vision*. The suggested parallel between the pagan myth and the biblical account of the descent of the Holy Spirit as a dove, announcing the birth of Christ, also carried with it the obvious implication of the imminent return of another social and political order antithetical to Christianity. Yeats's casual allusions to 'annunciation' were calculated to offend Catholic readers in Ireland, and the *Catholic Bulletin* obliged with an outraged response to the poet's 'Stinking Sonnet'.[18] Yeats later claimed that 'bird and lady took such possession of the scene that all politics went out of it', and there is certainly a strong indication that what Yeats ended up writing amounts to a powerful metaphorical account of the 'sudden blow' of inspiration and the mysterious conception of the poem itself.[19] However, the positioning of the poem at the centre of his great modernist volume *The Tower*, in the company of 'Meditations in Time of Civil War', and the careful italicized addition of the date of composition as 1923, make Yeats's non-political reading of his own poem seem highly unlikely. Declan Kiberd has offered a compelling post-colonial reading of 'Leda and the Swan', in which Yeats's mythologizing only thinly disguises the operations of British imperial power in Ireland, and in which the dropping by the 'indifferent beak' reveals his judgement 'on the callous and irresponsible suddenness of an unplanned and ill-prepared British withdrawal'.[20]

Yeats's theories of cyclical history, and of the rise and fall of civilizations, move inevitably towards tragic destruction, but find compensatory solace in the spiritual wisdom of the East. The late sonnet 'Meru' offers its own astringent reflections on humanity's desire for lasting monuments—a theme familiar in the sonnets of Shakespeare and Shelley. Strategically positioned as the final offering in a series of 'Supernatural Poems' in *Parnell's Funeral and Other Poems* (1935), 'Meru' looks back to the leisurely, civilized ways of Lady Gregory's Coole Park and forward to 'Lapis Lazuli' and other late poems of tragic joy. As 'things fall apart', Yeats finds an exemplary image of

---

17. Terence Brown, *The Life of W. B. Yeats* (Oxford: Blackwell, 1999), p. 296.
18. Brown, *The Life of W. B. Yeats*, p. 297.   19. *The Poems*, ed. Albright, p. 664.
20. Declan Kiberd, *Inventing Ireland* (London: Jonathan Cape, 1995), p. 315.

cold aesthetic detachment in the hermits who inhabit a mountain sacred in Hindu and Buddhist cosmology:

> Civilisation is hooped together, brought
> Under a rule, under the semblance of peace
> By manifold illusion; but man's life is thought,
> And he, despite his terror, cannot cease
> Ravening through century after century,
> Ravening, raging, and uprooting that he may come
> Into the desolation of reality:
> Egypt and Greece, good-bye, and good-bye, Rome!
> Hermits upon Mount Meru or Everest,
> Caverned in night under the drifted snow,
> Or where that snow and winter's dreadful blast
> Beat down upon their naked bodies, know
> That day brings round the night, that before dawn
> His glory and his monuments are gone. (151)

Civilization is 'hooped together', both in the spiralling gyres of time and as a temporary, man-made artefact, sustained by 'manifold illusion'. The poem adopts a Shakespearean rhyme scheme, but allows the syntax to run over the quatrain divisions in contemplation of ceaseless historical action, giving powerful emphasis instead to the turn from West to East. The octave exposes the destructive effects of incessant thought in Western tradition, as humanity perpetually creates and destroys civilization, finding only terror and desolation in its quest for fulfilment. The sestet, in sharp contrast, acknowledges the cold wisdom of 'Hermits upon Mount Meru or Everest, | Caverned in night under the drifted snow'. In a poetic form long dedicated to themes of transience, Yeats bids farewell, not just to the glory and monuments of places like Coole Park, but to mighty empires and civilizations, too: 'Egypt and Greece good-bye, and good-bye, Rome!' As Vendler notes, the sonnet is not Irish 'in any visible sense', but its central, valedictory line 'would be taken, by any Irish reader, as a farewell not only to the empires of Egypt, Greece, and Rome, but also to the British Empire'.[21] Anticipating the stoical wisdom of Yeats's self-declared epitaph in 'Under Ben Bulben', the sonnet casts a cold eye on life and death.

If Yeats gives the political sonnet a new visionary, prophetic complexion, bending it to the urgent impress of Irish nationalism, he also recreates the sonnet with such intense creative power that it confidently withstands and

---

21. Vendler, *Our Secret Discipline*, p. 177.

transmits the shocks of modernism. 'High Talk', written in the final months of his life, looks ruefully on the Romantic legacy of transcendence and inspiration and sees the modern artist, in contrast, parading on stilts and baring the artifice of his own laborious constructions. Speaking through the mask of Malachi Stilt-Jack, a weird composite of the tenth-century high king of Ireland and a local circus performer, Yeats presents the poet in a final frenzied act of imagination, in which he himself is transformed into metaphor:

> All metaphor, Malachi, stilts and all. A barnacle goose
> Far up in the stretches of the night; night splits and the dawn breaks loose;
> I, through the terrible novelty of light, stalk on, stalk on;
> Those great sea-horses bare their teeth and laugh at the dawn.   (177–8)

In place of the traditional elevated discourse of poetry, Yeats gives us a defiant, reckless, populist 'high talk', in which the barnacle geese and the sea horses at dawn are part of a freewheeling imaginative transmogrification of the world. Daniel Albright emphasizes the extraordinary modernist vision of the poem, acknowledging its 'essentially Surrealist state of referencelessness' and presenting it as a prime example of Yeats's 'seriously shapeless ways of writing' at the end of his career.[22] At the same time, the poem's strange and arresting mixture of the sublime and the grotesque owes much to the way in which it wilfully summons and deranges the traditionally elevated form of the sonnet, instructing it to speak in manic couplets and making it 'run wild' with extra feet. In his posthumous *Last Poems*, then, Yeats lays down a magnificent metamorphic sonnet as a lasting token of Irish inventiveness and as a challenge and a model for poets everywhere.

Patrick Kavanagh

Though steadfastly opposed to the heroics and histrionics of the Irish Literary Revival, Patrick Kavanagh brings to the sonnet a distinctive development of 'the Irish mode' to complement that of Yeats. 'Inniskeen Road: July Evening' was one of Kavanagh's earliest sonnets, first published in *The Ploughman and Other Poems* (1936), and it marks his quiet possession and mastery of the form.[23] The title is indicative of his early artistic

---

22. Daniel Albright, 'Yeats and Modernism', *The Cambridge Companion to W. B. Yeats*, ed. Marjorie Howes and John Kelly (Cambridge: Cambridge University Press, 2006), p. 74.
23. Patrick Kavanagh, *Collected Poems*, ed. Antoinette Quinn (Allen Lane, 2004).

acknowledgement of his own parish of Inniskeen in County Monaghan, and of his instinctive attachment in his early poetry to the particularities of place and time. Even so, for all its present-tense felicity, the poem has a wistful, ironic regard for Inniskeen and the solitude of rural Ireland. That Kavanagh, the farmer-cobbler, should have chosen the sonnet form, with all its associations with prestige and sophistication, as a means of exploring his ambivalence towards his own local culture is itself worth noting. The form is Shakespearean, but the rhythm derives from local speech and habitual observation.

> The bicycles go by in twos and threes—
> There's a dance in Billy Brennan's barn tonight,
> And there's the half-talk code of mysteries
> And the wink-and-elbow language of delight.
> Half-past eight and there is not a spot
> Upon a mile of road, no shadow thrown
> That might turn out a man or woman, not
> A footfall tapping secrecies of stone.
>
> I have what every poet hates in spite
> Of all the solemn talk of contemplation.
> Oh, Alexander Selkirk knew the plight
> Of being king and government and nation.
> A road, a mile of kingdom, I am king
> Of banks and stones and every blooming thing. (15)

The passing bicycles of the opening line create a brisk, excited immediacy, a sense of activity on Inniskeen Road, but also imply the perspective of a speaker who is slightly remote, perhaps overtaken and left behind. The dash at the end of the line has an explanatory function, but also effectively suggests continuing action. The repeated contraction—'There's a dance... | And there's the half-talk code'—together with the repeated conjunction at the beginning of lines 2 and 3 gives the first quatrain a relaxed, colloquial ease. The sonnet highlights the attractions of the local and the ordinary in the boldly alliterative 'Billy Brennan's barn', but there is also a secret delight and mystery that perhaps owes as much to the ban on dancing in conservative post-Independence Ireland as it does to the more mundane suggestions of romantic gossip.

Kavanagh uses the second quatrain of the sonnet with great fluency to clear the road and dramatically change the setting to one of stillness and silence. As Seamus Heaney points out in an early essay on Kavanagh, the repeated negatives in the second quatrain have the effect of seeming to reinvoke what they claim to deny:

> The power of the negated phrases, 'turn out a man or woman' and (especially) 'a footfall tapping secrecies of stone', works against the solitude and establishes a ghostly populous atmosphere, and this prepares us for the poet's double-edged feelings in the sestet of being at once marooned and in possession.[24]

The turn between octave and sestet is strongly marked, introducing for the first time the first-person voice of the poet. The possessive 'I have' is picked up and echoed in the 'I am' in the closing couplet of the sonnet, seeming to reinforce the dual notion of possession and self-possession in the sestet, but the entire sonnet is fraught with ambivalence and division. The solitude of the road is intensified in the solitude of the poet, caught as he is between the local 'language of delight' and 'the solemn talk of contemplation', fully embracing neither. In this respect, the sonnet is as much about the metaphorical road of the Irish poet as it is about the actual Inniskeen Road. Having once taken possession of that place imaginatively, the poet is seemingly banished from its everyday ordinariness. The tension is wonderfully captured in the deflationary closing rhyme of 'king' and 'thing'. The rhyme is given additional piquancy by the highly appropriate 'blooming', suggesting both a suitably conventional poetic response to the natural beauty of a summer's evening and a blunt colloquial expression of impatience and disgruntlement. Heaney's verdict on 'Inniskeen Road: July Evening' is characteristically astute and illuminating: 'It is a love poem to a place written towards the end of the affair and it is also one of the earliest and most successful of Kavanagh's many poems about the nature of the poetic life.'[25]

If Kavanagh seeks in this poem to find a new source of subject matter for the sonnet in the attractions and discomforts of Irish rural solitude, he does so partly by invoking English literary tradition in a quietly ironic and slightly parodic fashion. The sestet of the sonnet pulls away from the contemplative prospects of eighteenth-century English landscape poetry, taking as its cue the opening line of William Cowper's 'Verses supposed to be written by Alexander Selkirk' (1782): 'I am monarch of all I survey.' The speaker of Kavanagh's sonnet both reiterates Cowper's questioning of the claims of solitude and ironically identifies with the colonizing Robinson Crusoe

---

24. Seamus Heaney, 'From Monaghan to the Grand Canal: The Poetry of Patrick Kavanagh', *Preoccupations: Selected Prose 1968–1978* (London: Faber, 1980), p. 118.
25. Heaney, 'From Monaghan to the Grand Canal', p. 118.

(based on the fugitive sailor, Selkirk) in Daniel Defoe's novel of 1719. Given the uncertain predicament of the Irish Free State in 1936, there is every justification for rhyming 'nation' with 'contemplation' and for alternating these rhymes with 'spite' and 'plight'.

An ironic tendency to evaluate the local and the parochial according to the standards of an imposing literary tradition is also evident in the later sonnet, 'Epic', first published in *The Bell* (a journal) in November 1951. There is, in the first place, a calculated audaciousness in fitting the sonnet to the stuff of Homerian epic, but Kavanagh is unabashed in proclaiming the appeal and the adequacy of the local:

> I have lived in important places, times
> When great events were decided: who owned
> That half a rood of rock, a no-man's land
> Surrounded by our pitchfork-armed claims.
> I heard the Duffys shouting 'Damn your soul'
> And old McCabe, stripped to the waist, seen
> Step the plot defying blue cast-steel—
> 'Here is the march along these iron stones.'
> That was the year of the Munich bother. Which
> Was most important? I inclined
> To lose my faith in Ballyrush and Gortin
> Till Homer's ghost came whispering to my mind.
> He said: I made the *Iliad* from such
> A local row. Gods make their own importance. (184)

As Paul Muldoon remarks, 'The stand-off, or "temporary wrangle" has rarely been so brilliantly presented, at least in the lyric poem.'[26] The image of the feuding local families, the Duffys and the McCabes (whose names are as familiar as that of Billy Brennan), is seen initially against the massive scale of international politics and then against the backdrop of the Homeric epic, as the sonnet dwells upon the idea of 'importance'. 'Places' and 'times' are neatly aligned, so that the latter acquires some of the charge of the preceding adjective. Even allowing for Irish neutrality in the Second World War, 'the year of the Munich bother' provocatively plays down the importance of the international crisis. Muldoon is probably right to suggest a pun on 'Erin' in 'iron', so that 'march' comes to indicate not just a local boundary but an acute awareness of the Partition

---

26. Paul Muldoon, *To Ireland, I* (Oxford: Oxford University Press, 2000), p. 67.

that so decisively affected Kavanagh's County Monaghan as one of the Ulster counties positioned south of the new political border in 1921. 'March' also has uncomfortable militaristic associations that anticipate the outcome of the 'Munich bother', so further complicating what seems initially to be an obvious distinction between a local row and an international war.

'Epic' shows an increased confidence in Kavanagh's handling of the sonnet form. The first-person voice is strongly evident from the outset, and the octave-sestet division is centred neatly on the question of 'the Munich bother'. The rhyme scheme is both irregular (*abbacdcdefgfeg*) and imprecise ('owned' rhyming with 'land' and 'Gortin' opportunistically rhymed with 'importance'), both qualities producing an impression of local speech. At the same time, the literariness of the sonnet is evident, not just in the explicit reference to Book II of the Aeneid, but in the less obvious allusion to Browning's 'Dis Aliter Visum', through which it is mediated. The sonnet appears to insist on the importance of the local, but the closing line (in which poets now become God-like, as well as king-like in their making) effectively suggests that it is the mind of the maker that confers such importance.

At the time of writing 'Epic', Kavanagh had been living in Dublin for more than a decade. The move to an urban centre, from Monaghan to the Grand Canal, brought with it understandable anxieties about the role of the poet and his relationship with his subject matter. 'Epic' suggests that despite his fears of condescension from the Dublin literati towards the farmer-poet, Kavanagh was able to draw powerfully on his rural background. Antoinette Quinn considers 'Epic' to be his 'finest and most subtle defence of old-fashioned rural subject matter'.[27] Nevertheless, there are decisive changes in the later poetry, especially in the so-called Canal Bank Sonnets that were to appear in the volume *Come Dance with Kitty Stobling* (1960). The closing sonnet of 'Auditors In' suggests a new imaginative realm in the self and its spiritual destiny, though the style is rhythmically relaxed and comically irreverent: 'From the sour soil of a town where all roots canker | I turn away to where the self reposes | The placeless heaven that's under all our noses.' Seamus Heaney detects a critical transformation in the poetry after 'Epic', especially in terms of Kavanagh's consciousness

---

27. Antoinette Quinn, *Patrick Kavanagh: A Biography* (Dublin: Gill and Macmillan, 2001), p. 304.

of place and his gradual move away from the solid, physical presence of Monaghan life in his poetry:

> We might say that now the world is more pervious to his vision than he is pervious to the world. When he writes about places now, they are luminous spaces within his mind. They have been evacuated of their status as background, as documentary geography, and exist instead as transfigured images, sites where the mind projects its own force.[28]

The sonnets written after Kavanagh underwent emergency surgery in Dublin's Rialto Hospital in March 1955 are buoyant with linguistic energy and excitement, and with a new sense of dedication to the art of poetry. In this spirit of recovery, Kavanagh writes a new kind of love sonnet in which the 'common and banal' are transformed in the heat of passion and 'nothing whatever is by love debarred'. The opening of 'The Hospital' is calculatedly inauspicious and unprepossessing, though there is evident technical skill in the way that Kavanagh reels out such long and leisurely lines: 'A year ago I fell in love with the functional ward | Of a chest hospital.' The second quatrain, however, acknowledges the transforming power of love, and the promise and potential it offers to the aspiring poet. With almost Blakean intensity, the sonnet imaginatively recreates the hospital surroundings and discovers 'the inexhaustible adventure of a gravelled yard'. The turn is insistent: 'This is what love does to things.' The sestet proceeds to show how the quotidian world of the hospital bridge, the gate dented by a lorry, and the seat at the back of a shed are newly perceived and made worthy of poetry. For all its delight in the art of naming, 'The Hospital' reveals a shift from realist denotation to a modernist art of epiphany. The sonnet is modernized and transformed by Kavanagh as it rapidly adjusts to a contemporary urban locale. The celebrated function of the amatory sonnet is now critically redefined: 'For we must record love's mystery without claptrap, | Snatch out of time the passionate transitory.'

'October', first published in *Encounter* in January 1958, shows Kavanagh redefining self and place in a new mood of serenity and repose, while continuing to employ the sonnet form with great technical assurance:

> O leafy yellowness you create for me
> A world that was and now is poised above time,
> I do not need to puzzle out Eternity

---

28. Seamus Heaney, 'The Placeless Heaven: Another Look at Kavanagh', *The Government of the Tongue* (London: Faber, 1988), p. 5.

> As I walk this arboreal street on the edge of a town.
> The breeze, too, even the temperature
> And pattern of movement, is precisely the same
> As broke my heart for youth passing. Now I am sure
> Of something. Something will be mine wherever I am.
> I want to throw myself on the public street without caring
> For anything but the prayering that the earth offers.
> It is October over all my life and the light is staring
> As it caught me once in a plantation by the fox coverts.
> A man is ploughing ground for winter wheat
> And my nineteen years weigh heavily on my feet.   (218)

The sonnet is introspective without being either morbid or sentimental. The spirit of gratitude is strong enough to earn that opening lyric apostrophe. The sensuous delight in colour that Kavanagh celebrates in other sonnets of this period, including 'Canal Bank Walk', 'Yellow', and 'The One' is subdued and turned towards meditation on time and change. Even so, 'October' vividly captures the plenitude, as well as the depletion, of both the autumn morning and the later years of the poet's life.

The sonnet's leafy yellowness is a meeting place for the rural past and the urban present, just as 'this arboreal street on the edge of a town' is a liminal space, a placeless Heaven, in which the speaker might contemplate his former self. The yellow leaves, of course, derive from Shakespeare's Sonnet 73—'That time of year thou mayst in me behold'—and the form is essentially Shakespearean. Some of the rhymes are loosely deployed ('time'/'town', 'offers'/'coverts'), though this approximation makes the closing couplet, by way of contrast, seem all the more emphatic. The premature turn at the end of line 7 skilfully catches the ebb and flow of the speaker's hopes and anxieties, resting its certainty in a dubious 'something' before picking up that 'something' and reasserting a sense of confidence at the end of the octave: 'Something will be mine wherever I am.'

The speaker's wish to 'throw himself on the street' is both a declaration of disregard for the usual distinction between private and public behaviour, and a desire to avail himself of the 'prayering' (a strange Hopkins-like neologism, suggesting incitement to prayer) that the earth holds out always and everywhere. Alongside this melodramatic gesture, the sestet deftly places a memory of the speaker as shy and withdrawn ('in a plantation by the fox coverts'), and gently allows the October light to dissolve the years between. The sonnet ends movingly with an image from the past renewed and reinstated as part of the poet's continuous present.

The spirit of self-renewal and re-invention in the late sonnets was prompted in part by Kavanagh's convalescence on the banks of the Grand Canal in Dublin in the summer of 1955. The opening two sonnets in *Come Dance with Kitty Stobling* derive from that place and time, though neither is simply descriptive. 'Canal Bank Walk' envisages the speaker's rebirth in the waters of the canal and marks the occasion with a spirited linguistic renovation:

> Leafy-with-love banks and the green waters of the canal
> Pouring redemption for me, that I do
> The will of God, wallow in the habitual, the banal,
> Grow with nature again as before I grew.
> The bright stick trapped, the breeze adding a third
> Party to the couple kissing on an old seat,
> And a bird gathering materials for the nest for the Word,
> Eloquently new and abandoned to its delirious beat.
> O unworn world enrapture me, encapture me in a web
> Of fabulous grass and eternal voices by a beech,
> Feed the gaping need of my senses, give me ad lib
> To pray unselfconsciously with overflowing speech,
> For this soul needs to be honoured with a new dress woven
> From green and blue things and arguments that cannot be proven. (224)

The lyric expansiveness and exuberance of Kavanagh's born-again poetic spirit push against the perimeters of the sonnet form to the point where grammatical structure collapses and gives way to verbal improvisation. The opening line spills over with stresses and seems to fill the capacious self that is seeking renewal and transformation. The urban and industrial associations of the canal are momentarily effaced by a pervasive pastoral mysticism. The turn from octave to sestet seeks the reconciliation of word and world, fitting a newly discovered eloquence to a world that is endlessly renewable. The lyric apostrophe, 'O unworn world' is not wildly extravagant in a sonnet that is essentially a prayer, though the chiming of 'enrapture me, encapture me' suggests that the speaker hardly requires the 'ad lib' licence he craves in line 11. As Michael O'Neill has thoughtfully observed, there is, paradoxically, a strategically rehearsed dimension to Kavanagh's effusive spontaneity: 'Nothing is more self-conscious, though the self-consciousness is worn lightly, than the wish to "pray unselfconsciously."'[29] Even so, 'Canal

---

29. Michael O'Neill, *The All-Sustaining Air: Romantic Legacies and Renewals in British, American, and Irish Poetry since 1900* (Oxford: Oxford University Press, 2007), p. 127.

Bank Walk' fills the sonnet form with 'overflowing speech', especially in the superabundant syllables of the closing couplet. The great achievement of these late sonnets is in finding a vision that will hold in enthralled suspension both the ordinariness of 'the habitual, the banal' and the miraculousness of 'fabulous grass and eternal voices'. The alignment of 'green and blue things' (grass, sky, water) with 'arguments that cannot be proven' lifts the sonnet into a realm of pastoral mysticism.

The companion sonnet, 'Lines Written on a Seat on the Grand Canal, Dublin', immediately undercuts the formality of its title with a voice that is playfully exuberant and ironically disposed towards its own memorializing tendencies: 'O commemorate me where there is water, | Canal water preferably, so stilly | Greeny at the heart of summer.' The intensifying effects of 'stilly | Greeny' are repeated in the extravagant description of lock water that 'niagorously roars', and the same rhetorical enlargement is evident in the 'tremendous silence' and 'fantastic light' of midsummer. The Grand Canal has now become the home of the Muses, and poetic embellishment comes naturally: 'No one will speak in prose | Who finds his way to these Parnassian islands.' The sestet celebrates the canal as a place of epiphany, while quietly displacing the Yeatsian mythmaking that had dominated the poetry of earlier decades: 'Yeats's magnificent swan sailed by, head low with many apologies.' New mythologies now arrive, not from the Celtic Twilight, but on a barge from 'far-flung towns'. The closing lines of the sonnet quietly deflate the grandeur of Yeats's apocalyptic horseman in his 'Ben Bulben' epitaph, offering 'just a canal-bank seat for the passer-by'.

The linguistic exuberance and poetic playfulness of Kavanagh's late visionary mode have their apotheosis in the sonnet enigmatically titled 'The One'. The sonnet returns to the bogland of the early Monaghan poems, but with an astonishing stylistic virtuosity and technical daring:

> Green, blue, yellow and red—
> God is down in the swamps and marshes,
> Sensational as April and almost incred-
>   ible the flowering of our catharsis.
> A humble scene in a backward place
> Where no one important ever looked;
> The raving flowers looked up in the face
> Of the One and the Endless, the Mind that has baulked
> The profoundest of mortals. A primrose, a violet,

> A violent wild iris—but mostly anonymous performers,
> Yet an important occasion as the Muse at her toilet
> Prepared to inform the local farmers
> That beautiful, beautiful, beautiful God
> Was breathing His love by a cut-away bog.   (229)

The splotches of colour that might at first be seen as the randomly experimental gestures on the painter's canvas prove to be the flowering of a more profound development at the end of Kavanagh's journey as artist. 'A humble scene in a backward place' now provides the setting for 'the One and the Endless'. Kavanagh's handling of the sonnet line is so flexible and sinuous that the verse seems to slip effortlessly from sensation to revelation. Michael O'Neill's reading of 'The One' is acutely responsive to the effects of Kavanagh's sonnet on the eye and the ear, meticulously pointing out that the first line of the sonnet 'has about it a spondaic calm that is misleading (excitement will take over) and yet definitive. The line utters the colours as though speaking a laconic rosary chant.'[30] The verbal transfer from 'red' to 'God' across the opening lines, the audacious rhyming of 'red' with 'incredible' across the line-break, and the sudden lift from 'marshes' to 'catharsis' are all indicative of the liberating effects that Kavanagh eventually discovers in the sonnet form. 'The One' is Shakespearean, but radically innovative in its lyrical variations on the staple line of the sonnet, giving us only six syllables in the opening line. It runs line 8 across the turn between octave and sestet, so that the word 'baulked' looms large between 'the Mind' of God and the 'profoundest of mortals', and it then sets up the most idiosyncratic yet lyrically fulsome couplet. The triple repetition and provocative pseudo-rhyme are the climax of a complexly articulated sentence that winds through the sestet and finally presents us with local farmers about to learn 'That beautiful, beautiful, beautiful God | Was breathing His love by a cut-away bog'.

Seamus Heaney

Kavanagh's wayward but assured deployment of the sonnet was to prove immensely instructive and enabling for later Irish poets such as Seamus Heaney and Paul Muldoon. In his essay, 'From Monaghan to the Grand Canal', Heaney acknowledges 'something new, authentic and liberating' in

---

30. O'Neill, *The All-Sustaining Air*, p. 124.

Kavanagh's poetry.[31] His own early poetry, in *Death of a Naturalist* (1966) and *Door into the Dark* (1969), takes its bearings from Kavanagh's example, drawing resourcefully on the local landscape and the farm labour of County Derry for subject matter, and often looking to rural crafts and occupations for emblems of artistic creativity. In an essay on Kavanagh published in *The Listener* in 1979, Heaney claims that 'Kavanagh enhances our view of the world, and makes us feel that any task, in any place, is an important act, in an important place.'[32] Important, too, is the way that Kavanagh legitimizes the sonnet form for writers in Ireland, granting poets like Heaney the confidence and authority to employ the form for their own local and national interests, and to shape it with the energies and rhythms of their own vernacular speech.

Door into the Dark takes its title from one of Heaney's earliest sonnets, 'The Forge', in which the 'leather-aproned' blacksmith is a salutary figure of the artist at work.[33] The idea of the artist as blacksmith extends from Homer to Joyce, and Heaney's poem no doubt recalls the youthful determination of Stephen Dedalus 'to forge in the smithy of my soul the uncreated conscience of my race'.[34] It is Kavanagh, however, who inspires Heaney's confident depiction of local, rural labourers such as the blacksmith: 'Kavanagh forged not so much a conscience as a consciousness for the great majority of his countrymen... raising the inhibited energies of a subculture to the power of a cultural resource.'[35] 'The Forge' occupies a significant position in Heaney's developing career, serving as a manifesto for the kind of poetry he wished to write in the late 1960s. As well as possessing the sensuous, physical appeal and powerful linguistic compression that were to become the hallmarks of Heaney's early style ('the hammered anvil's short-pitched ring | The unpredictable fantail of sparks'), the sonnet also has a metaphysical function, a subtle and tentative enquiry into the realm of the unknown and the unexplored, which prompts it to reflect on its own imaginative origins and its own processes of composition. The opening line, 'All I know is a door into the dark', is Heaney's version of negative capability, suggesting a willingness to go forward and discover poetry in the dark places of the mind and memory.

31. Heaney, 'From Monaghan to the Grand Canal', p. 116.
32. 'After the Synge-song: Seamus Heaney on the Writings of Patrick Kavanagh', *The Listener*, 13 January 1972, pp. 55–6.
33. Quotations from the poems of Seamus Heaney are from *Opened Ground: Poems 1966–1996* (London: Faber, 1998).
34. James Joyce, *A Portrait of the Artist as a Young Man*, ed. Jeri Johnson (Oxford: Oxford University Press, 2000), p. 213.
35. Heaney, 'From Monaghan to the Grand Canal', p. 116.

The sonnet form is skilfully employed in a way that both captures and emulates the blacksmith's beating of iron. The admiring speaker imagines the anvil 'somewhere in the centre' of the forge, and it obligingly appears at the centre of the sonnet, between octave and sestet, with all its mystical and metaphorical significance on show: 'an altar | Where he expends himself in shape and music.' The rhyme scheme is hammered out, as if a Petrarchan sonnet was moulded and refined, but the word 'clatter' (recalling the lost sound of hooves on the street outside) has no adjacent rhyme in the sestet and so bends the sonnet back, in horseshoe-like fashion, towards 'altar' and 'water' in the octave. The insistent infinitive verbs in the closing line concentrate the energies of the sonnet impressively on both the authentic craft of art and its necessary inspiration, as the blacksmith goes inside, 'To beat real iron out, to work the bellows' (19).

Although 'The Forge' might not seem to have any obvious connection with the explicitly political sonnet, 'Requiem for the Croppies', also in *Door into the Dark*, both poems derive from Heaney's meditation on the 1798 Irish Rebellion. Michael Parker notes that Heaney had borrowed an anvil from a local forge and played the part of a blacksmith in a Bellaghy Dramatic Society play about the 1798 Rising.[36] In his candidly revealing conversation with Karl Miller, recorded in May 1999, Heaney confirms that there was a self-consciously subversive design in his use of the sonnet form for a poem celebrating the fiftieth anniversary of 1916 and its roots in the Rebellion of 1798: 'My poem about the croppies was particularly pleasing to me because it was a sonnet. It was an example, if you like, of an official English-poetry form, but one that incorporated what had been sub-cultural material during my growing-up—ballads about '98, and so on. This was a matter of deep political relevance, and it was important that it be acknowledged.'[37] Heaney's stress on the importance of bringing that material to the surface clearly echoes his remarks (already alluded to) on Kavanagh's skill in 'raising the inhibited energies of a sub-culture to the power of a cultural resource'. As Heaney observes, however, the power and potential scope of meaning in his sonnet were to acquire a charged intensity as the political conflict in the North began to escalate: 'By the mid-Seventies, to recite "Requiem for the Croppies" in Ireland in public would have been taken as a gesture of solidarity

---

36. Michael Parker, *Seamus Heaney: The Making of the Poet* (Basingstoke: Macmillan, 1993), p. 81.
37. Seamus Heaney, *Seamus Heaney in Conversation with Karl Miller* (London: Between the Lines, 2000), pp. 19–20.

with the Provisionals.'[38] Nevertheless, Heaney thought highly enough of the sonnet to include it in *Selected Poems 1965–1975* (1980), *New Selected Poems 1966–1987* (1990), and *Opened Ground: Poems 1966–1996* (1998).

> The pockets of our greatcoats, full of barley—
> No kitchens on the run, no striking camp—
> We moved quick and sudden in our own country.
> The priest lay behind ditches with the tramp.
> A people, hardly marching—on the hike—
> We found new tactics happening each day:
> We'd cut through reins and rider with the pike
> And stampede cattle into infantry,
> Then retreat through hedges where cavalry must be thrown.
> Until, on Vinegar Hill, the fatal conclave.
> Terraced thousands died, shaking scythes at cannon.
> The hillside blushed, soaked in our broken wave.
> They buried us without shroud or coffin
> And in August the barley grew up out of the grave.

'Requiem for the Croppies' is ambitious in the way that it experiments with voice in the sonnet form, both adopting the folk idiom of ballads like 'The Croppy Boy' and quietly articulating the redemptive ideals of Irish political elegy: 'They buried us without shroud or coffin | And in August the barley grew up out of the grave' (22). That the voice appears to come from the grave or from the ghost of a fallen rebel makes this early elegiac sonnet all the more remarkable.

In the early 1970s Heaney gave decisive reconsideration to the relevance and adequacy of the English lyric mode in the midst of escalating sectarian violence. The question that he repeatedly asks himself, as a kind of touchstone for these times, is taken from Shakespeare's Sonnet 65: 'How with this rage shall beauty hold a plea, | Whose action is no stronger than a flower?' The answer he provides comes not from Shakespeare's Sonnets, but from W. B. Yeats's 'Meditations in Time of Civil War'. Like Yeats, he must discover 'befitting emblems of adversity'. As well as finding 'images and symbols adequate to our predicament', Heaney faced the task of renovating the staple line of English lyric poetry typified most beautifully and melodiously (as the quotation from Shakespeare suggests) by the English sonnet.[39] In an interview with Frank Kinahan, Heaney explained his feelings of dissatisfaction

---

38. Heaney, *Seamus Heaney in Conversation with Karl Miller*, p. 20.
39. Heaney, *Preoccupations*, pp. 56–7.

towards the lyric mode: 'I thought that music, the melodious grace of the English iambic line, was some kind of affront, that it needed to be wrecked.' Similarly, in an interview that appeared in the *Irish Times* on 28 December 1973, Heaney told Harriet Cooke that he felt compelled 'to take the English lyric and make it eat stuff that it has never eaten before...like all the messy, and it would seem incomprehensible, obsessions in the North'.[40]

It is perhaps not surprising, then, that sonnets are conspicuously absent among the bleakly reflective and obliquely political poems of *Wintering Out* (1972). The volume does, however, present 'befitting emblems of adversity', most strikingly in the images of violated bodies preserved in bogland, the victims of Iron Age sacrificial rituals that Heaney encountered in his reading of *The Bog People* by P. V. Glob. As he explains in the 1974 essay, 'Feeling into Words', 'the unforgettable photographs of these victims blended in my mind with photographs of atrocities, past and present, in the long rites of Irish political and religious struggles'.[41] In one of the most memorable and controversial 'bog poems' in *North* (1975), he muses on the Medusa-like head of a girl exhumed from the fens of northern Denmark during archaeological excavations. 'Strange Fruit' is a sonnet, but one that displaces lyric gratification, including the satisfactions of rhyme. It takes its title from an anti-lynching song, first performed by Billie Holiday in 1939, in which the murdered victims are depicted as 'Black bodies swinging in the southern breeze, | Strange fruit hanging from the poplar trees'.[42]

Richard Rankin Russell offers a compelling account of the evolution of Heaney's 'Strange Fruit', noting how it began life as a poem titled 'Reliquary' (with a strong emphasis on Catholic martyrology) and how the sonnet form was crucial to its genesis.[43] In some respects, the poem displays the fascinated apprehension of the woman's physiognomy—skin, teeth, hair, nose, and eyes—characteristic of the Renaissance love sonnet, but this is a very strange love sonnet: 'Here is the girl's head like an exhumed gourd. | Oval-faced, prune-skinned, prune-stones for teeth.' While the octave concentrates with awed fixation on the 'terrible beauty' of the gruesome head, the sestet turns

---

40. Interview with Frank Kinahan, cited by Neil Corcoran in *Seamus Heaney* (London: Faber, 1986), p. 107. Interview with Harriet Cooke, *Irish Times*, 28 December 1973, p. 8.
41. Heaney, *Preoccupations*, pp. 57–8.
42. See David Margolick, *Strange Fruit: Billie Holiday, Café Society, and an Early Cry for Civil Rights* (Philadelphia: Running Press, 2000), pp. 25–7.
43. Richard Rankin Russell, *Seamus Heaney's Regions* (Notre Dame: University of Notre Dame Press, 2014), pp. 162–86.

to the Greek chronicler, Diodorus Siculus, who 'confessed | His gradual ease among the likes of this'. As if rejecting the prayerful veneration with which Heaney had approached the Tollund Man in *Wintering Out*, the head looks back in all its awful anonymity: 'Outstaring | What had begun to feel like reverence' (119).

North also includes a remarkable pair of sonnets, 'Act of Union', a condensed version of a sequence of four sonnets that originally appeared in *The Listener* on 22 February 1973 as 'A New Life'. The sonnets contemplate the difficult and painful birth of Ulster's 'heaving province', imagining the parliamentary Act of Union in 1800 as a sexual, as well as political, event, giving formal recognition to a long history of English male, imperial aggression towards Ireland's female body. The Act of Union effectively imposed direct rule over Ireland in the aftermath of the 1798 Rebellion, creating the United Kingdom of Great Britain and Ireland, and it is the legacy of this ill-fated 'union' that the sonnets consider. Although the familiar trope of Anglo-Irish relations as colonizing male and colonized female can be found in Gaelic poetry as early as the seventeenth century, Heaney gives it a striking new dimension by focusing so sensuously and insistently on the sexualized topography of the political partners, and by imagining the imperial voice of England addressing a heavily pregnant Ireland:

> To-night, a first movement, a pulse,
> As if the rain in bogland gathered head
> To slip and flood: a bog-burst,
> A gash breaking open the ferny bed.   (127)

The sonnet form is used with impressive resourcefulness, in a way that gives a powerful present-tense immediacy to the intractable stuff of history. The opening and closing lines of the first sonnet are noticeably taut and shortened, and the rhyme scheme plays full rhymes against near rhymes in tense unease ('pulse' and 'burst' against 'head and 'bed', and 'coast' and 'caress' against 'thrown' and 'grown'). The turn in the first sonnet is initiated with the imperious 'I am the tall kingdom over your shoulder', and this is picked up and replayed at the beginning of the second sonnet: 'And I am still imperially | Male, leaving you with the pain, | The rending process in the colony.' There is no turn in the second sonnet as it moves headlong in contemplation of the unruly child whose 'parasitical | And ignorant little fists' are already beating at the borders. As Neil Corcoran suggests, the conclusion of the poem is 'hopeless and exhausted, the rhyme of "pain" and "again" insisting on the apparent endlessness of political suffering in Irish history.'[44] The poem is at once prophetic and disillusioned:

> No treaty
> I foresee will salve completely your tracked
> And stretchmarked body, the big pain
> That leaves you raw, like opened ground, again. (127–8)

Of course, much depends on the word 'completely', but it might be added that what makes this an especially unsettling poem is the collision of despairing vision and aesthetic satisfaction. There is a potent irony in the way that the poem gathers force and delivers its devastating verdict on Ireland's future through an impressive stylistic control of the English sonnet, beautifully positioning the double caesura in a perfect line of closing iambic pentameter.

The 'opened ground' at the end of 'Act of Union' reappears in Heaney's 'Glanmore Sonnets', at the centre of his next volume, *Field Work* (1979), but this time the image is one of fertile openness to experience, of nourishment, replenishment, and reconciliation. In giving these ten pastoral sonnets such prominence in the book, Heaney signals a tacit return, not just to rural preoccupations, but also to the continuing possibilities of lyric grace and amplitude. Reaching back to the pastoral poetics of Horace and Virgil, and drawing sustenance from the close attachment to the land in the poetry of Wordsworth and Kavanagh, the sequence meditates on the nature of 'the good life', on the delicate balance of love and art, and on the fragile dream of peace.

The opening line of Sonnet I establishes the common field work of ploughing and poetry: 'Vowels ploughed into other: opened ground.' The sharp-pointed V resembles a ploughshare, while the caesura effectively marks the opening up of the line, preparing the ground for new poetic cultivation. The oddly unspecific 'other' invites a view of language that is physically palpable (with Irish vowel-based sounds ploughed into English consonant-based sounds), but it points more generally, perhaps, to the fundamental encounter of word and world. The mild February is full of promise and imagined plenitude, in contrast to the cold isolation of *Wintering Out* and *North*, but there is also in the opening sonnet a note of caution and tentativeness, a patient waiting in mist and silence, and an acute awareness of the fragility of both art and nature: 'The dream grain whirls like freakish Easter snows' (163).

44. Corcoran, *Seamus Heaney*, p. 121.

The close contiguity of poetry and place in 'Sensings, mountings from the hiding places' at the beginning of Sonnet II suggests the potent influence of Wordsworth. The prevailing paradigm of poet as ploughman recalls Heaney's vivid description of Wordsworth in compositional mode, 'to-ing and fro-ing like a ploughman up and down a field', and his remarks on the etymology of the word 'verse' in the same essay (in *Preoccupations*) are apposite here:' "Verse" comes from the Latin *versus* which could mean a line of poetry but could also mean the turn that a ploughman made at the head of the field as he finished one furrow and faced back into another.'[45] Sonnet II closes with a beautifully modulated and perfectly controlled illustration of poetic ploughing: 'Vowels ploughed into other, opened ground, | Each verse returning like the plough turned round.' At the same time as cultivating Wordsworthian soundings and resonances, the sonnet articulates a specifically Irish rural inheritance from the 'hedge-school of Glanmore', tutoring its voice in the echoes of the old Irish music of 'slug-horn and slow chanter'. Heaney contemplated calling his sonnet sequence 'Hedge-school Sonnets', and his allegiance to that unofficial, outlawed way of learning in rural Ireland is an indication that his poetic voice is not one that quiescently submits to English directives, but rather one 'That might continue, hold, dispel, appease' (164).

Heaney had moved south to the Glanmore estate in rural County Wicklow in August 1972, and his new surroundings appear to have induced a return to a more melodious iambic line and, specifically, to the sonnet. The first sonnet to be written was Sonnet III, in which a field of alliterative consonants is opened up to the swell of vowels amidst birdsong and twilight:

> This evening the cuckoo and the corncrake
> (So much, too much) consorted at twilight.
> It was all crepuscular and iambic.
> Out on the field a baby rabbit
> Took his bearings, and I knew the deer
> (I've seen them too from the window of the house,
> Like connoisseurs, inquisitive of air)
> Were careful under larch and May-green spruce.
> I had said earlier, 'I won't relapse
> From this strange loneliness I've brought us to.
> Dorothy and William—' She interrupts:
> 'You're not going to compare us two...?'
> Outside a rustling and twig-combing breeze
> Refreshes and relents. Is cadences.   (165)

---

45. Heaney, *Preoccupations*, p. 65.

The momentary temptation to liken Glanmore to Dove Cottage is firmly rebuffed. The domestic realism and novelistic dialogue bear close comparison with the iconoclastic style of *Modern Love*, and Meredith's sequence is invoked again in the startling image of husband and wife as 'breathing effigies' in Sonnet X. The subtle interplay of inside and outside scenes is also reminiscent of *Modern Love*. The rhyme scheme in Sonnet III is Shakespearean, though the rhymes themselves are delicately nuanced and relaxed, in keeping with the natural cadences of the sonnet's creative breeze. Elsewhere in the sequence, there are variants of both Italian and English sonnet forms.

Sonnet VII is extravagant in its deployment of rhyme, both wilfully pulling away from any obvious rhyme scheme and simultaneously striking the ear with such ingenious and innovative rhymes as 'penumbra' and 'tundra' and 'marvellous' and 'Faroes'. The sparkling rhymes are in keeping with the virtuosic recital of place names from the BBC Shipping Forecast and the attendant warning of a coming gale:

> Dogger, Rockall, Malin, Irish Sea:
> Green, swift upsurges, North Atlantic flux
> Conjured by that strong gale-warning voice
> Collapse into a sibilant penumbra.
> Midnight and closedown. Sirens of the tundra,
> Of eel-road, seal-road, keel-road, whale-road, raise
> Their wind-compounded keen behind the baize
> And drive the trawlers to the lee of Wicklow.
> *L'Etoile, Le Guillemot, La Belle Hélène*
> Nursed their bright names this morning in the bay
> That toiled like mortar. It was marvellous
> And actual, I said out loud, 'A haven,'
> The word deepening, clearing, like the sky
> Elsewhere on Minches, Cromarty, The Faroes.   (169)

The litany of place names recovers the early excitement of words as 'bearers of history and mystery' that Heaney writes about in *Preoccupations*. Recalling the 'exotic listing on the wireless', he wonders if his 'first sense of crafting words' was 'stirred by the beautiful sprung rhythms of the old BBC weather forecast: 'Dogger, Rockall, Mailn, Shetland, Faroes, Finisterre.'[46] As Bernard O'Donoghue points out in his excellent study of Heaney's language, Sonnet VII also skilfully parodies the old Irish *dinnseanchas* (place name poems) with Chaucerian variations (trochaic inversions) on the iambic pattern.

---

46. Heaney, *Preoccupations*, p. 45.

The sonnet includes 'a couplet marrying old English kennings with the "horseback, ass back, muleback" of Yeats's 'Lapis Lazuli'…before a run of French boat-names to complete the linguistic composite'.[47] Against the octave's 'wind-compounded keen' blowing in from far-flung places in the night, the sestet of Sonnet VII sets the 'bright names' of boats in the bay at morning, a clearing sky, and a heavenly haven. The word 'marvellous' anticipates the visionary and miraculous element of Heaney's later volume *Seeing Things* (1991), but the epiphanies in 'Glanmore Sonnets' are hard earned, invariably wrested out of darkness and drizzle.

Even the love sonnet that closes the sequence contemplates a cold and deathly exposure. The lovers are likened to Lorenzo and Jessica in *The Merchant of Venice* and Diarmuid and Grainne in Celtic myth, both comparisons suggesting danger and distress. The sonnet celebrates the pains as well as the pleasures of love, and although it ends with a powerful act of union, it also acknowledges an ultimate, unyielding sense of 'separateness':

> I dreamt we slept in a moss in Donegal
> On turf banks under blankets, with our faces
> Exposed all night in a wetting drizzle,
> Pallid as the dripping sapling birches.
> Lorenzo and Jessica in a cold climate.
> Diarmuid and Grainne waiting to be found.
> Darkly asperged and censed, we were laid out
> Like breathing effigies on a raised ground.
> And in that dream I dreamt—how like you this?—
> Our first night years ago in that hotel
> When you came with your deliberate kiss
> To raise us towards the lovely and painful
> Covenants of flesh; our separateness;
> The respite in our dewy dreaming faces.   (172)

At the turn is a dream within a dream, with Sir Thomas Wyatt's beautifully intimate address effecting a strange transition from the Donegal moss to the more mundane hotel, but also intensifying the ritualistic suggestions of holy water and incense in the biblical-sexual 'covenants of flesh'. The exposure implicit in 'raised ground' is mitigated by the erotic raising. It is the woman who initiates the love-making at the end of the sonnet, just as it is the woman who speaks those seductively intimate words in Wyatt's lyric, 'They

---

47. Bernard O'Donoghue, *Seamus Heaney and the Language of Poetry* (London: Harvester Wheatsheaf, 1994), p. 82.

flee from me': 'How like you this?' If 'kiss' rhymes with 'this', it also rhymes awkwardly with 'separateness'. The closing line of the sonnet suggests a further stage of dreaming, refreshed by dew, but the faces of the lovers show neither rest nor repose, only a temporary 'respite'.

If Heaney adds significantly to the tradition of the love sonnet and the topographical sonnet, infusing these with a knowledge and understanding of the Irish landscape and Irish speech, he subsequently revises and extends the tradition of the elegiac sonnet in his powerfully moving 'Clearances', published in *The Haw Lantern* in 1987. Written after the death of Margaret Heaney, the poet's mother, in 1984, these sonnets suggest a clearing away of many things. Historically, clearances involve the clearing of land and the chopping down of trees, and so at one level the poem draws on deep reserves of cultural memory and national loss. At a more intimate, personal level, the title suggests the painful processes of grief and adjustment after the death of a loved one. It recognizes what has been lost but also apprehends the new space in which life continues. In ways that both draw upon the long tradition of the English sonnet and at the same time subtly revise it, Heaney finds an appropriate medium for memory and grief in the tightly compressed and confined space of fourteen lines.

The third sonnet in the sequence is especially notable for its handling of the dynamics of the sonnet form, including the conventional turn between octave and sestet, to give shape and significance to memory.

> When all the others were away at Mass
> I was all hers as we peeled potatoes.
> They broke the silence, let fall one by one
> Like solder weeping off the soldering iron:
> Cold comforts set between us, things to share
> Gleaming in a bucket of clean water.
> And again let fall. Little pleasant splashes
> From each other's work would bring us to our senses.
>
> So while the parish priest at her bedside
> Went hammer and tongs at the prayers for the dying
> And some were responding and some crying
> I remembered her head bent towards my head,
> Her breath in mine, our fluent dipping knives—
> Never closer the whole rest of our lives.

From the outset, the sonnet is poignantly alert to the patterns of possession and dispossession that death distorts. Looking back from a desolate present on scenes of childhood closeness and companionship, the poem recalls how

'I was all hers'. An ordinary domestic event—peeling potatoes on a Sunday morning—is invested with special significance in the octave of the sonnet. The potatoes are 'things to share', associated with the happy sights and sounds of the kitchen: 'Gleaming in a bucket' and giving rise to 'Little pleasant splashes'. At the same time, they plangently recall what has been lost and broken. The potatoes falling in the water are likened to 'solder' and the word 'weeping' immediately suggest tears, as does the word 'splashes'. The repetition of the phrase 'let fall' (an echo of Robert Frost's 'After Apple Picking') takes on a ritualistic power that links the customary work of the kitchen with later patterns of grieving and the psychological need to let go. The strongly marked turn between octave and sestet completes the strange inversion of domestic and sacred rituals in the poem, so that potato peeling becomes religious and sacramental in its watery element, while the last rites of the Catholic Church take on the semblance of a domestic task, with the priest going 'hammer and tongs at the prayers for the dying'. This unexpected relationship between two powerful memories—one of abundant life and one of approaching death—gains its clarity and intensity precisely because of the formal possibilities afforded by the sonnet form.

Reflecting on the anguished final moments of death, the sonnet retrieves those other moments of life's early intimacy and attachment and grants them an archetypal, spiritual significance: 'her head bent towards my head, | Her breath in mine'. With the rueful wisdom that comes to characterize the parental elegies in *Human Chain*, the sonnet acknowledges the full meaning of that earlier memory and of those 'fluent dipping knives' only when it is too late to reinstate it or re-enact it: 'Never closer the whole rest of our lives' (309). The closing couplet works supremely well here, without any sentimentality or straining for effect. This is due, in part, to the surprising novelty of the knife-as-pen image, making knives emblematic of writing ('fluent' and 'dipping') in a heightened moment of severance. In large part, though, the couplet makes its impact because of the exemplary rhythmic control with which Heaney manages the sestet as a single sentence, pausing decisively with that devastating dash at the end of the penultimate line.

The fourth sonnet of 'Clearances' moves from the silent, rapt communion of mother and son at work to a tender recollection of how words were sometimes productive of friction and awkwardness between them. The sonnet is a powerfully condensed lesson in the divisive effects of language and education, tactfully exposing the rift between what is linguistically correct and what is well considered, and between the individualistic aspirations of a well-developed vocabulary and the social solidarity implicit in the local vernacular:

> Fear of affectation made her affect
> Inadequacy whenever it came to
> Pronouncing words 'beyond her'. *Bertold Brek.*
> She'd manage something hampered and askew
> Every time, as if she might betray
> The hampered and inadequate by too
> Well-adjusted a vocabulary.
> With more challenge than pride, she'd tell me, 'You
> Know all them things.' So I governed my tongue
> In front of her, a genuinely well-
> Adjusted adequate betrayal
> Of what I knew better. I'd *naw* and *aye*
> And decently relapse into the wrong
> Grammar which kept us allied and at bay.   (310)

The sonnet form is used here with a strong emphasis on its capacity for creating and exploring dialectical (as well as dialectal) tensions. The shift of focus from mother to son, and the potent irony of doing right by doing wrong, are deftly handled through the formal devices of the sonnet. Mother and son both indulge in the kind of knowing, upfront acting that Brecht approved of. If there is alienation hovering over these lines, there is also affection playing beneath and gently observing the subtle differences between 'affectation' and 'affect'. The different possibilities of the verb 'to manage' are also brought into play so that line 4 captures both the formal sense of management (as in 'stage management') and the more familiar sense of just coping. The rhyme scheme of Sonnet IV begins in a regular Shakespearean fashion (*ababcdcd* in the octave) before lapsing into irregularity (*effgeg* in the sestet) in a well-adjusted betrayal of the standard form. The relationship between octave and sestet is given maximum flexibility in accordance with the careful adjustments of discourse and address. The sentence structure and punctuation suggest a neat balance of 7 + 7, in keeping with the two-part role of mother and son, though technically the sonnet runs over the turn at precisely that moment when the mother tells her son: 'You | know all them things.' If the turn is initiated by the connective 'So', as it clearly is in Sonnet 3, then a further structural possibility arises. Here, there is another 'genuinely well-adjusted adequate betrayal' of the sonnet form as the sestet decently gives way to the mother's part in the octave.

If the tongue is governed in Sonnet 4, in an act of self-chastisement, it is given freedom to do the governing in the mystical spaces and silences of the closing sonnet. Kavanagh's late sonnets once again prove to be enabling and instructive. Significantly, it is in his essay on Kavanagh in *The Government of the Tongue* that Heaney recounts the story of how in 1939, the year he was born, his aunt planted a chestnut in a jam jar, and how 'over the years' he came to identify his own life with that of the chestnut tree. The eventual felling of the tree leads him to reflect on the space where the tree had once been: 'In my mind's eye I saw it as a kind of luminous emptiness, a warp and waver of light.'[48] The difference between this reimagined realm and the actual location of the absence leads him to speculate on the notion of a placeless heaven, as distinct from a heavenly place, and this is the starting point for his essay on changing conceptions of place in Kavanagh's work. In Sonnet 8, the fallen tree is a powerful emblem of loss and absence and deracination in the aftermath of his mother's death:

> I thought of walking round and round a space
> Utterly empty, utterly a source
> Where the decked chestnut tree had lost its place
> In our front hedge above the wallflowers.
> The white chips jumped and jumped and skited high.
> I heard the hatchet's differentiated
> Accurate cut, the crack, the sigh
> And collapse of what luxuriated
> Through the shocked tips and wreckage of it all.
> Deep-planted and long gone, my coeval
> Chestnut from a jam jar in a hole,
> Its heft and hush become a bright nowhere,
> A soul ramifying and forever
> Silent, beyond silence listened for.   (314)

The mourned chestnut tree falls across the division between octave and sestet, but the sonnet accommodates its 'collapse' and 'wreckage', and lifts it up again from 'a jam jar in a hole' to a transcendental 'bright nowhere'. The transition from a heavenly place to a placeless heaven is wonderfully adroit, with 'heft and hush' suggesting the magnificent solidity and leafy sway of the tree, but also delicately anticipating total emptiness and silence. The alternating rhymes in the octave give way to the gentle triplets and feminine endings in the sestet. The line break that tips 'forever' into 'silent' epitomizes

---

48. Heaney, *The Government of the Tongue* (London: Faber, 1988), p. 3.

the sonnet's capacity for giving shape and recognition to both the blank perception of irretrievable loss and the continual yearning for consolation.

A new lightness of touch and a new visionary intensity are brought to fruition in *Seeing Things* (1991). In the seven sonnets of 'Glanmore Revisited', Heaney returns to the estate in County Wicklow after a period of nearly twenty years to reconsider the place and the memories it holds. The closing sonnet, titled 'The Skylight', is emblematic of the letting in of light and air to a new ideal of poetry. The stubborn preference for 'The perfect, trunk-lid fit of the old ceiling' gives way at the turn to 'extravagant sky' and wondrous 'surprise' (350). The shift is neatly enacted in the resourceful blending of Italian and English sonnet forms, with the sturdy alternating rhymes of the octave tightening into resistant couplets and then suddenly giving way to the much looser, more relaxed rhymes of the sestet (*ababccdd efegfg*). The sonnet's allusion to the biblical parallel in which a sick man is lowered through the roof of a house to be healed and forgiven reinforces a concern throughout *Seeing Things* with crediting marvels and acknowledging miracles.

The mysticism in Heaney's later work is moving, conveyed in his account of poetic maturing in the sonnet 'Fosterling'.

> '*That heavy greenness fostered by water*'
> At school I loved one picture's heavy greenness—
> Horizons rigged with windmills' arms and sails.
> The millhouses' still outlines. Their in-placeness
> Still more in place when mirrored in canals.
> I can't remember not ever having known
> The immanent hydraulics of a land
> Of *glar* and *glit* and floods at *dailigone*.
> My silting hope. My lowlands of the mind.
>
> Heaviness of being. And poetry
> Sluggish in the doldrums of what happens.
> Me waiting until I was nearly fifty
> To credit marvels. Like the tree-clock of tin cans
> The tinkers made. So long for air to brighten,
> Time to be dazzled and the heart to lighten.   (357)

The 'heavy greenness' discerned by the schoolchild admiring Dutch landscape painting is a quality that might be attributed both to the weighty stuff of nationalist politics and to the early, watery imagery of a poetry preoccupied with bogland.[49] The cherished archaisms, 'glar' and 'glit', are suggestive of a

---

49. The epigraph to 'Fosterling' is taken from John Montague's early poem, 'The Water Carrier', first published in *Poisoned Lands* (London: MacGibbon & Kee, 1961).

land of mud and slime, while the word 'dailigone' is suggestive of the light that is daily gone at dusk. The sestet turns the sonnet from the sombre responsibility of the music of 'what happens' towards the visionary enlightenment of the music of what *might* happen, and from the poetry of earth and water to the poetry of air and light. There is a light-hearted recognition of the marvellous and of a recovered childhood wonder. This shining example of how to measure time and how to make art shows Heaney's continuing fidelity to the rural Ireland of his youth, while memorably fusing the influences of Shakespeare and Yeats. The resounding closing couplet looks back to the closing lines of Shakespeare's Sonnet 18, 'So long as men can breathe or eyes can see, | So long lives this, and this gives life to thee', while also recalling the 'brightening air' of 'The Song of Wandering Aengus' and the political instruction in 'Easter 1916' that 'Too long a sacrifice | Can make a stone of the heart'.

One important consequence of the 'lightening up' in Heaney's later poems is a new willingness to play experimentally with lyric forms, including the sonnet. As Jason Hall observes in his exemplary account of the poet's 'rhythmic contract', 'In the books following *The Haw Lantern*, Heaney displays much more formal variousness in his use of the sonnet.'[50] He claims, with ample justification, that the later Heaney demonstrates this new versatility in his handling of 'hybrid, in-between shapes' and 'nonce' or 'improvised' sonnets. There is a new imaginative territory in the 'Sonnets from Hellas' in *Electric Light* (2001), blending ancient and modern, local and international, and showing a relish for the sensuous, tactile stuff of lyric poetry. At the same time, in the fourth sonnet in the sequence, 'The Augean Stables', the pleasures of Greece are violently displaced by news of the murder of Sean Brown, a member of the GAA (Gaelic Athletic Association), close to Heaney's former home in Bellaghy. What is now imagined, as the actual intervenes, all too sensuously, in the realm of the mythological, is 'Hose water smashing hard back off the asphalt | In the car park where his athlete's blood ran cold'.

A roaming international intelligence alert to the challenges of modernity and globalization is evident in the later poems, even as Heaney turns back to reflect on where he started out in *District and Circle* (2006). The sonnet proves an ideal form for holding in suspension here and there, then and now, as Heaney embarks on a series of imaginative forays into his childhood past, transporting us through the streets of his district and circling around the

---

50. Jason David Hall, *Seamus Heaney's Rhythmic Contract* (Basingstoke: Palgrave Macmillan, 2009), p. 167.

memories it evokes, even entering the butcher's shop ('The Nod'), the hairdresser's makeshift salon ('A Clip'), and the tobacconist's store ('A Chow'). The London Underground provides a fitting setting for Heaney's encounter with his own poetic legacy and his own poetic creations in 'District and Circle' and 'The Tollund Man in Springtime' (both short sonnet sequences). The virtuosic handling of line, rhythm, and rhyme in these later sonnets is evidence, if we need it, of how far the sonnet has travelled, and of how it continues to be a vibrant and dynamic form for contemporary poets writing in English.

Paul Muldoon

Among the generation of Irish poets succeeding Seamus Heaney, Paul Muldoon has been the poet most obviously preoccupied with the experimental possibilities of the sonnet form. Muldoon's best-known sonnet, 'Why Brownlee Left', appears to take its bearings from familiar poems of Irish rural life and labour, including those of Patrick Kavanagh and Seamus Heaney, but it also owes something to the more mysterious and metaphysically speculative poetry of Louis MacNeice and Derek Mahon.[51] The opening lines recall Mahon's 'Going Home' (for Douglas Dunn): 'Why we died remains a mystery.'[52] Death is only one of a number of possible explanations for Brownlee's sudden disappearance, but surprisingly it is not one that tends to be given much prominence in critical discussions of this poem. The more usual way of reading 'Why Brownlee Left' is to suggest that the poem conjures up the idea of a dramatic departure prompted by yearnings for elsewhere, while holding in the balance the less romantic possibility that Brownlee (as his name suggests) is so thoroughly a part of his surroundings that he has ceased to have any other identity.

> Why Brownlee left, and where he went,
> Is a mystery even now.
> For if a man should have been content
> It was him; two acres of barley,
> One of potatoes, four bullocks,
> A milker, a slated farmhouse.
> He was last seen going out to plough
> On a March morning, bright and early.

---

51. Quotations from the poems of Paul Muldoon are from *Poems 1968–1998* (London: Faber, 2001).
52. Derek Mahon, *Poems 1962–1978* (Oxford: Oxford University Press, 1979), p. 61.

> By noon Brownlee was famous;
> They had found all abandoned, with
> The last rig unbroken, his pair of black
> Horses, like man and wife,
> Shifting their weight from foot to
> Foot, and gazing into the future. (84)

What makes this such a compelling poem, however, is the way in which its mysteries and ambiguities are held in suspense by the sonnet form. Even the metre is evasive, deftly shying away from the staple iambic pentameter of the English sonnet, varying both the stress patterns and the number of syllables in each line. The rhymes are also evasive, with 'early' pulling away from 'barley', and 'farmhouse' being placed at considerable distance, phonetically, from 'bullocks'. The deployment of rhymes conforms to neither Italian nor English patterns. The sonnet appears, in the manner prescribed by Thomas MacDonagh, to be fusing English lyricism with Irish metrics and versification. Bernard O'Donoghue claims that much of Muldoon's brilliant loose rhyming throughout his work functions as a variant on old Irish patterns. In particular, he draws attention to the seven-syllable opening of the sestet in 'Why Brownlee Left', which he sees as deriving from the Irish *deibidhe*, along with the practice of rhyming monosyllabic and disyllabic words, as with 'went' and 'content'.[53]

The apparent simplicity and deadpan style of the poem tend to conceal what is happening with the sonnet form. The octave both sets up narrative expectations and neatly contains within its orderly syntax the enumerated contents of Brownlee's supposed domestic contentment. The conventional turn, picking up and repeating Brownlee's name in the first line of the sestet, is strategically positioned at mid-day. If the sestet offers revelation, it also denies resolution. The expected turn to a new set of rhyme words in the sestet is abandoned, along with Brownlee's ploughshare. Oddly, the word 'famous' looks back to 'farmhouse', as if reinforcing the idea that Brownlee's escape is only an illusion. The word 'black' is given prominence in the sestet, in part because it has no obvious rhyme. It has to look back to 'bullocks' for a distant echo. The run-on line invites 'black shoes' or 'black boots', perhaps, but the sonnet gives us 'black | Horses', which for a moment appear with stately funereal presence, before our attention is diverted by the mundane domestic simile 'like man and wife'. Poetic feet and horses' feet happily coincide in the ostentatious enjambment, 'from foot to | Foot', while the

---

53. O'Donoghue, *Seamus Heaney and the Language of Poetry*, p. 33.

verbal participles, 'Shifting' and 'gazing', suspend the action in the present. The horses are gazing, *not* into the distance but into the future, as Brownlee presumably did, for better or worse, and the brilliantly enterprising half-rhyme of 'foot to' and 'future' both holds out and denies the possibility of fulfilment. Muldoon's sonnet subtly and slyly invites misreadings. Tim Kendall's book on Muldoon, for instance, includes the poem in full but mistakenly gives the final line as 'gazing into the distance'. For 'distance' read 'future'.[54]

Clair Wills claims that the strangest thing about the enigma in 'Why Brownlee Left' is 'surely that there is no enigma...the sestet's single sentence pulls inevitably towards the final image' of the horses as man and wife, and this, she says, is indicative of Brownlee's wish to 'deviate from the marital plot'.[55] This seems to wrap the poem up a little too neatly. The poem doesn't, of course, discount an alternative reading, in which conjugal togetherness is precisely what Brownlee is seeking. In this reading, Brownlee is the Irish bachelor descendant of Kavanagh's Maguire, finally taking leave of his rural solitude and his hunger for something more fulfilling. Whatever we make of Brownlee's destiny, the poem's purposeful poise clearly has much to do with its status as a sonnet. It seems to do much more than simply acknowledge the fact that the sonnet form can readily accommodate Irish rural subject matter in the manner of Kavanagh and Heaney. The sonnet itself seems crucially poised and gazing into the future, as if in readiness for the more radical innovations in later works such as 'The More a Man Has, the More a Man Wants'. If it replays a familiar Irish theme of leaving and parting, it also cleverly gives the slip to the ploughing poems of Kavanagh and Heaney, including 'The Glanmore Sonnets', in which the trope of poetry as ploughing is so strongly marked.

'Lull', another sonnet in *Why Brownlee Left*, similarly looks into the future while shifting from foot to foot. Reflecting obliquely on the IRA ceasefire, the poem considers both the beneficent calm implied by lull and the consequences of being lulled into a false sense of security.

> I've heard it argued in some quarters
> That in Armagh they mow the hay
> With only a week to go to Christmas.
> That no one's in a hurry
>
> To save it, or their own sweet selves.
> Tomorrow is another day,

---

54. Tim Kendall, *Paul Muldoon* (Bridgend: Seren, 1996), p. 69.
55. Clair Wills, *Reading Paul Muldoon* (Newcastle: Bloodaxe, 1998), p. 78.

>   As your man said on the Mount of Olives.
>   The same is held of County Derry.
>
>   Here and there up and down the country
>   There are still houses where the fire
>   Hasn't gone out in a century.
>
>   I know that eternal interim;
>   I think I know what they're waiting for
>   In Tyrone, Fermanagh, Down and Antrim.   (81)

As so often in Muldoon's work, a familiar colloquial voice invests with thoughtful reasoning what turns out to be palpable nonsense. Here, the language of proverb (making hay while the sun shines) is nicely confused with the commercial language of Christmas shopping. The octave underwrites the ethic of taking one's time with an appeal in the second quatrain to the Sermon on the Mount, but this, too, is made questionable by a relentless use of cliché and by a colloquial over-insistence on Christ's incarnation among us: 'Tomorrow is another day, | As your man said on the Mount of Olives.' Clearly, no one is in a hurry to save themselves, either spiritually or physically. 'Sweet selves' sarcastically picks up the suggestion of rotting hay, though of course to 'mow the hay' is, in any case, an absurdity, since hay (as Muldoon is careful to point out in his 1998 volume of that title) is grass that has already been mown.

The insistence that what goes on in Armagh also goes on in Derry seems to lend authority to the octave, but the geographical spread of that general principle throughout the sestet is cause for consternation rather than celebration. What initially looks like trust in providence begins to look like self-defeating enterprise, if not reckless intransigence. The houses where the fire 'hasn't gone out in a century' might be indicative of life-affirming tradition and continuity, but just as likely this is the fire, real or metaphorical, of burning sectarian passion. The rhyme scheme of the sonnet deftly captures its prevailing ambiguity and confusion. Hay and hurry appear to rhyme by virtue of their initial consonants and near vowel sounds, but hay and hurry rhyme more obviously with day and Derry in the second quatrain. Similarly, country and century might appear to set up a new rhyme in the sestet, but they also carry forward the earlier 'hurry'/'Derry' rhyme. There is no single or obvious way of transcribing the rhyme scheme. This is not just playful indulgence but a serious observation—as the troubling rhyme of interim and Antrim suggests—of how poetry is both a shaping by, and a shaping of, the politics of its time. The closing tercet of the sonnet balances the sure knowledge of the lull, whose paradoxical eternal interim invites despair, with the uncertain outcome of a widespread wish for change. The gathering place names add as much weight to misery as they do to hope. If Muldoon slyly introduces a phrase from another poem of ponderous waiting—'Whose woods these are I think I know'—he also creates something strikingly new in crossing the sonnet with the Irish *dinnseannchas* or place name poem.

Muldoon's 1983 volume *Quoof* uses the sonnet form with impressive versatility, exploiting both its lyric concentration and its narrative potential, as well as showing a new willingness to experiment with line length and deployment of rhyme. At the same time as experimenting with the form, Muldoon finds ways of making it accommodate the political realities of modern Ulster, including the continual threat of violence. 'The Sightseers' uses the sonnet form to set a scene of family togetherness on a Sunday afternoon in the summer against the memory of a night of violence. The new roundabout at Ballygawley is not a promising landmark, but for the speaker it offers an exciting alternative to visiting dead relatives.

> My father and mother, my brother and sister
> and I, with uncle Pat, our dour best-loved uncle,
> had set out that Sunday afternoon in July
> in his broken-down Ford
>
> not to visit some graveyard—one died of shingles,
> one of fever, another's knees turned to jelly—
> but the brand-new roundabout at Ballygawley,
> the first in mid-Ulster.
>
> Uncle Pat was telling us how the B-Specials
> had stopped him one night somewhere near Ballygawley
> and smashed his bicycle
>
> And made him sing the Sash and curse the Pope of Rome.
> They held a pistol so hard against his forehead
> there was still the mark of an O when he got home.   (110)

The flexible line length is well suited to the relaxed storytelling mode in which the sonnet begins. A staple twelve-syllable line is played off against a shorter six-syllable line at the end of the first two quatrains and the first tercet. The ominous closing line is the exception to this pattern. Although the longer line (with its emphasis on 'home') creates an illusory sense of resolution and relief, the peculiar rhymes elsewhere are strangely unsettling. 'Ford' in the opening quatrain rhymes distantly with 'forehead' in the closing tercet, while 'uncle', 'shingles', and 'B-Specials' chime awkwardly, and 'Ballygawley' rhymes with itself. 'July' finds an echo in 'jelly'. The only full rhyme in the sonnet is 'Rome' and 'home', but the rhyme is not ecumenically promising. The turn of the sonnet, while maintaining the temporal framework of the family day out, introduces Uncle Pat's unsettling memory of sectarian violence on the part of those who are supposed to be the upholders of law and order, the notorious B-Specials. The closing lines record the novelty of a salient detail without veering from the dispassionate anecdotal style that characterizes the rest of the narrative. The imprinted O of the pistol neatly reproduces the image of the roundabout, suggesting a pervasive sense of entrapment, as well as a more immediate cry of pain.

The title poem 'Quoof' is one of the strongest sonnets in the collection, although its apparent concerns are common enough in Muldoon's work: the father–son relationship, the journey from Ireland to America, the pleasures and pains of sexual relationships, the felicities and estrangements of language. There is a vulnerable, childlike playfulness in the images of the hot water bottle and the fabled yeti, but also a darker set of preoccupations establishing connections between sexual experience and linguistic experience, while leaving those connections tantalizingly unclear:

> How often have I carried our family word
> for the hot water bottle
> to a strange bed,
> as my father would juggle a red-hot half-brick
> in an old sock
> to his childhood settle.
> I have taken it into so many lovely heads
> or laid it between us like a sword.
>
> A hotel room in New York City
> with a girl who spoke hardly any English,
> my hand on her breast
> like the smouldering one-off spoor of the yeti
> or some other shy beast
> that has yet to enter the language.   (112)

There is a teasing corollary between the strange word for the hot water bottle ('quoof') and the strange bed to which it (the word, not the bottle) is carried. For the narrator, of course, this is not a strange word but a 'family word', and at one level the poem reflects on the intimacies and the estrangements that language can beget.

The sonnet form is used resourcefully to explore the nature of inclusive and exclusive uses of words. Narrative flexibility is achieved through an extended twelve-syllable line played off against a much shorter line ('as my father would juggle a red-hot half-brick | in an old sock'), but 'Quoof' also plays with the usual quatrain-tercet division of octave and sestet, choosing to divide the octave syntactically into two tercets and a couplet and the sestet into three couplets. The turn is sudden and abrupt, transporting us from the parochial 'childhood settle' to the cosmopolitan sophistication of 'A hotel room in New York City'. The lack of a main verb in the sestet gives the sexual encounter 'with a girl who spoke hardly any English' a strong sense of stasis or arrested movement. The rhymes appear to establish meaningful connections while simultaneously denying them, as the half rhyme of 'word' and 'sword' in the octave suggests. The sestet rhymes 'English' and 'language' as it contemplates the problems of communication. The rhyming of 'city' and 'yeti' with the internal rhyme 'yet to' sets up a pattern of expectation, but the sonnet slyly withholds the conventional rhyming satisfaction of the sonnet form, leaving us on the very threshold of entry into meaning.

The *tour de force* in Muldoon's work, as far as the sonnet form is concerned, is the closing, culminating poem of *Quoof*, 'The More a Man Has the More a Man Wants'. In this bewildering sequence of forty-nine phantasmagorical stanzas, Muldoon performs his most audacious and adventurous experiments with the sonnet and the sonnet sequence. The sonnet form buckles and bends, mutates and morphs, as it seeks to withstand the pressures of political violence and the multiple confusions of postmodern culture. Muldoon's extraordinary achievement is to fertilize and hybridize the sonnet through a sustained exposure of the form to, and interaction with, the widest possible range of other literary and cultural forms, from medieval myth to modern pop. Ovid has a cameo appearance in the poem's metamorphic shifts, while *Gawain and the Green Knight* and the Irish *Buile Suibhne* (recalling the fate of the mad King Sweeney) underwrite the quest motif. The presence of *Kidnapped*, *Treasure Island*, and *Alice and Wonderland* suggest that the poem is also an adventure story, while allusions to American Romanticism in the writings of Thoreau, Emerson, and Hawthorne serve as an ironic counterpoint to the disgraces and debasements of contemporary culture. If the sonnet sequence swells with the dense intertextual freight of earlier literary works, the individual sonnets within it are streamlined with a startling sparseness of technique that at times recalls the experimental canvasses of Pablo Picasso and Jackson Pollock. It is little wonder that critics of these sonnets have tended to resort to painterly terms as a way of explaining their formal devices and procedures, variously describing them as abstract, surrealist, and even cubist. So radically renovated and reworked are these sonnets, that the clever echo in line 5 of Sonnet 10—'*for thou art so possessed with murd'rous hate*'—sounds like a distant memory of the sonnet's own genetic origins in the work of Shakespeare (131). Amidst the sheer variety and abundance of literary and cultural allusions in the sonnet sequence, there are two principal organizing myths or frameworks, though these are employed in a parodic, debunking style that questions the very notion of myth as a totalizing cognitive structure. The first of these is the old Irish *aisling* or dream vision in which Ireland is figured as a beautiful enchantress, and the second is the Native American cycle of Trickster stories, adopted here from the legends of the Winnebago Indians. These two cultural types have their debased counterparts in the two anti-heroes, the Irish terrorist, Gallogly, and his alter ego or nemesis, the American Indian, Mangan Jones. The two figures continually merge and mutate. Gallogly, a derivation of Gallowglass (an early Gaelic mercenary), otherwise known as Golightly, is a shape-shifter who repeatedly and bafflingly turns into birds and beasts, while Jones is an avenging Apache (or is it Oglala Sioux?) who is 'busily tracing the family tree | of an Ulster man who had some hand | in the massacre at Wounded Knee' (134). The offending hand (carrying suggestions of the Red Hand of Ulster) reappears at the end of the poem as the self-destructive hand of the composite Gallogly/Jones.

For all the weight of literary and cultural allusion that the sequence carries, the sonnets themselves have a compelling immediacy and verbal excitement. Muldoon appears to have reinvented the sonnet as film script, endowing it with vivid sound effects and visual imagery. Gallogly is introduced to us in what appears to be the opening of a cinematic thriller rather than a sonnet:

> At four in the morning he wakes
> to the yawn of brakes,
> the snore of a diesel engine.
> Gone. All she left
> is a froth of bra and panties. (127)

All of the familiar resources of the sonnet, except for the staple fourteen lines, are radically overhauled so that the English lyric line gives way to a spoken voice much more vigorous and varied than we have seen before.

Rhyme, metre, line length, and syllabification are all dramatically revised in the interests of a new and urgent poetic perspective. Rhyme is used sparingly but resourcefully, while syntax is deployed for cinematic and dramatic effect, as with the strategic placing of the single word 'Gone' in the lines above. Sudden shifts of tense function like filmic cuts, as in the chilling depiction of the murder of a UDR corporal.

> The U.D.R. corporal had come off duty
> to be with his wife
> while the others set about
> a follow-up search.
> When he tramped out just before twelve
> to exercise the greyhound
> he was hit by a single high-velocity
> shot.
> You could, if you like, put your fist
> in the exit wound
> in his chest.
> He slumps
> in the spume of his own arterial blood
> like an overturned paraffin lamp.   (134–5)

The initial pluperfect tense seems amiably chatty, but the switch to the past tense initiated with the word 'When' prepares us for what is about to happen, just as the association of the greyhound with speed prepares us, strangely, for the high-velocity shot. That single, isolated word 'shot' is stunningly positioned at the end of the octave. A further disarming shift of tense occurs with the turn between octave and sestet. The sudden intimacy of the second-person address is intensified by the polite insertion of 'if you like' which exploits the modal instability of the auxiliary 'could', bizarrely changing the expression from colloquial astonishment at the fist-sized wound to one of dubious pleasure. The plump consonants in 'slump' and 'spume' and 'lamp' seem to swell the clinically specific 'arterial' blood. The rapid cut from the two-syllable line 'He slumps' to the eleven-syllable line that follows is characteristic of the filmic fluency that Muldoon is able to capture throughout the sequence. The paraffin lamp simile brilliantly signifies a life snuffed out and is all the more effective in its comparison of the slumped body of the UDR man with an inanimate household object. For all its apparent irregularity, the sonnet functions through a precise observation of the proper divisions inherent in the form. The octave-sestet division, the quatrain-tercet sub-divisions, and the characteristic turn are all used with devastating effect.

Muldoon explodes the lexical field of the sonnet, violently displacing the well-established vocabulary of love, nature, and religion, with a spiky, streetwise diction drawn from contemporary colloquial speech and consumerist jargon. The local specificities of vernacular English in 'scum', 'squats', and 'skedaddled' (all in the first sonnet) jostle with the widely travelled, flashy capitals of company names and brand names like Hertz and Avis, Esso and Mobil, Cortina and Citroën. Different linguistic registers are disconcertingly played off against each other with a level tonality that becomes increasingly difficult to gauge, especially when the subject is violence.

> Once the local councillor straps
> himself into the safety belt
> of his Citroën
> and skids up the ramp
> from the municipal car park
> he upsets the delicate balance
> of a mercury-tilt
> boobytrap.
> Once they collect his smithereens
> he doesn't quite add up.
> They're shy of a foot, and a calf
> which stems
> from his left shoe like a severely
> pruned-back shrub.   (138)

The sonnet form controls and contains the violence here with excruciating exactness. The repetition of 'Once' across the opening lines of the octave and the sestet powerfully acknowledges both the singularity and the frequency of this horrific event, while 'boobytrap' is cunningly deposited between the two constituent parts of the sonnet. Leaving aside the awful irony of the useless safety belt, the sonnet focuses with ruthless attention on what remains. The stiff formality of 'councillor', 'municipal', and 'mercury-tilt' is swiftly dispatched by the callous cliché of 'smithereens', 'doesn't quite add up', and 'shy of a foot' which are then given a further cruel twist with the hideous horticultural 'stems' and 'shrub'. If, at one level, the sonnet functions as an assault on what Seamus Heaney has called the 'civilised outrage' of public opinion,[56] including the sanitized 'coverage' of news bulletins, it also exposes the unfathomable gap between the actuality of sectarian violence and *any* attempt to depict it in language.

---

56. Heaney, 'Punishment', *Opened Ground*, p. 118.

'The More a Man Has the More a Man Wants' confronts us with shootings, bombings, hijackings, glue-sniffing, drug dealing, and armed thefts, and it cuts and compresses the sonnet form so that it shapes itself to the violent disorder of contemporary urban culture. At the same time, it reaches back to the revolutionary aspirations of United Ireland and the heroic endeavours of Wolfe Tone, Napper Tandy, and the Croppy Boys. Like Ciaran Carson's sonnets in *The Twelfth of Never*, it revels in the songs and stories of the 1798 Rebellion while parodically defusing them. Dante's Beatrice is transfigured as a heroine of the French Revolution, sympathetic to the Irish cause, though in a later incarnation she is a lager-drinking karaoke queen in Roxborough, near the Moy, and the blessing she gives is no blessing at all. Throughout the sequence, the sonnet is fruitfully crossed with the Irish *aisling* or dream-voyage popular in the eighteenth century:

> When who should walk in but Beatrice,
> large as life, or larger,
> sipping her one glass of lager
> and singing her one song.
> If he had to do it all over again
> he would let her shave his head
> in memory of '98
> and her own, the French, Revolution.
> The son of the King of the Moy
> met this child on the Roxborough
> estate. *Noblesse*, she said. *Noblesse
> oblige.* And her tiny nipples
> were bruise-bluish, wild raspberries.
> The song she sang was 'The Croppy Boy'.   (137)

Ciaran Carson, commenting on the 'here-and-now' demotic qualities of Muldoon's verse, observes how myth is exposed and undermined by its close juxtaposition with everyday speech: 'It doesn't pay homage to notional ideas of Ireland, to the received myths. It includes the myths, of course, and then sets them up against pub-talk and slabbering.'[57] Muldoon's sonnet sequence closes with a virtuosic rendering of pub-talk and slobbering, as Gallogly (transformed into Jones in a Jekyll and Hyde dénouement) is blown apart by a homemade bomb planted at a petrol station.

> It was this self-same pump attendant
> who dragged the head and torso

---

57. Interview with Ciaran Carson, in Steven Matthews, *Irish Poetry: Politics, History, Negotiation* (Basingstoke: Macmillan, 1987), p. 189.

> clear
> and mouthed an Act of Contrition
> in the frazzled ear
> and overheard
> those already-famous last words
> *Moose... Indian.*
> 'Next of all wus the han'.' 'Be Japers.'
> 'The sodgers cordonned-off the area
> wi' what-ye-may-call-it tape.'
> 'Lunimous.' 'They foun' this hairy
> han' wi' a drowneded man's grip
> on a lunimous stone no bigger than a...'
>
> 'Huh.'   (147)

The repeated mispronunciation and the shrugging, dismissive 'Huh' seem to offer little illumination, but the 'luminous stone' recalls the 'pebble of quartz' in Robert Frost's poem 'For Once, Then, Something', and both acknowledges the inevitable limitations and distortions of vision and asserts the need to go on looking. There is evidence enough in the sheer vitality and linguistic exuberance of Muldoon's sonnets to support his belief in F. W. Bateson's claims that 'the reading of poetry and the writing of poetry are both social duties, essential acts of citizenship'. On the one hand, he is tempted by the Keatsian notion that poetry 'should be a friend | To soothe the cares, and lift the thoughts of man', but on the other he 'disavows the notion of poetry as a moral force, offering respite or retribution'.[58] If poetry is a making of an artefact—a sonnet, say—it is also a making aware, a transforming and heightening of consciousness.

'Hard Drive', in *Moy Sand and Gravel* (2002), has continuities with 'Lull' in its ritual play with proverbs and place names, but this is very much a post-ceasefire poem, with the habitual past tense perhaps suggesting that things have moved on: 'I would drive through Seskinore.'[59] Unlikely as it might seem, all of these places, including Derryfubble, can be found on a map of contemporary Ireland. The act of driving and saying the names recalls Heaney's poem 'The Tollund Man' ('driving, | Saying the names | Tollund, Grauballe, Nebelgard'), but this is a poem of a different order, well beyond the wounding and self-wounding of *North*.[60] The sonnet is curtailed by the formal incantation of proverbs and place names. It drives straight over the

---

58. Paul Muldoon, 'Getting Round: Notes Towards an *Ars Poetica*', F. W. Bateson Memorial Lecture, *Essays in Criticism* 48 (1998), pp. 121, 127.
59. Paul Muldoon, *Moy Sand and Gravel* (London: Faber, 2002), p. 3.
60. Heaney, 'The Tollund Man', *Opened Ground*, p. 65.

turn, but does observe the traditional closing couplet of the Shakespearean sonnet. 'Keeping that wound green' recalls not only 'The Wearing of the Green' from 1798 and its echo at the end of Yeats's 'Easter 1916', but also the end of Derek Mahon's elegy for Louis MacNeice, 'rinsing the choked mud, keeping the colours new'.[61] This is a teasingly ambivalent line, testifying to both enduring nationalist fervour and the stubborn intransigence by which green might turn to gangrene. If the title acknowledges the hard drive of nationalist struggle, it also playfully undermines that suggestion with the alternative reading of 'Hard Drive' as the pre-programmed hard drive of contemporary computer-speak. Like other recent Muldoon poems, it seeks to circumvent some of the hardened oppositions and tensions of sectarian politics through a pervasive playfulness and ambivalence, signalling a changed political order but retaining a circumspect outlook nonetheless.

The title poem of *Horse Latitudes* (2006) is a sonnet sequence written in the context of the American invasion of Iraq in 2003. It maps a variety of places, all beginning with B, where major battles have taken place: Bannockburn, Bosworth Field, Blenheim, Bull Run, Burma. The missing place, which also happens to be the fourteenth in what would otherwise be a sonnet of sonnets, is Baghdad. All of the battles included in the sequence have involved the use of horses or mules. 'Intercut with those battle scenes', as Muldoon's 'Note on the Text' informs us, 'are accounts of a "battle" with cancer by a former lover, here named Carlotta, and a commentary on the agenda of what may only be described as the Bush "regime"'.[62] The opening sonnet in the sequence is 'Beijing':

> I could still hear the musicians
> cajoling those thousands of clay
> horses and horsemen through the squeeze
> when I woke beside Carlotta.
> Life-size, also. Also terra-cotta.
> The sky was still a terra-cotta frieze
> over which her grandfather still held sway
> with the set square, fretsaw, stencil,
> plumb line, and carpenter's pencil
> his grandfather brought from Roma.
> Proud-fleshed Carlotta. Hypersarcoma.

---

61. Mahon, 'In Carrowdore Churchyard', *Poems 1962–78*, p. 3.
62. Muldoon's 'Note on the Text' of 'Horse Latitudes' accompanies the first printing of the sonnets in his *Medley for Morin Khur* (London: Enitharmon, 2005), n.p. The sonnets were later reprinted in *Horse Latitudes* (London: Faber, 2006), with 'Beijing' on p. 3.

> For now our highest ambition
> was simply to bear the light of the day
> we had once been planning to seize.

Beijing is conjured up in the powerful image of the terracotta army of warriors and horsemen excavated in China in 1974, with that image also impressing upon us the ambitious making of an art that might survive the centuries. At the same time, the clay is an unignorable reminder of human mortality, just as the 'Life-size' figures ironically comment on Carlotta's imminent death. The grandfather is a planner and a craftsman who represents survival and inheritance, though his 'fretsaw' is an ominous image of pain and separation. The cruel rhyming of 'Roma' and 'Hypersarcoma' is indicative of losses and collisions that the sonnet is at pains to expose rather than conceal. Embedded in the desultory closing tercet are passing allusions to Andrew Marvell, invoking both 'An Horatian Ode upon the Return of Cromwell from Ireland' ('As if his highest plot | To plant the Bergamot') and 'To His Coy Mistress' (with its strong *carpe diem* theme).[63] The subtle shift of tense at the end of the sonnet cancels out the possibility of seizing the day, with the abject mood of the lines resulting in part from their delayed and distant rhymes. With a curiously elaborate rhyme scheme (*abcddcbeeffabc*), the sonnet contrives to return us to where we started, in clay. *Horse Latitudes* revitalizes the sonnet and the sonnet sequence. It brings together the principal functions that have preoccupied the sonnet since its inception, impressing upon us love poem, elegy, and polemic all at once. There is a playful swagger in the title of Muldoon's *Songs and Sonnets* (2012), with its knowing nod to John Donne and the English Renaissance lyric. Muldoon goes on writing some of the most inventive and provocative sonnets in the English language, and there is no sign of any abatement.

Ciaran Carson

Since the 1980s, and especially since the publication of *The Irish for No* (1987) and *Belfast Confetti* (1989), Ciaran Carson has acquired a reputation as a master of the long line, a poet who cannily crosses the English lyric with the endlessly digressive narratives and tall tales of the Irish storyteller

---

63. Andrew Marvell, *The Complete Poems*, ed. George deF. Lord (London: David Campbell, 1993), pp. 23, 56.

or *seanachie*. That long line is allied to an unflinching and remorseless way of seeing. Frequently it conveys the bewildering experience of mapping a city that keeps on changing, but it also suggests the relentless effort of an imagination that refuses to be quelled by violence, the existential persistence of a voice that goes on talking at the same time as it sceptically undermines its own ostensible desire for meaning and order. In the late 1990s, a new lyric intensity pervaded Carson's work and found its most creative expression in a prolific series of sonnets. Significantly, it was the twelve-syllable or alexandrine line of the French sonnet that Carson found most appealing. His versions of sonnets by Charles Baudelaire, Stéphane Mallarmé, and Arthur Rimbaud in *The Alexandrine Plan* (1998) provided the blueprint for the immensely ambitious sequence of seventy-seven alexandrine sonnets in *The Twelfth of Never* (1999). The earlier book, dedicated to Paul Muldoon, is a remarkable set of translations of late nineteenth-century French Symbolist and Decadent poetry with unmistakably Irish nuances and allusions.

The opening sonnet of *The Alexandrine Plan* opportunistically seizes on the Hibernian possibilities in the title of Rimbaud's 'Au-Caberet Vert', felicitously rendering it as 'the green bar' and cheekily turning the narrator from a bohemian French wanderer to a garrulous Irish rover.

> I'd ripped my boots to pieces on the pebbly roads
> Since Monday was a week. I walked into Kingstown.
> Found myself in the old Green Bar. I ordered loads
> Of cool ham, bread and butter. It was nearly sundown.
>
> Pleased as Punch, I stretched my legs beneath the shamrock
> Table. I admired the tacky '50s décor.
> Then this vacant waitress in a tit-enhancing frock
> Came on and wiggled up to me, her eyes galore
>
> With hints of smoochy kisses and her gorgeous platter
> Of green gherkins, slabs of ham and bread and butter,
> Rosy, garlic-scented ham; and then she filled my beer mug
>
> With a bright smile, and turned herself into a ray
> Of sunshine, like an unexpected Lady Day.
> I guzzled it all into me. *Glug. Glug. Glug. Glug.*[64]

The advantages of the alexandrine form are immediately apparent in the luxuriously long rambling opening line, playing off its plosive consonants against a variety of vowel sounds. Like the original, Carson's sonnet

---

64. Ciaran Carson, *The Alexandrine Plan* (Oldcastle: Gallery Press, 1998), p. 13. Further references are to this edition and page numbers are given within brackets in the text.

intersperses run-on lines with shorter syntactical units emulating the rhythms of actual speech. Rimbaud's 'Charlerois' is neatly translated as Kingstown (now Dun Laoghaire), conveniently resituating the sonnet in the Dublin environs, while 'la table | Verte' is ostentatiously rendered as 'the shamrock | Table'. In other respects, Carson dutifully acknowledges the technical resources and procedures of the Rimbaud sonnet, including the quatrain-tercet sub-divisions, line breaks, and syntax, and even the deployment of rhymes. The discipline of form permits some liberties of expression, including the nicely colloquial 'Pleased as Punch' for 'Bien heureux' and the blatantly anachronistic 'tacky '50s décor' for 'les sujets tres nifs'. The ironic re-employment of a familiar anglicized French word to assist with his translation is typical of Carson's ingenuity in these sonnets. His easy colloquialisms are strenuously serviceable. The versatile opening 'Came on', for instance, suggests both coming on duty and acting in a sexually provocative way, but it also retains the performative connotations of cabaret (coming on stage). Anticipating the generic modulations and transformations in *The Twelfth of Never*, 'The Green Bar' crosses the French sonnet with the Irish *aisling*. Having entered the Green Bar at sundown, the narrator finds himself blessed with the sunshine of 'an unexpected Lady Day', and consumes it with an appreciative pleasure. Carson closes his version of Rimbaud's sonnet with his own distinctive signature: a phonetic, onomatopoeic rendering of the verb to drink.

In his versions of poems by Mallarmé, Carson catches the yearning isolation and inwardness of the originals, as well as their penchant for vivid symbols of transcendence, including the familiar swan. 'The Sonneteer' ('Le Sonneur') depicts the writer as a 'lonely campanologist' turning out 'muted, brittle tinkles' on the bell of poetry and anticipating a suicidal death on the end of his own rope. Carson observes the confessional candour that marks the sudden turn between octave and sestet in Mallarmè's sonnet, but he also captures something of the desperate, self-defeating ironies of his near-contemporary, Derek Mahon: 'I am that man. Alas! Most nights I dangle on | An anxious tangled cable' (57). 'At the Sign of the Swan' reproduces the extravagant praise bestowed upon that favourite symbol of Mallarme, Baudelaire, and Yeats, brilliantly capturing the pervasive image of the bird as poet by deftly rhyming 'line' and 'sign' and playing on the phonetic similarity of 'sign' and 'Cygne': 'Beautiful ghost, condemned by his own brilliant line, | Engraved within a pond of icy crystallite, | He maintains the useless exile of a Swan, or sign' (51).

Carson's versions of sonnets by Baudelaire are infused with enticing allusions to popular film and song. 'À une passante' is translated as 'Brief Encounter', with another glance at the *aisling*: 'She stepped out from nowhere, slim and tall, dressed in black' (39). 'Le Possèdè' becomes 'Just Crazy about You' and brings the Parisian muse of Baudelaire's sonnet to the catwalk and the nightclub (73). 'The Dongless Bell' (an inspired translation of 'La cloche fêlèe') carries echoes of Elvis Presley ('I'm all shook up'), while 'Blue Grass' conveys the marijuana-induced melancholy of 'Parfum exotique', simultaneously evoking the recumbent rhythms of country music (83, 77). Carson's perceptive remark on the use of stock-phrases and clichés in country music illuminates his own rejuvenating linguistic practices in both *The Alexandrine Plan* and *The Twelfth of Never*. 'If "stock" at one point in its history meant a tree-trunk, it is augmented by a family tree of branching limbs and leafy ornament, and if "cliché" was a stereotype plate or a bank of type, then an impression taken from it can come out freshly-minted as an original print.'[65]

The Twelfth of Never is a cornucopia of cultural, political, and mythical allusion, ranging imaginatively over revolutionary France and Ireland in the 1780s and 1790s, the Napoleonic Wars, Imperial Japan, and the trenches of the First World War, occasionally surfacing in contemporary Ireland or the crowded streets of modern Tokyo.[66] Keats and Coleridge rub shoulders with Kavanagh and Mangan. The gaudy poppy and the humble potato are the salient emblems of the sonnet sequence, both of them productive of mind-expanding drugs and drink. The rising sun of the Japanese flag finds its counterpart in the rising moon of Irish revolutionary ballads. The sonnet form is repeatedly fused with the *aisling* and also with the vernacular idiom of Irish street songs and popular lyrics. The title of the volume acknowledges the popular idiom of improbability, but it also calls to mind the Loyalist commemoration of the Battle of the Boyne on the twelfth of July. At the same time, it evokes the undying love celebrated in the song by Paul Webster and Jerry Livingston, made famous in a recording by Johnny Mathis in 1957. The song shares with Irish ballads the pervasive imagery of roses, but it also asserts the continuity of both love and poetry: 'I'll love you 'til the poets run out of rhyme, | Until the Twelfth of Never and that's a long, long time.'[67]

---

65. Ciaran Carson, *Last Night's Fun: A Book About Music, Food and Time* (London: Pimlico, 1996), p. 157.
66. *The Twelfth of Never* was first published in 1999 by Picador (London) and The Gallery Press (Oldcastle).
67. See David Roberts, *British Hit Singles & Albums*, 19th edn (London: Guinness World Records Limited, 2006), p. 284.

Repeatedly, the sonnets in *The Twelfth of Never* dissolve the myths that have hardened around historical events and their monumental dates, allowing dream and fantasy to wash over the fixed and fossilized terrain of sectarian politics, and countering the violence of both revolutionary insurrection and imperial power with images of peace and sleep. By revisiting and revising popular myths, songs, and stories, exuberantly foregrounding their patently fictive qualities, Carson both acknowledges their durability and disarms them, consigning them to the realm of rhetoric rather than reality. Like Muldoon, Carson turns his parodic gaze on poetic tradition itself, mixing genres and registers and intertextual allusions with impressive ease and fluency.

'Spraying the Potatoes' transforms Kavanagh's celebrated images of Irish rural labour into a dark fantasy of political execution. The octave of the sonnet closely echoes Kavanagh's poem of the same title, right down to the knapsack-sprayer and the names of the flowering potato plants, but it turns the potato drills into a military metaphor: 'Knapsack sprayer on my back, I marched the drills | Of blossoming potatoes—Kerr's Pinks in a frivelled blue, | The Arran Banners wearing white.'[68] Kavanagh's 'axle-roll of a rut-locked cart' now signifies the ominous arrival of the tumbrel. The sestet presents the vision of a 'verdant man' being bound and taken to his execution. The blue and white of the potatoes seem to consort with the red of the troopers as the man in green swings from an oak tree: 'I watched him swing in his Derry green for hours and hours, | His popping eyes of apoplectic liberty | That blindly scanned the blue and white potato flowers.' The sonnet rehearses the nationalist sentiments of Irish political ballads associated with 1798, but it also declares its origins in other texts rather than in history, self-consciously foregrounding its own fictiveness in the slightly theatrical repetition of 'pop' in 'apoplectic' and in the rather arch and poetical use of 'scanned' in the final line.

The personification of Ireland as Roisin Dubh or Dark Rosaleen is a recurring motif in several sonnets which adopt the nationalist emblems of the Irish Rebellion of 1798 and present themselves as variants of the familiar *aisling*. The sonnet simply titled '1798' is a floral tribute to Dark Rosaleen, although the poppy appears to take precedence over the rose:

---

68. Ciaran Carson, *Collected Poems* (Gallery Press, 2008), p. 423. Further quotations from *The Twelfth of Never* are from this edition of the poems and page numbers are given within brackets in the text.

> I met her in the garden where the poppies grow,
> Quite over-canopied with luscious woodbine,
> And her cheeks were like roses, or blood dropped on snow;
> Her pallid lips were red with Papal Spanish wine.
>
> Lulled in these wild flowers, with dance and delight,
> I took my opportunity, and grasped her hand.
> She then disclosed the eyelids of her second sight,
> And prophesied that I'd forsake my native land.
>
> Before I could protest, she put her mouth to mine
> And sucked the broken English from my Gaelic tongue.
> She wound me in her briary arms of eglantine.
>
> Two centuries have gone, yet she and I abide
> Like emblems of a rebel song no longer sung,
> Or snowy blossoms drifting down the mountainside.   (377)

A principal source here is James Clarence Mangan's 'Dark Rosaleen', which acknowledges the support of Catholic Spain and praises Ireland as 'my flower of a flower'. Mangan's patriotic eulogy, 'To My Native Land' (1832) is also echoed in Carson's sonnet.[69] The collusion of roses and snow, however, suggests that nationalist sentiment is being tempered here with the ironic and circumspect intelligence that informs Louis MacNeice's much-admired 'Snow' (1935). Although the sonnet makes lavish use of the alexandrine line, its potent music also derives from the luscious English lyricism of Shakespeare's comedies. Line 2 is lifted straight from Act 2, Scene 2 of *A Midsummer Night's Dream* (lines 250–1). The rhyme scheme of the sonnet is Shakespearean in the octave (*ababcdcd*) but deviates in the sestet, avoiding a rhyming couplet by prematurely introducing the 'g' rhyme (*efegfg*). The turn coincides magnificently with the kiss of Dark Rosaleen, but the lingering Shakespearean 'eglantine' implies that she hasn't altogether succeeded in sucking the broken English from the poet's Gaelic tongue. '1798' powerfully conveys the seductive glamour of nationalist iconography, while also subtly decommissioning those rebel emblems, willingly exchanging them for the delicate Japanese image of snowy blossoms in a closing glimpse of peace. The recollection of 'a rebel song no longer sung' is a reminder that Carson's prolific bursts of sonnet writing took place in the aftermath of the ceasefire announced by the Provisional IRA at the end of August 1994. The uncertain

---

69. For James Clarence Mangan, 'Dark Rosaleen' and 'To My Native Land', see Stephen Regan (ed.), *Irish Writing: An Anthology of Irish Literature in English 1789–1939* (Oxford: Oxford University Press, 2004), pp. 140, 146.

pause, the sense of campaigns coming to an end, and the possibility of a new political order all seem to shape the sonnets that constitute *The Twelfth of Never*. Yet the very title of the volume warns against excessive optimism, while its 'Envoy' insists that 'every fairy story has its variorum' and that 'the printed news is always unreliable' (427).

Michael Longley and Eavan Boland

That the sonnet continues to provide space for reflection on the most pressing public and political concerns in Ireland was strongly affirmed by Michael Longley's 'Ceasefire', published in the *Irish Times* two days after the IRA ceasefire of 31 August 1994.[70] Although the title signifies the sonnet's immediate relevance, its subject matter is drawn from Book XXIV of the *Iliad*, in which Priam, the Trojan king, goes to Achilles to request the dead body of his son. Longley emphasizes a shared humanity in the tears of the two men, but also an unexpected gentleness and carefulness in the midst of the Trojan War.

> I
> Put in mind of his own father and moved to tears
> Achilles took him by the hand and pushed the old king
> Gently away, but Priam curled up at his feet and
> Wept with him until their sadness filled the building.
> II
> Taking Hector's corpse into his own hands Achilles
> Made sure it was washed and, for the old king's sake,
> Laid out in uniform, ready for Priam to carry
> Wrapped like a present home to Troy at daybreak.
> III
> When they had eaten together, it pleased them both
> To stare at each other's beauty as lovers might,
> Achilles built like a god, Priam good-looking still
> And full of conversation, who earlier had sighed:
> IV
> 'I get down on my knees and do what must be done
> And kiss Achilles' hand, the killer of my son.'

What is most remarkable here is the way in which the sonnet provides a formal means of isolating and intensifying that particular moment of mutual understanding in the epic literature of war. It is almost as if the sonnet provides

---

70. Michael Longley, *Collected Poems* (London: Jonathan Cape, 2006), p. 225. Further quotations are from this edition of the poems and page numbers are given within brackets in the text.

a poetic space for reflection that corresponds with the political function of the ceasefire. The numbering of the constituent parts of the sonnet—three quatrains and a couplet—suggests an element of narrative derived from its epic progenitor, but it also stresses the importance of a carefully staged ritual in which the weeping and the washing of the body contribute to a dignified honouring of the dead. Longley employs a stately line of twelve or thirteen syllables. The quatrains, each of which rhymes on lines 2 and 4, reinforce the strong sense of ritual observation in the sonnet and culminate in the closing couplet with its emphasis on 'what must be done'—a tentative move towards forgiveness. 'Ceasefire' recalls Yeats's 'Leda and the Swan' in its allusions to the Trojan War, but the voice is altogether more meditative and subdued. The sonnet is tempered by the communal grief and loss beneath its own critical moment of ceasefire, but its sombreness is alleviated by a characteristic gentleness and generosity of spirit.

There are moments in Longley's later sonnets when the prophetic Yeatsian strain can be heard, though always his own carefully considered response to classical precedents is foremost in the writing. 'The Vision of Theoclymenus' recalls the Homeric seer from Argos who prophesied the return of Odysseus and the slaughter of Penelope's suitors, and it allows his nightmare vision to resonate through history, right through to its own terrible moment of contemplation:

>   What class of a nightmare are you living through,
>   Poor bastards, your faces, knees, shrouded in darkness,
>   The atmosphere electric with keening—for it all
>   Ends in tears—the walls bloody, and the crossbeams
>   Like branches after a cloudburst dripping blood... (252)

The sonnet appears to turn ironically from perceived distress to a declaration of the seer's 'unimpaired' intelligence, but it also speaks eloquently of the continuing need for a poetry capable of registering the pain and suffering of war with compassion and understanding. The mounting violence here is countered elsewhere by Longley's instinctive turning to the pastoral, elegiac side of his classical education. 'The Beech Tree' begins with the attitude of a lover, subtly exchanging the fierce antinomies of Yeats's 'great-rooted blossomer', the chestnut tree, for Virgil's beech, and settling for a quiet sleep beneath its branches. The unrhymed sonnet gently unfolds in a single ruminating sentence, delighting in the pleasures of the senses and reacquainting the poet with his younger self as it moves inevitably towards its restful close:

>   Leaning back like a lover against this beech tree's
>   Two-hundred-year-old pewter trunk, I look up

>   Through skylights into the leafy cumulus, and join
>   Everybody who has teetered where these huge roots
>   Spread far and wide their motionless mossy dance,
>   As though I'd begun my eclogues with a beech
>   As Virgil does, the brown envelopes unfolding
>   Like fans their transparent downy leaves, tassels
>   And prickly cups, mast, a fall of vermilion
>   And copper and gold, then room in the branches
>   For the full moon and her dusty lakes, winter
>   And the poet who recollects his younger self
>   And improvises a last line for the georgics
>   About snoozing under this beech tree's canopy.   (281)

Longley's penchant for writing nature sonnets that meditate on his own mortality is not, in itself, unusual, and it places him in a tradition that includes Shakespeare's Sonnet 73 ('That time of year thou mayst in me behold') with its poignant imagery of falling leaves.[71] What lends his sonnets a distinctive character and appeal is their intense naturalistic attention to detail. The 'tassels' and 'prickly cups' of 'The Beech Tree' have a botanical exactness that stands out in relief against the urge to view the natural world as metaphor.

   The Ghost Orchid (1995) initiated a new formal inventiveness and lyric intensity in Longley's work, and the sonnet is clearly a favoured form in *The Weather in Japan* (2000) and *Snow Water* (2004). There are love sonnets ('Autumn Lady's Tresses'), bird sonnets ('Stonechat', 'Dipper', 'Robin'), elegiac sonnets ('The Snow Leopard'), sonnets on the aftermath of the Second World War ('The Bullet Hole', 'Sweetie Papers'), and sonnets for fellow poets, painters, and sculptors ('Poetry', 'Remembering the Poets', 'Woodsmoke'). The bird sonnets have a sharpness and liveliness of perception reminiscent of John Clare, and a similar care for the delicate relations between creatures and their environment. The single sentence of 'Stonechat' begins and ends with the bird, but sweeps out across the landscape just before sunset, gathering impressions in the changing light of autumn: 'A flicker on the highest twig, a breast | That kindles the last of the fuchsia flowers | And the October sunset still to come...' (296). Longley's imagination is repeatedly drawn to the sights and sounds of the Mayo townland of Carrigskeewaun, in the west of Ireland, where the poet can see himself more clearly as part of an intricate and evolving ecology. 'Flight Feathers' transports us, in three quatrains and a

---

71. William Shakespeare, *The Complete Sonnets and Poems*, ed. Colin Burrow (Oxford: Oxford University Press, 2008), p. 527.

closing couplet, from nesting boxes to resting places, meditating on 'all of the birds that have disappeared', and finally situating the poet close to a burial mound (itself subject to natural erosion), familiar from his other poems about the west of Ireland. The poet's 'breastbone' both links him with bird-life and exposes his vulnerability and precariousness in the natural scheme of things: 'The tide-digested burial mound has almost gone. | A peregrine is stooping high above my breastbone' (288).

Like Robert Frost, Longley has been able to take the sonnet form and quietly render it capable of expressing both a delighted vision of the variegated natural world and a pained apprehension of human suffering and loss. Fran Brearton notes astutely how Longley challenges traditional assumptions about the subject matter of the sonnet, habitually bringing to the form an unsettling darkness of mood and theme.[72] The point is well illustrated by 'The Miner', in which the poet's namesake, William Longley, appears in the Durham Miners' Book of Remembrance in Durham Cathedral, prompting a dark meditation on memory, consciousness, and ultimate extinction:

> When they turn the page tomorrow, William Longley
> Will disappear back into darkness and danger
> And crawl on hands and knees in the crypt of the world
> Under houses ands outhouses and workshops and fields.   (312)

As Brearton suggests, the sonnet's durability and persistence as a form makes it for Longley a particularly apt vehicle 'in which to shape an apprehension of mortality'.[73] At the same time, the elegiac tenor of Longley's verse is gently relieved by an extraordinary delicacy of perception, or by a casual, self-deflating humour. 'The Snow Leopard', another clearly demarcated four-part sonnet like 'Ceasefire' and 'Flight Feathers', moves stealthily towards a cold and passionate Yeatsian close, and in the absence of any traditional consolation in the face of death offers its own heavenly, metamorphic image of survival: 'The snow leopard that vanishes in a whirlwind of snow | Can be seen stalking on soft paws among the clouds' (264). In contrast, 'Robin' contemplates for a moment the powerful elegiac symbolism of Yeats in 'The Wild Swans at Coole' and then whimsically settles for a more naturalistic idiom: 'I would count the swans but it hurts my eyes' (297).

Eavan Boland, in her experiments with the sonnet, both registers the formidable influence of Yeats and shows her determination to move

---

72. Fran Brearton, *Reading Michael Longley* (Tarset: Bloodaxe, 2006), p. 257.
73. Brearton, *Reading Michael Longley*, p. 257.

beyond it.[74] Among her earliest work in *New Territory* (1967), 'Yeats in Civil War' recalls the sustaining, nurturing image of the honey-bee in *The Tower* (1928), and finds in the career of Yeats a dubious but unignorable model for her own generation of Irish poets:

> *Presently a strange thing happened:*
> *I began to smell honey in places*
> *Where honey could not be.*
>
> In middle age you exchanged the sandals
> Of a pilgrim for a Norman keep
> In Galway. Civil war started, vandals
> Sacked your country, made off with your sleep:
>
> Somehow you arranged your escape
> Aboard a spirit-ship which every day
> Hoisted sail out of fire and rape,
> And on that ship your mind was stowaway.
>
> The sun mounted on a wasted place,
> But the wind at every door and turn
> Blew the smell of honey in your face
> Where there was none. Whatever we may learn
>
> You are its sum, struggling to survive—
> A fantasy of honey your reprieve.   (19)

Although perhaps too readily associating Yeats with fantasy and escape, the sonnet speaks out of a readiness to learn, with the uneasy rhyme of its closing couplet balancing the struggles of Irish history against the compensating sweetness of imaginative endeavour. In her critical and editorial work, Boland has candidly described how, as a young, aspiring Irish poet, she resisted the sonnet form: 'I was sure it was un-Irish, un-local, too courtly for a new republic, too finished to ever find a new beginning in the literature I was trying to understand.' Boland places 'Leda and the Swan' at the head of the twentieth-century section of her anthology, *The Making of a Sonnet* (2009). She makes it clear in the introduction that it was the anti-heroic Kavanagh, rather than the heroic Yeats, who convinced her of the 'age-old resilience of the form'.[75]

---

74. Quotations from the poems of Eavan Boland are from *New Collected Poems* (New York: Norton, 2008), unless otherwise specified.
75. Edward Hirsch and Eavan Boland (eds), *The Making of a Sonnet* (New York: Norton, 2008), pp. 44, 48.

'Heroic', from *The Lost Land* (1998), uses the sonnet form with great inventiveness to explore a girl's divided feelings about growing up in an Irish national culture in which violent struggle and patriotic sacrifice go hand in hand with religious devotion. The idea of praying to statues amplifies a strong concern with desire in a sonnet essentially concerned, like much of Boland's work, with sex and history. Boland subtly explores the way in which heroic ideals are encapsulated in civic monuments, and the way in which they speak to the present, aware that the sonnet is, itself, a kind of monument:

> Sex and history. And skin and bone.
> And the oppression of Sunday afternoon.
> Bells called the faithful to devotion.
> I was still at school and on my own.
> And walked and walked and sheltered from the rain.
> The patriot was made of drenched stone.
> His lips were still speaking. The gun
> he held had just killed someone.
> I looked up. And looked at him again.
> He stared past me without recognition.
> I moved my lips and wondered how the rain
> would taste if my tongue were made of stone.
> And wished it was. And whispered so that no one
> could hear it but him. Make me a heroine.   (269)

The poem dutifully observes the constituent parts of the sonnet—couplet, tercet, quatrains—while at the same time pulling it apart. It instigates a turn between the notional octave and the notional sestet, implying both respect in the speaker's 'looking up' and a strong sense of being ignored and excluded in the statue's 'staring past'. The rhymes are similarly disposed, with the repeated 'on' and 'in' sounds of the line endings suggesting both an intimate attachment and a stifling lack of progress. The closing near-couplet is particularly telling, with 'no one' and 'heroine' defining the troubled process of identity formation where sexual politics and national politics are not easily reconciled.

Boland, along with Longley, Carson, and others, has helped to refashion the political sonnet by dissolving and defusing images of violence. She has also patiently re-worked the ekphrastic sonnet traditionally associated with male painters and their female subjects. In the sonnet 'On Renoir's *The Grape Pickers*' she notes how the women—plump, round, and shining—are depicted as sensuously akin to the fruit they are harvesting. The turn between octave and sestet pulls away from the group picture to highlight the individual life of one working woman—'But not this one: this red-headed woman'—and draws even further back from the painting's idealized shapes to imagine a woman exhausted and unfulfilled: 'When she wakes summer will be over' (114). The first published version of the sonnet in *Night Feed* (1982) observes the binary form, marking the octave-sestet division typographically, but in later printings the sonnet is split into five parts (1 + 3 + 4 + 5 + 1), so that its sporadic half rhymes ('harvesting'/'clustering'; 'shines'/'vine'; 'other'/'weather'; 'woman'/'plums') seem even more desolatory and incomplete.[76]

Allusions to other art works and a supple handling of formal devices are also hallmarks of the sonnets in Leontia Flynn's *Drives* (2008). Some of these sonnets are reflections on contemporary Belfast ('Leaving Belfast' and 'Poem for Christmas', for instance), but Flynn has excelled in the writing of sonnets that offer brief meditations on the lives (and deaths) of writers and artists, among them Samuel Beckett, Olive Schreiner, Marcel Proust, Elizabeth Bishop, Scott Fitzgerald, Alfred Hitchcock, and Ingmar Bergman. A double sonnet on Robert Lowell conveys the salient details of his life and art through poignant echoes of 'Water', 'Skunk Hour', and 'Home After Three Months Away'. Aptly rhyming 'rebellion' and 'tradition', the sonnet contemplates the 'twists and tangles' of Lowell's career, and dwells upon the ethics of turning 'the living details of a living life' into poetry: 'And imagine using those letters in his sonnets.'[77] If Flynn's sonnets are, in many ways, rooted in Belfast, they also have a far-reaching international significance in their imaginative exploration of so many literary lives.

Summarizing an illuminating account of the modern Irish sonnet in *The Oxford Handbook of Modern Irish Poetry*, Alan Gillis notes how 'Differing modulations of the Irish sonnet might ultimately signify struggles and transformations within the national cultural bloc, or psychic formation', but he wisely adds that 'any interpretation along such lines is always likely to be suspect'.[78] Gillis is, himself, a distinguished exponent of the sonnet form and his poems aptly convey his well-judged reading of the situation, playfully announcing and renouncing their Irish provenance at the same

---

76. Eavan Boland, *Night Feed* (Dublin: Arlen House, 1982), p. 46.
77. Leontia Flynn, *Drives* (London: Jonathan Cape, 2008), p. 36.
78. Fran Brearton and Alan Gillis (eds), *The Oxford Handbook of Modern Irish Poetry* (Oxford: Oxford University Press, 2012), p. 586.

time. 'The Green Rose' unsettles any easy assumptions we might make about Irish and English iconography, or about poetic tradition (the vivid title brings to mind both the red rose of Robert Burns and the dark rose of James Clarence Mangan). The sonnet is tentative about location and about the sources of creativity, giving both Belfast and Dublin a look-in: 'It might have been Lady Dixon Park | or Stephen's Green, maybe Killynether, | retreading leaves of grass.'[79] As in sonnets by Muldoon and Carson, the fixity normally associated with place names dissolves and what transpires is a poem that meditates as much on its own elusive and allusive procedures as on the world at large. The spirit of Whitman washes over the poem, and what the sonnet ultimately conveys is an intelligence that refuses to be contained. The form of the sonnet buckles and bends in the process, presenting us with four tercets and a couplet, a late turn in line 9 (nicely coinciding with Whitman's 'amplitude of time'), and a rhyme scheme that looks straightforward to begin with, but collapses in the struggle with its own art of containment. There is yet more evidence here that, as Gillis himself concludes, 'Indeed, the Irish sonnet has brought riches.'[80]

---

79. Alan Gillis, *The Green Rose* (Thame: Clutag, 2009), n.p.
80. Brearton and Gillis (eds), *The Oxford Handbook of Modern Irish Poetry*, p. 587.

5

The American sonnet

From the late eighteenth century onwards, the sonnet held a special fascination for American poets. The challenge of a prestige form with its roots in European Renaissance culture was compounded with a deeply felt urge to write about America at both a regional and a national level, and to modify inherited literary conventions in the light of a new social and political experience. Walt Whitman signals the attractions of a pioneering poetic expansiveness in keeping with the buoyant democratic spirit of the mid-nineteenth century, but there is also a persistent interest in traditional lyric forms, including the sonnet. While acknowledging the long and distinguished history of the European sonnet, American poets bring to the form a new freedom of speech, a new diction and syntax, and a new set of local and national preoccupations. Shakespeare's sonnets provide the obvious model, but it is Milton who exerts the greatest influence over a generation of writers for whom religious and political liberty is sacrosanct.

Henry Wadsworth Longfellow

Henry Wadsworth Longfellow's 'Milton' is one of the defining sonnets of its time, both acknowledging Milton's rhetorical power and renovating the sonnet form in a way that will make it relevant to the concerns of writers and readers in nineteenth-century New England.[1]

> I pace the sounding sea-beach and behold
> How the voluminous billows roll and run,
> Upheaving and subsiding, while the sun

---

1. Quotations from Longfellow's poems are from *The Poetical Works of Longfellow* (London: Oxford University Press, 1957). Page numbers are given within brackets in the text.

> Shines through their sheeted emerald far unrolled,
> And the ninth wave, slow gathering fold by fold
> All its loose-flowing garments into one,
> Plunges upon the shore, and floods the dun
> Pale reach of sands, and changes them to gold.
> So in majestic cadence rise and fall
> The mighty undulations of thy song,
> O sightless bard, England's Maeonides!
> And ever and anon, high over all
> Uplifted, a ninth wave superb and strong,
> Floods all the soul with its melodious seas. (711–12)

Here, Longfellow takes the Italian sonnet favoured by Milton and powerfully emulates the surging syntax of his predecessor. The poem is remarkable for the way it apprehends the unbounded nature of the ocean from the small sea-beach of the sonnet's fourteen lines. The strongly marked turn effectively aligns the power and the beauty of the ocean with the might and melody of Milton's song. Although the poem opens with an acoustic image of 'the sounding sea-beach', it quickly moves into a marvellous visual rendering of the sun shining on 'the sheeted emerald' of water and transforming the sand to gold. The octave-sestet link is then effectively made between the glorious sight of the sea and the mighty sound of the 'sightless bard' (Longfellow was himself to suffer partial loss of sight after 1843). From the bold first-person pronouncement in the opening line, the sonnet gathers momentum and follows Milton in running its sense across line endings. The enjambment is especially pronounced where a run-on line opens with a verb, as in lines 4, 7, and 14. The closing line gains its impact both from the mellifluous play of 'l' and 'o' and 's' sounds, and from the cumulative force of 'shines', 'plunges', and 'floods'.

The early American sonnet possesses a deeply engrained classicism that sometimes sits awkwardly alongside a determination to throw off the vestiges of European tradition and establish something new. As with the later efforts of Ezra Pound, however, the wish to 'make it new' often entails a profound engagement with the work of the past. It would be wrong to read these classical allusions purely as the symptoms of cultural anxiety among a group of writers who feel ambivalent towards a European literary inheritance. Longfellow, after all, was a prodigiously gifted linguist and translator, for whom classical literature was a vital and necessary part of a modern education. For other writers, though, a display of classical allusion only serves to clutter and impede the flow of the sonnet. Edgar Allan Poe's best-known sonnet, 'To Science' (1829), suffers badly in this respect. A high Romantic disdain for scientific enquiry is undermined in the sestet when Poe turns to the imagined figure of Science and asks, 'Hast thou not dragged Diana from her car? | And driven the hamadryad from the wood | To seek a shelter in some happier star?' Similarly, the exotic sensuousness of 'The summer dream beneath the tamarind tree' is disappointingly overshadowed by the presence of the naiad in the closing lines of Poe's allusive sonnet.[2]

Longfellow demonstrates in what was probably his final sonnet (found among his papers after his death) that it was entirely possible for American poets of his generation to use the form successfully without any self-conscious display of learning. 'The Cross of Snow' alludes to the domestic fire of 1861 that injured Longfellow and killed his second wife, though it wasn't composed until 1879. The poem is modelled on Milton's sonnet for his second wife, Katherine Woodcock, 'Methought I saw my late espoused saint', but the striking contrast of fire and snow gives Longfellow's poem an imposing originality and a moving elegiac power:

> In the long, sleepless watches of the night,
> A gentle face—the face of one long dead—
> Looks at me from the wall, where round its head
> The night-lamp casts a halo of pale light.
> Here in this room she died, and soul more white
> Never through martyrdom of fire was led
> To its repose; nor can in books be read
> The legend of a life more benedight.
> There is a mountain in the distant West
> That, sun-defying, in its deep ravines
> Displays a cross of snow upon its side.
> Such is the cross I wear upon my breast
> These eighteen years, through all the changing scenes
> And seasons, changeless since the day she died.　　(137)

Once again, Longfellow adopts a standard Petrarchan model (*abbaabbacd-ecde*). This time, however, the sonnet achieves a quiet dignity by firmly adhering to the quatrain and tercet divisions implicit in the rhyme scheme. The turn takes us unexpectedly from the night-time bedroom scene and the ghostly image of the dead woman to the 'sun-defying' mountain 'in the distant west'. The cross of snow, neatly transferred from the mountain to the

---

2. Edgar Allan Poe, 'To Science', *The Oxford Book of Sonnets*, ed. John Fuller (Oxford: Oxford University Press, 2000), p. 168.

speaker's breast, is an imposing emblem of continuing grief and chilled solitude. Longfellow shows superbly well how the tercet can be more rhetorically effective than the couplet, especially when the subject is grief. The adroit shift from 'changing' to 'changeless' in the closing line is carried out with an impeccable control of pace and punctuation.

It is likely that the emblem of the cross of snow was inspired by paintings and photographs of the Mountain of the Holy Cross in Colorado, which was widely regarded in the popular imagination as a mountain that carried snow in its heart all summer long. As Stephanie Burt notes, a photograph by Henry Jackson and a famous painting by Thomas Moran were displayed at the Centennial Exposition in Philadelphia in 1876 as 'patriotic icons of Manifest Destiny' and a spur to American expansion in the West. He argues convincingly, though, that the poem subscribes neither to political ideas of destiny nor to Christian ideals of resurrection: 'the "sun-defying cross" is ironic, found in an American nature that holds no sign and no promise that the dead shall live'.[3] What Longfellow shows us, like Milton before him, is how readily the sonnet lends itself to elegiac purposes, giving momentary expression to feelings too painful to be borne for very long, while also serving in its written form as a lasting memorial.

Jones Very, William Cullen Bryant, and John Greenleaf Whittier

The spiritual intensity associated with nineteenth-century American transcendentalism, and in particular the work of Ralph Waldo Emerson, finds a powerful creative outlet in the sonnets of Emerson's strange disciple, Jones Very. The son of a Salem sea captain, and a student at the Harvard Divinity School, Very was for a while a tutor in Greek at Harvard, but lost his job as a result of his perceived psychological instability and eccentric behaviour. As one commentator has noted, his poems were written mainly in 1838 and 1839, 'when he was in a state of permanent ecstasy, teetering on the brink of insanity'.[4] Even so, Jones makes a distinctive and original contribution to

---

3. Stephanie Burt and David Mikics, *The Art of the Sonnet* (Cambridge, MA: Harvard University Press, 2010), p. 204.
4. Christoph Irmscher, 'Linen Shreds and Melons in a Field: Emerson and his Contemporaries', *The Cambridge History of American Poetry*, ed. Alfred Bendixen and Stephanie Burt (Cambridge: Cambridge University Press, 2015), p. 206.

sonnet writing in America and justly deserves the generous space accorded him in David Bromwich's valuable anthology, *American Sonnets*.[5] The visionary quality of Very's sonnets is immediately evident in the extravagant declaration of witness with which so many of them open: 'I saw the spot where our first parents dwelt' ('The Garden'); 'I see them crowd on crowd they walk the earth' ('The Dead'); 'I saw, strange sight! The children sat at meat' ('The Children'). In other respects, though, Jones is a patient and attentive observer of nature, as in 'The Celandine', in which all the resources of the love sonnet are heaped upon the humble spring flower in a startling scene of transmutation: 'Still, still my eye will gaze long-fixed on thee, | Till I forget that I am called a man | And at thy side fast-rooted seem to be.' If Jones sometimes too readily turns the flowers and fruits of his experience into spiritual emblems, he nevertheless retains an appealing ecological sensitivity and also sets a standard for other American poets intent on writing about their own particular landscapes. His 'Barberry Bush' sonnet cautions the reader to leave alone the 'bitter fruit' of spring and wait for autumn's 'sweeter taste', but what outweighs the homiletic impulse of the poem is its vivid rendering of the actual barberry bush, 'Upon the hills of Salem, scattered wide'.[6]

The determination of American poets to write about their own sense of place and their own sense of belonging produces some notable and distinguished experiments with the sonnet form. William Cullen Bryant's stirringly patriotic sonnet, 'To Cole, the Painter, Departing for Europe', is a striking instance of this assertion of American artistic sensibility in the face of European tradition.

> Thine eyes shall see the light of distant skies:
> Yet, COLE! thy heart shall bear to Europe's strand
> A living image of thy native land,
> Such as on thine own glorious canvas lies;
> Lone lakes—savannas where the bison roves—
> Rocks rich with summer garlands—solemn streams—
> Skies, where the desert eagle wheels and screams—
> Spring bloom and autumn blaze of boundless groves.
> Fair scenes shall greet thee where thou goest—fair,
> But different—everywhere the trace of men,
> Paths, homes, graves, ruins, from the lowest glen

---

5. David Bromwich (ed.), *American Sonnets* (New York: Library of America, 2007), pp. 12–25.
6. Bromwich, *American Sonnets*, pp. 14, 16, 19, 12, 21.

> To where life shrinks from the fierce Alpine air,
> Gaze on them, till the tears shall dim thy sight,
> But keep that earlier, wilder image bright.[7]

In its adulation of the power and plenitude of nature, and in its tender regard for the longings of the human heart, Bryant's sonnet eloquently restates some of the familiar preoccupations of European Romanticism. In other respects, however, it displays a clear recognition of difference. As well as giving prominence to images drawn from the 'native land' he shares with Cole—the desert eagle and the bison roving in the savannahs—Bryant also attempts something new with the structure of the sonnet. His sonnet for Cole is neither English nor Italian, but a subtle reworking of both. The use of seven rhymes, including a rhyming couplet, is reminiscent of the Shakespearean sonnet, but the distribution of rhymes (envelope rather than alternate) is closer to the Petrarchan sonnet: *abbacddceffegg*. The turn appears to be conventional, but its force is withheld until line 10. 'Fair scenes shall greet thee where thou goest' seems to restate the opening farewell to Cole, but this is unexpectedly disrupted, so that the real turn occurs in line 10 with the emphatic phrase, 'But different'. The closing couplet is imbued with melancholy reflections on the 'paths, homes, graves, ruins' of European civilization, but the sonnet closes buoyantly and optimistically with a wilder, brighter image of America.

Longfellow's contemporary, John Greenleaf Whittier, displays a strong New England sensibility and a strong commitment to place in his good-luck sonnet, 'To a Cape Ann Schooner':

> Luck to the craft that bears this name of mine,
> Good fortune follow with her golden spoon
> The glazèd hat and tarry pantaloon;
> And wheresoe'er her keel shall cut the brine,
> Cod, hake and haddock quarrel for her line.
> Shipped with her crew, whatever wind may blow,
> Or tides delay, my wish with her shall go,
> Fishing by proxy. Would that it might show
> At need her course, in lack of sun and star,
> Where icebergs threaten, and the sharp reefs are;
> Lift the blind fog on Anticosti's lee
> And Avalon's rock; make populous the sea

---

7. William Cullen Bryant, 'To an American Painter', *American Poetry: The Nineteenth Century*, ed. John Hollander (New York: Library of America, 1993), vol. 1, pp. 160–1.

> Round Grand Manan with eager finny swarms,
> Break the long calms, and charm away the storms.[8]

The local place names are confidently brought into the realm of the mythological Avalon, but the sonnet does much more than this. What is also striking here is Whittier's brilliant synechdochic depiction of sailors in 'The glazed hat and tarry pantaloon' and his briskly colloquial rendering of fish in 'Cod, hake and haddock quarrel for her line'. The rhyme scheme is unusual, and so is the syntactical arrangement of the fourteen lines. Avoiding the usual quatrain subdivisions within the octave and sestet, Whittier structures the sonnet around syntactical units of varying line length (3 + 2 + 5 + 4). Like Bryant, he fashions a novel rhyme scheme that both resembles and resists European models: *abbaacccddeeff*. The triple vowel rhyme of 'blow' / 'go' / 'show' gives the sonnet tremendous momentum, allowing the voice to extend across the expected turn and all the way through to the caesura in line 12. The sonnet thereby gains additional force from the run-on half line that precedes the closing couplet.

Emma Lazarus, Frederick Goddard Tuckerman, and Trumbell Stickney

Although Whittier's use of the sonnet as a blessing or charm can be traced all the way back to Renaissance Europe, it also confirms in its recognition of the ship's crew that the sonnet has by this time moved significantly away from the exclusive domain of the court to become an appropriate poetic form for common lives and common destinies. As the nineteenth century progresses, the cultural influences that impinge upon the American sonnet tend to come from more local and less obvious places than the pages of Shakespeare and Milton. Any comprehensive account of the American sonnet must surely acknowledge that remarkable poem, 'The New Colossus', written by a Russian Jewish immigrant, Emma Lazarus, in 1883, to welcome the Statue of Liberty to New York Harbour. The sonnet was recited at the dedication of the statue in October 1886 and inscribed on a plaque that was later read by millions of visitors. The sestet of the poem contains those words that came to be seen as the very embodiment of American civic idealism and aspiring democracy: 'Give me your tired, your poor, | Your huddled

---

8. John Greenleaf Whittier, 'To a Cape Ann Schooner', *The Oxford Book of Sonnets*, ed. Fuller, p. 162.

masses yearning to breathe free, | The wretched refuse of your teeming shore.'[9] The sonnet's association with monuments goes back a long way to Shakespeare and Spenser and beyond, but 'The New Colossus' is unusual in its candid declaration of equality. A poetic form with its origins in the aristocratic, courtly circles of Renaissance Europe had now come to voice the aspirations of the homeless and the dispossessed, 'the wretched refuse' in search of liberty.

Emma Lazarus is not alone in using the sonnet as an imaginative bridge between the artistic achievements of the Old World and the teeming expectations of the New. The effort is perhaps more starkly and troublingly apparent in the work of the brilliant young Harvard classicist, Trumbull Stickney, who died at the age of 30 in 1904. Born in Geneva and educated in classical literature and history by his father, Stickney retained a powerful reverence for antique civilization, for the glorious Aegean, and for the majestic slopes of Lykaion, Helikon, and Simium. Nevertheless, it is Stickney who speaks on behalf of a new industrial democracy, candidly expressing solidarity and support for the downtrodden workers in the docks and factories of modern America. His sonnet 'Six O' Clock' registers the troubling political transition to modernity at the end of the nineteenth century through memorable images of an urban landscape in the fading light of winter:

> Now burst above the city's cold twilight
> The piercing whistles and the tower-clocks:
> For day is done. Along the frozen docks
> The workmen set their ragged shirts aright.
> Thro' factory doors a stream of dingy light
> Follows the scrimmage as it quickly flocks
> To hut and home among the snow's gray blocks.—
> I love you, human labourers. Good-night!
> Good-night to all the blackened arms that ache!
> Good-night to every sick and sweated brow,
> To the poor girl that strength and love forsake,
> To the poor boy who can no more! I vow
> The victim soon shall shudder at the stake
> And fall in blood: we bring him even now.[10]

---

9. Emma Lazarus, 'The New Colossus', *American Sonnets: An Anthology*, ed. David Bromwich (New York: Library of America, 2007), p. 48.
10. Trumbull Stickney, 'Six O'Clock', *Oxford Book of American Poetry* (Oxford: Oxford University Press, 2006), pp. 245–6.

The sonnet risks sentimentality in acknowledging the victimized labourer as a sacrificial Christ figure, but this does not detract from the imposing first-person declaration of love at the end of the octave, or from the simple but effective way in which the sestet picks up the closing 'good-night' of the octave and lets it echo throughout the rest of the sonnet.

The celebration of ordinary lives is one of the appealing characteristics of the sonnets of Frederick Goddard Tuckerman (a student of Jones Very at Harvard), though often Tuckerman invests the commonplace with a Decadent strangeness. Yvor Winters, who championed Tuckerman as 'one of the most remarkable American poets of the nineteenth century', astutely surmised that the sonnets were unusual in imbuing a New England landscape with a sensibility derived from French Symbolist poets, including Paul Verlaine. At the same time, it might be argued that the intense qualities of mystery and imagination in the sonnets derive in part from the example of Edgar Allan Poe. As Winters points out, the tenth sonnet in Tuckerman's 'First Series' of 1854–60 is 'one of the strangest and at the same time one of the most beautiful... It deals with a man of whom we know nothing except that he is obsessed with terror and anguish'.[11]

> An upper chamber in a darkened house,
> Where, ere his footsteps reached ripe manhood's brink,
> Terror and anguish were his lot to drink;
> I cannot rid the thought, nor hold it close
> But dimly dream upon that man alone:
> Now though the autumn clouds most softly pass,
> The cricket chides beneath the doorstep stone
> And greener than the season grows the grass.
> Nor can I drop my lids nor shade my brows,
> But there he stands beside the lifted sash;
> And with a swooning of the heart, I think
> Where the black shingles slope to meet the boughs
> And, shattered on the roof like smallest snows,
> The tiny petals of the mountain ash.   (7)

The architectural details—the 'darkened house' and the 'black shingles'—have an obvious Gothic intensity, but the mystery of the sonnet derives essentially from the unstated relationship between the speaker and the unnamed, terrified man. It is not just the anonymous man who is obsessed. The speaker's

---

11. Yvor Winters, Foreword to *The Complete Poems of Frederick Goddard Tuckerman*, ed. N. Scott Momaday (New York: Oxford University Press, 1965), p. xii. Quotations are from this edition of the poems.

'swooning of the heart' and his inability to 'rid the thought' suggest a powerful identification with the mysterious figure who is now presumably dead (though the nature of his death is tantalizingly concealed). The autumn clouds, the returning grass, and the tree blossom all contribute to the sonnet's pervasive elegiac mood. What generates much of the intrigue, however, is the sonnet's peculiar grammatical slippages occasioned in both the octave and the sestet by the word 'where'. In both instances, the effect is to draw attention to the house and simultaneously direct attention away from any significant revelation. The sestet directs the speaker's thoughts towards the meeting place of house and trees, where black shingles and the tiny petals 'shattered' on the roof provide a compelling suggestion of the young man's premature death. In keeping with Tuckerman's habitual method of leaving clues but refusing to offer conclusive evidence, the sonnet opens with a conventional Petrarchan quatrain (*abba*) but then refuses to observe any coherent rhyme scheme. The rhymes in the sestet are puzzlingly close to those in the octave. The 'house'/'close' rhyme is echoed in 'brows'/'boughs'/'snows', while the 'pass'/'grass' rhyme is picked up in 'sash'/'ash'/'house'. Line 11 calls attention to itself in an eccentric but revealing way by wilfully disregarding convention and repeating the 'b' rhyme of the octave. The sonnet presents us with a speaker whose thinking is obsessive.

Tuckerman's sonnet on the deserted home of two deceased sisters (from his 'Second Series' of sonnets, also composed between 1854 and 1860), provides further evidence of his penchant for strangeness and melancholy. Once again, the sonnet works through evasion, imprinting its sense of loss and decay in the architectural details of the house:

> Under the mountain, as when first I knew
> Its low dark roof and chimney creeper-twined,
> The red house stands; and yet my footsteps find,
> Vague in the walks, waste balm and feverfew.
> But they are gone: no soft-eyed sisters trip
> Across the porch or lintels; where, behind,
> The mother sat, sat knitting with pursed lip.
> The house stands vacant in its green recess,
> Absent of beauty as a broken heart.
> The wild rain enters, and the sunset wind
> Sighs in the chambers of their loveliness
> Or shakes the pane—and in the silent noons
> The glass falls from the window, part by part,
> And ringeth faintly in the grassy stones.   (26)

The speaker's memory holds clues to a narrative that is simultaneously revealed and concealed. The mother's 'pursed lip' and the description of the house as 'Absent of beauty as a broken heart' are poignantly suggestive of disappointment and unfulfilment. There is a curious tension in the poem, perhaps in keeping with the cravings of memory, between the waste and overgrown homestead and the animating effects of rain and wind. Twice we are told that the house 'stands', as if simply a vacant property, but the persistent present-tense verbs refuse to consign it to the past, even while the alliterative phrasing of 'glass falling faintly to grass' works as an insistent reminder of broken lives consigned to earth. Once again, Tuckerman begins conventionally enough with a Petrarchan quatrain (*abba*), only to break the pattern and scatter his rhymes at random. In style and outlook, Tuckerman is a post-Romantic writer, closer to Frost than to Longfellow. Even now, as Don Paterson claims, he is 'one of the most seriously undervalued poets of the nineteenth century'.[12]

As the century wore on, some of the most pressing social and political actualities of modern American life—industrialization, urbanization, immigration—would begin to impinge on the sonnet, transforming it from the favoured form of the privileged few to the instrument of popular and progressive opinion. English poets had, of course, already democratized the sonnet. The radical, republican tradition of Milton, Wordsworth, and Shelley had profoundly altered the sonnet's reach and capability, but American poets opened the sonnet further to a distinctive vernacular current and distinctive national and regional concerns. The process is evident in the nineteenth century in the sonnets of Henry Wadsworth Longfellow, John Greenleaf Whittier, James Russell Lowell, and William Cullen Bryant.

Edwin Arlington Robinson

Among the later poets who help to renovate and domesticate the sonnet in America, Edwin Arlington Robinson shows how well the form lends itself to the exploration of grief and loss in the lives of ordinary mortals, and how well it accommodates the modulations and inflections of a plain-speaking voice.[13] Like Robert Frost, Robinson is a renovator of poetic language who

---

12. Don Paterson, *101 Sonnets from Shakespeare to Heaney* (London: Faber, 1999), p. 106.
13. Quotations from the poems of Edwin Arlington Robinson are from *Collected Poems of Edwin Arlington Robinson* (New York: Macmillan, 1954).

strips away whatever seems superfluous or merely decorative and creates instead the impression of intimate speech. He brings to the sonnet a conviction that the form is flexible enough to accommodate the social actualities of his own time and place, and that its metrical patterns can be creatively aligned with his own distinctively New England voice. More than any other American poet, Robinson opens the sonnet to the lives of social misfits and outcasts—the strange, the lonely, the haunted, the defeated, and the disappointed. As Warner Berthoff has argued, 'Robinson is the poet of casualties; of broken lives and exhausted consciences; of separateness; and of the calm that comes with resignation and defeat—perhaps only with death.'[14] The poem that most clearly demonstrates Berthoff's description of Robinson is his well-known sonnet, 'Reuben Bright':

> Because he was a butcher and thereby
> Did earn an honest living (and did right),
> I would not have you think that Reuben Bright
> Was any more a brute than you or I;
> For when they told him that his wife must die,
> He stared at them, and shook with grief and fright,
> And cried like a great baby half that night,
> And made the women cry to see him cry.
>
> And after she was dead, and he had paid
> The singers and the sexton and the rest,
> He packed a lot of things that she had made
> Most mournfully away in an old chest
> Of hers, and put some chopped-up cedar boughs
> In with them, and tore down the slaughter-house.   (92)

That a butcher should assume prominence in a sonnet is, itself, worthy of comment, but what is most striking about this particular sonnet is its plain-speaking, intimately conversational idiom. The opening line is both abrupt and appealing, seeming to involve us in a narrative that is already underway. The implied tonal qualities of the opening are difficult to gauge. The voice seems matter-of-fact, yet it hints at profound emotional and psychological depths in Reuben Bright's response to his wife's death. The close proximity between Bright and brute (both phonetically and typographically) suggests what might be the main enquiry in the poem. The nature of Bright's occupation belies his capacity for deep feeling, but there is nevertheless

---

14. Warner Berthoff, 'The "New" Poetry: Robinson and Frost', *Edwin Arlington Robinson: A Collection of Critical Essays*, ed. Francis Murphy (Englewood Cliffs, NJ: Prentice Hall, 1970), p. 120.

something 'brutal' in his inability to speak. Bright only cries, 'like a great baby'. The 'chopped-up cedar boughs' that he places in his wife's belongings recall his occupation and his usual rough and ready exertion, but they also provide a poignant indication of his continuing love and care.

Here and elsewhere, Robinson adopts a Petrarchan octave but then follows it with a sestet that includes a closing couplet. There is a noticeable turn that coincides with the aftermath of the funeral service, though to some extent this is played down by the repeated use of the narrative conjunction 'And' throughout both octave and sestet. The cumulative force of the conjunction gathers in the final line, recounting Bright's destruction of his workplace in a studiously casual and understated delivery. That violent detail, however, is crucial in summing up the combination of outer brutal strength and inner human tenderness that characterizes Reuben Bright.

Robinson's preference is for gentle and subdued half rhymes, avoiding the resounding conclusiveness and proverbial neatness that sometimes accompanies the traditional closing couplet. At times, the language and the rhythm of the sonnet are so colloquial that we might take them for granted and forget what a great innovator Robinson can be at the level of diction and metre. The seemingly unexceptional line, 'He packed a lot of things that she had made' is a monosyllabic line of vigorous iambic pentameter, but the line that follows it pulls away from the metre and induces a more desultory lyricism: 'Most mournfully away in an old chest.' Like Frost, Robinson is adept at running the sense of what he says across line endings, generating subtle tonal shifts, and ultimately it is the enjambment in the sestet that makes this such a memorable and harrowing sonnet.

Robinson also shares with Frost a strong sense of spiritual quest, a journeying in which a New England Puritan inheritance is both carried forward and submitted to sceptical apprehension. The early sonnet 'Credo', from the aptly titled *Children of the Night* (1897), anticipates the metaphysical darkness in a good deal of Frost's writing, setting the apparent certitude of its Christian declaration against a deeply negative reading of the universe:

> I cannot find my way: there is no star
> In all the shrouded heavens anywhere;
> And there is not a whisper in the air
> Of any living voice but one so far
> That I can hear it only as a bar
> Of lost, imperial music, played when fair
> And angel fingers wove, and unaware,
> Dead leaves to garlands where no roses are.

> No, there is not a glimmer, nor a call,
> For one that welcomes, welcomes when he fears,
> The black and awful chaos of the night;
> For through it all—above, beyond it all—
> I know the far sent message of the years,
> I feel the coming glory of the Light.   (94)

As with Frost, the colloquial idiom and seeming nonchalance of the verse serve to intensify rather than diminish the 'black and awful chaos of the night'. Berthoff claims that for Robinson religion was 'a kind of optimistic desperation',[15] and this would seem to be borne out by the closing parallel lines of the sonnet, asserting what is known and felt. The sonnet sets up such a strongly negative apprehension of creation, especially in the reiterated 'No' of the sestet, that the closing lines appear unconvincing and slyly ironic in their welcoming of the Puritan 'coming glory of the Light'.

A much later sonnet, published in the 1920s, shows Robinson, like Tuckerman before him, to be adept in utilizing the stock devices of the American Gothic and adopting the compressed space of the sonnet for strange and oblique imaginings of lives cut short and tragically defeated. 'Haunted House' is a striking and dramatic instance of how the sonnet can take on the function of a short story and offer scope for atmospheric setting, emotional suspense, and narrative climax:

> Here was a place where none would ever come
> For shelter, save as we did from the rain.
> We saw no ghost, yet once outside again
> Each wondered why the other should be dumb;
> For we had fronted nothing worse than gloom
> And ruin, and to our vision it was plain
> Where thrift, outshivering fear, had let remain
> Some chairs that were like skeletons of home.
>
> There were no trackless footsteps on the floor
> Above us, and there were no sounds elsewhere.
> But there was more than sound; and there was more
> Than just an axe that once was in the air
> Between us and the chimney, long before
> Our time. So townsmen said who found her there.   (870)

As with 'Reuben Bright', the modified Petrarchan structure allows just enough expansiveness and just enough concealment. The simple rhymes induce an intimate and conversational mood, while the closing half-rhyme

---

15. Berthoff, *Edwin Arlington Robinson*, p. 122.

skilfully evades too neat a sense of closure. Unobtrusively, we move from the opening 'Here' to the closing 'there', as if stepping back in awe. Syntactically, the sonnet works by setting up assurances and then casually undermining them. The haunted house is a place where 'none would *ever* come... *save* as we did from the rain'. Likewise, 'we saw no ghost, *yet* once outside...' (emphasis added). The scene of gloom and rain is 'plain' enough to see, yet the chairs 'like skeletons of home' are eerily unsettling. The imprecision of what remains, of what is 'more than sound', is similarly disturbing, but the triumph of the sestet is in the fluid enjambment of the final four lines and the sudden, deadening halt of the caesura at the end of 'our time'. The closing, almost casual, observation—'So townsmen said who found her there'—is characteristically grim and laconic, gathering into the highly compressed form of the sonnet all the economy and understatement and mystery of the most haunted Gothic fiction.

Robert Frost

By the 1920s, Robinson had redefined the nature and function of the sonnet for modern American poets, but it is Robert Frost, more than any other modern American poet, who domesticates the sonnet and demonstrates its viability and versatility at a time when free verse seems likely to displace traditional lyric forms. Although his reputation rests largely on his extended narrative and dramatic poems, his sonnets amply demonstrate his lyric aptitude. The sonnet form has a particular attraction for Frost, offering room for playful, individual manoeuvre within traditional constraints. In this respect, his sonnets have a special role in promoting and illustrating Frost's habitual concern with 'the sound of sense' and the effects that might be derived from crossing conventional metrical stresses with the natural stresses of the speaking voice. Frost was drawn to the sonnet at the very outset of his career in the 1890s and went on to write some of his most accomplished sonnets in the 1930s and 1940s. Even if we discount a few fourteen-line poems that are simply fourteen-line poems and don't appear to utilize any other conventions of the sonnet form, there are over forty sonnets in the Library of America edition of his writings, and these include some of his best-known poems: 'Into My Own', 'Mowing', 'Meeting and Passing', 'The Oven Bird', 'Once by the Pacific', 'Acquainted with the Night', 'The

Investment', 'Design', 'The Silken Tent' and 'Never Again Would Birds' Song Be the Same'.[16]

Frost's earliest known sonnet, 'Despair', written in the 1890s, confirms Lionel Trilling's famous remark that at times Frost could be 'terrifying', though this is a very early piece and is not likely to have been one of the poems that Trilling had in mind:

> I am like a dead diver after all's
> Done, still held fast in the weed's snare below,
> Where in the gloom his limbs begin to glow
> Swaying at his moorings as the roiled bottom falls.
> There was a moment when with vainest calls
> He drank the water, saying, 'Oh let me go—
> God let me go,'—for then he could not know
> As in the sun's warm light on earth and walls.
>
> I am like a dead diver in this place.
> I was alive here too one desperate space,
> And near prayer in the one whom I invoked.
> I tore the muscles from my limbs and choked.
> My sudden struggle may have dragged down some
> White lily from the air—and now the fishes come.[17]

The unusual contraction and enjambment of 'all's Done' in the opening line of the sonnet suggests the boldness of Frost's stylistic endeavour and the risks he was prepared to take in establishing a new vernacular standard in American poetry. The white lily, pulled down from the surface into the water, is a striking and memorable image of life's fragility, while the diving fishes at the end reveal something of Frost's relish for high drama and moments of extremity.

Within a few years, the images of despair and drowning in this early sonnet would reappear in Frost's troubled perceptions of industrial workers

---

16. Thirty-seven sonnets are listed in H. A. Maxson, *On the Sonnets of Robert Frost* (Jefferson, NC and London: McFarland, 1997). A more expansive account is offered by Richard J. Calhoun in his essay, '"By Pretending They Are Not Sonnets": The Sonnets of Robert Frost at the Millennium', in Earl J. Wilcox and Jonathan N. Barron (eds), *Roads Not Taken: Rereading Robert Frost* (Columbia and London: University of Missouri Press, 2000), pp. 217–35. If we count 'Two Look at Two' as three consecutive blank verse sonnets, then the number of sonnets in Frost's collected poems is even higher. I am grateful to David Sanders and Richard Wakefield for bringing this point to my attention.
17. Robert Frost, *Robert Frost: Collected Poems, Prose and Plays*, ed. Richard Poirier and Mark Richardson (New York: Library of America, 1995), p. 506. Further references are to this edition of Frost's work.

in the town of Lawrence, Massachusetts. Another two early sonnets, 'The Mill City' and 'When the Speed Comes', were probably written in 1905 and 1906 respectively, but they derive from Frost's experience of working in the wool mills of Lawrence in the 1890s. 'The Mill City' complicates any easy account of Frost's poetic development by revealing a strongly urban sensibility at the very outset of his career and suggesting that the pastoral mode was not the only road Frost might have taken. It also calls into question any simple assumption that Frost's politics were solidly and naively conservative:

> It was in a drear city by a stream,
> And all its citizens were sad to me,—
> I could not fathom what their life could be—
> Their passage in the morning like a dream
> In the arc-light's unnatural bluish beam,
> Then back, at night, like drowned men from the sea,
> Up from the mills and river hurriedly,
> In weeds of labor, to the shriek of steam.
>
> Yet I supposed that they had all one hope
> With me (there is but one.) I would go out,
> When happier ones drew in for fear of doubt,
> Breasting their current, resolute to cope
> With what thoughts they compelled who thronged the street,
> Less to the sound of voices than of feet.[18]

The sonnet imagines the mill workers being drowned in the stream that drives the machinery, but 'the weeds of labor' that cling to them recall the 'weeds' snare' of the earlier sonnet, 'Despair'. The octave and the sestet are used effectively to capture both the speaker's sense of remoteness and difference from the workers ('I could not fathom what their life could be—') and his abiding sense of solidarity with them ('Yet I supposed that they had all one hope | With me'). That key phrase, 'I would go out', provides the starting point for so much of Frost's later work. It represents an epistemological stance, a desire to know and understand the world, but also a formal equivalent in terms of a willingness to experiment with sentence sounds and with what constitutes a line of poetry. The structure of 'The Mill City' makes use of both the typical envelope rhymes of the Italian octave and the rhyming

---

18. *Collected Poems, Prose and Plays*, ed. Poirier and Richardson, p. 509. See Tyler Hoffman's excellent reading of this sonnet in *Robert Frost and the Politics of Poetry* (Hanover and London: University Press of New England, 2001), pp. 25–6.

couplet of the English sestet, but the novelty of Frost's sonnet is that its conclusion effectively begins in line 10 and gathers momentum through the unwinding of a single complex sentence. This 'going out' becomes a hallmark in some of Frost's best-known sonnets, including 'Into My Own' and 'Acquainted with the Night'.

'Into My Own' was obviously a critically important poem for Frost. It was the first poem in his first book, *A Boy's Will*, in 1913. With the exception of 'The Pasture', the short poem that Frost liked to use as a frontispiece to his work, 'Into My Own' was retained as the first poem in *Collected Poems* (1930) and *Complete Poems* (1949), and it continues to be the opening poem in most selections of Frost's work published today. It was written in 1909 when Frost was 35 and first published in the *New England Magazine* with the title 'Into Mine Own' (an echo of Psalm 35:13). The revised title 'Into My Own' can be read as a colloquial expression—coming into one's own in the sense of growing up and achieving independence—but also as an excursion into those dark places of the heart and mind, an interior journey for which the journey through the dark woods (the first of many in Frost's poems) provides a compelling metaphor.

> One of my wishes is that those dark trees
> So old and firm they scarcely show the breeze,
> Were not, as 'twere, the merest mask of gloom,
> But stretched away unto the edge of doom.
>
> I should not be withheld but that some day
> Into their vastness I should steal away,
> Fearless of ever finding open land,
> Or highway where the slow wheel pours the sand.
>
> I do not see why I should e'er turn back,
> Or those should not set forth upon my track
> To overtake me, who should miss me here
> And long to know if still I held them dear.
>
> They would not find me changed from him they knew—
> Only more sure of all I thought was true.   (15)

What is so characteristic of this poem in terms of Frost's development as a writer is that it presents itself as a journey or quest in which the speaker is prompted to test the limits of knowledge and experience. Elsewhere in Frost's work, the desire to enter the darkness is met by a commitment to communal or social responsibilities, and the writing carries on, having weighed up its possible choices and alternatives. But this early poem seems stubborn and headstrong, perhaps in keeping with the title of the volume, *A Boy's Will*, which echoes Longfellow's 1858 poem, 'My Lost Youth': 'A boy's will is the wind's will, | And the thoughts of youth are long, long thoughts.'[19]

If the poem is distinctively American in its emphasis on individual venture and self-reliance (and perhaps slightly ironic towards that nineteenth-century American Romantic inheritance), it also retains a significant link with European Renaissance poetry in its choice of the sonnet form. It consists of fourteen lines, each of ten syllables, though the colloquial ease of the poem pulls away from any strict observance of the usual iambic stress. In keeping with the Shakespearean sonnet, there are three quatrains and a closing couplet, and these are typographically and syntactically distinct. Each quatrain is a single sentence. Like the Shakespearean sonnet, the poem has seven rhymes, but instead of the alternating rhyme scheme of the traditional sonnet, we find rhyming couplets all the way through, giving the sonnet a strong sense of progression and also providing a strong emphasis with the closing couplet.

At the very point where we might expect a turn—between the opening eight lines and the closing six—the sonnet explicitly denies a turn, establishing a happy agreement between its formal and thematic procedures: 'I do not see why I should e'er turn back'. 'Into My Own' is a cleverly modified sonnet, though Shakespeare is the main influence. The speaker's contemplation of 'the edge of doom' in line 4 recalls Shakespeare's Sonnet 116, 'Let me not to the marriage of true minds admit impediments', which celebrates the durability of love against the encroachments of time: 'Love alters not with his brief hours and weeks, | But bears it out even to the edge of doom.'[20] Where Shakespeare's sonnet values love above all else, Frost's sonnet wilfully leaves it behind and settles for solitary endeavour.

Frost's first book also contains three other notable sonnets, 'A Dream Pang', 'The Vantage Point', and 'Mowing'. Frost claimed that 'Mowing', probably written in the spring of 1900, was the best poem in the book. Part of its appeal is that it asserts the value of its own pastoral vision within a tradition that goes all the way back to Virgil, subtly echoing Shakespeare, Marvell, and Wordsworth. It shows a highly self-conscious preoccupation with the making of poetry, as well as the making of hay, as the striking infinitive verb at the end of the poem declares. The motivating impulse

---

19. *The Poetical Works of Longfellow*, pp. 308–9.
20. William Shakespeare, *The Complete Sonnets and Poems*, ed. Colin Burrow (Oxford: Oxford University Press, 2008), p. 613.

behind the poem is the idea that poetry is a labour of love: it must be sought and earned. For Frost, as well as for Marvell, the mower with his long scythe is both lover and labourer, resourcefully making hay while the sun shines:

> There was never a sound beside the wood but one,
> And that was my long scythe whispering to the ground.
> What was it it whispered? I knew not well myself;
> Perhaps it was something about the heat of the sun,
> Something, perhaps, about the lack of sound—
> And that was why it whispered and did not speak.
> It was no dream of the gift of idle hours,
> Or easy gold at the hand of fay or elf:
> Anything more than the truth would have seemed too weak
> To the earnest love that laid the swale in rows,
> Not without feeble-pointed spikes of flowers
> (Pale orchises), and scared a bright green snake.
> The fact is the sweetest dream that labor knows.
> My long scythe whispered and left the hay to make. (26)

Two definitions of poetry (or two models of creativity) vie for attention here. One tends towards the realm of idle fantasy and the 'easy gold' of ready-made mythology, while the other is factual and pragmatic. In between, there is a tentative, exploratory engagement with the world, a thoughtful acknowledgement of both vision and actuality. This is a post-Romantic poem in which the only sound beside the wood is a whisper, and even that has to be worked at and teased into being. The poem highlights its own epistemological dilemmas, its own fraught exploration of what can and cannot be known: 'I knew not well myself'. In contrast, Wordsworth's 'The Solitary Reaper' seems positively assured and buoyant in its capturing of earth's music. 'Mowing' is also a post-Darwinian poem, in which 'pale orchises' and 'a bright green snake' are signifiers of a world in which 'nature's holy plan' has been supplanted by nature's unfathomable processes of selection, reproduction, and adaptability.

Not surprisingly, the poem opts for the idiom of whisper rather than confident speech, and for limited perception rather than revelation or transcendence. Very likely, the penultimate line of the poem is an echo of Henry Thoreau's pronouncement that 'a true account of the actual is the rarest poetry',[21] and indeed the sestet of Frost's sonnet pragmatically cautions

---

21. Henry David Thoreau, *A Week on the Concord and Merrimack Rivers; Walden; Or, Life in the Woods; The Maine Woods; Cape Cod* (New York: Library of America, 1985), p. 266.

against any tendency to exceed the truth of things as they are: 'Anything more than the truth would have seemed too weak'. Frost himself encouraged the notion that a definition of poetry might be found in the penultimate line, 'The fact is the sweetest dream that labor knows', in which fact and dream, labour and sweetness, are held in fragile balance.[22] It is almost as if the poem leaves off trying to make too much of its own potential meanings and settles for a circumscribed art of the unknown and the unstated: 'My long scythe whispered and left the hay to make.'

Such a tentative art required a modified lyricism, and Frost's description of 'Mowing' as 'a talk song' is a revealing indication of how he skilfully manipulates the resources of the sonnet form. It is perhaps too fanciful to claim that one can hear the swishing of the scythe in the long sweeping lines and added stresses in 'Mowing', but not too fanciful to claim that 'One can hear the poet talking here: the rough-hewn, New England accent not tripping along or lunging from stress to stress but giving almost equal weight to each vowel sound.'[23] 'Mowing' is one of the best and earliest examples of what Frost came to call 'the sound of sense', in which the patterns of vernacular speech are crossed with the patterns of poetic metre. In his celebrated 'Fourth of July' letter to John Bartlett in 1913, Frost explains that 'the sound of sense' is 'the abstract vitality of our speech', and he goes on to insist that 'if one is to be a poet he must learn to get cadences by skilfully breaking the sounds of sense with all their irregularity of accent across the regular beat of the metre'. The sonnet is the ideal space in which to explore 'the mingling of sense-sound and word-accent', providing Frost with exactly the right combination of metrical constraint and vocal freedom that he was seeking.[24]

As Tyler Hoffman has argued, Frost's 'Fourth of July' letter, written at a crucial moment in international political relations, provides a strong indication of his patriotic fervour, 'as he frames his struggle to break free from outmoded (British) aesthetic procedures (while in England) as an act of American independence'.[25] As we shall see, Frost's handling of the sonnet proves immensely valuable to later poets seeking a similar poetic independence from British aesthetic procedures. Both Seamus Heaney and Derek Walcott have admired the dexterity of Frost's versification in 'Mowing'. Walcott says

---

22. Jay Parini, *Robert Frost: A Life* (London: Heinemann, 1998), p. 56.
23. Parini, *Robert Frost*, p. 77.
24. Frost, *Collected Poems, Prose and Plays*, p. 665.
25. Hoffman, *Robert Frost and the Politics of Poetry*, p. 188.

of this poem that 'a deftness, like a skipping stone, evades the predictable scansion by a sudden parenthesis, by a momentarily forgotten verb...and shifting, dancing caesuras'.[26] His point is amply illustrated by the subtle syntactical shifts between lines 9 and 12 of the sonnet. We might add, as well, that one of the other ways that the poem evades predictable scansion is through a heaping up of syllables so that certain lines spill over the neat containment of iambic pentameter: 'Anything more than the truth would have seemed too weak'. Only two lines in the sonnet have ten syllables; the others range from eleven to thirteen syllables. Voice, not metre, determines scansion; or rather, voice pulling away from metre determines scansion. Frost also goes against the grain by sedulously avoiding the neat division of the sonnet into three quatrains and a couplet, and furnishing the poem with a highly unusual distribution of rhymes (*abcabdecdefgfg*). The irregularity in both syntax and rhyme deepens the impression of the sonnet both observing and discarding convention.

Given Frost's promising engagement with the sonnet form in his first book of poems, it seems surprising that his great book of 1914, *North of Boston*, contains not a single sonnet. There are interesting and persuasive reasons for this that have to do with the amplitude of narrative and dramatic currents that Frost was exploring with impressive and prolific results in poems like 'The Death of the Hired Man' and 'Home Burial'. In *Mountain Interval* in 1916, Frost is once again drawn to the lyric intensity of the sonnet, and here we might mention 'Meeting and Passing', 'Hyla Brook', 'The Oven Bird', and 'Range-Finding'. At the same time, Frost's experiments with narrative in *North of Boston* impact on his later sonnets in highly productive ways. The new sonnets are noticeably relaxed and conversational, and we can hear this immediately in the opening lines of 'Meeting and Passing':

> As I went down the hill along the wall
> There was a gate I had leaned at for the view
> And had just turned from when I first saw you
> As you came up the hill. We met. But all
> We did that day was mingle great and small
> Footprints in summer dust as if we drew
> The figure of our being less than two
> But more than one as yet. Your parasol
> Pointed the decimal off with one deep thrust.

---

26. Derek Walcott, 'The Road Taken', *Homage to Robert Frost* (New York: Farrar, Straus, and Giroux, 1996), p. 99.

> And all the time we talked you seemed to see
> Something down there to smile at in the dust.
> (Oh, it was without prejudice to me!)
> Afterward I went past what you had passed
> Before we met and you what I had passed. (115)

'Meeting and Passing' is a virtuosic medley of Italian and English sonnet techniques, but one in which the sound of sense predominates. The rhyme scheme begins conventionally enough in the Petrarchan mould (*abbaabba*), but then veers off, not into the expected tercets of the Petrarchan sonnet but into something closer to the Shakespearean quatrain and rhyming couplet (*cdcdee*), with a strategic and emphatic repetition of the word 'passed'. The rhyme scheme invites us in the conventional way to regard the sonnet as both a two-part structure (octave and sestet) and a four-part structure (three quatrains and a couplet). However, the syntactical arrangement of the poem continually pulls away from this structure, insisting on its own emphatic speech patterns imposed through strong caesuras and marvellously fluent enjambment. The sonnet runs without pause over the traditional turn, while nevertheless marking a point of transition between meeting and passing in the vivid image of the parasol thrust in the earth—less a sexual thrust than a firm indication of division and separation. The parenthetical insertion '(Oh, it was without prejudice to me!)' has an unsettling presence in the momentum of the sonnet. How exactly are we to read that line? Even if it is perceived as feigned nonchalance or ironic disregard, it hints at an emotional disturbance within this otherwise controlled retrospective narrative. To say that this is a poem of courtship or a poem anticipating marriage is only to touch the surface. The 'something' in the dust is every bit as tantalizingly vague as the 'something' that the scythe whispers in 'Mowing'. The last two lines are also teasingly enigmatic, not only reversing the expected relationship of before and after, and playing with the possibilities of past and passing, but also denying the epigrammatic neatness and assurance traditionally guaranteed by the closing couplet of the sonnet. Here the brisk enjambment allows no pause for proverbial wisdom, while the repeated rhyme word both suggests activity—something has passed—and implies that nothing has changed. Significance is simultaneously granted and denied.

Robert Faggen has made the excellent point that 'Frost reserves the small, constrained form of the sonnet' for making 'some of his largest cosmological suggestions', and this is certainly true of 'Acquainted with the Night', which was probably written in Ann Arbor during Frost's residency at the University of Michigan in 1921–2.[27] This particular sonnet ought to rid us once and for all of those misleading, simplified accounts of Frost the farmer poet, the rustic versifier, and provider of homespun truths. 'Acquainted with the Night' is an urban poem, but it is also a remarkably sophisticated poem in terms of form and technique. It speaks of a deep compulsion to see the darkness of those places far beyond the city lights and city lanes, to sever all human relations; it articulates a deep sense of homelessness: not just physical homelessness, but metaphysical homelessness. The speaker in the sonnet is the archetypal man of sorrows, and the title echoes Isaiah 53:3: 'He was despised and rejected of men; a man of sorrows, and acquainted with grief.' At the same time, as Frank Lentricchia points out, there is a profoundly modern sensibility at work in the poem. It confronts what Wallace Stevens memorably termed 'the experience of annihilation'.[28]

> I have been one acquainted with the night.
> I have walked out in rain—and back in rain.
> I have outwalked the furthest city light.
>
> I have looked down the saddest city lane.
> I have passed by the watchman on his beat
> And dropped my eyes, unwilling to explain.
>
> I have stood still and stopped the sound of feet
> When far away an interrupted cry
> Came over houses from another street,
>
> But not to call me back or say good-by;
> And further still at an unearthly height,
> One luminary clock against the sky
>
> Proclaimed the time was neither wrong nor right.
> I have been one acquainted with the night.   (234)

'Acquainted with the Night' is one of Frost's 'terrifying poems about wandering off, losing the self, or belonging nowhere'.[29] Where it marks a significant advance over earlier poems like 'Into My Own', however, is in its

---

27. Robert Faggen, *Robert Frost and the Challenge of Darwin* (Ann Arbor: University of Michigan Press, 2001), p. 46.
28. Frank Lentricchia, *Robert Frost: Modern Poetics and the Landscapes of Self* (Durham, NC: Duke University Press, 1975), p. 77.
29. Richard Poirier, *Robert Frost: The Work of Knowing* (New York: Oxford University Press, 1977), p. 147.

unusual verbal tense: 'I have been one acquainted with the night.' In place of the subjunctive tense, the imagined 'wish' of 'Into My Own', we have the past perfect tense declaring that the speaker has been there: he has tested the limits of emotional and psychological experience. The past perfect tense also hints unnervingly at the recent nature of that experience and so does not rule out the possibility of a repeat performance. Indeed, that repetition is already implicit in the anaphoric structure of the poem: 'I have walked out...I have outwalked...I have looked down...I have passed by...', with each of these actions carrying an insistent double stress. The rhythm fluctuates as we move from the end-stopped lines in the opening tercet to the more fluent, run-on lines in succeeding stanzas. The lines beginning 'I have' gradually diminish from three to two to one in the first three stanzas, and then the opening line reappears at the end: 'I have been one acquainted with the night.' There is circularity as well as repetition.

What makes this such a striking poem, however, is that once again Frost chooses to employ the sonnet form, and once again he shows a strongly cosmopolitan interest in poetic form, going this time not so much to Shakespeare as to Dante. He retains the staple ten-syllable line, but employs four tercets and a rhyming couplet. The rhyme scheme is highly ornate: *aba bcb cdc dcd ded ee*. Each new stanza picks up the previous rhyme, interweaving the rhymes in the *terza rima* of Dante's *Divine Comedy* (an appropriate source in view of the purgatorial darkness that engulfs Frost's poem). The tension between this highly ornate design in the fabric of the poem and the seeming absence of intelligibility in the world it seeks to explain is tightly contained within the sonnet form.

One of the central poetic beliefs articulated by Frost in the later years of his career is the idea that poetry can serve as a creative defence against emptiness. Frost states this explicitly as a matter of poetic principle in essays and letters, most memorably in 'The Figure a Poem Makes' (the Preface to his *Collected Poems* of 1939), in which he famously remarks that poetry is 'a momentary stay against confusion'. Several poems are themselves declarations of the idea that poetry should end in 'a clarification of life'.[30]

Once again, the sonnet form proves valuable as a space for creative reflection amidst prevailing chaos and confusion. The point is well illustrated in 'Design', a sonnet that has justifiably been anthologized many times and remains one of the most challenging sonnets for critics of Frost's poetry:

---

30. Frost, *Collected Poems, Prose and Plays*, p. 234.

> I found a dimpled spider, fat and white,
> On a white heal-all, holding up a moth
> Like a white piece of rigid satin cloth—
> Assorted characters of death and blight
> Mixed ready to begin the morning right,
> Like the ingredients of a witches' broth—
> A snow-drop spider, a flower like a froth,
> And dead wings carried like a paper kite.
>
> What had that flower to do with being white,
> The wayside blue and innocent heal-all?
> What brought the kindred spider to that height,
> Then steered the white moth thither in the night?
> What but design of darkness to appall?—
> If design govern in a thing so small. (275)

This strangely beautiful and potentially terrifying sonnet was included in *A Further Range* in 1936, though an early manuscript version titled 'In White' was attached to a letter to Susan Hayes Ward dated 15 January 1912. The original title, with its artistic suggestions of 'A Study in White', recalls the playful titles of paintings by James Abbot McNeill Whistler, though the final version of the poem is a study in white more in keeping with the blankness and emptiness in the pages of Samuel Beckett. If at one level, the new title hints more subtly at ideas of artistic arrangement and design, it also brings into sharp relief two other conflicting notions of design: the classic argument for the existence of God based on purposeful design in nature (usually attributed to St Thomas Aquinas) and the contrary idea of evolutionary design (derived from Darwin).

The word 'white' appears five times in the sonnet: three times in the octave and twice in the sestet. It also functions as a key rhyme word, being deftly positioned so that the opening line of the sestet echoes the opening line of the octave. The speaker finds by chance (or is it by design?) a white spider (normally black) and a white heal-all flower (normally blue), with the spider clutching a white moth. The opening line seems innocently childlike in its jaunty nursery rhyme simplicity: 'I found a dimpled spider, fat and white.' However, as Randall Jarrell was quick to point out, 'this little albino catastrophe is too whitely catastrophic to be accidental, too impossibly unlikely ever to be a coincidence'.[31] Jarrell observes a diabolical event in the octave of the poem. The spider is holding up the moth like a white

---

31. Randall Jarrell, *Poetry and the Age* (New York: Knopf, 1953), p. 88.

communion host; the dead wings are 'carried' as if part of some sacrificial offering, while the witches' broth clearly recalls the evil goings-on in the opening pages of *Macbeth*. The description of the moth as 'a white piece of rigid satin cloth' has disturbing connotations of *rigor mortis*. At the same time, this macabre scene gains some of its intensity from grotesque and ironic humour: the irony in the name of the flower, for instance; the incongruous evocation of breakfast cereal advertisements in 'Mixed ready to begin the morning right'; and the grim pun in morning right/mourning rite. In fact, the sonnet works as a black joke about whiteness: it gives us anecdotal narrative, insidious questioning complications, and a truly awful punch line.

As a sonnet, 'Design' looks conventional enough in terms of its typographical octave-sestet division, its fairly smooth decasyllabic lines, and its simple monosyllabic rhymes (heal-all and appall are the significant exceptions). The formal logic of the poem posits empirical recognition and description of the ready-made ingredients in the octave against the insistent metaphysical questioning of the sestet. But in fact the uncertainty and the questioning are already implicit in the unlikely similes of 'A snow-drop spider, a flower like a froth, | And dead wings carried like a paper kite.' In other ways, too, the sonnet sets up formal expectations, only to undo them. The regular iambic pattern of the opening line is repeatedly undermined by double and triple stresses in compound nouns and adjectives like 'white heal-all' and 'snow-drop spider'. Most tellingly, perhaps, Frost withholds the satisfied resolution conventionally associated with the closing couplet of the English sonnet. A strong pause is created at the end of the penultimate line through the combined punctuation of a question mark and a dash, and the final line then slows down the pace even further by introducing additional stresses. The troubling question in which design is associated with darkness is suddenly intensified by what is possibly an even more alarming question, though strangely it also has the effect of offering comic relief. In the same way, the suggestions of evil in the alliterative 'design of darkness' are offset by the clever wordplay in 'appall'—both terrifying and making white.

The title and the closing lines of the sonnet encourage a reading in which the strange artistic design of the spider, the flower, and the moth is measured against discomforting notions of providential and evolutionary design. Is human existence subject to some malevolent design or is it possibly without design at all? In a thing so small, maybe we just can't tell. But what about the design that governs the sonnet form, which is itself 'a thing so small'?

The sonnet this time is remarkably inventive in terms of its rhyme scheme, relying on even fewer words than the Italian sonnet habitually uses. There are only three rhyme words in 'Design' and these are distributed so that we have *ab* rhymes in the octave and *ac* rhymes in the sestet. Not only that, but we end up with six rhyming couplets, if we count the turn between the octave and the sestet. The intricate structure of the sonnet is an integral part of Frost's relentless preoccupation with design.

Frost's later sonnets—those written and published in the 1930s and 1940s—are remarkable for the way in which they handle the technical challenges of the form with seemingly effortless brio. Richard Poirier suggests that Frost 'derives energy and excitement from the fact that literature is most "natural" when it is most self-aware of its status as a "made" or performed object, and when it reveals thereby some pathos and wonderment about its claims to existence'.[32] This is certainly true of 'The Silken Tent' and 'Never Again Would Birds' Song Be the Same', both of which are fundamentally concerned with human dilemmas and yet supremely self-reflexive and playfully poetic. Don Paterson justifiably gives prominence to 'The Silken Tent' as the opening poem in his *101 Sonnets from Shakespeare to Heaney*, praising it as 'one of the most brilliantly sustained conceits in the English language...as quietly virtuosic as they come'.[33]

> She is as in a field a silken tent
> At midday when a sunny summer breeze
> Has dried the dew and all its ropes relent,
> So that in guys it gently sways at ease,
> And its supporting central cedar pole,
> That is its pinnacle to heaven ward
> And signifies the sureness of the soul,
> Seems to owe naught to any single cord,
> But strictly held by none, is loosely bound
> By countless silken ties of love and thought
> To everything on earth the compass round,
> And only by one's going slightly taut
> In the capriciousness of the summer air
> Is of the slightest bondage made aware.   (302)

Originally titled 'A Praise for Your Poise', the poem was first published in the *Virginia Quarterly Review* in Winter 1939 and presented by Frost to his friend and secretary, Kay Morrison. It is, itself, a marvellously poised

---

32. Poirier, *Robert Frost*, pp. xii–xiii.   33. Paterson, *101 Sonnets*, p. 104.

performance. Frost deftly establishes an intricate relationship between the extravagant, exotic image of the suspended silken tent and the suspended syntactical space of the sonnet form. The virtuosity of the performance is a measure of the implicit praise for the woman's admirable ability to maintain her poise without apparent strain.

The opening line pays tribute to the woman simply for being what 'she is' and simultaneously initiates the extended simile of the silken tent. The eastern, biblical appeal of the silken tent and its cedar pole perhaps owes something to the 'Song of Songs', in which a bride is praised for being as beautiful 'as the tents of Kedar'. In other respects, however, the poem has subtle ties to the Renaissance love sonnet, and certain lines and phrases would not be out of place in the metaphysical poetry of the seventeenth century ('the sureness of the soul', 'To everything on earth the compass round'). The 'summer breeze' and 'summer air' gently recall the 'summer's day' and 'summer's lease' of Shakespeare's Sonnet 18.[34] The rhyme scheme, too, is Shakespearean, as are the repeated conjunctions at the beginning of lines 5, 7, and 12. The great technical achievement of 'The Silken Tent' is in creating the impression of verbal freedom and flexibility within the supporting structure of the sonnet form, so that we are not made aware of the slightest bondage until the end of the poem's magnificent single sentence.

The poem's midday summer setting helps to establish its preoccupation with poise, while the breeze in line 2 prepares us for the 'capriciousness' of summer air that tightens and tautens the guy ropes of the tent. The compactness of the sonnet form allows Frost to demonstrate the possibilities of the sound of sense: the voice pulls ever so gently against the opening iambs, relaxes into the smooth vowel sounds and sibilants of line 2, before tightening a little in the nicely balanced alliteration of line 3. The technical assurance of the sonnet is such that Frost is cunningly able to introduce the impression of a turn without actually losing any of the momentum generated by the fluent enjambment of the octave. 'But' calls attention to itself as the most obvious indication of a turn in the English sonnet, but its grammatical function in Frost's sonnet is to act as a smooth and transitory connective rather than a strongly marked conjunction. To the very end of the poem, the tension between the pull of the voice and the fabric of the sonnet-tent determines its shape and meaning. The introduction of an additional stress in line 12, for instance, highlights 'one's going', both emphasizing the play of

---

34. *The Complete Sonnets and Poems*, ed. Burrow, p. 417.

a single rope and suggesting the presence of a human consciousness within the poem. Who, if not the tent itself, is made aware of the virtues of being 'loosely bound'? The poem subtly communicates the value and validity of life's 'countless silken ties of love and thought' while offering itself as a supreme aesthetic instance of freedom within form.

A self-reflexive preoccupation with the form and function of poetry is also abundantly evident in 'Never Again Would Birds' Song Be the Same'. This mellifluous sonnet is both a meditation on our human origins and a light-hearted explanation of the lyric impulse in poetry. It teasingly takes hold of the biblical myth of the Garden of Eden, but also returns us to some pure, pre-verbal notion of poetic creation. If it mourns the loss initiated by Adam and Eve, it also celebrates their archetypal purpose in humanizing nature:

> He would declare and could himself believe
> That the birds there in all the garden round
> From having heard the daylong voice of Eve
> Had added to their own an oversound,
> Her tone of meaning but without the words.
> Admittedly an eloquence so soft
> Could only have had an influence on birds
> When call or laughter carried it aloft.
> Be that as may be, she was in their song.
> Moreover her voice upon their voices crossed
> Had now persisted in the woods so long
> That probably it never would be lost.
> Never again would birds' song be the same.
> And to do that to birds was why she came.   (308)

The poem considers the echo of Eve's voice in birdsong, of human meanings in nature, and so it is appropriate that this Shakespearean sonnet should open with an echo of a line in *Hamlet* (1.1.146) that Frost considered 'the most beautiful single line of English verse': 'So have I heard, and do in part believe it.'[35] There is a further echo of Hamlet's famous soliloquy, 'To be, or not to be', in the opening line of the sestet—'Be that as may be'—but Frost leaves behind metaphysical speculation and uncertainty about origins and destinations, and offers instead an idea of persistence and survival. In a fundamental way, the poem explores what T. S. Eliot called 'the auditory imagination', 'the feeling for syllable and rhythm, penetrating far below the

---

35. Parini, *Robert Frost*, p. 323. *The Norton Shakespeare*, ed. Stephen Greenblatt et al. (New York: Norton, 1997), p. 1672.

conscious levels of thought and feeling, invigorating every word; sinking to the most primitive and forgotten, returning to the origin and bringing something back'.[36] Eliot's account of the auditory imagination is valuable here, but it so happens that Frost had his own very similar theory of the sounds of poetry. Writing to Sidney Cox from Dymock, in Gloucestershire, in December 1914, Frost elaborated on 'the sound of sense', maintaining that there were sentence sounds that served as a kind of repertoire of meaning, regardless of their strict grammatical function: 'Just so many sentence sounds belong to man as just so many vocal runs belong to one kind of bird. We come into the world with them and create none of them. What we feel as creation is only selection and grouping. We summon them from Heaven knows where under excitement with the audile imagination.'[37]

What Frost identifies as 'sentence sound' is delivered in the 'oversound' that the 'daylong voice of Eve' has added to the song of birds: 'Her tone of meaning but without the words.' In the same letter, Frost claims that the sounds of poetry will not be forced into being: 'And unless we are in an imaginative mood it is no use trying to make them, they will not rise.'[38] This idea, too, is picked up in the sonnet, in the suggestion that there is an optimum creative mood, closely allied with love. Eve's voice had an influence on birds only 'When call or laughter carried it aloft'. That realization marks a crucial turn in the sonnet, from innocence to experience, from the garden to the woods. The biblical fall meant that birdsong would never be the same as in that paradisial moment of happiness, but what the sonnet is able to recover and advocate is the idea of poetry and song as a joyful apprehension of loss. The sonnet form is vitally important in holding together the poem's contrary perceptions and its complex grasp of temporal perspectives. The speaker of the poem appears, in the terms of Eliot's 'auditory imagination', to fuse 'the most ancient and the most civilised mentality', being simultaneously an intimate of Adam and Eve and a representative modern commentator.[39] The sonnet also crosses two sets of sounds: the pure and primitive eloquence of birds and the intellectual reasoning of the modern mentality suggested by those deftly placed linguistic qualifiers: 'Admittedly... Moreover... That probably....' The unusual pluperfect tense blurs any easy distinction between the 'then' and 'there' of the octave and the 'here' and

---

36. T. S. Eliot, *The Use of Poetry and the Use of Criticism* (London: Faber, 1964), pp. 118–19.
37. Frost, *Collected Poems, Prose and Plays*, p. 681.
38. Frost, *Collected Poems, Prose and Plays*, p. 681.
39. T. S. Eliot, *The Use of Poetry and the Use of Criticism*, p. 119.

'now' of the sestet. As readers, we are inducted into a 'never again' with only a mythical and intuitive sense of what we have lost.

The force of the final line, introduced by a conjunction but nevertheless retaining the clinching effect of the familiar closing couplet, is such that it functions both as a casual and playful afterthought *and* as a slightly awed apprehension of the sonnet's own continuing place in the evolution of song. The title of the poem and its echo in the penultimate line of the sonnet are similarly counterweighted, seeming to offer simultaneously the continuing possibility of joy ('probably it never would be lost') and the seeming desolation that something has, indeed, been lost. Seamus Heaney sums up this contrariness with characteristic lucidity:

> The poem's argument, as I read it, ought to lead to the conclusion that the changed note of the birds' song should be an occasion of joy, since it happened in Paradise and was effected by the paradisial voice of Eve. But that logic is complicated by the actual note of repining that we hear in the line 'Never again would birds' song be the same', a note that comes from the fact that we are now beyond Eden, at a great distance of time and space.

As Heaney attests, we slip in this late sonnet from what seems in the octave to be 'a heart-lifting truth' to what we know in the sestet is the heaviness of heartbreak.[40]

Frost has been widely praised for his skills in handling dramatic incidents and narrative voice, and these are qualities that make for expansiveness in poetry. Rather less attention has been given to Frost's achievements as a poet of lyric intensity, though undoubtedly this is the appeal of poems such as 'The Silken Tent' and 'Never Again Would Birds' Song Be the Same'. A reappraisal of these sonnets ought to persuade us of what Heaney felicitously terms 'the overbrimming technical joys' of Frost's poetry. As a writer who has undoubtedly learned a great deal from poems like 'Mowing' and 'The Silken Tent', he reminds us that Frost is, among other things, 'one of the most irresistible masters of the sonnet in the English language'.[41]

T. S. Eliot, E. E. Cummings, and Wallace Stevens

In the first decade of the twentieth century, shortly after Robert Frost had written his industrial mill sonnets, the young T. S. Eliot composed three experimental sonnets prompted by vivid images of women in mythology,

---

40. Seamus Heaney, 'Above the Brim', *Homage to Robert Frost*, pp. 79–80.
41. Heaney, *Homage to Robert Frost*, pp. 84–5.

painting, and literature. The poems were published in the *Harvard Advocate* in 1908 and 1909, and they show Eliot subtly adopting and exploring some of the Decadent motifs familiar in late nineteenth-century English poetry.[42] In all three sonnets, Eliot experiments with voice and perspective. The speaker in 'Circe's Palace' (Odysseus or one of his sailors) fears imminent death or transformation, while the enchantress herself, famed in Greek and Latin literature for changing men into swine and other animals, is seen only through her exotic surroundings and imagined by Eliot as a version the late Romantic and Decadent *femme fatale*. Almost certainly inspired by Maxfield Parrish's illustration of 'Circe's Palace' for the 1907 edition of Nathaniel Hawthorne's *Tanglewood Tales* (1853), the sonnet presents the absent Circe through the disconcerting images of a fountain that 'flows | With the voice of men in pain' and strange flowers that spring 'from the limbs of the dead' with petals 'fanged and red'. Adopting a *terza rima* sonnet form with brisk trimeter lines, Eliot neatly cuts the poem into two seven-line stanzas (*abacbcb dedfefe*), with the second of these showing men already changed into panthers, pythons, and peacocks: 'And they look at us with the eyes | Of men whom we knew long ago' (231–2).

The second sonnet, 'On a Portrait', appears to have been inspired by Edouard Manet's 1866 painting, *Woman with a Parrot*, with Dante Gabriel Rossetti's sonnets in *The House of Life* providing a model for the relationship between visual medium and verbal response. This time, the woman is serenely poised and aloof. Rather than threatening emasculation, she remains inscrutable and mysterious, removed from the modern urban life of those with 'restless brain and weary feet'. Although another destructive classical female figure is invoked, Eliot safely contains the reference with the kind of intellectualized, ironic detachment that characterizes the later poems in *Prufrock and Other Observations* (1917). With a studied and affected air of aesthetic cultivation, the speaker describes the woman in the portrait as 'evanescent' and thoughtful, 'as if one should meet | A pensive lamia in some wood-retreat'. The sonnet opens with a Petrarchan rhyme scheme, but modulates into its Shakespearean counterpart, with three distinct quatrains and a couplet (*abba abba cdcd ee*). The isolated rhyming couplet allows the sonnet to adopt a new angle of vision: 'The parrot on his bar, a silent spy, | Regards her with a patient curious eye' (232). While the poem hints at the

---

42. T. S. Eliot, 'Circe's Palace', *Harvard Advocate* 86.5 (25 November 1908), 'On a Portrait', *Harvard Advocate* 86.9 (26 January 1909), and 'Nocturne', *Harvard Advocate* 88.3 (12 November 1909). Page numbers refer to *The Poems of T. S. Eliot*, ed. Christopher Ricks and Jim McCue (Baltimore: Johns Hopkins University Press, 2015), vol. I.

close identification (and even erotic encounter) found in other artistic representations of women and birds, it also functions as an early experiment with shifts of perspective and attitude, of a kind that Eliot would later explore in 'La Figlia che Piange'.

The third of the *Harvard Advocate* sonnets, titled 'Nocturne', is one of several night pieces in Eliot's early work, but also one of several poems alluding to varieties of musical composition ('Preludes' and 'Rhapsody on a Windy Night' come to mind). The subject of the sonnet, however, is Shakespeare's *Romeo and Juliet*, seen through the playfully ironic perspective of Jules Laforgue, who had given similar sardonic treatment to *Hamlet*. Romeo (*'grand sérieux'*) is seen with 'Guitar and hat in hand', perhaps recalling Arthur Symons's memorable description of Laforgue as a poet who 'composes love-poems hat in hand'. It is Juliet, however, who takes centre stage, as the speaker rearranges the scene in a manner reminiscent of Eliot's later 'Portrait of a Lady':'I have some servant wait, | Stab, and the lady sinks into a swoon.' The stabbing coincides with the *volta* and gives the nonchalant speaker an opportunity to arrange the scene once more at the opening of the sestet: 'Blood looks effective on the moonlit ground—' (234–5). The rhyme scheme this time follows a common Petrarchan model (*abbaabbacdcdcd*), but the awkward rhymes ('importune'/'courteous moon', 'oblique'/'next week') are in keeping with the cynical theatricality of the poem.

By 1917, Eliot had come to think that there might not be much of a future for the sonnet. In 'Reflections on *Vers Libre*', he makes the crucial distinction between 'liberation from rhyme' and 'liberation *of* rhyme', anticipating that formal rhymed verse, including the heroic couplet, will continue to be written by modern poets. 'As for the sonnet', he adds, 'I am not so sure.'[43] That uncertainty hovers over his later composition of fourteen-line verses that might or might not be sonnets. The seduction of the 'typist home at teatime' by 'the young man carbuncular' in 'The Fire Sermon' section of *The Waste Land* (lines 235–48) is nimbly and efficiently conveyed in fourteen lines that neatly deploy the rhyme scheme and quatrain divisions associated with an English tradition of sonnet writing. The concealed sonnet is fittingly embedded in a section of Eliot's great modernist poem in which Tiresias enacts a turn, announcing that he has seen it all before, 'Enacted on this same divan or bed'.[44] If Eliot's debased sonnet appears as an

---

43. *Selected Prose of T. S. Eliot*, ed. Frank Kermode (London: Faber, 1975), p. 36.
44. T. S. Eliot, *The Complete Poems and Plays 1909–1950* (New York: Harcourt Brace & Company, 1980), p. 44.

ironic commentary on the amatory ideals that once sustained the poetry of the English Renaissance, it might also be read as continuous with the cynical vision that rises to the surface in Shakespeare's sonnets.

'The Dry Salvages', the third of Eliot's *Four Quartets*, opens with an unrhymed sonnet that winds like a river towards the sea, though a river more likely to be the Mississippi than the Duddon, in expansive lines and vernacular rhythms closer to Whitman than Wordsworth: 'I do not know much about gods; but I think that the river | Is a strong brown god—sullen, untamed and intractable, | Patient to some degree, at first recognised as a frontier.'[45] The odd near-rhyme ('river'/'frontier') only serves to remind us, as Christopher Ricks points out, that these fourteen lines summon 'an enduring power which (like the sonnet itself within literary tradition) can be "almost forgotten" in the modern world but which can be felt "waiting, watching and waiting", a "reminder"'.[46] A similar attitude to the sonnet prevails in the work of other modernist poets, including Ezra Pound and William Carlos Williams, as if the sonnet is both vestigial and latent, both an outmoded curiosity from a bygone literary culture and a form awaiting recovery and capable of great resilience.

The sonnets of E. E. Cummings often serve as a reminder of a half-forgotten tradition of writing, radically renovating the lyrical style and the courtly sentiment associated with poets like Sir Philip Sidney. 'My true love hath my heart' is newly minted in the sonnet beginning 'i carry your heart with me(i carry it in | my heart)'. Despite the trademark lower case informality and parenthetical aside, Cummings remains true, here and elsewhere, to the time-honoured metaphors of love: 'you are whatever a moon has always meant.'[47] What is surprising, then, is just how forcefully and remorselessly Cummings is also able to dismantle Petrarchan conventions and displace them with strikingly modern ways of talking about love and sex. The sonnet 'my girl's tall with hard long eyes' has more in common with the paintings of Modigliani than the poems of Petrarch, and its attitude to love is brazenly modern and unromantic: 'good for sleeping | is her long hard body filled with surprise | like a white shocking wire.' The sonnet promises yet more 'hard long' activity, but the sestet is cynically intent on undermining any prospect of actual love or even sexual pleasure:

---

45. Eliot, *The Complete Poems and Plays*, p. 130.
46. *The Poems of T. S. Eliot*, ed. Ricks and McCue, p. 274.
47. E. E. Cummings, *Complete Poems* (London: McGibbon & Kee, 1968), vol. 2, p. 766. Volume number and page number for further quotations will be given in brackets in the text.

> my girl's tall
> and taut, with thin legs just like a vine
> that's spent all of its life on a garden-wall,
> and is going to die.   When we grimly go to bed
> with these legs she begins to heave and twine
> about me,and to kiss my face and head.   (1.147)

The sonnet retains a superficial attachment to Petrarchan forms in its rhyme scheme (*abbacddcefegfg*), but otherwise it casts out convention with its overt physicality and sardonic self-regard. The long pause attendant on thoughts of death seems spurious, and the final line with its countervailing speed suggests that there is really no space for reflection.

By dismantling traditional lineation and capitalization, Cummings brings a visual novelty to the sonnet form. There is also an aural novelty in what he does with the form, since he decisively alters the speed of the sonnet, upsetting its usual stately decorum through a hectic jumbling of syntax and a wilful omission of punctuation. If he makes an outrageous assault on the love sonnet, he also explodes the patriotic sonnet, bearing down on it with unrelenting pressure:

> "next to of course god america i
> love you land of the pilgrims' and so forth oh
> say can you see by the dawn's early my
> country 'tis of centuries come and go
> and are no more what of it we should worry
> in every language even deafanddumb
> thy sons acclaim your glorious name by gorry
> by jingo by gee by gosh by gum
> why talk of beauty what could be more beaut-
> iful than these heroic happy dead
> who rushed like lions to the roaring slaughter
> they did not stop to think they died instead
> then shall the voice of liberty be mute?"
> He spoke.   And drank rapidly a glass of water   (1.268)

What initially looks like comic buffoonery, provocatively intent on deflating patriotic rhetoric, perhaps conceals more complex ironic attitudes. As David Bromwich suggests, the collision of different viewpoints and registers makes it difficult to gauge the tone of the poem, and also leaves the reader with a sneaking suspicion that Cummings actually relishes the patriotic hymns of his childhood: 'Sentimentality and sarcasm, panegyric and parody jostle so closely in his poetry that sometimes only a title, a limping or short-footed line, a curl of the lip or a turn of phrase will let you know for sure that a given poem is not offered piously but in ridicule or self-mockery.'[48] Here, of course, the quotation marks ensure a sufficient distance from the performance, and the isolated closing line comments coolly on a speaker in danger of overheating himself. At the same time, the poem is not simply or straightforwardly a mockery of national, heroic ideals. It uses the sonnet form very cunningly to hold in suspension snatches of patriotic songs and anthems—'My Country, 'Tis of Thee' and 'The Star-Spangled Banner'—with a plethora of clichés and platitudes, so that what is exposed, more specifically, is a particular kind of national consciousness. Bromwich notes astutely that the technique very likely derives from James Joyce's *Ulysses*, with its acute awareness of advertising techniques and public consumption of slogans.[49] Cummings writes a suitably deranged sonnet, starting out with a sprightly Shakespearean rhyme scheme, but cautiously avoiding a rhyming couplet and offering instead a single line of sobering intent.

In 1931, the year in which 'The Star-Spangled Banner' was formally adopted as the American national anthem, Wallace Stevens gave a new complexion to the modern American sonnet in 'Autumn Refrain', allegedly the only poem he wrote that year, and one in which poetic inspiration is itself the principal subject of meditation.[50] Resistant in his own way to insinuating rhetoric and easy poeticizing, Stevens writes a chastened lyricism that wonders if, in sensitively describing the world, it might only be repeating what has already been put in words. The title aptly catches this double act of both adding to the store of poetic tradition and holding back in a self-cancelling or self-postponing way. The poem embarks on its own striking attempt to render a personal experience of autumn, conscious of the 'measureless measures' of poetry already devoted to the subject:

> The skreak and skritter of evening gone
> And grackles gone and sorrows of the sun,
> The sorrows of sun, too, gone ... the moon and moon,
> The yellow moon of words about the nightingale
> In measureless measures, not a bird for me
> But the name of a bird and the name of a nameless air
> I have never—shall never hear. And yet beneath

---

48. David Bromwich (ed.), *American Sonnets: An Anthology* (New York: Library of America, 2007), pp. xxviii–xxix.
49. Bromwich, *American Sonnets*, p. xxx.
50. *The Collected Poems of Wallace Stevens* (New York: Vintage, 1982), p. 160.

> The stillness of everything gone, and being still,
> Being and sitting still, something resides,
> Some skreaking and skrittering residuum,
> And grates these evasions of the nightingale
> Though I have never—shall never hear that bird.
> And the stillness is in the key, all of it is,
> The stillness is all in the key of that desolate sound.

The acoustic harshness of 'skreak and skritter' boldly announces the poem's determination to do something new with poetic representations of the sights and sounds of evening, just as the invocation of the querulous 'grackles' initially distances the poem from the English nightingale and Keatsian inflections of autumn. At the same time, these crackling consonantal nouns call attention to themselves as words, and as words rather too archly unpoetic. The sonnet holds in imaginative suspension both the object of perception and the word that denotes it: 'the moon and moon'. Against Romantic ideals of harmonious correspondence between mind and world, the poem posits its own fractured structure, its own desultory belatedness. As John Hollander observes, the poem bears out its title, in that it 'employs only broken recurrences, true *refractions*, in its scattered repetitions of word and phrase'. All the accoutrements of loss 'lie about in bits of fractured echoic hearsay, in rumours of *rentrement*'.[51] Just as surely, though, 'Autumn Refrain' recalls and recovers the sonnet form, bringing it into service as a way of holding contrary and conflicting ideas together, even while it self-consciously repeats the poignant fears of Keats that 'I may never live', from his most autumnal sonnet, in 'I have never—shall never hear'. At precisely that mid-line point, the sonnet turns prematurely to contemplate an echo of itself in the remaining seven lines. In its conviction that 'something resides' in the face of 'everything gone', the poem moves resolutely towards the idea that poetry is self-generating and self-perpetuating, the aesthetic experience it affords calling for recognition of its own indubitable reality in 'all of it *is*'. The refrain of 'stillness' acknowledges a deep sense of that which is gone, while simultaneously insisting that all of it is 'still' going on. In contradistinction to the near rhymes of the opening, which play with sonnet conventions and then dissolve them, the overflowing closing line ingeniously sets up expectations and then exceeds them: 'The stillness is all in the key of that desolate sound.'

51. John Hollander, 'Breaking into Song: Some Notes on Refrain', *Lyric Poetry: Beyond New Criticism*, ed. Chaviva Hošek and Patricia Parker (Ithaca, NY: Cornell University Press, 1985), p. 83.

Paul Laurence Dunbar, Countee Cullen, Claude McKay, and Gwendolyn Brooks

Among the poems in Edwin Arlington Robinson's *Children of the Night* (1897) is a sonnet declaring that 'The poet is a slave', and that the sonnet, of all forms, demands commitment to the perfect word. It follows, then, that 'the sonnet-slave must understand | The mission of his bondage'.[52] For Paul Laurence Dunbar, who also published his earliest poems in the 1890s, the idea of the poet as a slave had more than metaphorical significance. Both of his parents were former slaves, his father having escaped to Canada from a plantation in Kentucky, later joining the 55th Massachusetts Infantry, the sister regiment of the celebrated 54th that suffered heavy losses under Colonel Robert Gould Shaw at Fort Wagner in 1863 (the subject of Robert Lowell's great elegy 'For the Union Dead'). Dunbar's 'Robert Gould Shaw' is an elegant Petrarchan sonnet that echoes Milton's 'On the Lord General Fairfax', asking in the octave what it was that called Shaw 'To lead th' unlettered and despisèd droves | To manhood's home and thunder at the gate'. If this response seems *too* lettered, *too* ready to bathe in 'Learning's light', the sestet powerfully bends the rhetoric of the political establishment to its own vision, lamenting that the freedom for which Gould and his soldiers fought remains unrealized: 'Since thou and those who with thee died for right | Have died, the Present teaches, but in vain!'[53] Dunbar's sonnet for Frederick Douglass (1903) again recalls Milton, both in its direct opening address and in its prominent allusion to *Paradise Lost*: 'Ah, Douglass, we have fall'n on evil days, | Such days as thou, not even thou didst know.'[54]

In addition to his well-crafted sonnets in standard written English, Dunbar wrote poems in a style that sought to capture the diction and rhythms of African American speech and song, initiating a debate about authenticity and the politics of language that has carried on for over a century. The poets associated with the Harlem Renaissance in the 1920s pushed this debate in various directions. While Langston Hughes wrote in the vernacular of his own black community, drawing on rhythms inspired by jazz and blues, Countee Cullen was intent on showing what he could

---

52. *Collected Poems of Edwin Arlington Robinson*, p. 95.
53. Paul Laurence Dunbar, 'Robert Gould Shaw', *Atlantic Monthly*, October 1900, p. 488.
54. Paul Laurence Dunbar, 'Douglass', *The Norton Anthology of African American Literature*, ed. Henry Louis Gates, Jr and Nellie Y. McKay (New York: Norton, 2004), p. 925.

achieve within the established literary tradition, while sardonically expressing surprise to find himself there at all. 'Yet Do I Marvel', published in *Color* (1925), seems comfortably conversant with European literary tradition and classical mythology, ostentatiously rhyming 'Tantalus' and 'Sisyphus'. A modified Shakespearean sonnet, the poem moves eloquently in its octave towards justifying the ways of God to man, but resorts in the sestet to three emphatic couplets declaring the maker's ultimate inscrutability: 'Yet do I marvel at this curious thing: | To make a poet black, and bid him sing!'[55] The debate over language and form had a subtle and complex relationship with the politics of conciliation and opposition, and there were no easy dividing lines. Claude McKay, who had left Jamaica for the United States in 1912, clearly saw the political benefits in voicing militant opposition in a literary form that carried great cultural prestige but (in the hands of Milton, Shelley, and others) was also an instrument of subversion. 'If We Must Die' was one of the foundational poems of the Harlem Renaissance and a powerful instance of how the sonnet might continue to speak on behalf of justice and equality in a cultural context far removed historically and geographically from that other, European Renaissance. It was prompted by the 'Red Summer' of race riots in American cities in 1919, following demobilization and competition for jobs at the end of the First World War, and it was first printed in the *Liberator*, a Communist newspaper edited by Max Eastman. The form is Shakespearean, but the octave strategically echoes Rupert Brooke's well-known sonnet, 'The Soldier': 'If we must die, let it not be like hogs.' The initial appeal to honour and nobility makes the spirited resistance of the closing couplet all the more powerful, as McKay calls on his 'kinsmen' to 'face the murderous, cowardly pack, | Pressed to the wall, dying, but fighting back!'[56]

'America', also published in the *Liberator* (1921), is a political sonnet couched in the idiom of a love poem addressed to a cruel mistress. The form, the bitter disillusionment, and the meditation on 'time's unerring hand' are all derived from Shakespeare, but McKay's sonnet responds to the epic challenge of America in brilliantly innovative ways, catching both the excited jazzy underworld of the Harlem Renaissance ('I love this cultured hell that tests my youth') and the overwhelming power of America's geographical and architectural might: 'Her bigness sweeps my being like a flood.' The sonnet

---

55. *The Norton Anthology of African American Literature*, ed. Gates and McKay, p. 1341.
56. Claude McKay, *Complete Poems*, ed. William J. Maxwell (Urbana and Chicago: University of Illinois Press, 2004), pp. 177–8. Further references are to this edition of the poems.

turns wilfully and prematurely in the eighth line to confront America 'as a rebel fronts a king in state', but its triumph is in the stoical calm with which it empties out all feelings of resentment and terror, as it moves towards its final moment of prophetic illumination. The familiar biblical allusion to 'seeing through a glass darkly' (1 Corinthians 13:12) is combined with Keats's 'Darkling I stand and listen', while confidently proclaiming the sure sense of selfhood that Aimé Césaire would later define as 'Négritude':

> Darkly I gaze into the days ahead,
> And see her might and granite wonders there,
> Beneath the touch of Time's unerring hand,
> Like priceless treasures sinking in the sand.

The closing allusion to Shelley's 'Ozymandias' fills out the resonant echoes of Shakespeare's Sonnet 107. McKay's distinctive contribution to the sonnet tradition, however, is not simply to restate a familiar preoccupation with power and mutability, but to do so as a Jamaican American standing on the streets of New York in 1921. Both 'America' and 'If We Must Die' were included in McKay's *Harlem Shadows* in that *annus mirabilis* of modernism, 1922, reminding us of the broader context of cultural decline and artistic experimentation in which he and other émigré writers moved, from New York to London to Paris. His city poems have a ghostly appeal reminiscent of Hart Crane, combining a sweeping and intense Romantic vision with a modernist apprehension of the new. In 'Dawn in New York', the poet once again goes 'darkly-rebel' to work, but also thrills to the spirit of the dawn. 'Manhattan's roofs and spires and cheerless domes' resemble, for a moment, those of Wordsworth's London, but New York is not sleeping, and the people who appear on the streets are 'Grotesques beneath the strong electric lights' (172–3).

McKay died in Chicago in 1948, and a year later Gwendolyn Brooks published the Pulitzer prizewinning volume of poems, *Annie Allen*, in which she imagines an African American girl growing up in the city and learning to understand the complex interplay of love and art and violence. The third section of the book, tracing Annie's development into 'Womanhood', contains a sonnet sequence titled 'The Children of the Poor', which calls attention to poverty and racial discrimination, while asking candidly about the appropriate form in which to voice such concerns. In the second sonnet, Annie speaks as an anxious mother, but her voice takes on a biblical and historical authority: 'What shall I give my children? Who are poor, | Who are adjudged the leastwise of the land.'[57] Even while crafting a sonnet that draws its rhetorical ballast from both Petrarch and Shakespeare, Brooks wonders aloud about the adequacy of her medium in such pressing circumstances. Contemplating the hand that might give and the unsure hand of the mother in the octave, the sonnet turns in the sestet to the hand of the artist: 'My hand is stuffed with mode, design, device. | But I lack access to my proper stone' (1634). The fourth sonnet is more militant and more outspoken about the place of art in a time of violence. The immediate context is the Second World War and its unstable aftermath, but the sonnet clearly looks back to the Harlem Renaissance, as if picking up its cue from McKay, and it just as surely looks forward to the galvanizing of the Civil Rights Movement in the 1950s and 1960s. The sonnet seems uncompromisingly to subordinate art to political expediency, but it also suggests a subversive interim strategy by which those who are excluded might occupy the privileged realm of high culture and turn it to their own devices:

> First fight. Then fiddle. Ply the slipping string
> With feathery sorcery; muzzle the note
> With hurting love; the music that they wrote
> Bewitch, bewilder.   (1634)

Brooks would later give more credence to the idea of art and literature playing an active and progressive role in transforming civil life, but here the artfully crafted sonnet speaks uncomfortably about letting hate take priority over harmony. Behind this rhetorical armature, however, what the sonnet subtly achieves is a defence of its own civilized space, an assertion of radical action that nevertheless ends, and rhymes, with grace.

Edna St Vincent Millay, Elizabeth Bishop, and Anne Stevenson

New York in the first few decades of the twentieth century had a powerfully liberating effect on Edna St Vincent Millay's handling of the sonnet form, though Greenwich bohemianism rather than Harlem Renaissance is the ethos that many of her poems evoke.[58] One of the most prolific sonnet

---

57. *The Norton Anthology of African American Literature*, ed. Gates, Jr and McKay, p. 1633. Further quotations are given in brackets within the text.
58. Quotations from the poems of Edna St Vincent Millay are from *Collected Sonnets*, ed. Elizabeth Barnett (New York: Harper and Row, 1988).

writers in modern America, Millay acquired her felicity with rhyme and metre at an early age, publishing her first poems in her teens, and then perfecting her craft as a student at Vassar College between 1913 and 1917. A cool, wayward, idiosyncratic talent takes possession of the sonnet in her first collection of poems, *Renascence* (1917), making us think for a moment that it might be Christina Rossetti or Rupert Brooke we are hearing, but then unmistakably letting us know that this is the work of a modern woman in a modern city:

> If I should learn, in some quite casual way,
> That you were gone, not to return again—
> Read from the back-page of a paper, say,
> Held by a neighbor in a subway train,
> How at the corner of this avenue
> And such a street (so are the papers filled)
> A hurrying man, who happened to be you,
> At noon today had happened to be killed,
> I should not cry aloud—I could not cry
> Aloud, or wring my hands in such a place—
> I should but watch the station lights rush by
> With a more careful interest on my face;
> Or raise my eyes and read with greater care
> Where to store furs and how to treat the hair. (5)

The sonnet is adept in imagining and describing the circumstances in which the speaker might learn 'in some quite casual way' about the death of a lover, dropping the occasional aside ('say') or parenthetical addition ('so are the papers filled') into its meditation on that unfortunate day. The Shakespearean form allows a small drama to unfold, but the quatrain divisions are effaced, so that a single sentence relentlessly follows the movement of the subway train towards its destination in the city. The subjunctive mood and the suspended syntax keep us in the dark until the imagined death at the end of the octave, with a temporal mid-point marker, 'At noon today', neatly anticipating the turn. The sestet fulfils the expectation created in the opening line of the octave ('If I should learn... I should not cry aloud'), but also leads us into an unexpected psychological revelation. What might look like callousness or flippancy might also be read as a stubborn determination to keep going, to stay in control, and to exercise emotional restraint in public. The closing line smacks of modern advertising culture, but it speaks more subtly about the art of preservation—both preserving furs and preserving appearances in a culture where open displays of grief might be considered unseemly. This is not a plangent self-elegy in the manner of Rossetti's 'Remember', but a poem more obviously focused on the survival of the speaker. As such, it vividly illustrates Peter Sacks's claim that American elegies are historically marked by an evasion or denial of grief. American elegies, he claims, are often 'rebellious, as if the poets were unusually resistant to the very submission that we now recognize as crucial to the work of mourning'.[59]

Advertising and consumerism shape the sexual politics of Millay's sonnets in strange and intriguing ways. Her best-known sonnet, 'What lips my lips have kissed, and where, and why', published in *The Harp-Weaver* in 1923, opens with a flamboyant declaration of sexual independence and frankness, as if love's transactions were part of a hectic consumer culture. There is a strong suggestion of spectacle and self-publicity in the provocative declaration of careless promiscuity, but also an unmistakable air of lamentation, communicating a keen sense of loss and disappointment:

> What lips my lips have kissed, and where, and why,
> I have forgotten, and what arms have lain
> Under my head till morning; but the rain
> Is full of ghosts tonight, that tap and sigh
> Upon the glass and listen for reply,
> And in my heart there stirs a quiet pain
> For unremembered lads that not again
> Will turn to me at midnight with a cry.
> Thus in winter stands the lonely tree,
> Nor knows what birds have vanished one by one,
> Yet knows its boughs more silent than before:
> I cannot say what loves have come and gone,
> I only know that summer sang in me
> A little while, that in me sings no more.   (42)

The poem marks a significant advance in terms of how women writers of the sonnet might represent sexual relationships, and Diana Henderson is surely right to claim that Millay broke through 'the conventions inhibiting female expressions of sexual desire with modernist bravado'.[60] At the same time, what is puzzling here is the way in which the sonnet reverts in its dispirited melancholy to ghostly echoes of tradition (Shakespeare's Sonnet 73 and

---

59. Peter Sacks, *The English Elegy: Studies in the Genre from Spenser to Yeats* (Baltimore: Johns Hopkins University Press, 1985), p. 314.
60. Diana Henderson, 'The Sonnet, Subjectivity and Gender', *The Cambridge Companion to the Sonnet*, ed. A. D. Cousins and Peter Howarth (Cambridge: Cambridge University Press, 2011), p. 62.

A. E. Housman's *A Shropshire Lad* come to mind). The sonnet form itself is not severely disrupted, and what proves to be most innovative and imposing is the tension created between the unconventional attitude to love and the decorously handled Petrarchan rhyme scheme. With the divided attitude of a Scott Fitzgerald novel, the sonnet captures both the excitement and the exhaustion of the jazz age. If it speaks of a boldly permissive and hedonist culture, it also gives a desultory voice to an underlying emptiness and hollowness.

Another Vassar graduate, Elizabeth Bishop, began writing sonnets in her late teens, while still at high school. 'Sonnet', written in 1928, shows the unmistakable influence of Edna St Vincent Millay in its expressive frankness and its decorous handling of the Petrarchan form:

> I am in need of music that would flow
> Over my fretful, feeling finger-tips,
> Over my bitter-tainted, trembling lips,
> With melody, deep, clear, and liquid-slow.[61]

The sestet, however, moves into the coastal landscape and the oceanic imagery so distinctive in Bishop's later work, picking up the cues in the musical 'flow' and 'liquid-slow' pleasures of the octave. The sonnet closes by subtly and mysteriously equating 'the magic made by melody' with 'the subaqueous stillness of the sea' and 'a moon-green pool'. Bishop returned to the sonnet form occasionally, with 'The Reprimand' in 1935 and 'The Wit' in 1956, and she played ambitiously with voice and perspective (mixing archaic and modern diction in a Hopkins-like effusion) in the experimental triad, 'Three Sonnets for Eyes', in 1933. Compared with Millay, though, she used the form very sparingly.

Bishop's slender 'Sonnet' (1979) was very likely the final poem she wrote in her long career, and it marks a radical departure from Millay's careful adherence to formal conventions. The poem immediately calls attention to itself by flagrantly breaking with just about every formal device traditionally associated with its title: octave-sestet division, quatrain divisions, line length, rhyme scheme, and metre:

> Caught—the bubble
> in the spirit-level,
> a creature divided;

---

61. Elizabeth Bishop, *Poems, Prose, and Letters*, ed. Robert Giroux and Lloyd Schwartz (New York: Library of America, 2008), p. 186. Further references are to this edition of Bishop's work.

> and the compass needle
> wobbling and wavering,
> undecided.
> Freed—the broken
> thermometer's mercury
> running away;
> and the rainbow-bird
> from the narrow bevel
> of the empty mirror,
> flying wherever
> it feels like, gay!   (180)

'Sonnet' is composed of two sentences, each exploring a state of being: caught and freed. 'Caught' initiates an unorthodox sestet concerned with restriction and containment, while 'Freed' announces a celebratory octave and also marks a sudden, unexpected turn. The poem is structured around emblematic instruments of measurement and judgement, which both reflect on states of existence and bear a special relationship to the art and craft of poetry: the spirit-level and the compass in the sestet, and the thermometer and the mirror in the octave. The opening lines appear to be coaxing the sonnet into rhyme by placing 'bubble', 'level', and 'needle' in close proximity, but the more obvious rhymes exist at some distance from each other: 'divided' and 'undecided', 'level' and 'bevel', and 'away' and 'gay'. By inverting octave and sestet, and by writing the sonnet in half lines of just two or three stresses, Bishop focuses attention on the perennial artistic challenge of finding freedom within confinement. The fluctuating, uncertain stuff of the heart and the spirit are both contained and given release in the sonnet's formal and structural devices. 'Caught' is a moment of immediate, sensuous apprehension for Bishop, as in her well-known poem 'The Fish' ('I caught a tremendous fish'), while freedom is equated with the moment of joyful artistic transformation and epiphany (33). Significantly, artistic fulfilment is found in what is broken and empty, both as potential subject matter and as aspects of a modern style that breaks with convention and empties itself of direct personal expression. The 'rainbow-bird', that sudden, mysterious flourish of colour that emanates from the bevel edge of a mirror, brilliantly and memorably captures the intense uplift of aesthetic pleasure and creative fulfilment.

In her illuminating study of Elizabeth Bishop's poetry, Anne Stevenson reflects on the extent to which Bishop was, herself, the 'divided creature' in her 'Sonnet'.[62] With Bishop's example so clearly before her, Stevenson has been equally committed in her own creative writing to finding the appropriate balance between poetic form and self-expression. Her 'Sonnets for Five Seasons', an elegiac sequence first published in 1979, shows her using the sonnet and the sonnet sequence with great resourcefulness and inventiveness.[63] Initially inscribed 'For C. L. Stevenson', the sonnets later appeared in *Selected Poems 1956–1986* with the simple dedication, 'For my father'. As its title suggests, the sequence records an unsettled and protracted year, in which natural, seasonal change is disturbed and grief itself becomes a season. The five sonnets are formally diverse and highly accomplished in their deployment of rhyme. The opening sonnet, 'This House', both draws on the familiar architectural idea of the sonnet as a room or building and employs the traditional elegiac motif of the house as a place of memory and rootedness. A place of communal mourning, as well, the house 'waits' for the impact of momentous change. The numbness of grief and loss is figured in the sudden onset of winter, in 'the stun of snow', in 'faceless fields', and in 'the soldered glare of lakes'. The sonnet is painfully aware, in its touching address to the dead father, that the impending freeze signifies a stubborn resistance to loss and a difficult readjustment to change: 'Is it wanting you here to want the winter in?' The act of speech induces a premature turn and divides the sonnet into two seven-line stanzas, subtly tilting the dynamics of the form towards stasis rather than progression. The long, lingering lines, initiated by the necessary inclusion of the title as part of the opening sentence ('This House | which represents you, as my bones do, waits...'), extend to as many as fourteen syllables, contributing to the sonnet's strange temporal lag. The rhyme scheme sets out as if following a predictable Shakespearean pattern, but the rhymes struggle to come into being ('waits'/'nights'; 'come'/'sun') and keep repeating themselves without establishing a clear pattern, even prompting a premature couplet. At the same time, the sestet strives to imagine a time of thaw when the bare elements might show through again: 'Stones. Sky. Streams. | Sun.' There is tentative hope, as well, in the vision of 'what might be swallows at the edge of sight' (124).

---

62. Anne Stevenson, *Five Looks at Elizabeth Bishop* (Tarset: Bloodaxe: 1998), p. 17.
63. Anne Stevenson, *Sonnets for Five Seasons*, first published in a limited edition (Hereford: Five Seasons Press, 1979) and reprinted in *Minute by Glass Minute* (Oxford: Oxford University Press, 1982). The quotations here are from *Selected Poems 1956–1986* (Oxford: Oxford University Press, 1987).

'Complaint', the second sonnet, invokes theology by imagining a letter to God, in which his people ponder the disturbed passage of the seasons, with 'a selfish winter' leaning 'so long, unfairly, on the spring', and then 'too much greed of seedy summer'. This time, the sonnet assumes a more stable octave-sestet division marked typographically on the page. The rhymes begin to shape a near-Shakespearean pattern, but then melt into each other, with the prominent '-er' and '-ing' endings in the opening quatrain flowing into the sestet. In a bold reversal of the conventional ascent of the spirit into heaven, the Lord 'falls to earth in large hot drops of rain', arousing new life and urging spring into being once again. If the speaker's closing observation, 'Thunder. Lightning. He can do anything', is a fearful acknowledgement of God's omnipotence, it is also a hopeful suggestion of the possibility of miracles (124). 'Between', originally the fourth sonnet in the sequence, is strategically positioned in later printings at the very centre, offering a philosophical reflection on water, a journey by canal boat that is also a journey of the spirit through the changing seasons. The fluent syntax runs over quatrain divisions and over the turn between octave and sestet, while the rhymes flow all the way to the final couplet in a beautifully sustained echoic pattern of '-o' and '-er' endings, and alliterative and assonantal chimes, finally issuing in the stirring rhyme of 'spring' and 'imagining'. The seasons continue in collision and confusion, so that 'this half-born English winter', 'what should be end of summer', and 'the anxious clouding of first spring' are difficult to distinguish from each other. Even so, the flow of water tends towards what is 'real' (125).

The transforming element in 'Stasis', the fourth sonnet, is light, and the sequence now settles more securely in autumn and ideas of the fall, as it moves steadily through August and September. The form, appropriately, is more secure, arranging its rhyme scheme in a neat Shakespearean pattern that alternates the heaviness of 'blood' and 'mad' and 'head' with the lightness of 'rest' and 'ghost' and 'amethyst', until the pattern comes to rest in 'dead' and 'dust' (125). What Freud terms 'the work of mourning', including the painful acceptance of loss and the need for psychic recovery, appears to be underway.[64] 'The Circle' brings the sequence to a close, with the 'imagination's white face' remembering the snow and searching for signs of renewal and recovery. A year on, the sonnet measures the distance between March and March. The new month, as winter turns to spring, is 'shambles,

---

64. Sigmund Freud, *On Murder, Mourning and Melancholia* (Harmondsworth: Penguin, 2005), p. 215.

shards', but there is an assurance of new life. The sonnet is carefully presented in typographically distinct quatrains and tercets. The rhymes are once again subtly deployed, with 'amber' preserving 'remembers' while also anticipating 'summer' (125–6). With a quietening of the spirit ('Ghost, be content'), the sonnet turns to an explicit recognition of the event it has so far only hinted at, and then to its necessary shift from past to present:

> You died in March when the air hurt the maples.
> Birches knelt under ice. Roads forgot
> their way in aisles of frost. There were no petals.
>
> Face, white face, you are snow in the green hills.
> High stones complete your circle where trees start.
> Granite and ice are colours of the heart.   (126)

The sestet reiterates the familiar elegiac motif of a late frost hurting life and interrupting the passage of the seasons, but it also adds novelty to the idea of the world in processional mourning through a subtle religious vocabulary ('knelt' and 'aisles'). With the repetition of 'white face', the imagination is reconciled to its object of loss. The heart is still frozen, but 'colours' allows for the possibility of change. 'Green hills' are showing through the snow, and the persistent 'High stones' serve as a fitting memorial. Despite the hardness and coldness of granite and ice, there is a promise of new beginnings in the felicitous rhyme of 'start' and 'heart'.

John Berryman, Robert Lowell, and Sylvia Plath

John Berryman's *Sonnets to Chris*, his iconoclastic sequence recording an illicit love affair, was composed in 1947 but discreetly withheld from publication. The collection was revised and expanded twenty years later and published as *Berryman's Sonnets* in 1967.[65] There is a startling modernity in the sonnets, not just in their American city settings and their echoes of university campus gossip, but also in their cryptic twists and turns, and in their mischievous black comedy. The stylistic hallmark of the later Berryman is evident in the contorted syntax, the parenthetical asides, the puzzling ellipses, the sudden exclamations, and the rhetorical questions. At the

---

65. Quotations from John Berryman's poems are from *Collected Poems 1937–1971*, ed. Charles Thornbury (London: Faber, 1989).

same time, the sequence looks back to the Renaissance sonnet and its time-honoured themes of love and death, desire and despair:

> I've found out why, that day, that suicide
> From the Empire State falling on someone's car
> Troubled you so; and why we quarreled. War,
> Illness, an accident, I can see (you cried)
> But not this: what a bastard, not spring wide!...
> I said a man, life in his teeth, could care
> Not much just whom he spat it on...and far
> Beyond my laugh we argued either side.
> 'One has a right not to be fallen on!...'
> (Our second meeting...yellow you were wearing.)
> Voices of our resistance and desire!
> Did I divine then I must shortly run
> Crazy with need to fall on you, despairing?
> Did you bolt so, before it caught, our fire?   (74)

Berryman revivifies the narrative, conversational possibilities of the sonnet, combining the rhythms of actual speech with occasional idiosyncrasies in diction and phrasing. For all their shock effects, his sonnets are decorously Petrarchan in their rhyme schemes, and they derive much of their energy and ingenuity from being playfully experimental while dutifully observing formal requirements and restrictions. A number of sonnets push against tradition at the level of theme and subject matter. Sonnet 15, clearly labelled 'After Petrarch and Wyatt', is awash with ships and storms, ensigns and ports, and sighs and tears, but it might in the end have as much to do with alcohol: 'And I begin now to despair of port' (78). Sonnet 103 wonders if a broken heart might still have currency in the modern love sonnet—'A "broken heart"... but *can* a heart break, now?'—and settles instead for an aching arm: 'Still, this is something' (122).

Berryman pays homage to his fellow American poets, too. Cummings and Pound feature in Sonnet 27 and give a contemporary appeal to a poem otherwise preoccupied with checking the poetic currency of light and flowers and stars: 'In a poem made by Cummings, long since, his | Girl was the rain, but darling you are sunlight.' It takes liberties with its Petrarchan rhyme scheme, first rhyming 'his' with 'iris', and then following that up by rhyming 'miss' with 'synchrisis' (84). Sonnet 71 plays with Renaissance tropes of loving and dying, giving religious solemnity to erotic imaginings, but the immediate precursor is Wallace Stevens's 'Sunday Morning': 'Our Sunday morning when dawn-priests were applying | Wafer and wine to the human wound, we laid | Ourselves to cure ourselves down.' The turn boldly announces with Stevens, 'Death is the mother of beauty', extending the apophthegm so that 'we die to be well'. Retaining the religious ritualism of the octave, Berryman gives fresh impetus to the old Renaissance topos of love's transience: 'What if our convalescence must be brief as we are, the matin meet the passing bell?' (106). Berryman's 115 sonnets (117 in *Collected Poems 1937–1971*) represent a major contribution to the development of the American sonnet and the modern sonnet more generally. As Stephanie Burt notes, *Berryman's Sonnets* is 'the closest a modern poet has come to the sonnet sequence as practised by Sidney—indeed, so close as to constitute pastiche'.[66] The final sonnet in the sequence is a triumphant instance of Berryman's intense fusion of traditional sonnet preoccupations with a playful, modernizing impulse:

> All we were going strong last night this time,
> the mots were flying & the frozen daiquiris
> were downing, supine on the floor lay Lise
> listening to Schubert grievous & sublime,
> my head was frantic with a following rime:
> it was a good evening, an evening to please,
> I kissed her in the kitchen—ecstasies—
> among so much good we tamped down the crime.
>
> The weather's changing. This morning was cold,
> as I made for the grove, without expectation,
> some hundred Sonnets in my pocket, old,
> to read her if she came. Presently the sun
> yellowed the pines & my lady came not
> in blue jeans & a sweater. I sat down & wrote.   (129)

Much of what Berryman presents here is well established in the love sonnet tradition by the time he takes up the form—the heady excitement, the changing weather of the morning after, the self-conscious poeticizing, and even the speaker's shamed awareness of his adulterous love as a crime—but there are touches of the unmistakable talent that would emerge later in the century, not least in the delicious rhyme of 'daiquiris' and 'ecstasies'. The jaunty syntax, the intimately confiding voice, and the informal ampersands look forward to Berryman's major work in *The Dream Songs* (1969).

---

66. Stephanie Burt, 'The Contemporary Sonnet', *The Cambridge Companion to the Sonnet*, ed. A. D. Cousins and Peter Howarth (Cambridge: Cambridge University Press, 2011), p. 257.

In the mid-1940s, while Berryman was adding sonnet to sonnet in what would become one of the most ambitious modern sequences, Robert Lowell was also trying his hand at the form, including ten sonnets in his first major collection of poems, *Lord Weary's Castle* (1946). Lowell's technique is tentative and exploratory, but his early sonnets read like a rehearsal for the great convergence of private and public themes that would follow in *Life Studies* (1959) and *For the Union Dead* (1964).[67] There are sonnets about New England towns, about the violence of the sea, about Napoleon and European history, as well as sonnets written 'after' Rimbaud, Valéry, Rilke, and Villon. 'Salem' and 'Concord' meditate on a lost sense of tradition and a New England whose strong sense of identity and distinctive religious and cultural values are being dissipated by 'Mammon's unbridled industry' (30). 'The North Sea Undertaker's Complaint', inspired by Pieter Bruegel's *Gloomy Day* (1565), is a powerful study of voice, atmosphere, and mood, but the most innovative sonnet in the book is 'In the Cage'—a lean, tetrameter sonnet that recalls Lowell's imprisonment as a conscientious objector in 1943, and in doing so looks forward to the candid, so-called 'confessional' style of *Life Studies*.

Life Studies includes the memorable, elegiac 'Words for Hart Crane', notable for the dramatic flourish with which it gives those words *to* Crane: 'Who asks for me, the Shelley of my age, | must lay his heart out for my bed and board' (159). It also perversely employs the sonnet form for one of the most distressing studies of marital discord and destructive lust, '"To Speak of Woe That Is in Marriage"'. The title is from Chaucer, but the epigraph from Schopenhauer makes it clear that this is a portrait of troubled, modern love. The long, languorous opening line and the promise of life in blossom is deceptive—'The hot night makes us keep our bedroom windows open. | Our magnolia blossoms. Life begins to happen'—and it makes the events that follow in mechanical rhyming couplets all the more wretched: 'My hopped up husband drops his home disputes, | and hits the streets to cruise for prostitutes' (190). The major sonnet in the book is 'Inauguration Day: January 1953', with which Lowell both adds to a growing tradition of New York sonnets and gives the form a revived political function in post-war American letters (it was published in the radical political quarterly, the *Partisan Review*, in 1953). The occasion was the election as American President

---

67. Unless otherwise indicated, quotations from the poems of Robert Lowell are from *Robert Lowell: Collected Poems*, ed. Frank Bidart and David Gewanter (New York: Farrar, Straus, and Giroux, 2003).

of Dwight 'Ike' Eisenhower, who had previously served as Supreme Commander of the Allied Forces in Europe, authorizing the destruction of Dresden (one of the events that prompted Lowell's refusal to register for the armed services ten years earlier). A cold, deathly atmosphere settles over New York City, as another war veteran, reminiscent of the Civil War general Ulysses S. Grant, assumes power over the nation:

> The snow had buried Stuyvesant.
> The subways drummed the vaults. I heard
> the El's green girders charge on Third,
> Manhattan's truss of adamant,
> that groaned in ermine, slummed on want....
> Cyclonic zero of the word,
> God of our armies, who interred
> Cold Harbor's blue immortals, Grant!
> Horseman, your sword is in the groove!
>
> Ice, ice. Our wheels no longer move.
> Look, the fixed stars, all just alike
> as lack-land atoms, split apart,
> and the Republic summons Ike,
> the mausoleum in her heart.   (117)

Grimly contemplating 'inauguration', the sonnet dwells on the significance of ceremonies and memorials, leading us from the snow-covered, 'buried' statue of Peter Stuyvesant, the Dutch Director General of the colony that became New York in 1664, towards Grant's tomb, the mausoleum at the 'heart' of the city and the nation. The modern city seems to take part in a demented ritual celebration, with the subways drumming the vaults and the elevated railway ('the El') charging on Third Avenue, as it cuts through a city marked by social inequality and in need of a truss to prop it up. The wiping out of city monuments by snow prompts thoughts of that other wiping out by death at Cold Harbor, when Grant took to himself a God-like role in determining the destinies of Union soldiers now 'interred'. Adapting the tetrameter line of his earlier dissident sonnet, 'In the Cage', Lowell pushes against the stately decorum of the Petrarchan rhyme scheme, refusing the conventional turn. The stubbornly resistant ninth line, 'Horseman, your sword is in the groove', plays sardonically with the multiple possibilities of 'groove', linking the horseman to the railway in the rush of history, making the unfashionable fashionable through the colloquial expression 'in the groove', and also implying a long-playing record of history with the needle ('sword') stuck in the groove. The fractured sestet seeks connection and movement through rhyme, but what it speaks of is fixity and unease. A future previously divined by cosmology is now dominated by modern astronomy and the threat of nuclear warfare. The hardening of 'Ice' into the 'Ike' of advertising culture perfects Lowell's edgy, agitated Cold War sonnet.

Over the next twenty years, Lowell would write and publish hundreds of sonnets, but he would also play metamorphically with the form, sometimes converting poems written in other verse forms into sonnets, or conversely letting sonnets assume another shape. The twenty-eight-line poem, 'Night Sweat', which appeared in editions of Lowell's *Selected Poems* from 1976 onwards, was conceived as two sonnets and originally published as such in *For the Union Dead* (1964). The sonnets have hybrid rhyme schemes, but the first (ending in a couplet) is more obviously Shakespearean and dwells on the theme of human mortality, while the second, more obviously Petrarchan, finds momentary relief and stability in the love of man and wife. The first sees the sweat of night as natural and right, the consequence of working hard towards fulfilment ('one life, one writing!'), but the delayed turn tips the sonnet into a darker existential mood:

> But the downward glide
> and bias of existing wrings us dry—
> always inside me is the child who died,
> always inside me is his will to die—.

The imperatives of life and writing are now subsumed in an anxious philosophical dualism, in which the spirit burns up the expendable resources of an already dying body: 'one universe, one body...in this urn | the animal night sweats of the spirit burn.' Echoing Christ's words in Matthew 16:23, the second sonnet seeks to dismiss encroaching despair ('Behind me! You!'), and looks for both light and a lightening of the spirit that might bring artistic renewal ('I dabble in the dapple of the day'). As Frank Bidart helpfully notes,[68] there is a logic in the construction of the two sonnets, in that we move from a sense of closure and containment in the first towards a glimpse of redemption in love, 'partly reinforced but partly denied by the cyclical final rhymes':

> my wife...your lightness alters everything,
> and tears the black web from the spider's sack,
> as your heart hops and flutters like a hare.
> Poor turtle, tortoise, if I cannot clear

---

68. Frank Bidart, *Robert Lowell: Collected Poems* (New York: Farrar, Straus, and Giroux, 2003), p. xiv.

> the surface of these troubled waters here,
> absolve me, help me, Dear Heart, as you bear
> This world's dead weight and cycle on your back. (375)

The deathward glide of the world seen in the Inauguration Day sonnet impinges now on the domestic with debilitating heaviness, but the sonnet itself is a clarification and a lightening, a dabbling in the dapple of the day, and indubitably a part of another, more creative, cycle.

'Water' was the opening poem in *For the Union Dead*, and it was initially printed as eight loosely rhymed quatrains, but Lowell continued to work on the poem, reshaping its thirty-two lines into one of the unrhymed blank verse sonnets that he favoured in the *Notebook* collections published in the late 1960s and early 1970s. The poem has its origins in Lowell's friendship with Elizabeth Bishop and refers to the time they spent together in Stonington, Maine. Lowell first mentions the poem in a letter to Bishop in March 1962, as 'one to you, unidentified…More romantic and gray than the whole truth, for all has been sunny between us'. Replying to the letter from Rio de Janeiro a few weeks later, Bishop offers a few corrections and suggestions ('Shouldn't it be a *lobster* town [?]'), but also praises Lowell for the poem's execution: '"The sea drenched the rock" is so perfectly simple but so good.' Lowell later reminded her that the closing image of the mermaid pulling barnacles from the wharf was a 'nightmare' vision that she herself had written to him about in September 1948.[69] When the poem was rewritten and printed as a sonnet for the first time, it appeared as one of 'Four Poems for Elizabeth Bishop'. It carried the title 'Water 1948' and the 'Maine lobster town' was named as Stonington. The original poem uses rhyme and rhythm to catch the oscillation of fixity and release suggested by rock and water, and it moves towards an airborne transcendence in the image of gulls, only to deflate the dream, as if throwing cold water on any suggestion of a closer union. The poem hints obliquely at sexual incompatibility. The effect of the sonnet, with its remote half rhymes, is to give greater weight to 'distance in time', as if monumentalizing the experience, and rendering it more obviously as memory. The final eight lines are cleanly re-cast as four:

> You dreamed you were a mermaid clinging to a wharfpile,
> trying to pull off the barnacles with your hands.
> We wished our two souls might return like gulls to the rock.
> In the end, the water was too cold for us.[70]

---

69. *Words in Air: The Complete Correspondence between Elizabeth Bishop and Robert Lowell*, ed. Thomas Travisano with Saskia Hamilton (London: Faber, 2008), pp. 390, 402, 405.
70. Robert Lowell, *Notebook* (London: Faber, 1970), p. 234.

In the context of *Notebook*, with its organizing sense of life's accidents converging in a single plot, the sonnet is apt to seem even more like a moment's monument. Perhaps for this reason, Lowell revised it again for publication in *History* (1973), this time adding 'distance in time' to the dedication, 'For Elizabeth Bishop (twenty-five years)', and simply titling it '1. Water'. The new title notes the passage of time since the poem's first conception, but awkwardly, and not altogether successfully, seeks to capture both the vivid present-tense experience of 1948 and the increased sense of distance from it: 'We wish our two souls might return like gulls to the rock. | In the end, the water was too cold for us.'[71]

By the time he embarked on the writing of multiple groups of blank verse sonnets in the late 1960s and early 1970s, Lowell had already demonstrated his skills in sonnet writing with consummate versions of Baudelaire, Rimbuad, Valéry, and Rilke in his masterly *Imitations* (1961). In *Notebook 1967–68* (1969) he was able to develop a method for holding together the diverse perceptions and experiences of people, places, and events that constituted his increasingly chaotic and complicated life. It was also a method that allowed him to move between different imaginative realms, both personal and political, without ever simplifying or ignoring the complex relations between them. Memories of friends and snatches of remembered conversations with fellow poets, among them John Berryman, Theodore Roethke, Elizabeth Bishop, T. S. Eliot, and Robert Frost, sit alongside bold characterizations of historical figures (Napoleon, Stalin) and political luminaries (J. F. Kennedy, Che Guevara), as Lowell works out his own painful place in history. The book meditates on the passing months and seasons without any firm teleology or clear sense of direction. Lowell's 'Afterthought' to the book is helpful insofar as it tells us what *not* to expect:

> Notebook 1967–68: as my title intends, the poems in this book are written as one poem, jagged in pattern, but not a conglomeration or sequence of related material. It is not a chronicle or almanac…This is not my diary, my confession, not a puritan's too literal pornographic honesty…My plot rolls with the seasons. The separate poems and sections are opportunist and inspired by impulse.[72]

The compulsion to carry on writing a life in sonnets proved irresistible, and the book was enlarged for a second printing in 1969. It appeared simply as

---

71. Robert Lowell, *History* (London: Faber, 1973), p. 196.
72. Robert Lowell, *Notebook 1967–68* (New York: Farrar, Straus, and Giroux, 1969), p. 159.

Notebook in 1970 and was once again enlarged and reprinted. Three closely related sonnet books then appeared in 1973. *For Lizzie and Harriet* incorporated the family sonnets from *Notebook*, while *History* included the more obviously public sonnets and added a substantial selection of new poems. *The Dolphin* was composed mainly of sonnets written for and about Lowell's new wife, Caroline Blackwood.

Some of the finest critics of twentieth-century poetry have been baffled and bemused by Lowell's sonnet-mania, while admiring the sheer energy and range and versatility of his achievements in the form. M. L. Rosenthal, who had been among the early admirers of *Life Studies* in 1959, came to see the sonnets as part of 'an intellectual and introspective journal...a collection of biting or tender moments of poetic realization and beautiful *apercus*—sprinkled among much work that is either unfinished or facile and far too often artistically disappointing'.[73] Marjorie Perloff felt that the sonnets steered a difficult passage between obscurity and triviality, and that Lowell's notorious technique of using transcripts of letters and telephone conversations with his former wife, Elizabeth Hardwick, placed the reader in the uncomfortable position of being a voyeur.[74] There are many notable instances of this tendency in *The Dolphin*, some of heartbreaking intensity, as when Lowell (living in England) writes of the intimacy that perseveres in separation, quoting a letter he has received from America ('In the Mail'): 'I love you, Darling, there's a black, black void, | as black as night without you. I long to see | your face and hear your voice, and take your hand' (671). Neil Corcoran offers one of the most instructive and persuasive accounts of the sonnets in *Notebook* and the later collections, claiming that the 'permanent air of risk, of recklessness and restlessness' in Lowell's work stems from his habitual refusal to conform to what is conventionally considered proper and fitting: 'Lowell *wants* us to be checked and blocked by his "sonnets" in our legitimate expectations of what sonnet form "ought" to do.'[75] It seems strange, then, that Lowell's recensions of the *Notebook* material should aim for greater unity and consistency, clearing the 'jumble or jungle', as he put it in *History*. He hopes that in the later book he has 'cut the waste marble from the figure'.[76] The dolphin, in the book of that title, has a powerful

---

73. M. L. Rosenthal, 'Our Neurotic Angel', *Agenda*, Robert Lowell Special Issue, 18.3 (1980), p. 43.
74. Marjorie Perloff, 'Robert Lowell's Last Poems', *Agenda* 18.3 (1980), pp. 107–8.
75. Neil Corcoran, 'Lowell *Retiarius*', *Agenda* 18.3 (1980), p. 77.
76. Lowell, *History*, p. 9.

symbolic presence that sharpens and concentrates the vision. As Corcoran notes, the volume is distinguished, too, by the way in which Lowell uses the imagery of fishing to establish a 'combative, uneasy relationship with his own art'.[77] The opening sonnet is a bitter-sweet reflection on the sorrows and joys of poetry, with equal measures of circumspection and conviction:

> The line must terminate.
> Yet my heart rises, I know I've gladdened a lifetime
> knotting, undoing a fishnet of tarred rope;
> the net will hang on the wall when the fish are eaten,
> nailed like illegible bronze to the futureless future. (645)

In 'Dolphin', the closing poem in the volume, Lowell confesses to having 'plotted perhaps too freely with my life' (708). The sonnet issues a stern refusal of compassion for the poet, while clearly manifesting what Seamus Heaney identifies as his thirst for accusation. Heaney hears two kinds of music: 'the bronze note, perhaps even the brazen note, of artistic mastery' and 'the still, sad music of human remorse', superbly balanced in the final memorable line: 'my eyes have seen what my hand did.'[78] With the weight of feeling spilling over into that fifteenth line, Lowell seemed to mark the end of his long attachment to the sonnet.

Sylvia Plath was among the students who attended Lowell's writing course in Boston in 1959, though by that time she was already moving decisively away from the sonnet form that had captured her interest and sharpened her skills at the outset of her writing career.[79] Most of Plath's unusual and variegated sonnets were written during her student years at Smith College, Massachusetts, between 1950 and 1955. The earliest of these, 'To Spring', dated 1 September 1951, is a worthy exercise on a conventional theme, not altogether successful in its adjectival evocation of the season, with 'honeyflavored morning' and 'watergilded lawn' straining for effect. Plath retained only the closing couplet when she re-wrote the sonnet as 'April Aubade': 'Again we are deluded and infer | that somehow we are younger than we were' (312). 'Sonnet: To Eva', written just two months later, is altogether more striking in its choice of subject matter (the complicated

---

77. Corcoran, 'Lowell *Retiarius*', p. 81.
78. Heaney, 'A Memorial Address', *Agenda* 18.3 (1980), p. 25.
79. Unless otherwise indicated, quotations from the poems of Sylvia Plath are from *The Collected Poems* (New York: Harper and Row, 1981).

operations of the mind), with its calculated theatricality and its violent diction looking forward to 'Lady Lazarus' and 'Daddy':

> All right, let's say you could take a skull and break it
> The way you'd crack a clock; you'd crush the bone
> Between steel palms of inclination, take it,
> Observing the wreck of metal and rare stone.
>
> This was a woman: her loves and stratagems
> Betrayed in mute geometry of broken
> Cogs and disks, inane mechanic whims,
> And idle coils of jargon yet unspoken.
>
> Not man nor demigod could put together
> The scraps of rusted reverie, the wheels
> Of notched tin platitudes concerning weather,
> Perfume, politics, and fixed ideals.
>
> The idiot bird leaps up and drunken leans
> To chirp the hour in lunatic thirteens.   (304–5)

In a letter to her mother on 8 November 1951, Plath offered a brief précis, confessing to having written the sonnet when she should have been preparing for her Religion exam:

> I'm enclosing a sonnet composed when I should have been reading the mass. It's supposed to be likening the mind to a collection of minute mechanisms, trivial and smooth-functioning when in operation, but absurd and disjointed when taken apart. In other words, the mind as a wastebasket of fragmentary knowledge, things to do, dates to remember, details, and trifling thoughts. The 'idiot bird' is to further the analogy of clock-work, being the cuckoo in said mechanism. See what you can derive from this chaos.[80]

The Shakespearean sonnet form, typographically displayed in its constituent quatrains and couplet, neatly contains the sense of chaos and fragmentation Plath alludes to, much as she claims the mind does. At the same time, the sonnet is darker and more disturbed than Plath herself allows, with themes of death ('This was a woman') and madness ('idiot', 'lunatic') intruding into her work at this early stage. There are clear signs of the later Plath of *Ariel* in the performative opening, with the colloquial 'All right' effectively pushing the first line of the sonnet beyond the conventional ten syllables. The sound patterning also looks forward to the later Plath, with internal rhyme ('take...break') and forceful alliteration ('crack...clock...crush') acquiring a strong sonic charge within the confines of the sonnet form.

80. Sylvia Plath, *Letters Home*, ed. Aurelia Plath (London: Faber, 2010), p. 82.

Of the sonnets that eventually appeared in Plath's *Collected Poems*, the most notable are 'Conversation among the Ruins', based on the eponymous painting by Girogio de Chirico (1927); 'Mayflower', a patriotic tribute to America's Puritan ancestors; and 'Aftermath', in which the classical heroine Medea is invoked within a modern scene of domestic destruction. 'Mayflower' was written in 1957, the year Plath returned to America with her husband, Ted Hughes, and spent the summer on Cape Cod. The sonnet reflects on the name of the famous ship that in 1620 transported English pilgrims to New England. In the white flower of the hawthorn, it finds an appropriate emblem for the blessings that attend the hardships and struggles endured by the pilgrims:

> Throughout black winter the red haws withstood
> Assault of snow-flawed winds from the dour skies
> And, bright as blood-drops, proved no brave branch dies
> If root's firm-fixed and resolution good.
> Now, as green sap ascends the steepled wood,
> Each hedge with such white bloom astounds our eyes
> As sprang from Joseph's rod, and testifies
> How best beauty's born of hardihood.
>
> So when staunch island stock chose forfeiture
> Of the homeland hearth to plough their pilgrim way
> Across Atlantic furrows, dark, unsure—
> Remembering the white, triumphant spray
> On hawthorn boughs, with goodwill to endure
> They named their ship after the flower of May.   (60)

A simple Petrarchan structure (*abbaabba cdcdcd*) and a clearly demarcated turn allow the sonnet to convey its message of survival and endurance with quiet dignity. Even so, the hallmarks of Plath's mature style can be discerned in the strongly contrasting imagery ('black winter...red haws'), the alliterative similes ('bright as blood-drops'), and the powerful visual vocabulary ('astounds our eyes'). A very different and much more disturbing idea of survival prevails in 'Aftermath', which alludes to the remains of a house fire and sees the occupant of the building as a descendant of the abandoned Medea:

> Mother Medea in a green smock
> Moves humbly as any housewife through
> Her ruined apartments, taking stock
> Of charred shoes, the sodden upholstery:
> Cheated of the pyre and the rack,
> The crowd sucks her last tear and turns away.   (114)

The sonnet employs a hybrid rhyme scheme and relies mainly on a choked nine-syllable line. If it ruefully contemplates the tragic predicament of a modern Medea, it also turns its fire on the 'The peanut-crunching crowd' who later inhabit 'Lady Lazarus' and here present themselves as 'hunters after an old meat, | Blood-spoor of the austere tragedies'.

Ted Berrigan and James Merrill

In the early months of 1963, shortly after Plath's death, a 28-year-old aspiring writer from Tulsa, Ted Berrigan, composed the largest part of a striking avant-garde sequence that would become known simply as *The Sonnets*. Having based himself in New York, Berrigan began to absorb the multifarious cultural influences in that great city of modern art, including the poetry of Frank O'Hara and John Ashbery, the paintings of Andy Warhol and Jackson Pollock, and the music of John Cage. He studied Dadaism and Surrealism, and he tried in poetry to apply the techniques of collage, pop art, cartoons, and movies to the art of writing. Berrigan shows in his experimental sequence just how capacious and accommodating the sonnet form can be. As Alice Notley observes, 'It's about friends and loves but it's also about painting, music, architecture, philosophy, novels, the movies, and cultural icons.'[81] The poems carry forward some of the great themes associated with sonnet history—love, sleep, time, death—but they take on a new and radical complexion. They also significantly extend what we traditionally think of as a sequence, with lines and groups of lines being compulsively repeated and replayed. More than any other poet working in America at this time, Berrigan experimented with the sound of the sonnet, fusing conventional poetic lines and phrases with the most casual colloquial voice.

Berrigan also amply demonstrates what Stephanie Burt has identified as 'the dailiness' of the contemporary sonnet, as with the opening of Sonnet XXXVI (after Frank O'Hara):

> It's 8:54 a.m. in Brooklyn it's the 28th of July and
> it's probably 8:54 in Manhattan but I'm
> in Brooklyn I'm eating English muffins and drinking
> pepsi and I'm thinking of how Brooklyn is New
> York city too...[82]

---

81. Ted Berrigan, *The Sonnets*, with an introduction and notes by Alice Notley (Harmondsworth: Penguin, 2000), p. vi.
82. Burt, ed. Cousins and Howarth, p. 256. Berrigan, *The Sonnets*, p. 33. Further references are to this edition of the poems.

In other respects, though, Berrigan's sonnets are anything but ordinary. A number of sonnets open in the casual style of a letter, only to confound us and baffle us: 'DEAR CHRIS | it is 3:17 a.m. in New York city, yes, it is | 1962, it is the year of parrot fever...' (69). Formally, the sonnets are characterized by an experimental use of irregular line length, a frequent use of ellipsis (indicated by gaps in the text), and by various idiosyncracies, including the ampersand and single, unclosed brackets and speech marks. They are largely unrhymed and unpunctuated. There is a high degree of spatial and temporal disjunction in the sonnets, so that we lurch imaginatively from place to place and time to time. In Sonnet LXXVII, quoted above, we are transported from New York City to Brandenburg in the first four lines. The sonnets are also densely allusive, in ways that make them seem strangely and unexpectedly melodious at times, as when we slip from a Berryman-like confession, 'I am writing to you to say that | I have gone mad', to a lyrical Stevens-like desire to 'master the day, and | portion out the night'. Like many earlier sonnet sequences, however, this one is keenly aware of its own sonnet qualities, and paradoxically it performs its most daring tricks by working *with*, as well as *against*, the expectations associated with the form. Sonnet LXXVII closes with what initially sounds like a lyrical mode of address but drifts into comic absurdity as it upsets the traditional seasonal chronology of the genre. The comic wordplay (sonnet replacing bonnet) combines with a subversive glance back at the Easter poems of Edmund Spenser and George Herbert: 'My darling, it is nearly time. Dress | the snowman in the Easter sonnet we made for him | when scissors were in style' (69).

Scissors clearly were in style when Berrigan was composing these sonnets, and some of them were literally cut out of other sonnets and pasted by hand on to a new page. The collage technique was inspired by the New York artist, Joe Brainard, to whom *The Sonnets* is dedicated, and references to Brainard's art works and diaries appear in a number of the poems. Sonnet XV and Sonnet LIX contain exactly the same fourteen lines, but arranged in a different order. The later sonnet, it turns out, is the original, and the earlier sonnet in the sequence has been generated through a particular procedure: line 2 becomes line 14, line 4 becomes line 13, line 6 becomes line 12, and so on, until line 14 becomes line 8, where the conventional octave would be expected. Both sonnets contain an extract from Brainard's diary for August 1962, one in fragmented form and the other verbatim: 'Today | I am truly horribly upset because Marilyn | Monroe died, so I went to a matinee B-movie | and ate King Korn popcorn' (54). Berrigan invokes a figure who appears in neither the collage nor the diary entry: the poet-doctor William Carlos Williams, who had died even more recently than Marilyn Monroe (4 March 1963). Sonnet LIX is both a gentle riposte to Williams, who had deemed the sonnet dead, and a reassertion of its vitality as one of the great lyric forms of love poetry. It closes with the words, '"I LOVE YOU" | and the sonnet is not dead' (54). For all their experimental bravado and traducing of tradition, Berrigan's sonnets lay their claim on our attention by engaging with, rather than simply rejecting, well-established formal and thematic conventions. Sonnet LXXX opens with a familiar reflection on human transience—'How strange to be gone in a minute'—followed by a roll call of dead friends. The insertion of gaps between the names of these friends creates an impression of silence and solemnity, as it does with the tribute paid to the New York architect, Louis Sullivan, later in the sonnet. Even in the midst of textual incoherence, where strangeness melts into banality, the stirring of deep feeling ('whose grief I would most assuage') is poignant and imposing (71).

Ted Berrigan's sonnets have a continuing vitality for contemporary American poets. They represent a level of formal experimentation that explodes the constituent parts of the sonnet at the level of line, metre, syntax, rhyme, and rhythm, but they nevertheless bear some resemblance to familiar antecedents and they repeat a time-honoured formula in using the sequence as a method of aggregation. In different ways, James Merrill has also provided an enduring model of contemporary sonnet writing, showing how the form can readily accommodate deeply personal psychological fractures and tensions, at the same time registering a distinctive post-war American cultural climate. His sequence of seven sonnets, 'The Broken Home', published in *Nights and Days* in 1966, invites comparison with Lowell's *Life Studies* in its retrospective analysis of child–parent relations, but the mood is calmer and cooler, and the technique is altogether more restrained. Like Lowell, Merrill has a fondness for reiterated words and phrases, and for tightly clustered images that set up patterns of analogy and association, but the verbal tension is relieved in comic wit and gentle irony.

'The Broken Home', itself a euphemism for a child's traumatic experience of loss, works towards a finer apprehension of linguistic precision, with its characteristic wordplay often debunking cliché and inviting a deeper apprehension of what lies beneath the surface of casual description. There is nothing flagrantly experimental in the Berrigan sense, but each of the seven sonnets tries out a different formal arrangement at the level of line and metre, as if trying to repair the broken home. In the opening sonnet, the speaker, 'Crossing the street', catches sight of 'the parents and the child | At their window, gleaming like fruit'. The vision is a reminder of his own fruitlessness, just as his own room on the floor below is both 'Sunless' and son-less. What 'stirs' and 'quickens' in his life, however, is poetry, the 'tongue of fire'. The closing sonnet will return us to the window frame and to this elemental imagery of heat and flame with a renewed perspective.[83]

Sonnets 2 to 5 explore the child's anguished relationship with his parents in overlapping frames of reference that are at once historical, mythological, and psychological. There is a brilliant economy of style in the fractured narrative of the sequence. The father, 'who had flown in World War I', is both a business man and a romantic dreamer, who 'Might have continued to invest his life | In cloud banks well above Wall Street and wife' (197), while the mother, a child of the suffragette movement, is expected to be content 'giving birth, | Tending the house, mending the socks' (198). The Petrarchan conceit of shipwreck is neatly updated in the speaker's crisp and clichéd recognition of 'A marriage on the rocks' (198). There is a powerful Oedipal and mythical presentation of the child's relationship with his mother in Sonnet 4, which recalls how the boy and his dog, an Irish setter called Michael, crawl into the bedroom and disturb the mother while she is sleeping: 'Her eyes flew open, startled strange and cold' (198). The sequence returns to that memory in the final sonnet: 'A child, a red dog roam the corridors, | Still, of the broken home' (199). If there is an inescapable sense of everything 'still' going on, there is also an attempted 'stilling' of the feelings in the space of the sonnet. It seems entirely fitting that the 'real house' has become a boarding school, where 'Someone at last may actually be allowed | To learn something'. That someone, standing in for the poet, might also now look out of the window, 'cool with the unstiflement of the entire story' and 'Watch a red setter stretch and sink in cloud' (200). There is a childlike amusement here in the dog and the sun becoming one, but there is also a serious cooling off and a relaxed letting go.

Marilyn Hacker, Rita Dove, and Shane McCrae

Recent contemporary poets in America have generally been less given to technical experimentation with the sonnet form than either Berrigan or

---

83. James Merrill, *Collected Poems*, ed. J. D. McClatchy and Stephen Yenser (New York: Knopf, 2001), p. 197. Further references are to this edition of the poems.

Merrill, and more inclined to test the boundaries of its subject matter, especially where sexual relationships are concerned. Marilyn Hacker's collection of sonnets and occasional villanelles, *Love, Death, and the Changing of the Seasons* (1986), documents the speaker's turbulent love affair with a younger woman.[84] It takes its epigraphs from Shakespeare's Sonnet 73 and Pound's 'The River-Merchant's Wife: A Letter', combining the sonnet form and the epistolary poem, and acknowledging the mood of intense and expectant love in these earlier models. Hacker's sonnets, however, are flagrantly demotic and erotic, as the title 'Lesbian Ethics, or: Live Girl-Girl Sex Acts' neatly forewarns us. The sonnets are in eight sections, with individual poems sometimes numbered or titled, sometimes not. They are agitated, rowdy, restless sonnets, that shuttle us between New York and Paris, sometimes purporting to be written mid-air, as with the mini-sequence titled 'The Dark Night of the 747'. The sonnets mix Petrarchan and Shakespearean rhyme schemes, often prompting comedy through the sheer pace and energy of speech: 'After eight nights of sleeping with you, one | without you, and O damn it, I miss you. | I'd have to say how much and where I'd kiss you.' The excited couplet here is quickly deflated as the love talk runs on 'into your answering machine, It's on; | you're out' (73). For all its hustle and bustle, *Love, Death, and the Changing of the Seasons* invokes a familiar array of sonnet preoccupations, in keeping with its title. The closing sonnet, the most sombre in the book, invokes Shakespeare's Sonnet 73 as an ironic commentary on its own desolate solitariness: 'Did you love well what very soon you left?' (212).

Rita Dove and Shane McCrea are prolific sonnet writers who have used the form in distinctive ways to explore parental love (a theme that Hacker also attends to, amidst so much else). Dove's adaptation of the ancient Greek myth of Demeter and Persephone in *Mother Love* (1995) recalls Plath's 'Mother Medea', but her handling of myth is altogether more gentle and assuaging. Most of the poems in the volume are sonnets, but they are typographically diverse, with some in traditional octave-sestet patterns, some in paired seven-line stanzas, and others in irregular groupings of couplets and tercets. Dove's concern, as she makes clear in her foreword, is not to 'violate' the sonnet in the service of American speech or the interests of modern love, but rather to find comfort and consolation within it. She sees the Demeter

---

84. Marilyn Hacker, *Love, Death, and the Changing of the Seasons* (New York: Norton, 1986). All quotations are from this volume.

and Persephone 'cycle of betrayal and recognition' as 'ideally suited' to the form, as 'all three—mother-goddess, daughter-consort and poet—are struggling to sing in their chains'.[85] Both Demeter and Persephone speak through the poet in a language that economically embraces contemporary culture and ancient myth, as with the urgently titled 'Missing': 'I am the daughter who went out with the girls, | never checked back in and nothing marked my "last | known whereabouts," not a single glistening petal' (62).

McCrea, who acknowledges Plath's 'Lady Lazarus' as a powerful formative influence, also shares with Dove the deep sustaining tradition of African American poetry represented by Claude McKay, Langston Hughes, and Gwendolyn Brooks. The poems in *Mule* (2011) are candid in their treatment of racial and class discrimination (three poems carry the title 'Mulatto'), though the sonnets in the book fasten mainly on marriage and divorce. The broken marriage is revisited in a series of stops and starts, with similar titles, in parenthesis, catching both the past-tense of the event and various fitful attempts to keep it going: '[We married on a battlefield]', '[We married on a speeding train]', '[We married in the front yard]'.[86] McCrea is skilfully at ease with the stylistic ploys found in Berrigan's sonnets—the fractured lines, the lack of punctuation, the syntactical slippages, the insertion of textual gaps—but his technique is less a matter of foregrounding the artifice of writing than finding an adequate way of denoting painful separation between the estranged lovers and their autistic child: 'Our son has autism married in the back | Seat of a taxi slipping in the wind | We'll never have you said another child' (28). McCrea shows that the contemporary sonnet can be both radically experimental and lyrically expressive. Even when confronting desolation and disappointment, the contemporary American sonnet seems as buoyant as ever in its resourceful inventiveness.

---

85. Rita Dove, *Mother Love* (New York: Norton, 1995), p. xii. Further references are given in brackets within the text.
86. Shane McCrea, *Mule* (Cleveland, OH: Cleveland State University Poetry Center, 2011). Page numbers are given in brackets within the text.

6

The modern sonnet

There are good reasons for beginning a study of the modern English sonnet with 'The Soldier', from Rupert Brooke's '1914' sequence of war sonnets. It is difficult to think of any sonnet that has been so lauded in public on its initial appearance, yet so derided in its critical afterlife. An eloquent expression of English patriotism and an exemplary display of the sonnet's rhetorical resources, 'The Soldier' came to stand for all that modernism would denounce, including lyric eloquence, Georgian pastoralism, and the unrestrained expression of personal feeling. If, in some ways, 'The Soldier' illustrated an ideal fit between poetic form and public occasion when it was first published and read in 1914, it also registered how easily, and disturbingly, the sonnet form could become the vehicle for ready-made poetical attitudes. Brooke's poem would very quickly appear jarringly and appallingly naive. 'The Soldier' is therefore a crucial test case in the history of the sonnet. Part of its critical legacy is the reaction it prompted among other soldier poets—Charles Sorley, Wilfred Owen, and Ivor Gurney among them—whose work would in turn ensure that the sonnet re-emerged in the hands of later poets such as W. H. Auden, Geoffrey Hill, and Tony Harrison. Tempered by the experience of modern warfare, the sonnet would be a far more robust, ironic, and resilient form than ever before.

Rupert Brooke

The excessive critical attention given to 'The Soldier' and the mythologizing of Rupert Brooke after his death in the Aegean have concealed the true extent of his achievements as a writer of sonnets. By 1914, Brooke had been writing sonnets for ten years, and some of this work drew its inspiration from his travels in Germany, Canada, America, New Zealand, and the South Seas. As well as demonstrating a cosmopolitan sensibility, many of the sonnets are notable for their candid exploration of modern subject matter and for their playful experimentation with form. As Kenneth Millard has shown, Brooke's poetry warrants serious consideration for the place it occupies 'in the early twentieth-century rejection of Victorian romanticism'.[1] The earliest sonnets are decadent depictions of thwarted love and troubled dreams, reminiscent of the fin-de-siècle lyrics of Ernest Dowson and W. B. Yeats: 'Long had I dwelt in dreams and loneliness, | Until thy sad voice sighed through the dusk to me...'[2] As late as 1912, there is still a poetic extravagance derived in part from Swinburne's 'A Leave Taking', but it now begins to sound like the parody of aesthetic attitudinizing that T. S. Eliot and Ezra Pound perfected: 'She will not care. She'll smile to see me come, | So that I think all Heaven in flower to fold me.' The opening of this particular sonnet (casually or perhaps ironically titled 'Unfortunate') does, in fact, sound uncannily like the Eliot of 'Preludes': 'Heart, you are restless as a paper scrap | That's tossed down dusty pavements by the wind...' (61).

Several of the early sonnets show a spirited defiance of conventional poetic subject matter, and a willed determination to incorporate diction, rhymes, and syntax that would sound harsh or dissonant to contemporary readers. 'Sonnet: in Time of Revolt', written in January 1908, light-heartedly and ironically adopts a title recalling the political sonnets of Milton and Shelley. A juvenile protest against the poet's uncle (Alan Brooke, Dean of King's College, Cambridge) 'Sonnet: in Time of Revolt' promises a political meditation, but offers instead a deflationary comic rebellion of youth against avuncular authority. Brooke smuggles into the sonnet 'by God!' and 'Damn' (155). The octave is a Browning-like display of exclamations, quotations, italicization, capitalization, and ellipsis, giving the sonnet a striking dramatic momentum. The sestet, however, is even more remarkable in the way that it dramatizes the precocious intellect of the speaker through a lexical collocation that pulls awkwardly against the lyrical expectations of the form:

>You say I am your brother's only son.
>I know it. And, 'What of it?' I reply.
>My heart's resolvéd. *Something must be done.*
>*So* shall I curb, so baffle, so suppress
>This too avuncular officiousness,
>Intolerable consanguinity.   (155)

---

1. Kenneth Millard, *Edwardian Poetry* (Oxford: Clarendon Press, 1991), p. 156.
2. Rupert Brooke, *Poetical Works*, ed. Geoffrey Keynes (London: Faber, 1946), p. 188. Further quotations from the poems are from this edition.

The archly accented word 'resolvéd', the emphatic italics, the seemingly careless rhyme of 'reply' and 'consanguinity', and the compression of the final decasyllabic line into just two words—all suggest the kind of studied, ironic speech acts that Eliot was developing around the same time under the influence of Jules Laforgue.

An early sonnet titled 'Dawn' (1907) invokes the romantic associations of love and longing with the early morning light, but the subtitle '(From the train between Bologna and Milan, second class)' prepares us for an assault on the traditional aubade: 'Opposite me two Germans snore and sweat.' The repetition of this unpromising opening line (with 'snore' and 'sweat' reversed) at the end of both the octave and the sestet reinforces the tedious and joyless nature of the journey. The turn is equally unpromising: 'One of them wakes, and spits, and sleeps again.' The diction in 'Dawn' seems calculated to undermine any suggestion of transforming light—'sullen swirling gloom', 'dim water', 'night's foetor'—and when dawn eventually breaks, it only intensifies the general foulness inside the train: 'A wan light through the train | Strikes on our faces drawn and white. Somewhere | A new day sprawls' (162).

'A Channel Passage', written in December 1909, develops the technique of setting up romantic expectations traditionally associated with the sonnet form, only to undermine them. The poem was initially titled 'A Shakespearean Love Sonnet', but very likely it also started out as a parody of English sea poems. Swinburne had published a poem with the same title in 1899, and Alfred Austin had published 'Three Sonnets Written in Mid-Channel' (1898). In juxtaposing lovesickness and seasickness, Brooke demonstrates the comic potential of the sonnet, though much of this depends on the simple rhymes, the colloquial tenor, and the heavily punctuated lines:

> The damned ship lurched and slithered. Quiet and quick
>   My cold gorge rose; the long sea rolled; I knew
> I must think hard of something, or be sick;
> And could think hard of only one thing—*you*!   (113)

A further demythologizing of love takes place in the paired sonnets, 'Menelaus and Helen' (1909), in which Brooke skilfully fuses Petrarchan and Shakespearean rhyme schemes (125–6). The familiar poetic imaginings of Helen of Troy, 'lonely and serene', are rehearsed in the first sonnet and then demolished in the second, in which Helen 'becomes a scold, | Haggard with virtue' and Menelaus a garrulous bore. If Brooke is responding in part to the 'resolute Victorian virtues' espoused in Tennyson's 'Ulysses', he also appears to be drawing on the example of Meredith's *Modern Love* (a sonnet sequence he knew well, according to Christopher Hassall), in his disenchanting account of 'the long connubial years'.[3]

In his determination to dispense with idealized concepts of love, Brooke was prepared to experiment radically with the sonnet form, as in 'Sonnet Reversed' (1911). By inverting octave and sestet, he formally registers what Larkin ironically terms 'the long slide to happiness'.[4] Opening with a rhyming couplet evocative of radiant marital harmony, the sonnet then 'works its way through to an octave expository of the long anti-climax of a petit-bourgeois existence':

> Hand trembling towards hand; the amazing lights
> Of heart and eye. They stood on supreme heights.
> Ah, the delirious weeks of honeymoon!
>   Soon they returned, and, after strange adventures,
> Settled at Balham by the end of June.
>   Their money was in Can. Pacs. B. Debentures,
> And in Antofagastas. Still he went
>   Cityward daily; still did she abide
> At home. And both were really quite content
>   With work and social pleasures. Then they died.
> They left three children (besides George, who drank):
>   The eldest Jane, who married Mr Bell,
> William, the head-clerk in the County Bank,
>   And Henry, a stock-broker, doing well.   (159)

Again, Meredith appears to be the source of the ironic deflation, as well as the licence taken with the sonnet form, but the satirical exposure of suburban dreariness looks forward to Auden. The disclosure of loan stocks in the Canadian Pacific Railway and government bonds in South America crates an effective dissonance where a turn might be expected, while the euphemistic 'doing well' and 'really quite content' conceal a deep dissatisfaction. Brooke's potential as a satirist and his skilful employment of the sonnet form for a comedy of manners is seen again in the 1912 sonnet, 'In Freiburg Station', in which the simple device of opening and closing the sonnet with the same wry social observation intensifies the speaker's disdain

---

3. Christopher Hassall, *Rupert Brooke: A Biography* (London: Faber, 1964), pp. 167, 230.
4. *Philip Larkin: The Complete Poems*, ed. Archie Burnett (London: Faber, 2012), p. 80.

and disbelief: 'In Frieburg station, waiting for a train, | I saw a Bishop with puce gloves go by' (74).

Several early sonnets confirm the satirical tendency in Brooke's writing, but the enigmatic 'Seaside' sonnet reveals a darker, psychologically complex side to a poet who had already begun, in a proto-modernist way, to question the adequacy of lyric form as an expression of the innermost self (152). Straying away from the usual convivialities of the seaside, the sonnet confronts the possibility of a radical disjunction between mind and world:

> Swiftly out from the friendly lilt of the band,
>   The crowd's good laughter, the loved eyes of men,
>   I am drawn nightward; I must turn again
> Where, down beyond the low, untrodden stand,
> There curves and glimmers outward to the unknown
>   The old unquiet ocean. All the shade
> Is rife with magic and movement. I stray alone
>   Here on the edge of silence, half afraid,
>
> Waiting a sign. In the deep heart of me
> The sullen waters swell towards the moon,
> And all my tides set seaward.
>   From inland
> Leaps a gay fragment of some mocking tune,
> That tinkles and laughs and fades along the sand,
> And dies between the seawall and the sea.   (15)

The sonnet coincided with Brooke's decision in 1908 to sign the Fabian List, committing himself to its socialist principles, including equal citizenship for men and women, and the abolition of private property (so that 'the idle class now living on the labour of others will necessarily disappear').[5] It was a momentous decision, and Laskowski is probably right to detect in the sonnet some residual anxiety about personal vocation and direction.[6] The poem moves from companionship and solidarity towards isolation and uncertainty. Even so, this seems to be a sonnet that works on a wide existential plane, looking back to 'Dover Beach' and forward to 'The Idea of Order at Key West'. Hassall considers 'Seaside' to be the first poem Brooke wrote that was securely his own, and he gives a detailed account of the extensive revisions

---

5. One of the leading principles of the Fabian Programme of 1886. See Paul Adelman, *The Rise of the Labour Party 1880–1946*, 3rd edn (London: Routledge, 1996), p. 105.
6. William E. Laskowski, *Rupert Brooke* (New York: Twayne, 1994), pp. 46–7.

it underwent.[7] What emerges is a sonnet distinguished by its prevalent littoral or liminal images, reflecting on the space between self and others, mind and world, sea and land, silence and sound. The negative prefixes ('untrodden', 'unknown', 'unquiet') intensify the mysterious quality of the sonnet and its uncertain signification. Structurally, the composition is unusual, with the turn enacting the process of 'Waiting for a sign' and the broken eleventh line signalling the divide between land and sea. The rhyme scheme contributes to the pervasive uncertainty through the irregular patterning of the octave (*abbacdcd*) and the delayed final rhyme in the sestet (*efgfge*).

The picture of Brooke that emerges just prior to the publication of the 1914 sonnets is a complicated one, not easily reconciled with the image of the romantic, patriotic dreamer widely publicized after his death. It should certainly caution us against any outright condemnation of Brooke's 'ignorant nobilities' based primarily on a reading of 'The Soldier'.[8] We need to bear in mind the full extent of Brooke's writing career (short as it was), including his determined efforts to produce a new kind of lyric poetry that would sometimes be harshly dissonant and satirical. There is evidence of Brooke's enthusiasm for modernist art, including the work of the Post-Impressionist painters, and evidence also of political sympathies that far exceeded the narrow English nationalism with which he is usually associated. Edward Marsh recalls in his memoir that Brooke strongly defended the cause of workers during the Dublin lockout and sent funds to support their families. He wrote to Marsh from New Zealand: 'When the *Times* begins saying that the employers are in the wrong, they must be very unpardonably and rottenly so indeed.'[9] The poems written by Brooke as he sailed across the Pacific in 1913 and early 1914, including the Hawaiian sonnet 'Waikiko', have prompted Roger Ebbatson to challenge the familiar stereotyping of Brooke and to consider instead his 'fundamentally conflictual sense of Englishness'.[10]

In terms of the direction that Brooke was taking English lyric poetry, it is clear that by 1914 he had made significant gains in modifying the sonnet so that it would be more responsive to modern experience. One of his final sonnets, 'The Treasure', coincides with the outbreak of war and serves as a

---

7. Hassall, *Rupert Brooke*, pp. 417, 151–3.
8. Samuel Hynes, *Edwardian Occasions: Essays on English Writing in the Early Twentieth Century* (New York: Oxford University Press, 1972), p. 144.
9. *The Collected Poems of Rupert Brooke, with a Memoir* (London: Sidgwick and Jackson, 1918), p. cvi.
10. Roger Ebbatson, *An Imaginary England: Nation, Landscape and Literature, 1840–1920* (London: Ashgate, 2005), p. 317.

preface to the 1914 sequence. As if querying the historical associations of the sonnet with permanence and preservation, 'The Treasure' has an opening sestet that registers sudden death and a closing octave abruptly cut short. Contrary to what the title might suggest, with its connotations of hoarding memories like treasure, the sonnet is unusual and imposing in its unsentimental treatment of death and its candid apprehension of the sudden end of beauty, 'The rainbow and the rose', and the sudden loss of consciousness, 'Behind the gateways of the brain' (24).

As 'The Treasure' reveals, the outbreak of war threw into sharp perspective the role and function of lyric poetry, including its capacity for preserving idealized images of beauty and its facility for expressing personal thoughts and feelings. Brooke, who had been edging towards a counter-aesthetic, gradually developing a more impersonal style of writing, was now confronted with circumstances in which death was more than a poetic trope. The 1914 sonnets show him, as if having exhausted his imagination and his range of technical resources, reverting to the most conventional poetic images of death. Four sonnets—'Peace', 'Safety', and two titled 'The Dead'—rehearse familiar euphemisms of death in war as sleep and noble sacrifice. To enter battle is to turn from a sick world, 'as swimmers into cleanness leaping' (19), and to pour out 'the red | Sweet wine of youth' (21). Rhetorically, the poems are far more strident, far more declamatory in their public address, than any of the poems Brooke had previously written: 'Now, God be thanked who has matched us with His hour' (19), 'Blow out, you bugles, over the rich Dead!' (21). The immediate context for the writing of these sonnets, apart from the declaration of war in August 1914, was the invitation to publish some poems in the *New Numbers* quarterly journal, edited by Lascelles Abercrombie and Wilfred Gibson, and associated with the Dymock Poets in Gloucestershire. This partly explains the pastoral idiom and the populist sentiment in the '1914' sonnets, but it also seems that with the outbreak of war Brooke seized the opportunity for giving full vent to the rhetorical possibilities of the sonnet, having previously contented himself with the ironic discrepancy between the vast potential of the form and an often unprepossessing subject matter.

War gave Brooke the opportunity to reanimate the traditional associations of the sonnet with love, loyalty, and service, imbuing the ethic of self-sacrifice with a strong sense of religious devotion. The fifth and final sonnet in the sequence, 'The Soldier', is calmly reassuring in its deployment of lyric devices that can be traced all the way back to the English Renaissance and the poetry of Sidney and Spenser. Initially titled 'The Recruit', the sonnet dramatizes the contemplation of a premature death from the perspective of youth and inexperience, but part of its enduring appeal is the creation of a speaking voice that is at once confident and confiding:

> If I should die, think only this of me:
>   That there's some corner of a foreign field
> That is for ever England. There shall be
>   In that rich earth a richer dust concealed;
> A dust whom England bore, shaped, made aware,
>   Gave, once, her flowers to love, her ways to roam,
> A body of England's, breathing English air,
>   Washed by the rivers, blest by suns of home.
>
> And think, this heart, all evil shed away,
>   A pulse in the eternal mind, no less
>   Gives somewhere back the thoughts by England given;
> Her sights and sounds; dreams happy as her day;
>   And laughter, learnt of friends; and gentleness,
>   In hearts at peace, under an English heaven.   (23)

The eloquence of 'The Soldier' is such that we might easily overlook its essentially performative quality and consequently fail to appreciate the dramatic devices concealed in the rich earth of its rhetoric. Although the opening line appears reflective and conditional, it involves a command, an instruction to remember, which is intensified through the formal device of the turn: 'And think.' The sonnet's dubious proposition that the earth will be richer for the dust of an English soldier and thereby forever English is made to sound reasonable through simple devices of repetition, ranging from lexical reiteration ('rich...richer dust...rich') to carefully patterned alliteration ('foreign field...sights and sounds...dreams happy as her day'). The repetition functions most obviously in relation to England and its mutation into things that are English, but it also works more subtly, as with the shifting verbal emphasis on 'Gave', 'Gives', and 'given'. Syntactical variation allows for a combination of enjambment and mid-line pauses, with the caesura being used strategically, especially in line 3. The deftly placed commas, working as connectives, give a balanced, harmonious movement to the octave, while the more heavily punctuated lines of the sestet induce a slow, contemplative close. Although the octave of 'The Soldier' adopts a Shakespearean rhyme scheme, the sestet is Petrarchan. Brooke has the good judgement not to rhyme 'heaven' too obviously with any other word and sedulously avoids a rhyming couplet. Instead, 'heaven' hovers over 'hearts at peace', ushered in after a perfectly placed pause in the closing line.

The rhetorical power of 'The Solider' is amplified through literary allusion and quotation, with echoes of the Bible, Shakespeare, and Keats lending gravitas to the verse. The opening line recalls the late sonnet by Keats, 'When I have fears that I may cease to be', but it also looks back to the famous St Crispin's Day speech in *Henry V* (4.3): 'If we are marked to die, we are enough | To do our country loss.' The glorification of England recalls Old John of Gaunt's defence of the realm in *Richard II* (2.1): 'This blessed plot, this earth, this realm, this England | This nurse, this teeming womb of royal kings.'[11] The sonnet's consolatory belief in the enriching return to earth of the soldier's body has its roots in both classical and biblical sources, and in the fertility rituals that shape elegiac poetry. There are numerous literary sources that sanction Brooke's burial rites, including Don Sebastian's speech in John Dryden's *Don Sebastian, King of Portugal: A Tragedy* (1689): 'I beg no pity for this mouldring Clay! | For if you give it Burial, there it takes | Possession of your Earth.'[12] A more immediate influence, however, was Hilaire Belloc's fantasy, *The Four Men* (1911), in which the narrator is moved to verse, contemplating the idea of communion with the earth: 'He does not die... that can bequeath | Some influence to the land he knows.'[13]

Charles Sorley and Siegfried Sassoon

Among the first readers of Brooke's '1914' sonnets were the poets Edward Thomas and Charles Sorley. In a letter to Robert Frost, written shortly after the announcement of Brooke's death on 23 April 1915, Thomas reports, 'All the papers are full of his "beauty" and an eloquent last sonnet beginning "If I should die."' He tactfully avoids any comment on Brooke's patriotism, simply repeating his earlier point, 'He was eloquent'.[14] Sorley, however, makes it clear that he disapproves of the attitude behind Brooke's 'fine

---

11. William Shakespeare, *The Norton Shakespeare*, ed. Stephen Greenblatt (New York: Norton, 1997), pp. 1499, 967.
12. John Dryden, *Don Sebastian, King of Portugal: A Tragedy* (London: J. Tonson, 1689; 1735), p. 37.
13. Hilaire Belloc, *The Four Men: A Farago* (London: Thomas Nelson, 1911), p. 309.
14. Edward Thomas to Robert Frost, 3 May 1915, *Elected Friends: Robert Frost and Edward Thomas to One Another*, ed. Matthew Spencer (New York: Handsel Books, 2003), p. 51.

words', and claims in a letter written on 28 April 1915 that the sonnet sequence has been 'overpraised':

> He is far too obsessed with his own sacrifice, regarding the going to war of himself (and others) as a highly intense, remarkable and sacrificial exploit, whereas it is merely the conduct demanded of him (and others) by the turn of circumstances, where non-compliance with this demand would have made life intolerable...He has clothed his attitude in fine words: but he has taken the sentimental attitude.[15]

As John H. Johnston notes, Sorley's criticism is acute and makes clear that 'he, at least, did not regard Brooke as the spokesman for any general mood'. Johnston is inclined to see the outlook of the '1914' sonnets as largely driven or determined by Brooke's prior commitment to the lyrical standards of his day: 'Brooke was not really free to choose; his commitment to the attitudes and techniques of Georgian lyricism was such that he could hardly deal with the war in any other way. To have admitted fact or necessity or expedience among his spiritualized motivations would have been to destroy a semi-private fantasy of heroic self-sacrifice and moral regeneration.'[16] As we have seen, however, Brooke could, on occasion, be technically adventurous and provocative in his handling of the sonnet form, as well as unconventional in his outlook. The urgent and exceptional circumstances of war prompted Brooke to write one of the most polished rhetorical performances in the history of the English sonnet; its eloquence would be widely acknowledged, even if its sentiments would be seen by later generations as 'something of a reproach and an embarrassment'.[17]

That a different attitude to the war could be taken as early as 1914 is evident in Sorley's own extraordinary sonnets.[18] The earliest of these (written in September 1914) takes its ironically inflected title from the Acts of the Apostles (17:23): 'Whom therefore we ignorantly worship' (72). The sonnet cuts through the heroic narratives of war that prevail in public to acknowledge the fundamental instinct—the blind faith and anxious trust in God—that operates in private: 'Unheard, unnamed, unnoticed, crucified

---

15. *The Letters of Charles Sorley* (Cambridge: Cambridge University Press, 1919), p. 263.
16. John H. Johnston, *English Poetry of the First World War: A Study in the Evolution of Lyric and Narrative Form* (Princeton: Princeton University Press, 1964), p. 35.
17. Johnston, *English Poetry of the First World War*, p. 36.
18. Quotations from Sorley's poems are from *The Collected Poems of Charles Hamilton Sorley*, ed. Jean Moorcroft Wilson (London: Cecil Woolf, 1985). Page numbers are given within brackets in the text.

| To our unutterable faith, we wait.' The closing lines both resist any hasty declarations of heroism and, in their insistent negatives, dissociate themselves from the call for action. Sorley sarcastically noted, 'I think it should get a prize for being the first poem written since August 4th that isn't patriotic' (73). A later sonnet, 'To Germany' (written some time before April 1915), is notable for its complete absence of either patriotic fervour or moral justification in its attitude to the war. Once again, there is an appalled recognition of blindness, incomprehension, and inarticulacy:

> You are blind like us. Your hurt no man designed,
> And no man claimed the conquest of your land.
> But gropers both through fields of thought confined
> We stumble and we do not understand.   (70)

'To Germany' is not a protest poem, though its title alone suggests a daring departure from the nationalist fervour of the time. It does, however, make connection with that earlier tradition of political sonnets generated largely by Milton and Wordsworth, in which political circumspection and disquietude are candidly voiced. More radically committed than Brooke to overturning conventional lyric cadences, Sorley is not averse to introducing the odd discordant word that suddenly disrupts a line of verse. The purposeful awkwardness is reminiscent of Hardy, as with this skilfully compressed acknowledgement of German expansionism: 'You only saw your future bigly planned.'

It seems likely that Sorley's 'Two Sonnets' (dated June 1915) and the sonnet beginning 'When you see millions of the mouthless dead' (probably written shortly before his death in October 1915) were composed in reaction to Brooke's '1914' sonnets and designed as part of a counter-sequence. The first of the 'Two Sonnets', originally titled 'Death and the Downs', contrasts strongly with Brooke's radiant images of death as noble sacrifice and ultimate peace (87–8). The opening lines both invoke and declare their distance from familiar religious and literary personifications of death: 'Saints have adored the lofty soul of you. | Poets have whitened at your high renown.' In place of Brooke's reassuring association of death with home and England, Sorley offers a 'straight and steadfast signpost' that points to an unknown place: 'A homeless land and friendless, but a land | I did not know and that I wished to know' (87). The 'wish' is closer in its strange compulsion and psychological curiosity to the work of Edward Thomas and Robert Frost than to the 1914 sonnets of Rupert Brooke. The second sonnet is even more ruthlessly demystifying in choosing images of mundanity with which to record the ordinariness and blankness of death: 'Such, such is Death: no triumph: no defeat: | Only an empty pail, a slate rubbed clean' (88). The sonnet is inverted so that the two tercets of the opening sestet query idealized notions of death, while the octave rises to a climax and then a sudden anti-climax, with the delayed turn in the final three lines switching alarmingly to a sudden second-person address: 'And your bright Promise, withered long and sped, | Is touched, stirs, rises, opens and grows sweet, | And blossoms and is you, when you are dead.' The traditional elegiac consolation associated with flowers is brutally displaced here in the imposing image of violent, premature blossoming in war.

Sorley's final sonnet, 'When you see millions of the mouthless dead', was found among his belongings after his death in France in 1915, and is written as if addressed to another soldier who has yet to undergo the mental anguish and recurring nightmares of the speaker (91). The sonnet clearly counters 'The Soldier', envisaging death on a massive, terrifying scale, rather than idealizing the individual casualty:

> When you see millions of the mouthless dead
> Across your dreams in pale battalions go,
> Say not soft things as other men have said,
> That you'll remember. For you need not so.
> Give them not praise. For, deaf, how should they know
> It is not curses heaped on each gashed head?
> Nor tears. Their blind eyes see not your tears flow.
> Nor honour. It is easy to be dead.
> Say only this, 'They are dead.' Then add thereto,
> 'Yet many a better one has died before.'
> Then, scanning all the o'ercrowded mass, should you
> Perceive one face that you loved heretofore,
> It is a spook. None wears the face you knew.
> Great death has made all his for evermore.

Unlike the 'rich dead' of Brooke's sonnets, the dead are figured here as horrifying and haunting, with the near proximity of 'millions' and 'battalions' reinforcing the overwhelming impression of slaughter on a massive scale. The sonnet pulls away from any suggestion that death in war might be mitigated by the remembrance of an individual face, with 'mouthless' signifying both disfigurement and terminal silence. The grotesque and ghostly apparition of the opening lines is given shocking reiteration in the 'spook' of the penultimate line. Sorley inveighs against remembrance, undermining the buoyant imperatives of 'The Soldier' with repeated negatives and matter-of-fact assertions. The turn appears, for a moment, to offer something worth saying in response to the terrible realization that 'It is easy to be dead.' Instead, it is bluntly, unflinchingly, factual—'They are dead'—and the classics are invoked not to console but to counsel against any special valediction for the individual death: 'Yet many a better one has died before.' The mode of address in Sorley's work, sensitively pitched between hectoring and pleading, sets the tone for a good deal of First World War writing that follows, including some of the most memorable poems of Siegfried Sassoon and Wilfred Owen.

Siegfried Sassoon is not usually thought of as a writer of sonnets, though he had, in fact, shown a strong attraction to the form in poems written before 1914, including those in *Sonnets* (1909), *Sonnets and Verses* (1909), and *Twelve Sonnets* (1911). His later experiments with the form produced some accomplished war poems, including 'Glory of Women', 'Trench Duty', and 'Dreamers'.[19] There are distinctive qualities that he brings to the sonnet in time of war—a shocking realism, a strong sense of narrative, a colloquial voice, biting satirical wit—but all of these tendencies would eventually require a broader canvas. What the sonnet offers Sassoon in the first instance is technical discipline, especially in composing rhymed quatrains. 'A Subaltern' (March 1916) provides a good example of how Sassoon aims for a colloquial line, but at the same time packs in as much observation as possible, reinforcing the grimness of the scene through obvious alliterative effects:

> He told me he'd been having a bloody time
> In trenches, crouching for the crumps to burst,
> While squeaking rats scampered across the slime
> And the grey palsied weather did its worst.   (25)

By the end of the war, Sassoon's indignation found expression in a brisk satirical style, and in a repeated contrast between the misery of trench warfare and the domestic comfort of the misinformed at home. 'Remorse' opens abruptly and effectively with a soldier 'Lost in the swamp and welter of the pit', but the sonnet loses momentum as it carries the story of Germans

---

19. Quotations from Sassoon's poems are from *The War Poems*, ed. Rupert Hart-Davis (London: Faber, 1983). Page numbers are given within brackets in the text.

'Screaming for mercy' over the turn and into the sestet (118). Attracted by the rhetorical impact of the Shakespearean closing couplet, Sassoon doubles the effect at the end of 'Remorse', but risks bathos:

> Lost in the swamp and welter of the pit,
> He flounders off the duck-boards; only he knows
> Each flash and spouting crash,—each instant lit
> When gloom reveals the streaming rain. He goes
> Heavily, blindly on. And, while he blunders,
> 'Could anything be worse than this?'—he wonders,
> Remembering how he saw those Germans run,
> Screaming for mercy among the stumps of trees:
> Green-faced, they dodged and darted: there was one
> Livid with terror, clutching at his knees...
> Our chaps were sticking 'em like pigs... 'O hell!'
> He thought—'there's things in war one dare not tell
> Poor father sitting safe at home, who reads
> Of dying heroes and their deathless deeds.'

The problem here is that the sonnet form is used mechanically, with the calculated effect of the rhymes looking crude and simplistic. Elsewhere, in such poems as 'Two Hundred Years After' and 'In the Church of St Ouen', Sassoon shows subtlety and restraint in developing the sonnet's capacity for historical reflection and genuine pathos. 'Two Hundred Years After' shows how well Sassoon could adopt his narrative skills to the sonnet form, in this instance opening with a rhyming couplet that calls for the listener's attention and delaying the turn for maximum effect by opting for a 10 + 4 division rather than the usual 8 + 6 arrangement:

> Trudging by Corbie Ridge one winter's night,
> (Unless old hearsay memories tricked his sight)
> Along the pallid edge of the quiet sky
> He watched a nosing lorry grinding on,
> And straggling files of men; when these were gone,
> A double limber and six mules went by,
> Hauling the rations up through ruts and mud
> To trench-lines digged two hundred years ago.
> Then darkness hid them with a rainy scud,
> And soon he saw the village lights below.
> But when he'd told his tale, an old man said
> That *he'd* seen soldiers pass along that hill;
> 'Poor silent things, they were the English dead
> Who came to fight in France and got their fill.' (55)

The poem looks back two hundred years to the battle of Blenheim (1704) and recalls Robert Southey's anti-war poem, 'The Battle of Blenheim' (1796) in which an old man (Kaspar) explains to his children that English soldiers came to 'put the French to rout', adding, 'But what they fought each other for | I could not well make out.' Sassoon's sonnet works through indirection, not only in looking back to the earlier conflict, but in introducing an anonymous spectator who tells his tale to the old man. It retains its air of mystery and speculation, partly through atmospheric effects such as the 'winter's night', 'the quiet sky', and 'a rainy scud', and partly through the metaphorical darkness and silence undoing any glorification of English military history.

Sassoon persisted with the sonnet, and some of his most memorable achievements are in those poems that succeed in dramatizing experience in the trenches, using the resources of the form to animate sketches of life at the Front. 'Trench Duty' boldly employs a series of rhyming couplets, suddenly upsetting the pattern at the turn, as the sestet reaches the account of a raid on German posts, and then returning to a rhyming couplet at the close:

> Shaken from sleep, and numbed and scarce awake,
> Out in the trench with three hours' watch to take,
> I blunder through the splashing mirk; and then
> Hear the gruff muttering voices of the men
> Crouching in cabins candle-chinked with light.
> Hark! There's the big bombardment on our right
> Rumbling and bumping; and the dark's a glare
> Of flickering horror in the sectors where
> We raid the Boche; men waiting, stiff and chilled,
> Or crawling on their bellies through the wire.
> 'What? Stretcher-bearers wanted? Some one killed?'
> Five minutes ago I heard a sniper fire:
> Why did he do it?... Starlight overhead—
> Blank stars. I'm wide-awake; and some chap's dead.   (124)

Here, the couplets work purposefully to convey activity and anxiety while the use of strongly marked pauses and run-on lines (especially those that quietly efface quatrain and octave-sestet divisions) manage to avoid mechanical effect. 'Hark' is apt to sound archaic against 'the big bombardment' that follows, and the monosyllabic flatness of 'some chap's dead' is too obviously contrived, but in other respects the sonnet makes resourceful use of reported speech, ellipsis, and caesurae to create a dramatic impression of what the title casually refers to as 'Trench Duty'. As Patrick Campbell notes, 'Trench

Duty' demonstrates how capable Sassoon was of concentrating particular effects, especially sounds and sensations, 'in a trench-scape where the starry night is complemented by "candle-chinked" light and the "flickering horror" of the guns'. The imagery of light is telling. 'Starlight overhead' is not a promising omen as it brings exposure and danger to soldiers in the trenches. 'Blank stars' displace the 'lucky stars' associated with thanks and relief. They act as 'both agency and witness as another soldier loses his life'.[20]

Wilfred Owen, Edmund Blunden, and Ivor Gurney

Sassoon's example and his practical assistance were to prove invaluable in bringing to maturity the war poems of Wilfred Owen. Even so, many of the characteristics of Owen's mature verse can be seen taking shape at an early stage in his career, and his experiments with the sonnet form are crucially important in the development of both familiar thematic concerns and distinctive stylistic qualities. The sonnet had a special attraction for Owen, encouraging his disciplined handling of the pentameter line (especially in the construction of quatrains) and also exercising his facility with rhyme. He wrote over forty sonnets between 1910 and 1918, the earliest of which are strongly influenced by Shakespeare and Keats.[21] As Owen went into battle, perennial themes of love, beauty, and death worked out in sonnet form would become intensified or ironized, while rhyme and rhythm would be subtly adjusted to accommodate a dissonant music.[22]

Owen's earliest sonnet, 'Written in a Wood, September 1910', is explicit in declaring its devotion to Keats, but it is also candid about the lyrical appeal of the sonnet form itself. Composed some 'ninety autumns' after the death of Keats in Rome in 1821, the sonnet anticipates its author's own early demise. Within the 'leafy grots' of the wood (a borrowing of the 'lofty grot' in *Endymion* 2.921), the poet imagines Keats arriving, 'To hear the sonnets of its minstrel choir'. The association of birds with choirs recalls Shakespeare's

---

20. Patrick Campbell, *Siegfried Sassoon: A Study of the War Poetry* (London: McFarland, 1999), p. 185.
21. For valuable insights into Owen's indebtedness to Keats, see Emma Suret, 'John Keats, Wilfred Owen, and Restriction in the Sonnet', *English* 66.253 (2017), 145–62.
22. Unless otherwise indicated, all quotations from Owen's poems are from *The Complete Poems and Fragments*, ed. Jon Stallworthy (London: Chatto & Windus; Oxford: Oxford University Press, 1983), vol. 1. Page numbers are given within brackets in the text.

Sonnet 73 and its 'Bare ruined choirs, where late the sweet birds sang', and indeed the theme of chastened mortality and inevitable decay owes as much to Shakespeare as it does to Keats.[23] At the same time, Owen's premonition of his own death is softened by the anticipation of a shared poetic afterlife: 'Ah ninety times again, when autumn rots | shall birds and leaves be mute and all unseen, | Yet shall I see fair Keats, and hear his lyre' (7). The rhyme scheme is unorthodox, with an additional *b* rhyme upsetting the Petrarchan structure (*abbabbabcdecde*), and a gentle variation of the rhyme ('swell'/'gale'/'yell'/'hale'/'dell') looking forward to the more pronounced pararhyme of the later poems.

Owen's 'Sonnet, Written at Teignmouth, on a Pilgrimage to Keats's House' is modelled on Keats's 'Sonnet Written in the Cottage where Burns was Born', but the elegiac tenor of the poem anticipates the pervasive mourning of the war poems. The sestet gives a strong indication of how Owen's poetic skills would develop, especially in the expression of elegiac sentiment through a purposeful pathetic fallacy, drawn in part from Milton's 'Lycidas' and Shelley's 'Adonais'. The idea of nature mourning the death of a loved one is a well-established convention in elegiac verse, but Owen complements it with his own distinctive assonantal and alliterative effects: 'Eternally may sad waves wail his death' (10). The troubled pastoral vision and the tight compression of the lines are characteristic of his later poems, including 'Spring Offensive': 'While mournfully wail the slow-moved mists and rain.' The Keatsian 'wail' reappears in 'The Poet in Pain', in which Owen writes of his refusal to quench his 'remorseless ache' on behalf of 'speechless sufferers', recalling 'The weariness, the fever, and the fret' of Keats's 'Ode to a Nightingale':

> Rather be my part
> To write of health with shaky hands, bone-pale,
> Of pleasure, having hell in every vein,
> Than chant of care from out a careless heart,
> To music of the world's eternal wail.[24]

The Keatsian ideal of a poet in empathy with the sufferings of the world no doubt informs Owen's determination to record 'the pity of war', but his

---

23. William Shakespeare, *The Complete Sonnets and Poems*, ed. Colin Burrow (Oxford: Oxford University Press, 2008), p. 527.
24. John Keats, *Poetical Works*, ed. H. W. Garrod (Oxford: Oxford University Press, 1970), p. 207. Owen, *The Complete Poems and Fragments*, ed. Stallworthy, vol. I, p. 111.

commitment to the role of the poet as healer and comforter is evident at an early stage in his career. It occurs, for instance, in the dark sonnet 'On My Songs', in which the poet, 'Singing his frightened self to sleep', reaches out to others similarly distressed: 'Listen; my voice may haply lend thee ease.' As Owen's letters to his mother reveal, the sonnet was inspired by James Russell Lowell's sonnet, 'To the Spirit of Keats', in which the New England poet pays tribute to Keats's skill in bringing 'hope secure to him who lonely cries'. Along with other early sonnets, 'On My Songs' takes on a powerful new dimension when read in the context of the First World War.[25] This and other sonnets were revised by Owen at Criaglockhart and Scarborough in ways that give their memories of pain and grief a striking wartime relevance. Jon Stallworthy's meticulous editing of the poems reveals that the empathetic line, 'One night, if thou shouldst lie in this same room', initially drafted in 1913, was later changed to 'One night, if thou shouldst lie in this Sick room', probably at Craiglockhart at the end of 1917.[26] That small amendment reverberates throughout the poem, opening up a different and disturbing way of reading the poet's 'own weird reveries' and his abject confession of 'Singing his frightened self to sleep'.

Although there are some apparent echoes of Rupert Brooke's '1914' sequence in Owen's sonnets, as well as some striking differences in outlook, it seems that Owen did not read 'The Soldier' and its companion pieces until 1916. Owen's own '1914' sonnet was drafted in France in the winter of that year and revised some time between October 1917 and January 1918. At one point, perhaps after reading 'The Soldier' in 1916, he considered titling his own sonnet '1915', as if to put some distance between his work and Brooke's, and thereby discouraging comparison. The emphatic 'now' (in lines 1, 6, and 13) recalls the opening line of Brooke's sequence, 'Now, God be thanked', but the apprehension of war is altogether more unsettling and disturbing:

> War broke: and now the Winter of the world
> With perishing great darkness closes in.
> The foul tornado, centred at Berlin,
> Is over all the width of Europe whirled,

---

25. Wilfred Owen, *Collected Letters*, ed. Harold Owen and John Bell (London: Oxford University Press, 1967), p. 160. *Poetical Works of James Russell Lowell*, ed. Thomas Hughes (London and New York: Macmillan, 1896), p. 23. Owen, *The Complete Poems and Fragments*, ed. Stallworthy, vol. 1, p. 113.
26. *The Complete Poems and Fragments*, ed. Stallworthy, vol. 2, p. 267.

> Rending the sails of progress. Rent or furled
> Are all Art's ensigns. Verse wails. Now begin
> Famines of thought and feeling. Love's wine's thin.
> The grain of human Autumn rots, down-hurled.
> For after Spring had bloomed in early Greece,
> And Summer blazed her glory out with Rome,
> An Autumn softly fell, a harvest home,
> A slow grand age, and rich with all increase.
> But now, for us, wild Winter, and the need
> Of sowings for new Spring, and blood for seed.   (116)

The sacrificial 'blood for seed' and the declaration that 'Love's wine's thin' recall Brooke's 'red | Sweet wine of youth'. Owen's attitude, however, suggests a mood of resignation and a sense of inevitability markedly different from Brooke's euphoric heralding of death in the image of 'swimmers into cleanness leaping'. Like Brooke, Owen invokes both Shakespeare and Keats in his meditation on transience and death. Although the form is predominantly Petrarchan, it closes with a rhyming couplet, and line 12 echoes Shakespeare's Sonnet 97: 'The teeming autumn big with rich increase.'[27] The autumnal imagery is intensified through the sonnet's insistent allusions to Keats's ode 'To Autumn', but the urgent awareness of impending winter shows that Shelley was a powerful influence as well. The opening line echoes *The Revolt of Islam* (9.25): 'This is the winter of the world;—and here | We die', while the closing lines are reminiscent of 'Ode to the West Wind'. Owen had initially considered 'Bleed!' as a rhyme word, along with the variant closing line, 'That if Spring come again there may be seed.'[28]

The opening line of the sonnet 'With an Identity Disc', drafted on 23 March 1917, does appear to respond to Brooke and 'The Soldier': 'If ever I had dreamed of my dead name | High in the heart of London' (96). The poem fastens on the image of a soldier's identity disc as all that might remain of him after death, but poetic identity, as well as memory, is clearly one of its main concerns. Like 'The Soldier', it echoes Keats's sonnet, 'When I Have Fears that I May Cease to Be', but its longing for 'the quiet place of Keats' and the cypresses that 'keep in shade' is both a precise reference to the poet's burial place in Rome and a preference for an undemonstrative poetic character, reminiscent of one whose name was 'writ in water'.[29] Owen seems

---

27. *The Complete Sonnets and Poems*, ed. Burrow, p. 575.
28. *The Complete Poems and Fragments*, ed. Stallworthy, vol. 2, p. 271. Percy Bysshe Shelley, *The Revolt of Islam* (London: John Brooks, 1829), p. 205.
29. Andrew Motion, *Keats* (London: Faber, 1997), p. 564.

to have been much more genuinely attracted to late nineteenth-century Decadent and Symbolist verse than Brooke. Very likely, as Dominic Hibberd points out, Owen acquired a knowledge of French Symbolist poetry, especially that of Paul Verlaine, during the two years he spent in France, between September 1913 and August 1915, prior to enlisting.[30] Among Owen's manuscript drafts is a transcription of Verlaine's sonnet, 'Mon rêve familier', probably made in 1914, and the ghostly, erotic vision and the melancholy lyricism of the French poem are blended intoxicatingly with the Keatsian influence in a number of poems, including 'Autumnal' and 'On a Dream'.

One of Owen's most compelling early sonnets, 'The Unreturning', suggests that he was probably familiar with Verlaine's poetry as early as 1912. The attempted conversation with the dead is strangely reminiscent of 'Mon rêve familier': 'There watched I for the Dead; but no ghost woke. | Each one whom life exiled I named and called.' Among the sonnets Owen revised at Craiglockhart and Scarborough in 1917–18, 'The Unreturning' might plausibly be read as a nightmare vision of the war dead, but its original motivation appears to have been religious. The sonnet's failure to communicate with the dead raises questions about Christian belief in resurrection: 'I dreaded even a heaven with doors so chained' (107). The word 'unreturning' returns in a sonnet titled 'Happiness', written early in 1917. Owen claimed in a letter to his mother in August of that year that the closing lines were 'the *only lines* of mine that carry the stamp of maturity': 'The former happiness is unreturning: | Boys' griefs are not so grievous as youth's yearning, | Boys have no sadness sadder than than our hope.'[31]

'Happiness' was one of several sonnets written in 1916–17 on a poetic subject agreed by Owen and his cousin, Leslie Gunston, with the poet Olwen Joergens. Other suggested topics included colour, music, sunrise, love, and beauty. 'Purple', one of the earliest sonnets relating to this poetic friendship, suggests that the powerful mingling of Keats and Verlaine was pervasive. Hibberd claims that Owen had intended to collect his sonnets under the title, 'Certain Sonnets of Wilfred Owen', and that in 1917 he was contemplating 'Sonnets on Silence' as a possible title.[32] On 22 August 1917, he wrote to his mother after a meeting with Sassoon, confiding in her that 'Certain old sonnets of mine did not please S. at all.'[33] Even so, it appears

---

30. Dominic Hibberd, *Owen the Poet* (Basingstoke: Macmillan, 1986), pp. 30–3, 41.
31. *Collected Letters*, ed. Owen and Bell, p. 482.
32. Hibberd, *Owen the Poet*, p. 63.
33. *Collected Letters*, ed. Owen and Bell, p. 487.

that in early 1918 he fair-copied most of his sonnets and began to arrange them in a numbered sequence.

Notwithstanding Owen's remarks about coming to maturity as a poet in early 1917, one of the key transitional sonnets in his work is 'A New Heaven', subtitled 'To — On Active Service', and probably written in September 1916. Taking its title from Revelation 31:1, the sonnet lists in its octave those fabled heavens of the imagination—Mecca, Asgard, Nirvana—from which the soldier-poet seems forever banned. With the sharp ironic counterpoint that came to be seen as characteristic of Owen's later work, the sestet turns to the image of dead soldiers ferried over the English Channel rather than the Styx. Anticipating 'Anthem for Doomed Youth', the sonnet imagines the soldiers mythologized and worshipped as heroes ('To us, rough knees of boys shall ache with rev'rence'), only to undercut this institutionalized mourning with a more personal and persuasive note of pity, returning us at the same time to the realm of childhood: '—There our own mothers' tears shall heal us whole' (82).

A powerful elegiac impulse coupled to an ironic awareness of the inadequacy and irrelevance of conventional rites of mourning was to prompt what is arguably Owen's most moving and most memorable sonnet, 'Anthem for Doomed Youth'.

> What passing-bells for these who die as cattle?
>   Only the monstrous anger of the guns.
>   Only the stuttering rifles' rapid rattle
> Can patter out their hasty orisons.
> No mockeries now for them; no prayers nor bells;
>   Nor any voice of mourning save the choirs,—
> The shrill, demented choirs of wailing shells;
>   And bugles calling for them from sad shires.
>
> What candles may be held to speed them all?
>   Not in the hands of boys but in their eyes
> Shall shine the holy glimmers of goodbyes.
>   The pallor of girls' brows shall be their pall;
> Their flowers the tenderness of patient minds,
> And each slow dusk a drawing-down of blinds. (99)

The textual origins of 'Anthem for Doomed Youth' can be found in two abandoned poetic fragments composed in the late summer of 1917, both of which allude to 'Bugles saddening the evening air'. It seems likely that the poem was prompted by the anonymous Prefatory note to *Poems of Today: An Anthology* (1916), addressed to 'boys and girls' of the day and drawing their attention to how the various themes of the book mingle with 'the music of Pan's flute, and of Love's viol, and the bugle-call of Endeavour, and the passing-bells of Death'.[34] The various manuscript drafts of 'Anthem for Doomed Youth' show how extensively and persistently Owen labored over the sonnet form, but they also clearly reveal how the poem took shape under the guidance of Sassoon. As well as providing the title (initially suggesting 'Anthem for Dead Youth' and later adding the more evocative 'Doomed'), Sassoon also encouraged greater compression and precision in the writing of the sonnet. In the penultimate line, for instance, Owen had tried out various adjectives and possessives—silent, sweet-white, mortal, all men's, rough men's, comrades'—but the final draft benefits from Sassoon's gently restrained alternative: 'the tenderness of *patient* minds.'[35] The earliest draft is unrhymed, except for the closing couplet, but Owen worked assiduously to produce a form that, strictly speaking, is Spenserian rather than Shakespearean, with an additional couplet in lines 10–11: *ababcdcd effegg*. The octave-sestet division is clearly marked with the opening rhetorical question ('What passing-bells for these who die as cattle?') being echoed and intensified in line 9: 'What candles may be held to speed them all?'

The sonnet is structured around ideas of substitution and opposition, with the conventional tropes of mourning—bells, orisons, choirs, candles, palls, flowers, and blinds—displaced by explicit images of death in warfare. One of Owen's own inspired revisions was the amendment of 'you who die in herds' to 'these who die as cattle', intensifying the brutal undermining of the heroic individual death depicted in Brooke's sonnet. Rather than employing the octave-sestet division to enforce the opposition between convention and actuality, Owen extends the act of substitution across all fourteen lines, using the quatrains and couplets to create a sustained antithesis that finds release in the beautiful diminuendo of the final lines. Working within the disciplined form of the sonnet undoubtedly prompted Owen to produce those highly compressed alliterative effects which later became a hallmark of his style: the onomatopoeic realization of gunfire in 'the stuttering rifles' rapid rattle'; the grim pun in 'the pallor of girls' brows shall be their pall'; and the skilfully controlled deceleration enabled by the plosives in the final line: 'And each slow dusk a drawing-down of blinds.'

---

34. *Poems of Today: An Anthology* (1916), cited by Jon Stallworthy in Owen, *The Complete Poems and Fragments*, vol. 1, p. 99.
35. *The Complete Poems and Fragments*, ed. Stallworthy, vol. 2, p. 249.

For all of the deflationary scepticism with which it greets traditional images of consolation, the sonnet retains the solemnity and dignity customarily associated with an anthem. As Owen wrote to his mother, the title that Sassoon suggested for the poem was 'Just what I meant it to be'.[36] The elegiac mood and richness of texture draw upon the example of Keats's 'Odes', with line 7 clearly echoing 'To Autumn': 'Then in a wailful choir the small gnats mourn.' The cancelled word 'requiem' recalls the music of the nightingale—'To thy high requiem become a sod'—and that opposition of high and low, of imaginative figure and crude actuality, provides the basic structural principle of Owen's poem.[37] At the same time, as Hibberd has convincingly shown, the imagined 'requiem' is in keeping with the predominantly Catholic liturgical qualities of the sonnet, reinforced perhaps by Owen's enthusiasm for English and French Decadence.[38] His point is borne out in a letter from Bordeaux, written by Owen to his sister in May 1914, in which he describes an 'imposing Funeral Service' and recalls 'The gloom, the incense, the draperies, the shine of many candles, the images and ornaments'. In the same letter, he notes that the melancholy mourning of a bass voice was 'as fine as the Nightingale—(bird or poem)'.[39]

'Dulce et Decorum Est' was also written at Craiglockhart under the influence of Siegfried Sassoon in the autumn of 1917. Sassoon's unglamorous idiom of war and his fondness for unromantic similes is immediately evident: 'Bent double, like old beggars under sacks, | Knock-kneed, coughing like hags, we cursed through sludge' (140). Critical analysis of the poem has tended to concentrate on the implications of the Latin tag and the caustic address to the perpetrators of the 'old Lie'. The manuscript drafts show that the poem was initially addressed to Jessie Pope, author of *Simple Rhymes for Stirring Times*.[40] Understandably, 'Dulce et Decorum Est' has become a test case for those critics who share the opinion of W. B. Yeats that 'passive suffering is not a theme for poetry', and for those who wonder whether the poem, for all its imploring rhetoric, ultimately alienates its readers through its vehement excess of detail: 'If you could hear, at every jolt, the blood | Come gargling from the froth-corrupted lungs...' (140). Seamus Heaney responds judiciously to this debate by firmly but sympathetically acknowledging those

---

36. *Collected Letters*, ed. Owen and Bell, p. 496.
37. *Poetical Works*, ed. Garrod, pp. 219, 208.
38. Hibberd, *Owen the Poet*, pp. 111–12.
39. *Collected Letters*, ed. Owen and Bell, p. 248.
40. *The Complete Poems and Fragments*, ed. Stallworthy, vol. 2, p. 294.

moments in Owen's work when the exposure of suffering threatens to outweigh the transcendent impulse of song.[41]

Too insistent an emphasis on the shocking imagery of the poem and its disturbing rhetorical immediacy has been at the expense of a more appreciative criticism of its formal achievements. The extent of Owen's technical control is evident in his incisive reworking of an original thirty-two lines, so that what emerges is a concealed double sonnet. 'Dulce et Decorum Est' emerges from Owen's experimentation (following Sassoon's example) with narrative form and voice. What makes it such an imposing poem, however, is the tension that derives from the crossing of this narrative urgency with the lyrical compression required by the sonnet form. Pursuing a Shakespearean rhyme scheme and a neat arrangement of three quatrains, the first sonnet abruptly denies the expected paired *g* rhyme and the traditional closing couplet. Instead, it initiates a further turn, from the cry of 'Gas! Gas!' in line 9 to the nightmare vision of lines 15–16: 'In all my dreams, before my helpless sight, | He plunges at me, guttering, choking, drowning' (140). With brilliant economy of style, Owen both presents these lines as part of an isolated central observation and makes them serve as the first two lines of a second sonnet. The connecting rhyme word, the repeated 'drowning', recalls with devastating effect the simple description of the work in a letter Owen sent to his mother in October 1917: 'Here is a gas poem.'[42]

There is a radical disjunction at the centre of 'Dulce et Decorum Est', with the opening two lines of the second sonnet pulling away from the past-tense recollection of the gas attack into a shocking present-tense dreamscape and a nightmare vision of the injured soldier: 'In all my dreams, before my helpless sight, | He plunges at me, choking, guttering, drowning.' The remaining twelve lines are all the more striking for the way in which they function as a single sentence. Twice invoking the solemn subjunctive mood of Rupert Brooke ('If I should die...'), Owen urges his readers to consider the reality of war before pronouncing on the virtues of patriotic sacrifice: 'If in some smothering dreams you too could pace... If you could hear, at every jolt...' (140). Like 'The Soldier', 'Dulce et Decorum Est' considers the patriotic idea that it might be sweet and decorous to die for one's country, but it responds with an extreme ferocity of diction and a fractured form that ends abruptly, mid-line, with the verb to die.

---

41. W. B. Yeats, *The Oxford Book of Modern Verse 1892–1935* (Oxford: Oxford University Press, 1936), p. xxxiv. Seamus Heaney, *The Government of the Tongue* (London: Faber, 1988), p. xiv.
42. *Collected Letters*, ed. Owen and Bell, p. 499.

Owen's experimentation with the sonnet form as a space where dramatic events and narrative detail might be developed suggests one direction in which his work was tending in 1917. Another direction is evident in the lyric and elegiac intensity of poems like 'Futility', where death and destruction are approached with greater subtlety and obliquity than in 'Dulce et Decorum Est', and where lyric resources are made to withstand the pressure of war. 'Futility', written in May 1918, is not generally regarded as a sonnet, but its fourteen short lines appear to be a calculated departure from the conventional sonnet form. The manuscript reference to a soldier whose home is in Wales and the careful placing of the imperative 'Think' suggest that Owen might well have been writing a sonnet in reply to Rupert Brooke's example in 'The Soldier'. The title, the closing apostrophe, and the employment of a short line (mainly octosyllabic) are derived from Tennyson's *In Memoriam* ('O life as futile, then, as frail'), but the skilful pararhyme ('star'/'stir', 'tall'/'toil') is unmistakably Owen's own.[43]

Tennyson also hovers over the poem that is generally considered to be Owen's final sonnet, 'Hospital Barge', written at Scarborough in December 1917:

> Budging the sluggard ripples of the Somme,
> A barge round old Cérisy slowly slewed.
> Softly her engines down the current screwed,
> And chuckled softly with contented hum,
> Till fairy tinklings struck their croonings dumb.
> The waters rumpling at the stern subdued;
> The lock-gate took her bulging amplitude;
> Gently from out the gurgling lock she swum.
>
> One reading by that calm bank shaded eyes
> To watch her lessening westward quietly.
> Then, as she neared the bend, her funnel screamed.
> And that long lamentation made him wise
> How unto Avalon, in agony,
> Kings passed in the dark barge which Merlin dreamed. (127)

In a letter written to his mother in May 1917, Owen reveals that he had travelled with another injured soldier along the Somme Canal, close to the

---

43. *The Complete Poems and Fragments*, ed. Stallworthy, vol. 1, p. 158. For the Tennyson allusion, see *In Memoriam*, lvi, line 25, in *The Poems of Tennyson*, ed. Christopher Ricks (London: Longmans, 1969), p. 912.

military hospital in Cérisy. The letter vividly links the dream-like landscape of 'Hospital Barge' with the winter landscape of 'Futility' (the two poems were published together in the *Nation* in June 1916), at the same time as invoking Spenser and Tennyson:

> The scenery was such as I never saw or dreamed of since I read the *Fairie Queene*. Just as in the Winter when I woke up lying on the burning cold snow I fancied I must have died & been pitch-forked into the Wrong Place, so, yesterday, it was not more difficult to imagine that my dusky barge was wending up to Avalon, and the peace of Arthur, and where Lancelot heals him of his grievous wound.[44]

The 'dusky barge' links the poem and the letter to Tennyson and 'The Passing of Arthur', which Owen had read in *The Holy Grail and Other Poems* (1870). Compared with 'Dulce et Decorum Est', the sonnet works in a quiet and undemonstrative way, lifting us from 'the sluggard ripples of the Somme' into the contemplative, magical realm of the literary imagination, only to break that spell with the screaming funnel of the barge and the sombre allusion to the death of Arthur. Against the repetition of 'softly' and the delicate move across octave to sestet, from 'gently' to 'quietly', the screaming funnel and the isolated word 'agony' at the end of the penultimate line have a powerful contrasting effect. The division between octave and sestet is also the point at which the sonnet turns from casual description to personal witness. 'One reading' carefully avoids a direct first-person perspective, but nevertheless implicates the poet/speaker as both onlooker and participant. The wisdom that the sonnet imparts is obliquely transmitted through Merlin's dream, but like 'Strange Meeting', it poignantly prophesies the poet's own death in war.

Those poets who survived the war, among them Siegfried Sassoon, Edmund Blunden, and Ivor Gurney, would continue to write (reflectively, bitterly, compulsively) about the experience of war, and the sonnet would continue to be a versatile form for recovering and recording troubled, shell-shocked memories. Blunden's frequently anthologized sonnet, 'Vlamertinghe: Passing the Château, July 1917', has an alarming present-tense immediacy, though it wasn't published until 1928. Like Owen, Blunden registers disturbance through a violated pastoral idiom, through insistent rhetorical questions, and through an ironic use of literary allusion. Here, the opening echo of Keats's

---

44. *Collected Letters*, ed. Owen and Bell, p. 457.

'Ode to a Grecian Urn' is a prelude to imminent slaughter rather than eternal beauty:

> And all her silken flanks with garlands drest—
> But we are coming to the sacrifice.
> Must those flowers who are not yet gone West?
> May those flowers who live with death and lice?
> This must be the floweriest place
> That earth allows; the queenly face
> Of the proud mansion borrows grace for grace
> Spite of those brute guns lowing at the skies.
>
> Bold great daisies' golden lights,
> Bubbling roses' pinks and whites—
> Such a gay carpet! poppies by the million;
> Such damask! such vermilion!
> But if you ask me, mate, the choice of colour
> Is scarcely right; this red should have been duller.[45]

As in other Blunden poems, the human ordering of nature in gardens and farms is threatened with destruction. The repetition of 'flowers' and the over-emphatic 'floweriest' in the octave prepare us for the excessive display of daisies, roses, and poppies in the sestet, the floral beauty of the garden both contrasting with the grim truth of war and simultaneously serving as a massive funeral wreath. The disrupted sonnet form is integral to the meaning. What looks like an emerging Shakespearean rhyme scheme is not allowed to progress, and slips into a smoothly deceptive triplet ('place'/'face'/'grace'), while also keeping open the possibility of a half-rhyme with 'lice'. The final word of the octave, 'skies', looks back ominously to 'sacrifice' for its rhyme. Blunden also disrupts line length, knocking syllables off the pentameter line. The irregularities are carried through to the sestet, in which we have three couplets with unruly variant lines. The closing couplet asserts the vernacular wisdom of a British soldier against the effusive display of flowers and all that the blossoms might suggest in terms of beauty or consolation. The sonnet doesn't explicitly mention blood, since it can take for granted a literary symbolism that by the end of the war had become a cliché.

The technique of violating pastoral ideals with the brutal imagery of war is powerfully employed in the poetry of Ivor Gurney. The title of Gurney's first volume of poems, *Severn and Somme* (1917), points to a persistent dual focus on the meadows and rivers of England and the battlefields of France.

---

45. Edmund Blunden, *Undertones of War* (Harmondsworth: Penguin, 2000), p. 208.

Although the volume closes with a sequence of five sonnets titled 'Sonnets 1917', dedicated 'To the Memory of Rupert Brooke', both the style and the attitude suggest dissent rather than emulation.[46] In 1915, writing to his friend Marion Scott, he expresses doubts about Brooke's achievements in his war sonnets: 'Great poets, great creators, are not much influenced by immediate events; these must sink in to the very foundations and be absorbed. Rupert Brooke soaked it in quickly and gave it out with as great ease.' In Gurney's case, 'the sinking in' would be painful and prolonged. Embarking on his own sonnets in 1917, he told Scott that they would be 'a sort of counterblast' to Brooke's 1914 sonnets: 'They are the protest of the physical against the exalted spiritual; of the cumulative weight of small facts against one large. Of informed opinion against uninformed.'[47] The second sonnet in Gurney's 1917 sequence is simply titled 'Pain', and it recalls both the compression and the desolation of Hopkins's late sonnets. It registers the violence of war on the sensitive spirit with an ellipsis that would become a hallmark of Gurney's style: 'Pain, pain continual; pain unending; | Hard even to the roughest, but to those | Hungry for beauty...' (36). John Lucas notes perceptively that Gurney manages to incorporate dissident, disturbing viewpoints into the sequence by wrapping it in more conventional and acceptable sentiments, especially in the closing sonnet, 'England the Mother'.[48] Even so, there is a powerful, unignorable protest in Gurney's acknowledgement of 'Men broken, shrieking even to hear a gun' (36).

The ethic of service to England that Gurney articulates is strikingly different from that of 'The Soldier'. Indeed, Gurney speaks emphatically of 'Servitude' in the sonnet of that title, and of an oppressive, class-ridden system rather than an idealized 'giving': 'If it were not for England, who would bear | This heavy servitude one moment more?' Gurney's England is enshrined in the ideal of community and fellowship rather than individualized heroism: 'Only the love of comrades sweetens all' (37). As Lucas suggests, that comradeship was based on a desire to build a better, more peaceful world, and it was sustained by 'a radicalism which required him to make poetry very different from most of what he saw around him'.[49] Patiently undoing the

---

46. Ivor Gurney, *Collected Poems*, ed. P. J. Kavanagh (Oxford: Oxford University Press, 1982). Unless otherwise indicated, references are to this edition of the poems.
47. Ivor Gurney, *Collected Letters*, ed. R. K. R. Thornton (Ashington: MidNAG; Manchester: Carcanet, 1991), pp. 29, 210.
48. John Lucas, *Ivor Gurney* (Tavistock: Northcote House, 2001), pp. 10–11.
49. Lucas, *Ivor Gurney*, p. 32.

grandeur and eloquence that Brooke had reinvested in the sonnet, Gurney writes 'To England—A Note', once again questioning the patriotic ideal of service: 'I watched the boys of England where they went | Through mud and water to do appointed things.' The Petrarchan form is dutifully observed, but the direction of the sonnet is towards a recognition of the misfit between lyric form and warfare, just as the soldiers 'In the height of battle tell the world in song | How they do hate and fear the face of War'.[50]

It is in the 1920s, however, that Gurney produces his most radically innovative sonnets. 'Strange Hells', 'The Not Returning', and 'On Somme', as their titles suggest, all disturbingly record the 'sinking in' of war. In September 1922, after trying to commit suicide, Gurney was certified insane and admitted to a private asylum in Gloucester, before being transferred to the City of London Mental Hospital at Dartford, where he spent the rest of his life. 'Strange Hells', probably written shortly before he was committed to Barnwood Mental Hospital in Gloucester, coincides with this period of mental and emotional turbulence, but the sonnet is remarkable in its assertion that the frequency and ferocity of the 'strange hells' of war were less than 'one would have expected'.[51] What Gurney refuses to mitigate in the sonnet is the burning indignity and shame of soldiers readjusting to civic routine:

> There are strange Hells within the minds War made
> Not so often, not so humiliatingly afraid
> As one would have expected—the racket and fear guns made.
> One Hell the Gloucester soldiers they quite put out;
> Their first bombardment, when in combined black shout
> Of fury, guns aligned, they ducked low their heads
> And sang with diaphragms fixed beyond all dreads,
> That tin and stretched-wire tinkle, that blither of tune;
> 'Apres la guerre fini' till Hell all had come down,
> Twelve-inch, six-inch, and eighteen pounders hammering Hell's thunders.
>
> Where are they now on State-doles, or showing shop patterns
> Or walking town to town sore in borrowed tatterns
> Or begged. Some civic routine one never learns.
> The heart burns—but has to keep out of face how heart burns.

---

50. Ivor Gurney, *Severn & Somme* and *War's Embers*, ed. R. K. R. Thornton (Manchester: Carcanet, 1997), p. 28.
51. The version of 'Strange Hells' printed here is the one included by Philip Larkin in *The Oxford Book of Twentieth-Century English Verse* (Oxford: Clarendon Press, 1973; 1974), p. 265.

The sonnet carries forward from 1917 an enduring image of soldiers singing through war, but with the word 'tune' the rhymes 'come down' and the word 'thunders' is noticeably left unrhymed. The rhyme scheme is, in any case, unorthodox, opening with a stubbornly insistent triplet, 'made'/'afraid'/'made', and closing with two couplets. The octave-sestet division is jettisoned in favour of a late turn, with the closing quatrain initiating a short but stinging recognition of the humiliating civilian aftermath of war. The syntax, sprawling and unruly at the start, is given tighter rein in the quatrain. The enjambment of 'borrowed tatterns | Or begged' is neatly delivered, as is the double rhyme (internal as well as end rhyme) between 'learns' and 'burns'. The sonnet is outspoken and uncompromising in its revelation of smouldering resentment, as well as lasting sorrow, among demobilized soldiers.

That Gurney's sonnets were not merely erratic, not merely the fractured utterances of a shell-shocked consciousness, is evidenced by those occasions when he felt that it might be fitting to produce a more conventional lyric verse. 'The Golden Age' looks back from its own time of 'cold forms' to the kind of democratic English commonwealth that William Morris dreamed of. The sestet builds towards that ideal in a sweeping single sentence:

> O for some force to swing us back there to some
> Natural moving towards life's love, or that glow
> In the word to be glow in the State, that golden age come
> Again, men working freely as nature might show,
> And a people honouring stage-scenes lit bright with fine sound
> On a free soil, England happy, honoured and joy-crowned.   (158)

There is no delusion here. The poem is fully cognizant of the 'cold-blooded unfree' life of the present and of the force that might be necessary to change it. In the sonnets alone there is sufficient evidence to support the claim that Gurney is 'one of the most original, extraordinary, and *essential* of twentieth-century poets'.[52]

W. H. Auden

It was W. H. Auden who, more than any other poet writing in the twentieth century, adopted and modernized the sonnet as a form highly suited to the

---

52. Lucas, *Ivor Gurney*, p. ix.

peculiar cultural and psychological pressures of the time, and also ensured its continued use as an instrument of subtle political enquiry and debate. Auden was a prolific and accomplished sonnet writer, and his various experiments with the form include three sonnet sequences: a sequence of love poems sent to Christopher Isherwood in 1934; the sonnets 'In Time of War', an integral part of *Journey to a War* (1939); and 'The Quest', published in *The Double Man* in 1940. In addition, he wrote numerous occasional sonnets, often relating to particular places or people, by turns erotic, sardonic, satirical, moral, philosophical, and theological. He showed himself to be an astute and discerning critic of the sonnet, lecturing and writing on Shakespeare's sonnets, and editing the excellent Signet edition of Shakespeare's sonnets in 1964. It was in the sonnets 'In Time of War', later reprinted as 'Sonnets from China', that Auden excelled, both forging a link with earlier sonnet writers, including the generation of 1914–18, and refining the sonnet form so that it would become the perfect device for capturing the unremitting tension between historical forces and the individual conscience.

Auden claimed that his first poem had been a Wordsworthian sonnet on Blea Tarn in the Lake District, but only a line and a half are known to exist: 'and in the quiet | Oblivion of thy waters let them stay.'[53] Among his *Juvenilia: Poems 1922–1928* there are ten sonnets which tentatively explore the interests, obsessions, and preoccupations that would shape the later work: an attraction to obscure and deserted landscapes; a fascination with exceptional individuals, including other writers; clandestine, erotic encounters; the psychological dramas of family history; and political intrigue. 'Rookhope (Weardale, Summer 1922)' is notable for its early admiration of the lead-mining district of County Durham, close to Auden's cherished Alston, and of the lives of those who once worked there. A regular Shakespearean sonnet, probably written in April 1924, the poem uses its turn resourcefully to move from local description to personal involvement—'Yet—I have stood by their deserted shafts'—and towards a mystical communion in which the poet is able 'To glimpse the spirit which engendered these' (54). The mystic spirit perceived in wind and rain undoubtedly owes much to the influence of Richard Jefferies, who is the subject of a slightly later sonnet, written in May 1925, the first of Auden's numerous sonnet tributes, including those to A. E. Housman, Edward Lear, and Arthur Rimbaud. 'Richard Jefferies'

---

53. W. H. Auden, *Juvenilia: Poems 1922–1928*, ed. Katherine Bucknell (Princeton: Princeton University Press, 1994), p. 3.

begins as a Shakespearean sonnet, but its sestet is Petrarchan. The turn is effectively delayed until line 10, so that the celebration of Jefferies's uncanny sensitivity to the vibrant energies of nature, even as he lay dying, can be given maximum impact:

> What more? When dying he could praise the light
> And watch larks trembling over fields of corn
> Until the whole sky sang, with eyes as bright
> As kestrel perched upon the splintered oak,
> A sentinel, dark, motionless, at dawn.   (92)

The fluently articulated syntax (a single sentence drawn out over five lines of the sonnet) and the carefully modulated music of the final line suggest the influence of another follower of Richard Jefferies, Edward Thomas.

Auden's startling originality can be seen in the unrhymed sonnet, 'Control of the Passes was, he saw, the key', which was included in *Poems* (1928), published while he was at Oxford, and later reprinted as 'The Secret Agent':

> Control of the Passes was, he saw, the key
> To this new district, but who would get it?
> He, the trained spy, had walked into a trap
> For a bogus guide, seduced with the old tricks.
>
> At Greenhearth was a fine site for a dam
> And easy power, had they pushed the rail
> Some stations nearer; they ignored his wires.
> The bridges were unbuilt and trouble coming.
>
> The street music seemed gracious now to one
> For weeks up in the desert; woken by water
> Running away in the dark, he often had
> Reproached the night for a companion
> Dreamed of already. They would shoot, of course,
> Parting easily who were never joined.   (239)

'Greenhearth' is possibly Greenhurth, not far from Alston, but the sonnet depends on intrigue and anonymity rather than recognition. The poem might well allude to the closing of the Alpine passes into France and Italy by Mussolini in August 1927, but again the identification of specific places and events seems inappropriate to a sonnet that operates primarily in the realm of political and sexual fantasy. The 'unbuilt bridges' in the final line of the octave are figures of psychological, as well as political, isolation, and they suggest (as does the dreaming in the sestet) that repression and frustration are primary motives. John Fuller helpfully points out that 'Love is forced to act as a secret agent because the individual does not consciously recognize his desire (the spy) and represses it. "They", who ignore his wires, and eventually shoot him, represent the conscious will, the Censor, which represses the individual's emotional desires.' The last line, taken from the Old English poem, 'Wulf and Eadwacer' ('the monologue of a captive woman addressed to her outlawed lover') supports the supposition that 'the situation is one of unconsummated love'.[54]

In the summer of 1933, Auden embarked upon a sequence of love sonnets, which he sent to Christopher Isherwood the following year. The compositional history is complicated, but it seems that the original opening sonnet began with the line, 'The earth turns over, our side feels the cold', which later became 'Through the Looking-Glass'. The initial impulse behind the sequence appears to have been Auden's love for a 14-year-old boy whose portrait had been painted by the art master at the Downs School in the Malverns. A version of the sequence appears as Section XVIII of 'Poems 1931–36' in *The English Auden*.[55] Most of the sonnets are Shakespearean and the overall design of the sequence, as well as its intimate modes of address, are clearly indebted to Shakespeare's example. Shakespeare's finely discriminating moral intelligence and complex dramatization of the ego made him, for Auden, the most modern of artists, with an enduring capacity for engaging readers in the unfathomable mystery of personality and its 'millions of strange shadows'.[56] The Shakespearean sonnet appealed to Auden much as the dramatic monologue appealed to T. S. Eliot. It was a form in which the most private thoughts and feelings could acquire artistic impersonality. For this reason, he had little interest in the identities of the young man and the Dark Lady. The mystery and obscurity of the sonnets were, he believed, an integral part of their artistic accomplishment and lasting appeal.

The sonnets in Auden's early sequence are revealing stylistically in that they show him savouring the lyric potential of the Shakespearean sonnet (in such smoothly crafted lines as 'Turn not towards me lest I turn to you'), even while endeavouring to distort and fracture the staple iambic line. Among the rhetorical skills gleaned from Shakespeare's sonnets is the intimate pause created by a well-placed caesura. The opening line quoted above is replayed as the closing line, with a delicate but decisive difference: 'Turn not towards

---

54. John Fuller, *W. H. Auden: A Commentary* (London: Faber, 1998), p. 15.
55. *The English Auden: Poems, Essays and Dramatic Writings 1927–39* (London: Faber, 1977).
56. *The Complete Sonnets and Poems*, ed. Burrow, p. 487.

me, lest I turn to you' (146). There is tenderness and devotion in these early sonnets, but fear, jealousy, and disappointment prevail, so that like their Shakespearean counterparts they constitute a dramatization of what Auden neatly summed up as 'the anxiety into which the behaviour of another person can throw you'.[57]

The sonnets are very likely addressed to the same young man who inspired Auden's moving lyric, 'Lay your sleeping head, my love', and the same gentle imperatives move through the verse:

> Turn not towards me lest I turn to you:
> Stretch not your hands towards your harm and me
> Lest, waking, you should feel the need I do
> To offer love's preposterous guarantee
> That the stars watch us... (146)

Fuller's comments on the later poem are instructive here: 'It achieves the beauty of its effect by the way in which the moment of happiness is weighed gravely and consciously against an awareness of all that can threaten it.'[58] The innocence of the recipient is presented from the speaker's guarded, unillusioned perspective, his knowledge of 'the power which corrupts the heart'. The second sonnet in the sequence prepares the young man for inevitable disappointment with a mixture of ironic distance and troubled concern: 'Soon enough you will | Enter the zone where casualties begin' (146). The obliquity and obscurity of the sonnets arise from their self-conscious dramatization of the psychological confusions and uncertainties of a clandestine love. They function as a sublimation and displacement of desire. The allegorical landscapes of the sonnets constitute a kind of *paysage moralisé* through which the lover's progress is charted: 'Upon the mountains of our fear I climb... | Soon on a lower alp I fall and pant' (149). This is especially evident, as Fuller notes, in a sonnet that was originally included in the sequence, but later numbered separately as XIX in 'Poems 1931–6': 'To settle in this village of the heart, | My darling, can you bear it?' (154). Here, it becomes clear that changing conceptions of house and home are intimately related to questions of commitment within relationships.[59] Is it possible to establish a new ideal of community, without this turning to promiscuity and 'the shy encounter | With the irresponsible beauty of the stranger'? In this troubled sonnet, love finds no rhyme at all. The closing

---

57. Auden, *Lectures on Shakespeare*, ed. Arthur Kirsch (London: Faber, 2000), p. 93.
58. Fuller, *W. H. Auden*, p. 264.   59. Fuller, *W. H. Auden*, p. 168.

sonnet, later titled 'Meiosis', considers the erotic impulse and 'the little death' against the biological processes of fertilization, chromosome reduction, and the evolution of the species. This time, love finds a tentative, unanchored rhyme in 'The flood on which all move and wish to move' (150).

In 1937, Auden and Isherwood were commissioned by their publishers to write a travel book about the East, and prompted by the outbreak of the Sino-Japanese War in August of that year, they decided to visit China. They sailed to Hong Kong in January 1938 and made their way to Shanghai, returning to London in July, via Japan, Canada, and the United States. *Journey to a War* (1939) is a remarkable work of travel literature and photography, combining Isherwood's loosely written, entertaining diary of events with Auden's tightly compressed and intellectually commanding sonnets and verse commentary. The book includes a dedicatory sonnet to E. M. Forster and five prefatory sonnets of embarkation and journeying, as well as the twenty-seven sonnets that constitute the sequence 'In Time of War'. Tonally and structurally, the sonnets provide a contrast with the self-deprecating ironies of the diary, in which Isherwood records how the two writers enjoyed the pleasures of the British Ambassador's private villa ('Number One House') as the Japanese tightened their hold on Shanghai: 'In our world, there are the garden-parties and the night-clubs, the hot baths and the cocktails, the singsong girls and the Ambassador's cook.'[60] One of the functions of the sonnets, initiated by the dedicatory sonnet 'To E. M. Forster', is to strip away privilege and prejudice, and to face the reality of political events with the moral compunction of the inner life:

> Here, though the bombs are real and dangerous,
> And Italy and King's are far away,
> And we're afraid that you will speak to us,
> You promise still the inner life shall pay.   (11)

As Tony Sharpe points out, 'In Time of War' involves a learning process in which 'privileged insulation falls away in a revelation that is simultaneously of personal vulnerability and personal responsibility'.[61] The journey is, itself, a dominant metaphor in the book, and the ship is a microcosm of class society complacently going about its business: 'It is our culture that with such calm progresses | Over the barren plains of a sea.' The alexandrine line

---

60. W. H. Auden and Christopher Isherwood, *Journey to a War* (New York: Random House, 1939), p. 252. Page references are to this edition.
61. Tony Sharpe, *W. H. Auden* (London: Routledge, 2007), p. 54.

of 'The Ship' effectively conveys Auden's far-reaching vision and sense of journeying into the unknown, while also bringing the sonnet to an unnerving close: 'no one guesses | Who will be most ashamed, who richer, and who dead' (20).

'In Time of War' has been praised as 'Auden's most profound and audacious poem of the 1930s'.[62] As well as bringing to the course of human history a comprehensive analysis and a depth of moral understanding, the sequence employs the sonnet form in radically new and inventive ways. Stan Smith has shown how Auden skilfully turns the conventions of the love sonnet inside-out, 'evacuating the personal' and using it instead 'as a vehicle for an objective history of the species'. The opening twelve sonnets function not as an anodyne survey of human development and representative human types, but as a trenchant critique of prevailing political systems and values: 'By taking the personalized, self-regarding lover of the sonnet sequence, and dispersing him into the multitude of collective subjects who make a history, Auden deconstructs the political and literary traditions of bourgeois individualism.'[63] The sequence traces three broad epochs of political disappointment and failure, from the end of the Roman Empire, through medieval Christianity, to the modern machine age. The sonnets open, however, with the dawning of creation and the capacity for choice that distinguishes mankind from other living organisms. 'Fish swam as fish, peach settled into peach', but 'finally there came a childish creature' whose versatility and adaptability are traits of weakness as well as power: 'Who by the lightest wind was changed and shaken, | And looked for truth and was continually mistaken' (259).

The tight containment of individual sonnets, combined with the progression of the sequence, is perfectly suited to Auden's ambitious condensation of human history. We move through whole epochs of learning and advancement, from the development of agriculture to the monastic tradition, and on towards industrialization and urbanization, but with each stage of development there are troubling complexities and uncertainties within the human subject. Sonnet VIII is a brilliant synoptic rendering of the growth of cities, the measurement of time, the documentation of learning and culture, and the regulation of money and credit. With the great human achievements of the Enlightenment, however, come contradictions that steadily undermine the ideal of equality, inducing a condition of alienation and disenchantment:

---

62. Edward Mendelson, *Early Auden* (New York: Viking, 1981), p. 348.
63. Stan Smith, *W. H. Auden* (Oxford: Blackwell, 1985), pp. 109–10.

> He turned his field into a meeting-place,
> And grew the tolerant ironic eye,
> And formed the mobile money-changer's face,
> And found the notion of equality.
>
> And strangers were as brothers to his clocks,
> And with his spires he made a human sky;
> Museums stored his learning like a box,
> And paper watched his money like a spy.
>
> It grew so fast his life was overgrown,
> And he forgot what once it had been made for,
> And gathered into crowds and was alone,
>
> And lived expensively and did without,
> And could not find the earth which he had paid for,
> Nor feel the love that he knew all about.   (266)

The plain diction, the simple past tense, the repeated anaphoric conjunctions, and the almost comic, childlike rhymes ('clocks'/'box', 'made for'/'paid for'), all make for what looks initially like a straightforward allegory of human progress. Throughout the sequence, however, any notion of advancement and learning is subtly undermined by a corrosive, ironic awareness of a corresponding human diminishment and ignorance. Beneath the apparently simple, allegorical narrative are moral and psychological depths and complexities: the loneliness of the crowd, the lost sense of value, the disturbing disjunction of thought and feeling.

If Shakespeare provides the model and inspiration for Auden's early love sonnets, it is Rainer Maria Rilke who stands imposingly behind the sonnets in *Journey to a War*. Rilke's obliquity and comprehensiveness, his simultaneous looking back and looking forward, and his enquiries into the nature of being in a time of war leave a strong imprint on Auden's sequence. Sonnet XXIII pays tribute to Rilke, acknowledging his completion of the *Duino Elegies* at Château de Muzot after the First World War. Rilke's patient waiting is structurally embodied in the sonnet's syntactical interruption between octave and sestet:

> To-night in China let me think of one,
> Who through ten years of silence worked and waited,
> Until in Muzot all his powers spoke,
> And everything was given once for all...   (281)

In the 1936 edition of Rilke's *Sonnets to Orpheus*, which Auden read and absorbed, J. B. Leishman notes astutely that 'no other writer gives us such thrilling intimations of that inheritance on whose threshold we are standing, and which our civilisation may be about to enter, if it does not perish through its own destructive forces'.[64] Sonnet XIII of 'In Time of War' clearly echoes the opening of Rilke's Sonnet 7 ('Rühmen, das ists!'), with its determination to carry on singing in the face of history: 'Certainly praise: let the song mount again and again | For life as it blossoms out in a jar or a face.' Against this reassurance of lyric plenitude, the sestet reminds us that 'History opposes its grief to our buoyant song'. This mid-point sonnet sets the celebration of human happiness against 'the morning's injured weeping' and prepares us for the 'here' and 'now' of the sonnets that follow (271).

Sonnet XIV is alarming in its immediate declaration of the certainty of suffering and the reality of pain. The searchlights in the night-time sky are both a metaphorical exposure of repression and a frightening illumination of Japanese pilots involved in the aerial bombardment of China:

> Yes, we are going to suffer, now; the sky
> Throbs like a feverish forehead; pain is real;
> The groping searchlights suddenly reveal
> The little natures that will make us cry... (272)

The poetic voice here tends towards the sardonic while keeping open an attitude of pity towards the deluded and the complacent, as well as the more obvious victims of abusive power. Sonnet XV is similarly disarming in its tonal complexity, ironically linking the Japanese pilots with the privileged bourgeoisie: 'Engines bear them through the sky: they're free | And isolated like the very rich' (273). The main function of the sonnet, however, is to remind us of the helplessness of the poor, and to reassert the preoccupation of the sequence with the unending conflict between choice and necessity. Echoing the title of Louis MacNeice's 1938 collection of poems, *The Earth Compels*, Sonnets XIV and XV suggest, to the contrary, that the earth might well be at the mercy of 'The intelligent and evil'. In the case of the Japanese pilots, 'They chose a fate | The islands where they live did not compel' (273).

Even when appearing to meditate on abstract ideas, Auden's sonnets are powerfully concentrated on actual events and situations in China. Sonnet XVII notes how suffering displaces all other considerations, isolating the injured in their pain, but it also draws upon details of the visit that Auden and

---

64. J. B. Leishman (ed.), Introduction to Rainer Maria Rilke, *Sonnets to Orpheus* (London: Hogarth Press, 1936), pp. 11–12.

Isherwood made to a military hospital in Shang-kui: 'They are and suffer; that is all they do: | A bandage hides the place where each is living' (275). At the same time, the theatre of war is not confined to China, and as the sequence progresses it turns its gaze simultaneously on East and West. As Auden and Isherwood journeyed to a war in the early months of 1938, they received reports from Europe that Franco's forces had retaken Teruel from the Republicans in the Spanish Civil War, and that Hitler's troops had marched into Austria. Sonnet XVI, probably the most frequently quoted sonnet in the sequence, begins by directing its attention to the wartime exigencies of 'here', but closes with a compelling recognition of evil in other places. The opening simile—'Here war is simple like a monument'—belies its own obviousness, since starkness and memorializing are both implied in the monument, but do not necessarily cohere in a single attitude (274). Indeed, the symbols and ideas of war are at some distance from its reality throughout the sonnet. The sestet serves to close the gap between abstraction and actuality, asserting that some ideas are true and presumably worth dying for: 'But ideas can be true although men die.' In the same spirit, it now gives an urgent immediacy to those 'Flags on a map' that had previously seemed the remote and concealing signifiers of a war going on:

> And maps can really point to places
> Where life is evil now:
> Nanking; Dachau.

In a sequence in which concluding rhymed couplets are generally eschewed, the insistence on contemporary coincidences of geography and politics is all the more striking. The curtailment of the sonnet in a final line of just four syllables is a technique borrowed from Rilke's *Sonnets to Orpheus*, but here Auden achieves both a premonitory abbreviation and a steady focusing of attention over the tercet, unambiguously acknowledging *world* war in the linking of the Nanking massacre and the Nazi concentration camps. John Fuller notes how the contraction acts as both a stifling of emotion and a powerful memorial: 'The effect is at once choked and funereal...The silence is pregnant. Yet the short line itself acts musically, tolling like a bell.'[65]

Having returned to England in the summer of 1938, Auden completed 'In Time of War' and the 'Verse Commentary' that accompanies it in *Journey to a War*, and then spent part of the winter (December 1938 to January 1939) in Brussels, where he embarked on a new series of sonnets reflecting on the

---

65. John Fuller, *The Sonnet* (London: Methuen, 1972), p. 35.

motives of art and the ethical and political responsibilities of the poet. 'Brussels in Winter', in which the stranger coldly contemplates the modern city, serves as a prelude to these musings:

> Wandering the cold streets tangled like old string,
> Coming on fountains silent in the frost,
> The city still escapes you; it has lost
> The qualities that say 'I am a Thing.'
>
> Only the homeless and the really humbled
> Seem to be sure exactly where they are,
> And in their misery are all assembled;
> The winter holds them like the Opera.
>
> Ridges of rich apartments rise to-night
> Where isolated windows glow like farms,
> A phrase goes packed with meaning like a van,
>
> A look contains the history of a man,
> And fifty francs will earn the stranger right
> To warm the heartless city in his arms.[66]

The sonnet is 'a threnody of urban desolation', but in its search for the heart in a heartless world it also probes the fundamental conflicts in Auden's imagination, between private and public morality, and between the individual conscience and civic responsibility.[67] The octave and the sestet invert the typical associations of rich and poor, giving the homeless a sense of sureness and togetherness in the incongruous simile of the opera house, while (in a similarly incongruous simile) the hierarchy associated with 'rising' apartments is undermined by the association with farms. The sexual suggestiveness of 'A phrase' and 'A look' is confirmed in the final line of the sonnet, effectively linking the rich apartments with prostitution and revealing the cold city to be a place where love is a debased financial transaction. The role of the stranger is an ambivalent one, with the closing lines suggesting a wish for some more fulfilling and sustaining relationship.

The idea that art might begin in deprivation and assume the role of transforming what is broken and incomplete informs the sonnets for Arthur Rimbaud, A. E. Housman, and Edward Lear. 'Rimbaud' begins with the troubled child's exposure to 'The nights, the railway-arches, the bad sky', and asserts that 'the cold had made a poet' (181). Housman, too, is presented as a

---

66. W. H. Auden, *Collected Poems*, ed. Edward Mendelson (London: Faber, 1991), p. 178. Further references are to this edition of the poems.
67. Mendelson, *Early Auden*, p. 362.

writer hurt into poetry by circumstance: 'Heart-injured in North London, he became | The leading classic of his generation.' With a distinctly unromantic view of poetic inspiration, Auden peers into the murky and obscure psychological origins of creativity, finding in Housman's verse a volatile mix of emotional repression and socio-economic distinctions: 'his private lust | Something to do with violence and the poor.' The sonnet form allows Auden to conduct an intense case study of each poet, and also to hold in tension the strange oppositions that governed them. If Rimbaud's dream of a new self necessitates his eventual estrangement from poetry, Housman's struggle with feeling manifests itself in a 'dry-as-dust' pedantry (182). It seems likely that the two sonnets titled 'The Novelist' and 'The Composer' were written to counter and relieve the bleak psychological theorizing of art in the Rimbaud and Housman poems, and that the unnamed exemplary artists that Auden had in mind were his friends, Christopher Isherwood and Benjamin Britten. The poet has much to learn from the novelist and the composer, both of whom exercise a Christ-like humility in facing the world's hurt, with one having to 'suffer dully all the wrongs of Man' and the other prepared to pour out 'forgiveness like a wine' (180–1). Mendelson thoughtfully connects these sonnets to Brussels by suggesting that in Auden's mind 'An artist's conciliation with his gift corresponded to a citizen's concern for his city.'[68] The sonnet for Edward Lear presents a poet and artist who is reconciled with his tears and guided by them to produce a comic art. The final, isolated line of the sonnet depicts the fearful, isolated voyager now become the settling place for other travellers: 'And children swarmed to him like settlers. He became a land' (183).

It was in Brussels that Auden wandered into the Musée Royaux des Beaux Arts and, having viewed the paintings of Breughel, was inspired to write not only one of his greatest short poems but his boldest experiment with the sonnet form. 'Musée des Beaux Arts' extends the act of witness that Auden had begun in China, where war's collateral and haphazard injuries frequently went unnoticed and unremarked:

> About suffering they were never wrong,
> The Old Masters: how well they understood
> Its human position; how it takes place
> While someone else is eating or opening a window or just
>   walking dully along...

---

68. Mendelson, *Early Auden*, p. 361.

The inverted word order of the opening line makes absolutely clear at one level what the poem is 'about', but as John Fuller points out, there is 'a rich double meaning' in the opening word, subtly implying that it might well be Breughel's 'very circuitousness of approach...that Auden is interested in'.[69] The popular title of the painting, *Landscape with the Fall of Icarus*, spells out its apparent message by relegating the astonishing sight of 'a boy falling out of the sky' to some marginal space and foregrounding the landscape itself instead. The poem is more speculative about the seeming unconcern of the workaday world in its response to disaster, assuming that the ploughman 'may | Have heard the splash' and conjecturing that 'the expensive delicate ship...must have seen | Something amazing', but it nevertheless works towards a concluding image of life going 'calmly on' (179). The ramifications of what the poem is 'about', however, are complex and wide-ranging, and extend well beyond the ethical 'human position' or perspective on suffering to questions that have to do with the seemingly callous but necessary detachment of art and poetry. They also extend beyond what the conventional sonnet of fourteen lines might be expected to contain.

'Musée des Beaux Arts' is an extended sonnet of twenty-one lines. Although it contains half as many lines again as the conventional sonnet, it organizes these in verse sections of 13 + 8, rather than 14 + 7 (a sonnet and a half) or 12 + 9 (in proportion to the usual octave-sestet division). Even so, it clearly acknowledges the function of the conventional sonnet turn, and it does so precisely at that moment when it notes, 'In Breughel's *Icarus*, for instance: how everything turns away | Quite leisurely from the disaster'. The rhyme scheme, which appears quite casual and even erratic, steadfastly refuses to follow the quatrain patterns of the Shakespearean sonnet, even though it superficially resembles them: *abcadedbfgfge hhijkkij*. The centrally positioned 'e' rhyme both holds together the meandering lines of the opening verse and phonetically anticipates the closely related 'h' and 'i' rhymes, with 'tree' gently leading on to 'away', 'may', and 'cry' (179). The casual gait of lines 3–4, with the enjambment adding to the impression of dalliance, is altogether fitting in a poem in which 'life's tendency to overspill art's containment' is a serious consideration.[70]

After 'Musée des Beaux Arts', Auden's most radical and ambitious experiments with the sonnet form are to be found in his sequence, 'The Quest', first published in *The New Republic* in November 1940, with a helpful prefatory

---

69. Fuller, *W. H. Auden: A Commentary*, p. 266.   70. Sharpe, *W. H. Auden*, p. 91.

note: 'The theme of the quest occurs in fairy tales, legends like the Golden Fleece and the Holy Grail, boys' adventure stories and detective novels. These poems are reflections upon certain features common to them all.'[71] Auden's interest in quest literature can be detected at a very early stage in his career, as far back as the 1928 sonnet, 'The Secret Agent'. What makes 'The Quest' distinctive in its handling of the archetypal journey towards truth and knowledge is its unnerving combination of teasing playfulness and dark surrealist fantasy. The trials, tribulations, and transformations of the sequence conjure up *Alice in Wonderland* as if written by Franz Kafka, as Herbert Greenberg shrewdly notes.[72] Auden's abiding interest in Freudian and Jungian notions of psychic integration are now complemented by a renewed commitment to Christian ideals of faith and salvation, and by a strong attraction to existentialist ideas of authentic being and selfhood. Among the influences shaping Auden's conception of the quest are Charles Williams's history of Christian spirituality in *The Descent of the Dove* (1939) and Søren Kierkegaard's memorable image of the lonely walker in the dark in his *Journals* (1st English edn, 1938).

The twenty sonnets in 'The Quest' chart the individual pursuit of psychic integration and wholeness, acknowledging the obstacles presented by illusion, temptation, and presumptuousness. As Mendelson points out, Auden modelled the poem on his earlier sonnet sequence, 'In Time of War', but also devised it as a corrective. 'In Time of War' depicts psychological or political types that persist across centuries, but 'The Quest' is more obviously concerned with individuals and groups ('he' and 'they') facing difficult existential choices, and might therefore be regarded as 'a set of parables about consciousness and decision'.[73] The cryptic, riddling qualities of the sequence are more pronounced when the sonnets are simply arranged by number, without the titles assigned them in 1940, and Auden was compelled to make some local revisions. The opening sonnet, originally titled 'The Door', is an obvious case in point. In the 1945 edition of *The Collected Poetry of W. H. Auden*, the opening line of 'The Door' declares: 'Out of it steps the future of the poor, | Enigmas, executioners and rules.'[74] Later, Auden neatly amended the line, effacing any distinction between the speaker and 'the poor' while clarifying

---

71. Fuller, *W. H. Auden: A Commentary*, p. 336.
72. Herbert Greenberg, *Quest for the Necessary: W. H. Auden and the Dilemma of Divided Consciousness* (Cambridge, MA: Harvard University Press, 1968), p. 111.
73. Edward Mendelson, *Later Auden* (London: Faber, 1999), p. 135.
74. W. H. Auden, *The Collected Poetry of W. H. Auden* (New York: Random House, 1945), p. 251.

the central image of the now unnamed poem: 'Out of it steps our future, through this door | Enigmas, executioners and rules' (285). From the outset, Auden experiments with the resources of the sonnet, finding freedom within discipline as he earnestly plays with different arrangements of rhyme, line length, stanzaic patterning, and metre. As John Adames shows in his illuminating account of Auden's sonnet variations, 'The elasticity of the sonnet allows him to journey to the furthest edge of our epistemological frontiers without collapsing into nihilism and chaos.'[75]

Sonnet III, originally titled 'Crossroads', has twenty-one lines, but it differs from 'Musée des Beaux Arts' in its 6 + 6 + 9 arrangement, which subtly retains the bipartite ratio of the Italian sonnet through its rhyme scheme: *aabcbc ddecec fghifgigh*. The sonnet considers 'quays and crossroads' as 'places of decision and farewell', traditionally associated with uncertainty as well as dispersal. It invokes the Christian instruction that 'salvation' (later amended to 'vocation') is earned through a period of suffering (figured in the archetypal 'Bad Lands'), but it also playfully questions the formulaic 'one year and a day' employed in nursery rhymes (Edward Lear's 'The Owl and the Pussycat') and Arthurian legend (*Sir Gawain and the Green Knight*). In this respect, a thematic concern with the duration of the journey is fittingly recorded in the extended sonnet form (286). Other sonnets (Sonnet 15, 'The Lucky' and Sonnet 19, 'The Waters') employ a 6 + 6 + 2 arrangement, which allows Auden to evade the impression of logical progression associated with the three quatrains and closing couplet of the Shakespearean sonnet and instead 'immerse the reader in a series of oblique and riddling circumstances'.[76] Sonnet XIX, originally titled 'The Waters', is highly effective in its formal variations, with its brisk iambic tetrameter conveying the ease with which 'Poet, oracle and wit' are all led astray while fishing for truth in the waters of knowledge and perception (295). The poem reverts to a decasyllabic line at the end, but the closing couplet (despite its intimations of Humpty Dumpty) is provocatively enigmatic rather than epigrammatic: 'The waters long to hear our question put | Which would release their longed-for answer, but.' The closing sonnet, originally 'The Garden', moves towards a final sense of completion and transformation—'All journeys die here; wish and weight are lifted'—but this ultimate state of innocence and

---

75. John Adames, 'The Frontiers of the Psyche and the Limits of Form in Auden's "Quest" Sonnets', *Modern Language Review* 92 (1997), 574.
76. Adames, 'The Frontiers of the Psyche', p. 576.

freedom is attainable only through what Auden sees as a surrendering of the will, a shifting of 'the centre of volition' (296), and an acceptance of the difficult existential terrain of modern civilization.

Philip Larkin, Elizabeth Jennings, and Geoffrey Hill

Among the poets strongly influenced by Auden's impressive command of the sonnet form were Philip Larkin, Elizabeth Jennings, and Geoffrey Hill. Although Larkin published very few sonnets in his mature collections of poetry, just two in *The Less Deceived* (1955) and two in *High Windows* (1974), he wrote over thirty sonnets in the late 1930s and early 1940s, five of which appeared in *The North Ship* (1945). Auden's dramatization of moral choices, his metaphors of navigation, and his mounting sense of urgency in *Journey to a War* had a profound shaping effect on the young Larkin's own adventurous sonnets 'in time of war'. One of the earliest of these, 'Ultimatum', was published in *The Listener* in December 1940, and included by Larkin in a tentative collection of his own *Further Poems* ('Nine poems of depression and dismay'), with the pleased remark, 'Nicely obscure'.[77] Following Auden's example in Sonnet XIX of *In Time of War* ('But in the evening the oppression lifted'), 'Ultimatum' opens abruptly with a conjunction: 'But we must build our walls, for what we are | Necessitates it, and we must construct | The ship to navigate behind them, there.' As Richard Bradford notes, the poem 'reads like a thesaurus of Auden's phrasings and metrical orchestrations'.[78] At the same time, Larkin's sonnet shows considerable technical skill and originality, opting for a 7+3+4 division, rhyming *ababcdc dee ffgg*. The three closing couplets are handled subtly and adroitly, with enjambment and simple half rhymes ('Peace'/'pass', 'boy'/'by', 'now'/'no') keeping the movement of the verse confidently under control. 'Observation', another Audenesque sonnet whose title (like that of 'Ultimatum') has both private and militaristic connotations, was published in the *Oxford University Labour Club Bulletin* in November 1941. The sonnet registers the extent to which war necessitates a mask, insisting on a brave face, but also the way in which it conditions basic emotional responses ('Range-finding laughter, and ambush of tears'). Like

---

77. *Philip Larkin: The Complete Poems*, ed. Burnett, pp. 103, 481.
78. Richard Bradford, cited in *Philip Larkin: The Complete Poems*, ed. Burnett, p. 481.

'Ultimatum', it is 'nicely obscure', though its exposure of 'a government of medalled fears' and its closing assertion that 'nothing can be found for poor men's fires' no doubt appealed to Larkin's Labour Club acquaintances (105).

Auden's technique of conducting an impersonal, almost clinical, inspection of the anonymous subject can be seen at work in 'Two Sonnets', composed by Larkin in the first few months of the Second World War. The paired sonnets present a troubled 'he'—both self and other—in a dialectical exploration of the mental landscapes of 'The Conscript' and 'The Conscientious Objector'. Larkin wrote to his friend James Sutton in April 1941, admitting his 'fatal gift for pastiche...odd phrases just like Auden', and noting that the first of these sonnets 'shows how well I assimilated Auden's sonnet style'. The opening line, 'So he evolved a saving fiction as | The moving world abraised him' (157), recalls the opening sonnet of Auden's 'In Time of War': 'So from the years the gifts were showered.'[79] Once again, Larkin employs an ambitious run of three closing couplets (*eeffgg*). The second poem is essentially a Petrarchan sonnet (*abbacddc efegfg*), but its rhymes are playful and ambitious, with the balanced disyllabic rhyme of 'revolve' and 'resolve' in the octave contrasting with the uneven syllabification of 'nights' and 'stalactites' in the sestet (157). Both sonnets, however, dramatize the private, individual consciousness within a wartime context where public, collective ideals prevail. The troubled figure of the conscript reappears in a slightly later sonnet, 'Conscript', dedicated to Sutton. The form is Shakespearean (typographically presented as 4+4+4+2), but the oblique allegorical circumstances in which the conscript is abstracted from 'The details of his own defeat and murder' clearly derive from Auden (7). Archie Burnett, the editor of Larkin's *Complete Poems*, helpfully notes, among the debts to Auden, 'the mystery-laden narrative set in the past, the vague identities preserved by pronouns ("he", "they"), and the matter-of-fact reporting of portentous events'.[80]

The full extent of Auden's influence on Larkin's early sonnets can be seen in those poems that move beyond the immediate wartime context to consider individual psychology, probing both the Freudian unconscious and the shaping effects of religion, education, culture, and politics. Larkin was clearly pleased with the sonnet beginning 'Having grown up in shade of Church and State', stating with ironic self-regard, 'It is one of the few perfect

---

79. Auden and Isherwood, *Journey to a War*, p. 259.
80. *Philip Larkin: The Complete Poems*, ed. Burnett, p. 339.

sonnets I have ever come across.'[81] In reality, he was a severe and exacting critic of his own work, claiming in a later draft foreword to an unpublished collection that 'almost any single line by Auden would be worth more than the whole lot put together'.[82] Even so, there are startling glimpses of Larkin's own distinctive preoccupation with failure and remorse in another early sonnet, written as an undergraduate student at Oxford in 1940:

> Nothing significant was really said,
> Though all agreed the talk superb, and that
> The brilliant freshman with his subtle thought
> Deserved the praise he won from every side.
> All but one declared his future great,
> His present sure and happy; they that stayed
> Behind, among the ashes, were all stirred
> By memory of his words, as sharp as grit.
>
> The one had watched the talk: remembered how
> He'd found the genius crying when alone;
> Recalled his words: 'O what unlucky streak
> Twisting inside me, made me break the line?
> What was the rock my gliding childhood struck,
> And what bright unreal path has led me here?'   (178)

As Stan Smith notes in his excellent analysis of this sonnet, 'nothing' is 'an unusual, but quintessentially Larkinesque word with which to start a poem', but Auden had already done this in Sonnet XXV of 'In Time of War': 'Nothing is given: we must find our law... | We have no destiny assigned us.'[83] Larkin seems to have been especially drawn to Auden's insistence on distinguishing 'conventional assumptions of self and role from the existential aloneness of the exceptional individual'. Smith shows convincingly how the poem's movement from glittering success to miserable failure draws on techniques that were well established in Auden's work, including 'the rhetorical questions and reversals, often in a second, internally distantiated voice within the poem's main discourse', and 'the exclamatory "O" with which the direct reported speech breaks into the narrative'.[84] The turn in the sonnet coincides with a shift of perspective from 'all' and 'they' to the single 'one' who voices his dissenting opinion, and then to the tormented

---

81. *Philip Larkin: The Complete Poems*, ed. Burnett, pp. 171, 676.
82. *Philip Larkin: The Complete Poems*, ed. Burnett, p. 682.
83. Stan Smith, 'Something for Nothing: Late Larkins and Early', *English* 49.195 (2000), 262.
84. Smith, 'Something for Nothing', p. 261.

complaint of the 'brilliant' speaker himself. Larkin was to perfect these shifts of perspective superbly well in poems like 'Mr Bleaney' and 'The Old Fools', and the skilful pararhyme (which looks back through Auden to Wilfred Owen) was also to become a marked feature in his later style. Most revealing, perhaps, in terms of Larkin's characteristic deflation of illusionary ideals and his fondness for negative prefixes is the startling image of the 'bright unreal path'.

Larkin's earliest known sonnet, 'Winter Nocturne', written in 1938, is reminiscent of eighteenth-century pastoral poetry in its evocative, atmospheric details of dusk, wind, and rain, and probably derives (as its closing line suggests) from Thomas Gray's 'Elegy Written in a Country Churchyard': 'Dark night creeps in, and leaves the world alone' (99). The title, however, suggests more modern influences, and might well have been prompted by T. S. Eliot's fondness for musical titles such as 'Preludes' and 'Rhapsody on a Winter Night'. Eliot is unmistakably present in the 1939 sonnet, 'Street Lamps', which draws its desolate urban setting and its strange personification of street lamps from the poems already alluded to, but also borrows its evening sky and slinking animal from 'The Love Song of J. Alfred Prufrock':

> When night slinks, like a puma, down the sky,
>   And the bare, windy streets echo with silence,
> Street lamps come out, and lean at corners, awry,
>   Casting black shadows, oblique and intense;
> So they burn on, impersonal through the night,
>   Hearing the hours slowly topple past
> Like cold drops from a glistening stalactite,
>   Until grey planes splinter the gloom at last;
> Then they go out.
>   I think I noticed once
>   —'Twas morning—one sole street lamp still bright-lit,
> Which, with a senile grin, like an old dunce,
>   Vied the blue sky, and tried to rival it;
> And, leering pallid though its use was done,
> Tried to cast shadows contrary to the sun.   (100)

The Shakespearean sonnet form is cleverly concealed by the typographical layout of the poem and its fractured ninth line, aptly coinciding with the burning out of the street lamps. The turn accordingly announces the arrival of morning and introduces the speaker (a descendant of the arch, observant aesthetes who inhabit the poems of Baudelaire and Laforgue). If the sonnet looks back to French Symbolism through the poems of Eliot, it also has more than a touch of surrealist fantasy about it. Larkin was clearly determined, as he was with his borrowings from Auden, to move beyond pastiche, and there is a knowing, ironic intelligence that tilts the sonnet towards parody. 'Eliotian but amusing' was how Larkin described another experimental poem written around this time.[85] The strong presence of Eliot is all the more surprising, given the emphatic dislike of modernism and 'foreign' literature that Larkin declared in essays and interviews later in his career.

Throughout the late 1940s and early 1950s, Larkin composed a number of sonnets, including 'Neurotics', 'To Failure', and 'To My Wife', exploring those themes that would later become his hallmark: vision and perspective, illusory or confounded choices, regret and remorse, the disappointment of desire, and the jealously guarded autonomy of the writer/artist. Auden and Eliot continue to be immensely fertile influences, but the direction in which Larkin's mature work would go is clearly evident in 'Spring', included in *The Less Deceived* (1955). Written in 1950, and originally titled 'Spring and bachelors', the sonnet is a vivid re-working of a traditional Romantic poetic subject—the seasons: 'Green-shadowed people sit, or walk in rings, | Their children finger the awakened grass.' The green shadows perhaps derive from Virginia Woolf's novel *The Waves*, but people walking in rings recalls *The Waste Land*, and there is further evidence of Eliot's impact in the speaker's Prufrockian caricature of himself amidst abundant and sensuous new life, 'Threading my pursed-up way across the park, | An indigestible sterility.' The empirical, agnostic individual who inhabits 'Church Going' is present here, insisting that distance and difference from the popular celebration of spring and all its suggestions of rebirth and regeneration brings a compensating clarity of vision: 'And those she has least use for see her best' (40). The achievement of 'Spring', however, is that it uses the dialectical possibilities inherent in the sonnet form to hold in tension two different and divided viewpoints: those of the romantic idealist and the pragmatic materialist. As James Booth notes, the sonnet opens with a Shakespearean octave (*abab cdcd*), but forestalls any neat closure by pre-empting the closing couplet in the sestet, which rhymes *effgeg*.[86]

'Whatever Happened?', written slightly later than 'Spring', explores a subject that clearly interested Larkin, and one that has never been fully explicated in critical studies of his work: the nature of psychological repression. As

---

85. *Philip Larkin: The Complete Poems*, ed. Burnett, p. 514.
86. James Booth, *Philip Larkin: The Poet's Plight* (Basingstoke: Palgrave Macmillan, 2005), p. 14.

Larkin put it in a letter to Patsy Strang in November 1953: 'it treats of the way in which the mind gets to work on any violent involuntary experience & transforms it out of all knowledge.'[87] The use of the shipping metaphor to suggest a psychological journey recalls Auden's sonnet sequence 'In Time of War', but Larkin's sexual suggestiveness has a distinctively comic, ribald quality: 'Panting... With trousers ripped... We toss for half the night... What can't be printed... Such coastal bedding.' What is also distinctively Larkin's own is the seriousness with which he addresses the ambivalent idea, at the centre of the poem, that 'Perspective brings significance'. As with 'Lines on a Young Lady's Photograph Album', the poem recognizes photography as an art that is both faithful and disappointing in its perspectives. Here, photography is equated with an attitude of detachment and disengagement: 'All's kodak-distant.' In the realm of psychology, however, this remoteness amounts to an unhealthy repression that finds its violent release in dreams. The poem pursues its psychological investigation through successive stages of detachment represented in four tercets and a closing couplet—*aba bcb cdc ded ee*—constituting a *terza rima* sonnet reminiscent of Robert Frost's 'Acquainted with the Night'. Provoking an effective shift of perspective at the very end, the couplet tends towards a relaxed, common sense view of 'whatever happened', only to re-introduce a note of terror in a casual, parenthetical aside: 'Curses? The dark? Struggling? Where's the source | Of these yarns now (except in nightmares, of course)?' (34).

The sonnet form lent itself especially well to Larkin's intense explorations of loneliness and isolation. 'Friday Night in the Royal Station Hotel' and 'The Card-Players', both published in *High Windows* in 1974, are concerned at an elemental level with existential notions of survival, though they inhabit strikingly different imaginative worlds. Both are studies in mood: one pensive and melancholic, the other buoyant and zestful. 'Friday Night in the Royal Station Hotel' was written in 1966 and first published in a provincial English newspaper. Larkin was casually dismissive: 'I had a sonnet in the Sheffield *Morning Telegraph* last Saturday, which is how some people *start*, I suppose.'[88] Although allegedly based on an actual hotel, The Royal Station Hotel in Hull, the sonnet is notable for its strangely abstract treatment of loneliness and silence at the end of a working week. Every detail works towards the larger, generalized condition of emptiness. The precise observation that chairs are

---

87. *Philip Larkin: The Complete Poems*, ed. Burnett, p. 367.
88. *Philip Larkin: The Complete Poems*, ed. Burnett, p. 451.

'coloured differently' only seems to reinforce the fact that they are 'empty', just as the initially inviting 'open doors' lead on to 'A larger loneliness of knives and glass', with the particular detail of the unused dining utensils adding poignancy and tangibility to the deserted scene. The physical furnishings of the hotel are themselves emblematic of the general condition: silence is 'laid like carpet', and corridors are 'shoeless' (without shoes to be polished, but also without the sound of footsteps). Larkin subtly intimates the poem's preoccupation with duration in its 9 + 5 typographical arrangement. The poem spills over the usual octave boundary as 'Hours pass', and enacts a turn 'as lights burn' and '*Night comes on*'. The italicized words with which the poem closes, initiated by '*Now*', are a typographical representation of the act of 'writing home', itself an existential response to the predicament of loneliness amidst the engulfing darkness (80–1).

'The Card-Players' is a work of comic grotesquerie, as the allegorical names and strongly physical actions in the poem attest: 'Jan van Hogspeuw staggers to the door | And pisses at the dark.' At the same time, it has an underlying existential seriousness in its depiction of coarse humanity contending with the storm. Larkin was attracted to the subject of the card-players (a popular image of fortune and destiny in Dutch and Flemish genre painting of the seventeenth century) as early as 1965, but initially considered 'poems about works of art' to be illicit. His letters reveal that the Flemish painter he especially admired was Adriaen Brouwer (1605–38). The poem alludes to paintings such as *Scene at the Inn* and *Peasants Smoking and Drinking*, as well as *The Card Players*.[89] The fundamental contrast of inner and outer scenes is suggested in a letter to Monica Jones in May 1965: 'One man is flat out on the floor, having spewed (dogs are licking it up), another is pissing out of the back door. The candlelight shows patched clothes, broken cupboards: outside is mud, wind, winter. *But you are all right*' (original emphasis).[90] Larkin's not so clean, well-lighted place offers temporary respite from history and a dark, directionless present ('Wet century-wide trees | Clash in surrounding starlessness above | This lamplit cave'), recalling Louis MacNeice's 'firelit cave equipped with drinks and books' in *Autumn Sequel*. As Roger Day notes, the poem is 'somewhat unexpectedly, a sonnet rhyming *abbacd-dcefeggf*, but with 'one final, isolated line' offering a near rhyme on 'trees' and

---

89. *Philip Larkin: The Complete Poems*, ed. Burnett, p. 457.
90. *Philip Larkin: The Complete Poems*, ed. Burnett, p. 456.

'peace'.[91] It wilfully subverts the amatory associations of the Petrarchan sonnet by having the *volta* coincide with the moment when someone 'croaks scraps of songs | Towards the ham-hung rafters about love'. In the penultimate line, Jan van Hogspeuw 'Gobs at the grate, and hits the queen of hearts'. The closing isolated line is an exuberant declaration of resistance *against* isolation, reminiscent of the exclamatory cries of French Symbolist poetry: 'Rain, wind and fire! The secret, bestial peace!' (84).

Having been a prolific writer of sonnets in the war years, Larkin used the form sparingly in his later work. The waning influence of Auden partly explains this, but very likely the aspiring novelist in Larkin demanded a more expansive, narrative method, as with 'Church Going', 'The Whitsun Weddings', and 'To the Sea'. At the same time, the sonnets have an important function in providing Larkin with moments of intense concentration and clarification at critical stages in his career. For Elizabeth Jennings, however, the sonnet was a vital and necessary form that she went on using throughout her long career. Although closely associated with Larkin and the Movement poets in the 1950s and 1960s, largely by virtue of her commitment to traditional verse forms and a clear, well-ordered syntax, Jennings was always a distinctive individualist. The diverse imaginative geographies of her early poetry (much of it written in Italy) defy the commonplace critical notion that Movement poetry is narrowly English and provincial. Her poems of journeying are often subtle explorations of selfhood and self-knowledge, philosophical reflections on how we relate to the world and to others. 'A Sense of Place', first published in *A Way of Looking* (1955), is alert to the changing views afforded by perspective. An inverted sonnet, the poem is less a candid declaration of love than a clear-sighted recognition of how love conditions our vision and informs the way we see and appreciate a place:

> Now we cannot hold a sense of place
> Entirely by ourselves, we need to share,
> Look round for hands to touch, for eyes to bear
> Upon the same horizon that we love,
> Until we cannot part the hands, the eyes
> From the loved view and the close love we prize.

---

91. Roger Day, '"That Vast Moth-eaten Musical Brocade": Larkin and Religion', *Critical Essays on Philip Larkin: The Poems*, ed. Linda Cookson and Bryan Loughrey (Harlow: Longman, 1989), pp. 100–1.

> And when the eyes, the hands are gone we accuse
> The place, say the horizon is at fault,
> Thinking it has withdrawn a glory we felt,
> Finding in it not in ourselves the loss.
> Yet when the sharer is with us again
> And the whole landscape seems renewed, rebuilt,
> Not mountains or the sun are what we praise
> But his mood shared with us, his sense of place.[92]

There is a structural logic in the division of sestet and octave, with the turn initiating the loss of a shared sense of place, before briefly restoring it with an understanding of what John Ruskin termed 'pathetic fallacy': a perception of landscape coloured by mood.[93] The poem differs markedly from what we might expect of a conventional love sonnet. While openly acknowledging 'the loved view and the close love we prize', it addresses the implied lover in the third person with a judicious sense of distance and disengagement. 'Place' and 'love' ought to rhyme, but 'place' is rhymed instead with 'prize' and 'praise', while 'love' finds only a forlorn phonetic similarity in 'loss'.

Jennings experiments with the sonnet form in translation, including *The Sonnets of Michelangelo* (1961) and versions of 'Evening Prayer' and 'The Sly One' by Rimbaud in *Lucidities* (1971). Once again, the wide European range of her interests puts the lie to charges of insularity associated with the Movement writers. Even so, the disappointment and loss anticipated in 'A Sense of Place' continue to pervade her work. 'A Sonnet', in *Relationships* (1972), is notable for its emotional candour: 'Run home all clichés, let the deep words come | However much they hurt and shock and bruise.' The earlier sonnet had dwelt upon the complex correlation of love and place, but now the view is one of utter darkness, dangerously close to cliché: 'Once the stars shone within a sky I knew. | Now only darkness is my sky, my view' (282). Recovery is found in the 'Sources of Light' sonnets in *Celebrations and Elegies* (1982), which shimmer with a devotional intensity reminiscent of Herbert, Vaughan, and Hopkins:

> Gold, all shimmerings, and all excess
> Of light, entrances most of us. We cry
> At the world's dazzle when we're born but this
> Only reveals how sensitive we lie

---

92. Elizabeth Jennings, *The Collected Poems* (Manchester: Carcanet, 2012), p. 31. Further references are to this edition of the poems.
93. John Ruskin's essay on 'On Pathetic Fallacy' is ch. 12 in vol. 3 of *Modern Painters*. See *The Works of John Ruskin* (London: George Allen, 1903–12), vol. 5, pp. 201–20.

> Under our first shafts of the sun. We grow
> Into the well-worn gold, the reach of shine.   (497)

In her later work, Jennings turns increasingly to music and painting in search of parallels to inform and extend her own creative endeavours. 'Tribute to Turner', in a volume simply titled 'Tributes' (1989), aptly explores within the sonnet form how 'bonds and limits' might 'keep off sprawl and chaos'. The poem marvels at the aesthetic satisfaction afforded by the sublime depiction of 'fire and flood and steam', compounding danger and delight in a neatly alliterative close: 'And what seems peril has the power to please' (552). Among the tributes is a poem of praise and lament for Philip Larkin, wondering if the silence of his later years was 'the quiet of desperation' (551). Larkin's presence is still there in a late sonnet in one of her final collections, *In the Meantime* (1996). 'Having it Both Ways' uses the dynamics of the octave and sestet to set up an apparent freedom, 'What liberty we have when out of love', and then to question its adequacy, 'But how long can we live within this state?' Here, in the quick move from declaration to interrogation, Jennings shares with Larkin both a sceptical apprehension of the illusory freedoms we create and a compassionate understanding of our compulsion for contrary states of being: 'Don't we miss the slow encroachment of | Possessive passion? Don't we half-await | Its cruel enchantments which no longer have | Power over us? (737).

Compared with the immediately engaging and readily intelligible poetry of Philip Larkin and Elizabeth Jennings, the work of Geoffrey Hill appears self-consciously scholastic, obstinately antiquarian, and excessively elaborate. All three poets, however, exercise what Jennings sees as a 'watchful care over the chosen past' (550). Larkin and Hill, especially, seem intent on observing custom and ritual, carefully distinguishing that which might be worth preserving. As Seamus Heaney has argued, both poets reveal a distinctive post-war consciousness in the way that they establish 'a continuity with another England' and seek 'to keep open the imagination's supply lines to the past'.[94] Christopher Ricks reminds us that Hill belongs to a slightly later generation than Larkin (he was just 15 years old when the war ended in 1945), and so was among those poets whose adult consciousness coincided with an awakening to the atrocities of Auschwitz and Belsen.[95]

---

94. Seamus Heaney, 'Englands of the Mind', *Preoccupations: Selected Prose 1968–78* (London: Faber, 1980), p. 151.
95. Christopher Ricks, *The Force of Poetry* (Oxford: Clarendon, 1984), p. 287.

The sonnets of Geoffrey Hill have a major place in twentieth-century poetry in the way that they take a form habitually associated with love and religious devotion and resolutely expose it to violence and terror on an unparalleled scale. Even by the ambitious standards of Auden's 'In Time of War' sequence, these are sonnets that look on history with a fierce intensity and rapt concentration. The vision is all the more unsettling, given the equally intense concern for poetic ornamentation and stylistic elaboration. If this makes for an uncomfortable friction between acknowledged atrocity and the sensuous pleasures of style, it also prompts imposing questions about the authority and responsibility of poetry in the modern world. Hill's sonnets are essentially elegiac, with the important qualification that they repeatedly question their own elegiac impulse and undermine their own assuaging rhetoric. The title of Hill's first volume of poems is *For the Unfallen* (1959), which implies those still living, but it cannot help but summon images and memories of the fallen dead, especially those of two world wars. At the same time, it has a theological application to the blessed and the innocent and the morally upright, anticipating Hill's fascination with the lives of saints and martyrs in his later volumes.

'Requiem for the Plantagenet Kings' is printed immediately opposite 'Two Formal Elegies, For the Jews in Europe', unmistakably announcing continuities in Hill's vision of political violence in Europe from the Middle Ages to the present. In both cases, what can be known and understood is not easily gleaned from the opaque rhetoric and the slippery syntax. From the outset of the 'Requiem', there is some doubt about the person or persons 'For whom' war is waged (God, the people, or the kings themselves?).[96] The opening quatrain is typographically set off from the rest of the sonnet, as if constituting a formal announcement, but its declarations are riven with ambivalence, paradox, and concealment, as it winds its way around the dubious conception of 'good' and 'just' wars. The English Channel is 'possessed' in the multiple sense of being disturbed, filled with possessions, and territorially governed. The remaining ten lines of the sonnet shift to the present tense and ironically depict the effigies of the Plantagenet kings 'set in trust' where all is untrustworthy, and 'secure' in a history of bloodshed. Where the turn should be, at line 9, the sonnet sees in the 'supine stationary'

---

96. Geoffrey Hill, *Broken Hierarchies: Poems 1952–2012*, ed. Kenneth Haynes (Oxford: Oxford University Press, 2013), p. 15. Quotations from the poems are taken from this edition and page numbers are given in brackets in the text.

forms of the dead kings a powerful deception, as well as a grotesque contradiction between their ambition for worldly power and their expectation of eternal life:

> At home, under caved chantries, set in trust,
> With well-dressed alabaster and proved spurs
> They lie; they lie; secure in the decay
> Of blood, blood-marks, crowns hacked and coveted,
> Before the scouring fires of trial-day
> Alight on men...

As if distrustful of its own 'well-dressed alabaster', the sonnet denies the expected Shakespearean couplet, leaving the unruly 'sea' unrhymed and closing instead on the heavy rhyme of 'head' and 'dead'. The ending is all the more effective for the way in which it both enacts a surging triumphalism and simultaneously undermines it:

> ...before sleeked groin, gored head,
> Budge through the clay and gravel, and the sea
> Across daubed rock evacuates its dead.

If 'trial-day' gives this apocalyptic imagery a somewhat subdued impression, conjuring up medieval rituals of law and order, the word 'evacuates', so closely associated here with the sea, carries strong suggestions of Dunkirk and the dead and wounded of the Second World War.

'Funeral Music', in *King Log* (1968), extends the elegiac mood and vision of the earlier book, but it brings to the sonnet sequence a new kind of historical witness and assessment, and a new kind of harshness in its handling of lyric form. In 'Funeral Music: An Essay', appended to *King Log*, Hill describes the sequence as 'a commination and an alleluia for the period popularly but inexactly known as the Wars of the Roses', and the voices of vengeance and celebration implied here mingle in strange and unsettling ways.[97] The sequence carries an 'oblique' dedication to the Duke of Suffolk, the Earl of Worcester, and Earl Rivers, men of letters, as well as men of arms. All were beheaded for their part in the political intrigues and bitter feuding of the later fifteenth century, and these nobles are seen by Hill to 'haunt the mind vulnerable alike to admiration and scepticism'.[98] The force of that divided attitude is immediately borne out in the opening sonnet, which depicts a culture that supplements high-minded idealism and religious devotion

---

97. Geoffrey Hill, *King Log* (London: André Deutsch, 1968), p. 67.   98. Hill, *King Log*, p. 67.

with a relish for the most gruesome physical violence. John Tiptoft, Earl of Worcester, exemplifies the values of his class in the moment of his decapitation, calling for three strokes of the axe in honour of the Blessed Trinity:

> Processionals in the exemplary cave,
> Benediction of shadows. Pomfret. London.
> The voice fragrant with mannered humility,
> With an equable contempt for this World,
> 'In honorem Trinitas'. Crash. The head
> Struck down into a meaty conduit of blood.
> So these dispose themselves to receive each
> Pentecostal blow from axe or seraph,
> Spattering block-straw with mortal residue.
> Psalteries whine through the empyrean. Fire
> Flares in the pit, ghosting upon stone
> Creatures of such rampant state, vacuous
> Ceremony of possession, restless
> Habitation, no man's dwelling-place.   (47)

From the outset, 'Funeral Music' enacts a grotesque ceremony of dying and remembrance, with 'Processionals' and 'Benediction' suggesting both religious liturgy and ritual execution, as well as drawing attention to the poem's own ceremonial summoning of the dead. The 'exemplary cave' is at once a place of philosophical reflection for Neo-Platonist scholars, a church or cathedral, a dark place of imprisonment, such as Pomfret or the Tower of London, and the poem itself. If the poem acknowledges an apparent humility and unworldliness in the face of death, it also registers a less appealing set of qualities in 'mannered' (affected rather than polite), and 'dispose' and 'receive' (rather too passive and contrived to win much admiration). There is an ironic deflection, not without compassion, in the closing acknowledgement of the scene of death as 'no man's dwelling-place', but the poem's prevailing attitude to the religiose ceremonies of death is carried in the prominent word 'vacuous'. Once again, 'possession' works on a number of levels, signifying the possession of souls in heaven but also demonic uncontrol and hunger for power, while 'rampant' suggest both heraldic order and wild frenzy.

The discordant 'whine' of 'Psalteries' registers the poem's sceptical vision of a belief system in which violent politics and Christian sublimation are mutually reinforcing. It also initiates what Hill himself describes as 'a florid grim music broken by grunts and shrieks'.[99] Looking back to a period of

---

99. Hill, *King Log*, p. 67.

English history shortly before the great flowering of the Renaissance sonnet and sonnet sequences, 'Funeral Music' qualifies the spirit of devotion in that literature with an extraordinary emphasis on suffering and pain. Although the sequence is largely unrhymed, it makes extensive use of consonantal and assonantal chimes and echoes, sometimes in alliterative phrases broken across the line, as with 'Fire | Flares in the pit' or 'the future | Flashed back at us' (47, 48). The sequence has 'the ornate heartlessness of much mid-fifteenth-century architecture' in its combination of decorative beauty and stiff impersonality, but the likeness is relevant, too, in so far as the sequence 'avoids any overt narrative or dramatic structure'.[100] Although events are 'recalled', what results is a frozen tableau that nevertheless has lasting significance. There is a disconcerting array of voices, with the ghosts of history sometimes presented as 'we' and sometimes as 'they', and with the voice of the poet-historian sometimes mingling with them in a sombre moment of witness, as with the terrible Battle of Towton on Palm Sunday, 1461:

> Recall the cold
> Of Towton on Palm Sunday before dawn,
> Wakefield, Tewkesbury: fastidious trumpets
> Shrilling into the ruck; some trampled
> Acres, parched, sodden or blanched by sleet,
> Stuck with strange-postured dead. Recall the wind's
> Flurrying, darkness over the human mire.   (48)

The poet's 'recall' here is not simply a matter of dramatic mimesis, an attempt to recreate the battle scene in realistic detail. It is too obviously saturated with his own sensuous and self-conscious ruminations on the carnage and destruction. The harsh acoustic 'Shrilling', the dissonant internal rhyme of 'ruck' and 'stuck', the curious aesthetic observation of 'the strange-postured dead', and the momentary attention to natural phenomena amidst the mire all declare a continuity with First World War poetry, especially that of Wilfred Owen. Towton is presented as 'a holocaust', giving the sequence an immense historical significance that reverberates across centuries, its 'ornate and heartless music punctuated by mutterings, blasphemies and cries for help'.[101] Religious oaths shade into cursing in Sonnet 3, which opens with stern and earnest preparations for battle—'They bespoke doomsday and they meant it by | God'—and ends with the victims of slaughter lying down among the carnage, 'gasping "Jesus"' (49).

100. Hill, *King Log*, p. 67.   101. Hill, *King Log*, p. 68.

'Funeral Music' is unusual among sonnet sequences for the way it casts itself in relation to history, simultaneously declaring both its own belatedness (too late to avert the history it announces) and a strong sense of futurity (reflecting on a history not yet known and written). A strange parenthetical insertion in Sonnet 2, where the consciousness of poet-historian merges with that of a victim of history, wonders about the 'Ultimate recompense' of being able to see into the future (48). The sequence meditates on its own possible misrepresentation of the past from the perspective of those whose lives it claims an interest in: 'not as we | Desire life but as they would have us live' (54). It is in the midst of these philosophical reflections on futurity and the reconciling perspectives of eternity that the closing sonnet suddenly turns against itself and issues a final cry, speaking on behalf of all unfinished lives:

> Then tell me, love,
> How that should comfort us—or anyone
> Dragged half-unnerved out of this worldly place,
> Crying to the end 'I have not finished'. (54)

In that startling return to the scene of execution with which the sequence opens, the sonnet implicates itself in a tradition of sonnet writing that goes back to *Astrophil and Stella* (whose confiding address it echoes here), and at the same time confesses the difficulty of finding comfort (and therefore formal closure) in its own moment of history.

'Lachrimae', the first of two sonnet sequences in *Tenebrae* (1978), is steeped in the devotional literature and music of the Counter Reformation, but like 'Funeral Music' it approaches the rituals of the past with both intimate familiarity and critical detachment. If it functions as a glorious imitation of religious and artistic meditations on the Passion, it also takes liberties with its sources and redirects the flowing of tears in the light of its own agonized secular humanism. Hill's title is taken from John Dowland's 'Lachrimae, or Seaven Teares, Figured in Seaven Passionate Pavans' (1604), a collection of consort music for lute and viols, but the epigraph from St Robert Southwell's 'Mary Magdalen's Funeral Tears' (1591) both maintains his fascination with martyrology and suggests a broad concern with the objects of passion and love in art. The sonnet sequence is clearly modelled on seventeenth-century devotional poetry, with its strongly Petrarchan influences, its fusing of worldly and spiritual themes, and its striking deployment of paradox, irony, and wordplay. The opening sonnet, 'Lachrimae Verae', emulates the traditional yearning for spiritual truth in its octave and answers this with a harsh counter-truth in its sestet:

> Crucified Lord, you swim upon your cross
> and never move. Sometimes in dreams of hell
> the body moves but moves to no avail
> and is at one with that eternal loss.
>
> You are the castaway of drowned remorse,
> you are the world's atonement on the hill.
> This is your body twisted by our skill
> into a proper patience for redress.
>
> I cannot turn aside from what I do;
> you cannot turn away from what I am.
> You do not dwell in me nor I in you
>
> however much I pander to your name
> or answer to your lords of revenue,
> surrendering the joys that they condemn.   (121)

As well as accepting the challenge of the conventional Petrarchan sonnet form, Hill produces a virtuoso rendition of the devotional lyric of tears, with the figure of the crucified Christ both 'swimming' in the tearful eyes of the onlooker and appearing, arms outstretched, as a swimmer on the Cross. The paradox of stillness and movement both captures Christ's quiet submission to sacrifice and comments on the unmoved spectator. At the same time, the sonnet subtly distinguishes between Christ's passion and its representation in the fixity of icons, in which it is itself implicated as poetic form. The swimming motif is repeated in the image of Christ as 'castaway', both rejected and isolated on Calvary. There is a punning echo of 'at one', as well as an echo of the poet's name, in 'atonement on the hill', along with a self-conscious alignment of the 'twisted' ways of art and craft with the twisted body of Christ on the Cross. The acknowledgement of 'a patience proper for redress' associates a meditative art with Christ's patience for sinners and gives the idea of 'redress' as reparation a physical manifestation in the reclothing of the undressed body of the crucifixion. The sestet rather too ostentatiously announces the turn of the sonnet with a declaration of the speaker's own inability to 'turn aside from what I do'. The initial suggestion of being fixed in meditation, unable to turn away from the spectacle of Christ's broken body, gives way to the more insistent meaning of being unable to repent. The sestet also turns on an ironic echo of T. S. Eliot's 'Ash Wednesday' ('Because I do not hope to turn again'), from which the sonnet declares its difference.[102] The speaker is acutely and critically conscious of his own tendency to 'pander' to institutionalized Christianity, and of his own habitual 'surrendering' of joy. The closing tercets establish a decisive distance between Hill's 'Lachrimae' and its source texts in the way that they summon, but ultimately dispel, the idea of spiritual colloquy: 'You do not dwell in me nor I in you.' The sonnet's scepticism is powerfully registered in the resounding rhyme of 'you' and 'revenue', subordinating the older, reverential suggestions of a spiritual 'return' to the baser instincts of economic gain.

Although each sonnet in the sequence offers itself as a spiritual exercise or meditation on the Passion, it also questions its own status as a reconstruction of a devotional form that might now be defunct. Hill announces the modernity of his sequence in other ways: by deliberately undoing Dowland's arrangement (beginning, rather than ending, his sequence with 'Lachrimae Verae'), and by explicitly inverting the terms of Southwell's epigraph, opening Sonnet 5, 'Pavana Dolorosa', not with 'Passions I allow, and loves I approve', but with 'Loves I allow and passions I approve' (123). He provocatively follows this with a paradoxical perception of 'Ash-Wednesday feasts, ascetic opulence', hinting at the possible self-serving, narcissistic elements of martyrdom, and implicating the poet of sorrows as a 'Self-seeking hunter of forms'. The closing sonnet, 'Lachrimae Amantis' ('tears of a lover'), is an imitation of a poem by the Spanish Renaissance poet and playwright, Lope de Vega (1562–1635). Hill keeps in place the poem's scriptural allusions to the heart's reluctant admission of the saviour, including Revelation 3:20 ('Behold, I stand at the door, and knock'), but he gives his own intensely self-scrutinizing recognition to the kind of modern sensibility that earnestly keeps itself 'religiously secure' from religious belief (124).

The second sonnet sequence in *Tenebrae*, 'An Apology for the Revival of Christian Architecture in England', is undoubtedly Hill's most ambitious and most controversial experiment with the sonnet form. As well as possessing 'one of the most immediately unappealing poetic titles' in modern literary history, the sequence seems so powerfully preoccupied with Victorian medievalism and Gothic revivalist ideals as to merit the occasional charges of nostalgic fantasy and feudalistic nationalism. It illustrates superbly well what Hugh Haughton has termed 'the fraught anachronism' of Hill's poetry: 'the

---

102. T. S. Eliot, 'Ash Wednesday', *The Complete Poems and Plays 1909–1950* (New York: Harcourt Brace & Company, 1980), p. 60.

imaginative pull of the past for a poet obsessed above all by the persistence of what has been lost, and the impossibility of reappropriating it: the idea of continuity—and the stark fact of distance'.[103] The title recalls Augustus Pugin's 1843 defence of Christian architecture as the ideal expression of national sentiment and belief, and as an organic connection with the landscape and its ordered community, going back to the Middle Ages. The epigraphs from Samuel Taylor Coleridge and Benjamin Disraeli assert the idea of 'the spiritual, Platonic old England' (typified by Sidney and Shakespeare and other poets) in opposition to 'the New World' of industrialism and commerce. As the sequence proceeds, however, its poetic vision of pastoral England articulated through titles alluding to Shakespeare, Marvell, Keats, and Tennyson is steadily compromised and complicated by less appealing reminders of national glory, including three sonnets all titled 'A Short History of British India'. In this respect, Hill's title functions as an ironic undermining of Pugin's 'apologia', and an assertion of the more obvious contemporary use of 'apology', in keeping with the desire for atonement and expiation elsewhere in his work.

If 'An Apology' is even more disconcertingly anachronistic than Hill's previous sonnet sequences, it is also considerably sharper in conception and design, with a tightly organized set of images and motifs. Fire and ice co-exist in fierce tension ('the chilly fountains burn'), both elements involved in seasonal and symbolic rituals, as autumn turns to winter and decay gives way to a cold, illuminating clarity (125). As Jonathan Bolton has shown, the sequence has a cruciform plan in keeping with its architectural title, alternating between images of verticality, such as the Gothic spire and belfry, 'which rise out of the English soil and extend upward to God', and images associated with 'the horizontal movement of history and the expansion of empire, which extends outward away from England and God'.[104] The sequence is also constructed around alternating examples of the ennobling and destructive effects of passion, and contrasting ideas of love and lust. The opening sonnet, 'Quaint Mazes', recalls Titania's complaint in *A Midsummer Night's Dream* (2.1) that the land is overgrown and neglected, and it initiates

---

103. Hugh Haughton, 'How Fit a Title: Title and Authority in the Work of Geoffrey Hill', in *Geoffrey Hill: Essays on his Work*, ed. Peter Robinson (Milton Keynes: Open University Press, 1985), pp. 129, 131.
104. Jonathan Bolton, 'Empire and Atonement: Geoffrey Hill's "An Apology for the Revival of Christian Architecture in England"', *Contemporary Literature* 38.2 (1997), 293.

a meditation on the powerful appeal of revivalist ideologies of decay and renewal: 'It is the ravage of the heron wood; | it is the rood blazing upon the green' (125).

The enduring image of the English country house is central to Hill's vision of 'Platonic England', even as the sequence makes clear its inseparable relationship with the exploitative politics of empire. Sonnet 9, 'The Laurel Axe', both acknowledges the symbolic power of the house as an emblem of English aristocratic life and implies that it is now, itself, the object of the falling axe:

> Autumn resumes the land, ruffles the woods
> with smoky wings, entangles them. Trees shine
> out from their leaves, rocks mildew to moss-green;
> the avenues are spread with brittle floods.
>
> Platonic England, house of solitudes,
> rests in its laurels and its injured stone,
> replete with complex fortunes that are gone,
> beset by dynasties of moods and clouds.
>
> It stands, as though at ease with its own world,
> the mannerly extortions, languid praise,
> all that devotion long since bought and sold,
>
> the rooms of cedar and soft-thudding baize,
> tremulous boudoirs where the crystals kissed
> in cabinets of amethyst and frost.   (129)

The sonnet tends towards an elegiac manner reminiscent of Yeats writing about Coole Park, but decisively holds back from any indulgence; if autumn is synonymous with loss, it also affords an opportunity for clear vision, as 'Trees shine | out from their leaves'. However embedded in history and nature it might appear, the house that 'rests in its laurels' also unmistakably rests *on* its laurels, destined to be no more than a literary fiction. The vagueness of its 'complex' fortunes and mysterious 'dynasties' cannot conceal that the house is a place of violence as well as beauty. The sestet appears to reinforce an impression of powerful persistence ('It stands...'), but what it presents is a remorseless process of diminishment, with the closing tercet skilfully scaling down the house to the billiards room, the boudoir, a cabinet, and finally crystals of stone or ice (hard and cold, but also the appropriate remains of a scientific, acquisitive culture). Rhetorical grandeur ends in a sibilant whisper. The rhymes hold back from any satisfying fullness or completion, most obviously in the closing couplet that refuses to be a closing couplet, holding its tantalizing kiss at a chilly distance from fulfilment.

The sonnet and the sonnet sequence prove highly amenable to Hill's design, both allowing for the vertical rise and fall of human aspirations in each constituent poem, and denoting the horizontal movement of history outwards from England. At the minute level of diction, metre, line, and syntax, the sonnet suits Hill's intense historical reflections extremely well, granting him the licence for magnificent lyrical flourishes and rhetorical declarations, but also providing a tightly controlled space for jarring discordances and antinomies, beguiling changes of tone and texture, and densely impacted allusions. The compression of meaning that the sonnet produces through its formal devices contributes significantly to the 'hermeneutic ellipsis' that makes Hill's work at once mysteriously beguiling and intellectually challenging.[105]

The closing sonnet in 'An Apology', 'The Herefordshire Carol', promises closure and completion, but its final brilliant epiphany emerges from a complex vision of transformation, in which renewal and repair are subject to incessant ruin and disfigurement:

> So to celebrate that kingdom: it grows
> greener in winter, essence of the year;
> the apple-branches musty with green fur.
> In the viridian darkness of its yews
>
> it is an enclave of perpetual vows
> broken in time. Its truth shows disrepair,
> disfigured shrines, their stones of gossamer,
> Old Moore's astrology, all hallows,
>
> the squire's effigy bewigged with frost,
> and hobnails cracking puddles before dawn.
> In grange and cottage girls rise from their beds
>
> by candlelight and mend their ruined braids.
> Touched by the cry of the iconoclast,
> how the rose-window blossoms with the sun!   (131)

Amidst the paradoxical and ambivalent realization of the 'kingdom' (both old England and an abstraction of political and cultural values), there is a final, disillusioned acknowledgement of repeated betrayals and injustices,

---

105. Haughton, *Geoffrey Hill: Essays on his Work*, p. 129.

but also a shimmer of hope for the future. Amidst so much falsity, illusion, and fiction there is also dynamic historical change. The frozen image of the squire is immediately followed by more positive images of enterprising workers. As Henry Hart points out, the poem shares the intense vision made possible by 'wintry purification' in T. S. Eliot's *Four Quartets*, but its final vision is not so much one of 'contraries unified' as one of conflicting opposites held in suspension.[106] The image of a stained-glass 'rose-window' seeming to blossom in the animating light of the sun is perceived most intensely in the moment of threatened loss and destruction. The perception colours the entire sequence, suggesting in retrospect that the imagined ideal of Platonic old England is inseparable from, and perhaps even the inevitable product of, its long and troubled history.

Tony Harrison

The poetry of Tony Harrison, like that of Geoffrey Hill, illuminates the dark recesses of human history, bringing the imagination into powerful contact with the conflicts and cruelties of the past, while also staring into the midst of unending violence and oppression. Harrison shares with Hill persistent memories of an English childhood in which celebration of the war's ending is overshadowed by the incomprehensible scale of suffering at Auschwitz and Hiroshima and elsewhere. His muted celebratory 'Sonnets for August 1945' recall 'a dark, scorched circle on the road' (an emblem of continuous conflict and warfare) on the morning after bonfires have burned for Victory over Japan.[107] Since the 1990s, Harrison's work has been prompted by an anguished meditation on war in Bosnia and Iraq. Though always strongly internationalist (his early 'Curtain Sonnets' derive from his time in Russia and Czechoslovakia in the 1960s and 1970s), Harrison's outstanding achievement in modern poetry has been to voice the painful and corrosive effects of English social class in a compelling sequence of highly innovative and idiosyncratic sixteen-line sonnets.

If Hill is inspired by the Plantagenet kings, Harrison is moved by the popular radicalism of the English working class. The title of Harrison's sonnet sequence, *from The School of Eloquence*, acknowledges that long tradition of

---

106. Henry Hart, *The Poetry of Geoffrey Hill* (Carbondale, IL: Southern Illinois University Press, 1986), p. 244.
107. Tony Harrison, *The Gaze of the Gorgon* (Newcastle upon Tyne: Bloodaxe Books, 1992), p. 9.

political struggle identified by E. P. Thompson in *The Making of the English Working Class* (1963), connecting the poet's own hunger for articulation with the aspirations of radical, republican organizations like the London Corresponding Society in the 1790s. Reading Harrison's sonnets can be a painful experience, though discomfort comes less from the learned and allusive references he shares with Hill than from the caustic stuff of class-consciousness and divisive social attitudes. At the same time, there is a compensating aesthetic satisfaction to be found in the sheer virtuosity of Harrison's poetic manoeuvres. The sonnets are by turns ostentatiously intellectual and intimately personal, often switching registers unexpectedly. The formal tension generated by an awkward alignment of educated discourse and local vernacular speech is, itself, indicative of Harrison's strong sense of dislocation and deracination. Where Hill inclines to obliquity and obscurity, Harrison seizes the opportunity for implicating his readers in the dramatization and exposure of deeply felt grievances and injustices.

The opening sonnet in *from The School of Eloquence*, 'On Not Being Milton', recalls Thomas Gray's acknowledgement of unrecorded and unremarked poetic talent, 'some mute inglorious Milton', in his 'Elegy Written in a Country Churchyard'. In a celebration of the struggle for articulate speech, Harrison aligns linguistic achievement with political emancipation, taking inspiration from the struggles of the industrial working class in Victorian Britain, as well as from colonial and post-colonial liberation movements. The sonnet is dedicated to two Mozambique poets and political activists, Sergio Vieira and Armando Guebuza, and it looks to the example of Aimé Césaire and his declaration of 'negritude' in his *Cahier d'un retour au pays natal* (1939). Harrison's reflection on 'growing black enough to fit my boots' is both a declaration of solidarity with Césaire, insisting against all prejudice and opposition upon his rights as a poet, and also a grim reminder of the alternative forms of labour then available to the northern working class in mining and other industrial occupations. The motivating impulse in the poem is its profound awareness of language as power, and of the various means, including physical coercion, by which the lowly and the unruly have historically been reduced to silence or inarticulacy: 'The stutter of the scold out of the branks | of condescension.'[108] The linguistic rebellion of 'glottals' and 'morphemes' has a parallel in the Luddite destruction of machinery,

---

108. Tony Harrison, *Selected Poems* (London: Penguin, 1987), p. 112. Further references are to this edition of the poems.

though Harrison notes with irony that the Leeds-built sledge hammers used to destroy the weaving frames in the textile industry in Yorkshire were made by the same Enoch Taylor who built the frames. The sonnet opens with a fiery declaration of poetic vocation, in which the flames are simultaneously emblematic of literary censorship (the burning of books), revolutionary struggle, and Pentecostal inspiration:

> Read and committed to the flames, I call
> these sixteen lines that go back to my roots
> my *Cahier d'un retour au pays natal*,
> my growing black enough to fit my boots.
>
> The stutter of the scold out of the branks
> of condescension, class and counter-class
> thickens with glottals to a lumpen mass
> of Ludding morphemes closing up their ranks.
> Each swung cast-iron Enoch of Leeds stress
> clangs a forged music on the frames of Art,
> the looms of owned language smashed apart!
>
> Three cheers for mute ingloriousness!
>
> Articulation is the tongue-tied's fighting.
> In the silence round all poetry we quote
> Tidd the Cato Street conspirator who wrote:
>
> *Sir, I Ham a very Bad Hand at Righting.*

The advantage of using sixteen lines rather than fourteen is that it gives Harrison the liberty to deploy the extra syllables in cunningly strategic ways, both building on the traditional sonnet form and departing from it when the need arises. Harrison's use of the Meredithian sonnet gives him licence to clang his own 'forged music on the frames of Art', asserting a claim for cultural recognition on behalf of the disempowered and the dispossessed. While supremely adept in handling the traditional quatrain, Harrison delights in demolishing and rebuilding conventional verse, frequently isolating a single line for special emphasis, as he twice does here. His technique involves both a formal recognition of the sonnet as 'highly wrought' language and a desire to include within that frame a set of fragments and verbal dissonances: 'lines which are directly from the speech of my parents, for example, or from forgotten victims of the class history of Britain, like Tidd the Cato Street Conspirator'.[109] For all its overt literariness and allusiveness, the sonnet gives

---

109. Tony Harrison, Interview with Stephen Regan at the National Theatre, London, 28 March 1996, broadcast as 'The Sonnet', BBC 2, 20 January 1998.

closing emphasis and distinction to a single line of writing: '*Sir, I Ham a very Bad Hand at Righting.*' There is pathos, as well as felicity, in the rightness of Richard Tidd's bad writing. Accompanying the fearful memory of the Cato Street Conspirator, there is a touching acknowledgement of his deferential politeness and his inexpert 'hamming' performance.

For all its apparent denial of Milton, Harrison's work aspires to the greatness of a poet who could fill the sonnet with polemical vigour but also use it feelingly and elegiacally to honour departed friends and loved ones. Harrison is candid about the extent of Milton's influence:

> I've probably been drawn to Milton more than to any other writer of sonnets. As Wordsworth says, 'In his hands the thing became a trumpet.' He took a form that we associate with love and the courtly style, and he made it speak publicly and politically. He gave it weight and mass. This doesn't mean that he wasn't able to write privately. He ranges from the public sonnets of 'Avenge thee O Lord thy slaughtered saints', 'A book was writ of late called *Tetrachordon*', and 'I did but prompt the age to quit their clogs', to 'Methought I saw my late espoused saint' and 'When I consider how my life is spent', with their wonderfully inward and private claims. For me, it was a revelation that this form could have mass and weight, as well as tenderness.

In the same interview, Harrison speaks positively of the 'enabling current' which comes from taking on a form already well established and associated with Milton, Wordsworth, Hopkins, and others: 'It gives me confidence to overcome the sense of futility that I often feel about how effective, how valid, or how civilizing poetry can be.' If the sonnet inducts the writer into visionary company, it also provides the perfect form for the poetry of loss. Harrison insists upon the virtues of concentration and intensity that sonnet writing involves: 'It's about concentration, it's about paring away what is unnecessary, but it's also momentary... it celebrates the moment of love, and it celebrates those emotions which we cannot bear holding on to for very long... the intensity can only be short lived.' Harrison speaks eloquently for many sonnet writers in his account of how form relates to feeling: 'Strong, powerful emotions are very hard to articulate and measure without some kind of form, and form for me has never been something which inhibits feeling; it has always been something which allows me to examine and explore, and even develop and understand, feeling. I've never thought of it as a constriction or a corset.'[110]

110. Tony Harrison, Interview, 28 March 1996.

The sonnets titled *from The School of Eloquence* are primarily elegies for Harrison's mother and father, infused with a sorrowful awareness that it was only after their deaths that he was able to write in a poetic language that they might have understood. Eschewing the cultural *bricolage* of the sonnet 'On Not Being Milton', the double sonnet 'Book Ends' resorts to plain diction, with the only quotations being fragments of speech that Harrison remembers from conversations with his parents. The title cleverly positions father and son, sitting in close domestic proximity, but in reality separated by a weight of learning and unable to communicate: 'only our silence made us seem a pair'. The sense of an ending pervades the poem, with its abrupt opening line dropping a syllable so as to maximize the stress on 'Baked', phonetically anticipating the closing, spluttering 'books'. The deadening dental consonants modulate into the gentler plosives of the second line and its desolate sundering of domestic comfort: 'Baked the day she suddenly dropped dead | we chew it slowly that last apple pie.' Harrison uses the dynamics of the sixteen-line sonnet superbly well here, setting the lines in alternately rhymed pairs until he contemplates his father's desolate bleakness in the isolated line 13: 'Your life's all shattered into smithereens.' The first of the two sonnets closes with a delayed turn and a dismal tercet:

> Back in our silences and sullen looks,
> for all the Scotch we drink, what's still between 's
> not the thirty or so years, but books, books, books.   (126)

The unpoetic 'smithereens' and its opportunistic rhyme with the fitting but ungainly 'between 's' recalls the spirited rhymes and teasing contractions of John Berryman, but the effect in Harrison's sonnet is one of calculated gaucheness, wilfully disrupting any possibility of lyric smoothness in the penultimate line.

Sonnet II of 'Book Ends' accentuates the division between father and son, between customary and educated ways of being, in its pained reflection on what might constitute 'the right words' for the mother's gravestone. As the brisk rhyme between 'terse' and 'verse' suggests, and as the usually inarticulate father is quick to point out, there are times when poetry fails in the civic roles that might be expected of it, by seeming superfluous or irrelevant in the face of life's pressing needs: '*Come on, it's not as if we're wanting verse. | It's not as if we're wanting a whole sonnet!*' Now, it seems, the division created by books finds a finer distinction in words, and the father gets the upper hand in perfecting the art of the painful cut: '*You're supposed to be the bright boy at description | and you can't tell them what the fuck to put!'* The sonnet plays arrestingly with the various colloquial uses and meanings of 'wanting' and 'getting', from needing and desiring to having and possessing. Aspiration, as well as urgency, is implied in the isolated monosyllabic line: 'I've got to find the right words on my own.' The line hints at the separation induced through education, as well as implying a determined independence of thought and feeling, but it also prepares us for the realization that the sonnet is, in retrospect, mourning the loss of both parents. The poem closes uncomfortably, with 'my own' anchored in 'their stone':

> I've got the envelope that he'd been scrawling,
> mis-spelt, mawkish, stylistically appalling
> but I can't squeeze more love into their stone. (127)

The final 'got' denotes inheritance, with the scrawled envelope as a sad objective correlative of both mis-communication and continuing attachment. Inverting the familiar saying about the difficulty of squeezing blood from a stone, the sonnet ends ruefully by reflecting on its own inadequacy, as elegiac inscription, in conveying deep personal feeling.

A selection of fifty sonnets appearing in *from The School of Eloquence* was published as *Continuous* in 1981, a year after the death of Harrison's father. As one of its epigraphs, the volume carries the opening and closing lines of 'Ad Patrem', in which Milton movingly addresses his father and offers his poems in dedication: 'I do not know what I can more fittingly offer in return for your gifts to me, though my greatest gifts could never match yours, much less can yours be equalled by the barren gratitude expressed in mere words.' Milton's filial verse ends with a self-conscious meditation on the poet's own 'youthful poems and diversions', hoping that they might be saved from 'dark oblivion' and one day 'see the light'.[111] Harrison's sonnets are 'continuous' in that they carry on a dialogue with ghosts. The implication is that they will never be finished. The title poem, 'Continuous', evokes a strong sense of connection and continuity between father and son through a shared love of cinema (where films were shown continuously throughout the day), and through poignant images of circularity, including the father's wedding ring and the 'looped' music played at his funeral. The sonnet juxtaposes the memory of the cinema organist disappearing from sight at the start of the film with the father descending into the flames of the crematorium. The Cagney film in question,

---

111. John Milton, *Poetical Works*, ed. Douglas Bush (Oxford: Oxford University Press, 1969), p. 101.

White Heat (1949), has a chilling relevance for the poet contemplating 'the blinding light' of his father's incineration, suggesting a contemporary analogy for Shelley's 'white radiance of Eternity'.[112] If the sonnet has a turn, it occurs, as with 'Book Ends', in a line that swells with recognition of what it is to be 'on my own':

> James Cagney was the one up both our streets.
> His was the only art we ever shared.
> A gangster film and choc ice were the treats
> that showed about as much love as he dared.
>
> He'd be my own age now in '49!
> The hand that glinted with the ring he wore,
> *his* father's, tipped the cold bar into mine
> just as the organist dropped through the floor.
>
> He's on the platform lowered out of sight
> to organ music, this time on looped tape,
> into a furnace with a blinding light
> where only his father's ring will keep its shape.
>
> I wear it now to Cagneys on my own
> and sense my father's hands cupped round my treat—
>
> they feel as though they've been chilled to the bone
> from holding my ice cream all through *White Heat*.   (143)

The four quatrains and two couplets maintain a steady narrative progression, intensifying with the moment of transfer from father to son, 'I wear it now...'. The rhymes are simple and unforced, and the only obvious cultural allusion is to the gangster film. The sonnet is written in a demotic idiom that the father might have appreciated, exemplified most fittingly in 'the one up both our streets', simultaneously registering togetherness and the rare nature of its occurrence. The doubleness of the sonnet, both recognizing tender moments of intimacy and regretting their repressed, unspoken form, is powerfully captured in the caring but deathly image of the father's cold hands around the ice cream, 'keeping it for me', as Harrison explains, 'going through the fire of cremation'. Without any obtrusive metaphysics, 'Continuous' gently dwells upon questions of belief: 'It's about as far as I can get in establishing continuity between life and death, between the beliefs

---

112. Percy Bysshe Shelley, *The Major Works*, ed. Zachary Leader and Michael O'Neill (Oxford: Oxford University Press, 2003), p. 545.

I have and the views my father struggled to believe in: the real sense of my father being present, even when he's dead.'[113]

'Marked with D' shows how deftly Harrison employs the double-edged legacy of Milton, turning from an intimate twelve-line elegiac remembrance to an angry denunciation of England and its divisive class society in the closing quatrain. Although the sonnet employs a religious vocabulary, it is principally concerned with language, class, and education. The image of bread is at once a prominent allusion to the work of Harrison's father and a Christian symbol of communion and resurrection. The title is taken from a popular nursery rhyme ('Pattercake, pattercake, baker's man') and recalls the practice of marking bread with initials and symbols. D is for Dad as well as Death, and it also stands for Dunce. The sonnet neatly conflates two sets of images, from work and from death. The dead father's flesh is 'chilled dough', and his cremation recalls the oven at which he worked; his ashes are like flour, enough 'for one small loaf'. Recalling how his father used to light the ovens, Harrison both sets up a Pentecostal image of tongues of fire (of gifted speech universally understood) and immediately undermines it by giving priority to the literal rather than metaphorical associations of the image:

> When the chilled dough of his flesh went in an oven
> not unlike those he fuelled all his life,
> I thought of his cataracts ablaze with Heaven
> and radiant with the sight of his dead wife,
> light streaming from his mouth to shape her name,
> 'not Florence and not Flo but always Florrie'.
> I thought how his cold tongue burst into flame
> but only literally, which makes me sorry,
> sorry for his sake there's no Heaven to reach.
> I get it all from Earth my daily bread
> but he hungered for release from mortal speech
> that kept him down, the tongue that weighed like lead.
>
> The baker's man that no one will see rise
> and England made to feel like some dull oaf
> is smoke, enough to sting one person's eyes
> and ash (not unlike flour) for one small loaf.   (155)

Once again, the sixteen-line form allows space for a steady progression of ideas, beginning with an extended line in which the additional syllables mitigate against an otherwise shocking and abrupt announcement. The two-part structure has the 'weight and mass' that Harrison admires in Milton's sonnets, allowing the turn between twelve lines and four to effect a shift from sorrow to anger, subtly prepared by the repetition of 'sorry' across lines 8 and 9, where the conventional *volta* would be. The domestic diction of breadmaking reinforces the poignancy of the working-class father's 'hunger' for articulate speech and aspiration for social betterment, without losing the transcendental appeal of 'the bread of heaven'. 'The baker's man that no one will see rise' very effectively combines the earthly and heavenly associations of bread, as does the earlier reference to 'daily bread' (an explicit allusion to The Lord's Prayer or 'Our Father'). The sting of the closing quatrain derives from pained regret at the father's limited opportunities on earth, coupled with an uncompromising scepticism towards his belief in eternal life.

Jamie McKendrick notes in a brief but illuminating summary of Harrison's poetry that the battle played out in the sonnets between upbringing and education induces a 'sense of elegiac arrest'. The poetry 'holds in painful suspension a permanent ambivalence', as it grapples with 'the terms of British class conflict', which are seen to be 'entrenched and static'.[114] Harrison's sonnets certainly acknowledge their own obsessive circularity as they repeatedly return to childhood and adolescence, both celebrating class solidarity and articulating the painfulness of class division within his own family relationships. However, there is both a stubbornly inherent predicament and an energetic renewal of response in Harrison's depiction of these sonnets as *Continuous* (the title he chose for his 1981 selection of the poems). At the same time, since the 1980s, the sonnets in the continuing work titled *from The School of Eloquence* have focused their attention on the repercussions of political violence and war, as well as social class. 'Sonnets for August 1945', published in *The Gaze of the Gorgon* (1992), is a short sequence bringing together poems published elsewhere and situating them alongside his fierce Gulf War poems, 'A Cold Coming' and 'Initial Illumination'. The opening sonnets recall 'the circle of scorched cobbles' after the VJ bonfire celebrations of 15 August 1945 (when Harrison was 8 years old), while powerfully acknowledging the interminable burning of the fires of Hiroshima and Nagasaki. Harrison continues to render the urgency of his insights in the fractured,

---

114. Jamie McKendrick, 'Contemporary Poetries in English, circa 1980 to the Present 2', *The Cambridge History of English Poetry*, ed. Michael O'Neill (Cambridge: Cambridge University Press, 2010), p. 1001.

disrupted syntax of his sixteen-line sonnets. The mordantly titled 'First Aid in English' reflects on the benefits of the grammar book in providing collective nouns, before conceding that 'there's no aid in English, first or last, | For a [Fill in the Blank] of genocide | or more than one [Please Tick] atomic blast'. Harrison's confrontation of the unspeakable gives his work immense stature in the twenty-first century, moulding and remoulding the sonnet as a poetic form resilient enough to register the pressures of both personal and global disintegration.

Douglas Dunn, Edwin Morgan, and Kathleen Jamie

Like Tony Harrison, Douglas Dunn has infused the melodic structure of the sonnet with his own vernacular style—a style perfected in the urban demotic of *Terry Street* (1969)—and he, too, has adopted the sonnet as a form well-suited to the writing of elegies. An early sonnet, 'Modern Love', might be expected to follow the sixteen-line pattern of Meredith's iconoclastic sequence, but it settles for a subtle adjustment of the fourteen-line Shakespearean model, gently drifting into blank verse, in keeping with its relaxed and ruminative mood. In place of Harrison's neo-classical insistence on full rhymes, Dunn shows a preference for unobtrusive half rhymes, the initial rhyme of 'house' and 'silence' delicately catching the poem's subdued domestic aura, before it slips into unrhymed pentameter: 'It is summer, and we are in a house | That is not ours, sitting at a table | Enjoying minutes of a rented silence.' There are no moments of dramatic confrontation, jealousy, or anger. Dunn's modern love sighs with relief at its own existence, content enough with the way things are. The sonnet turns from 'no hope' into 'happiness' with a resigned but realistic awareness of the pragmatics of love: 'Our lives flap, and we have no hope of better | Happiness than this, not much to show for love | Than how we are, or how this evening is...'. The calculated bathos of 'Looking forward to a visit from the cat' confirms a way of seeing that happily settles for a quiet, quotidian contentment.[115]

The intimate domestic details that conjure up a life are given poignant expression in the sonnets included in *Elegies* (1985), dedicated to the poet's wife, the artist and curator, Lesley Balfour Dunn, who died in 1981. The

---

115. Douglas Dunn, *New Selected Poems 1964–2000* (London: Faber, 2003), p. 22.

tensions and paradoxes that have traditionally shaped the elegy as a poetic genre are powerfully concentrated in the sonnet form. *Elegies*, like other imposing works of mourning, from Milton's 'Lycidas' to Hardy's 'Poems of 1912–13', is riven with contradiction, recognizing both the need to remember and the need to forget. While staring into a painful emptiness, the volume conjures up ghostly appearances and consoling fictions. Within the most forlorn utterance of loss, there is a vestigial religious vocabulary, so that secular observations and activities take on the semblance of sacred ritual and longing. Several sonnets in *Elegies* dwell on the temporary consolations of art, or on the fragile, fleeting beauty of objects such as the decorative mobiles of aeroplanes and birds in 'A Silver Air Force' and 'Sandra's Mobile'. 'The Kaleidoscope' is a hybrid sonnet that starts out with a Petrarchan quatrain but modulates into a Shakespearean sonnet with a strong closing couplet:

> To climb these stairs again, bearing a tray,
> Might be to find you pillowed with your books,
> Your inventories listing gowns and frocks
> As if preparing for a holiday.
> Or, turning from the landing, I might find
> My presence watched through your kaleidoscope,
> A symmetry of husbands, each redesigned
> In lovely forms of foresight, prayer and hope.
> I climb these stairs a dozen times a day
> And, by the open door, wait, looking in
> At where you died. My hands become a tray
> Offering me, my flesh, my soul, my skin.
> Grief wrongs us so. I stand, and wait, and cry
> For the absurd forgiveness, not knowing why.

The opening infinitive, with its distant echo of *Astrophil and Stella* ('With how sad steps, O Moon, thou climbst the skies!'), embraces both laborious ritual and hopeful longing. The ascendant, affirmative action of the opening line gently subsides into the subjunctive and the illusory: 'Might be to find you . . . As if preparing for a holiday.' The bearing of a tray is preparation for a ritual Offertory and then Communion, in which the speaker's own body and soul await a blessing and transformation. The repeated 'wait' is both touchingly reverential (echoing Milton's celebrated line, 'They also serve who only stand and wait') and ultimately futile. The sonnet is candidly agnostic in its declaration of the absurd and inexplicable nature of death, but also insistently drawn to the consoling rituals of prayer. The image of the kaleidoscope serves to focus the sonnet's disparate perceptions, promising to reorder and reshape what is, in actuality, an irreparably fractured life. In structural terms, however, what gives coherence to the sonnet is its carefully organized syntax and its punctilious control of rhythm and pace. The opening line of the sestet, 'I climb these stairs a dozen times a day', reiterates and develops the opening line of the octave, while the caesura of the penultimate line, the hanging 'cry' produced by the enjambment, and the momentary pause in the closing line all contribute to the restrained but devastating confession of hurt and bewilderment.

'A Silver Air Force' and 'Sandra's Mobile' are crafted with a loving care for colour, light, and shape, as fitting elegies for a woman who was herself 'a constant artist'. In both poems, the artistic mobile is a thing of fragile beauty, gently stirring on air and breath until it moves no more, but it is also in each case an emblem of the poet's hopes and fears. A playful distraction to begin with, the toy planes and birds take on a metaphysical significance in the poet's retrospective imaginings, a conceit in which life is 'Hanging from threads'. The models of things in flight provide a way of recalling some of the most intimate and painful moments of togetherness, as well as being poignant reminders of imminent loss. 'A Silver Air Force' opens with a simple preterite, but then follows it in line 2 with a strategically weak and hesitant rhyme word, the prepositional form of 'to' vainly attempting to ward off the awful infinitive:

> They used to spin in the light, monoplanes,
> Biplanes, a frivolous deterrent to
> What had to happen.   (18)

If the silver planes recall the heroic struggles of the Second World War in the popular saying, 'a wing and a prayer', they also bring to mind the catastrophic images of defeat depicted in Hollywood films, 'shot down, shot down in flames'. The poet imagines himself as a wartime pilot, but his 'scramble' carries fear as well as heroic endeavour, and it extends beyond his immediate care for his wife to the war-torn sky of his own existence when she is gone:

> I watched, and thought, 'What will become of me
> When she is dead?' I scramble in my dreams
> Again, and see these secret Spitfires fly
> As the inevitable aces of the sky,
> Hanging from threads, a gentle violence.   (18)

Dunn uses the architectonics of the sonnet with impressive skill. 'A Silver Air Force' has a Shakespearean octave, but scrambles nervously over the expected turn to the sestet with the word 'Again' and lifts its hopes once more with a close pairing of the two buoyant rhyme words, 'fly' and 'sky'. The rhyming couplet brings the sonnet to an illusory highpoint, only to come back down to earth with a delayed turn in line 11, 'But day by day they fell...'. Against the steady expectation of four quatrains suggested by the rhyme scheme, the sonnet plays off the increasing tautness of three sentences (sense units) of six, five, and three lines. The close of the sonnet eschews the Shakespearean rhyming couplet, separating the strained rhyme of 'violence' and 'distance' with the unignorable 'crashed', and isolating the gentle but remorseful 'White strings of hope a summer blueness washed' (18). If the summer blue reiterates the suggestions of heaven in 'God's distance', it also allows the elegiac blue of eternal loss to run like a dye into the pristine white of former hopes.

'Sandra's Mobile' observes the Shakespearean model more closely than 'A Silver Air Force', though once again Dunn makes imposing use of the tension that comes from playing off the quatrain structure established by the rhyme scheme with a varying syntactical pattern of five, three, four, and two lines. It, too, initially pulls back from the lyrical fluency that the sonnet is apt to set in motion, placing the weak prepositional 'to' at the end of a line (rhyming it this time with 'blue' rather than 'blew'), and following it with a feminine rhyme ('colour' and 'duller') that suggests diminishment. The sestet shows consummate control over the painful divulgence of loss, with the ebb and flow of feeling transmitted through the interplay of enjambment and strong mid-line pauses. Like Harrison, Dunn is skilful in heightening and intensifying the emotional tenor of a sonnet with fragments of recorded speech. Here, the imperative 'Blow' initiates a current of hope but also testifies to a final exhalation of breath:

> "Blow on them, Love." Those silent birds winged round
> On thermals of my breath. On her last night,
> Trying to stay awake, I saw love crowned
> In tears and wooden birds and candlelight.
> She did not wake again. To prove our love
> Each gull, each gull, each gull, turned into dove. (21)

As with Shakespeare's sonnets, 'Love' is both person and concept, a word forever seeking and fulfilling rhyme. The closing couplet subtly echoes Shakespeare's Sonnet 116 ('If this be error and upon me proved'), with 'prove' approvingly anticipating the rhyme of 'love' and 'dove'. The insistent repetition, as 'each gull' comes into sight, gives credence to love in the face of death, with the final turn of the sonnet and the appearance of the dove acknowledging both the sacredness of that love and a peaceful departure.

Although *Elegies* includes poems that draw on Dunn's native Scotland (the closing poem is 'Leaving Dundee'), the sonnets in the collection are not obviously those of a Scots poet. Edwin Morgan's sonnets are much more explicitly rooted in Scotland, though his ten 'Glasgow Sonnets' (1973) appear to draw on the gritty urban realism of Dunn's *Terry Street*. The opening sonnet paints a grim picture of Glasgow tenements in the 1970s as vandalized, rat-infested places, where lives are laid to waste in boredom and unemployment. There is neither sentimentality nor sanctimoniousness in Morgan's depiction of the city, but neither is there a monotonous excess of descriptive detail. Instead, the scene is strangely animated (or not quite animated) by a pervasive imagery of wind, steam, and air:

> A mean wind wanders through the backcourt trash.
> Hackles on puddles rise, old mattresses
> puff briefly and subside. Play-fortresses
> of brick and bric-a-brac spill out some ash.
> Four storeys have no windows left to smash,
> but the fifth a chipped sill buttresses
> mother and daughter the last mistresses
> of that black block condemned to stand, not crash.
> Around them the cracks deepen, the rats crawl.
> The kettle whimpers on a crazy hob.
> Roses of mould grow from ceiling to wall.
> The man lies late since he has lost his job,
> smokes on one elbow, letting his coughs fall
> thinly into an air too poor to rob.[116]

The sonnet as an elegant court form is now filled with 'backcourt trash', and that uninviting image sets the scene for the 'brick and bric-a-brac' and the 'black block' that follow. Ambitiously pursuing a Petrarchan rhyme scheme, the sonnet struggles between 'trash' and 'ash' and 'smash' and 'crash' to find what might rhyme with 'old mattresses'. The turn coincides with deepening cracks and crawling rats, and the one potential blossoming of beauty decays into 'Roses of mould'.

While Edwin Morgan's sonnets from Scotland range fantastically from pre-historic settings to imagined futures, Kathleen Jamie's experiments in the genre tend lovingly and respectfully to the natural world and to a delicate

---

116. Edwin Morgan, *New Selected Poems* (Manchester: Carcanet, 2000), p. 82.

and threatened eco-system, in which humans, birds, and rivers are all part of a shared landscape. The sonnet has a special significance in showing how adaptation and renewal might be achieved within existing structures. 'Swallows' is exemplary in this respect, with the pared-down quatrains, the short, unrhymed lines, and the unpunctuated close suitably suggesting freedom in flight and a way of moving 'at ease' in the world. The poet's 'battened | heart', contrasting with this ease, recalls Donne's battered heart and Hopkins's 'heart in hiding', but there is promise and hope in the fluent brilliance of birds that 'stream out into light'.[117] In 'Moult', the way in which discarded feathers are reminders of a complex design in nature, each a part 'of the pattern the outstretched | wing displays', becomes a model for a sustaining vision of co-operation and interaction. The sonnet registers its preoccupation with randomness and pattern in nature by unexpectedly settling into rhyme and letting the earlier word 'coverts' echo in 'the covenant they undertake, | wind and kittiwake' (38).

As Michael O'Neill has noted with reference to *The Tree House* (2004), the sonnet takes on a special role in articulating Jamie's ecological and environmental concerns: 'at once old and resilient, the form answers the needs of a poet who wishes to keep faith with the natural world and to renew or re-comprehend her vision of it'.[118] The observation applies equally well to the sonnets in the later volume, *The Overhaul* (2012), especially those in the sequence, 'Five Tay Sonnets'. In these meditations on the life of Scotland's longest river and the life that goes on around it, Jamie presents a contemporary Scots version of the picturesque English river sonnet that was popular in the eighteenth century. The opening sonnet, welcoming the return of a pair of ospreys to a riverside nest in the pine trees, is infused with Scots words and sayings that give the poetry a distinctive phonetic appeal. The allusion to 'a teuchit storm' links the bleak spring weather to the arrival of another bird, the lapwing or peewit, while the address to the ospreys in the sestet, 'So redd up your cradle, on the tree-top, | claim your teind from the shining | estates of the firth', mixes a nursery rhyme idiom with the historical discourse of land management and maintenance. The local speech with which the sonnet closes typifies the vigilant and caring attitude to the environment that Jamie seeks to promote: '*that's them, baith o' them, they're in.*'[119]

---

117. Kathleen Jamie, *The Tree House* (London: Picador, 2004), p. 18. Page numbers for other poems in the collection are given in brackets in the text.
118. Michael O'Neill, 'Form in *The Tree House*', *Kathleen Jamie: Essays and Poems on her Work*, ed. Rachel Falconer (Edinburgh: Edinburgh University Press, 2015), p. 103.
119. Kathleen Jamie, *The Overhaul* (London: Picador, 2012), p. 5.

Andrew McNeillie, Don Paterson, and Carol Ann Duffy

Andrew McNeillie, editor of the literary journal *Archipelago*, has given a fresh and exhilarating impulse to the sonnet as a form ideally suited to unstable, metamorphic notions of identity and place. Born in North Wales, the son of the distinguished Scots writer Ian Niall, McNeillie also has strong attachments to Ireland (his year on Inis Mór is vividly recorded in his memoir, *An Aran Keening*, 2001). A keen naturalist, his poems look out from middle England across the sweeping landscapes and seascapes of the British Isles, dwelling on the visionary ideal of an archipelagic imagination. His sonnets are respectfully traditional in attending to the time-honoured duties of praise and lament, but they are also attuned to the contemporary politics of devolution within a fractured United Kingdom, buckling and bending as they take the measure of conflicting ideas of language, nationality, and culture. His third collection of poems, *Slower* (2006), makes extensive and varied use of the sonnet and the sonnet sequence. The book includes elegiac sonnets for Vernon Watkins, Dylan Thomas, and Edward Thomas, and for the Welsh painter, Carey Morris. It explores the youthful Welsh writer's coming to consciousness in a verse memoir in sonnets, 'Portrait of the Poet as a Young Dog', and it mourns the sinking of the *Princess Victoria* ferry on its way from Stranraer to Larne in January 1953, in a striking sequence of allusive, meditative sonnets titled 'Arkwork'.

McNeillie's twenty-eight 'Glyn Dŵr Sonnets' lift the Welsh prince (Owen Glendower) from the margins of Shakespeare's history plays and allow his legendary presence to shape a sustained and impassioned study of language, politics, and poetics. Musing over personal memories, snatches of conversation, favourite quotations, and scraps of history, the sequence is a record of a mind vitally responsive to its own place and time. The writing of poetry is, itself, a subject of intense enquiry, with the Welsh hero inspiring a verse that steps back from full exposure to create an impression of mystery and inscrutability: 'To keep them wondering what | it is you're up to, haunting the page at | the edge of sense.' If, like *from The School of Eloquence*, the sequence considerably extends the resources of the sonnet by infusing it with many different, previously unheard, sounds and voices, it does so partly by capturing the music of *Cymraeg* (the Welsh language) in English, 'aspiring to *cynefin*' (a Welsh word that pleasingly embraces 'dwelling' and 'being').[120] The spirit

---

120. Andrew McNeillie, *Slower* (Manchester: Carcanet, 2006), pp. 27–8.

of Gerard Manley Hopkins, an enthusiastic experimenter with Welsh metrical forms and sound patterns such as the *Cywydd* and *Cynghannedd*, hovers benignly over the sequence.

On matters of language, education, and culture, McNeillie can be as combative and cuttingly ironic as Harrison, as with his strictures on the 'imperialist sweetness and shite' of 'St Matthew Arnold' in his 1866 lectures 'On the Study of Celtic Literature':

> Meanwhile, back at the Eisteddfod,
> as high above the Irish sea he stood
> pontificating about the need to drive
> the 'English wedge' into the very Welsh-
> Welsh heart of Wales, the natives strove
> to judge the best essay on: 'What it means to be English'. (31)

In this sestet of a hybrid sonnet, Arnold is allowed a moment's elevation in a rhyming couplet, before his cultural authority is undermined. The force of the sonnet, however, resides in its closing imperfect rhyme of 'Welsh' and 'English'. Celtic connections course through the searching archipelagic sonnet, 'The Emerald Isle Express' (a reference to the boat-train connecting Dublin with London via Holyhead, and also connecting contemporary writers like McNeillie with Yeats and Joyce). The child's excited interest in trains and journeys is allied to a growing understanding of words and puns, seeing how 'destiny' and 'nation' inhere in 'destination'. Learning 'how poems and railways' work involves an understanding of networks and an appreciation of 'the allure of elsewheres'. In keeping with the stress given throughout the sequence to the inevitable imprint of place, 'The Emerald Isle Express' shows identity to be fluid, forever running its course 'on that fine line between nation and mental states' (39).

Don Paterson has been among the most ardent practitioners of the sonnet, and he has also been an influential anthologist and controversial critic of the form. As his excellent Faber collection, *101 Sonnets from Shakespeare to Heaney* (1999), makes clear, he has both a deep appreciation of the musicality of the sonnet, and a lively critical discernment of its narrative and dramatic possibilities. While noting the special achievements of Scottish sonneteers, from William Drummond of Hawthornden and Alexander Montgomerie to Robert Garioch and Norman MacCaig, he is just as likely to take his inspiration from Rimbaud or Rilke. His first collection of poems, *Nil Nil* (1993), includes the sonnet 'Morning Prayer (*after Rimbaud*)', a version of 'Oraison du soir', but also the strange and disconcerting 'Exeunt', a series of four sonnets in which characters and situations are assembled with naturalistic detail and psychological acuity in various dramatic encounters and exits. 'The Electric Brae' brilliantly cuts from the oxygen tent on a hospital ward to the patient's delirious recollection of a journey across the Scottish landscape in his father's 'clapped-out Morris Minor' car. The patient's overworked heart and lungs are described in musical terms ('the pounding of a terrible jug band'), while the oxygen tent unexpectedly opens onto the landscape at the sonnet's turn: 'The windscreen presents | The unshattered myth of a Scottish spring.' The sonnet is dramatically suspended between life and death: 'Everything is still. | He frees the brake: the car surges uphill.'[121]

In *Landing Light* (2003), Paterson shows himself to be a fine and moving sonneteer of paternal love. With a combination of light-hearted wit and worldly gravitas reminiscent of the seventeenth-century metaphysical poets, 'Waking with Russell' imagines father and son as besotted lovers. The conceit of a shared smile spreads from the opening image of man and child waking 'face-to-face' to the closing image of a kiss pledged forever. Like Dunn, Paterson is adept at playing off the energies of syntax against the exigencies of rhyme. The sonnet appears to take an early turn after six lines, as if inverting octave and sestet, only to show how the poet, lost like Dante halfway through his life's journey, discovers new life:

> Dear son, I was *mezzo del cammin*
> And the true path was as lost to me as ever
> When you cut in front and lit it as you ran.

The lines here run across the expected division between octave and sestet, acquiring a positive charge from the suggestion of the child taking over and being father to the man. The true turn comes later:

> See how the true gift never leaves the giver:
> Returned and redelivered, it rolled on
> Until the smile poured through us like a river.

The intimacy of the sonnet is also a matter of intricacy at the level of rhyme: 'giver' and 'river' find a happy chime in 'redelivered', but also look back to 'lovers'. The musicality of the sonnet is such that it might be said to have only two rhymes, opening with 'began' and closing with 'forever'.[122]

---

121. Don Paterson, *Nil Nil* (London: Faber, 1993), p. 6.
122. Don Paterson, *Landing Light* (London: Faber, 2003), p. 5.

'The Thread' also uses a metaphysical style of conceit in a poem of paternal love, picking up the popular expression 'hanging to the world by a thread' and giving that image of perilousness a novel twist in the idea of a child caught and recovered 'by the thread of his one breath'. The thread extends in more positive ways to connect and hold together a family:

> Jamie made his landing in the world
> so hard he ploughed straight back into the earth.
> They caught him by the head of his one breath
> and pulled him up. They don't know how it held.
> And so today thank what higher will
> brought us to here, to you and me and Russ,
> the great twin-engined swaying wingspan of us
> roaring down the back of Kirrie Hill
>
> and your two-year-old lungs somehow out-revving
> every engine in the universe.
> *All that trouble just to turn up dead*
> was all I thought that long week. Now the thread
> is holding all of us: look at our tiny house,
> son, the white dot of your mother waving.   (6)

The form is Petrarchan, with the rhymes in the sestet neatly threaded so that they effect a swift reversal (*cdeedc*) from impending disaster. The rhyme word 'dead' is caught and held by 'thread'. The image of flight lifts the sonnet away from the crash landing of the opening line towards the buoyant take-off of the turn and the child's recovery. If the 'tiny house' and 'the white dot' of the mother 'waving' are images of near loss, and of a life given a new and terrifying perspective, they are also images of togetherness, recovery, and elevation.

Paterson's intensely powerful *Orpheus* (2006), his version of Rilke's enigmatic *Sonette an Orpheus* (1923), sharpens his conviction that sonnets and sonnet sequences are peculiarly well suited to the exploration of existential dilemmas. His fourteen-part Afterword to *Orpheus* provides an illuminating introduction to Rilke's lyric masterpiece, and also clarifies his own ardent interest in the sonnet form. What generates the German poet's sonnets, according to Paterson (and what drives his own poetic practice), is 'sheer wondering enquiry'.[123] The figure of Orpheus, he claims, is emblematic of our own 'conscious foreknowledge' of death, our own state of ghosthood,

---

123. Don Paterson, *Orpheus: A Version of Rilke's 'Die Sonette an Orpheus'* (London: Faber, 2006), p. 67. Further references are given in page numbers within brackets in the text.

having 'descended to the land of the shades' and returned to 'the living present' (68). In Orpheus, Rilke discovers 'the ideal possessor of the "double realm"' and a model of how to live with the paradox of human consciousness (69). Paterson's version of the sonnets to Orpheus takes on the mystery and the urgent summons of the original work, while deftly shaping it to reflect his own concern with the 'moral education and comfort' that poetry might provide.[124] An empathetic language of instruction is given lyric expression in Paterson's grave and lucid sonnets, culminating in the equanimity of 'Being': 'Our senses cannot fathom this night, so | be the meaning of their strange encounter; | at their crossing, be the radiant centre' (59).

Sheer wondering enquiry motivates the remarkable achievement of Paterson's *40 Sonnets* (2015), in which the flux of consciousness is matched by a bold adventurousness with form. *Orpheus* closes with 'Being' and *40 Sonnets* opens with 'Here', conjuring up what Larkin memorably termed 'the million-petalled flower | Of being here'.[125] What it is to be, and to be here, prompts multiple unanswerable questions, reinvigorating the sonnet as a space for meditation, as with 'The Air': 'When will the air stop breathing? Will it all | come to nothing, if nothing came to this?'[126] Several of the poems are existential musings ('Souls') or ontological riddles ('Seven Questions about the Journey'), but these are grounded and relieved by mordant satirical reflections on social institutions ('To Dundee City Council') and on poetry itself ('Requests'). Sometimes the sonnets give shape to the push and pull of existence in an apt metaphor such as the stalled lift in 'A Powercut' or the stalled wooden roundabout in 'The Roundabout', once again reminding us of Paterson's fondness for the metaphysical conceit. What all of the poems share, however, is a willingness to challenge and exceed what might be thought of as conventional subject matter for the sonnet. 'Mercies' is an elegiac love sonnet for a dog 'put down' that uses its premature turning in line 7 to intensify its meditation on love and loss:

> So I turned her face to mine,
> and seeing only love there—which, for all
> the wolf in her, she knew as well as we did—
> she lay back down and let the needle enter. (43)

---

124. 'Leading Light', An Interview with Don Paterson by Nicholas Wroe, *Guardian*, 25 November 2006, p. 11.
125. Philip Larkin, *The Complete Poems*, ed. Burnett, p. 81.
126. Don Paterson, *40 Sonnets* (London: Faber, 2015), p. 3.

There is a strategic turning, too, in 'The Roundabout', which turns back to Rilke and the verities of being in its recognition of the need to keep going: 'there was nothing in the world to prove our turning | but our light heads, and the wind's lung' (44). Although Paterson distances himself from 'spiritual writing' that communicates 'belief', his own wondering sonnets have an orison-like quality (emphatically so in 'Funeral Prayer'), and what they frequently utter is the miraculousness of utterance itself.

Among Paterson's *101 Sonnets from Shakespeare to Heaney* is the sonnet titled 'Prayer' by another poet born in Scotland, Carol Ann Duffy. Very little critical attention has been given to Duffy's Celtic connections, but memories of leaving Glasgow in her childhood, and recollections of an Irish Catholic upbringing and education, undoubtedly shape the strong preoccupation in her poetry with ideas of displacement. There is a pervasive longing for both physical and spiritual connectedness in her work, and in many ways the sonnet has proved an amenable form for her sorrowful reflections on distance, separation, and loneliness. At a fundamental level, the recitation of poetry becomes a way of filling a metaphysical emptiness, but the sonnet, with its well-established history as a devotional form, lends itself especially well to her needs: 'Poetry and prayer are very similar. I write quite a lot of sonnets and I think of them almost as prayers: short and memorable, something you can recite.'[127]

Unlike George Herbert's 'Prayer', however, Duffy's 'Prayer' is written in spite of itself: a prayer that emerges unexpectedly from the inability to pray and from a declared condition of faithlessness. What makes the poem unusual is that prayer arises without intercession, in the usual sense of being addressed to someone (God, Our Lady, the Saints) or offered up on behalf of someone (friends, loved ones, those in need). Even so, the prayer-like sounds that can be heard in trees, in trains, in piano music, in the calling of a child's name, and in the shipping forecast have a prayer-like function in providing moments of uplift, revelation, comfort, and consolation:

> Some days, although we cannot pray, a prayer
> utters itself. So, a woman will lift
> her head from the sieve of her hands and stare
> at the minims sung by a tree, a sudden gift.
>
> Some nights, although we are faithless, the truth
> enters our hearts, that small familiar pain;

---

127. Carol Ann Duffy, Poetry Archive <http://www.poetryarchive.org>.

THE MODERN SONNET   371

> then a man will stand stock-still, hearing his youth
> in the distant Latin chanting of a train.
>
> Pray for us now. Grade 1 piano scales
> console the lodger looking out across
> a Midlands town. Then dusk, and someone calls
> a child's name as though they named their loss.
>
> Darkness outside. Inside, the radio's prayer—
> Rockall. Malin. Dogger. Finisterre.

The sonnet form provides a space for litany and ritual in its quatrains and in its closing couplet, even though the parallel structure of 'Some days... a woman', 'Some nights... a man' speaks of arbitrariness rather than coherent destiny. The emphatic turn seems like an assertion of belief, contradicting the octave, but while it recognizes the common plight of 'us' all, it has a strangely disconnected presence, more a fragment or an echo of prayer than the thing itself. The form is Shakespearean, but the repetition of a rhyme on the word 'prayer', picking up the opening *a* rhyme, gives it an additional intensity. This isn't the first sonnet to hear a prayer for navigation in the shipping forecast (Seamus Heaney's 'Glanmore Sonnets' tune in to 'Dogger, Rockall, Malin, Irish Sea'), but as Paterson points out, it does have a special poignancy, not least because of its meditation on final things in 'Finisterre'.[128]

In *Feminine Gospels* (2002), Duffy extends the project (begun in *The World's Wife* in 1999) of giving prominence to women's experience by rewriting and revising those myths and stories in which it has generally been obscured or ignored.[129] New myths are presented, sometimes in the form of tall tales masquerading as gospel truth, and sometimes as striking versions or subversions of biblical and classical narratives. 'Wish' draws on female resurrection myths, including the story of the Corpse Bride and the classical legend of Proserpine, as well as the gospels. The opening is abrupt and startling:

> But what if, in the clammy soil, her limbs
> grew warmer, shifted, stirred, kicked off
> the covering of earth, the drowsing corms,
> the sly worms...   (63)

An inverted sonnet, the sestet dispels what initially looks like a Gothic indulgence in the macabre and closes with a positive longing for the woman

---

128. Don Paterson (ed.), *101 Sonnets from Shakespeare to Heaney* (London: Faber, 1999), p. 120.
129. Carol Ann Duffy, *Feminine Gospels* (London: Picador, 2002). Page numbers are given in brackets in the text.

returned from the dead: 'I wish.' The octave pictures such a resurrection—'Her bare feet walk along the gravel path | between the graves'—before reverting to the stark subjunctive with which the sonnet began. The closing lines recall the gospel story (Matthew 28:8) of how the women attending Christ's burial rolled away the stone from his tomb, and finding it empty, ran in fear and joy. At the same time, they testify to the continuing struggle for women's freedom: 'If I can only push open this heavy door | she'll be standing there in the sun, dirty, tired, | wondering why do I shout, why do I run.' The rhymes are cleverly disguised, sometimes working as chimes ('limbs'/'corms', 'woken'/'run'), but also planted in a series of internal rhymes ('corms'/'worms', 'sun'/'run').

'North-West', the sonnet that immediately follows 'Wish', elevates the ordinary stuff of local lives in 'hidden streets' and 'rented rooms' to mythic status. The title is unspecific, but the references to 'Pier Head' and to a well-known song by the Beatles suggest that the city in question is Liverpool, and that the ferry in line 2 is crossing the Mersey. Already a legendary event in popular song, the Mersey ferry ride now takes on the semblance of an underworld crossing of the Styx:

> However it is we return to the water's edge
> where the ferry grieves down by the Pier Head,
> we do what we always did and get on board.
> The city drifts out of reach . . .   (64)

The sonnet is a lament for lost and unfulfilled lives, and for a city now dominated by tourism and the heritage industry. The rhyming couplets struggle towards co-ordination, with only 'wave' and 'grave' managing a full rhyme at the heart of the sonnet. The closing couplet is whimsical, ironic, and elegiac in its recall of the Beatles hit single from 1963, 'She Loves You': 'Above our heads the gulls cry *yeah yeah yeah*. | Frets of light on the river. Tearful air.'

The sonnets in *Rapture* (2005), including the title poem, represent a notable departure in Duffy's work, both celebrating a new-found connection in love and experimenting excitedly with the formal possibilities of rhyme and rhythm.[130] There is a greater flexibility than previously with line length and typography. 'Forest' is a rapturous celebration of the pains and pleasures of new love, its abundant syllables spilling over in four restless tercets and a couplet: 'Thorns on my breasts, rain in my mouth, loam on my bare feet,

---

130. Carol Ann Duffy, *Rapture* (London: Picador, 2005). Page numbers are given in brackets in the text.

rough | bark grazing my back, I moaned for them all...' The speaker of the title poem, 'Rapture', is both lover and beloved, whose 'thinking' connects with a long tradition of poetry and song, from Andrew Marvell ('To His Coy Mistress') to The Merseybeats ('I Think of You'):

> Thought of by you all day, I think of you.
> The birds sing in the shelter of a tree.
> Above the prayer of rain, unacred blue,
> not paradise, goes nowhere endlessly.   (4)

If the image of sky recalls Larkin's 'High Windows' in its negation of paradise, it is only a passing resemblance. The Shakespearean form is honoured, despite a late turn, and (with an echo of Sonnet 29) the sullen earth is reconnected with heaven once again: 'Then love comes, like a sudden flight of birds | from earth to heaven.' In a poetry so habitually given to distance and detachment, there is a sudden pleasure in the prospect of hearts and minds united, and in the buoyant display of the sonnet reinvigorated as the most potent lyric expression of love: 'Huge skies connect us, joining here to there. | Desire and expression on the thinking air.'

Wendy Cope and Eleanor Brown

The subversion and re-writing of popular myths and stories in Duffy's poetry has an appealing comic dimension, but her sonnets have tended to be elegiac and devotional. Other women writers, however, have seen the comic potential in appropriating a poetic form long associated with male prowess and seductive eloquence. Wendy Cope is adept in exploiting the narrative and dramatic qualities of the sonnet form in the interests of comedy, playfully adjusting voice and tone in ways that humorously undermine the conventions of the love lyric. Using the persona of the hapless contemporary poet, Jake Strugnell, she parodies some well-known sonnets, including the love sonnet by Sir Philip Sidney popularly known as 'The Bargain'. 'Strugnell's Bargain' opens with Sidney's eloquent declaration of love, but rapidly deflates the noble sentiments of the original:

> My true love hath my heart and I have hers—
> We swapped last Tuesday and we felt elated—
> But now, whenever one of us refers
> To 'my heart' things get rather complicated.
> Just now, when she complained 'My heart is racing',

'You mean my heart is racing,' I replied.
'That's what I said.' 'You mean the heart replacing
Your heart, my love.' 'Oh piss off, Jake!' she cried.
I ask you, do you think Sir Philip Sidney
Got spoken to like that? And I suspect
If I threw in my liver and a kidney,
She'd still address me with as scant respect.
Therefore do I revoke my opening line:
My love can keep her heart and I'll have mine.[131]

The structure of the sonnet is used here in a manner similar to the telling of a joke, with a narrative proposition, a complicating development, and a punchline. The amatory ideals of intimate exchange and unity collapse in a farcical literal-mindedness, but the comedy owes much to the manipulation of rhythm and rhyme. The fluency of the opening line is immediately undercut by the deadening slackness of 'We swapped last Tuesday' and the awkward rhyme of 'elated' and 'complicated'. The quatrains are used resourcefully for dialogue, with Jake's dismissal appropriately coinciding with the close of the octave. Although the rhyme of 'Sidney' and 'kidney' first appears in 'A Cooking Egg' by T. S. Eliot, it retains its novelty and surprise, with the bathos here arising from the unromantic appreciation of the heart as just another bodily organ.[132] Cope relishes the opportunity to seal the sonnet with a snappy couplet, exploiting precisely those qualities of epigrammatic neatness and brisk denouement that other writers have avoided.

'Faint Praise' extends Cope's comic appropriation of the sonnet form by having her speaker address a male companion with a heavy measure of sarcasm that blatantly undermines the traditional associations of the sonnet with worship and extravagant admiration.

Size isn't everything. It's what you do
That matters, darling, and you do quite well
In some respects. Credit where credit's due—
You work, you're literate, you rarely smell.
Small men can be aggressive, people say,
But you are often genial and kind,
As long as you can have things all your way

---

131. 'Strugnell's Bargain' was printed as a Headland 'Poetry Live' Card by Headland Publications in 1987 and reprinted in *Unauthorized Versions: Poems and their Parodies*, ed. Kenneth Baker (London: Faber, 1990), p. 325.
132. T. S. Eliot, *The Complete Poems and Plays 1909–1962* (London: Faber, 2002), p. 36.

And I comply, and do not speak my mind.
You look all right. I've never been disgusted
By paunchiness. Who wants some skinny youth?
My friends have warned me that you can't be trusted
But I protest I've heard you tell the truth.
Nobody's perfect. Now and then, my pet,
You're almost human. You could make it yet.[133]

The sonnet makes compelling use of the rhetorical device known as asteism or back-handed compliment. Cope excels in the art of the comic put-down with a skilfully modulated speech that conceals contempt beneath genteel politeness. Although the sonnet carefully observes the Shakespearean quatrain and couplet divisions, it creates a lively momentum through a relaxed colloquial voice and frequent stops and starts (six lines have a strong caesura or mid-line break). The comedy derives, to a large extent, from the playful use of line arrangement, especially the element of surprise that accompanies line endings, as with the deflationary effect of the line break between lines 2 and 3: 'you do quite well | In some respects.' Once again, the closing couplet aims for comic effect through an obvious clinching rhyme, though what makes this such a striking sonnet is its sustained reversal of roles, with the male partner being the unenviable recipient of casual condescension and an ironized use of familiar endearments like 'darling' and 'my pet'.

'The Sitter' is a memorable instance of comic ekphrasis, drawing on a long tradition of poems about paintings, including Rossetti's arcane Pre-Raphaelite picture sonnets, and subtly subverting the tradition by allowing the uncomfortable sitter in the painting to speak. The subject, a nude figure in a painting by the Bloomsbury artist, Vanessa Bell, speaks her mind in a resentful but ultimately triumphant monologue:

Depressed and disagreeable and fat—
That's how she saw me. It was all she saw.
Around her, yes, I may have looked like that.
She hardly spoke, she thought I was a bore.
Beneath her gaze I couldn't help but slouch.
She made me feel ashamed. My face went red.
I'd rather have been posing on a couch
For some old rake who wanted me in bed.
Some people made me smile, they made me shine,
They made me beautiful. But they're all gone,

133. Wendy Cope, *Two Cures for Love: Selected Poems 1979–2006* (London: Faber, 2008), p. 33.

> Those friends, the way they saw this face of mine,
> And her contempt for me is what lives on.
> Admired, well-bred, artistic Mrs Bell,
> I hope you're looking hideous in Hell.[134]

What works especially well here is the way in which the vocabulary and the rhythms of everyday speech are easefully adapted to the four quatrains and the closing couplet of the Shakespearean sonnet. The syntax and the rhymes have a plaintive simplicity that gathers force and finds a satisfying outlet in the rhyming couplet, with its faux polite compliment and its forthright alliterative insult.

The comic potential of the sonnet is given free rein in Eleanor Brown's sparkling sequence, 'Fifty Sonnets', in her début collection, *Maiden Speech* (1996). By turns elated and dejected, the sonnets constitute a 'dissection' of modern love reminiscent of Meredith's sequence, but without its tragic consequences. While confessing her own vulnerability, Brown's speaker reveals a saving toughness and resilience, as well as an abundance of wit and sarcasm. The sonnets draw on both Petrarchan and Shakespearean models, frequently combining them. Conversational and engaging throughout, they are quick to observe ironic parallels and contrasts between their own amatory exploits and those of illustrious literary predecessors. The red dress in Sonnet 3 prompts an allusion to *La Vita Nuova*, but there is no doubt about which of the lovers takes the initiative:

> When Dante first saw Beatrice, she wore
> a red dress—probably not much like mine.
> Allowing, though, for accident (design,
> and taste, and length, and Lycra), what he saw
> was more or less what you saw on that night
> when I decided you were mine. My dress
> was red in its intent and—more or less—
> red in its consequence. And I was right
> to wear it, and play 'queen' with those poor boys
> who didn't know quite what was going on,
> and deferentially provided noise
> of admiration and desire. These gone,
> certain of these, and certain of your bed,
> we left; and the rest is taken as read.[135]

---

134. Cope, *Two Cures for Love*, p. 5.
135. Eleanor Brown, *Maiden Speech* (Newcastle upon Tyne: Bloodaxe, 1996), p. 20. Page numbers for other poems in the collection are given in brackets in the text.

Rhyme, rhythm, and syntax, including the enjambment and use of parenthesis, make the speaker's declaration of intent seem casual but forthright. The assertion of 'When I decided you were mine' gains force from the preceding rhyme of 'mine' and 'design'. The sestet closes with a further assertion, 'And I was right', while the octave moves assuredly above 'those poor boys' towards certainty. The mid-line pause after 'we left' is so strongly marked that the punning remainder of the line seems self-consciously superfluous.

Surprising and unpredictable, Brown's sonnets explore a failed relationship with exhilarating pace and fluency. Sonnet XXXIII seems intent on rehearsing the familiar motifs of Petrarchan and Renaissance love poetry, as if preparing to debunk them, only to reinstate their value and validity:

> Wings, flames, and arrows? Storms, and crowns, and chains?
> Sighs, tears and throbbings? Death? One perfect rose?
> All the fantastic trappings; all the old
> tried trusted true trivial trite but true
> accepted, true, rejected, true, much-sworn,
> forsworn, outworn, ill-fated, date things,
> that *must* some time have sounded real and fine—
> maybe it is a foolishness of mine
> not to say simply that my heart took wings;
> burned with desire; shattered before your scorn;
> would willingly have made a king of you,
> if not a god; saw life in red and gold...
> a foolishness to say that I suppose
> I underwent the normal aches and pains.   (35)

Here, the mirrored rhyme scheme (*abcdefggfedcba*) enacts the process of reversal, with the rhymes meeting in a couplet that grants some truth and reality to 'the fantastic trappings' of Petrarchan tradition. The sequence sustains its narrative and dramatic power, not least because it so carefully observes the methods of its predecessors while simultaneously subverting them.

Ken Edwards, Tony Lopez, and Robert Hampson

It would be wrong to assume that there has been no radical rejection of the sonnet among British avant-garde poets, comparable to that of William Carlos Williams and other modern American experimenters. Tom Pickard is guaranteed a *frisson* of excitement at live readings of his work when he delivers a short lyric beginning, 'Fuck the sonnet, I piss upon it | And those who seek to launch | A sinking reputation on it.' The comic rhymes expose what Pickard sees as the easy facility of the sonnet and its inflated prestige. His poem is just half a sonnet, provocatively titled 'To goad my friggin peers'.[136] This antipathy to the sonnet links Pickard's sinewy work to that of another iconoclastic northerner, Basil Bunting, who allegedly edited his school copy of Shakespeare's sonnets, 'cutting out the inessential bits, straightening the syntax and so on to reveal the essence of the poems'. According to Richard Caddel, Bunting repeated the exercise in the late 1920s for the benefit of Dorothy Pound.[137]

Even among those experimental poets fiercely opposed to conventional lyric techniques, the sonnet has a strangely compelling attraction. In seeking to push the sonnet to breaking point, contemporary British poets in the past two decades have discovered how to 'make it new' through modernist and postmodernist techniques of fracture, dissonance, and collage. Sternly opposed to organicist ideas of the sonnet taking shape in the heat of inspiration and achieving formal unity, those poets associated with *The Reality Street Book of Sonnets* (2008) tend to demystify the form, simply taking fourteen lines as a convenient starting point or framework for an assemblage of ideas. This proceduralist approach is often self-consciously playful or conducted in the spirit of a game, while carrying with it some ghostly semblance of earlier sonnets and sonnet sequences through echo and allusion. The lyric 'I' is displaced or subordinated within the overarching project of construction, while the lyric expectations associated with the staple iambic pentameter line are consistently undermined by discordant rhythmic variations. Ken Edwards has produced a book of ninety-eight sonnets titled *eight + six* (2003), in which he experiments wildly with typography (layout, spacing, and line length), as well as with language and voice.[138] The opening sonnet, 'Darkly Slow', is reminiscent of Berryman in its eccentric flouting of grammar, its repeated use of the ampersand, and its dark psychological subtext, but Edwards has his own special fondness for English pub talk:

---

136. Tom Pickard, *Winter Migrants* (Manchester: Carcanet, 2016), p. 62.
137. Basil Bunting, 'Shakespeare's Sonnets Edited', *Sharp Study and Long Toil*, Basil Bunting Special Issue, *Durham University Journal*, ed. Richard Caddel (1995), pp. 48–52. Helen Vendler, following Massimo Bacigalupo's account of Bunting's apprenticeship in *Pound in Rapallo*, claims that it was Ezra Pound who instructed the Northumbrian poet to 'go through Shakespeare's Sonnets correcting the inversions, and removing all the "superfluous words"'. See *The Art of Shakespeare's Sonnets* (Cambridge, MA: Harvard University Press, 1997), pp. 8–10.
138. Ken Edwards, *eight + six* (London: Reality Street, 2003). Page numbers are given in brackets in the text.

Bring back the persons! I
Ups & says
     they are bipolar & splendid
The jogger in the park, the murderer in the dark
They're so lonely, they speculate, give em something to do
The imaginary persons right here
Wherever that may be, beloved, awed
And in a cloud (a crowd)
       he she & you
Catching the eye ordering a round for the unknowables

Bring em all back, I don't want to see them go
One's at a university in the snow
Another on a beach, one praying for the souls in woe
Oh sad poet please be on your toes
The boat casts off, the buddleia grows
And what's behind the moment's horizon no-one knows. (9)

The sonnets are made to swallow a mass of unedifying material from the world of corporate finance and business management, from new information technologies, and from bleak despoliated landscapes. Against the stultifying influence of contemporary public discourse, the vitality and playfulness of the sonnets are liberating. Like the coteries of poets that Edwards imagines, his sonnets are 'variously and severally assembled', with the same title sometimes being applied to six or seven sonnets. 'Many to Many: Big Story' runs to 137 words in two prose-like sections of eight and six lines, whereas 'His Last Gasp (2)' is a minimalist construction of just twenty-one words:

          but isn't
    matter
      nowhere
  Bright

      know

              the air
   Which isn't
         person
   know   Oh air
       adventure given
  To
    Want is   to
      illuminate

A sonnet of this kind invites a radically different reading experience from what we might expect of a Shakespeare sonnet. The spatial arrangement suggests omission or concealment and at the same time encourages visual and phonetic connections. The near-repetition of 'know...the air' in 'know...Oh air' seems to emerge from 'nowhere'. 'Bright' anticipates 'illuminate' in a poem that playfully foregrounds the reader's 'adventure' with words (61).

Compared with the sonnets in *eight + six*, those in *False Memory* by Tony Lopez are densely compacted (110 unbroken and largely unrhymed quatorzains), but they share a common poetic outlook. Like Edwards, Lopez is sensitively attuned to the white noise of contemporary civilization, and to the continuous bombardment of the ear by discordant language uses, especially public announcement systems, instruction manuals, tabloid newspaper articles, advertising rhetoric, and scientific reports. A single line will sometimes appear as an arbitrary but striking reminder of the multiple discourses of everyday life, including the railway station announcement that manages to be both geographically specific and ubiquitous: 'Running seven minutes late out of Berwick-upon-Tweed.'[139] Amidst this welter of discursive practices, literature sometimes appears as just one more rhetorical performance, and fragments of both classical and modern texts co-exist with the spawning clichés of business and bureaucracy: 'no-risk enrolment', 'enclosed renewal-notice', 'audit trails', 'non-core assets', and 'pump-priming write-offs' (2, 8, 24, 39, 46). The pastoral terrain of earlier poetry functions as a distant memory, or glimmers briefly in the vestiges of unspoiled nature amidst a landscape of business parks and nuclear waste processors. A characteristic feature of *False Memory* is its habitual use of sudden and bewildering shifts in register, sometimes mid-line, creating what Lopez terms 'choreographed collisions'[140] of different kinds of language:

> When did the blue skies start to gather clouds?
> How long have we poor shepherds lived and dreamed
> Within these shady incremental pay-scales?   (30)

These linguistic collisions sometimes occur abruptly or (as happens here) they come about through a subtle slippage from one idiom to another. The jargon of 'blue-sky thinking' prompts metaphorical clouds, which lead in turn to the slippage from 'shade' to 'shady'. If, at times, the 'officialese' is oppressive,

---

139. Tony Lopez, *False Memory* (Bristol: Shearsman Books, 2012), p. 8. Page numbers are given in brackets in the text.
140. Lopez, *False Memory*, p. x.

there is a redeeming comic irony that exposes the deep cultural divisions in contemporary society and points to the likely sources of alienation.

In his perceptive introduction to *False Memory*, Robert Hampson elucidates the structural patterns in the book, noting how recurring motifs within the eleven sections enable the poems to 'speak to each other'. He also helpfully clarifies the linguistic processes by which the poems are able to appear simultaneously coherent and discontinuous: 'They are coherent on the levels of syntax and punctuation, but semantically discontinuous.' An impersonal instruction will modulate mysteriously into a more intimate, personal idiom, though one very likely drawn from literature or myth, and then re-emerge with a teasing ambivalence:

> This application form should be accompanied
> By voice-mail and personal calls. Fair Athena,
> It's easier if we don't see one another
> And fold back separate pages.   (63)

Hampson notes, as well, how often the poems not only cite but re-contextualize literary fragments, and how they take on a positive function by implicating readers in 'a tradition of engagement and re-interpretation'.[141] The closing sonnet seems to end, like all the others, with utter inconsequence, though it does comically invite dissent from the reader: 'Tick if you | Would prefer not to receive this material.' It opens, however, with a disconcerting image of mist drifting over the tideways of the Thames, 'the pool of London', gently relieved by a comic misremembering of Philip Larkin's memorable journey to London in 'The Whitsun Weddings': 'An uncle running up to bowl | Someone sampling smut.' The 'sampling' here fits comfortably into the cultural context suggested by the preceding line: 'Through a headset' (110). False memory takes many forms, but it brings with it sustaining flashes of recognition.

Robert Hampson's own innovative sonnets are a lively and entertaining 'sampling' of the diverse linguistic uses and cultural practices that inform and define contemporary society, briskly mixing literary and artistic allusions with the idiom of the free market and corporate enterprise. His sequence of fourteen sonnets, 'Reworked Disasters or: Next checking out the Chapmans' Goyas', cleverly combines the sublimity of John Keats's sonnet, 'On First Looking into Chapman's Homer' with the grotesquerie of the controversial art works produced by the Chapman brothers, Jake and Dinos. The title alludes to Francisco Goya's series of etchings, *The Disasters of War*, which

---

141. Robert Hampson, Introduction to *False Memory*, pp. xiii, xv.

the Chapman brothers reworked into a series of three-dimensional plastic models, *Great Deeds against the Dead* in 1994, and a life-size sculpture depicting torture and disfigurement in 1997. In this respect, Hampson's sequence takes as its main 'resources' two art works that are themselves indebted to prominent literary and artistic sources. 'Reworked Disasters' alludes to the re-working of old mines in England's industrial past, while commenting in a comic, self-deprecating way on its own artistic aspirations. Each of the fourteen sonnets takes as a heading, or as a starting point, a phrase from lines 1–5 and 13–14 of Keats's Chapman sonnet. While presenting a startling collage of materials, including quotations from the songs of Elkie Brooks and the investigative journalism of Diana Washington Valdez, the sonnets have a serious political focus on global warfare, imperialism, and torture. The opening sonnet, 'much have I travelled', might initially conjure up images of hiking and mountain climbing—'the surface is rugged | limitless clouds above | limitless ranges of hills'—but it takes us quickly 'into the killing zone'.[142] In keeping with the sonnets by Lopez in *False Memory*, Hampson's sonnets are linguistically discontinuous, but they are even more radically experimental in dispensing with punctuation altogether and noticeably veering away from the decasyllabic line. Nevertheless there are vestiges of coherence in the way that the sonnets speak with each other through a series of allusions to Homer's *Odyssey* (as a foundational epic text of warfare). Sonnet 9, 'oft of one wide expanse', mixes discourses from literature, literary theory, finance, corporate law, and waste disposal:

> junks all the issues
> in their holdings
> ghost ships in harbour
> like so much dirty laundry
> asbestos & toxic metals
> articulate the space
> a mode of reading
> with regard to ownership
> opens up markets
> sets a deadline for institutions
> law & disclosure
> updates & distracted
> with off-shore accountants
> about to go global

---

142. Robert Hampson, 'Reworked Disasters or: Next checking out the Chapmans' Goyas', *The Reality Street Book of Sonnets*, ed. Jeff Hilson (London: Reality Street, 2008), p. 158.

In the absence of punctuation, the connections between and across the individual lines are tenuous, depending largely on the opportune placing of a preposition or the convenient addition of a verb to a noun phrase. Even so, the sonnet ironically links its title to contemporary globalization and playfully invites its readers to 'articulate the space' with 'a mode of reading' suitably and creatively engaged with the hermeneutic challenges it presents.[143]

Andrew Motion and Alice Oswald

In its more conventional lyric mode, the sonnet has had immense popularity in contemporary British poetry as a form that still enables intense concentration on the perennial subject matter of love, death, nature, war, and religious belief. Changing attitudes to time-honoured themes continue to prompt new and striking variations in the way the sonnet is handled. Among those poets who have continued to use the sonnet in its traditional lyric mode, while also renovating and reinvigorating the form, Andrew Motion and Alice Oswald are deserving of special attention, one finding new possibilities in the sonnet some twenty-five years after the publication of his first book of poems, and the other giving the sonnet imposing prominence in her first published collection.

Andrew Motion, whose elegies in *The Pleasure Steamers* (1978) are among the most moving and candidly confessional in post-war British poetry, has sought over the course of his writing career to extend and revitalize traditional lyric modes. In *Public Property* (2002) and *The Cinder Path* (2009), he turns to the sonnet as the instrument of elegy, drawing deeply on the lyric influence of poets from John Keats to Robert Frost, but also adventurously shaping the sonnet form by repeatedly playing off the resources of actual speech against the formal requirements of rhyme, rhythm, metre, and line length. One of his notable achievements has been the refinement of the long conversational sentence, so that the sonnet recovers and reasserts one of its primary functions as a speech act, while acting upon the reader or listener with as little apparent artifice or design as possible. 'In Memory of Mervyn Dalley', a sequence of eight sonnets, opens with a recollection of

---

143. Sonnet 9 is printed here with the permission of Robert Hampson.

Auden's 1939 elegy 'In Memory of W. B. Yeats', but only to set itself apart as a rather different, low-keyed poem of mourning:

> I was going to quote whoever it was said
> *It was your last afternoon as yourself.*
> But in truth that afternoon came weeks ago.

The sonnet sequence modestly avoids the large-scale public announcement of death that Auden strives for in his elegy, while nevertheless registering the fact that even the most seemingly private sentiments in poetry become public property. The opening sonnet addresses its subject in an intimate conversational style, moving from what looks like a premature turn in line 3 ('But in truth...') to the actual turn marked by the phrase 'years back' in line 9, steadily gathering momentum in a twelve-line sentence that carries us to the close. While acknowledging the octave-sestet division, the sonnet erases quatrain and couplet divisions in favour of fluid colloquial speech with only sporadic or accidental rhymes. In its conversation with the dead man, the sonnet recalls the events of his 'last afternoon', noting how seemingly mundane things—'the plain page of a newspaper', 'an absolutely ordinary gin', and the 'bobbing-head routine' of a collar dove—'became the final proof of everything | you were and now could never be again— | relics which stayed as you were carried off.'[144]

The most striking innovation in the sequence for Mervyn Dalley is the use of the sonnet as a single-sentence speech act. The second sonnet combines a highly lyrical use of rhyme (especially in the couplets of the octave) with lines of varying length and metre (some of just two or three syllables). At the same time, the unbroken sentence retains the effect of actual speech: 'That bright day, | your last day, | a breeze | visible in no other trees | found within its reach | the copper beech | flourishing beneath your room...' (73). In a sonnet sequence that functions primarily as a compressed narrative of one man's life, including his work as a naval engineer during the Second World War, the copper beech has a powerful symbolic resonance, a version of the traditional motif of nature partaking in the process of mourning. In a strange moment of inversion, the gloom of old leaves clinging to the tree is dispersed and the man's 'last day' coincides with the waking of new leaves like eyes 'without the gift of sight'. If the image of leaves is briskly shaken

---

144. Andrew Motion, *Public Property* (London: Faber, 2002), p. 73.

out of its usual autumnal role into an emblem of blindness in the face of what the future holds, it also functions at the end of the sequence as an emblem of seeing in the aftermath of death. The tree becomes an anthropomorphic figure of nature's seeming involvement and ultimate unconcern: 'The copper beech swung round its million eyes | and met my gaze, and blinked, and looked away' (77).

In 'Harry Patch', five unrhymed sonnets tell the life story of the man who came to be known as 'The Last Fighting Tommy'. Each sonnet is a single sentence contributing to a small five-act drama (initially titled 'The Five Acts of Harry Patch') tracing Patch's long life from his childhood in Combe Down, near Bath, to his final days in a nursing home in Wells. At the time of his death in 2009, Patch was the oldest man in Europe and the last surviving soldier to have fought in the trenches of the First World War. Early in 2008, Motion (then Poet Laureate) was commissioned by the BBC to record a film interview with Patch and write a poem about his life. Some of the biographical details are extracted from Patch's memoir, written with Richard Van Emden, *The Last Fighting Tommy* (2007), including the memories of his father's garden and masonry business, his encounter with a dying soldier who asks to be shot, and his work on the building of the Wills Tower in Bristol after the war. The sonnet sequence skilfully arranges the details of Patch's life so that events in his early years anticipate the experience of war, while everything that follows the war seems unavoidably affected by it.

The opening sonnet recalls the schoolboy Patch wittily responding to a teacher's question about the definition of a curve: 'A curve is a straight line caught bending.' If this subtly hints at what happens to the line of the sonnet as it curves through the life of its subject, it also transports the reader imaginatively to the front line of battle. The picture of the young boy crawling along potato furrows 'on all fours, stomach hard to the ground' anticipates his service as a soldier in the trenches of Ypres. The child's crouched posture, hiding from his parents as he goes in search of apples, plums, and pears on his father's fruit trees, suddenly resembles that of the old man surviving for over a century: 'if only it were possible to stand upright | in so much clear light.' The flash in the 'bright eyes' of his mother and father at the start of the sequence is linked to the flash of a light coming on at the end. Wisely avoiding the risks of either an intrusive first-person narrative or an impersonal third-person account, the sonnet sequence repeats the intimate second-person address of 'In Memoriam Mervyn Dalley', sympathetically recreating Patch's life story through turns of speech he might have used: 'catch a packet... unless needs must... no puff in the lungs.'[145]

Sonnet V of 'Harry Patch' amply demonstrates Motion's expressed desire to use the unrhymed sonnet as the basis for 'a whole life poem'. What he sought was a form that would appear 'circuitously slowed down, like the mechanics of ancient memory, but also headlong as if driven by compulsions'.[146] Each line, freed from the strict requirements of rhyme and metre, spills over to eleven or twelve syllables, allowing for rumination while propelling the narrative forward: 'You grow a moustache, check the mirror, notice | you're forty years old, then next day shave it off, check the mirror again—and find you're seventy, but life is like that now...' (9).

The single sentence structure allows for rapid compression and seamless transitions from one time period to another. The present tense, persisting until the very end of the sonnet, initially suggests a scene from Patch's First World War service as a Lewis gunner. The 'nurses on night duty', introduced with a simple conjunction, appear to be part of the same scene (9). It is only with the detail of the linen cupboard and the switching on of a light that the sonnet shows the scene to be a nursing home, with the war being relived inside the old man's head, and the sudden flash alarmingly reminding him of gunfire and explosions. The blacked out window, ostensibly protecting Patch from painful memories, nevertheless recalls the Blackout of a later war and also hints at the final extinction of memory itself.

'London Plane', also in *The Cinder Path*, plays a further variation on the possibilities of sentence structure in the sonnet, with each of its fourteen lines being a separate sentence or isolated clause ending with a period. On the surface, the sonnet appears to be a strictly factual, unelaborated account of a tree in London having to be cut down: 'They felled the plane that broke the pavement slabs.' The matter-of-fact narrative recalls another poem in which a tree has fallen, 'As the Team's Head-Brass': 'The blizzard felled the elm whose crest | I sat in.'[147] Like Edward Thomas's meditation on loss and possible recovery, 'London Plane' astutely watches work going on and notes those events that might be cause for hope even while they hint at disappointment.

---

145. Andrew Motion, *The Cinder Path* (London: Faber, 2009), pp. 5, 8. Further page numbers are given in brackets in the text.
146. Andrew Motion, 'Harry Patch: A Century's Life Shaped by Four Months at War', *Daily Telegraph*, 8 March 2008.
147. Edward Thomas, *Selected Poems and Prose* (Harmondsworth: Penguin, 1981), p. 256.

When the tree is reduced to a stump, a wren sits on it 'once'. The sonnet closes ambivalently, with the wind fulfilling its poetic role as both creator and destroyer: 'All afternoon the street was strewn with bits. | That night the wind got up and blew it bare' (26).

If 'London Plane' tends towards the elegiac without explicitly articulating its sense of loss, then 'Raven', closely associated with the death of the poet's father in 2006, functions as a half-comic anticipatory elegy, recalling a boyhood conversation about the calls of birds. The sunlight pouring on to a blazing fire in the middle of a winter's day creates a ghostly scene in which 'flames look tissue or not there at all'. The father suddenly 'appears', just as the rhyme scheme, imperceptible at first, emerges after that word 'appears' to complete an octave that is neither Petrarchan nor Shakespearean: *abcdabcd*. The recollection of the father 'interrupting me again', a typically boyish complaint, takes on a darker tone as the later psychological motive for the poem being written at all. The correction in the closing line, 'The raven's cough? You mean the raven's croak', both affectionately restores the father's authority and symbolically invokes the shadow of old age and death (46).

Like Andrew Motion, Alice Oswald has been attracted by the lyric intensity of the sonnet, as well as its versatility and adaptability. In her hands, the sonnet functions as a form well disposed to solitary musings and imagined conversations. The nine sonnets in her first book of poems, *The Thing in the Gap-Stone Stile* (1996), are notable for the seemingly effortless way in which they both acknowledge and transform the traditional subject matter of the form, dealing variously with love, landscape, and spiritual devotion. The first sonnet in the collection is Shakespearean in its rhyme scheme and its exploration of temporal consciousness: 'When I sit up this late, breathing like so | into the growing soap-ball of my silence...'.[148] What makes the sonnet unusual is its apparent loss of heart and its struggle to voice emotions close to despair. Few poets since Meredith have used the sonnet so creatively for the exploration of desolate feeling, turning the form away from its customary association with artifice and extravagance in love towards emptiness and exhaustion. The sestet is subdued, but there is an evident need for the speaker to carry on talking, despite the protestations of having nothing to say, with the final quatrain allowing little room for breath until the word

---

148. Alice Oswald, *The Thing in the Gap-Stone Stile* (Oxford: Oxford University Press, 1996), p. 9.

'survive'. The closing couplet, unable to find any uplift, is distinguished mainly by its muted, monotone uncertainty:

> I chose to think of you but I can't say
> whether it's peace or makeshift that I live
> in this last zero of the millionth day
> which ends like this, just breathing to survive.
> And I don't know and so I haven't said
> whether it's you or nothing in my head.

The repeated 'whether' finds a creative outlet in the repeated 'weather' of 'Sea Sonnet', the first of three poems bearing this title. The artist's palette is clearly displayed in what initially looks like an oriental miniature, but the subtle use of the verb 'japans' both darkens and deepens the poem. As with Wallace Stevens, the boundaries between art and nature, mind and world, dissolve in a poetry of intense perception. At the same time, an ardent vocabulary of the soul and a careful apprehension of the sacredness of nature suggest connections with the metaphysical poetry of Henry Vaughan and Thomas Traherne:

> Green, grey and yellow, the sea and the weather
> instantiate each other and the spectrum
> turns in it like a perishable creature.
> The sea is old but the blue sea is sudden.
>
> The wind japans the surface. Like a flower,
> each point of contact biggens and is gone.
> And when it rains the senses fold in four.
> No sky, no sea—the whiteness is all one.
>
> So I have made a little moon-like hole
> with a thumbnail and through a blade of grass
> I watch the weather make the sea my soul,
> which is a space performed on by a space;
>
> and when it rains, the very integer
> and shape of water disappears in water.   (17)

The abstract nature of 'instantiate' and 'integer' in the second and second from last lines of the sonnet ought to signal that this is not in any obvious sense a topographical poem, but one in which philosophical categories of the real and the self are imaginatively explored and the demarcations between them gently erased. Even so, there is a child-like simplicity in 'biggens', as the wind stirs the water, and in the curious act of looking through a blade of grass.

The sonnet moves from a watchful awareness of the world's contingency and its changing appearances towards a revelation of the self as similarly contingent and protean. It seeks to understand the correspondence of world and self in space and time, with the repeated phrase 'and when it rains' enacting the process of knowledge. In the octave, the world asserts itself against the senses, while the sestet, with its clearly marked turn to the self, proposes a way of seeing and being in the world. The 'moon-like hole' both catches the crescent-like shape of the thumbnail's imprint and associates the perceiver with the moon's controlling power over the sea. The rhyme scheme is suitably fluid and circular (*abab abab cdcd aa*), so that the *-er* rhyme in 'weather' and 'flower' is picked up in 'water' in the closing couplet. The disappearance of the horizon, the merging of sky and sea, is mirrored in the dissolution of the self.

The second 'Sea Sonnet' develops the correspondence between seascape and mindscape by imagining the sea as 'made'. This time, while the sea is granted its own material force and substance, it is also seen to be coextensive with the fluid and mysterious processes of language and thought:

> The sea is made of ponds—a cairn of rain.
> It has an island flirting up and down
> Like a blue hat. A boat goes in between.

The unlikely pairing of sea and rock is enabled by the phonetic cohesion of 'cairn' and 'rain', but the tricks of language, as well as its exciting possibilities, are immediately exposed in the slippage from 'floating' to 'flirting', while the simile 'Like a blue hat' is striking for its strange dissimilitude rather than its exactness. The movement of the boat momentarily registers the navigation of the poem between its different spheres of existence, earth and water, language and thought, and its different points of perception. Like the imagined cairn, the sonnet is made through a process of accretion, structurally displayed in four loosely rhymed tercets and a couplet: *aaa bbb ccc ddd ee*. Language and thought resort to paradox and myth in seeking to embody the sea—'The sea crosses the sea, the sea has hooves'—or else find a happy suspension in ambivalence, as with the teasing conjoining of the physical and philosophical in the 'hypostases of holes' in which rain water disappears. With the boat's arrival on the island, a new perspective is established, from which the sea is sublimely itself, beyond any further simile: 'and then the boat arriving on the island | and nothing but the sea-like sea beyond' (18).

If Wallace Stevens hovers over the sea sonnets, then Theodore Roethke inspires the exuberantly sensuous and enchantingly mystical 'Prayer'. The simple declarative syntax elevated to ritual is reminiscent of Roethke's villanelle, 'The Waking', and so, too, is the deep sense of communion and kinship with elemental processes.

> Here I work in the hollow of God's hand
> with Time bent round into my reach. I touch
> the circle of the earth, I throw and catch
> the sun and moon by turns into my mind.
> I sense the length of it from end to end,
> I sway me gently in my flesh and each
> point of the process changes as I watch;
> the flowers come, the rain follows the wind.
>
> And all I ask is this—and you can see
> how far the soul, when it goes under flesh,
> is not a soul, is small and creaturish—
> that every day the sun comes silently
> to set my hands to work and that the moon
> turns and returns to meet me when it's done. (38)

There is a tightness and compactness to 'Prayer', initiated by the stirring alliterative music of the opening lines, by the modified Petrarchan rhyme scheme (*abbaabba cddcee*), and by the repeated motif of the sun and moon turning and returning. The sonnet's turn is from a cosmic sense of unity to a more modest reckoning of daily needs and duties, engineered by the parenthetical insertion of the sestet (reminiscent, once again, of the metaphysical poets), in which the soul is brought down to a manageable size. The extended syntax and the undemonstrative half rhyme of 'moon' and 'done' ensure that the sonnet ends gently and harmoniously, and that the prayer offered up is neither extravagant nor sentimental.

As Jahan Ramazani has wisely observed, 'the secular cast of modernity has made prayer one of the creations that the modern literary mind turns to and examines', and it might be added that the modern sonnet exhibits a peculiarly intense relationship with prayer in its tendency both to embrace it and refute it, to 'echo and invert it'.[149] Even in its most striking contemporary manifestations, the sonnet is well endowed with the rhetorical qualities often associated with prayer: its figurative richness, its ritualistic intensity, and its apostrophic and petitionary forms of address. Nevertheless, the sonnet firmly retains its own aesthetic priorities and its own formal deliberations, often

---

149. Jahan Ramazani, *Poetry and its Others: News, Prayer, Song, and the Dialogue of Genres* (Chicago and London: University of Chicago Press, 2014), p. 183.

invoking prayer in a spirit of metaphysical wonder and imaginative exploration rather than theological certitude.

To move from Andrew Motion's elegiac sonnets for the veteran soldier Harry Patch to Alice Oswald's prayerful meditations on the earth is to acknowledge, close-up, how poetry seems to occupy a zone between news and prayer, perhaps even interfusing them. The modern sonnet, especially, exhibits those intergeneric and dialogic qualities that Ramazani highlights in his study of poetry and 'its others', particularly in its relationships with journalism, prayer, and song. In the sonnets of Rupert Brooke and Wilfred Owen, W. H. Auden and Philip Larkin, Elizabeth Jennings and Kathleen Jamie, we can readily observe how poetry both responds to contemporary events in the world, sometimes resembling the discourse of 'the news', and also engages with the realm of the ineffable, sometimes assuming 'the ceremonial qualities' of prayer.[150] As we have seen, the sonnet is an intensely self-questioning artefact, continually alert to its own formal constraints and transgressions. If it declares its place in a long-evolving history of poetic form and takes its authority and sustenance from that, it also repeatedly demonstrates its own restless and inexhaustible inventiveness.

150. Ramazani, *Poetry and its Others*, p. 125.

Epilogue
The sonnet and its travels

If the sonnet is distinguished among poetic forms for its durability and longevity, it also has claims to being one of the most widely travelled. Its versatility and adaptability can be measured historically, through its extraordinary persistence among poetic forms, but also geographically, through the expansive terrain in which it has made itself at home. The focus of this book has been primarily on the sonnet in Britain, Ireland, and America, and on the sonnet written in English, but the form exists in many other places and many other languages. It has a venerable reputation throughout Europe, with highpoints of achievement and notable practitioners, including Lope de Vega (1562–1635) in Spain; Luís de Camões (1524–80) in Portugal; Pierre de Ronsard (1524–85) in France; Andreas Gryphius (1616–64) in Germany; and Maria Gustava Gyllenstierna (1672–1737) in Sweden. A roll call of modern practitioners of the sonnet would include Charles Baudelaire and Paul Verlaine, Rainer Maria Rilke and Rudolf Alexander Schröder, Eugenio Montale, Jean Cassou, and Pablo Neruda, to name but a few.

Throughout its history, the sonnet in English has asserted its claims to global vision, often provocatively embracing a world-wide perspective seemingly disproportionate to its size. Shakespeare memorably opened the sonnet to the enthralling prospect 'Of the wide world dreaming on things to come', and that imaginative vista reappears over and over again in the history of the sonnet, most notably in the poems of Keats, in the 'wide expanse' of Chapman's Homer and 'the wide world' confronting the solitary mind in the poignant self-elegy, 'When I have fears that I may cease to be'.[1] The appeal of the sonnet as a global form is given a playfully novel turn in a poem that has frequently been anthologized, though very likely for sentimental reasons: 'Letty's Globe' by Charles Tennyson Turner. The sonnet depicts a

---

1. John Keats, *Poetical Works*, ed. H. W. Garrod (Oxford: Oxford University Press, 1970), pp. 38, 366.

EPILOGUE: THE SONNET AND ITS TRAVELS

child coming to know her home and what lies beyond it through 'a coloured sphere | Of the wide earth':

> When Letty had scarce passed her third glad year,
> And her young artless words began to flow,
> One day we gave the child a coloured sphere
> Of the wide earth, that she might mark and know,
> By tint and outline, all its sea and land.
> She patted all the world; old Empires peeped
> Between her baby fingers; her soft hand
> Was welcome at all frontiers. How she leaped,
> And laughed and prattled in her world-wide bliss!
> But when we turned her sweet unlearned eye
> On our own isle, she raised a joyous cry,
> 'O yes! I see it, Letty's home is there!'
> And, while she hid all England with a kiss,
> Bright over Europe fell her golden hair.[2]

It is far too easy to dismiss the sonnet for what might look like collusion with Victorian imperialist ideology. As John Fuller notes, Letty's 'epiphanic but Aryan "golden hair" seems at once to bless and defy the frontier-conscious Europe of the early nineteenth century'.[3] There is nothing heavy-handed here; rather the 'soft hand' that 'patted all the world' and is 'welcome at all frontiers' traces the globe in innocent curiosity, just as the 'unlearned eye' is set against a knowledge of 'old Empires'. The function of the sonnet is both to acknowledge and to efface, for a brief moment of 'world-wide bliss', the boundaries of England, Europe, and Empire. It does so by stealthily traversing the boundaries of the sonnet form itself, first by running on over the first quatrain and ending syntactically with line 5, and then by allowing Letty's excited leaping to propel the poetry over the expected division between octave and sestet, delaying the turn until line 10. In a cunningly self-referential move, the turn coincides with the moment Letty turns to England, and 'turned' is given additional prominence through an internal rhyme with 'unlearned'. Syntactically, then, the sonnet is arranged in units of $5 + 4 + 3 + 2$ rather than $4 + 4 + 4 + 2$. Its curious rhyme scheme (*ababcdcdeffgeg*) sets up expectations of an English, rather than Petrarchan, sonnet, but the pattern is dissolved after the delayed turn and we are denied the full satisfaction of a rhyming couplet.

---

2. *The Oxford Book of Sonnets*, ed. John Fuller (Oxford: Oxford University Press, 2000), p. 165.
3. *The Oxford Book of Sonnets*, ed. Fuller, p. xxx.

Often the sonnet uses its structural divisions, not so much as an indication of articulated units of thought as imaginary thresholds that might transport us into new realms of thought and feeling. In this respect, the geographical terrain of the sonnet is consonant with the exploration of the mind itself and with the opening up of infinite expanses of knowledge. It is not surprising that a strongly spatial emphasis is given to the sonnet in the nineteenth century, when a greater ease of travel coincides with new vistas of artistic, as well as scientific, exploration. Baudelaire is thought to have composed his sonnet 'A Une Dame Créole' ('To a Creole Lady') on his way home to Paris from Ile Bourbon during a voyage on the Indian Ocean in 1841. Purportedly addressed to Mme Autard de Bragard, the poem is one of the earliest of *Les Fleurs du Mal* (published twenty years later), and it brings to the conventional love sonnet a strongly exotic and orientalist tinge:

> In scented countries by the sun caressed
> I've known, beneath a tent of purple boughs,
> And palmtrees shedding slumber as they drowse,
> A creole lady with a charm unguessed.

In the sestet, however, the sonnet ironically shifts its gaze back from colonial France and its seemingly infinite poetic possibilities to 'the land of glory | Along the Seine or Loire'. Here, the creole lady's role would be to 'ornament some mansion famed in story', though she would breed 'a thousand rhymes in poets' hearts'.[4] The image of poets tamed and subdued like slaves is in keeping with the hyperbolic figuring of love extending back to Petrarch and his contemporaries, but in the colonial politics of the 1840s it has a very real and troubling presence. Slavery in the French colonies would not be abolished for another seven years. For all their libertarian tendencies, Baudelaire's sonnets are sometimes uncomfortably complicit with the existing political regime.

The publication of *Les Fleurs du Mal* in nineteenth-century Paris is nevertheless one of the crucial moments in the travels of the sonnet. Writing to Armand Fraisse, a reviewer of the book, in February 1860, Baudelaire explains why the sonnet should be regarded seriously, and in doing so he provides one of the most succinct and compelling accounts of its special formal qualities, acknowledging both 'la beauté pythagorique' (its mathematical precision and numerical logic) and 'la beauté du metal et du mineral bien travaillés' (the malleability and adaptability of the form, akin to well-worked metal

---

4. Charles Baudelaire, *Poems of Baudelaire: Les Fleurs du Mal*, translated by Roy Campbell (London: The Harvill Press, 1954), p. 84. Campbell titles the poem 'To a Colonial Lady'.

and stone).[5] His letter constitutes one of the most incisive descriptions of the architectonics of the sonnet:

> What is then the imbecile (perhaps a well-known man) who deals so lightly with the Sonnet, and does not see its Pythagorean beauty? The idea comes out more intensely because its form is compressed; everything can fit into the Sonnet, buffoonery, gallantry, passion, dream, philosophic meditation. It has the beauty of well-worked metal or stone. Have you noticed that a sliver of sky, seen through a basement window, or between two chimneys, two rocks, through the entrance of an arcade, etc., gives a more profound idea of infinity than a wide panorama viewed from the top of a mountain?[6]

Baudelaire immediately grasps the paradox of unlimited scope within a tightly confined space, subtly intimating that the sonnet's intense compression allows a privileged vision of the world, a deeper awareness of infinity than more expansive forms permit. The point is made again by Théophile Gautier in his 'Notice' to the 1868 edition of *Les Fleurs du Mal*, in which he acknowledges how 'a mighty concept can move freely in these methodically organised fourteen lines'. Even so, Gautier has misgivings about the liberties that Baudelaire takes with the sonnet form, quoting against him his own critique of poets who allow themselves 'free-thinking sonnets, that is to say unorthodox and happily transgressing' the rules and regulations of rhyme. Gautier's campaign against irregular and illegitimate sonnets was in vain, but we owe to him the appealing nomenclature of *sonnets libertins*, a term that happily describes the vast majority of sonnets written since the end of the nineteenth century.[7]

Among the celebrated sonnets in *Les Fleurs du Mal*, 'Correspondences' pursues that 'profound idea of infinity' ('l'expansion des choses infinies') that Baudelaire claims the form makes possible, transporting us from the pleasures of the senses to the mysteries of the soul.[8] Baudelaire was unorthodox and transgressive in more obvious ways than Gautier suggests, of course, composing sonnets that flirted provocatively with the exotic, the macabre, and the grotesque. To Baudelaire must go the credit for having brazenly established a new set of standards for the love sonnet, displacing conventional nineteenth-century pieties in favour of a love in which 'teeth and talons are

---

5. Charles Baudelaire, *Correspondance 1: 1832–1860*, ed. Claude Pichois (Paris: Gallimard, 1973), pp. 674–7.
6. I am grateful to David Darbyshire for his help in translating Baudelaire's letters.
7. Théophile Gautier, 'Notice' to Charles Baudelaire, *Les Fleurs du Mal* (Paris: Calmann-Lévy, 1868), p. 43.
8. Charles Baudelaire, *Poems of Baudelaire: Les Fleurs du Mal*, p. 8.

the fashion' and in which the heart has become a place of 'ulcerated passion'.[9] At the same time, the depths of remorse, confession, and penitential suffering in Baudelaire's poems endeared him to modern British and American poets, among them T. S. Eliot and Robert Lowell. In his influential *Imitations* (1961), Lowell translated five sonnets by Baudelaire, including 'The Ruined Garden' and 'The Flawed Bell', along with other major achievements in the genre, such as Arthur Rimbaud's 'Eighteen Seventy' sonnet sequence and Paul Valéry's 'Helen'.[10] Lowell's encounter with the nineteenth-century French sonnet would be vitally important in stimulating his own obsessive use of the form and encouraging the exploration of intensely personal subject matter within a strictly circumscribed space.

Roy Campbell, one of the most influential modern translators of Baudelaire, was born in South Africa in 1901, where he founded the literary journal *Voorslag*, intended as a 'whiplash' on the South African colonial sensibility. Although his edition of the *Poems of Baudelaire: Les Fleurs du Mal* was not published until 1952, Campbell was profoundly influenced by the French poet, as he reveals in his Translator's Note: 'I have been reading Baudelaire since I was fifteen, carried him in my haversack through two wars, and loved him longer and more deeply than any other poet.' There are few better examples of the sonnet's modern internationalism than 'The Zebras' (1930), in which Campbell's desire to capture the beauty of the South African landscape combines with the passionate sensuousness of Baudelaire's love poems:

> From the dark woods that breathe of fallen showers,
> Harnessed with level rays in golden reins,
> The zebras draw the dawn across the plains
> Wading knee-deep among the scarlet flowers.
> The sunlight, zithering their flanks with fire,
> Flashes between the shadows as they pass
> Barred with electric tremors through the grass
> Like wind along the gold strings of a lyre.
> Into the flushed air snorting rosy plumes
> That smoulder round their feet in drifting fumes,
> With dove-like voices call the distant fillies,
> While round the herds the stallion wheels his flight,
> Engine of beauty volted with delight,
> To roll his mare among the trampled lilies.[11]

---

9. Baudelaire, *Poems of Baudelaire*, p. 45.
10. Robert Lowell, *Imitations* (New York: Farar, Straus, and Cudahy, 1961; London: Faber, 1962).
11. Roy Campbell, *The Collected Poems of Roy Campbell* (London: The Bodley Head, 1949; 1955), p. 30.

Campbell uses the sonnet form with a contrastive power and delicacy reminiscent of the French poet's handling of the form: the 'flanks with fire' and 'electric tremors' are derived from Baudelaire's sonnets on cats, and the vivid flower imagery is also characteristic of *Les Fleurs du Mal*. In other respects, though, Campbell is highly innovative in maximizing the compression of the form, employing a rhyme scheme with four couplets (*abbacddceefggf*), and exploiting every line phonetically and semantically. The unusual 'zithering' maintains the buzzing sound of 'zebras', while simultaneously suggesting (in the imagined plucking of strings) both the play of sunlight (previously figured in the equestrian image of 'golden reins') and the thrill of music (in 'the gold strings of a lyre'). The interplay of sunlight and shadows is likened to the 'barred' pattern of the zebra, while 'rosy plumes' vividly catches the colour and texture of the breath snorted from the animal's nostrils against the rising sun.

The rhyme scheme employed for 'The Zebras' is put to use in another well-known sonnet, 'The Serf', popularized through its inclusion in *The Oxford Book of Modern Verse*, edited by W. B. Yeats, in 1936. Like Yeats, Campbell was attracted to the autocratic, right-wing politics of the 1930s (he supported Franco in the Spanish Civil War), but at a national level he is apt to idealize the African labourer, much as Yeats romanticizes the Irish peasantry. Even so, 'The Serf' is surprisingly radical in its political vision, and formally effective in the way that it begins its turn after a strong mid-line caesura and then unwinds a single sinuous sentence that finds its satisfaction in the cumulative destruction of the closing line:

> But as the turf divides
> I see in the slow progress of his strides
> Over the toppled clods and falling flowers,
> The timeless, surly patience of the serf
> That moves the nearest to the naked earth
> And ploughs down palaces, and thrones, and towers.[12]

Campbell's achievement here is to reconnect the sonnet with its popular, democratic heritage, echoing Shakespeare and Shelley as he does so. At the same time, it might be argued that the very form of the sonnet, with its eloquent standard English, too easily contains and aestheticizes the already antiquated figure of 'the serf' whose heart is 'insult torn'. A later generation of poets writing back from the margins of Empire would seek a different formal articulation of that far cry from Africa.

12. Campbell, *The Collected Poems of Roy Campbell*, p. 30.

The opening of one of Allen Curnow's best-known poems initially appears to be such a cry—'Weeping for bones in Africa I turn | Our youth over like a dead bird in my hand'—but this elegiac sonnet issues from New Zealand. 'In Memoriam 2 / Lieutenant T. C. F. Ronalds' was written for Curnow's cousin, who was killed in April 1943 as the Eighth Allied Army moved into Enfidaville, near Tunis. As the speaker turns over his shared youth in an act of meditation, the sonnet itself turns prematurely, questioning its own motives, but nevertheless giving emphasis to its cry: 'And why should my report | Cry one more hero...?' Curnow avoids any unseemly glorification of the soldier's death and any suggestion that some corner of a foreign field is thereby enriched, but he does allow the sonnet to search for common ground between New Zealand and North Africa, even if this amounts to no more than the telling of tall tales: 'But O if your blood's tongued it must recite | South Island feats, those tall snow-country tales | Among incredulous Tunisian hills.'[13] As well as facilitating the imaginative transportation from the southern to the northern hemisphere, the sonnet meets the generic expectations of elegy in registering both the need for impassioned speech and its ultimate collapse in bewildered disbelief.

While Curnow was publishing his poems in Christchurch, the young Derek Walcott was coming to consciousness as a writer in Castries, St Lucia, seeking ways of representing his own Caribbean landscapes and experiences in the English literary models inherited from a colonial education. When fire ravaged Castries in 1948, the 18-year-old writer turned to the sonnet as a form that might capture the intensity of the occasion and memorialize its devastating effects on the physical structures of the city, as well as on the religious faith of its inhabitants. 'A City's Death by Fire' was instrumental in launching Walcott's poetic career (it appeared in his *25 Poems*, published in Trinidad the same year), and it signalled a serious determination to give St Lucia prominence in art and literature. The poem clearly shows the influence of 'A Refusal to Mourn the Death, by Fire, of a Child in London' by Dylan Thomas (1946), especially in its religious symbolism, its emphatic wordplay, and its air of proclamation. At the same time, it demonstrates a bold and original handling of the sonnet form:

> After that hot gospeller had levelled all but the churched sky,
> I wrote the tale by tallow of a city's death by fire;

---

13. Allen Curnow, *Early Days Yet: New and Collected Poems 1941–1997* (Manchester: Carcanet, 1997), p. 225.

Under a candle's eye, that smoked in tears, I
Wanted to tell, in more than wax, of faiths that were snapped like wire.[14]

The expansive lines and the alert first-person pronoun capture the urgency of a tale that must be told. The rhyme scheme begins conventionally enough (*abab*) but modulates into the unexpected (*cbcb*), and then (coinciding with a questioning sestet) into increasing uncertainty. As the poem seeks to rebuild belief after 'the baptism by fire', it strategically positions 'faiths' between 'fails' and 'breath', giving it the possibility of rhyming with either. The most prominent rhymes in the poem, however, are those that emanate from 'fire'.

In his 'Tales of the Islands', a sonnet sequence first published in the Caribbean literary journal *Bim* in 1958, Walcott experimented with a range of different voices and viewpoints that would capture the cultural melange of St Lucia and the surrounding islands. He wrote to Frank Collymore, the editor of the journal, that he had been trying to give the sonnets 'a certain factual, biographical plainness'. His aim was 'to dislocate the traditional idea of the sonnet as a fourteen line piece of music' and establish a prose-like 'dispassionate observation'.[15] As the title of the sequence implies, there is a loose narrative and anecdotal framework, with each of the ten sonnets presented as a 'chapter', sometimes carrying a brief epigraph. The sonnets are powerfully evocative vignettes of St Lucian people, places, and cultural traditions. *Chapter I / La rivière dorée* is set in Choiseul and contrasts the sensuous appeal of the river 'rushing cool | Through gorges of green cedars' with the spiritual transcendence of the 'stone cathedral'. *Chapter III / La belle quit fut* introduces us to the eccentric Miss Rossignol who 'lived in the lazaretto | For Roman Catholic crones', one of a number of local characters who inhabit the tales and fuel their mix of gossip and superstition (22–3).

The most striking innovation in Walcott's sonnets, though, is the introduction of different tones and dialects representative of the islands, including what is often described as 'the broken French' of St Lucian Creole or patois, the West Indian English used throughout the islands, and the standard English associated with a colonial education, as well as with the language of English literature. Walcott's revisions of the sonnets show him deftly bringing these different linguistic registers of class and culture into ironic alignment with each other. *Chapter VI* opens and closes with contrasting rituals—the

---

14. Derek Walcott, *Collected Poems* (New York: Farrar, Straus, and Giroux, 1986), p. 6.
15. J. Edward Chamberlin, *Come Back to Me my Language: Poetry and the West Indies* (Urbana and Chicago: University of Illinois Press, 1993), pp. 117–18.

music of steel bands and voodoo—both commonly associated with the Caribbean. The sonnet originally began:

> Garçon, that was a fête... I mean they had
> Free whisky and they had some fellows beating
> Steel from one of the bands in Trinidad...[16]

When 'Tales of the Islands' was published in Walcott's first major book of poems, *In a Green Night* (1962), the sixth sonnet was subtly revised to highlight the rhythms of local speech even more emphatically:

> Poopa, da' was a fête! I mean it had
> Free rum free whisky and some fellars beating
> Pan from one of them band in Trinidad... (24–5)

The Jamaican poet and critic John Figueroa claimed that this sonnet, in particular, marked 'the real beginnings of the use of dialect in West Indian poetry', and Ted Chamberlin in his landmark study of poetry and the West Indies claimed that 'Walcott's achievement here was to establish West Indian languages within an English literary tradition'.[17] It was as if Walcott had first to demonstrate his originality in the handling of a prestige European poetic form, before giving full vent to an independent poetic voice. Tellingly, the closing sonnet of the sequence, *Chapter X / 'Adieu foulard'*, is less a tale and more a prayerful meditation, full of watching and self-conscious reflections on the art of writing, as the speaker travels by air to Barbados. It is also a love sonnet for St Lucia, and Walcott would once again give it prominence in his work by incorporating it into the closing lines of Part Three of his ambitious verse autobiography, *Another Life* (1973): 'I watched the island narrowing, the fine | writing of foam around the precipices, then | the roads as small and casual as twine' (257). Often, in this way, sonnets provide the impulse for new works of a different scope and magnitude. They travel into new imaginative formations.

There is perhaps no better example of the sonnet's travels, in both international and inter-generic terms, than Vikram Seth's verse novel in sonnets, *The Golden Gate* (1986). Here, an Indian novelist and poet fastens enthusiastically upon the sonnet form devised by Alexander Pushkin for *Eugene Onegin* (1833), using the Russian–English translation provided by a British

---

16. Chamberlin, *Come Back to Me my Language*, p. 118.
17. Bruce King, *Derek Walcott: A Caribbean Life* (Oxford: Oxford University Press, 2000), p. 183. Chamberlin, *Come Back to Me my Language*, p. 119.

diplomat, Sir Charles Johnston, in 1977. Seth arranges his San Francisco comedy of manners in thirteen books, comprising a total of 590 sonnets in iambic tetrameter, rhyming *AbAbCCddEffEgg* (where the capital letters stand for feminine rhymes), and he extends the form to the preliminary Acknowledgements, Dedication, and Contents, as well as to his closing note About the Author. The combination of a brisk metre and an intricate rhyme scheme calls for great agility, especially when extended over the thirteen books of Seth's experimental novel. 'Pushkin in Silicon Valley', as Marjorie Perloff dubbed it, follows the fortunes of a young computer scientist, John Brown, and his Bay area friends in what is primarily a light-hearted, comic mode. At times, however, the mood darkens and individual sonnets seem uncertainly positioned between comic satire and elegy. In 13.11, for instance, John arrives at the hospital where his partner, Jan, is in a coma, and he strives 'To induce the starched and startled nurses | With incoherent tears and curses' to let him in. He is told that he will have to ask permission from their supervisor: '"She'll be down soon," they sighed and fled. | She came. But Jan by then was dead.' The difficulty here is that repeated rhyming couplets impel the sonnet towards comedy, while the brisk tetrameter verse doesn't allow much room for tonal variation. Where these sonnets do succeed is in capturing, in brief impressionist glimpses, both the cityscape of San Francisco ('the city's glittering grid. The Transamerica Pyramid') and the magnificence of the Pacific coastline ('With wharves and cypresses and pines').[18]

Versions, imitations, and translations ensure that the sonnet continues to travel widely. It seems fitting to end with an elegiac sonnet in which a contemporary Irish poet looks back to Petrarch, to the closing sonnet of the *Rime Sparse*. This is 'Exequy *(from the Italian of Petrarch)*' by Derek Mahon:

> The eyes of which I spoke so warmly once,
> the face and figure, shoulders, hands and knees
> that once deranged my rational faculties
> and made me different from the usual bunch;
> the quick inviting smile and generous breast,
> the streaming hair with its angelic glow
> that seemed to make a paradise below,
> are now a whisper of insentient dust.
> Yet I live on, in grief and self-disdain,
> bereft of the light I loved so earnestly,
> as if on a lost ship in a storm at sea.

18. Vikram Seth, *The Golden Gate* (London: Faber, 1986), pp. 286, 281, 257.

> Now there will be no more love poetry:
> the vital flow has dried up in the vein
> and the strings whimper in a minor key.[19]

Petrarch's sonnet has been translated and imitated many times, but rarely with such haunting gravity. Strictly speaking, what Mahon has written here is an adaptation, and it appears in an aptly titled collection of such poems, *Echo's Grove* (2013). In his foreword to the book, Mahon candidly confides that he has 'taken many liberties, in the hope that the results will read *almost* like original poems in English, while allowing their sources to remain audible'. Petrarch's original is often regarded as a sonnet of recantation. It mourns the loss of wasted time and addresses its regrets to God, the King of Heaven ('Re del Cielo'). There is none of this in Mahon's subdued reflections, which register a grievous loss—a loss of light equated here with the inspiration so vital to poetry. Petrarch's rhymes (*abba abba cdc dcd*) are subtly amended to *abbacddc efffef*, but the sonnet retains a strong turn and a clear sense of division between its closing tercets. It also holds on to the familiar Petrarchan navigation conceit, though significantly the speaker in the original longs to die in peace and in port ('mora in pace et in porto'), while Mahon's speaker lives on, as if still lost at sea. With a final twist that signals his sonnet's ultimate concern with the lifeblood of poetry itself, Mahon hears an echo in 'et se la stanza | fu vana' ('if my stay has been in vain') and writes it down as 'vein'. The whimpering strings in the final line are entirely his own. Mahon's 'Exequy' is a startling invention of farewell. In the moment of carrying out its funeral rites, it shimmers with the possibility of renewal. Even as it turns from love poetry to elegy in a plaintive minor key, it speaks eloquently of the persistence and durability of the sonnet over centuries. In its subtle adaptation of Petrarch, it acknowledges and invigorates the sonnet as a form pre-eminently associated with love and loss, and it reminds us that poems will be born of other poems. Every sonnet has an echo and what it says is 'I live on'.

---

19. Derek Mahon, *Echo's Grove* (Oldcastle: Gallery Books, 2013), p. 70.

Bibliography

SONNET ANTHOLOGIES

Allen, Michael J., ed. *The Anthem Anthology of Victorian Sonnets*, 2 vols. London: Anthem Press, 2011.
Boland, Eavan and Edward Hirsch, eds. *The Making of a Sonnet: A Norton Anthology*. New York: Norton, 2008.
Briggs, A. P. D., ed. *English Sonnets*. London: Dent, 1999.
Bromwich, David, ed. *American Sonnets*. New York: Library of America, 2007.
Evans, Maurice, ed. *Elizabethan Sonnets*, revised by Roy Booth. London: Dent, 1994.
Feldman, Paula R. and Daniel Robinson, eds. *A Century of Sonnets: The Romantic-Era Revival, 1750–1850*. New York and Oxford: Oxford University Press, 1999.
Fuller, John, ed. *The Oxford Book of Sonnets*. Oxford: Oxford University Press, 2000.
Hale, John, ed. *Sonnets of Four Centuries, 1500–1900*. Dunedin, New Zealand: University of Otago, 1992.
Hilson, Jeff, ed. *The Reality Street Book of Sonnets*. Hastings: Reality Street, 2008.
Hunt, Leigh and S. Adams Lee, eds. *The Book of the Sonnet*, 2 vols. Boston: Roberts Brothers, 1867.
Klein, Holger, ed. *English and Scottish Sonnet Sequences of the Renaissance*, 2 vols. Hildesheim: Georg Olms, 1984.
Lee, Sidney, ed. *Elizabethan Sonnets*, 2 vols. London: Constable, 1904.
Lever, J. W., ed. *The Elizabethan Love Sonnet*. London: Methuen, 1956.
Levin, Phillis, ed. *The Penguin Book of the Sonnet*. New York: Penguin, 2001.
Main, David M., ed. *A Treasury of English Sonnets*. Manchester: Ireland & Co., 1880.
Paterson, Don, ed. *101 Sonnets from Shakespeare to Heaney*. London: Faber, 1999.
Russell, Matthew, ed. *Sonnets on the Sonnet*. London: Longmans, Green & Co., 1898.
Sharp, William, ed. *Sonnets of This Century*. London: Walter Scott, 1886.
Taylor, Walt, ed. *English Sonnets*. London: Longmans, Green & Co., 1947.
White, Gertrude M. and Joan G. Rosen, eds. *A Moment's Monument: The Development of the Sonnet*. New York: Charles Scribner's Sons, 1972.
Withers, Carl, ed. *The Penguin Book of Sonnets*. New York: Penguin, 1943.

CRITICAL STUDIES OF THE SONNET

Adames, John. 'The Frontiers of the Psyche and the Limits of Form in Auden's "Quest" Sonnets', *Modern Language Review* 92 (1997), 573–80.
Adames, John. 'The Sonnet Mirror: Reflection and Revaluations in Seamus Heaney's "Clearances"', *Irish University Review* 27 (1997), 276–86.

Bolton, Jonathan. 'Empire and Atonement: Geoffrey Hill's "An Apology for the Revival of Christian Architecture in England"', *Contemporary Literature* 38.2 (1997), 287–306.

Booth, Stephen. *Shakespeare's Sonnets*. New Haven: Yale University Press, 1977.

Burt, Stephanie and David Mikics. *The Art of the Sonnet*. Cambridge, MA: Harvard University Press, 2010.

Burman, Lars. *Den Svenska Stormaktstidens Sonett*. Stockholm: Almqvist and Wiskell International, 1990.

Chapman, Alison. 'Sonnet and Sonnet Sequences', in *A Companion to Victorian Poetry*, ed. Richard Cronin, Alison Chapman, and Antony H. Harrison. Oxford: Blackwell, 2002, pp. 99–114.

Cousins, A. D. *Shakespeare's Sonnets and Narrative Poems*. Harlow: Longman, 2000.

Cousins, A. D. and Peter Howarth, eds. *The Cambridge Companion to the Sonnet*. Cambridge: Cambridge University Press, 2011.

Crosland, T. W. H., *The English Sonnet*. London: Secker, 1917.

Cruttwell, Maurice. *The English Sonnet*. London: Longman, 1966.

Distiller, Natasha. *Desire and Gender in the Sonnet Tradition*. Basingstoke: Palgrave Macmillan, 2008.

Donow, Herbert S. *The Sonnet in England and America: A Bibliography of Criticism*. London and Westport, CT: Greenwood, 1982.

Edmondson, Paul and Stanley Wells. *Shakespeare's Sonnets*. Oxford: Oxford University Press, 2004.

Ferry, Anne. *The 'Inward' Language: Sonnets of Wyatt, Sidney, Shakespeare, Donne*. Chicago: University of Chicago Press, 1983.

Fineman, Joel. *Shakespeare's Perjured Eye: The Invention of Poetic Subjectivity in the Sonnets*. Berkeley: University of California Press, 1986.

Fuller, John. *The Sonnet*. London and New York: Methuen, 1986.

Gibbs, Donna. *Spenser's Amoretti: A Critical Study*. Aldershot: Scolar Press, 1990.

Going, William T. *Scanty Plot of Ground: Studies in the Victorian Sonnet*. The Hague: Mouton, 1976.

Harris, Daniel. *Inspirations Unbidden: The 'Terrible Sonnets' of Gerard Manley Hopkins*. Berkeley: University of California Press, 1982.

Hodgson, Andrew. 'Form and Feeling in John Clare's Sonnets', *John Clare Society Journal* 31 (2012), 51–66.

Holmes, John. *Dante Gabriel Rossetti and the Late Victorian Sonnet Sequence: Sexuality, Belief and the Self*. Aldershot: Ashgate, 2005.

Houston, Natalie M. 'Reading the Victorian Souvenir: Sonnets and Photographs of the Crimean War', *Yale Journal of Criticism* 14 (2001), 353–83.

John, Lisle Cecil. *The Elizabethan Sonnet Sequences*. New York: Columbia University Press, 1938.

Johnson, Anthony L. 'Formal Messages in Keats's Sonnets', in *The Challenge of Keats: Bicentenary Essays 1795–1995*, ed. Allan C. Christensen, Lilla Maria Crisafulli Jones, Giuseppe Galigani, and Anthony L. Johnson. Amsterdam: Rodopi, 2000, pp. 95–111.

Kerrigan, John. 'Wordsworth and the Sonnet: Building, Dwelling, Thinking', *Essays in Criticism* 35 (1985), 45–75.
Kingsley-Smith, Jane. '"Let Me Not to the Marriage of True Minds": Shakespeare's Sonnet for Lady Mary Wroth', *Shakespeare Survey* 69 (2010), 277–91.
Kleinhenz, Christopher. *The Early Italian Sonnet: The First Century, 1220–1321*. Lecce: Milella, 1986.
Leishman, J. B. *Themes and Variations in Shakespeare's Sonnets*. New York: Harper and Row, 1961.
Lever, J. W. *The Elizabethan Love Sonnet*. London: Methuen, 1956; 1978.
Marotti, Arthur. '"Love Is Not Love": Elizabethan Sonnet Sequences and the Social Order', *ELH* 49.2 (1982), 396–428.
Martz, Louis. 'The *Amoretti*: "Most Goodly Temperature"', in *Form and Convention in the Poetry of Edmund Spenser*, ed. W. Nelson. New York: Columbia University Press, 1961, pp. 146–68.
Maxson, H. A. *On the Sonnets of Robert Frost*. London and Jefferson, NC: McFarland, 1997.
Nardo, Anna K. *Milton's Sonnets and the Ideal Community*. Lincoln, NE: University of Nebraska Press, 1979.
Oppenheimer, Paul. *The Birth of the Modern Mind: Self, Consciousness, and the Invention of the Sonnet*. New York: Oxford University Press, 1989.
Parker, Tom. *Proportional Form in the Sonnets of the Sidney Circle*. Oxford: Oxford University Press, 1998.
Paterson, Don. *Reading Shakespeare's Sonnets: A New Commentary*. London: Faber, 2010.
Pattison, Mark, ed. *Milton's Sonnets*. London: Kegan Paul, 1892.
Phelan, Joseph. *The Nineteenth-Century Sonnet*. Basingstoke: Palgrave Macmillan, 2005.
Regan, Stephen. 'Robert Frost and the American Sonnet', *Robert Frost Review* 14 (2005), 13–35.
Regan, Stephen. 'The Victorian Sonnet, from George Meredith to Gerard Manley Hopkins', *Yearbook of English Studies* 36.2 (2006), 17–34.
Robinson, Daniel. 'Reviving the Sonnet: Women Romantic Poets and the Sonnet Claim', *European Romantic Review* 6 (1995), 98–127.
Roche, Thomas. *Petrarch and the English Sonnet Sequences*. New York: AMS Press, 1989.
Roche, Thomas P., Jr. *Petrarch in English*. London: Penguin, 2005.
Scott, Janet G. *Les Sonnets Elisabéthains*. Paris: Honoré Champion, 1929.
Sinfield, Alan. 'Sexual Puns in Astrophil and Stella', *Essays in Criticism* 24.4 (1974), 341–55.
Smith, Rosalind. *Sonnets and the English Woman Writer, 1560–1621*. Basingstoke: Palgrave Macmillan, 2005.
Spiller, Michael R. G. *The Development of the Sonnet: An Introduction*. London and New York: Routledge, 1992.
Spiller, Michael R. G. *The Sonnet Sequence: A Study of its Strategies*. New York: Twayne, 1997.

Spiller, Michael R. G. *Early Modern Sonneteers: From Wyatt to Milton*. Tavistock: Northcote House, 2001.
Stanivuković, Goran. 'Portrait Miniature Painting, the Young Man of Shakespeare's Sonnets, and Late Elizabethan Aesthetics', *English Studies* 95.4 (2014), 367–91.
Suret, Emma. 'John Keats, Wilfred Owen, and Restriction in the Sonnet', *English* 66.253 (2017), 145–62.
Tomlinson, Charles. *The Sonnet: Its Origin, Structure and Place in Poetry*. London: John Murray, 1874.
Vaganay, Hugues. *Le Sonnet en Italie et en France au XVIe siècle*. Lyons: au siege des Facultés Catholiques, 1902; reprinted Geneva: Slatkine, 1966.
Van Remoortel, Marianne. *Lives of the Sonnet, 1787–1895*. Farnham: Ashgate, 2011.
Vendler, Helen. *The Art of Shakespeare's Sonnets*. Cambridge, MA: Harvard University Press, 1997.
Wagner, Jennifer Ann. *A Moment's Monument: Revisionary Poetics and the Nineteenth-Century English Sonnet*. London: Associated University Presses, 1996.
Warley, Christopher. *Sonnet Sequences and Social Distinction in Renaissance England*. Cambridge: Cambridge University Press, 2005.
Weiser, David K. 'Berryman's Sonnets: In and Out of the Tradition', *American Literature* 55.3 (1983), 388–404.
Wilkins, E. H. 'The Invention of the Sonnet', *Modern Philology* 13 (1915), 463–94.

PRIMARY SOURCES

Arber, Edward, ed. *Tottel's Miscellany: Songs and Sonnettes by Henry Howard, Earl of Surrey, Sir Thomas Wyatt the Elder, Nicholas Grimald and Uncertain Authors* [1557]. London: Constable, 1914.
Arnold, Matthew. *Arnold: The Complete Poems*, ed. Kenneth Allott. 2nd edn by Miriam Allott. London: Longman, 1965; 1979.
Auden, W. H. *The Collected Poetry of W. H. Auden*. New York: Random House, 1945.
Auden, W. H. *Collected Poems*, ed. Edward Mendelson. New York: Random House, 1976.
Auden, W. H. *Juvenilia: Poems 1922–1928*, ed. Katherine Bucknell. Princeton: Princeton University Press, 1994.
Auden, W. H. *Lectures on Shakespeare*, ed. Arthur Kirsch. London: Faber, 2000.
Auden, W. H. and Christopher Isherwood. *Journey to a War*. New York: Random House, 1939.
Baudelaire, Charles. *Poems of Baudelaire: Les Fleurs du Mal*, translated by Roy Campbell. London: The Harvill Press, 1954.
Berrigan, Ted. *The Sonnets*, ed. Alice Notley. Harmondsworth: Penguin, 2000.
Berryman, John. *Collected Poems 1937–1971*, ed. Charles Thornbury. London: Faber, 1989.
Bishop, Elizabeth. *Poems, Prose and Letters*, ed. Robert Giroux and Lloyd Schwartz. New York: Library of America, 2008.
Blunden, Edmund. *Undertones of War* (1928). Harmondsworth: Penguin, 2000.

Boland, Eavan. *New Collected Poems*. New York: Norton, 2008.
Boland, Eavan. *Night Feed*. Dublin: Arlen House, 1982.
Bowles, William Lisle. *Fourteen Sonnets, Elegiac and Descriptive, Written During a Tour*. London: Dilly, 1789. Facsimile edn, introduced by Jonathan Wordsworth. Oxford: Woodstock Books, 1991.
Brooke, Rupert. *The Collected Poems of Rupert Brooke, with a Memoir*. London: Sidgwick and Jackson, 1918.
Brooke, Rupert. *The Poetical Works of Rupert Brooke*, ed. Geoffrey Keynes. London: Faber, 1946; 1970.
Brown, Eleanor. *Maiden Speech*. Newcastle upon Tyne: Bloodaxe, 1996.
Browning, Elizabeth Barrett. *The Poetical Works of Elizabeth Barrett Browning*. Edinburgh: W. P. Nimmo, Hay, and Mitchell, 1903.
Browning, Robert. *Robert Browning: The Major Works*, ed. Adam Roberts and Daniel Karlin. Oxford: Oxford University Press, 2005.
Burke, Edmund. *Reflections on the Revolution in France*, ed. L. G. Mitchell. Oxford: Oxford University Press, 1993.
Campbell, Roy. *The Collected Poems of Roy Campbell*. London: The Bodley Head, 1949; 1955.
Carson, Ciaran. *The Alexandrine Plan*. Oldcastle: Gallery Press, 1998.
Carson, Ciaran. *Collected Poems*. Oldcastle: Gallery Press, 2008.
Clare, John. *Selected Poems*, ed. J. W. Tibble and Anne Tibble. London: Dent, 1975.
Clare, John. *Major Works*, ed. Eric Robinson and David Powell, with an Introduction by Tom Paulin. Oxford: Oxford University Press, 2008.
Coleridge, Samuel Taylor. *Samuel Coleridge Taylor: Major Works*, ed. H. J. Jackson. Oxford: Oxford University Press, 2008.
Coleridge, Samuel Taylor. *Coleridge's Responses*, Vol. 1: *Coleridge on Writers and Writing*, ed. Seamus Perry. London: Continuum, 2008.
Cope, Wendy. *Two Cures for Love: Selected Poems 1979–2006*. London: Faber, 2008.
Crabbe, George. *The Complete Poetical Works*, ed. Norma Dalrymple-Champneys and Arthur Pollard, 3 vols. Oxford: Clarendon Press, 1988.
Cummings, E. E. *Complete Poems*. 2 vols. London: MacGibbon & Kee, 1968.
Curnow, Allen. *Early Days Yet: New and Collected Poems 1941–1997*. Manchester: Carcanet, 1997.
Donne, John. *John Donne*, ed. John Carey. Oxford: Oxford University Press, 1990.
Dove, Rita. *Mother Love*. New York: Norton, 1995.
Drummond, William. *The Poetical Works of William Drummond of Hawthornden*, ed. L. E. Kastner, 2 vols. Manchester: Manchester University Press, 1913.
Duffy, Carol Ann. *Feminine Gospels*. London: Picador, 2002.
Duffy, Carol Ann. *Rapture*. London: Picador, 2005.
Dunn, Douglas. *Elegies*. London: Faber, 1985.
Dunn, Douglas. *New Selected Poems 1964–2000*. London: Faber, 2003.
Edwards, Ken. *eight + six*. London: Reality Street, 2003.
Eliot, T. S. *The Use of Poetry and the Use of Criticism*. London: Faber, 1964.
Eliot, T. S. *Selected Prose of T. S. Eliot*, ed. Frank Kermode. London: Faber, 1975.

Eliot, T. S. *The Complete Poems and Plays 1909–1950*. New York: Harcourt Brace & Company, 1980.
Eliot, T. S. *The Poems of T. S. Eliot*, ed. Christopher Ricks and Jim McCue, vol. 1. Baltimore: Johns Hopkins University Press, 2015.
Flynn, Leontia. *Drives*. London: Jonathan Cape, 2008.
Frost, Robert. *Robert Frost: Collected Poems, Prose and Plays*. New York: Library of America, 1995.
Gillis, Alan. *The Green Rose*. Thame: Clutag, 2009.
Greville, Fulke. *Selected Poems*, ed. Neil Powell. Manchester: Carcanet, 1990.
Gurney, Ivor. *Collected Poems of Ivor Gurney*, ed. P. J. Kavanagh. Oxford: Oxford University Press, 1982.
Gurney, Ivor. *Collected Letters*, ed. R. K. R. Thornton. Manchester: Carcanet, 1991.
Gurney, Ivor. *Severn & Somme* and *War's Embers*, ed. R. K. R. Thornton. Manchester: Carcanet, 1997.
Hacker, Marilyn. *Love, Death, and the Changing of the Seasons*. New York: Norton, 1986.
Harrison, Tony. *Selected Poems*. London: Penguin, 1987.
Harrison, Tony. *The Gaze of the Gorgon*. Newcastle upon Tyne: Bloodaxe, 1992.
Heaney, Seamus. *Opened Ground: Poems 1966–1996*. London: Faber, 1998.
Herbert, George. *The Works of George Herbert*, ed. F. E. Hutchinson. Oxford: Clarendon Press, 1941.
Hill, Geoffrey. *Selected Poems*. London: Penguin, 2006.
Hill, Geoffrey. *Broken Hierarchies: Poems 1952–2012*, ed. Kenneth Haynes. Oxford: Oxford University Press, 2013.
Ingram, John Kells. *Sonnets and Other Poems*. London: Adam and Charles Black, 1900.
Jamie, Kathleen. *The Tree House*. London: Picador, 2004.
Jamie, Kathleen. *The Overhaul*. London: Picador, 2012.
Joyce, James. *A Portrait of the Artist as a Young Man*, ed. Jeri Johnson. Oxford: Oxford University Press, 2000.
Kavanagh, Patrick. *Collected Poems*, ed. Antoinette Quinn. London: Allen Lane, 2004.
Keats, John. *Poetical Works*, ed. H. W. Garrod. Oxford: Oxford University Press, 1970.
Keats, John. *John Keats: The Major Works*, ed. Elizabeth Cook. Oxford: Oxford University Press, 2001.
Larkin, Philip. *The Complete Poems*, ed. Archie Burnett. London: Faber, 2012.
Larkin, Philip, ed. *The Oxford Book of Twentieth-Century English Verse*. Oxford: Clarendon Press, 1973.
Longfellow, Henry Wadsworth. *The Poetical Works of Longfellow*. London: Oxford University Press, 1957.
Longley, Michael. *Collected Poems*. London: Jonathan Cape, 2006.
Lopez, Tony. *False Memory*. Bristol: Shearsman Books, 2012.
Lowell, Robert. *Collected Poems*, ed. Frank Bidart and David Gewanter. New York: Farrar, Straus, and Giroux, 2003.

McCrea, Shane. *Mule*. Cleveland, OH: Cleveland State University Poetry Center, 2011.
McKay, Claude. *Complete Poems*, ed. William J. Maxwell. Urbana and Chicago: University of Illinois Press, 2004.
McNeillie, Andrew. *Slower*. Manchester: Carcanet, 2006.
Mahon, Derek. *Poems 1962–1978*. Oxford: Oxford University Press, 1979.
Mahon, Derek. *Echo's Grove*. Oldcastle: Gallery Books, 2013.
Marvell, Andrew. *The Complete Poems*, ed. George deF. Lord. London: David Campbell, 1993.
Meredith, George. *The Poems of George Meredith*, ed. Phyllis Bartlett, 2 vols. New Haven: Yale University Press, 1978.
Meredith, George. *Modern Love*, ed. Stephen Regan. Peterborough: Monitor House, 1988.
Merrill, James. *Collected Poems*, ed. J. D. McClatchy and Stephen Yenser. New York: Knopf, 2002.
Millay, Edna St Vincent. *Collected Sonnets*, ed. Elizabeth Barnett. New York: Harper and Row, 1988.
Milton, John. *Milton's Sonnets*, ed. E. A. J. Honigmann. London: Macmillan, 1966.
Milton, John. *John Milton*, ed. Stephen Orgel and Jonathan Goldberg. Oxford: Oxford University Press, 1991.
Milton, John. *Milton: Poetical Works*, ed. Douglas Bush. Oxford: Oxford University Press, 1996.
Milton, John. *Milton: The Complete Shorter Poems*, ed. John Carey. Harlow: Longman, 1997.
Morgan, Edwin. *New Selected Poems*. Manchester: Carcanet, 2000.
Motion, Andrew. *Public Property*. London: Faber, 2002.
Motion, Andrew. *The Cinder Path*. London: Faber, 2009.
Muldoon, Paul. *Poems 1968–1998*. London: Faber, 2001.
Muldoon, Paul. *Moy Sand and Gravel*. London: Faber, 2002.
Muldoon, Paul. *Horse Latitudes*. London: Faber, 2006.
Owen, Wilfred. *The Complete Poems and Fragments*, ed. Jon Stallworthy, 2 vols. London: Chatto & Windus; Oxford: Oxford University Press, 1983.
Owen, Wilfred. *Collected Letters*, ed. Harold Owen and John Bell. London: Oxford University Press, 1967.
Pater, Walter. *Appreciations, with an Essay on Style*. London: Macmillan, 1907.
Paterson, Don. *Nil Nil*. London: Faber, 1993.
Paterson, Don. *Orpheus: A Version of Rilke's 'Die Sonette an Orpheus'*. London: Faber, 2006.
Paterson, Don. *Selected Poems*. London: Faber, 2012.
Paterson, Don. *40 Sonnets*. London: Faber, 2015.
Petrarca, Francesco (Petrarch). *Petrarch's Lyric Poems*, ed. and translated by Robert M. Durling. Cambridge, MA: Harvard University Press, 1976.
Petrarca, Francesco (Petrarch). *Selections from the Canzoniere and Other Works*, ed. and translated by Mark Musa. Oxford: Oxford University Press, 1999.

Petrarca, Francesco (Petrarch). *Canzoniere*, ed. and translated by Anthony Mortimer. London: Penguin, 2002.
Pickard, Tom. *Winter Migrants*. Manchester: Carcanet, 2016.
Plath, Sylvia. *The Collected Poems*. New York: Harper and Row, 1981.
Plath, Sylvia. *Letters Home*, ed. Aurelia Plath. London: Faber, 2010.
Rilke, Rainer Maria. *Sonnets to Orpheus*, ed. J. B. Leishman. London: Hogarth Press, 1936.
Robinson, Edwin Arlington. *The Collected Poems of Edwin Arlington Robinson*. New York: Macmillan, 1954.
Rossetti, Christina. *Poems and Prose*, ed. Simon Humphries. Oxford: Oxford University Press, 2008.
Rossetti, Dante Gabriel. *The Complete Poetical Works of Dante Gabriel Rossetti*, ed. William Michael Rossetti. Boston: Little, Brown, and Co., 1907.
Ruskin, John. *The Works of John Ruskin*, 39 vols. London: George Allen, 1903–12.
Sassoon, Siegfried. *The War Poems of Siegfried Sassoon*, ed. Rupert Hart Davis. London: Faber, 1983.
Seth, Vikram. *The Golden Gate*. London: Faber, 1986.
Seward, Anna. *The Collected Poems of Anna Seward*, ed. Lisa L. Moore, 2 vols. Abingdon: Routledge, 2016.
Shakespeare, William. *The Sonnets and a Lover's Complaint*, ed. John Kerrigan. Harmondsworth: Penguin, 1986; 1999.
Shakespeare, William. *The Sonnets and a Lover's Complaint*, ed. Martin Dodsworth. London: Dent, 1995.
Shakespeare, William. *The Complete Sonnets and Poems*, ed. Colin Burrow. Oxford: Oxford University Press, 2002.
Shelley, Percy Bysshe. *Percy Bysshe Shelley: The Major Works*, ed. Zachary Leader and Michael O'Neill. Oxford: Oxford University Press, 2003.
Sidney, Sir Philip. *Sir Philip Sidney: The Major Works*, ed. Katherine Duncan-Jones. Oxford: Oxford University Press, 2008.
Smith, Charlotte. *The Poems of Charlotte Smith*, ed. Stuart Curran. New York and Oxford: Oxford University Press, 1993.
Sorley, Charles Hamilton. *The Collected Poems of Charles Sorley*, ed. Jean Moorcroft Wilson. London: Cecil Woolf, 1985.
Sorley, Charles Hamilton. *The Letters of Charles Sorley*. Cambridge: Cambridge University Press, 1919.
Spenser, Edmund. *The Poetical Works of Edmund Spenser*, 3 vols. Vol. 1: *Spenser's Minor Poems*, ed. Ernest de Sélincourt. Oxford: Clarendon Press, 1910.
Stevens, Wallace. *The Collected Poems of Wallace Stevens*. New York: Vintage, 1982.
Stevenson, Anne. *Selected Poems 1956–1986*. Oxford: Oxford University Press, 1987.
Tennyson, Alfred. *The Poems of Tennyson*, ed. Christopher Ricks, 3 vols. Harlow: Longman, 1987.
Thomas, Edward. *Selected Poems and Prose*. Harmondsworth: Penguin, 1981.
Tuckerman, Frederick Goddard. *The Complete Poems of Frederick Goddard Tuckerman*, ed. N. Scott Momaday. New York: Oxford University Press, 1965.

Verlaine, Paul. *Selected Poems*, translated by C. F. MacIntyre. Berkeley and Los Angeles: University of California Press, 1948.
Walcott, Derek. *Collected Poems*. New York: Farrar, Straus, and Giroux, 1986.
Wordsworth, Dorothy. *Journals of Dorothy Wordsworth*, ed. Mary Moorman. London: Oxford University Press, 1971.
Wordsworth, William. *The Sonnets of William Wordsworth*. London: Edward Moxon, 1838.
Wordsworth, William. *Poems in Two Volumes, and Other Poems, 1800–1807*, ed. Jared Curtis. Ithaca, NY: Cornell University Press, 1983.
Wordsworth, William. *William Wordsworth*, ed. Stephen Gill. Oxford: Oxford University Press, 1984.
Wroth, Mary. *The Poems of Lady Mary Wroth*, ed. Josephine A. Roberts. Baton Rouge: Louisiana State University Press, 1983.
Wroth, Mary. *Lady Mary Wroth: Poems*, ed. R. E. Pritchard. Keele: Keele University Press, 1996.
Wyatt, Thomas. *Collected Poems*, ed. Joost Daalder. London: Oxford University Press, 1975.
Yeats, W. B., ed. *The Oxford Book of Modern Verse*. Oxford: Clarendon Press, 1936.
Yeats, W. B. *The Poems*, ed. Daniel Albright. London: Dent, 1992.
Yeats, W. B. *W. B. Yeats*, ed. Edward Larrissy. Oxford: Oxford University Press, 1997.

SECONDARY SOURCES

Abbott, Claude Colleer, ed. *The Correspondence of Gerard Manley Hopkins and Richard Watson Dixon*. London: Oxford University Press, 1955.
Alexander, Gavin. *Writing after Sidney: The Literary Response to Sir Philip Sidney, 1586–1640*. Oxford: Clarendon Press, 2006.
Armstrong, Isobel. *Victorian Poetry: Poetry, Poetics and Politics*. London: Routledge, 1993.
Avery, Simon and Rebecca Stott. *Elizabeth Barrett Browning*. Harlow: Longman, 2003.
Barrell, John. *Poetry, Language and Politics*. Manchester: Manchester University Press, 1998.
Bate, Walter Jackson. *John Keats*. Cambridge, MA: Harvard University Press, 1963.
Bates, Catherine. *The Rhetoric of Courtship in Elizabethan Language and Literature*. Cambridge: Cambridge University Press, 1992.
Bateson, F. W. *English Poetry: A Critical Introduction*. London: Longman, 1950; 1966.
Bell, Vereen. *Robert Lowell: Nihilist as Hero*. Cambridge, MA: Harvard University Press, 1983.
Bendixen, Alfred and Stephanie Burt, eds. *The Cambridge History of American Poetry*. Cambridge: Cambridge University Press, 2015.
Bolton, Jonathan. 'Empire and Atonement: Geoffrey Hills' "An Apology for the Revival of Christian Architecture in England"', *Contemporary Literature* 38.2 (1997), 287–306.

Booth, James. *Philip Larkin: The Poet's Plight*. Basingstoke: Macmillan, 2005.
Brearton, Fran. *Reading Michael Longley*. Tarset: Bloodaxe Books, 2006.
Brewster, Scott. *Lyric*. London and New York: Routledge, 2009.
Bristow, Joseph, ed. *The Victorian Poet: Poetics and Persona*. London: Croom Helm, 1987.
Brodsky, Joseph, Seamus Heaney, and Derek Walcott. *Homage to Robert Frost*. New York: Farrar, Straus, and Giroux, 1996.
Brooks, Cleanth. *The Well Wrought Urn*. London: Dennis Dobson, 1949.
Brown, Terence. *The Life of W. B. Yeats*. Oxford: Blackwell, 1999.
Caddel, Richard, ed. *Sharp Study and Long Toil*, Basil Bunting Special Issue of *Durham University Journal*. Durham: Durham University, 1995.
Campbell, Matthew. *Rhythm and Will in Victorian Poetry*. Cambridge: Cambridge University Press, 1999.
Campbell, Patrick. *Siegfried Sassoon: A Study of the War Poetry*. London: McFarland, 1999.
Caplan, David. *Questions of Possibility: Contemporary Poetry and Poetic Form*. New York: Oxford University Press, 2005.
Chamberlin, J. Edward. *Come Back to Me my Language: Poetry and the West Indies*. Urbana and Chicago: University of Illinois Press, 1993.
Cline, C. L., ed. *The Letters of George Meredith*, 3 vols. Oxford: Clarendon Press, 1970.
Colie, Rosalie. *The Resources of Kind*. Berkeley: University of California Press, 1973.
Cookson, Linda and Bryan Loughrey, eds. *Critical Essays on Philip Larkin: The Poems*. Harlow: Longman, 1989.
Corcoran, Neil. 'Lowell Retiarius', *Agenda*, Robert Lowell Special Issue, 18.3 (1980), 75–85.
Corcoran, Neil, ed. *English Poetry Since 1940*. Harlow: Longman, 1993.
Corcoran, Neil. *The Poetry of Seamus Heaney: A Critical Guide*. London: Faber, 1998.
Corcoran, Neil, ed. *The Cambridge Companion to Twentieth-Century English Poetry*. Cambridge: Cambridge University Press, 2007.
Cousins, A. D. *Shakespeare's Sonnets and Narrative Poems*. Harlow: Longman, 2000.
Cronin, Richard, Alison Chapman, and Antony Harrison, eds. *A Companion to Victorian Poetry*. Oxford: Blackwell, 2002.
Curran, Stuart. *Poetic Form and British Romanticism*. New York and Oxford: Oxford University Press, 1986.
Deane, Seamus. *Strange Country: Modernity and Nationhood in Irish Writing since 1790*. Oxford: Clarendon Press, 1997.
Dubois, Martin. *Gerard Manley Hopkins and the Poetry of Religious Experience*. Cambridge: Cambridge University Press, 2017.
Dubrow, Heather. *Echoes of Desire: English Petrarchism and its Counterdiscourses*. Ithaca, NY: Cornell University Press, 1995.
Dubrow, Heather. *The Challenges of Orpheus: Lyric Poetry and Early Modern England*. Baltimore: Johns Hopkins University Press, 2008.
Eagleton, Terry. *How to Read a Poem*. Oxford: Blackwell, 2007.
Ebbatson, Roger. *An Imaginary England: Nation, Landscape and Literature, 1840–1920*. London: Ashgate, 2005.

Eliot, T. S. *The Use of Poetry and the Use of Criticism*. London: Faber, 1964.
Faggen, Robert. *Robert Frost and the Challenge of Darwin*. Ann Arbor: University of Michigan Press, 2001.
Falconer, Rachel, ed. *Kathleen Jamie: Essays and Poems on her Work*. Edinburgh: Edinburgh University Press, 2015.
Fernie, Ewan. *Shame in Shakespeare*. London: Routledge, 2002.
Fernie, Ewan. *The Demonic: Literature and Experience*. London: Routledge, 2013.
Forster, Leonard. *The Icy Fire: Five Studies in European Petrarchism*. Cambridge: Cambridge University Press, 1969.
Fowler, Alastair. *Kinds of Literature*. Oxford: Oxford University Press, 1982.
Fredeman, William E. 'Rossetti's "In Memoriam": An Elegiac Reading of the House of Life'. *Bulletin of the John Rylands Library* 47 (1965), 298–341.
Freud, Sigmund. *On Murder, Mourning and Melancholia*. Harmondsworth: Penguin, 2005.
Fuller, David. *The Life in the Sonnets*. London: Continuum, 2011.
Fuller, John. *W. H. Auden: A Commentary*. London: Faber, 1998.
Fussell, Paul. *Poetic Meter and Poetic Form*. New York: Random House, 1965.
Gill, Stephen. *William Wordsworth: A Life*. Oxford: Oxford University Press, 1990.
Greenberg, Herbert. *Quest for the Necessary: W. H. Auden and the Dilemma of Divided Consciousness*. Cambridge, MA: Harvard University Press, 1968.
Greenblatt, Stephen. *Renaissance Self-Fashioning*. Chicago: University of Chicago Press, 1980.
Greene, Roland. *Post-Petrarchism: Origins and Innovations of the Western Lyric Sequence*. Princeton: Princeton University Press, 1991.
Guibbory, Achsah, ed. *The Cambridge Companion to John Donne*. Cambridge: Cambridge University Press, 2006.
Hadfield, Andrew. *Edmund Spenser: A Life*. Oxford: Oxford University Press, 2012.
Hall, Jason David. *Seamus Heaney's Rhythmic Contract*. Basingstoke: Palgrave Macmillan, 2009.
Hanke, Michael and Michael Spiller, eds. *Ten Shakespeare Sonnets: Critical Essays*. Trier: Wissenschaftlicher Verlag Trier, 2006.
Harrison, Antony. *Christina Rossetti in Context*. Chapel Hill, NC: University of North Carolina Press, 1988.
Hart, Henry. *The Poetry of Geoffrey Hill*. Carbondale, IL: Southern Illinois University Press, 1986.
Hassall, Christopher. *Rupert Brooke: A Biography*. London: Faber, 1964.
Heaney, Seamus. *Preoccupations: Selected Prose 1968–1978*. London: Faber, 1980.
Heaney, Seamus. 'A Memorial Address', *Agenda*, Robert Lowell Special Issue, 18.3 (1980), 23–8.
Heaney, Seamus. *The Government of the Tongue*. London: Faber, 1988.
Henderson, Diana E. *Passion Made Public: Elizabethan Lyric, Gender, and Performance*. Ithaca, NY: Cornell University Press, 1995.
Hibberd, Dominic. *Owen the Poet*. Basingstoke: Macmillan, 1986.
Hoffman, Tyler. *Robert Frost and the Politics of Poetry*. Hanover and London: University Press of New England, 2001.

Holmes, Olivia. *Assembling the Lyric Self: Authorship from Troubadour Song to Italian Poetry Book*. Minneapolis: University of Minnesota Press, 2000.
Hošek, Chaviva and Patricia Parker, eds. *Lyric Poetry: Beyond New Criticism*. Ithaca, NY: Cornell University Press, 1985.
Hough, Graham. *The Last Romantics*. London: Duckworth, 1949.
Howes, Marjorie and John Kelly, eds. *The Cambridge Companion to W. B. Yeats*. Cambridge: Cambridge University Press, 2006.
Huggins, Nathan Irvin. *Harlem Renaissance*. New York: Oxford University Press, 1973.
Hurley, Michael D. and Michael O'Neill. *Poetic Form: An Introduction*. Cambridge: Cambridge University Press, 2012.
Hynes, Samuel. *Edwardian Occasions: Essays on English Writing in the Early Twentieth Century*. New York: Oxford University Press, 1972.
Jarrell, Randall. *Poetry and the Age*. New York: Knopf, 1953.
Johnston, John H. *English Poetry of the First World War: A Study in the Evolution of Lyric and Narrative Form*. Princeton: Princeton University Press, 1964.
Kalstone, David. *Sidney's Poetry*. Cambridge, MA: Harvard University Press, 1965.
Kelly, John and Eric Domville, eds. *The Collected Letters of W. B. Yeats*, Vol. 1: *1866–1895*. Oxford: Oxford University Press, 1986.
Kennedy, William J. *Authorizing Petrarch*. Ithaca, NY: Cornell University Press, 1994.
Kent, David A., ed. *The Achievement of Christina Rossetti*. Ithaca, NY: Cornell University Press, 1987.
Kermode, Frank, ed. *Selected Prose of T. S. Eliot*. London: Faber, 1975.
Kerr, Douglas. *Wilfred Owen's Voices: Language and Community*. Oxford: Oxford University Press, 2006.
Kiberd, Declan. *Inventing Ireland*. London: Jonathan Cape, 1995.
King, Bruce. *Derek Walcott: A Caribbean Life*. Oxford: Oxford University Press, 2000.
Kuenz, Jane. 'Modernism, Mass Culture and the Harlem Renaissance: The Case of Countee Cullen'. *Modernism/Modernity* 14 (2007), 507–15.
Laskowski, William. *Rupert Brooke*. New York: Twayne, 1994.
Leavis, F. R. *Revaluation*. Harmondsworth: Penguin, 1994.
Leighton, Angela. *Victorian Women Poets: Writing Against the Heart*. Hemel Hempstead: Harvester, 1992.
Lentricchia, Frank. *Robert Frost: Modern Poetics and the Landscapes of Self*. Durham, NC: Duke University Press, 1975.
Lucas, John. *England and Englishness*. London: Hogarth Press, 1990.
Lucas, John. 'England in 1830—Wordsworth, Clare, and the Question of Poetic Authority', *Critical Survey* 4.1 (1992), 62–6.
Lucas, John. *Ivor Gurney*. Tavistock: Northcote House, 2001.
MacDonagh, Thomas. *Literature in Ireland: Studies Irish and Anglo-Irish*. London: T. Fisher Unwin, 1916.
McGann, Jerome J. *Dante Gabriel Rossetti and the Game That Must Be Lost*. New Haven: Yale University Press, 2000.

McLaughlin, Martin and Letitizia Panizza, eds. *Petrarch in Britain: Interpreters, Imitators, and Translators over 700 Years*, Proceedings of the British Academy 146. Oxford: Oxford University Press, 2007.
Marotti, Arthur F. *Manuscript, Print and the English Renaissance Lyric*. Ithaca, NY: Cornell University Press, 1995.
Martz, Louis. *The Poetry of Meditation*. New Haven: Yale University Press, 1954.
Matthews, Steven. *Irish Poetry: Politics, History, Negotiation*. Basingstoke: Macmillan, 1987.
Maynard, John. *Victorian Discourses on Sexuality and Religion*. Cambridge; Cambridge University Press, 1993.
Mazzotta, Giuseppe. *The Worlds of Petrarch*. Durham, NC: Duke University Press, 1992.
Mendelson, Edward. *Early Auden*. New York: Viking, 1981.
Mendelson, Edward. *Later Auden*. London: Faber, 1999.
Millard, Kenneth. *Edwardian Poetry*. Oxford: Clarendon Press, 1991.
Miller, J. Hillis. *The Linguistic Moment*. Princeton: Princeton University Press, 1995.
Milroy, James. *The Language of Gerard Manley Hopkins*. London: André Deutsch, 1977.
Moffett, Judith. *James Merrill: An Introduction to the Poetry*. New York: Columbia University Press, 1984.
Motion, Andrew. *Keats*. London: Faber, 1997.
Muldoon, Paul. 'Getting Round: Notes Towards an *Ars Poetica*', F. W. Bateson Memorial Lecture, *Essays in Criticism* 48.2 (1998), 107–28.
Muldoon, Paul. *To Ireland, I*. Oxford: Oxford University Press, 2000.
Murphy, Francis, ed. *Edward Arlington Robinson: A Collection of Critical Essays*. Englewood Cliffs, NJ: Prentice Hall, 1970.
Norbrook, David. *Poetry and Politics in the English Renaissance*. Oxford: Oxford University Press, 1984; 2002.
Nowottny, Winifred. *The Language Poets Use*. London: Athlone Press, 1962.
O'Donoghue, Bernard. *Seamus Heaney and the Language of Poetry*. London: Harvester Wheatsheaf, 1994.
O'Neill, Michael. *Percy Bysshe Shelley: A Literary Life*. Basingstoke: Macmillan 1989.
O'Neill, Michael. *The All-Sustaining Air: Romantic Legacies and Renewals in British, American, and Irish Poetry since 1900*. Oxford: Oxford University Press, 2007.
O'Neill, Michael, ed. *The Cambridge History of English Poetry*. Cambridge: Cambridge University Press, 2010.
Owen, Harold and John Bell, eds. *Wilfred Owen: Collected Letters*. London: Oxford University Press, 1967.
Parini, Jay. *Robert Frost: A Life*. London: Heinemann, 1998.
Parker, Michael. *Seamus Heaney: The Making of the Poet*. Basingstoke: Macmillan, 1993.
Paulin, Tom. *Minotaur: Poetry and the Nation State*. London: Faber, 1992.
Paulin, Tom. *The Secret Life of Poems*. London: Faber, 2008.

Perloff, Marjorie. 'Robert Lowell's Last Poems', *Agenda*, Robert Lowell Special Issue, 18.3 (1980), 104–14.
Poirier, Richard. *Robert Frost: The Work of Knowing*. New York: Oxford University Press, 1977.
Ramazani, Jahan. *Poetry of Mourning: The Modern Elegy from Hardy to Heaney*. Chicago: University of Chicago Press, 1994.
Ramazani, Jahan. *Poetry and its Others: News, Prayer, Song, and the Dialogue of Genres*. Chicago: University of Chicago Press, 2014.
Rebholz, A. C. *The Life of Fulke Greville*. Oxford: Clarendon Press, 1971.
Rees, Joan. *The Poetry of Dante Gabriel Rossetti: Modes of Self-Expression*. Cambridge: Cambridge University Press, 1991.
Regan, Stephen. *Philip Larkin*. Basingstoke: Macmillan, 1992.
Regan, Stephen, ed. *Philip Larkin*. New Casebooks. Basingstoke: Macmillan, 1997.
Regan, Stephen, ed. *Irish Writing: An Anthology of Irish Literature in English 1789–1939*. Oxford: Oxford University Press, 2004.
Ricks, Christopher. *The Force of Poetry*. Oxford: Clarendon Press, 1984.
Ricks, Christopher. *True Friendship: Geoffrey Hill, Anthony Hecht, and Robert Lowell Under the Sign of Eliot and Pound*. New Haven and London: Yale University Press, 2010.
Riede, David. *Dante Gabriel Rossetti and the Limits of Victorian Vision*. Ithaca, NY: Cornell University Press, 1983.
Roberts, Andrew Michael. *Geoffrey Hill*. Tavistock: Northcote House, 2004.
Robinson, Peter, ed. *Geoffrey Hill: Essays on His Work*. Milton Keynes: Open University Press, 1985.
Rosenthal, M. L. 'Our Neurotic Angel', *Agenda*, Robert Lowell Special Issue, 18.3 (1980), 34–45.
Russell, Richard Rankin. *Seamus Heaney's Regions*. Notre Dame: University of Notre Dame Press, 2014.
Ryan, Kiernan. *Shakespeare*, 3rd edn. Basingstoke: Palgrave Macmillan, 2002.
Sacks, Peter. *The English Elegy: Studies in the Genre from Spenser to Yeats*. Baltimore: Johns Hopkins University Press, 1985.
Schalkwyk, David. *Shakespeare, Love and Service*. Cambridge: Cambridge University Press, 2008.
Sessions, William A. *Henry Howard, the Poet Earl of Surrey: A Life*. Oxford: Oxford University Press, 1999.
Sharpe, Tony. *W. H. Auden*. London: Routledge, 2007.
Sharpe, Tony, ed. *W. H. Auden in Context*. Cambridge: Cambridge University Press, 2013.
Silkin, Jon. *Out of Battle: The Poetry of the Great War*, 2nd edn. Basingstoke: Macmillan, 1998.
Smith, A. J. *Literary Love: The Role of Passion in English Poems and Plays of the Seventeenth Century*. London: Edward Arnold, 1983.
Smith, Stan. *W. H. Auden*. Oxford: Blackwell, 1985.

Spencer, Matthew, ed. *Elected Friends: Robert Frost and Edward Thomas to One Another.* New York: Handsel Books, 2003.
Stallworthy, Jon. *Wilfred Owen.* London: Oxford University Press and Chatto & Windus, 1974.
Stevenson, Anne. *Five Looks at Elizabeth Bishop.* Tarset: Bloodaxe, 1998.
Thornton, R. K. R., ed. *Ivor Gurney: Collected Letters.* Manchester: Carcanet, 1991.
Travisano, Thomas with Saskia Hamilton, eds. *Words in Air: The Complete Correspondence between Elizabeth Bishop and Robert Lowell.* London: Faber, 2008.
Vendler, Helen. *The Poetry of George Herbert.* Cambridge, MA: Harvard University Press, 1983.
Vendler, Helen. *The Odes of John Keats.* Cambridge, MA: Harvard University Press, 1983.
Vendler, Helen. *Coming of Age as a Poet: Milton, Keats, Eliot, Plath.* Cambridge, MA: Harvard University Press, 2003.
Vendler, Helen. *Our Secret Discipline: Yeats and Lyric Form.* Cambridge, MA: Harvard University Press, 2007.
Waller, Gary. *English Poetry of the Sixteenth Century.* London and New York: Macmillan, 1986.
Weinberg, Bernard. *A History of Literary Criticism in the Italian Renaissance*, 2 vols. Chicago: University of Chicago Press, 1961.
Welland, D. S. R. *Wilfred Owen: A Critical Study*, London: Chatto & Windus, 1960.
White, Norman. *Hopkins: A Literary Biography.* Oxford: Clarendon, 1992.
Widdowson, H. G. *Practical Stylistics.* Oxford: Oxford University Press, 1992.
Wilcox, Earl J. and Jonathan N. Barron, eds. *Roads Not Taken: Rereading Robert Frost.* Columbia and London: University of Missouri Press, 2000.
Williams, Ioan, ed. *Meredith: The Critical Heritage.* London: Routledge and Kegan Paul, 1971.
Wilson, Katharina, ed. *Women Writers of the Renaissance.* Athens, GA: University of Georgia Press, 1987.
Woudhuysen, Henry. *Sir Philip Sidney and the Circulation of Manuscripts 1580–1640.* Oxford: Clarendon Press, 1996.
Wright, George. *Shakespeare's Metrical Art.* Berkeley: University of California Press, 1988.
Yeats, W. B., ed. *The Oxford Book of Modern Verse.* Oxford: Clarendon Press, 1936.

Index

Adames, John 329
adaptability 11–12
address 11
Alabaster, William 58
Albright, Daniel 168
aposiopesis 66
apostrophizing 26–7
argumentation 6
Armstrong, Isobel 132–3
Arnold, Matthew 106, 140–3, 366
  'Continued' 142
  Culture and Anarchy 124
  'East London' 142
  Marguerite poems 143–4
  'Quiet Work' 140
  'The Scholar-Gipsy' 140
  'Thyrsis' 140
  'To a Republican Friend, 1848' 141–2
  'West London' 142–3
attitude 11
Auden, W. H. 13–14, 315–31, 334, 391
  love sonnets 318–20
  'A. E. Housman' 316, 325–6
  'Brussels in Winter' 325
  'Control of the Passes was, he saw, the key' ('The Secret Agent') 317–18, 328
  'Crossroads' 329
  'The Door' 328–9
  'The Garden' 329–30
  'In Memory of W. B. Yeats' 384
  'In Time of War' ('Sonnets from China') 316, 320–4, 328, 331–2, 335
  Journey to a War 320–4, 330
  Juvenilia: Poems 1922–1928 316
  'Lear' 316, 325–6
  'The Lucky' 329
  'Musée des Beaux Arts' 326–7
  'The Quest' 327–30
  'Richard Jefferies' 316–17
  'Rimbaud' 316, 325
  'Rookhope (Weardale, Summer 1922)' 316
  'Through the Looking-Glass' 318
  'To E. M. Forster' 320
  'The Waters' 329
Austin, Alfred 288
autobiography 6, 9

Barnes, Barnabe, *A Divine Centurie of Spirituall Sonnets* 58
Barrell, John 52, 74, 77
Bateson, F. W. 18, 204
Baudelaire, Charles 207, 209, 275, 393, 397–8
  'A Une Dame Créole' ('To a Creole Lady') 395
  'Correspondences' 396
  Les Fleurs du Mal 395–8
Beckett, Samuel 245
The Bell (journal) 171
Belloc, Hilaire, *The Four Men* 294
Berrigan, Ted, *The Sonnets* 280–2
Berryman, John 275
  'After Petrarch and Wyatt' 269
  Berryman's Sonnets (*Sonnets to Chris*) 268–70
  The Dream Songs 270
Berthoff, Warner 231
Bidart, Frank 273
Bim (journal) 399
Bishop, Elizabeth 264–6, 275
  'The Fish' 265
  'The Reprimand' 264
  'Sonnet' (1928) 264
  'Sonnet' (1979) 264–6
  'Three Sonnets for Eyes' 264
  'The Wit' 264

Blackwood, Caroline 276
Blunden, Edmund 311–12
  'Vlamertinghe: Passing the Château, July 1917' 311–12
Boland, Eavan 215–18
  'Heroic' 217
  The Lost Land 217
  The Making of a Sonnet 216
  New Territory 216
  Night Feed 218
  'On Renoir's *The Grape Pickers*' 217–18
  'Yeats in Civil War' 216
Boleyn, Anne 18
Bolton, Jonathan 347
Bonnycastle, J., *Introduction to Astronomy* 114
Booth, James 334
Bowles, William Lisle 87–8, 94
  'At Bamborough Castle' 88
  Fourteen Sonnets 87–8
  'On Dover Cliffs' 88
  'To Evening' 88
  'To the River Itchin, near Winton' 85, 88
  'To Time' 88
Boyle, Elizabeth 33, 36
Bradford, Richard 330
Brainard, Joe 281–2
Brearton, Fran 215
Breton, Nicholas 58
brevity 1–2, 13
Bridges, Robert 153, 157
Britten, Benjamin 326
Bromwich, David 224, 255–6
Brooke, Rupert 14, 286–95, 303–4, 309, 313, 391
  'A Channel Passage' 288
  'Dawn' 288
  'The Dead' 292
  'In Freiburg Station' 289–90
  'Menelaus and Helen' 288–9
  'Peace' 292
  'Safety' 292
  'Seaside Sonnet' 290–1
  'The Soldier' 259, 286, 292–4, 304
  'Sonnet: in Time of Revolt' 287–8
  'Sonnet Reversed' 289
  'The Treasure' 291–2

  'Unfortunate' 287
  'Waikiko' 291
Brooks, Cleanth 98–9
Brooks, Gwendolyn 260–1, 285
  Annie Allen 260
  'The Children of the Poor' 260–1
Brouwer, Adriaen 336
Brown, Eleanor
  'Fifty Sonnets' 376–7
  Maiden Speech 376
Browning, Elizabeth Barrett
  'Finite and Infinite' 130
  'Grief' 130
  'How do I love thee? Let me count the ways.' 131–2
  'If I leave all for thee' 130
  'Love' 130
  'My letters! All dead paper, mute and white!' 131
  'On a Portrait of Wordsworth by R. B. Haydon' 130
  Poems (1844) 130
  'The Poet' 130
  'The Prisoner' 130
  Sonnets from the Portuguese 13–14, 129–33
  'The Soul's Expression' 130
  'Tears' 130, 133
  'Yes, call me by my pet-name' 130
Browning, Robert 123, 128–30
  'Dis Aliter Visum' 172
  'Now' 128–9
Bruegel, Pieter, 'Gloomy Day' 271
Bryant, William Cullen, 'To Cole, the Painter, Departing for Europe' 224–5
Bryskett, Lodovick 40
Buchanan, Robert, 'The Fleshly School of Poetry' 137
Bunting, Basil 378
Burke, Edmund 94
  Reflections on the Revolution in France 99–100
Burnett, Archie 331
Burns, Robert 219
  'Sonnet upon Sonnets' 2
Burrow, Colin 44
Burt, Stephanie 130, 223, 270, 280

Bush, Douglas 72
Byron, George Gordon (Lord Byron),
    'On Chillon' 111

Caddel, Richard 378
Camões, Luís de 130, 392
Campbell, Patrick 300–1
Campbell, Roy 396–7
    'The Serf' 397
    'The Zebras' 396–7
canzone 5
Carey, John 78
Carson, Ciaran 203, 206–12
    '1798' 210–11
    The Alexandrine Plan 207–9
    'At the Sign of the Swan' 208
    Belfast Confetti 206
    'Blue Grass' 209
    'Brief Encounter' 209
    'The Dongless Bell' 209
    The Irish for No 206
    'Just Crazy about You' 209
    'The Sonneteer' 208
    'Spraying the Potatoes' 210
    The Twelfth of Never 203, 207, 209–12
Cassou, Jean 392
Catholic Bulletin 166
Césaire, Aimé 260
    Cahier d'un retour au pays natal 351
Chamberlin, Ted 400
Chapman, George 113
Chapman, Jake and Dinos 381–2
Chirico, Girogio de, 'Mayflower' 279
Clare, John 117–22
    and politics 120–1
    'Emmonsails Heath in Winter' 118–20
    'England 1830' 120–1
    'The Nightingale' 117–18
    Poems Descriptive of Rural Life and Scenery 118
    'Sonnet: "I Am"' 121–2, 157
    'To the Memory of John Keats' 117
Clarke, Charles Cowden 112
Clough, Arthur Hugh 141–2
Coleridge, Samuel Taylor 80, 87, 94, 126
    'Frost at Midnight' 140

'Hymn Before Sun-Rise, in the Vale of Chamouni' 113–14
'Sonnet: To the River Otter' 85, 88–90
'To The Evening Star' 102
Collymore, Frank 399
Colonna, Vittoria 129
Constable, Henry 58
convention 4
Cooke, Harriet 181
Cope, Wendy 373–6
    'Faint Praise' 374–5
    'The Sitter' 375–6
    'Strugnell's Bargain' 373–4
Corcoran, Neil 182–3, 276–7
couplet 8
court society 5–6, 8, 19
Cowper, William 170
Cox, Sidney 250
Crabbe, George 118
Crane, Hart 260
Cromwell, Oliver 72, 75, 77–8
Cullen, Countee 258–9
    Color 259
    'Yet Do I Marvel' 259
Cummings, E. E. 254–6, 269
    'my girl's tall with hard long eyes' 254–5
    '"next to of course god america i"' 255–6
Curnow, Allen, 'In Memoriam 2 / Lieutenant T. C. F. Ronalds' 388
Curran, Stuart 94, 102, 114

da Lentino, Giacomo 5
Dante Alighieri 6, 110, 133, 135
    Beatrice 6, 133
    Divine Comedy 6, 244
    Vita Nuova 6, 7, 136, 376
d'Arezzo, Guittone 7
Day, Roger 336–7
Deane, Seamus 164
Della Casa, Giovanni, *Rime e Prose* 72
de Sade, Laura 7
Devereux, Penelope 22
devotional sonnets *see* religious sonnets
diplomacy 19, 29
Dixon, Richard Watson 151

Donne, John 10, 17, 364
  'At the round earth's imagined
    corners' 59–60
  'Batter my heart, three-personed
    God' 61
  'La Corona' 58–9
  'Death be not proud' 60–1
  Holy Sonnets 14, 59–61
  Songs and Sonnets 10
Dove, Rita, *Mother Love* 284–5
Dowland, John 344, 346
Dowson, Ernest 287
Drayton, Michael, *Ideas Mirrour (Idea)* 9–10, 42
Drummond, William 66–9
  'The Booke of the World' 68
  Flowers of Sion 66, 68
  Poems 66, 69
  'To spreade the azure Canopie of Heauen' 67
Dryden, John, *Don Sebastian, King of Portugal: A Tragedy* 294
Dubrow, Heather 69
Duffy, Carol Ann 370–3
  Feminine Gospels 371
  'Forest' 372–3
  'North-West' 372
  'Prayer' 370–1
  Rapture 372
  'Rapture' 373
  'Wish' 371–2
  The World's Wife 371
Dunbar, Paul Laurence 258
  'Douglass' 258
  'Robert Gould Shaw' 258
Dunn, Douglas 359–63
  Elegies 359–63
  'The Kaleidoscope' 360–1
  'Leaving Dundee' 363
  'Modern Love' 359
  'Sandra's Mobile' 360, 362–3
  'A Silver Air Force' 360–2
  Terry Street 359, 363
Dunn, Lesley Balfour 359

Eastman, Max 259
Ebbatson, Roger 291
Edwards, Ken 78–80
  'Darkly Slow' 378–9
  eight + six 378

  'His Last Gasp (2)' 379–80
  'Many to Many: Big Story' 379
Eliot, T. S. 147, 165, 249–50, 251–4, 275, 287–8, 333–4, 396
  'Ash Wednesday' 345
  'Circe's Palace' 252
  'A Cooking Egg' 374
  'The Dry Salvages' 254
  Four Quartets 254
  'La Figlia che Piange' 253
  'The Love Song of J. Alfred Prufrock' 333
  'Nocturne' 253
  'On a Portrait' 252–3
  'Portrait of a Lady' 253
  'Preludes' 253
  Prufrock and Other Observations 252
  'Reflections on *Vers Libre*' 253–4
  'Rhapsody on a Windy Night' 253
  'The Waste Land' 253, 334
Elizabeth I, queen of England 56
eloquence 5–6
Emerson, Ralph Waldo 223
Encounter (journal) 173
Englishman's Magazine 126
English sonnet 9–11, 15, 21
European Magazine 82
Examiner 112–13

Faggen, Robert 241–3
Fairfax, Thomas 72, 77
Figueroa, John 400
Fineman, Joel 46 n. 32
Flynn, Leontia, *Drives* 218
form of the sonnet 1–5
Forster, E. M. 320
Fraisse, Armand 394
Frederick II, Emperor 5
French Revolution 81, 94, 99–100
Frost, Robert 14, 232, 234–51, 275, 296
  'Acquainted with the Night' 234, 237, 243–4, 335
  'After Apple Picking' 188
  A Boy's Will 237–8
  Collected Poems 237
  Complete Poems 237
  'The Death of the Hired Man' 241
  'Design' 235, 244–7
  'Despair' 235–6

'A Dream Pang' 238
'The Figure a Poem Makes' 244
'For Once, Then, Something' 204
'Fourth of July' letter to John
    Bartlett 230
A Further Range 245
'Home Burial' 241
'Hyla Brook' 241
'Into My Own' 234, 237–8
'Meeting and Passing' 234, 241–2
'The Mill City' 236–7
Mountain Interval 241
'Mowing' 234, 238–41
'Never Again Would Birds' Song Be
    the Same' 235, 247, 249–51
North of Boston 241
'The Oven Bird' 234, 241
'The Pasture' 237
'Range-Finding' 241
'The Silken Tent' 235, 247–9
'The Vantage Point' 238
Fuller, John 7, 317–19, 324, 327, 393

Gascoine, George 10–11
Gautier, Théophile 395
genre theory 12–13
Gentleman's Magazine 81
Gillis, Alan 218–19
    'The Green Rose' 219
Gill, Stephen 105
Glob, P. V., *The Bog People* 181
Godwin, William 85
Goldberg, Jonathan 78 n. 57
Gonne, Maud 161
Goya, Francisco, *The Disasters of
    War* 381–2
Gray, Thomas, 'Elegy Written in a
    Country Churchyard' 333, 351
Greenberg, Herbert 328
Greenblatt, Stephen 19
Greville, Fulke, *Caelica* 40–3
Gryphius, Andreas 392
Guebuza, Armando 351
Gunston, Leslie 305
Gurney, Ivor 14, 311–15
    'England the Mother' 313
    'The Golden Age' 315
    'On Somme' 314
    'Pain' 313
    'The Not Returning' 314

'Servitude' 313
Severn and Somme 312–13
'Sonnets 1917' 313
'Strange Hells' 314
'To England–A Note' 314
Gyllenstierna, Maria Gustava 393

Hacker, Marilyn
    'The Dark Night of the 747' 284
    'Lesbian Ethics, or: Live Girl-Girl
        Sex Acts' 284
    *Love, Death, and the Changing of the
        Seasons* 284
Hadfield, Andrew 38
Hall, Jason 192
Hallam, Arthur Henry 126
Hampson, Robert 381
    'Reworked Disasters or: Next checking
        out the Chapmans' Goyas'
        381–3
Hardwick, Elizabeth 276
Harlem Renaissance 258–61
Harris, Daniel 157
Harrison, Tony 2, 13–14, 350–9
    'Book Ends' 354–5
    'A Cold Coming' 358
    'Continuous' 355–7
    Continuous 355, 358
    'Curtain Sonnets' 350
    'First Aid in English' 359
    The Gaze of the Gorgon 358
    'Initial Illumination' 358
    'Marked with D' 357–8
    'On Not Being Milton' 351–3
    from *The School of Eloquence* 14, 350–1
    'Sonnets for August 1945' 350,
        358–9
Harvard Advocate (journal) 252
Hassall, Christopher 289–91
Haughton, Hugh 346–7
Hawthorne, Nathaniel, *Tanglewood
    Tales* 252
Heaney, Margaret 187
Heaney, Seamus 172–3, 177–93, 202, 240,
    308–9, 339
    on Robert Frost 251
    on Robert Lowell 277
    'Act of Union' 182–3
    'The Augean Stables' 192
    'A Chow' 193

INDEX

Heaney, Seamus (*cont.*)
  'Clearances' 187–91
  'A Clip' 193
  Death of a Naturalist 178
  District and Circle 192–3
  'District and Circle' 193
  'Dogger, Rockall, Malin, Irish Sea' 185–6
  Door into the Dark 178–9
  Electric Light 192
  'Fear of affectation made her affect' 188–90
  'Feeling into Words' 181
  Field Work 183
  'The Forge' 178–9
  'Fosterling' 191–2
  'From Monaghan to the Grand Canal' 177–8
  'Glanmore Revisited' 191
  'Glanmore Sonnets' 183–7, 195, 371
  The Government of the Tongue 190
  The Haw Lantern 187
  Human Chain 188
  'I dreamt we slept in a moss in Donegal' 186–7
  'I thought of walking round and round a space' 190–1
  'A New Life' 182
  New Selected Poems 1966–1987 180
  'The Nod' 193
  North 181–2, 204
  Opened Ground: Poems 1966–1996 180
  Preoccupations 184–5
  'Requiem for the Croppies' 179–80
  Seeing Things 186, 191
  Selected Poems 1965–1975 180
  'The Skylight' 191
  'Sonnets from Hellas' 192
  'Strange Fruit' 181–2
  'This evening the cuckoo and the corncrake' 184–5
  'The Tollund Man' 204
  'The Tollund Man in Springtime' 193
  'When all the others were away at Mass' 187–8
  Wintering Out 181–2
Henderson, Diana 69, 134, 263
Henry VIII, king of England 8, 18
Herbert, George 57–9, 61–6, 155, 281
  'The Answer' 65–6
  'My God, where is that ancient heat towards thee' 62–3
  'Prayer (I)' 63–4
  'Redemption' 64–5
  'Sure, Lord, there is enough in thee to dry' 62–3
  The Temple 63
Herbert, William 69
Herbet, Magdalen 58–9
Hibberd, Dominic 305, 308
Hill, Geoffrey 14, 330, 339–50
  'An Apology for the Revival of Christian Architecture in England' 346–50
  For the Unfallen 340
  'Funeral Music' 341–4
  'The Herefordshire Carol' 349–50
  King Log 341
  'Lachrimae' 344–6
  'The Laurel Axe' 348–9
  'Quaint Mazes' 347–8
  'Requiem for the Plantagenet Kings' 340–1
  Tenebrae 344, 346
  'Two Formal Elegies, For the Jews in Europe' 340
historical formalism 12
Hoffman, Tyler 240
Hollander, John 257
holy sonnets *see* religious sonnets
Homer 113–14
  Iliad 212
  Odyssey 382
Hopkins, Gerard Manley 2, 14, 60, 150–7, 364, 366
  'As kingfishers catch fire' 153
  'The Caged Skylark' 153
  'Felix Randal' 124, 155–7
  'God's Grandeur' 152–3
  'Hurrahing in Harvest' 152–3
  'I wake and feel the fell of dark' 157
  'The Lantern out of Doors' 153
  'Let me be to Thee' 152
  'Myself unholy' 152
  'On the Origin of Beauty' 151
  'Pied Beauty' 152–3
  "The Sea and the Skylark' 153
  'See how Spring opens' 152–3
  'sonnets of desolation' or 'terrible sonnets' 152

'Spelt from Sibyl's Leaves' 152, 157
'The Starlight Night' 153
'That Nature is a Heraclitean Fire' 152
'The Windhover' 1, 152–5
'Tom's Garland' 124, 152, 157
'To seem the stranger lies my lot' 157
Horace 77
Housman, A. E. 316, 325–6
   A Shropshire Lad 264
Hughes, Langston 258, 285
Hunt, Leigh 112
Hyde, Douglas 162

iambic pentameter 2
Ingram, John Kells 159
   'Memories of the Dead' 159
   'National Presage' 159
innovation 4
intimacy 2–3
Irish Times 181
Isherwood, Christopher 14, 316, 318, 320, 324, 326
Italian sonnet 5–8, 15, 151

James I, king of England 56
Jamie, Kathleen 363–4, 391
   'Five Tay Sonnets' 364
   'Moult' 364
   The Overhaul 364
   'Swallows' 364
   The Tree House 364
Jarrell, Randall 245
Jefferies, Richard 316–17
Jennings, Elizabeth 330, 337–9, 391
   Celebrations and Elegies 338
   'Having it Both Ways' 339
   In the Meantime 339
   Lucidities 338
   Relationships 338
   'A Sense of Place' 337–8
   'A Sonnet' 338
   The Sonnets of Michelangelo 338
   'Sources of Light' 338–9
   'Tribute to Turner' 339
   A Way of Looking 337
Joergens, Olwen 305
Johnston, John H. 295
Jones, Monica 336
Jones, Robert 103
Joyce, James, *Ulysses* 256

Kavanagh, Patrick 12, 168–79, 190, 193, 195
   'Auditors In' 172
   Canal Bank Sonnets 172
   'Canal Bank Walk' 174–6
   Come Dance with Kitty Stobling 172, 175
   'Epic' 171–2
   'The Hospital' 173
   'Inniskeen Road: July Evening' 168–71
   'Lines Written on a Seat on the Grand Canal, Dublin' 176
   'October' 173–4
   'The One' 174, 176–7
   The Ploughman and Other Poems 168
   'Yellow' 174
Keats, John 13–14, 83, 111–17, 126, 294, 301
   and politics 111–13
   and Wilfred Owen 301–5, 308
   'Bright Star' 140
   Endymion 301
   'The Fall of Hyperion' 138
   'Ode to Melancholy' 125
   'Ode to a Nightingale' 302
   'On First Looking into Chapman's Homer' 113–14, 158, 381–2, 392
   'On Peace' 111–12
   'To Autumn' 304, 308
   'When I have fears that I may cease to be' 3–4, 115–16, 304, 392
   'Written on the Day that Mr Leigh Hunt Left Prison' 112–13
Kendall, Tim 195
Kerrigan, John 96
Kiberd, Declan 166
Kierkegaard, Søren 328
Kinahan, Frank 180–1

Laforgue, Jules 253, 288
Lamb, Charles 90
Landor, Walter Savage 91
landscape, exploration of, in romantic sonnets 80–2, 86
Larkin, Philip 14, 289, 330–7, 339, 369, 391
   'The Card-Players' 335–7
   'Church Going' 334, 337
   'The Conscientious Objector' 331
   'The Conscript' 331
   'Friday Night in the Royal Station Hotel' 335–6

Larkin, Philip (*cont.*)
   'Having grown up in shade of Church and State' 331–2
   High Windows 330, 335
   'High Windows' 373
   The Less Deceived 330, 334
   'Lines on a Young Lady's Photograph Album' 335
   'Mr Bleaney' 333
   'Neurotics' 334
   The North Ship 330
   'Nothing significant was really said' 332–3
   'Observation' 330–1
   'The Old Fools' 333
   'Spring' 334
   'Street Lamps' 333–4
   'To Failure' 334
   'To My Wife' 334
   'To the Sea' 337
   'Ultimatum' 330
   'Whatever Happened?' 334–5
   'The Whitsun Weddings' 337
   'Winter Nocturne' 333
Laskowski, William E. 290
Lawrence, Edward 72
Lazarus, Emma, 'The New Colossus' 226–7
Lear, Edward 316, 325–6
Leavis, F. R. 110
Leishman, J. B. 322–3
Lentricchia, Frank 243
Lever, J. W. 36
Liberator (newspaper) 259
The Listener (magazine) 178, 182, 330
Locke, John 94
Lok (Locke), Anne, *A Meditation of a Penitent Sinner* 9, 58
Lok, Henry 58
Longfellow, Henry Wadsworth 220–3
   'The Cross of Snow' 222–3
   'Milton' 220–1
   'My Lost Youth' 238
   'To Science' 222
Longley, Michael 212–15
   'The Beech Tree' 213–14
   'Ceasefire' 212–13
   'Flight Feathers' 214–15
   The Ghost Orchid 214
   'The Miner' 215
   'Robin' 215
   'The Snow Leopard' 215
   Snow Water 214
   'Stonechat' 214
   'The Vision of Theoclymenus' 213
   The Weather in Japan 214
Lope de Vega, Félix 346
Lopez, Tony, *False Memory* 380–1
love sonnets 6–7, 124
   Auden 318–20
   Baudelaire 395–6
   Dante Gabriel Rossetti 136–7
   Drayton 9–10
   Elizabeth Barrett Browning 13–14, 129–33
   Greville 40–3
   Jennings 337–8
   Meredith 143–50
   Petrarch 15–20
   Robert Browning 128–9
   Sidney 22–33
   Spenser 33–40
   Tennyson 126–9
   Wyatt 15–20
   Yeats 160–1
Lowell, James Russell, 'To the Spirit of Keats' 303
Lowell, Robert 218, 271–7
   'I. Water' 275
   'Concord' 271
   The Dolphin 276–7
   'The Dolphin' 277
   For Lizzie and Harriet 276
   For the Union Dead 271, 273–4
   History 275–6
   Imitations 275, 396
   'Inauguration Day: January 1953' 271–2
   'In the Cage' 271–3
   'In the Mail' 276
   Life Studies 271
   Lord Weary's Castle 271
   'Night Sweat' 273–4
   'The North Sea Undertaker's Complaint' 271
   Notebook 274–6
   'Salem' 271
   Selected Poems 273
   '"To Speak of Woe That Is in Marriage"' 271
   'Water 1948' 274
   'Water' 274–5
   'Words for Hart Crane' 271

Loyola, Ignatius 58
Lucas, John 110, 313

McCrea, Shane 284–5
   Mule 285
MacDonagh, Thomas 158–60, 194
McGann, Jerome 137–8
McKay, Claude 259–60, 285
   'America' 13, 259–60
   'Dawn in New York' 260
   Harlem Shadows 260
   'If We Must Die' 259–60
MacNeice, Louis 193, 205
   Autumn Sequel 336
   The Earth Compels 323
   'Snow' 211
McNeillie, Andrew 365–6
   'Arkwork' 365
   'The Emerald Isle Express' 366
   'Glyn Dŵr Sonnets' 365–6
   'Portrait of the Poet as a Young Dog' 365
   Slower 365
Mahon, Derek 193, 205, 208
   Echo's Grove 402
   'Exequy' 401–2
Mallarmé, Stéphane 207–8
Manet, Edouard, 'Woman with a Parrot' 252
Mangan, James Clarence 219
   'Dark Rosaleen' 211
   'To My Native Land' 211
Marotti, Arthur 30, 40, 43
Marsh, Edward 291
Martz, Louis 36, 58
Marvell, Andrew 17, 77
   'An Horatian Ode upon the Return of Cromwell from Ireland' 206
   'To His Coy Mistress' 206
Mendelson, Edward 326, 328
Meredith, George 2, 14, 151
   political sonnets 150
   'Behold me striking the world's coward stroke' 147
   'By this he knew she wept with waking eyes' 144–5
   Modern Love 124, 143–50, 185, 289
   'Outside the Crowd' 150
   'This was the woman; what now of the man?' 147

'The Warning' 150
'We saw the swallows gathering in the sky' 149
'What are we first?' 146–7
Merrill, James 282–3
   'The Broken Home' 282–3
   Nights and Days 282
metre 2
Millard, Kenneth 287
Millay, Edna St Vincent 13–14, 261–4
   The Harp-Weaver 263
   'If I should learn, in some quite casual way' 262–3
   Renascence 262
   'What lips my lips have kissed, and where, and why' 263
Miller, J. Hillis 99
Miller, Karl 179
Milroy, James 156
Milton, John 13, 68–9, 71–9, 113, 121, 153
   Italian influences 72
   political sonnets 75–6
   and Tony Harrison 353
   and Wordsworth 91–2, 100–1, 103–4
   'L'Allegro' 111–12
   'A book was writ of late called *Tetrachordon*' 76
   'How soon hath time the subtle thief of youth' 72–3
   'Lycidas' 302
   'Methought I saw my late espousèd saint' 78–9, 222
   'On his blindness' 73–5
   'O nightingale, that on yon bloomy spray' 71–2
   'On the Late Massacre in Piedmont' 75–6, 126, 139
   'On the Same' 76–7
   Paradise Lost 84, 101, 258
   sonnet to Cromwell 72, 77–8
   sonnet to Fairfax 72, 77, 258
   sonnet to Vane 72, 77–8
   'Whither the Muse or Love call thee his mate' 84
Mitford, Mary Russell 130
Montale, Eugenio 393
Moore, George 163
Morgan, Edwin, 'Glasgow Sonnets' 363
Morris, Jane 135

Motion, Andrew 113, 383–7
  The Cinder Path 383, 386
  'Harry Patch' 385–6
  'In Memory of Mervyn Dalley' 383–5
  'London Plane' 386–7
  The Pleasure Steamers 383
  Public Property 383
  'Raven' 387
Movement poets 337
Moxon, Edward 126
Muldoon, Paul 171, 193–206
  'Beijing' 205–6
  'Hard Drive' 204–5
  Horse Latitudes 205–6
  'Lull' 195–7
  'The More a Man Has, the More a Man Wants' 195, 199–204
  Moy Sand and Gravel 204
  Quoof 197, 199
  'Quoof' 198–9
  'The Sightseers' 197–8
  Songs and Sonnets 206
  'Why Brownlee Left' 193–5
musicality 2–3

narrative 6, 9
Nashe, Thomas 23
Neruda, Pablo 392
New England Magazine 237
The New Republic (magazine) 327
Norbrook, David 41–2
Notley, Alice 280

octave 1, 5, 7–8
O'Donoghue, Bernard 185–6, 194
O'Neill, Michael 107–8, 120, 175, 177, 364
Orgel, Stephen 78 n. 57
origins of the sonnet 5–11
Oswald, Alice 383, 387–90
  'Prayer' 389–90
  'Sea Sonnets' 388–9
  The Thing in the Gap-Stone Stile 387
Owen, Wilfred 14, 60, 301–11, 391
  and Keats 301–5, 308
  and Sassoon 305, 307–8
  and Shakespeare 302–4
  '1914' 303–4
  'Anthem for Doomed Youth' 306–8
  'Dulce et Decorum Est' 308–9
  'Futility' 310–11

'Happiness' 305
'Hospital Barge' 310–11
'A New Heaven' 306
'On My Songs' 303
'The Poet in Pain' 302–3
'Purple' 305
'Sonnet, Written at Teignmouth, on a Pilgrimage to Keats's House' 302
'Spring Offensive' 302
'Strange Meeting' 311
'The Unreturning' 305
'With an Identity Disc' 304
'Written in a Wood, September 1910' 301–2
Oxford University Labour Club Bulletin 330

Paine, Thomas 85
Parker, Michael 179
paronomasia 48
Parrish, Maxwell 252
Partisan Review (magazine) 271
Paterson, Don 230, 247, 366–71
  40 Sonnets 369
  'The Air' 369
  'Being' 369
  'The Electric Brae' 367
  'Exuent' 366–7
  'Funeral Prayer' 370
  'Here' 369
  Landing Light 367
  'Mercies' 369
  'Morning Prayer' 366
  Nil Nil 366
  Orpheus 368–9
  'The Powercut' 369
  'Requests' 369
  'The Roundabout' 369–70
  'Seven Questions about the Journey' 369
  'Souls' 369
  'The Thread' 368
  'To Dundee City Council' 369
  'Waking with Russell' 367
Pater, Walter 137–8, 151
patronage 52, 54–5
Paulin, Tom 156
Pembroke, William Herbert, 3rd Earl of 57
Perloff, Marjorie 276, 401
persuasion 1, 5–6
Petrarchan sonnet 7–8, 25, 67, 69, 71, 143

Petrarch, Francis 6–7, 83, 133, 135, 401–2
  Rime Sparse (Canzoniere) 6–8, 15–21, 24, 401
Phillips, Edward 69
Pickard, Tom 377–8
Plath, Sylvia 13–14, 277–80
  'Aftermath' 279–80
  'April Aubade' 277
  Collected Poems 279
  'Conversation among the Ruins' 279
  'Daddy' 278
  'Lady Lazarus' 278, 280, 285
  'Mayflower' 279
  'Sonnet: To Eva' 277–8
  'To Spring' 277
Poe, Edgar Allan 221–2
Poirier, Richard 247
politics and political sonnets 11–14, 75–6, 80–1, 124
  Arnold 140–3
  Browning 128
  Clare 120–1
  Heaney 179–80, 181
  Keats 111–13
  Meredith 150
  Rossetti 139
  Shelley 109–10
  Sidney 29–32
  Tennyson 126
  Wordsworth 93–4, 102–6
  Wyatt 19
Pope, Jessie 308
Pound, Dorothy 378
Pound, Ezra 221, 254, 269, 287
  'The River-Merchant's Wife: A Letter' 284
Powell, Mary 78 n. 57
Powell, Neil 43
prosody 8
prospect (or topographical) sonnets 90, 94–6
Pugin, Augustus 347
Pushkin, Alexander 400

quatrain 5, 7
Quinn, Antoinette 172

Ramazani, Jahan 12, 390–1
The Reality Street Book of Sonnets 378
reasoning, sonnet as instrument of 6, 8

religious sonnets 57–69
  Donne 14, 59–61
  Herbert 57–9, 61–6, 155
rhetoric 6
rhyme 2–3
Rich, Lady Penelope 30
Ricks, Christopher 126, 254, 339
Rilke, Rainer Maria 275, 322, 366, 392
  'Sonnets to Orpheus' 322–4, 368–9
Rimbaud, Arthur 275, 316, 325–6, 338, 366, 396
  'Au-Cabaret Vert' 207
  'Charlerois' 208
  'Oraison du soir' 366
river sonnets 85, 87–90, 94–5, 99, 364
Robertson, William, *History of America* 114
Robinson, Edwin Arlington 230–4
  Children of the Night 233, 258
  'Credo' 232–3
  'Haunted House' 233–4
  'Reuben Bright' 231–2
Roethke, Theodore 275, 289–90
  'The Waking' 390
Romantic movement 80–2
Ronsard, Pierre de 160, 392
Rosenthal, M. L. 276
Rossetti, Christina 133–5
  'Come back to me, who wait and watch for you' 134
  'Later Life: A Double Sonnet of Sonnets' 134–5
  'Monna Innominata' 133–4
  'Remember' 134, 263
  'Rest' 134
  'Youth gone, and beauty gone if ever there' 134
Rossetti, Dante Gabriel 135–9
  and politics 139
  sonnets for pictures 137–8
  'At the Sunrise in 1848' 139
  'Body's Beauty' 138
  The House of Life 135–9, 252
  'Nuptial Sleep' 136–7
  'On Refusal of Aid Between Nations' 139
  'Proserpina' 137–8
  'A Sonnet is a moment's monument' 135–6
  'Soul's Beauty' 138
  'Vox Ecclesiae, Vox Christi' 139

Ruskin, John 338
Russell, William Rankin 181
Ryan, Kiernan 56

Sacks, Peter 263
Sand, George 130
Sassoon, Siegfried 298–301, 311
   and Wilfred Owen 305, 307–8
   'Dreamers' 298
   'Glory of Women' 298
   'In the Church of St Ouen' 299
   'Remorse' 298–9
   'A Subaltern' 298
   'Trench Duty' 298, 300–1
   'Two Hundred Years After' 299–300
Schalkwyk, David 51
Schröder, Rudolf Alexander 392
Scott, Marion 313
sequences 9, 22
sestet 2, 5, 7–8
Seth, Vikram, *The Golden Gate* 400–1
Seward, Anna 80–2
   'On the damp margin of the sea-beat shore' 82
   'Sonnet: To the Poppy' 82
   'Sonnet to France on her Present Exertions' 81
Shakespeare, William
   Hamlet 249
   Henry V 84, 294
   King Lear 114–15
   A Lover's Complaint 45
   Richard II 294
   Romeo and Juliet 253
   sonnets 3, 9, 13, 43–57, 136, 192, 220, 301, 304, 392
      17 'Who will believe my verse in time to come' 46
      18 'Shall I compare thee to a summer's day?' 46–50, 248
      25 'Let those who are in favour with their stars' 50–1
      29 'When in disgrace with Fortune and men's eyes' 51–2, 373
      37 'As a decrepit father takes delight' 54
      53 'What is your substance, whereof are you made' 54–5
      55 'Not marble, nor guilded monuments' 53, 55–6
      64 'When I have seen by Time's fell hand defaced' 53–4
      65 'How with this rage shall beauty hold a plea' 180
      73 'That time of year thou mayst in me behold' 174, 214, 263, 284, 301–2
      97 'How like a winter has my absence been' 304
      104 'To me, fair friend, you never can be old' 2
      107 'Not mine own fears, nor the prophetic soul' 4, 55–7, 134, 260
      115 'Those lines that I before have writ do lie' 55
      116 'Let me not to the marriage of true minds admit impediments' 238, 362
      126 'O Thou, my lovely boy, who in thy power' 44
      127 'In the old age black was not counted fair' 44
      152 'In loving thee thou know'st I am forsworn' 44
Shakespearean sonnet 9, 45, 151, 318
Sharpe, Tony 61
Shelley, Percy Bysshe 13, 106–10, 122, 128, 141–2
   and politics 109–10
   'Adonais' 302
   'Defence of Poetry' 6
   'Ode to the West Wind' 110, 141, 304
   'On the Extinction of the Venetian Republic' 107
   'On Sitting Down to Read *King Lear* Once Again' 114–15
   'Ozymandias' 1, 108–9, 260
   'Political Greatness' 139
   The Revolt of Islam 304
   'Sonnet: England in 1819' 109–10, 121, 141
   'Sonnet: On Launching Some Bottles Filled with Knowledge into the Bristol Channel' 107–8
   'Sonnet: To a Balloon, Laden with Knowledge' 107–8
   'To Wordsworth' 106–7
Siddall, Elizabeth 135
Sidney, Robert 69–70
Sidney, Sir Henry 31

Sidney, Sir Philip 10, 34, 41
   Astrophil and Stella 9, 13, 22–33, 45–6, 70, 134, 158, 360
      ambition 29–31
      apostrophizing 26–7
      as autobiography 23
      diction 25–7
      kissing, pleasures of 29
      and politics 29–32
      rhyme scheme 25, 27–8
      sexual desire 28–30
      syntax 25–8
Sigerson, George 158
Skinner, Cyriack 72
Smith, Charlotte Turner 80, 82–5, 87, 95
   'Composed during a walk on the Downs' 85
   Elegaic Sonnets 82–5
   'Oh! place me where the burning noon' 83
   'On the departure of the nightingale' 83–4
   'To a nightingale' 83
   'To spring' 84
   'Written in the church-yard at Middleton in Sussex' 85
Smith, Stan 321, 332
Sorley, Charles Hamilton 294–8
   'Death and the Downs' 296
   'To Germany' 296
   'Two Sonnets' 296–7
   'When you see millions of the mouthless dead' 296–8
   'Whom therefore we ignorantly worship' 295–6
Southampton, Henry Wriothesley, Earl of 57
Southey, Robert 90
   'The Battle of Blenheim' 300
Southwell, St Robert 344, 346
Spenser, Edmund 161–2, 281
   Amoretti 9, 33–40
      calendrical structure 36–7
      courtship and marriage as theme 36–7
      rhyme scheme 35, 39
      Sonnet 3 36
      Sonnet 8 34
      Sonnet 12 37
      Sonnet 16 37
      Sonnet 34 35
      Sonnet 45 34–5
      Sonnet 62 36
      Sonnet 68 37
      Sonnet 75 37–9
      Sonnet 76 37
      Sonnet 86 39
      Sonnet 89 39–40
   Epithalamion 33, 39
   The Faerie Queene 40, 115
   View of the Present State of Ireland 161–2
Spiller, Michael 8, 26, 39, 46, 74
Stallworthy, Jon 303
Stevenson, Anne 265–8
   'Sonnets for Five Seasons' 266–8
Stevens, Wallace 243, 388–9
   'Autumn Refrain' 256–7
   'Sunday Morning' 269–70
Stickney, Trumbull, 'Six O'Clock' 227–8
Stott, Rebecca 131
strambotto 5
Strang, Patsy 335
stress patterns 2
structure 2, 5, 7–9, 20
Surrey, Henry Howard, Earl of 8–9, 15, 20–2, 45
   and Petrarch 20–1
   'Set me whereas the sun doth parch the green' 20–1
Sutton, James 331
Swinburne, Algernon Charles 288
   'A Leave Taking' 287
Symons, Arthur 253

Tasso, Torquato, *Sonneti Eroici* 72
Tennyson, Alfred 13, 123, 125–8
   and politics 126
   love sonnets 126–9
   'As when with downcast eyes we muse and brood' 127
   'Check every outflash' 125–6
   'If I were loved, as I desire to be' 126
   In Memoriam 126–7, 310
   'The Lady of Shalott' 125
   'The Lotus-Eaters' 126
   'Mariana' 125
   'Me my own Fate to lasting sorrow doometh' 125
   'Now sleeps the crimson petal' 128–9
   'The Passing of Arthur' 311

Tennyson, Alfred (*cont.*)
  Poems (1832) 125–6
  Poems, Chiefly Lyrical 125
  The Princess 127
  'Sonnet On the Result of the Late Russian Invasion of Poland' 126
  'Sonnet written on hearing of the outbreak of the Polish Insurrection' 126
  'Ulysses' 289
Tennyson, Charles 125
tercet 5, 7
Thomas, Dylan, 'A Refusal to Mourn the Death, By Fire, of a Child in London' 398
Thomas, Edward 294, 296, 317
  'As the Team's Head-Brass' 386
Thompson, E. P., *The Making of the English Working Class* 351
Thoreau, Henry 239
Tighe, Mary 159
Tóibín, Colm 161
topographical (or prospect) sonnets 90, 94–6
Tottel, Richard, *Songes and Sonettes* (*Tottel's Miscellany*) 9, 21–2
Traherne, Thomas 388
Trilling, Lionel 235
troubadour poets 5
Tuckerman, Frederick Goddard 228–30
  'An upper chamber in a darkened house' 228–9
  'Under the mountain, as when first I knew' 229–30
Turner, Charles Tennyson, 'Letty's Globe' 393–4

Valéry, Paul 275, 396
Vane, Henry 72, 77–8
Vaughan, Henry 388
Vendler, Helen 3, 45, 55, 115, 159, 163–4, 167
Verlaine, Paul 305, 392
  'Mon rêve familier' 305
Very, Jones 223–4
  'Barberry Bush' 224
  'The Celandine' 224
  'The Children' 224
  'The Dead' 224
  'The Garden' 224

Vieira, Sergio 351
Virginia Quarterly Review 247
Voorslag (journal) 396

Wagner, Jennifer Ann 123–4
Walcott, Derek 240–1, 398–400
  Another Life 400
  'A City's Death by Fire' 398–9
  In a Green Night 400
  'Tales of the Islands' 399–400
Ward, Susan Hayes 245
Warton, Thomas, 'To the River Loden' 87
Watson, Thomas, *Hekatompathia* 9
Whistler, James Abbott McNeill 245
White, Norman 153–4
Whitman, Walt 220
Whittier, John Greenleaf, 'To a Cape Ann Schooner' 225–6
Wilcox, Helen 57
Williams, Charles, *The Descent of the Dove* 328
Williams, Helen Maria 80, 85–6
  'Sonnet: To the Curlew' 86
  'Sonnet: To the Strawberry' 86
  'Sonnet: To the Torrid Zone' 86
  'Sonnet: To the White Bird of the Tropic' 86
  'Sonnet to the Calbassia Tree' 86
Williams, William Carlos 254, 282, 377
Wills, Clair 195
Wollstonecraft, Mary 86
Woodcock, Katherine 78
Wordsworth, Dorothy 97
Wordsworth, Jonathan 87
Wordsworth, William 13–14, 80, 90–108, 123, 140, 184
  Milton's influence on 91–2, 100–1, 103–4
  and politics 93–4, 102–6
  '1830' 105–6
  'Calais, August, 1802' 103
  'Composed after a Journey across the Hamilton Hills, Yorkshire' 95
  'Composed by the Sea-Side, near Calais' 102–3
  'Composed Upon Westminster Bridge' 96–100
  'Composed in the Valley, near Dover, on the Day of Landing' 103–4

'Ecclesiastical Sonnets' 90, 105
'Ere we had reached the wished-for place' 95–6
'Gipsies' 140
'How sweet it is, when mother Fancy rocks' 95
'I grieved for Buonaparte' 103
'It is a beauteous evening' 100–2
'Lines written a few miles above Tintern Abbey' 101, 107
'London 1802' 100, 102, 104, 107
Lyrical Ballads 90, 93, 98
'Miscellaneous Sonnets' 94–5, 100, 105
'Nuns fret not at their Convent's narrow room' 92–3, 113
'Ode: Intimations of Mortality' 107
The Prelude 14, 90
'River Duddon Series' 85, 90, 94–5
'The Solitary Reaper' 239
'Some Souls (for such there needs must be)' 94
'Sonnets Dedicated to Liberty' 94, 99–100, 102–5, 107
'The world is too much with us' 100–1
Wright, George 46
Wroth, Lady Mary 22, 69–70, 129
    Pamphilia to Amphilanthus 69–70
Wyatt, Sir Thomas 8–9, 15–20, 186–7
    and diplomacy 19, 29
    and Petrarch 15–20
    and politics 19
    rhyme scheme 19–20, 25
    and sonnet structure 20
    'The long love that in my thought doth harbour' 15–17
    'Whoso list to hunt' 17–20

Yeats, W. B. 2, 158–68, 176, 192, 215–16, 287, 308
'At the Abbey Theatre' 162–3
'Easter 1916' 192, 205
'The Fascination of What's Difficult' 160
'The Fisherman' 162
'The Folly of Being Comforted' 160–1
The Green Helmet 162
'The Harp of Aengus' 160
'High Talk' 159, 168
In the Seven Woods 161
'In the Seven Woods' 161–2
'Lapis Lazuli' 166, 186
Last Poems 160, 168
'Leda and the Swan' 1, 164–6, 213, 216
'Meditations in Time of Civil War' 166, 180
'Meru' 166–7
'Never Give all the Heart' 160–1
'No Second Troy' 162
'Notoriety' 163
Parnell's Funeral and Other Poems 166
'Remembrance' 159
Responsibilities 163
'The Second Coming' 164
'September 1913' 163
The Shadowy Waters 160
'The Song of Wandering Aengus' 192
The Tower 166
'Under Ben Bulben' 167
A Vision 163, 166
'When You are Old' 160